Paris

THE ROUGH GUIDE

There are more than one hundred and fifty Rough Guide titles
covering destinations from Amsterdam to Zimbabwe

Forthcoming titles include

Argentina • Croatia • Ecuador • Money Online • Switzerland

Rough Guide Reference Series

Classical Music • Drum 'n' Bass • English Football • European Football
House • The Internet • Jazz • Music USA • Opera • Reggae
Rock Music • Techno • World Music

Rough Guide Phrasebooks

Czech • Dutch • Egyptian Arabic • European Languages • French
German • Greek • Hindi & Urdu • Hungarian • Indonesian
Italian • Japanese • Mandarin Chinese • Mexican Spanish • Polish
Portuguese • Russian • Spanish • Swahili • Thai • Turkish • Vietnamese

Rough Guides on the Internet

www.roughguides.com

Rough Guide Credits

Text Editor:	Olivia Eccleshall
Series Editor:	Mark Ellingham
Editorial:	Martin Dunford, Jonathan Buckley, Jo Mead, Kate Berens, Amanda Tomlin, Ann-Marie Shaw, Paul Gray, Chris Schüler, Helena Smith, Judith Bamber, Kieran Falconer, Orla Duane, Ruth Blackmore, Sophie Martin, Jennifer Dempsey, Geoff Howard, Claire Saunders, Anna Sutton, Gavin Thomas, Alexander Mark Rogers (UK); Andrew Rosenberg, Andrew Taber (US)
Online Editors:	Alan Spicer, Kate Hands (UK); Geronimo Madrid (US)
Production:	Susanne Hillen, Andy Hilliard, Link Hall, Helen Ostick, James Morris, Julia Bovis, Michelle Draycott, Cathy McElhinney
Picture Research:	Eleanor Hill, Louise Boulton
Cartography:	Melissa Flack, Maxine Burke, Nichola Goodliffe, Ed Wright
Finance:	John Fisher, Neeta Mistry, Katy Miesiaczek
Marketing & Publicity:	Richard Trillo, Simon Carloss, Niki Smith, David Wearn (UK); Jean-Marie Kelly, SoRelle Braun (US)
Administration:	Tania Hummel, Charlotte Marriott

Acknowledgements

Thanks to Yvanne Artur of the French Government Tourist Office, James Daunt of Daunt Books, Hamid Saadia, Jerôme Pins, Bettina Daly, Hervé Bethuel, Anaïs and Elodie, and Justine Scott-McCarthy.

At Rough Guides, thanks to Olivia Eccleshall; Jonathan Buckley; Henry Barrkman and Melanie Ross for Basics research; Kingston Presentation Graphics for cartography; Helen Ostick for meticulous typesetting; and Russell Walton for sharp-eyed proofreading.

The publishers and authors have done their best to ensure the accuracy and currency of all information in *The Rough Guide to Paris*; however, they can accept no responsibility for any loss, injury, or inconvenience sustained by any traveller as a result of information or advice contained in the guide.

This seventh edition published April 1999 by Rough Guides Ltd, 62–70 Shorts Gardens, London WC2H 9AB. Reprinted April 2000.
Previous editions published 1987, 1989, 1991, 1993, 1995 and 1997.

Distributed by the Penguin Group:
Penguin Books Ltd, 27 Wrights Lane, London W8 5TZ.
Penguin Books USA Inc, 375 Hudson Street, New York 10014, USA.
Penguin Books Australia Ltd, 487 Maroondah Highway, PO Box 257, Ringwood, Victoria 3134, Australia.
Penguin Books Canada Ltd, 10 Alcorn Avenue, Toronto, Ontario, Canada M4V 1E4.
Penguin Books (NZ) Ltd, 182–190 Wairau Road, Auckland 10, New Zealand.

Printed in England by Clays Ltd, St Ives PLC
Typography and original design by Jonathan Dear and The Crowd Roars.
Illustrations throughout by Edward Briant.

480pp. Includes index.

A catalogue record for this book is available from the British Library.

ISBN 1-85828-407-4

Paris

THE ROUGH GUIDE

Written and researched by
Kate Baillie, Tim Salmon,
Margo Daly and Rachel Kaberry

THE ROUGH GUIDES

Help us update

We've gone to a lot of trouble to ensure that this seventh edition of the *Rough Guide to Paris* is completely up-to-date and accurate. However, things do change: hotels and restaurants come and go, opening hours are notoriously fickle, and prices are extremely volatile. We'd appreciate any suggestions, amendments or contributions for future editions of the guide. We'll credit all letters and send a copy of the next edition (or any other *Rough Guide*) for the best.

Please mark all letters "Rough Guide to Paris Update" and send to: Rough Guides, 62–70 Shorts Gardens, London WC2H 9AB or Rough Guides, 375 Hudson St, 3rd Floor, New York, NY 10014.

Email should be sent to:
mail@roughguides.co.uk

Online updates about Rough Guide titles can be found on our Web site at *www.roughguides.com*

Readers' letters

Many thanks to all the readers who wrote in with comments on the last edition:

Paul Alford, Mary Bailes, Vikki Balchin, Victoria Bayman, Richard Bevans, Stanley Blenkinsop, G. Boyd-Hall, R.H. Bradbery, Mrs R. Britton, Colin D. Byatt, Eric Carlson, Malcolm Churchill, Brian Conroy and Louise Garrett, Desmond Coughlan, Eddy le Couvreur, P.G. Cox, Paola Cremonini, Philip Denton, C.D. Earl, Julie Farquhar, Ann Feltham, Dermot Foley, Christopher Furniss, Timothy Galligan, Peter Grencis, Lois J. Gent, W.K. Hamilton, D. Hanson, Lisa Harkey, Meg Howarth, Rita and Rolfe Herber, Douglas Jackson, J.P.M. Jarvis, Paul Keniger, Nicholas Kennedy, Nicholas Kotarski, N. Kutty, Joanne Lahiff, H.D. Lewis, Lucy Liddell, Deirdre Madden, Malcolm, Ian Mardon, Bill Martin and Sandra Mason, Alan Matthias, Tommy McGibney, Howard Millbank, Gavin Mooney, Richard S. Moore, Andrew and Wendy Morrow, Mr and Mrs Nick Muir, Helen Pearce, Bridget Pegna, Maria Shepherdson, Tim Simpkins, Helen Smith, J.A. Smith, Ashley Spell, Julie Summers, Taku Tada, Alan Tomlinson, Andrew Thomson, Simon Vicary, Maria Warren, Rose White, Brigitte Whitehead, Michael Wilks and Sue Hogg, Bryony Williams, Phil Wood, Bill Wright, Penny Wright, Sue Wright, Alison Yates, and Michael Yorke.

Rough Guides

Travel Guides • Phrasebooks • Music and Reference Guides

We set out to do something different when the first Rough Guide was published in 1982. Mark Ellingham, just out of university, was travelling in Greece. He brought along the popular guides of the day, but found they were all lacking in some way. They were either strong on ruins and museums but went on for pages without mentioning a beach or taverna. Or they were so conscious of the need to save money that they lost sight of Greece's cultural and historical significance. Also, none of the books told him anything about Greece's contemporary life – its politics, its culture, its people, and how they lived.

So with no job in prospect, Mark decided to write his own guidebook, one which aimed to provide practical information that was second to none, detailing the best beaches and the hottest clubs and restaurants, while also giving hard-hitting accounts of every sight, both famous and obscure, and providing up-to-the-minute information on contemporary culture. It was a guide that encouraged independent travellers to find the best of Greece, and was a great success, getting shortlisted for the Thomas Cook travel guide award, and encouraging Mark, along with three friends, to expand the series.

The Rough Guide list grew rapidly and the letters flooded in, indicating a much broader readership than had been anticipated, but one which uniformly appreciated the Rough Guides' mix of practical detail and humour, irreverence and enthusiasm. Things haven't changed. The same four friends who began the series are still the caretakers of the Rough Guide mission today: to provide the most reliable, up-to-date and entertaining information to independent-minded travellers of all ages, on all budgets.

We now publish more than 100 titles and have offices in London and New York. The travel guides are written and researched by a dedicated team of more than 100 authors, based in Britain, Europe, the USA and Australia. We have also created a unique series of phrasebooks to accompany the travel series, along with the acclaimed series of music guides, and a best-selling pocket guide to the Internet and World Wide Web. We also publish comprehensive travel information on our Web site: *www.roughguides.com*

Contents

Part Four: Beyond the City 373

Part Five: Contexts 413

Index 441

List of maps

MAP SYMBOLS

—•—	Railway	⊠	Post office
═══	Main road	ⓘ	Tourist office
───	Minor road	▬	Building
▥▥▥	Steps	✈	Airport
▀▀▀▀	Wall	🅿	Parking
··········	River	Ⓜ	Metro station
-----	Chapter division boundary	Ⓡ	RER station
▬✛	Church	Ⓣ	Tram stop
✡	Synagogue	⫶⫶	Cemetery
		▨	Park

Introduction

I t's little wonder that so many wistful songs have been penned over the years about France's capital. What city experiences could be more seductive than sitting in the gardens of Notre-Dame beneath the drifting cherry blossom, strolling the riverside quais on a summer evening, sipping coffee and cognac in the early hours to the sound of the blues, or exploring the ancient alleyways and cobbled lanes of the Latin Quarter and Montmartre? Paris has no problem living up to the painted images and movie myths with which we're all familiar.

Nor does Paris falter in its reputation as a great hive of artistic and intellectual stimulation. World-class art collections at the Louvre and Musée d'Orsay, as well as the great many smaller museums devoted to individual artists and collectors, underscore an impressive roster of talents linked to the city – Delacroix, Ingres, Seurat, Degas, Van Gogh, Picasso, Braque and Gris are but a few. The new National Library, open to all, embodies a cultural attitude that both proclaims Parisian cleverness and invites you to share in it. And it is only the latest in a line of grand and often ground-breaking modern buildings – the Pompidou Centre, the Arab World Institute, among others – that assert modern architecture and design.

For the greatest work of art has to be the city itself. Two thousand years of shaping and reshaping have resulted in monumental buildings, sweeping avenues, grand esplanades and historic bridges. The fabric of the city has been fortunate throughout its history, spared the ravages of flood and fire and saved from Hitler's intended destruction. And it survives with a sense of continuity and homogeneity, as new sits comfortably against a backdrop of old, old against new – the glass Pyramid against the grand fortress of the Louvre, the Column of Liberty against the Opéra Bastille. Time has acted as judge as buildings once swathed in controversy – the Eiffel Tower, the Sacré-Cœur, the Pompidou Centre – have in their turn become symbols of the city. Yet for all the tremendous pomp and

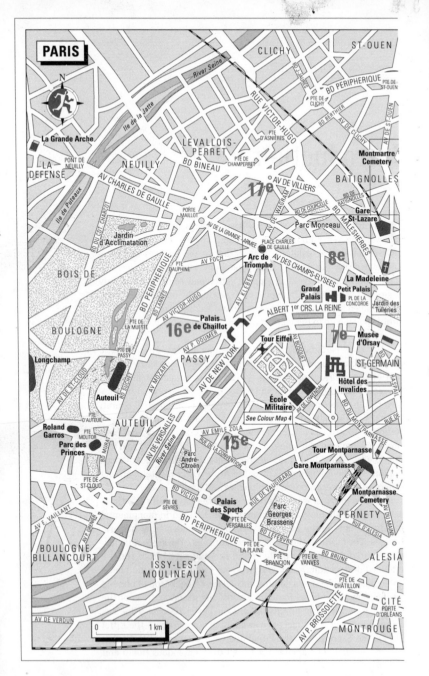

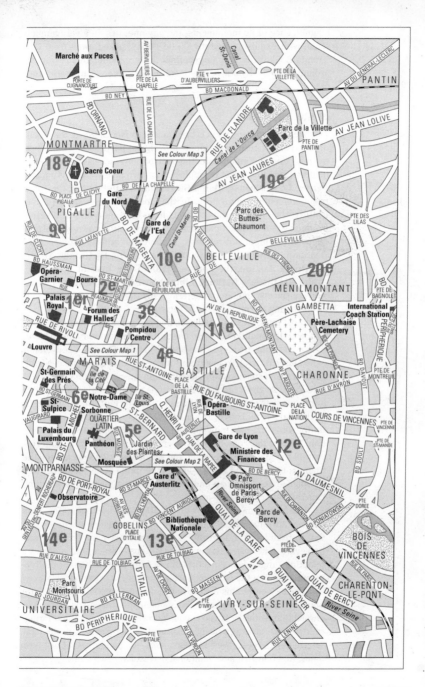

magnificence of its monuments, the city operates on a very human scale, with exquisite, secretive little nooks tucked away from the Grands Boulevards and very definite little communities revolving around games of boules, the local boulangerie, charcuterie and café.

Some highlights

The backdrop of the streets is predominantly Neoclassical, the result of nineteenth-century development designed purposefully to reflect the power of the French state. But each period since has added, more or less discreetly, novel examples of its own styles – with **Auguste Perret**, **Le Corbusier**, **Mallet-Stevens** and **Eiffel** among the early twentieth-century innovators. In the closing decades of the same century, the architectural additions have been on a dramatic scale, producing new and major landmarks, and recasting down-at-heel districts into important centres of cultural and consumer life. **Beaubourg** (the Pompidou Centre), **La Villette**, **La Grande Arche**, the **Opéra Bastille**, the **Louvre Pyramid**, the **Institut du Monde Arabe** and the new **National Library** have all expanded the dimensions of the city, pointing it determinedly towards the future as well as enhancing the monuments of the past.

Paris' **museums and galleries** number among the world's finest, and, with the tradition of state cultural endowment very much alive, their collections are among the best displayed. The art of conversion – the Musée d'Orsay from a train station, the **Cité des Sciences** from abattoirs, and spacious well-lit exhibition spaces from mansions and palaces – has given the great collections unparalleled locations. The Impressionists at the **Musée d'Orsay** and **Marmottan**, the moderns at the **Palais de Tokyo**, the ancients in the **Louvre**, **Picasso** and **Rodin** with their own individual museums – all repay a visit. In addition, there's the contemporary scene in the **commercial galleries** that fill the Marais, St-Germain, the Bastille and the area around the Champs-Élysées, and an ever-expanding range of museums devoted to other areas of human endeavour – science, history, decoration, fashion and performance art.

Few cities can compete with the thousand and one **cafés**, **bars** and **restaurants** – from ultra-modern and designer-signed, to palatial, to traditional and scruffy – that line every Parisian street and boulevard. The restaurant choice is not just French, but includes a tempting range of cuisines that draws from every ethnic origin represented among the city's millions and caters to every pocket.

The city entertains best at night, with a deserved reputation for outstanding **film** and **music**. Paris' cinematic prowess is marked by annual film festivals. Music is equally revered, with nightly offerings of excellent jazz, top-quality classical, avant-garde experimental, international rock, West African *soukous* and French-Caribbean *zouk*, Algerian *raï*, and traditional *chansons*.

If you've time, venture out of the city to one of the worthy attractions detailed in Part Four of the guide. The region surrounding the capital – the Île de France – holds cathedrals and châteaux that bear comparison with anything in Paris itself – **Chartres**, **Versailles** and **Fontainebleau**, for example. An equally accessible excursion from the capital is that most un-French of attractions, **Disneyland Paris**, which is covered in its own separate chapter.

When to go

The best time to visit Paris is largely a question of personal taste. The city has a more reliable **climate** than Britain, with uninterrupted stretches of sun (or rain) year round. However, while it maintains a vaguely southern feel for anyone crossing the English Channel, Mediterranean it is not. Winter temperatures drop well below freezing, with sometimes biting winds. If you're lucky, spring and autumn will be mild and sunny; in summer it can reach the 30s°C (80s°F).

In terms of pure aesthetics, winter sun is the city's most flattering light, when the pale shades of the older buildings become luminescent without any glare, and the lack of trees and greenery is barely relevant. By contrast, Paris in high summer can be choking, with the fumes of congested traffic becoming trapped within the high narrow streets, and the reflected light in the city's open spaces too blinding to enjoy.

If you visit during the **French summer holidays**, from July 15 to the end of August, you will find that large numbers of Parisians have fled the city. It's quieter then, but a lot of shops and restaurants will be closed. There is, too, the **commercial calendar** to consider – fashion shows, trade fairs and the like. Paris hoteliers warn against September and October, and **finding a room** even at the best of times can be problematic. Early spring, autumn if you book ahead, or the midwinter months will be most rewarding.

Basics

Basics

Getting there from Britain

The quickest way of reaching Paris from Britain is by plane, though air travel is now rivalled closely by the Channel Tunnel rail link, which has cut the 340-kilometre London–Paris journey to just three hours. The standard rail- or road-and-sea routes are significantly more affordable, but can be uncomfortable, and if you're going for just a short break, the added journey time could drastically eat into your holiday.

By air

Paris is just fifty minutes' flying time **from London**. Prices are, out of necessity, now highly competitive with those of Eurostar. As often as not, if you live outside London, you'll find it pays to go to the capital and fly on to Paris from there.

Direct flights from British **regional airports** do exist, however, and are detailed below; though they are generally more expensive than fares from London, prices sometimes compare favourably, particularly with British Midland, who fly direct from Leeds-Bradford, and East Midlands.

Shopping for tickets

Deals on flights to Paris change all the time. To find the best ones, you should shop around, ideally a month or so before you plan to leave. A good place to look for **discount fares** to Paris is the classified travel sections of the Saturday editions of the *Independent* and *Daily Telegraph*, and Sunday editions of the *Observer*, *Times* and *Independent*; if you're in London, check the back pages of the listings magazine *Time Out*, or the *Evening Standard* or the free travel mag *TNT*, found outside main-line train stations. **Independent travel specialists** STA Travel and Campus Travel offer deals for students and anyone under 26, or can simply sell a scheduled ticket at a discount price, as can the French agents Nouvelles Frontières. We list contact numbers for these and other travel specialists in the box overleaf.

Charter flights are, in theory, supposed to be sold in conjunction with accommodation, but it's possible just to buy the air ticket at a discount through your travel agent – Nouvelles Frontières are again worth contacting on this front. Bear in mind that any travel agent can sell

---

Airlines

Air France
1st Floor, 10 Warwick St, London W1R;
www.airfrance.fr (☎0181/742 6600).

Brit Air
239 Longbridge House, Gatwick Airport,
Crawley, West Sussex RH6.
Reservations with Air France.

British Airways
156 Regent St, London W1R;
www.britishairways.com (☎0345/222111).

British Midland
Donington Hall, Castle Donington, Derby DE4;
www.iflybritishmidland.com (☎0345/554554).

KLM UK
www.airuk.co.uk (direct sales ☎0990/074074).

Specialist agencies for independent travel

Campus Travel
52 Grosvenor Gardens, London SW1;
www.campustravel.co.uk
(☎0171/730 3402).
Student/youth travel specialists with branches in Birmingham, Brighton, Bristol, Cambridge, Edinburgh, Glasgow, Manchester and Oxford, plus in YHA shops and on university campuses all over Britain.

Council Travel
28a Poland St, London W1V; www.ciee.org
(☎0171/437 7767).
Specialists in student/youth travel, with several offices in France.

Masterfare
19–21 Connaught St, London W2
(☎0171/262 0599).
Discount agent with competitive deals.

Nouvelles Frontières
2–3 Woodstock St, London W1R;
www.nouvelles-frontieres.com
(☎0171/629 7772).
French travel agency.

STA Travel
86 Old Brompton Rd, London SW7;
www.statravel.co.uk
(Telesales ☎0171/361 6161).
Worldwide specialists in low-cost flights and tours for students and under-26s. Offices all

over, including Brighton, Bristol, Cambridge, Glasgow, Leeds, Manchester, Newcastle and Oxford; on university campuses in Aberdeen, Canterbury, Cardiff, Coventry, Durham, Loughborough, Nottingham, Sheffield and Warwick; and abroad.

Thomas Cook
45 Berkeley St, London W1X;
www.tch.thomascook.com
(Telesales ☎0990/666222,
Flights Direct ☎0990/101520).
Long-established one-stop travel agency for package holidays or scheduled flights, with bureau de change (issuing Thomas Cook travellers' cheques), own travel insurance and car rental. Found on High Streets across the UK.

Trailfinders
215 Kensington High St, London W6
(☎0171/937 5400).
One of the best-informed and most efficient agents for independent travellers, with offices in Birmingham, Bristol, Glasgow and Manchester.

Travel Bug
125 Gloucester Rd, London SW7;
www.travel-bug.co.uk
(☎0171/835 2000).
Offers large range of discounted tickets; branch in Manchester.

you a **package deal** with a tour operator (see box opposite), and these can be an exceptional bargain.

British Airways, Air France, Brit Air and British Midland are the **main carriers** to France from Britain, offering scheduled flights and **Apex** (Advance Purchase Excursion) fares, the latter of which must be reserved one or two weeks in advance depending on the airline and must include one Saturday overnight stay. Your return date must be fixed when purchasing, and no subsequent changes are allowed. Of the proliferation of **no-frills airlines** offering cheap scheduled flights to European cities from smaller airports (like Stansted and Luton) via direct sales, so far only KLM UK fly to Paris (from Stansted). There

are no advance purchase conditions with KLM UK, but obviously the earlier you book the greater your chance of taking advantage of special offers.

The snapshot fare prices we quote below include airport taxes of between £12 to £20 depending on airline and routing.

Flights

Flights to Paris can cost as little as £75 from London even with the big airlines – Air France, British Airways and British Midland – though you could expect to pay up to £150 for an economy return. There is no particular peak time when fares are more likely to be inflated, and special offers are frequent. To get the cheaper fares, you simply need to ring around well in advance.

Air France fly to Paris Charles de Gaulle (Paris CDG) five to nine times daily from Heathrow and weekdays only from London City Airport (four flights daily Mon–Fri); also daily from Manchester, Birmingham, Edinburgh and Glasgow. **British Airways** fly to Paris CDG five times daily from Gatwick; and from Heathrow seven times daily to Paris CDG and six times daily to Paris Orly. BA also fly directly to Paris CDG from Newcastle (2 daily), Birmingham (3–5 daily), Manchester (2–5 daily), Glasgow (Mon–Sat 1–2 daily), Aberdeen (2–3 daily) and Edinburgh (2–3 daily). There's also a **British Midland** service to Paris CDG from Heathrow (6–7 daily), and directly from Leeds-Bradford (1–3 daily; fares from £99) and East Midlands (1–4 daily). The cheapest option, flying from Stansted, is to fly **KLM UK**, who head for Paris four times daily (from £75); as the airline operates from virtually all British airports to a variety of destinations, regional passengers can get through flights via Stansted or Amsterdam. A flight from Edinburgh to Paris via Amsterdam, for example (with a 1hr 45min stopover and 2hr 30min flying time), costs around £152.

STA Travel (see box opposite) specializes in flights for **under-26s**; the various airlines all have different policies on discounts for full-time students who are over 26 – British Airways, for example, allows discounts for students under 34. Current return price to Paris CDG is £80. Campus Travel student/youth charter returns to Paris start at £78 with British Midland, but you'll need to arrive and depart midweek. Both STA and Campus Travel also offer limited special offers.

Packages

Any travel agent will be able to provide details of the many operators running **package tours** to Paris, which can work out to be a competitively priced way of travelling, especially if you're flying

---

Packages

The following is a selection from the wide range of companies selling travel plus accommodation packages to Paris from outside London, either on direct regional charter flights, or including the fare to the capital to catch a flight from London in the overall price, or offering special deals on ferry crossings.

Allez France (☎01903/742345). *Two-night Paris packages from all major British airports from £159.*

British Airways Holidays (☎0870/242 4245). *Good for Paris accommodation and flight packages from regional airports.*

French Holiday Service (☎0171/355 4747). *Can book the largest range of package holidays in France.*

Hoverspeed (☎0990/240241). *Two-night packages with car/hovercraft for £100 per person, staying in a two-star hotel.*

Kirker Europe (☎0171/231 3333). *Specialists in quality short breaks in characterful hotels within walking distance of major sights. Departures from most regional airports, with arrival transfers included. Two-night packages from £195–291 depending on accommodation.*

Paris Travel Service (☎01992/456000). *Good for regional flights and rail deals via London. Wide range of packages: for example, flight from Manchester and 3 nights' basic accom-modation for £173, or the same accommodation but travelling with Eurostar from London for £187.*

Sally Short Break Holidays (☎0181/427 4445). *Ferry for car and two adults plus two-star hotel in central Paris from £142 per person for 5 nights' accommodation.*

Time Off (☎0990/846363 or 0345/336622). *Short breaks to Paris by air or Eurostar (and Orient Express packages) in comfortable central accommodation. Two nights in a one-star hotel, travelling by Eurostar, from £151.*

Travelscene Ltd (☎0181/427 4445). *Short breaks in all grades of accommodation, by air, Eurostar or car/shuttle or car/ferry. Two nights in a two-star hotel by Eurostar from £119, by air from £145 and £82 self-drive.*

VFB Holidays (☎01242/240300). *Flights from regional destinations including Newcastle, Glasgow and Bristol. Two nights in two-star hotel plus flight from Gatwick from £235, or £179 by ferry and car.*

from a regional airport (see box on p.5). Some are straightforward travel-plus-hotel affairs, whereas others are city breaks that include meals and set itineraries. A package will often include transfers to and from your hotel or a rental car, which can leave you more time to enjoy your stay. In addition to the addresses in the box overleaf, bear in mind that most of the ferry companies (see box on p.9) also offer their own travel and accommodation deals.

By train

The Channel Tunnel has slashed travelling time by train from London to Paris and has also led to a multitude of cut-rate deals on regular train and ferry or hovercraft fares via Calais, Boulogne or Dieppe.

Eurostar

Eurostar operate high-speed passenger trains daily from London Waterloo to Paris Gare du Nord via Ashford in Kent and the Channel Tunnel in exactly three hours. There are at least fifteen trains a day, on weekdays and Saturday, running from around 5am to just before 6pm (to just before 7pm Fri & Sat), and on Sunday, running from just

after 8am to just before 8pm. There is a separate direct train to Disneyland Paris (one daily summer and school holidays; Sat & Sun only in winter; 3hr)

Expensive first-class **fares** are aimed at business travellers and include meals. Standard Class return fares to Paris range from £79 (weekend day-trip) to £220, but frequently advertised special offers can go as low as £59. Otherwise, the cheapest ticket to Paris is the "Excursion", a return ticket that can be purchased up to 30min before departure and must include a Saturday night, with fixed outward and return dates and no refunds; it's usually less than £99. However, Excursion tickets are limited, and you'll have a greater chance of getting one if you book at least a week or more in advance. A more realistic average price for a high-season ticket with changeable departure and return times, bought close to your departure date, is £115. Return fares to Disneyland Paris range from £89 to £149 for adults, and your kids will set you back £54 each if they're aged 4–11, £79 if they're any older. There are concessions for those under 26 (student discounted tickets are only available from STA, Campus Travel and Wasteels, not directly from Eurostar), over 60, or for holders of an international rail pass.

Useful train and bus addresses in the UK

Eurolines
52 Grosvenor Gardens, London SW1; *www.eurolines.co.uk* (Bookings & enquiries ☎ 0990/143219 or Luton ☎ 01582/404511). *Tickets can also be purchased from any National Express agent:* ☎ 0990/808080.

Eurostar
Waterloo International Station, London SE1 (Telesales☎ 0990/186186). *Tickets can also be purchased at Ashford International Terminal, Kent, and the Eurostar ticket shop, 102–104 Victoria St, London SW1 (Mon–Fri 9am–5.30pm, Sat 9am–3.45pm).*

Eurotrain
Campus Travel, 52 Grosvenor Gardens, London SW1 (☎ 0171/730 3402). *Plus regional Campus Travel offices.*

Eurotunnel
Customer Services Centre (☎ 0990/353535).

Hoverspeed SeaTrain Express
Telesales (☎ 0990/240241).

International Rail Centre
Victoria Station, London SW1(☎ 0990/848848).

Rail Europe (SNCF French Railways)
179 Piccadilly, London W1V. *Same phone as International Rail Centre.*

Wasteels
By Platform 2, Victoria Station, London SW1V (☎ 0171/834 7066).

Note that addresses and telephone numbers may not be in the same location: some airlines and agents use a single telephone-sales number for several offices. Note also that ☎ 0345 and ☎ 0990 are nationwide numbers charged at a local rate.

Tickets can be bought directly by phone from Eurostar (see box opposite), from most travel agents, from all main rail stations in Britain or through SNCF (Société Nationale des Chemins de Fer – the French Railway) in London, from the Waterloo International and Ashford ticket offices and from the Eurostar shop. You can get **through-ticketing** – including the tube journey to Waterloo International – if you travel on GNER or Virgin train services from Manchester and Edinburgh, or on the Alphaline Rail Service from South Wales, Avon and West Wiltshire, for around an extra £30. There's still no sign of the promised direct high-speed Eurostar services from the north of England, Scotland and the Midlands.

Rail and sea

Crossing the Channel **by sea** works out slightly cheaper than using the Channel Tunnel, but takes considerably longer and is obviously less convenient unless you live down south. You can catch one of the many trains from London Victoria to connect with cross-Channel ferries or hovercrafts, with an onward train service on the other side. However, the **Hoverspeed SeaTrain Express** is now the only combined train/sea ticket package to Paris available. Trains depart once daily from London Charing Cross at 8.55am for Folkestone, connecting with a high-speed Seacat to Boulogne, with another train connection to Paris Gare du Nord, arriving at 5.17pm. **Tickets** cost £44 one way or £59 return (no youth price available); return tickets last up to two months.

Rail passes

If you plan to use the rail network to visit other regions of France, there are several **rail passes** you might consider buying.

The **Eurodomino Freedom pass**, available from the International Rail Centre at London Victoria, or from Rail Europe (SNCF), Wasteels or Eurotrain, offers unlimited rail travel through France for any three (£105), five (£145) or ten (£220) days within a calendar month; passengers **under 26** pay £85, £115 and £185 respectively. A **child** fare (4–11-year-olds) is half the adult price. The pass also entitles you to reductions on rail/ferry links to France.

InterRail passes cover eight European "zones" and are available for either 22-day or one-month periods; you must have been resident in Europe for at least six months before you can buy the

pass. The passes for those over 26 have now been extended to cover the same territory as for those under 26 so that the only difference now is the price. France is in the zone including Belgium, the Netherlands and Luxembourg. A 22-day pass to travel this area is £159/£229 (under/over 26); a two-zone pass valid for a month is £209/279; a three-zone, £229/309 and an all-zones £259/349. The pass is available from the same outlets as the Eurodomino (see above) and from STA Travel. InterRail passes do not include travel between Britain and the Continent, although InterRail Pass holders are eligible for discounts on rail travel in Britain and Northern Ireland and cross-Channel ferries.

The InterRail pass and the Eurodomino Freedom Pass both give a discount on the London–Paris Eurostar service.

By bus

Eurolines run regular bus/ferry services from Victoria coach station in London to Paris. Prices are very much lower than for the same journey by train, with adult return fares in July and August and around Christmas currently at £49; off-peak fares are around £5 cheaper. Regional return fares from England and Wales are available, as are student and youth discounts. As well as ordinary tickets on its scheduled coach services, Eurolines offers a **pass** for Europe-wide travel, for either thirty days (over 26 £199; youth pass £159) or sixty days (over 26 £249; youth pass £199). **Tickets** are available from the company direct (see box opposite), from National Express agents and from most High-Street travel agents.

By car

The most convenient way of taking your car across to France is to drive down to the **Channel Tunnel**, load your car on the train shuttle, and be whisked under the Channel in 35 minutes, emerging at Sangatte on the French side, just outside Calais. From there, it's little more than three hours' drive to Paris on the fast autoroutes A26 and A1 (tolls payable); Le Havre is even closer and also offers autoroute all the way.

Car and train

The Channel Tunnel entrance is off the M20 at junction 11A, just outside Folkestone, and the sole operator, **Eurotunnel**, offers a continuous service with up to four departures per hour (only

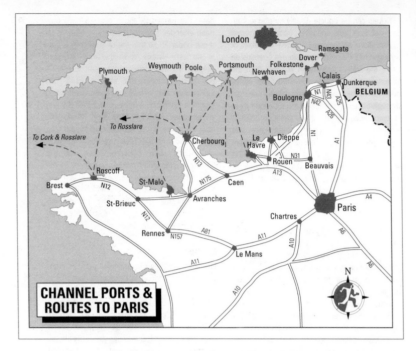

CHANNEL PORTS & ROUTES TO PARIS

one per hour midnight–6am; 24-hour recorded departure info ☎0891/555566). Because of the frequency of the service, you don't have to buy a ticket in advance (though it's advisable to do so in mid-summer or during school holidays; in any case you must arrive at least 25min before departure); the usual loading time is just ten minutes.

Tickets are available through Eurotunnel's Customer Service Centre or from your local travel agent. Fares are calculated per car, not passengers. Rates depend on the time of year, time of day and length of stay (the cheapest ticket is for a day-trip, followed by a five-day return); it's cheaper to travel between 10pm and 6am, while the highest fares are reserved for weekend departures and returns in July and August. As an example, a five-day trip at an off-peak time starts at £95 (passengers included) in the low season and goes up to £135 in the peak period.

By car and ferry/hovercraft

The cheapest cross-Channel options for most car travellers are the **ferry** or **hovercraft** (or high-speed catamaran) links between **Dover and Calais** and **Folkestone and Boulogne**. However, if your starting point is further west than London, it may well be worth heading direct to one of the south coast ports and catching one of the ferries to Normandy or Brittany – Newhaven to Dieppe, Portsmouth to Cherbourg/Le Havre/Caen/St Malo, Weymouth to St Malo, Poole to Cherbourg and Plymouth to Roscoff. If you're coming from the north of England or Scotland, opting for the Hull–Zeebrugge (Belgium) crossing overnight with North Sea Ferries makes economic sense.

Ferry prices vary according to the season and, for motorists, the size of car. The popular Dover–Calais routing costs just over £62 one-way for a car and two adults in low season, but cheaper deals are regularly available. Return prices are substantially cheaper than one-way fares, but generally need to be booked in advance.

You can either contact the companies direct to reserve space in advance (essential at peak season), or any competent travel agent can do it for you. The ferry companies will also often

Ferry companies in Britain

Brittany Ferries	☎ 0990/360360	P&O European Ferries	☎ 0990/980555
Condor Ferries	☎ 01305/761551	P&O North Sea Ferries	☎ 01482/377177
Hoverspeed	☎ 0990/240241 or	P&O Stena Line	☎ 0990/980980
	☎ 0990/595522	Sea France	☎ 0990/711711

offer **special deals** on three-, five- and ten-day returns, or discounts for regular users who own a property abroad. The tour operator **Eurodrive** (☎ 0181/324 4000) can also arrange discounts on ferry crossings and the Eurotunnel for people taking their cars to France, and can book accommodation en route to Paris at competitive rates.

Lift-shares

To arrange a **lift-share**, consult the notice boards of specialist **travellers' bookshops** or put up your own notice. Nomad Books at 781 Fulham Rd, London SW6 (☎ 0171/736 4000) has a particularly good notice board downstairs. The travel magazine **Wanderlust** has a useful "Connections" page worth consulting for possible lift-shares/trav-

el companions; you can also advertise for free (up to 35 words; £5 for a box number if you don't want your address or phone published). Address mail to: Connections, *Wanderlust*, PO Box 1832, Windsor, Berks SL4 6YP.

Coming back, contact the French **ride-share organization** Allostop Provoya, based at 8 rue Rochambeau (on square Montholon), 17009 Paris (Mon–Fri 9am–7.30pm, Sat 9am–1pm & 2–6pm; M° Cadet/Poissonnière; ☎ 01.53.20.42.42, fax 53.20.42.44; *allostop@ecritel.fr*). You'll be asked to pay a registration fee (30F for a journey less than 200km, 50F if less than 400km, 60F if less than 500km and a maximum of 70F if more than 500km; or you can buy a 180F membership card good for eight trips over two years); plus 22 centimes for every kilometre of the journey.

Getting there from Ireland

If you want to fly direct to Paris from Dublin or Belfast, you'll be limited by the choice available, or you may have to catch a routing through London or Amsterdam.

In the **Irish Republic**, Aer Lingus fly direct from Cork and Dublin to Paris CDG (respectively once and five times daily) with a few seats at IR£129 return and a standard fare of IR£199. Ryanair offer three flights daily from Dublin to Beauvais Tillé airport, just under 65km northwest of Paris for £97.50 (a connecting bus costing around IR£5 will take you into the centre of Paris; 1hr). Go Holidays organizes charter flights (from April to September) from Dublin,

---

USEFUL ADDRESSES IN IRELAND

AIRLINES

Aer Lingus
40 O'Connell St, Dublin (☎ 01/844 4777).
46 Castle St, Belfast BT1 (☎ 0645/737747).
www.aerlingus.ie
Branches also in Cork and Limerick.

British Airways
60 Dawson St, Dublin (☎ 1800/626747).

9 Fountain Centre, College St,
Belfast (☎ 0345/222111).
www.british-airways.com

Ryanair
Phoenix House, Conyngham Rd,
Dublin 8 (☎ 01/609 7800).

AGENTS AND OPERATORS

Budget Travel
134 Lower Baggot St,
Dublin (☎ 01/661 1866).

Joe Walsh Tours
8–11 Baggot St, Dublin (☎ 01/876 3053).
31 Castle St, Belfast (☎ 01232/241144).
Discounted flight agent.

NIR Travel
28–30 Great Victoria Street Station, Belfast
(☎ 01232/230671).
InterRail agents.

Thomas Cook
11 Donegall Place, Belfast (☎ 01232/554455).
118 Grafton St, Dublin (☎ 01/677 1721).
Package holiday and flight agent, which can

also arrange travellers' cheques, insurance and car rental.

Trailfinders
4 Dawson St, Dublin 2 (☎ 01/677 7888).
Comprehensive flight and travel agent with deals on hotels, insurance, tours and car rental.

USIT
Aston Quay, O'Connell Bridge,
Dublin (☎ 01/679 8833).
Fountain Centre, College St,
Belfast (☎ 01232/324073).
www.usit.ie
Student and youth specialists. Also branches in Athlone, Coleraine, Cork, Derry, Galway, Jordanstown, Maynooth and Waterford.

Shannon and Cork to Paris from £179 return.
Alternatives via Britain are unlikely to be attractive
considering the additional time factor and the cost
of a flight from Dublin to Britain. For up-to-date
details, contact USIT, specialists in student/youth
travel, or Trailfinders (see box opposite).

In **Northern Ireland**, British Airways fly directly
from Belfast City Airport to Paris Charles de Gaulle.
Otherwise, a routing through London or
Amsterdam is the best option. The Paris Travel
Service (☎01992/456000), based just outside
London, offers package deals including flights
from Belfast.

By car and ferry

The cheapest way of getting to France from
Ireland – though far from the quickest – is by
ferry on three routes: from Cork to Roscoff, and
Rosslare (outside Wexford) to Roscoff and
Cherbourg.

Ferry **prices** vary according to season and, for
motorists, the size of their car; note that return
prices are substantially cheaper but generally

need to be booked in advance. Brittany Ferries
prices vary from around IR£95 to IR£260 for a
small car and two adults one-way; **foot passengers** will pay between IR£30 and IR£60. With
Irish Ferries, the corresponding rates are
IR£99–275 and IR£75. Often ferry companies will
offer special deals on return fares for a specified
period, so check first. You can either contact the
companies direct to reserve space in advance
(essential at peak season if you're driving), or any
competent travel agent at home can do it for
you. For details of routes and fares, contact the
ferry companies listed below.

Getting there from the USA and Canada

Getting to Paris from the USA or Canada is straightforward. The city is the only French transatlantic gateway and has direct flights from more than thirty major North American cities. Nearly a dozen different scheduled airlines operate flights, making Paris also one of the cheapest destinations in Europe.

Shopping for tickets

Apart from special offers, the cheapest ticket on a scheduled flight is a non-refundable **Apex** fare, which normally entails booking 21 days in advance of flying, travelling midweek, and staying for at least seven days.

You can normally cut costs further by going through a specialist flight agent – either a **consolidator**, who buys up blocks of tickets from the airlines and sells them at a discount, or a **discount agent**, who deals in blocks of tickets offloaded by the airlines, and often offers special student and youth fares and a range of other travel-related services such as travel insurance, rail passes, car rental, tours and the like. The independent travel specialists **STA Travel** and **Council Travel** are two of the most reliable agents, but not surprisingly the French group **Nouvelles Frontières** has some good offers.

You'll find other agents advertised in the travel sections of the *New York Times, Washington Post* and *Los Angeles Times*. Bear in mind, though, that penalties for changing your plans can be stiff, and that these companies make their money by dealing in bulk – don't expect them to answer lots of questions. Some agents specialize in **charter flights**, which may be cheaper than anything available on a scheduled flight, but again departure dates are fixed and withdrawal penalties are high (check the refund policy). If you travel a lot, **discount travel clubs** are another option – the annual membership fee may be worth it for benefits such as cut-price air tickets and car rental.

A further possibility is to see if you can arrange a **courier flight**, although the hit-or-miss nature of these makes them most suitable for a single traveller who travels light and has a very flexible schedule. Round-trip journeys to Paris are available for around $350, with last-minute specials (booked within three days of departure) as low as $150. Now Voyager (☎212/431-1616) and Discount Travel International (☎212/362-3636) arrange such flights to Europe from JFK, Newark and Houston. Tickets are issued on a first-come, first-served basis, and there's no guarantee that the Paris route will be available at the specific time you want.

Don't automatically assume that tickets purchased through a travel specialist will be cheapest – once you get a quote, check with the airlines and you may turn up an even better deal. Be advised also that the pool of travel companies is swimming with sharks – exercise caution and never deal with a company that demands cash up front or refuses to accept payment by credit card.

Fares are dependent on **season**, and are highest from around early June to the end of August, when everyone wants to travel; they drop during the "shoulder" seasons, September–October and April–May, and you'll get the best deals during the low season, November to March (excluding

---

Discount agents, consolidators and travel clubs in North America

Council Travel 205 E 42nd St, New York, NY 10017 (☎1-800/226-8624).
Nationwide US student travel organization with branches in 40 US cities, including Austin, Boston, Chicago, Minneapolis, San Francisco, Seattle, Washington DC.

Travel Savings Club 4501 Forbes Blvd, Lanham, MD 20706 (☎1-800/444-9800).
Discount travel club.

Flight Centre S Granville Street, Vancouver (☎1-604/739-9539).
Discount airfares from a choice of Canadian cities.

High Adventure Travel Inc. 253 Sacramento St, Suite 600, San Francisco, CA 94111 (☎1-800/428-8735) *www.highadv.com Round-the-world ticket specialists.*

Interworld Travel 800 Douglass Rd, Miami, FL 33134 (☎305/443-4929).
Consolidator.

New Frontiers/Nouvelles Frontières 12 E 33rd St, New York, NY 10016 (☎800/366-6387). 1001 Sherbrook East, Suite 720, Montréal, H2L 1L3 (☎514/526-8444).
French discount travel firm; also markets

charters to Paris and Lyon. Other branches in LA, San Francisco and Québec City.

STA Travel 10 Downing St, New York, NY 10014 (☎1-800/777-0112 or 212/627-3111).
Worldwide specialist in independent travel with offices in the Los Angeles, San Francisco and Boston areas. French branches in Paris and Grenoble.

Travac Tours 989 Sixth Ave, New York, NY 10018 (☎1-800/872-8800).
Consolidator and charter broker.

Travel Cuts 187 College St, Toronto, ON M5T 1P7 (☎416/979-2406).
Canadian student travel organization with branches all over the country.

Travelers Advantage 3033 S Parker Rd, Suite 900, Aurora, CO 80014 (☎1-800/548-1116).
Discount travel club.

Unitravel 1177 N Warson Rd, St Louis, MO 63132 (☎1-800/325-2222).
Consolidator.

Worldwide Discount Travel Club 1674 Meridian Ave, Miami Beach, FL 33139 (☎305/534-2082).
Discount travel club.

Christmas). Note that Friday, Saturday and Sunday travel tends to carry a premium.

Flights from the USA

The most comprehensive range of flights from the US is offered by **Air France**, the French national carrier, which flies non-stop to Charles de Gaulle airport from selected cities (see box overleaf), in most instances daily. However, Air France does tend to be expensive.

The **major American competitors** tend to be cheaper, but offer fewer non-stop routes. Of those offering non-stop routes, American, TWA, Delta and United have the biggest range. American flies to Paris Orly non-stop from Dallas, Miami and Chicago and has good connections from cities all over the country. TWA flies non-stop to Paris Charles de Gaulle from St Louis and JFK; Delta flies non-stop from Atlanta, New York and Cincinatti; and United flies non-stop from San Francisco, Chicago and Washington DC. AOM French Airlines offers the best rate non-stop from

LA; Tower Air offer the best non-stop rate from New York. For details of other airlines plying the US to Paris route, see the box overleaf.

The lowest discounted scheduled fares you're likely to get in low/high season flying midweek to Paris are US$473/900 from Chicago, US$500/814 from Houston, US$575/947 from Los Angeles, US$395/757 from New York and US$490/767 from Washington DC.

Flights from Canada

The strong links between France and Québec's Francophone community ensure regular air services from Canada to Paris. Air France and Air Canada offer **non-stop services** to Paris from the major Canadian cities. There are also some excellent **charter deals**: Air Transit Holidays, a Canadian charter operation, is worth trying for its wide selection of non-stop summer and shoulder-season flights to Paris from Vancouver and Toronto. (Toronto–Paris round-trip, for instance, is CDN$449–660; Vancouver–Paris CDN$759–1000.)

Airlines in North America

Only gateway cities are listed for each airline; other routings are always possible using connecting flights.

Air Canada (☎1-800/776-3000; ☎1-800/555-1212 in Canada). *Daily non-stop to Paris from Toronto and Montréal. Direct flights from Vancouver.*

Air France (☎1-800/237-2747; ☎1-800/667-2747 in Canada). *Non-stop to Paris from Atlanta, Boston, Chicago, Cincinatti, Houston, Los Angeles, Miami, Montréal, New York (JFK and Newark), San Francisco, Toronto and Washington DC.*

American Airlines (☎1-800/433-7300). *Daily non-stop to Paris from Chicago, Dallas and Miami.*

AOM French Airlines (☎1-310/338-9613). *Non-stop from Los Angeles to Paris three to five times a week depending on the season.*

British Airways (☎1-800/247-9297). *From Montréal, Toronto and Vancouver, and many US cities, to London, with connections to Paris and Nice.*

Continental Airlines (☎1-800/231-0856). *Daily non-stop to Paris from New York and Houston.*

Delta Airlines (☎1-800/241-4141; ☎1-800/555-1212 in Canada). *Daily non-stop to Paris from New York, Cincinnati and Atlanta.*

Iceland Air (☎1-800/223-5500). *Baltimore (BWI), Boston, Halifax, Minneapolis/St Paul, New York (JFK) and Orlando to Reykjavik and on to Paris.*

KLM (☎1-800/374-7747). *Many North American cities to Amsterdam, with connections to Paris, Lyon, Marseille and Nice among other French destinations.*

Northwest Airlines (☎1-800/447-4747). *Detroit to Paris.*

PIA Pakistan International Airways (☎1-800/221-2552). *Non-stop service from New York to Paris three to five times a week.*

Tower Air (☎1-800/221-2500). *Daily non-stop from New York to Paris.*

TWA (☎1-800/982-4141). *Daily non-stop from New York and St Louis to Paris.*

United Airlines (☎1-800/538-2929). *Daily non-stop to Paris from Chicago, San Francisco and Washington DC.*

US Airways (☎1-800/622-1015). *Daily non-stop from Philadelphia to Paris.*

Virgin Atlantic Airways (☎1-800/862-8621). *Flights to London from Boston, JFK, Miami, Newark, Orlando and Washington DC.*

Canada 3000/Fiesta West is another charter company and good source of information. The lowest discounted scheduled fares for midweek travel to Paris will be around CDN$825/1249 from Montréal and Toronto, and CDN$1115/1639 from Vancouver and CDN$1003/1353 from Halifax on Iceland Air. **Travel Cuts** and **Nouvelles Frontières** are the most likely sources of good-value discounted seats; call for details as flights vary from season to season.

Package tours

Dozens of tour operators offer reasonably priced packages to Paris and the surrounding countryside. Many can put together very **flexible deals**, sometimes amounting to no more than a flight and accommodation; if you're planning to travel in moderate or luxurious style, and especially if your trip is geared around special interests, such

packages can work out cheaper than the same arrangements made on arrival. A **tour** is inevitably more confining than independent travel, but it can help you make the most of time if you're on a tight schedule; and if Paris is your first stop on a longer trip, a tour can ensure a worry-free first few days while you're finding your feet.

Many **airlines** have reasonably priced packages including round-trip airfare, hotel, some sightseeing tours and, in the case of fly-drive packages, a rental car. Delta Airlines offers a seven-day fly-drive package to Paris starting at US$628 for New York departures. British Airways has a seven-day Paris tour starting at US$771, including transatlantic airfare via London, hotels and sightseeing. American Airlines offer a seven-day England–France fly-drive package, including Channel Tunnel crossing, from US$1016 per person for hotel, breakfast, rental car and Channel

Tour operators in North America

Abercrombie & Kent (☎1-800/323-7308). *Canal and barge journeys, walking tours.*

American Airlines Fly Away Vacations (☎1-800/321-2121). *Package tours, fly-drive programmes.*

British Airways Holidays (☎1-800/359-8722). *Package tours, fly-drive programmes.*

Canada 3000/Fiesta West *Discount charter flights, cars, hotels, package tours through BCAA TeleCentre (☎1-800/663-1956 in Canada) or travel agents.*

CBT Bicycle Tours (☎1-800/736-BIKE). *European bike tours, some starting or ending in Paris.*

Contiki Tours (☎1-800/CONTIKI). *European vacations (most including Paris) for under-35s.*

Cosmos Tourama (☎1-800/221-0090). *Paris city-breaks.*

Delta Vacations (☎1-800/872-7786). *Packages, escorted tours and fly-drive programmes.*

EC Tours (☎1-800/388-0877). *City packages.*

ETT Tours (☎1-800/551-2085). *Independent tours and city packages.*

France Vacations (☎1-800/332-5332). *Flight/hotel packages through AOM French Airlines.*

The French Experience (☎1-800/28-FRANCE). *Self-drive tours, apartment rentals.*

International Study Tours (☎1-800/833-2111). *Culture/art tours.*

New Frontiers/Nouvelles Frontières (☎1-800/366-6387). *City packages and à la carte accommodation.*

---

tickets. American also has a variety of hotel/sightseeing packages (airfare from the US not included), such as its seven-day Paris package for US$800, and the "Paris Stopover", which starts at US$52 per person for one night's hotel and breakfast. AOM French Airlines offers a six-day Paris package for $659, including return airfare from Los Angeles, hotels and breakfast.

For other possibilities, see the box above or make enquiries at a travel agent (remember, bookings made through a travel agent cost no more than going through the tour operator).

Getting there from Australia and New Zealand

Most people travelling to Paris from Australia and New Zealand will choose to travel via London. There are, however, alternative stopover points in Europe, often available at economical fares. Most airlines can add on a Paris leg to any Australia/New Zealand–Europe ticket.

Fares to Paris vary according to the **season**, and seasons vary slightly depending on the airline, but in general, low season lasts from mid-January to the end of February, and from 1 October to the end of November; high season is from mid-May to the end of August, and from the beginning of December to mid-January. Seasonal fare increases are between A/NZ$200–400.

From Australia

There's a host of airlines operating a service between major cities in **Australia** via their home ports to Paris. **Discount** agents should be able to get you at least ten percent off the following low-season published fares. Conditions may apply to the following such as booking three months in advance: Alitalia/Qantas (via Milan) A$1395; KLM (via Amsterdam), JAL (Tokyo), Lufthansa (Frankfurt), Olympic (Athens) A$1530; Thai International (Bangkok), Singapore Airlines, Qantas A$1670; Thai A$1792 (2 stops); British Airways (via

---

Airlines in Australia and New Zealand

Aeroflot Level 24/44 Market St, Sydney (☎02/9262 2233). *No NZ office.*

Air France 64 York St, Sydney (☎02/9244 2100); 2nd Floor, Dataset House, 143 Nelson St Auckland (☎09/303 3521); 6th Floor, Trustbank Building, 229 Queen St, Auckland (☎09/379 4457).

British Airways Level 26, 201 Kent St, Sydney (☎02/9258 3300); 154 Queen St, Auckland (☎09/356 8690).

Cathay Pacific Level 12, 8 Spring St, Sydney (☎02/9931 5500; Local-call rate ☎13/1747); 11f Arthur Andersen Tower, 205–209 Queen St, Auckland (☎09/379 0861).

Garuda 55 Hunter St, Sydney (☎02/9334 9944); 120 Albert St, Auckland (☎09/366 1855).

JAL Floor 14, Darling Park, 201 Sussex St, Sydney (☎02/9272 1111); Floor 12, Westpac

Tower, 120 Albert St, Auckland (☎09/379 9906).

KLM 5 Elizabeth St, Sydney (☎02/9231 6333; Toll-free ☎1800/505 747). *No NZ office.*

Lufthansa/Lauda-air 143 Macquarie St, Sydney (☎1300/655 727); Lufthansa House, 36 Kitchener St, Auckland (☎09/303 1529).

Malaysian Airlines 16 Spring St, Sydney (Local-call rate ☎13/2627); Floor 12, Swanson Centre, 12–26 Swanson St, Auckland (☎09/373 2741).

Qantas Chifley Square, cnr Hunter & Phillip streets, Sydney (☎13/1211); Qantas House, 154 Queen St, Auckland (☎09/357 8900).

Thai Airways 75–77 Pitt St, Sydney (☎1300/651 960); Kensington Swan Building, 22 Fanshawe St, Auckland (☎09/377 3886).

London) A\$1885; Air France (on to 87 destinations within France) A\$1903; Qantas/Air France A\$1980 (3 stops).

Airpasses, coupons and discounts on further flights within Europe vary with airlines, but the basic rules are that they must be pre-booked with the main ticket, are valid for three months, and are available only with a return fare with the one airline – for example, you have to fly to France with British Airways alone to be eligible for their airpass deals. Air France offers a **Euroflyer** for use in France and Europe at A\$120 each flight; British Airways have a zone system: around A\$135 for each flight within France, A\$200 each for single flights to and

around Germany, Italy and Belgium. Both airlines also arrange **fly-drive packages**; check with an agent for current deals as prices are variable.

From New Zealand

From Auckland, the best discounted deals are: Japanese Airlines (NZ\$2200, with an overnight stop in Tokyo), Malaysian Airlines (NZ\$2300) and Garuda (NZ\$2250). For **stopovers** in Europe, British Airways charge NZ\$2399 via London; Qantas/Alitalia are slightly less at NZ\$2300 via Rome and London. For **side-trips** within Europe, Qantas/Lufthansa have a four-coupon deal on a six-month fare for NZ\$2600.

Red tape and visas

Citizens of EU (European Union) countries, and thirty-one other countries, including Canada, the United States, Australia, New Zealand and

Norway, do not need any sort of visa to enter France, and can stay for up to ninety days. All other passport holders must obtain a visa before arrival. Obtaining a visa from your nearest French consulate is fairly automatic, but check their hours before turning up, and leave plenty of time, since there are often queues (particularly in London in summer).

Three types of **visa** are currently issued: a transit visa, valid for two months; a short-stay (*court séjour*) visa, valid for ninety days after the date of issue and good for multiple entries; and a long-stay (*long séjour*) visa, which allows for multiple stays of ninety days over three years, but which is issued only after an examination of an individual's circumstances. EU citizens (or other non-visa citizens) who **stay longer than three months** are officially supposed to apply for a **Carte de Séjour**,

---

French embassies and consulates overseas

Australia
492 St Kilda Rd, Melbourne, VIC 3001 (☎03/9820 0921); 31 Market St, Sydney, NSW 2000 (☎02/9261 5779).

Canada
Embassy: 42 Promenade Sussex, Ottawa, ON K1M 2C9 (☎613/789 1795).

Consulates: 1 place Ville Marie, Bureau 22601, Montréal, Québec H3B 4S3 (☎514/878-4385); 25 rue St-Louis, Québec QC G1R 3Y8 (☎418/694-2294); 130 Bloor St W, Suite 400, Toronto, ON M5S 1N5 (☎416/925-80441); 1201-736 Granville St, Vancouver, BC V6Z 1H9 (☎604/681-4345); 250 Lutz St, PO Box 1109, Moncton, New Brunswick, EIC 8B6 (☎506/857-4191).

Ireland
36 Ailesbury Road, Dublin 4 (☎01/260 1666).

New Zealand
1 Williston St, PO Box 1695, Wellington (☎04/472 0200).

UK
French Consulate General (visas section) 6a Cromwell Place, London SW7 (☎0171/838 2051 or premium rate ☎0891/887733). *Visa applications Mon–Fri 9–10am & 1.30–2.30pm.* 11 Randolph Crescent, Edinburgh (☎0131/220 6324 or premium rate ☎0891/600215). *Visa applications Mon–Fri 9.30am–1pm.*

USA
Embassy: 4101 Reservoir Rd NW, Washington, DC 20007 (☎202/944-6000).

Consulates: Park Square Building, Suite 750, 31 St James Ave, Boston, MA 02116 (☎617/542-7374); 737 N Michigan Ave, Olympia Centre, Suite 2020, Chicago, IL 60611 (☎312/787-5360); 2727 Allen Parkway, Suite 976, Houston, TX 77019 (☎713/528-2181); 10990 Wilshire Boulevard, Suite 300, Los Angeles, CA 90024 (☎310/235-3200); 934 Fifth Ave, New York, NY 10021 (☎212/606-3689); One Biscayne Tower, Suite 1710, 2 Biscayne Blvd, Miami, FL 33131 (☎305/372-9799); 540 Bush St, San Francisco, CA 94108 (☎415/397-4330); 4101 Reservoir Rd NW, Washington, DC 20007 (☎202/944-6000).

---

for which you'll have to show proof of income at least equal to the minimum wage (at least 6700F per month). However, EU passports are rarely stamped, so there is no evidence of how long you've been in the country. If your passport does get stamped, you can cross the border – to Belgium or Germany, for example – and re-enter for another ninety days legitimately.

Customs

With the Single European Market you can bring in and take out most things as long as you have paid tax on them in an **EU country** and they are for personal consumption. Customs may be suspicious if they think you are going to resell goods (or break the chassis of your car). Limits still apply to drink and tobacco bought in duty-free shops: 200 cigarettes, 250g tobacco or 50 cigars; one litre of spirits or two litres of fortified wine, or two litres of sparkling wine; two litres of table wine; 50gm of perfume and 250ml of toilet water.

Americans can bring home up to $400 worth of goods purchased overseas duty-free, including a litre of alcohol or wine, 200 cigarettes and 100 cigars. If you carry back between $400 and $1000 worth of stuff you'll have to go through the red lane and pay ten percent of the value in duty; above $1000 and the duty depends on the items. For the full rundown on customs

niceties, request a copy of the pamphlet *Know Before You Go* from the US Customs Service, PO Box 7407, Washington, DC 20044. Their information line (☎ 202/927-6724) lists other publications for travellers, but they must be requested by mail.

Canadians are exempt from paying duty on up to $300 worth of goods after spending seven days out of the country (or $100 worth after a trip lasting two to six days). Those goods may include up to 1 litre of spirits or wine, 24 355ml bottles of beer and 200 cigarettes. For more details, call ☎ 1-800/461-9999 and request a copy of the government's *I Declare* brochure.

Travellers returning to **Australia** can bring in $400 worth of "gifts" duty-free (for under-18s this is reduced to $200), not including personal purchases such as clothing which don't incur duty, plus 250 cigarettes or 250g of tobacco and one bottle of alcohol (beer, wine or spirits). **New Zealand** permits $700 worth of "gifts", plus six 750ml bottles of wine or beer (4.5 litres in all), 1125ml of spirits; 200 cigarettes, or 250g tobacco, or 50 cigars, or a mixture of these not exceeding 250g. In both countries, certain goods must be declared for inspection and may be prohibited: these include cordless phones purchased overseas, artefacts containing wood or other plant material, and foodstuffs.

Health and insurance

TRAVEL INSURANCE COMPANIES AND AGENTS

Citizens of all EU and Scandinavian countries are entitled to take advantage of French health services under the same terms as residents, if they have the correct documentation. British citizens need form E111, available from post offices. Non-EU citizens have to pay for most medical attention and are strongly advised to take out some form of travel insurance.

Under the French Social Security system, every hospital visit, doctor's consultation and pre-scribed medicine incurs a charge. Although all employed French citizens are entitled to a refund of 70–75 percent of their medical and dental expenses, this can still leave a hefty shortfall, especially after a stay in hospital (accident victims even have to pay for the ambulance that takes them there).

To find a **doctor**, stop at any *pharmacie* and ask for an address, or look under Médecins Qualifiés in the Yellow Pages of the Parisian phone directory. To qualify for Social Security refunds, make sure the doctor is a médecin conventionné. An average consultation fee would be between 110F and 150F. You will be given a Feuille de Soins (statement of treatment) for later documentation of insurance claims. Prescriptions should be taken to a *pharmacie* where they must be paid for; the medicines will have little stickers (*vignettes*) attached to them, which you must remove and stick to your Feuille de Soins, together with the prescription itself. **Centre Médical Europe** (44 rue Amsterdam, 9e; M° Liège; ☎01.42.81.93.33; Mon–Fri 8am–7pm, Sat 8am–6pm) has a variety of different practitioners charging low consultation fees.

TRAVEL INSURANCE COMPANIES AND AGENTS

BRITAIN AND IRELAND

Age Concern (☎01883/346964)

American Express (☎0800/700737)

Campus Travel or **STA** in Britain (see box on p.4 for addresses) and **USIT** in Ireland (see box, p.10)

Columbus Travel Insurance (☎0171/375 0011)

Endsleigh Insurance (☎0171/436 4451)

Frizzell Insurance (☎01202/292333)

Marcus Hearne & Co (☎0171/739 3444)

Snowcard Insurance Services (☎01327/262805)

Worldwide (☎01892/833 338)

USA AND CANADA

Access America (☎1-800/284-8300)

Carefree Travel Insurance (☎1-800/323-3149)

International Student Insurance Service (ISIS) – sold by STA Travel (☎1-800/777-0112)

Travel Assistance International (☎1-800/821-2828)

Travel Guard (☎1-800/826-1300)

Travel Insurance Services (☎1-800/937-1387)

AUSTRALIA AND NEW ZEALAND

Australian Federation of Travel Agents (☎02/9264 3299)

Cover More (☎02/9202 8000)

Ready Plan (☎1300/555 017)

In serious emergencies you will always be admitted to the nearest **hospital** (*hôpital*), either under your own power or by ambulance, which even French citizens must pay for; many people call the fire brigade (*pompiers*) instead, who are equipped to deal with medical emergencies and are the fastest and most reliable emergency service. For a list of phone numbers to call in a **medical emergency**, consult the Directory of this *Guide*, p.368.

As getting a refund entails a complicated bureaucratic procedure, and in any case does not cover the full cost of treatment, it's always a better idea to take out ordinary **travel insurance**, which generally allows full reimbursement, less the first few pounds or dollars of every claim, and also covers the cost of repatriation.

If you're travelling in your own car, you may want to have breakdown cover which includes **personal insurance**.

British cover

When considering any insurance policy, check carefully that it will cover you in case of an accident. Note also that very few insurers will arrange on-the-spot payments in the event of a major expense or loss; you will usually be reimbursed only after going home. In all cases of loss or theft of goods, claims can only be dealt with if a report is made to the local police (the Commissariat de Police) within 24hr and a copy of the report (*constat de vol*) sent with the claim.

Most policies are broadly similar, but before signing up you should always read the small print to see what's covered: often money and credit cards are covered only if stolen from your person. If you have any other insurance policies – house and contents insurance, for example – you'll find some of the optional extra cover in travel insurance only duplicates what you already have at home.

Bank and **credit cards** often have certain levels of medical or other insurance included, especially if you use them to pay for your trip. This can be quite comprehensive, anticipating anything from lost or stolen baggage and missed connections to charter companies going bankrupt. Barclaycard, for example, automatically insures anything you've purchased with the card for 100 days, gives travel insurance if you pay for your holiday with the card and has a free International Rescue Service of legal advice, translation assistance, money transfer, contacting relatives and accompanying children home.

Nearly all travel agents and tour operators will offer you insurance when you book your flight or holiday, and some will insist you take it. There are moves, however, to ban travel packages that compel you to take the agents' own policy. If you shop around with banks or **specialist insurance companies**, you can often find better value travel insurance schemes, such as those offered by Columbus Travel Insurance, who offer a month's cover in Europe from around £26.50. (ISIS policies, from STA Travel or branches of Endsleigh Insurance, are also usually good value.)

North American cover

Before buying an insurance policy, check that you're not already covered. **Canadian** provincial health plans typically provide some overseas medical coverage, although they are unlikely to pick up the full tab in the event of a mishap. Holders of official **student and youth cards** (see p.27) are entitled to accident coverage and hospital inpatient benefits – the annual membership is far less than the cost of comparable insurance. **Students** may also find that their student health coverage extends during the vacations and for one term beyond the date of last enrolment. Bank and credit cards (particularly American Express) often provide certain levels of medical or other insurance, and travel insurance may also be included if you use a major credit or charge card to pay for your trip. **Homeowners'** or **renters' insurance** often covers theft or loss of documents, money and valuables while overseas.

After exhausting the possibilities above, you might want to contact a specialist travel insurance company; your travel agent can usually recommend one (or see the box opposite). Policies vary: some are comprehensive, while others cover only certain risks (accidents, illnesses, delayed or lost luggage, cancelled flights, etc). In particular, ask whether the policy pays medical costs up front or reimburses you later, and whether it provides for medical evacuation to your home country. For policies that include lost or stolen luggage, check exactly what is and isn't covered, and make sure the per-article limit will cover your most valuable possession.

The best premiums are usually to be had through student/youth travel agencies. ISIS policies, for example, cost US$60 for fifteen days,

Alternative medicine

Acupuncture

Association Française d'Acupuncture, 3 rue de l'Arrivée, 15ᵉ (Mᵒ Montparnasse-Bienvenüe; ☎01.43.20.26.26).

Chiropractic

American Chiropractice Center, 119 rue de l'Université, 7ᵉ (Mᵒ Invalides; ☎01.45.51.38.38).

Homeopathy

Académie d'Homéopathie et de Médecines Douces, 2 rue d'Isly, 8ᵉ (Mᵒ St-Lazare; ☎01.43.87.60.33).

Most pharmacies sell homeopathic medicines

US$110 for a month, US$165 for two months, US$665 for a year.

Most North American travel policies apply only to items lost, stolen or damaged while in the custody of an identifiable, responsible third party – hotel porter, airline, luggage consignment, etc. Even in these cases you will have to contact the local police within a certain time limit to have a complete report made out so that your insurer can process the claim.

Australasian cover

Travel insurance is put together by the airlines and travel agent groups such as UTAG, AFTA, Cover More and Ready Plan in conjunction with insurance companies. They are all similar in premium and coverage, however Ready Plan give the best value for money coverage. A typical policy will cost A$190/NZ$220 for a month, A$270/NZ$320 for two months and A$330/NZ$400 for three months.

Disabled travellers

Paris has no special reputation for providing ease of access or facilities for disabled travellers. The way cars park on pavements makes wheelchair travel a nightmare, and the métro system has endless flights of steps. Museums, however, are getting much better; the Cité des Sciences has won European awards for its accessibility to those with sight, hearing and mobility disabilities. The Comédie Française, the Théâtre National de l'Odéon, the planetarium at the Palais de la Découverte and the Studio St-Séverin cinema have special equipment into which to plug hearing aids.

Up-to-date **information** is best obtained from organizations at home before you leave or from the French disability organizations (see box opposite) – the Paris tourist office touts various unreliable and dated guides.

Access in Paris by Gordon Couch and Ben Roberts, published in Britain by Quiller Press and available from the London-based organization

RADAR (£6.95; post & packing £4 extra), is a thorough **guide** to accommodation, monuments, museums, restaurants and travel to the city. The Holiday Care Service has an information sheet on accessible **accommodation** in France.

Eurostar offers an excellent deal for wheelchair-users. There are two spaces in the First Class carriages for wheelchairs, each with an accompanying seat for a companion. **Fares** are a flat rate £72 return from Paris and London (with fully flexible dates) and though it's not absolutely guaranteed, you will normally get the First Class meal as well. No advance bookings are necessary, though the limited spaces make it wise to reserve ahead and arrange the special assistance which Eurostar offer at either end. Most of the cross-Channel **ferry companies** offer good facilities, though up-to-date information about access is difficult to obtain. As for **airlines**, British Airways has a better-than-average record for treatment of disabled passengers, and from North America,

Useful contacts for travellers with a disability

Paris

APF (Association des Paralysés de France) 17 bd Auguste-Blanqui, 13ᵉ (☎01.40.78.69.00). *A national organization providing useful information including lists of new and accessible accommodation. Their guide* Où Ferons-Nous Étape *(Where Will We Stay), costing 85F, provides details of accessible places to stay throughout France, and is available at the office or by post to a French address.*

CNRH (Comité National Français de Liaison pour la Réadaptation des Handicapés), 236bis rue Tolbiac, 13ᵉ (☎01.53.80.66.66). *Information service whose various useful guides include* Paris-Île de France: Guide Touristique pour les Personnes à Mobilitée Réduite, *available in English for 60F.*

UK

Holiday Care Service 2nd Floor, Imperial Building, Victoria Rd, Horley, Surrey RH6 (☎01293/774535, fax 784647; minicom ☎01293/776943). *Information on all aspects of travel, including free lists of accessible accommodation in France, plus details about financial help for holidays.*

RADAR (Royal Association for Disability and Rehabilitation) 12 City Forum, 250 City Rd, London EC1(☎0171/250 3222,

fax 0171/250 0212; minicom ☎0171/250 4119). *A good source of advice on travel abroad, they produce a guide on European holidays (£5 inc. p&p) alternate years. You can also obtain the useful publication* Access in Paris *(see opposite) through them.*

Tripscope The Courtyard, Evelyn Rd, London W4 (☎0181/994 9294). *Phone-in travel information and advice service for those with mobility difficulties.*

North America

Twin Peaks Press Box 129, Vancouver, WA 98666 (☎360/694-2462 or 1-800/637-2256). *Publishes excellent travel guides including the* Directory of Travel Agencies for the Disabled *(US$19.95).*

Australia and New Zealand

ACROD (Australian Council for Rehabilitation of the Disabled), PO Box 60, Curtin, ACT 2605, (☎02/6282 4333); 24 Cabarita Rd, Cabarita, NSW 2137 (☎02/9743 2699). *Provides lists of travel agencies and tour operators for people with disabilities.*

Disabled Persons Assembly, PO Box 10, 138 The Terrace, Wellington (☎04/472 2626). *Provides lists of travel agencies and tour operators for people with disabilities.*

Virgin and Air Canada come out tops in terms of disability awareness (and seating arrangements) and might be worth contacting first for any information they can provide.

The French Government Tourist Office in London has a free booklet on disabled access to hotels, called *Paris, Île de France: Hôtels et Residences de Tourisme*. For more information, plus first-hand accounts by disabled travellers to France, see the Rough Guide special *Able to Travel/Nothing Ventured*, and contact the organizations below.

Getting around

If you are physically handicapped, **taxis** are obliged by law to carry you and to help you into the vehicle, also to carry your guide dog if you are blind. The suburban agencies **GiHP** (Mon–Fri 7.30am–8pm; ☎01.41.83.15.15) and **Le Kangourou** (Mon–Fri 9am–6pm; ☎01.47.08.93.50) have taxicabs and

minibuses fully adapted to wheelchairs; 24-hour advance notice is usually needed.

For travel on the **buses**, **métro** or **RER**, the RATP offers accompanied journeys for disabled people not in wheelchairs – Service d'Accompagnement – which operates Monday to Friday from 8am to 6pm (and costs more than 60F an hour). You have to book your minder on ☎01.42.71.20.53 or 01.48.93.06.23 a day in advance. Blind passengers can request a free companion from the volunteer organization Auxiliaires des Aveugles (☎01.43.06.39.38).

For **wheelchair-users**, some RER stations are accessible, though only a very few, like Vincennes and Marne-la-Vallée (for Disneyland), can be used autonomously, while others, including Châtelet-les-Halles, Denfert-Rochereau, Gare de Lyon and Grande Arche de la Défense require an official to work the lift for you. The new

Météor métro line (14) opened in October 1998 and is designed to be easily accessible by all. One bus line, #20, linking Gare de Lyon and Gare St-Lazare, via Opéra, has specially designed, lower floors for wheelchair-users. A leaflet, *Handicaps et Déplacements en Région Île-de-France*, outlining such transport details is available free at main métro/RER stations. A Braille métro **map** is obtainable from L'Association Valentin Haüy (AVH), 5 rue Duroc, 7ᵉ (☎01.44.49.27.27). Aihrop (Mon–Fri 8am–noon & 1.30–6pm; ☎01.40.24.34.76) arranges transport to and from the airports and within the city.

Cars with hand controls can be rented from Hertz with 48 hours' advance notice (in France call ☎08.00.05.33.11).

Information and maps

French Government Tourist Offices (see list below) give away large quantities of **maps** and glossy brochures for every region of France, including lists of hotels and campsites. For Paris, these include everything from useful fold-out leaflets detailing sights, markets, shops, museums, ideas for excursions, useful phone numbers and opening hours, to lists of Paris' gardens and squares, and of course maps. For the clearest picture of the layout of the city the best map you can buy is Michelin no. 10, the 1:10,000 *Plan de Paris*. More convenient is the pocket-sized *Falkplan*, which folds out only as you need it, or, if you're staying any length of time, one of the various bound, book-form street plans (such as the Michelin *Paris Plan*), which have a street

---

French Government Tourist Offices

Australia
Level 22/25 Bligh St, Sydney, NSW 2000 (☎612/9231 5244, fax 9221 8682).

Canada
1981 av McGill College, Suite 490, Montréal, QC H3A 2W9 (☎514/288-4264, fax 845-4868).

30 St Patrick St, Suite 700, Toronto, ON M5T 3A3 (☎416/593-4723, fax 979-7587).

Ireland
10 Suffolk St, Dublin 2 (☎01/679 0813, fax 679 0814).

UK
178 Piccadilly, London W1V 0AL (☎0891/244123, 50p per minute premium rate; fax 0171/493 6594).

USA
444, Madison Ave, 16th Floor, New York, NY 10022 (☎212/838-7800, fax 838-7855).

676 N Michigan Ave, #3360, Chicago, IL 60611-2819 (☎312/751-7800, fax 337-6339).

9454 Wilshire Blvd, Suite 715, Beverly Hills, CA 90212-2967 (☎310/271-6665 or 272-2661, fax 276-2835).

Note that New Zealand does not have a French Government Tourist Office.

Map outlets

UK

Blackwell's Map and Travel Shop, 53 Broad St, Oxford OX1 (☎01865/792792; *bookshop.blackwell.co.uk*).

Daunt Books, 83 Marylebone High St, London W1M 3DE (☎0171/224 2295); 193 Haverstock Hill, London NW3 4QL (☎0171/794 4006).

Heffers Map Shop, 3rd Floor, in Heffers Stationery Department, 19 Sidney St, Cambridge CB2 (☎01223/568467; mail-order available; *www.heffers.co.uk*).

National Map Centre, 22–24 Caxton St, London SW1 (☎0171/222 2466; *www.mapsworld.com*).

Newcastle Map Centre, 55 Grey St, Newcastle upon Tyne NE1 (☎0191/261 5622).

James Thin Melven's Bookshop, 29 Union St, Inverness IV1 (☎01463/233500; mail-order available; *www.jthin.co.uk*).

John Smith and Sons, 57–61 St Vincent St, Glasgow G2 (☎0141/221 7472; mail-order available; *www.johnsmith.co.uk*).

Stanfords, 12–14 Long Acre, London WC2E (☎0171/836 1321; *sales@stanfords.co.uk*). *Maps by mail or phone order are available on the above number and via email. Other branches in London are located within Campus Travel at 52 Grosvenor Gardens, SW1W (☎0171/730 1314), and within the British Airways offices at 156 Regent St, W1R (☎0171/434 4744); and outside London at 29 Corn St, Bristol BS1 (☎0117/929 9966).*

The Travel Bookshop, 13–15 Blenheim Crescent, London W11 (☎0171/229 5260; *www.thetravelbookshop.co.uk*).

Ireland

Easons Bookshop, 40 O'Connell St, Dublin 1 (☎01/873 3811; mail-order available).

Fred Hanna's Bookshop, 27–29 Nassau St, Dublin 2 (☎01/677 1255).

Hodges Figgis Bookshop, 56–58 Dawson St, Dublin 2 (☎01/677 4754; mail-order available).

Waterstone's, Queens Building, 8 Royal Ave, Belfast BT1 (☎01232/247355); 7 Dawson St, Dublin 2 (☎01/679 1415); 69 Patrick St, Cork (☎021/276522).

USA

Adventurous Traveler Bookstore, PO Box 1468, Williston, VT 05495 (☎1-800/282-3963).

The Complete Traveler Bookstore, 199 Madison Ave, New York, NY 10016 (☎212/685-9007); 3207 Fillmore St, San Francisco, CA 92123 (☎415/923-1511).

Map Link Inc, 30 S La Petera Lane, Unit #5, Santa Barbara, CA 93117 (☎805/692-6777).

Phileas Fogg's Books & Maps, #87 Stanford Shopping Center, Palo Alto, CA 94304 (☎1-800/533-FOGG).

Rand McNally, 444 N Michigan Ave, Chicago, IL 60611 (☎312/321-1751); 150 E 52nd St, New York, NY 10022 (☎212/758-7488); 595 Market St, San Francisco, CA 94105 ☎415/777-3131); 1201 Connecticut Ave NW, Washington, DC 20003 (☎202/223-6751). For other locations, or for maps by mail order, call ☎1-800/333-0136 (ext 2111).

Sierra Club Bookstore, 6014 College Ave, Oakland, CA 94618 (☎510/658-7470).

Travel Books & Language Center, 4931 Cordell Ave, Bethesda, MD 20814 (☎1-800/220-2665).

Traveler's Bookstore, 22 W 52nd St, New York, NY 10019 (☎212/664-0995).

Canada

Open Air Books and Maps, 25 Toronto St, Toronto, ON M5R 2C1 (☎416/363-0719).

Ulysses Travel Bookshop, 4176 St-Denis, Montréal (☎514/843-9447).

World Wide Books and Maps, 736 Granville St, Vancouver, BC V6Z 1E4 (☎604/687-3320).

Australia and New Zealand

Map Land, 372 Little Burke St, Melbourne (☎03/9670 4383).

The Map Shop, 16a Peel St, Adelaide (☎08/8231 2033).

Perth Map Centre, 884 Hay St, Perth (☎08/9322 5733).

Specialty Maps, 58 Albert St, Auckland (☎09/307 2217).

Travel Bookshop, Shop 3, 175 Liverpool St, Sydney (☎02/9261 8200).

index, bus-route diagrams, useful addresses, and show car parks and one-way streets – all a great deal more useful than the tourist office's free handout. The information desk at Roissy airport does, however, provide a helpful free map.

The Internet

The appearance of the first cybercafés in Paris in 1996 caused a wave of media excitement, but France has actually been relatively slow to take up **Internet** connections. This is due in part to its familiarity with Minitel, which is far too slow to link up to even the slowest normal modem, and the fact that ownership of personal computers is very low. An additional problem is the dominance of the English language on the Net.

France Telecom launched its own online service in 1996 and has been busy selling a Minitel programme for PCs, and many French towns (and top Paris museums) now have sites on the World Wide Web. You can get into a list of all French servers via the Centre National de Research Scientifique on *www.urec.fr/* or visit the Ministry of Culture's site on *web.culture.fr/*.

It is, however, still considered pretty cool to have an email address as part of your coordonnées (contact details), and most analysts believe France will have to junk the Minitel box altogether if it's going to take part in the Internet revolution.

Some interesting or useful sites are detailed in the box below. You can stay online while travelling at the handful of cybercafés, as well as several shops and libraries that offer Internet access detailed in the guide. Try Vidéothèque de Paris (p.316); Virgin Megastore (p.340); Web Bar (p.272); and cybercafé Latino (p.275). It's easy to open a free Internet account with Hotmail or Yahoo to send and receive email while you're away: head for *www.hotmail.com* or *www.yahoo.com* to find out how.

Web sites

Many useful Web sites are listed throughout "Basics", particularly those of tour operators to provide an alternative to receiving brochures. Below are some more general, fun or interesting sites; they're in English unless stated otherwise.

www.fr-holidaystore.co.uk
France Holiday Store 98 is a useful site for planning a package deal to Paris.

www.jazzfrance.com
Brilliant bilingual site for jazz fans with everything from venues and festivals covered, and an up to date diary. Links to music stores.

www.parisfranceguide.com
The Web site of the free *Living in France* magazine has plenty of tips on how to set yourself up over there.

www.pariscope.fr
Mostly French with a bit of English, this is a rendering of the popular weekly Parisian listing mag online.

www.paris.org
The Web site of the Paris tourist office with impressive detail on Paris and France – though unfortunately not all as up-to-date as it could be. Recent essays on Paris to read, photographs of French classes of the world to peruse (lots of American and Japanese schoolkids) and links to other sites including universities and a national ballet diary.

www.lemonde.fr
In French only; a version of the highbrow daily newspaper.

www.webbar.fr
The Web site of Paris' best cybercafé, with details of the events it hosts – from art exhibitions to DJ-nights, and even cyber exhibitions on the site itself.

Costs and money

Like all capital cities, Paris has the potential to be very expensive, certainly more so than the rest of France, but it compares favourably to the standards set by other North European cities because of the relatively low cost of accommodation and eating out. If you are one of two people sharing a comfortable central hotel room, you can manage a reasonably snug existence, including restaurant lunch and dinner, museum and café stops, on 600F per person per day (around £62/US$107). At the bottom line, by watching the pennies, staying at a hostel (120F for B&B), being strong-willed about cups of coffee and drinks, and admiring monuments and museums from the outside, you could survive on as little as 250F (around £26/US$45) a day, including a cheap restaurant meal – less if you limit eating to street snacks or market food.

For two or more people, hotel **accommodation** can be almost as cheap as hostels, but a sensible average estimate for a comfortable double room would start from 300F (though perfectly adequate but simple doubles can be had from 160F). Single-rated and -sized rooms are often available, beginning from 140F in a cheap hotel. Breakfast at hotels is normally an extra 30F, for coffee, croissant and orange juice, about the same as you'd pay in a bar (where you'll normally find the coffee and ambience more agreeable).

As for other food, you can spend as much or as little as you like. There are large numbers of reasonable, if not very exciting, **restaurants** with three- or four-course menus for between 75F and 150F; the lunchtime *menu* is nearly always cheaper and you can get a filling midday *plat du jour* (dish of the day) of hot food for under 60F. **Picnic fare**, obviously, is much less costly, especially when you buy in the markets and cheap supermarket chains; generous take-away baguette sandwiches from cafés and boulangeries are not extortionate (ranging from 12–30F).

Wine and **beer** are both very cheap in supermarkets; buying wine from the barrel at village co-op cellars will give you the best value for money. The mark-up on wine in restaurants is high, though the house wine in cheaper establishments is still very good value. **Drinks in cafés** and bars are what really make a hole in your pocket: black coffee, wine and draught lager (*un demi*, around a half pint, costs from 15F) are the cheapest drinks to order, while mixed drinks or cocktails cost from 40F. The least expensive coffee or tea with milk if you need quick refreshment is just 7F at *McDonald's* or other fast-food establishments, while at a café a *café crème* costs from 12–30F. Glasses of tap water are free. Remember that it's cheaper to be at the bar than at a table in cafés and most expensive to sit outside on the terrace.

Transport within the city is inexpensive. The *Carte Orange*, for example, with a 75F weekly ticket (see p.56 for more details) gives you a week's unlimited travel on buses and métro/RER in central Paris.

Reductions and freebies

Museums and monuments have become a lot more expensive in recent years and are likely to prove one of the biggest wallet-eroders. If you are a full-time student, it's worthwhile carrying the **ISIC Card** (International Student Identity Card) to gain entrance **reductions** (usually about a third off). The card is universally accepted as ID, while the student card from your home institution is not. The main tourist office and youth travel agencies like USIT will sell you a **Carte Jeune** (with your passport as proof) for 120F, valid for a year, which will get you all the reductions for under-26s in France and elsewhere in Europe.

For **children and teenagers**, the range of reductions can be quite bewildering as each institution has its own policy. In many museums under-18s are free; all monuments are free for under-12s. Universally, however, under 3-year-olds are free, and usually under-4s and less often under-8s. Half-price or reduced admission is normally available for 5- to 18-year-olds. Some more **commercial attractions**, however, begin to charge adult rates at twelve.

For those **over 60 or 65**, depending on the institution (regardless of whether you are still working or not), reductions are available, though not as widely as they were a couple of years ago. You will need to carry your passport around with you as proof of age.

Whatever your age, if you are going to do a lot of museum duty, it is worth considering buying a **museum card** (details on p.61). Some museums have free or half-price admission on Sundays, and museums or exhibition spaces with no entry charge at all do still exist.

Cinemas often have reduced-price admission on Monday or Wednesday; and **churches**, **cemeteries** and, of course, **markets** are free (except for some specialist annual antique and book markets). Most **parks** are free but some gardens within have small charges, usually around 10F, to enter. **Libraries** and the cultural centres of different countries put on films, shows and exhibitions for next to nothing (details in the listings mags); most libraries themselves are free but some have entry charges – in such cases a day-pass might cost 20F or 30F. Other free **cultural offerings** appear regularly, from bands in the streets to firework shows, courtesy of the Mairie de Paris (publicized in *Paris Le Journal* – see p.56).

Budget-watchers need to be most wary of café-lounging and nightlife; drinks in flash pubs and bars can quickly become a major expense.

Money

The most sensible strategy is to take more than one means of payment and keep them separate. It's always a good idea to have a small amount of French currency on you when you arrive.

Currency and the exchange rate

French currency is the **franc** (abbreviated as F or sometimes FF), divided into 100 **centimes**. Francs come in notes of 500, 100, 50 and 20F, and there are coins of 20, 10, 5, 2 and 1F, and 50, 20, 10 and 5 centimes. During most of 1998, the exchange rate hovered around 9.5F to the pound stirling, 5.5F to the US dollar, 3.5F to the Canadian dollar, 3.5F to the Australian dollar, and 3F to the New Zealand dollar. For the most current exchange rates, consult the useful **Currency Converter Internet site**: *www.oanda.com.*

Travellers' cheques

Travellers' cheques are one of the safest ways of carrying your money. Worldwide, they're available from almost any major bank (whether you have an account there or not), and from special American Express or Thomas Cook offices, usually for a service charge of one to two percent. Check with your own bank first as they may offer cheques free of charge provided you meet certain conditions. The most widely recognized brands are **Visa** and **American Express**, which most banks will change. American Express travellers' cheques can be cashed at post offices. **French franc travellers' cheques** can be worthwhile: they can often be used as cash, and you should get the face value of the cheques when you change them, so commission is only paid on purchase. Banks being banks, however, this is not always the case.

Eurocheques, available to Europeans with an annual charge of between £4 and £8 and commission of between 1.6 and 2 percent, are no longer such a good idea for France as many banks and post offices now refuse to cash them. You can still use the card, however, in ATMs (cash machines) and as a debit card, and write out cheques in francs in hotels and restaurants, etc.

Visa TravelMoney Cards

The latest way of carrying your money abroad is with a **Visa TravelMoney Card**, or **Visa Cash Card** in the US, a sort of electronic travellers' cheque. The temporary disposable debit card is "loaded up" with an amount between £100 and £5000 and can then be used (in conjuction with a PIN number) in any Automatic Teller Machine (ATM) carrying the Visa sign in France (and 112 other countries). When your funds are depleted, you simply throw the card away. It's recommended you buy at least a second card as backup in case your first is lost or stolen, though like travellers' cheques the cards can be replaced if such mishaps occur. Up to nine cards can be bought to access the same funds – useful for couples/families travelling together. Charges are 2 percent commission with a minimum charge of £3.

In Britain, the cards are sold by Thomas Cook; you can go into any office or order the card by telephone (call ☎01733/318900) using a debit or credit card, and your card will be sent out the next day by registered post. For more information, consult the Visa Web site (*www.visa.com*).

Credit and debit cards

Credit cards are widely accepted. Visa – known as the Carte Bleue in France – is almost universally recognized; Access, Mastercard – sometimes called Eurocard – and American Express rank a bit lower. It's always worth checking first, however, that restaurants and hotels will accept your card; some smaller ones won't despite the sign. Be aware, also, that French cards have a smart chip and machines may reject the magnetic strip of British, American or Australasian cards, even if they are valid. If your card is refused because of this, we suggest you say *"Les cartes britanniques/americaines/canadiennes/de Nouvelle Zealand ne sont pas cartes à puce, mais à piste magnetique. Ma carte est valable et je vous serais très reconnaissant(e) de demander la confirmation auprès de votre banque ou de votre centre de traitement."*

You can also use credit cards for **cash advances** at banks and in ATMs. The charge tends to be higher, for example 4.1 percent instead of the 1.5 percent at home for Visa cards. The PIN number should be the same as the one you use at home, but check with your credit card company before you leave. Also, because French credit cards are smart cards, some ATMs baulk at foreign plastic and tell you that your request for money has been denied. If that happens, just try another machine. All ATMs give you the choice of instructions in French or English.

Post offices will give cash advances on Visa credit cards if you are having a problem using them in ATMs.

Debit cards can also be used in ATMs or to pay for goods and services where there's an "edc" (European acceptance) sign or if the card carries the appropriate Visa symbol. You will be charged around 1 percent or a minimum of £1.50 to use your debit card in an ATM, so don't constantly take out small sums. And don't rely on ATMs as your sole source of money, as a lost, stolen or malfunctioning card would leave you with nothing – always have some spare currency or travellers' cheques as a backup.

Changing money

Standard **banking hours** are Monday to Friday from 9am to 4 or 5pm. Some close at midday (noon/12.30pm–2/2.30pm); some are open on Saturday 9am to noon. All are closed on Sunday and public holidays. They will have a notice on the door if they do currency exchange, and **rates and commission** vary from bank to bank, so shop around. The usual procedure is a 1–2 percent commission on travellers' cheques and a flat rate charge on cash – a 30F charge for changing 200F is not uncommon. Be wary of banks claiming to charge no commission at all; often they are merely adjusting the exchange rate to their own advantage.

Rue de la Paix and other streets around the Opéra-Garnier in the 1er arrondissement are full of **banks**; the Banque de France tends to be the most competitive. Rates are inevitably poorer at **money-exchange bureaux** (bureaux de change). There are also **automatic exchange machines** at the airports and train stations and outside many money exchange bureaux. They accept £10 and £20 notes as well as dollars and other European currency notes, but offer a very poor rate of exchange.

The Euro

The new European Monetary Union currency, the **Euro**, will replace the French franc sometime in the year 2002. In January 1999 businesses in France began to show prices in Euros as well as francs, part of a plan to familiarize the public with the idea and worth of the new money well in advance.

Post and phones

You can send **faxes** from post offices: the official French word is *télécopie*, but "fax" is commonplace. You can also use Minitel (see opposite) at post offices, change money, and make photocopies and phone calls. To post your letter on the street, look for the bright yellow post boxes.

The French term for the **post office** is "la poste", or "les PTT"; look for the bright yellow signs. They generally open from 9am to 7pm Monday to Friday, and 9am to noon on Saturday. However, Paris' **main office**, at 52 rue du Louvre, 1er (M° Étienne Marcel), is open 24 hours (for all postal services but not banking and money changing). It's the best place to have your mail sent, unless you have a particular branch office in mind. Poste restante letters should be addressed (preferably with the surname first, underlined and in capitals) to Poste Restante, 52 rue du Louvre, 75001 Paris.

To **collect your mail**, you need a passport or other convincing ID, and there'll be a small charge of 3F for every letter. You should ask for all your names to be checked, as filing systems are not brilliant.

Inside post offices you will now find a row of yellow-coloured *guichet automatiques* – automatic machines with instructions available in English with which you can weigh packages and buy the appropriate stamps (*timbres*) with small change; sticky labels and tape are also dispensed. A machine can change notes into coins, so there's no need to queue for counter service. Standard letters (20g or less) and postcards within France and to European Union countries cost 3F, to North America 4.40F and to the Antipodes 5.20F. For sending letters, remember that you can also buy stamps with less queuing from tabacs.

Phones

You can make international **phone calls** from any telephone box (*cabine*) and can receive calls where there's a blue logo of a ringing bell. A 50-unit (40.60F) and 120-unit (97.50F) **phonecard** (called a *télécarte*) is essential, since coin boxes are being phased out. Phonecards are available from tabacs and newsagents as well as post offices, tourist offices and some train station ticket offices. You can also use credit cards in many call boxes. Coin-only boxes do still exist in cafés, bars, hotel foyers and rural areas; they take 50 centimes, 1F, 5F or 10F pieces; put the money in after lifting up the receiver and before dialling. You can keep adding more coins once you are connected.

Local calls are timed in France. Off-peak charges (for local, long-distance and international calls) apply on weekdays between 7pm and 8am, and after noon on Saturday until 8am Monday.

For calls within France – local or long-distance – dial all ten digits of the number. Numbers beginning with ☎08.00 are free numbers; those beginning with ☎08.36 are premium-rate (from 2.23F per minute), and those beginning with 06 are mobile and therefore also expensive to call. The major **international calling codes** are given in the box opposite; remember to omit the initial 0 of the local area code from the subscriber's number.

A **convenient** way of making international calls is to use a **calling card**, opening an account

TELEPHONING

IDD CODES

From France dial ☎ 00 + IDD code + area code minus first 0 + subscriber number
Britain ☎ 44
Ireland ☎ 353
USA and Canada ☎ 1
Australia ☎ 61
New Zealand ☎ 64

From Britain to Paris: dial ☎ 00 33 + nine-digit number (leaving out the first 0)

From the USA and Canada to Paris: dial ☎ 011 33 + nine-digit number (leaving out the first 0)

From Australia to Paris: dial ☎ 011 33 + nine-digit number (leaving out the first 0)

From New Zealand to Paris: dial ☎ 044 33 + nine-digit number (leaving out the first 0)

From Paris to elsewhere in the city you must dial all ten-digits including the initial 01.

TIME

France is one hour ahead of Britain, six hours ahead of Eastern Standard Time (eg New York), and nine hours ahead of Pacific Standard Time (eg Los Angeles). Australia is eight to ten hours ahead of Paris, depending on which part of the continent you're in.

USEFUL NUMBERS WITHIN FRANCE

Telegrams By phone: internal ☎ 36.55; external ☎ 08.00.33.44.11 (all languages)
Time ☎ 36.99
International operator ☎ 00.33 followed by the relevant country code.

International directory assistance For Canada & US ☎ 00.33.12.11; for all other countries ☎ 19.33.00, followed by the country code
French directory assistance ☎ 12

---

before you leave home; calls will be billed monthly to your credit card, to your phone bill if you are already a customer or to your home address. However, rates per minute on these cards are many times higher than the cost of calling from a public phone in France, with flat rates only. But since all of these cards are free to obtain, it's certainly worth getting one at least for emergencies. You dial a free number (make sure you have with you the relevant number for France), your account number and then the number you wish to call. The drawbacks are that the free number is often engaged and you have to dial a great many digits.

The best value calling card is offered by Interglobe (☎ 0171/972 0800), followed by AT&T (☎ 0500/626262), Cable and Wireless Calling Card (☎ 0500/100505), Swiftcall Global Card (☎ 0800/769 1444) and the most expensive rates with British Telecom's BT Charge Card (☎ 0800/345600 or 345144).

If you need to make many foreign calls from France, several companies in Paris offer **cheap-rated phonecards**, such as the bargain-basement store Tati who sell a 50F or 100F Intercall

Carte Téléphone (☎ 08.00.51.79.43; see "Shopping" chapter on p.332 for Tati addresses) for calling overseas which you can use on a public or private telephone; a 50F card gives you, for example, 15 minutes to Australia, 32 minutes to Canada or the USA and 29 minutes to the UK. These rates work out much cheaper than using France Telecom from a public phone.

To avoid payment altogether, you can, of course, make a reverse charge or **collect call** – known in French as *téléphoner en PCV*. This can also be done through the operator in the UK, by dialling the Home Direct number ☎ 08.00.89.00.33 and asking for a "reverse charge call"; to get an English-speaking operator for North America, dial ☎ 00.00.11.

Minitel

The majority of phone subscribers in Paris (and almost everywhere in France) have **Minitel**, a dinosaurial online computer allowing access through the phone lines to directories, databases, chat lines, etc. You will also find them in **post offices**. Most organizations, from sports federations to government institutions to gay groups, have a code consisting of numbers and letters to call up information, leave messages, make reservations and so on. You dial the number on the phone, wait for a fax-type tone, then type the letters on the keyboard. Lastly, press *Connexion Fin*

(the same key also ends the connection). If you're computer-literate and can understand basic keyboard terms in French (*retour* – return, *envoi* – enter, etc), you shouldn't find them hard to use. Be warned that most services cost more than phone rates.

The media

British **newspapers**, the *Washington Post*, *New York Times* and the *International Herald Tribune* are widely on sale on the same day. The free monthly *Paris Free Voice* (www.parisvoice.com) produced by the American Church at 65 quai d'Orsay, 7e, has good listings, ads for flats and courses, and interesting articles on current events. It's available from the church and from English-language bookshops. *France USA Contacts*, a free American fortnightly available in various cafés, restaurants, shops and colleges, is also useful for flats, jobs, travel, alternative medicine, therapy and the like.

The **listings magazines** *Pariscope* (3F) and *L'Official des Spectacles* (2F) come out on Wednesdays and are indispensable for knowing what's on. *Pariscope*, in particular, has a huge and comprehensive section on films and a small English section with weekly entertainment highlights, restaurant reviews and a special interest page put together by *Time Out*.

Of the **French daily papers**, *Le Monde* is the most intellectual; it is widely respected, but is somewhat austere, making no concessions to such frivolities as photographs. *Libération*, founded by Jean-Paul Sarte in the 1960s, is moderately left-wing, independent, and more colloquial, with good, if choosy, coverage, while rigorous left-wing criticism of the French government comes from *L'Humanité*, the Communist Party paper. The other nationals, and the local paper *Le Parisien*, are all firmly right-wing in their politics: *Le Figaro* is the most respected. The top-selling national is *L'Équipe*, dedicated to sports coverage.

Weeklies of the *Newsweek/Time* model include the wide-ranging and socialist-inclined *Le*

Nouvel Observateur, its right-wing counterpoint *L'Express*, the boringly centrist *L'Événement de Jeudi* and the newcomer with a bite, *Marianne*. The best investigative journalism is in the weekly satirical paper *Le Canard Enchaîné*. *Charlie Hebdo* is a sort of *Private Eye* or *Spy Magazine* equivalent. *Paris-Match* provides gossip about stars and the royal families.

Monthlies include the young and trendy – and cheap – *Nova*, with excellent listings of cultural events; the glossy *Paris Capitale*, with fashion, culture and listings; and *Actuel*, which is good for current events. There are, of course, the French *Vogue*, *Marie-Claire* and *Elle*, and the relentlessly urban *Biba*, for women's fashion and lifestyle.

"Moral" **censorship** of the press is rare. On the newsstands you'll find pornography of every shade, as well as covers featuring drugs, sex, blasphemy and bizarre forms of grossness. You'll also find French **comics** (*bandes dessinées*) that often indulge such adult interests: wildly and wonderfully illustrated, they are considered to be quite an artform – whole shops are devoted to them (see p.327 of the "Shopping" chapter).

TV and radio

French TV has six terrestrial channels: three public (France 2, Arte/La Cinquième and FR3); one subscription (Canal Plus, with some unencrypted programmes); and two commercial open broadcasts (TF1 and M6). In addition there are the **cable** networks, which include France Infos (French news), CNN, the BBC World Service, BBC Prime (*Eastenders*, etc), Planète, which specializes in documentaries, Paris Première (lots of VO – *version originale* – films), and Canal Jimmy

(*Friends* and the like in VO). There are two **music channels**, the American MTV and the far superior French-run MTM.

The main French **news broadcasts** are at 8.30pm on Arte and at 8pm on F2 and at TF1.

With a radio, you can tune into English-language news on the BBC World Service on 648kHz or 198kHz long wave from midnight to 5am (and Radio 4 during the day). The Voice of America transmits on 90.5, 98.8 and 102.4FM. You can also listen to the news in English on Radio France International (RFI) for an hour (3–4pm) on 738kHz AM. For radio news in French, there's the state-run France Inter (87.8FM), Europe 1 (104.7FM), or round-the-clock news on France Infos (105.5FM).

For more on Parisian television and film, see Chapter 15.

Business hours and holidays

Most shops, businesses, information services, museums and banks in Paris stay open all day. The exceptions are the smaller **shops** and enterprises, which may close for lunch sometime between 12.30pm and 2pm. Basic hours of business are from 8 or 9am to 6.30 or 7.30pm Monday to Saturday for the big shops and Tuesday to Saturday for smaller shops (some of the smaller shops may open on Monday afternoon). You can always find boulangeries and food shops that do stay open, however, on days when others close – on Sunday normally until noon.

Restaurants, bars and cafés also often close on Sunday or Monday. It's common for bars and cafés to stay open to 2am, and even extend hours on a Friday and Saturday night, closing earlier on Sunday, but it's unusual to find a restaurant that will serve a meal after 10pm. And most small businesses, including some hotels, take a **holiday** between the middle of July and the end of August.

The standard **banking** hours are 9am–4/5pm, closed Saturday and Sunday; for more details, see p.29.

Museums open between 9 and 10am and close between 5 and 6pm. Summer times may differ from winter times; if they do, both are indicated in the listings of the guide. Summer hours usually extend from mid-May or early June to mid-September, but sometimes they apply only during July and August, occasionally even from Palm Sunday to All Saints' Day. Don't be caught out by museum **closing days** – usually Monday or Tuesday and sometimes both. **Churches** and cathedrals are almost always open all day, with charges only for the crypt, treasuries or cloister, and little fuss is made about how you're dressed.

One other factor can disrupt your plans. There are thirteen **national holidays** (*jours fériés*), when most shops and businesses, though not necessarily museums or restaurants, are closed. **May** in particular is a big month for holidays, when Ascension Day normally falls, as sometimes does Pentecost, added to May Day and Victory Day. It makes a peaceful time to visit as people clear out of town over several weekends, but many businesses are erractically open. Just about everywhere, including museums, is closed on May 1. July 14 heralds the beginning of the French holiday season and people leave town en masse between then and the end of August. The public holidays are:

January 1 New Year's Day

Easter Sunday

Easter Monday

Ascension Day (forty days after Easter)

Pentecost or Whitsun (seventh Sunday after Easter, plus the Monday)

May 1 May Day/Labour Day

May 8 Victory in Europe Day

July 14 Bastille Day

August 15 Assumption of the Virgin Mary

November 1 All Saints' Day

November 11 1918 Armistice Day

December 25 Christmas Day

Festivals and events

With all that's going on in Paris, festivals – in the traditional "popular" sense – are no big deal. But there is an impressive array of arts events and an inspired internationalist jamboree at the Fête de l'Humanité.

The tourist office produces a biannual *Saisons de Paris – Calendrier des Manifestations,* which gives details of all the mainstream events; otherwise, check the listings and other Paris magazines (see p.32).

Many Parisian quartiers like Belleville and Montmartre have *portes ouvertes* (open doors) weeks when artists' studios are open to the public and some festivities are laid on – keep an eye open for posters and flyers.

January
La Grande Parade de Montmartre (January 1) New Year's Day parade from place Pigalle to place Jules-Joffrin.

La Mairie de Paris vous invite au concert A week of two concert tickets for the price of one.

Festival Mondial du Cirque de Demain International circus festival at the Cirque d'Hiver Bouglione (☎01.48.04.30.30).

February
Foire à la Feraille de Paris Antiques and bric-a-brac fair in the Parc Floral de Paris (☎01.40.62.95.95).

Salon de l'Agriculture (end of February to beginning of March) The biggest agricultural show in the world at the Parc des Expositions (☎01.49.09.60.00).

March
Salon de Mars International antiques, primitive and contemporary art fair by the Eiffel Tower (☎01.44.94.86.80).

Banlieues Bleus (mid-March to mid-April) International jazz festival in the towns of Seine-Saint-Denis (Blanc-Mesnil, Drancy, Aubervilliers, Pantin, St-Ouen, Bobigny); info on ☎01.42.43.56.66.

Festival Exit International festival of contemporary dance, performance and theatre at Créteil; information from Maison des Arts, place Salvador-Allende, 9400 Créteil (☎01.45.13.19.19).

Festival de Films des Femmes (end of March/beginning of April) Women's film festival at Créteil; information from Maison des Arts, place Salvador-Allende, 9400 Créteil (☎01.49.80.38.98).

Festival d'Art Sacré de la Ville de Paris (end of March to beginning of April) Concerts and recitals of church music in Paris' churches and concert halls (☎01.45.61.54.99). Also in November/December (see p.36).

Foire du Trône (end of March to end of May) Funfair located in the 12e, Pelouse de Reuilly and Bois de Vincennes.

April
Poisson d'Avril (April 1) April Fools' Day with spoofs in the media and people sticking paper fishes on the backs of unsuspecting fools.

Marathón International de Paris The Paris Marathon departs from Place de la Concorde, arrives at the Hippodrome de Vincennes 42km later.

Foire de Paris (end April/beginning of May) Food and wine fair at the Parc des Expositions, Porte de Versailles (☎01.49.09.60.00).

May
Fête du Travail (May 1) May Day with marches and festivities in eastern Paris and around place de la Bastille.

La Mairie de Paris vous invite au théâtre A week of two theatre tickets for the price of one.
Finale de la Coupe de France French football championships final at the Parc des Princes (☎01.44.31.73.00).

Internationaux de France de Tennis (last week of May and first week of June) The French Open tennis championships at Roland Garros (☎01.47.43.48.00).

June

Finale du Championnat de France de Rugby French rugby championships final at the Parc des Princes (☎01.48.74.84.75).

Fête de la Musique (June 21) Live bands and free concerts throughout the city (☎01.40.03.94.70).

Feux de la Saint-Jean (around June 21) Fireworks for St-Jean's Day at the Parc de la Villette and quai St-Bernard.

Gay Pride Gay and Lesbian Pride march (☎01.47.70.01.50).

Féte du Cinéma (end of June) Three days of 10F cinema tickets after you have paid one full-price entry.

Course des Garçons er Serveuses de Café (late June/early July) Waiters and waitresses race through the streets of Paris carrying trays laden with alcohol. Depart from and arrive at the Hôtel de Ville, 1er (☎01.46.33.89.89).

Halle That Jazz (end of June to beginning of July) Jazz festival at Grande Halle de la Villette (☎01.40.03.75.75).

Foire St-Germain (June to July) Concerts, antique fairs, poetry and exhibitions in the 6e (☎01.40.46.75.12).

July

La Goutte d'Or en Fête (first week) Music festival of rap, reggae, raï with local and international performers (☎01.53.09.99.22).

Bastille Day (July 14 and evening before) The 1789 surrender of the Bastille is celebrated in official pomp, with parades of tanks down the Champs-Élysées, firework displays and concerts. At night there is dancing in the streets around place de la Bastille to good French bands.

Jazz à la Villette (early July) Big-name jazz and blues performers at the Grande Halle of the Parc de la Villette, less conventional acts at the Cité de la Musique (☎01.44.84.44.84).

Arrivée du Tour de France Cyclistes (third or fourth Sunday) The Tour de France cyclists cross the finishing line in the avenue des Champs-Élysées.

Paris Quartier d'Été Music, cinema, dance and theatre events around the city (☎01.44.83.64.40).

Festival de Cinéma en Plein Air (July 15–Aug 15) Open-air cinema at Parc de la Villette (☎01.40.03.75.03).

Festival Musique en l'Île (July to September) Classical music festival (☎01.44.62.70.90).

September

Fête de l'Humanité (second weekend) Sponsored by the French Communist Party and *L'Humanité* newspaper, this annual three-day event just north of Paris at La Courneuve attracts people in their tens of thousands and of every political persuasion. Food and drink (all very cheap), and music and crafts from every corner of the globe, are the predominant features, rather than political platforms. Each French regional CP has a vast restaurant tent with its specialities; French and foreign bands play on an open-air stage; and the event ends on Sunday night with an impressive firework display. (M° La Courneuve, then bus #177 or special shuttle from RER). Info on ☎01.49.22.72.72.

Journees du Patrimonie (mid-September weekend) A France-wide event where normally off-limits buildings – like the Palais de l'Elysée where the President resides – are opened to a curious public (☎01.44.61.20.00).

Nouveau Festival International de Danse de Paris (end of September to beginning of October) State-of-the-art international dance festival based at the Théâtre du Châtelet (☎01.40.28.28.40).

Festival d'Automne (end of September to end of December) Theatre and music festival including companies from Eastern Europe, America and Japan; multilingual productions; lots of avant-garde and multimedia stuff, most of it very exciting (☎01.53.45.17.17).

October

Fêtes des Vendanges (first or second Saturday) The grape harvest festival in the Montmartre vineyard, at the corner of rue des Saules and rue St-Vincent (☎01.42.52.42.00).
Foire Internationale d'Art Contemporain

(FIAC) International contemporary art show by the Eiffel Tower (☎01.49.90.47.80).

Prix de l'Arc de Triomphe Horse flat racing with high stakes at Longchamp (☎01.49.10.20.30).

November

Festival d'Art Sacré de la Ville de Paris (end of November to end of December) Concerts and recitals of church music in Paris' churches and concert halls (☎01.45.61.54.99).

Mois de la Photo (biennial – even years) Photographic exhibitions are held in museums, galleries and cultural centres throughout the city (☎01.44.78.75.00).

Festival FNAC-Inrockuptibles (early Nov) Dubbed *Les Inrocks*, a rock festival featuring lots of new names at various venues around town, put on by the book and record chain-store FNAC (see p.326 for addresses). FNAC have a good track record for funding the arts, including a public campaign launched in autumn 1998 against a

growing number of political attacks on multiculturalism in France due to the increasing power of the Front National.

Marjolaine (early Nov) Environmental/ecological festival with more than 400 stalls in the Parc Floral, Bois de Vincennes. Everything from organic produce to Greenpeace stands (☎01.45.56.09.09).

Lancement des Illuminations des Champs-Élysées (end of November) Jazz bands, the Republican Guard and an international star turning on the Christmas lights down the Champs-Élysées.

Concours International de Danse de Paris (end of November/beginning of December) Prestigious dance competition at the Opéra Comique (☎01.45.22.28.74).

December

Le Nouvel An (December 31) New Year's Eve means fireworks, drinking and kissing, notably on the Champs-Élysées.

Women's Paris

Paris is an easy city for women to feel comfortable in. The areas you're likely to frequent at night will be full of people; the last métro home is rarely empty; streets are well lit; and

Parisians are rather more inclined than Brits or Americans to get involved if scenes get heavy. That's not to say that unpleasant things don't happen, but there's no reason to feel less safe here than you would in any other large European city.

Young women can expect a certain amount of harassment (see opposite) but also plenty of opportunities for being pleasantly chatted up.

Political correctness is completely alien to the French, partly because it doesn't work in the French language and partly because philosophically and culturally it's a nonsense to them. Attitudes to seduction and sex are much more ingrained than in Anglo-Saxon cultures, though the balance of power between the sexes is no better – some would say worse. You may well be shocked by the sexism of advertising images but at the same time impressed by the confidence and individualism of so many French women.

Feminism in France

During the Socialist government's first term in the early 1980s, Yvette Roudy's new **Women's Ministry** spent five years getting long-overdue equal pay and opportunity measures through parliament. Some funding was given to women's groups, but the main emphasis was on legislation, including the provision of socialized health coverage for abortion. A law against degrading, discriminatory or violence-inciting images of women in the media was, however, thrown out by the National Assembly.

Meanwhile, the MLF (*Mouvement de Libération des Femmes* – **Women's Liberation Movement**) had been declared by the media to be dead and buried. There were no more Women's Day marches, no major demonstrations, no direct action. Feminist bookshops and cafés started closing, publications reached their last issue, and polls showed that young women leaving school were only interested in men and babies. As the Socialist policies ran out of steam, cuts in public spending and traditional ideas about the male breadwinner sent more and more women back to their homes and hungry husbands.

Under Chirac and the Gaullists, the Ministère des Droits des Femmes (Ministry of Women's Rights) was renamed as the Ministère des Droits de l'Homme (Ministry of the Rights of Man). The full title of the ministry included "the feminine condition" and "the family", but the irony of the implacably male gender-bias of the French language went generally unremarked. The first woman prime minister, **Edith Cresson** (1991–92), had a disastrous time in office, but was rarely attacked on grounds of gender. Feminist *députés* in parliament did all they could to keep women's issues prominent, but received no support from their colleagues and little from the movement outside.

Feminist intellectuals – always the most prominent section of the French women's movement – have continued their *seminaires*, erudite publications and university Feminist Studies courses, while at the other end of the scale, women's refuges and rape crisis centres are still maintained, with some funding from the ministry. The MLF is occasionally seen on the streets, but disorganized and in much diminished numbers.

More recently, a key mobilizing issue has again been **abortion**, with French women fearing the influence of the powerful US anti-abortion lobby on European public opinion. When a French company applied for a licence for the abortion pill RU486, French pro-lifers initially forced them to withdraw it, threatening its employees with violence, even death. The male Minister for Health, however, declared RU486 to be "the moral property of women". It has since been used by tens of thousands of women for terminations that are far safer and simpler than those by surgical methods. How much the minister was influenced by the needs of the French pharmaceutical industry rather than the needs of women is a matter of opinion, but it was a significant victory nevertheless.

Feminists continue to be active in unions and political parties; male bastions in the arts and media have been under attack; in business and local government leading roles have been taken by a few women; and there has even been talk of the possibility of a woman president in the future. Women have also been very visible in the street protests against the government, though gone are the days when International Women's Day would see crowds of women marching.

Sexual harassment and assault

Much of the eyeing-up and comments that you're likely to experience can be ignored and will not lead to serious annoyance. However, lack of familiarity with linguistic and cultural clues can sometimes make it difficult to judge a situation correctly.

A "*Bonjour*" or "*Bonsoir*" on the street is almost always a pick-up line: if you return the greeting, you've left yourself open to a persistent monologue and a difficult brush-off job. On the other hand, it's not unusual to be offered a drink in a bar if you're on your own and *not* to be pestered afterwards, even if you accept. This is rarer in Paris than elsewhere in the country, but don't assume that any overture by a Frenchman is a predatory come-on. It's perfectly possible to chat and even flirt, then say goodbye without any hassle at all.

If you are the victim of rape or any violent crime, it's advisable to contact your consulate (see p.43) before going to the police – the police don't have a good reputation for dealing with violence against women. See also the Directory of the guide (p.368) for other contacts offering support in the event of a crisis.

Feminist contacts and information

French culture remains stuck with myths about femininity that disable women to a far greater extent than in Britain, Holland or the USA. There is, however, a strong network for Parisian lesbians, and havens for non-lesbian feminists do exist, such as those listed below.

Maison des Femmes

163 rue de Charenton, 12e (☎01.43.43.41.13, fax 01.43.43.42.13; M° Reuilly-Diderot/Gare de Lyon). Wed & Fri 4–7pm; café Fri 7–10pm.

A women's meeting place run by Paris Féministe, who produce a monthly bulletin and organize a range of events and actions. Many women's organizations and solidarity groups use the Maison as a base; SOS Sexism, the anti-sexism group; the European network for women's rights, Coordination Européenne des Femmes; women's aid and rape crisis; ARCL (Les Archives, Recherches et Cultures Lesbiennes; see opposite) and other lesbian groups; artists and intellectual groups like Rupture who meet to discuss Feminist theory.

This is by far the best place to come if you want to make contact with the women's movement. Though English speakers can't be guaranteed, you can count on a friendly reception. There's a cafeteria, which serves drinks and dinner most Friday evenings, as well as a library (Fri 7–10pm); plus open days with exhibitions and concerts or discos, workshops and self-defence classes, discussions and film shows.

Bibliothèque Marguerite Durand

3rd floor, 79 rue Nationale, 13e (☎01.45.70.80.30; M° Tolbiac). Tues–Sat 2–6pm. The first official feminist library in France, this carries the widest selection of contemporary and old periodicals, news clippings files, photographs, posters and etchings, documentation on current organizations, as well as books on every aspect of women's lives, past and present (some in English). It's a very pleasant place to sit and read, and admission is free. In order to consult publications you need to fill out a form and produce identification – the staff are very helpful.

Media

There is no national feminist magazine or paper in France; instead nearly every group produces its own publication. Some are stapled, photocopied handouts issued at random intervals; others are regular, well-printed serials, with many of them linked to particular political parties.

• **L'Annuaire**, biannual directory of feminist, lesbian and gay groups, venues and publications produced by the lesbian cultural research organization *ARCL*; 70F from Maison des Femmes and women's bookshops; available for reference at the Bibliothèque Marguerite-Durand.

• **Paris Féministe** (see Maison des Femmes, above) is a monthly carrying detailed listings for events and groups in Paris.

• **Paris Plurielle** is a women's radio programme on 106.3MHz each Tuesday 7–8.30pm.

Gay and lesbian Paris

Paris is one of Europe's major centres for gay men. There are numerous bars, clubs, restaurants, saunas and shops. In the central street of the Marais, rue Ste-Croix-de-la-Bretonnerie, every other address is very visibly gay. Lesbians have much less choice here commercially, but there are networks of feminist groups and specific publications that cater for the well-organized lesbian community (see opposite).

The high spots of the calendar are the annual **Gay Pride** parade and festival and the **Bastille Day Ball**. Gay Pride is normally held on the Saturday closest to the summer solstice. It starts from the Bastille, and is a major carnival for both lesbians and gays. The Bastille Day Ball (July 13 10pm–dawn) is a wild open-air dance on the quai de la Tournelle, 5e (M° Pont Marie), and is free for all to join in.

For a long time the emphasis of the gay community in Paris tended towards providing the requisites for a hedonistic lifestyle, rather than any very significant political campaigning. With the legal age of consent set at 15, and discrimination and harassment non-routine, protest was not a high priority.

Matters have changed, here as elsewhere, since the advent of AIDS (SIDA in French). The resulting homophobia, though not as extreme as in Britain or middle America, has nevertheless increased the suffering in the group statistically most at risk. A group of gay doctors and the association AIDES (Association pour l'Entraide et l'Information SIDA) have consistently provided sympathetic counselling and treatment, and the gay press has done a great deal to disseminate the facts about AIDS and to provide hope and encouragement.

A second factor has been the success of the gay community in the Marais; a recent backlash has been manifest in the form of increasing complaints against bars and clubs over noise and infraction of licensing laws, with the police taking speedy and sometimes heavy-handed action.

In general, however, the French consider sexuality to be a private matter. On the whole, gays tend to be discreet outside specific gay venues, parades and the prime gay area between the

Hôtel de Ville, the Bastille and Arts et Métiers. Gay-bashing is very uncommon.

Contacts and information

ARCL (Les Archives, Recherches et Cultures Lesbiennes; ☎01.46.28.54.94), based at the Maison des Femmes (see opposite). ARCL publish a biannual directory of lesbian, gay and feminist addresses in France, *L'Annuaire* (70F), and organize frequent meetings around campaigning, artistic and intellectual issues. In addition, they produce a regular newsletter, and run a Feminist/Lesbian archive–library at the Maison des Femmes which you can consult Fri 7–10pm.

Centre Gai et Lesbienne, 3 rue Keller, 11e (M° Ledru-Rollin; ☎01.43.57.21.47, fax 01.43.57.27.93; *www.cglparis.org*). The main information centre for the gay, lesbian, bisexual and transexual community in Paris (open Mon–Sat 2–8pm; *Café Positif* for HIV-positive people and their friends Sun 2–7pm). The centre publishes a free map/guide to gay and lesbian Paris, and a monthly magazine, *3 Keller*. It's also the meeting place for numerous campaigning, identity, health, arts and intellectual groups.

David & Jonathan, 92bis rue Picpus, 12e (M° Michel-Bizot; ☎01.43.42.09.49). Gay Christian organization.

GAGE, c/o Les Mots à la Bouche – see overleaf (☎01.48.93.16.93). Gay and lesbian students' group, meeting every week at a local bar – ask at the bookshop for the latest location.

Lesbian and Gay Pride, 27 rue du Faubourg, 9e (☎01.47.70.01.50, fax 01.45.23.10.66). Organizes the Gay Pride march in Paris.

Maison des Femmes (see under "Women's Paris" opposite).

Minitel 36.15 GAY is the Minitel number to dial for information on groups, contacts, messages, etc.

Media

FG (Fréquence Gaie) 98.2 FM 24hr gay and lesbian radio station with music, news, chats, information on groups and events, etc.

Gageure Small monthly mag for gay students, produced and distributed by GAGE (see overleaf).

Gai Pied publishes the annual *Guide Gai Pied*, which is the most comprehensive gay guide to France, carrying a good selection of lesbian and gay addresses, with an English section; 79F from newsagents and bookshops. More info on *www.gaipied.fr*

e.m@le magazine. Free gay and lesbian paper with small ads, lonely hearts, services, etc.

Lesbia. The most widely available lesbian publication, available from most newsagents. Each monthly issue features a wide range of articles, listings, reviews, lonely hearts and contacts.

Les Mots à la Bouche, 6 rue Ste-Croix-de-la-Bretonnerie, 4ᵉ (☎01.42.78.88.30; Mᵒ Hôtel-de-Ville). The main gay and lesbian bookshop, with exhibition space and meeting rooms; a selection of literature in English, too. Lots of free listing mags and club fliers to pick up, and one of the helpful assistants usually speaks English. See also p.328. Mon–Thurs 11am–11pm, Fri & Sat 11am–midnight, Sun 2–8pm.

3 Keller and **Le Plan Officiel**. Centre Gai et Lesbienne's publications (see overleaf).

SOS

Association des Médecins Gais (AMG; gay doctors' organization), 45 rue Sedaine, 11ᵉ (Mᵒ Bréguet-Sabin); ☎01.48.05.81.71; Wed 6–8pm, Sat 2–4pm.

Écoute Gaie (helpline), ☎01.44.93.01.02; daily 6pm to 10pm.

Racism

France has a deservedly bad reputation for racist attitudes and behaviour. A survey on French attitudes to race, commissioned by the French government and published in June 1998, resulted in a statistical 38 percent of the population declaring themselves racist, double the figures for similar surveys in Britain and Germany. Percentage votes for the **Front National** were fifteen percent in the last parliamentary elections, and support for the neo-fascist, racist party, headed by **Jean-Marie Le Pen**, is growing. Its heartland is in Provence and the Côte d'Azur, where by 1997 four cities had Front National Mayors. The alliance with conservatives has led to changes in educational, cultural and sporting programmes to suit Front National policies; their fundamental priority is the withdrawal of benefits to immigrants who have not yet been granted French citizenship. The jubilant mood in France after the 1998 World Cup victory of its multi-cultural team (see box opposite) forced Le Pen to modify some of his statements.

However, the warm glow after the World Cup has yet to transform France into a racially tolerant nation, and for the moment, if you are black or Arab, or look as if you might be, your chances of avoiding unpleasantness are very low. Hotels claiming to be booked up, police demanding your papers, and abuse from ordinary people are all horribly frequent. In addition, being black, of whatever ethnic origin, can make entering the country difficult. Changes in passport regulations have put an end to outright refusal to let some holiday-makers in, but customs and immigration officers can still be obstructive and malicious. In North African-dominated areas of Paris such as the Goutte d'Or, identity checks by the police are common and not pleasant. The clampdown on illegal immigration (and much tougher laws), along with the Algerian-based terrorist attacks in the city in 1995, have resulted in a significant increase in police stop-and-search operations. Carrying your passport at all times is a good idea (and you are legally required to have some identification on you in any case).

There are many **antiracist organizations** including SOS Racisme, 28 rue des Petits-Écuries, 10ᵉ (☎01.53.24.67.67; Mᵒ Chateau d'Eau). Though it doesn't represent the majority of immigrants and their descendants in France (for rioting kids in

Football unites France?

For the abandoned section of the population, the World Cup may have been an ephemeral opening, an illusion of fraternity. But such illusions are useful; they can alter people's minds.

Laurent Joffrin, *Libération*, July 1998

France's hosting of the **1998 World Cup** in July 1998 was marred in its early stages by ticket scandals that left many foreign fans without seats, and by widespread English and German football hooliganism. But it finished with France's biggest street party since the end of World War II as it celebrated victory over Brazil in the brand new Stade de France at St-Denis on the edge of Paris – and a feeling of unprecedented racial unity flooded the country.

Of the thirty-two teams that made it to the World Cup, France's was the most **diverse ethnically**. Half of the squad's 22 players were of foreign extraction: Patrick Vieira was born in Senegal, Marcel Desailly in Ghana, Christian Karembeu in New Caledonia, Lilian Thuram and Bernard Lama in Guadeloupe, where both Thierry Henry and Bernard Diomède's parents were from, Zinedine Zidane's parents immigrated from Algeria, David Trezeguet's father is Argentinian and both Alain Boghossian and Youri Djorkaeff are of Armenian extraction. Yet only two of these players were really born outside "France", whose overseas *départements* make it truly a global nation; the others mainly originate from ex-French colonies. For the first time, the national team really reflected how France looks in the 1990s.

On the evening of July 12, 1998, France frenziedly celebrated its multi-ethnic football team's 3–0 win against Brazil. The hero of the match was **Zinedine "Zizou" Zidane**, the Marseille-born son of Algerian parents. Just two days before Bastille Day, the traditional celebration of French nationalism, the *rouge-blanc-bleu* flags were already out in force, but for the first time those carrying them along the Champs-Élysées were just as likely to be the marginalized young blacks and "Beurs" (French-born North Africans) from the *"quartiers difficiles"* on the edge of Paris. The wild scenes, with black, white and *beurs* embracing in the streets, were a revelation in a country exposed in a national survey published the fortnight before as having the most racist attitudes in Europe (and fifteen percent of Front National votes in the last parliamentary elections).

The French President, **Jacques Chirac**, had been an enthusiastic supporter of the team throughout the competition, gaining media attention and popularity in the opinion polls as the cameras cut to him happily waving his *Allez les Bleus* scarf and chanting the team players names as they made their victory jog. He used the Bastille Day press conference as a political platform to warn the right wing to drop support for the Front National's policies of racial discrimination, and to praise France's "tricolour and multi-colour" World Cup win. He stated that suspicion of immigrants went against French principles of democracy, humanism and republicanism. Chirac bestowed the Legion of Honour on **Aimé Jacquet**, the French coach, and applauded his strength against National Front demands for exclusion of immigrants from the team.

Paris' suburbs, it's an irrelevant middle-class outfit), SOS Racisme has done a great deal over the last few years to raise consciousness amongst young white French people. If you speak French,

they will give you support should you be the victim of a **racist assault** (phone first, as opening times vary). The police are unlikely to be sympathetic – your consulate may be more helpful.

Trouble and the police

Petty theft is bad in the crowded hang-outs of the capital, as in most major cities; the métro and Les Halles are notorious pickpocket grounds. It makes sense to take the normal precautions: not flashing wads of notes or travellers' cheques around; carrying your bag or wallet securely; and never letting cameras and other valuables out of your sight. But the best security is having a good insurance policy, keeping a separate record of cheque numbers, credit card numbers and the phone numbers for cancelling them, and the relevant details of all your valuables.

Cars with foreign number plates are standard prey. Vehicles are rarely stolen, but tape-decks and luggage left in cars make tempting targets. Good insurance is the only answer, but even so, try not to leave any valuables in plain view. If you have an **accident** while driving, officially you have to fill in and sign a **constat à l'aimable** (jointly agreed statement); car insurers are supposed to give you this with the policy, though in practice few seem to have heard of it. For **non-criminal driving offences** such as speeding, the police can impose an on-the-spot fine.

If you need to **report a theft**, go along to the commissariat de police of the arrondissement in which the theft took place, where they will fill out a constat de viol. The first thing they'll ask for is your passport, and vehicle documents if relevant. Although the police are not always as co-opera-

tive as they might be, it is their duty to assist you if you've lost your passport or all your money.

Should you be **arrested** on any charge, you have the right to contact your consulate (see box opposite). People caught **smuggling or possessing drugs**, even a small amount of marijuana, are liable to find themselves in jail, and consulates will not be sympathetic. This is not to say that hard-drug consumption isn't a visible activity: there are scores of kids dealing in poudre (heroin) in Paris, and the authorities are unable to do much about it.

Free legal advice over the phone (in French) is available from SOS Avocats (☎01.43.29.33.00; Mon–Fri 7–11.30pm; closed Aug).

Emergency number to call for police ☎ 17

The police

French police (in popular argot, les flics) are barely polite at the best of times, and can be extremely unpleasant if you get on the wrong side of them. In Paris, the city police force has an ugly history of cockups, including sporadic shootings of innocent people and brutality against "suspects" – often just ordinary teenagers and black people. You can be stopped at any time and asked to produce ID. If that does happen to you, it's highly inadvisable to be difficult or facetious. The police can also be rather sensitive on political issues: a group of Danish students wearing "Chirac Non!" T-shirts against the French nuclear tests in the Pacific were surrounded in force to their hotel and made to change.

The **two main types** of police – the Police Nationale and the Gendarmerie Nationale – are for all practical purposes indistinguishable. The **CRS** (Compagnies Républicaines de Sécurité), on the other hand, are an entirely different proposition. They are a mobile force of paramilitary heavies, used to guard sensitive embassies, "control" demonstrations, and generally intimidate the populace on those occasions when the public authorities judge that it is stepping out of line. Armed with guns, CS gas and truncheons, they have earned themselves a reputation for brutality over the years, particularly at those moments when the tensions inherent in the long civil war of French politics have reached boiling point.

Work and study

EU nationals can legally work in France, while most North Americans and Australasians (specialists aside) who manage to work and live in Paris do so on luck, brazenness and willingness to live in pretty grotty conditions. An exhausting combination of bar and club work, freelance translating, data processing, typing, busking, providing novel services like home-delivery fish'n'chips, teaching English or computer programming, dancing or modelling are some of the ways people get by. Great if you're into self-promotion and living hand-to-mouth, but if you're not, it might be wise to think twice – and remember that unemployment in France is very high.

Anyone staying in France for more than three months must have a **carte de séjour**, or residency permit – citizens of the EU are entitled to one automatically. France has a **minimum wage** (the SMIC – *Salaire Minimum Interprofessional de Croissance*); indexed to the cost of living, it's currently around 40F an hour (for a maximum 169-hour month). By law, all EU nationals are entitled to exactly the same pay, conditions and trade union rights as French nationals. Employers, however, are likely to pay lower wages to temporary foreign workers who don't have easy legal resources, and make them work longer hours. It's also worth noting that if you're a full-time non-EU student in France (see p.45), you can get a non-EU **work permit** for the following summer as long as your visa is still valid.

If you're looking for secure employment, it's important to begin planning before you leave home. A few **books** that might be worth consulting are *Work Your Way Around the World* by Susan Griffiths (Vacation Work), *A Year Between* and *Working Holidays* (both Central Bureau), and *Live and Work in France* by Victoria Pybus (Vacation Work).

Finding a job in a **French language school** is best done in advance. In Britain, jobs are often advertised in the *Guardian*'s "Education" section (every Tues) and in the weekly *Times Educational Supplement*. Late summer is usually the best time. You don't need fluent French to get a post, but a degree and a TEFL (Teaching English as a Foreign Language) qualification will almost certainly be required. Vacation Work, 9 Park End St, Oxford OX1 1HJ (☎01865/241978, fax 790885) publishes the useful *Teaching English Abroad* (£10.99 plus £1.50 post and packaging) while the British Council's Website (*www.britcoun.org/english/engvacs.htm*) has a list of English-teaching vacancies. If you apply for jobs from home, most schools will fix up the necessary papers for you. EU nationals don't need a work permit, but getting a *carte de séjour* and social security can still be tricky should employers refuse to help. It's quite feasible to find a teaching job once you're already in France, but you may have to accept semi-official status and no job security. For the addresses of schools, look under *"Écoles de Langues"* in the *Professions* directory of the phone book. Offering **private lessons** (via university notice boards or classified ads), you'll have lots of competition.

For **temporary work** check the ads in the *Paris Free Voice* and *France USA Contacts* (see p.32) and keep an eye on the notice boards at the Anglophone churches: the American Church in Paris (65 quai d'Orsay, 7e; M° Invalides); St George's English Church (7 rue Auguste-Vacquerie, 16e; M° Charles-de-Gaulle/Étoile); St Michael's Anglican Church (5 rue d'Aguesseau, 8e; M° Madeleine); and the American Cathedral (23 av George V, 8e; M° Alma-Marceau). You could also try the notice boards located in the offices of CIDJ at 101 quai Branly, 15e (Mon–Sat

10am–6pm; M° Bir-Hakeim), and CROUS, 39 av Georges Bernanos, 5e (RER Port-Royal), both youth information agencies which advertise a number of temporary jobs for foreigners.

The **national employment agency**, ANPE (Agence Nationale pour l'Emploi), advertises temporary jobs in all fields and, in theory, offers a whole range of services to job-seekers; though it's open to all EU citizens, it is not renowned for its helpfulness to foreigners. Non-EU citizens will have to show a work permit to apply for any of their jobs. It's worth getting in touch with **CIEE (Council on International Educational Exchange)** who can arrange three-month work programmes for US, Canadian and Australasian students and recent graduates, as well as help Britons find work. Although they do have an office in Paris, at 1 place de l'Odéon, 6e (☎01.44.41.74.74; M° Odéon), it's better to arrange things in advance: in Britain, they're based at 52 Poland St, London W1V 4JQ (☎0171/478 2000; *www. ciee.org*), and they have offices in North America and Australia. Other possible sources include the "Offres d'Emploi" (Job Offers) in *Le Monde*, *Le Figaro* and the *International Herald Tribune*, and notice boards at English bookshops. Vac-Job, 46 av Réné-Coty, 14e (☎01.43.20.70.51), publishes the annual *Emplois d'Été en France* (*Summer Jobs in France*), which may be useful.

Some people have found jobs **selling magazines** on the street and **leafleting** just by asking people already doing it for the agency address. The American/Irish/British **bars and restaurants** sometimes have vacancies. You'll need to speak French, look smart and be prepared to work very long hours. Obviously, the better your French, the better your chances are of finding work.

Although **working as an au pair** is easily set up through any number of agencies (lists are

---

French bureaucracy: a warning

French officialdom and bureaucracy can damage your health. That Gallic shrug and *"Ce n'est pas possible"* is not the result of training programmes in making life difficult for foreigners: they drive most French citizens mad as well. Sorting out social security, long-stay visas, job contracts, bank accounts, tenancy agreements, university enrolment or any other financial, legal or state matter, requires serious commitment. Your reserves of patience, diligence, energy

(both physical and mental) and equanimity in the face of bloody-mindedness and Catch-22s will be tested to the full. Expect to spend days repeatedly visiting the same office and considerable sums on official translations of every imaginable document. Before you throw yourself into the Seine in despair, remember that others are going through it, too, and sharing the frustration may well help: the American Church (see above) is the place for such contacts.

available from French embassies or consulates, and there are lots of ads in *The Lady* in the UK), this sort of work can be total misery if you end up with an unpleasant employer, with conditions, pay and treatment the next worst thing to slavery. If you're determined to try – and it can be a very good way of learning the language – it's better to apply once in France, where you can at least meet the family first and check things out. However, you can arrange it first through an agency. As initial numbers to ring, in Britain try Avalon Au Pairs (☎01344/778246), in the US the American Institute for Foreign Study (☎203/869-9090), or in Paris itself Accueil Familial des Jeunes Étrangers (☎01.42.22.50.34; 690F joining fee). These have positions for female au pairs only and will fill you in on the general terms and conditions (never very generous); you shouldn't get paid less than 1650F a month (on top of board and lodging and some sort of travelpass).

Claiming benefit in Paris

Any EU citizen who has been signing on for **unemployment benefit** for a minimum period of four to six weeks at home, and intends to continue doing so in Paris, needs a letter of introduction from their own social security office, plus an E303 certificate of authorization (be sure to give them plenty of warning to prepare this). You must register within seven days with the Agence Nationale pour l'Emploi (ANPE), whose offices are listed under *Administration du Travail et de l'Emploi* in the Yellow Pages or ANPE in the White Pages.

It's possible to claim benefit for up to three months while you look for work, but it can often take that amount of time for the paperwork to be processed (also see warning opposite). Pensioners can arrange for their **pensions** to be paid in France, but cannot receive French state pensions.

Studying

It's relatively easy to be a student in Paris. Foreigners pay no more than French nationals (around 2000F registration fee) to enrol in a course, but there's also the cost of supporting yourself. Your *carte de séjour* and – for EU nationals – social security will be assured, and you'll be eligible for subsidized accommodation, meals and all the student reductions. Few people want to do undergraduate degrees abroad, but for higher degrees or other diplomas, the range of options is enormous. Strict entry requirements, including an exam in French, apply only for undergraduate degrees.

Generally, French universities are much less formal than British ones, and many people perfect their fluency in the language while studying. For full details and prospectuses, go to the Cultural Service of any French embassy or consulate (see p.18 for the addresses).

Embassies and consulates can also give details of **language courses**, which often combine with lectures on French "civilization" and are usually very costly. In Britain, the French Institute, 17 Queensbury Place, London SW7 2DT (☎0171/838 2148), is a cultural centre which has a cinema and a library where you can come to pick up a list of language courses in France (library hours Tues–Fri noon–7pm & Sat noon–6pm); otherwise send a letter requesting the list accompanied by a self-addressed envelope. Courses at the non-profit making **Alliance Française** (101 bd Raspail, 6e; ☎01.45.44.38.28; M° St-Placide), are reasonably priced (from about 1500F per month) and well regarded, while the **Sorbonne** (47 rue des Écoles, 5e; ☎01.40.46.22.11), has special six-month courses aimed at foreigners. Saying you studied French at the latter may impress your friends, but there are no prerequisites and the courses are very old-fashioned and grammar-based. You'll find ads for lesser language courses in the *Paris Free Voice*.

Part 2

The City

Chapter 1

Introducing the city

Geography, history and function have combined to give Paris a remarkably coherent and intelligible structure. The city lies in a basin surrounded by hills. It is very nearly circular, confined within limits of the **boulevard périphérique**, which follows the line of the most recent, nineteenth-century fortifications. Through its middle, the **River Seine** flows east to west in a satisfying arc. At the hub of the circle, in the middle of the river, anchors the island from which all the rest grew: the **Île de la Cité** (covered in Chapter 2). Here, the city's oldest religious and secular institutions – the cathedral and the royal palace – overlook the river, which was itself both the city's raison d'être and its lifeline.

The royal palace of the **Louvre** lies on the north or **Right Bank** (*rive droite*) of the Seine. To the northwest runs the longest and grandest vista of the city – **La Voie Triomphale** (Chapter 3) – comprising the Tuileries gardens, the Champs-Élysées, the Arc de Triomphe, and the Grande Arche de la Défense, each an expression of royal or state power across the centuries. To the north and east of the Voie Triomphale, clamped in an arc around the river, you'll find the commercial and financial quarters (covered in Chapter 4): the stock exchange, the Bank of France, the fashion and leather trades, jewellers, remnants of the medieval guilds, and what remains of the fruit, vegetable and meat market that was based in **Les Halles**. Just to the east of Les Halles, the **Marais** (Chapter 5) was the first really prestigious address for leading courtiers and businessmen in the seventeenth century; with the **Bastille** next door, it's now one of the liveliest areas of the city.

The south bank of the river, on the other hand, **Left Bank** (*rive gauche*; Chapter 6), developed quite differently. It owes its existence to the cathedral school of Notre-Dame, which spilled over from the Île de la Cité and became the university of the Sorbonne, attracting scholars and students from all over the medieval world. Ever since, it has been the traditional domain of the intelligentsia – of academics, writers, artists and the liberal professions, and of the cinema.

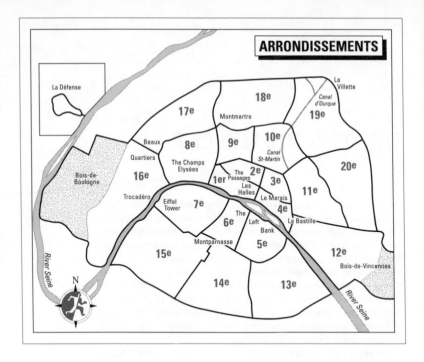

The city is divided into twenty **arrondissements**, whose spiral arrangement provides a fairly accurate guide to its historical growth. Centred on the Louvre, they wind outwards in a clockwise direction. The inner hub of the city comprises arrondissements 1er to 6^e, and it's here that most of the major sights and museums are to be found. The outer or higher-number arrondissements were mostly incorporated into the city in the nineteenth century, those to the east accommodating mainly the poor and the working-class, while those to the west held the aristocracy and the newly rich. Most of them were outlying villages that were gradually absorbed by the expanding city – some, such as **Belleville** (Chapter 10), **Montmartre** (Chapter 9) and **Passy** (Chapter 11), have succeeded in retaining something of their separate village identity.

These historical divisions substantially retain their validity to this day. The Right Bank still connotes business and commerce, the Left Bank arts and letters; west means bourgeois and smart, east means working-class, immigrant and scruffy. In recent years, however, such neat arrangements have been increasingly disturbed as rising property values open up their traditional quartiers to gentrification.

One thing Paris is not particularly well endowed with is **parks**. The largest, the **Bois de Boulogne** (Chapter 11) and the **Bois de Vincennes** (Chapter 10), at the western and eastern limits of the city, do possess small pockets of interest, but are largely anonymous

THE CITY: CHAPTER 1

sprawls. More enjoyable recreational spaces in Paris are the small squares and *places*, the quais along the banks of the Seine, and the bits of unexpected greenery encountered as you wander the streets. For a real break from the bustle of the city, it is best to try an out-of-town excursion, to the château of Vaux-le-Vicomte, for example, or the forest of Fontainebleau (see Chapter 18).

At its widest point, Paris is only about 12km across, which, at a brisk pace, is not much more than two hours' **walk**. By far the best way to discover Paris, walking is very pleasant as long as you're away from the main roads. This marvellous compactness leaves little space for dross and tedium, for lifeless and interminable residential areas – on the contrary, any walk across the city is action-packed. You move swiftly from villagey Montmartre to the sleaze of Barbès, from the high-powered elegance of the Faubourg-St-Honoré to the frenetic and downmarket commercialism of Les Halles. You exchange vast subterranean shopping and entertainment complexes for chaotic and colourful quartiers, where West African textiles and teapots from the Maghreb are piled high behind narrow counters; you leave the maelstrom of the Right Bank expressway to find yourself alone by the brown waters of the Seine.

Arriving in Paris

Whatever your point of arrival, it's no great problem getting to any part of Paris. The **train stations** are all very central with direct access to the fast and efficient métro and RER network; the main **bus station**, just outside the city proper, is close to a métro station. From the two **airports**, Roissy Charles de Gaulle and Orly, there are trains, buses or taxis to get you to the centre of the city.

By air

The two main Paris **airports** dealing with international flights are Roissy Charles de Gaulle and Orly with two terminals Orly Sud and

*Disneyland
Paris is linked
by bus from
both Charles
de Gaulle and
Orly airports;
for details of
these services,
plus train
links from the
centre to the
purpose-built
Marne-La-
Vallée TGV, see
p.397.*

Orly Ouest, linked by shuttle bus but easily walkable. Ouest (West) is used for domestic flights, while Sud (South) handles international flights. Both airports have money exchanges and information desks providing good, free maps and accommodation listings.

Aéroport Roissy Charles de Gaulle

BA, Air France and most transatlantic flights touch down at **Roissy Charles de Gaulle** Airport, known familiarly as Charles de Gaulle (though you'll see the additional Roissy on most official signs) and abbreviated to CDG or Paris CD. The airport has two main terminals – Aérogare 1 and Aérogare 2 (CDG1 and CDG2, the latter subdivided into 2A, 2B, 2C, 2D and 2F). It lies 23km to the northeast of the city, and is connected to the centre by several means of transport. Line B of the **RER** (the suburban train network; see p.58) runs from the Aéroport CDG1 station and Aéroport CDG2 TGV station (there is direct access from CDG 2 to the station, while passengers arriving at CDG1 must take a free shuttle to the RER); an express service called **Roissyrail** links to Gare du Nord, Châtelet-les-Halles, St-Michel and Denfert Rochereau (every 15min from 5am until midnight), where you can transfer to the métro. Taking about thirty minutes to Gare du Nord, this is the quickest route and costs 47F second class. The indirect service (same price), which takes in suburban stops, operates continuously between 4.56am and 11.55pm, and takes only about five minutes more, but is not designed to accommodate luggage. **Leaving Paris** for Charles de Gaulle, from Gare du Nord all but the first train leave from platform 43, where helpful English-speaking staff at an information desk, indicated by a large question mark (daily 7am–7pm), can tell you at which of the two CDG airport stations to disembark for your airline; if it's closed, check the airline code on your ticket against the information board here.

By bus from the airport, the cheapest service is run by **Roissy Bus** (45F), which connects CDG2 with the Opéra-Garnier on the corner of rues Auber and Scribe (RER Auber & Mº Opéra) every 15 minutes from 5.45am to 11pm; journey time is approximately 45 minutes. Alternatively, the **Air France Bus** offers three services with differing routes, times and prices (information in English ☎01.41.56.89.00). The green-coded line 2 (60F one way, 105F return) leaves from CDG2 every twelve minutes from 5.40am to 11pm, terminating at Porte Maillot métro on the northwest edge of the city, stopping at avenue Carnot, outside Charles-de-Gaulle-Étoille RER/métro between the Arc de Triomphe and rue Tilsitt. The orange-coded line 5 leaves from CDG1 but takes the same route as line 2 and costs the same (every 20min 6am–11pm). The yellow-coded line 4 (70F one way, 120F return) departs from both CDG1 and CDG2 every half hour from 7am to 9.30pm, terminating near Gare Montparnasse and stopping at Gare du Lyon. Journey times vary from 25 minutes to more than an hour during rush hour. **Leaving Paris** to get to the airport, the green-coded line 2 (for CDG2) and orange-coded route 5 (CDG1) buses departs from avenue Carnot, right outside the RER exit of Charles-de-Gaulle-Étoile, and from Porte Maillot. The yellow-coded line 4 (for both CDG1 and CDG2) leaves from 2 bis bd Diderot outside Gare du Lyon and near Gare Montparnasse at rue du Commandant-René-Mouchotte in front of the *Méridien Hotel*.

Taxis into central Paris cost at least 205F, plus a small luggage supplement (6F per piece of luggage), and should take between fifty minutes and one hour. The **Airport Shuttle**, a minibus door-to-door airport service into central Paris, with no extra charge for luggage, can work out to be more reasonable than a taxi (89F per head if there are more than two people, 120F for a single person). For advance bookings (English-speaking) call ☎01.45.38.55.72, fax 01.43.21.35.67.

Aéroport d'Orly

Orly Airport, 14km south of Paris, has three connections to RER lines and a choice of buses. **Orlyrail** is a bus–rail link to central Paris; a shuttle bus goes to RER station Pont de Rungis (line C), from where the Orlyrail train leaves every fifteen minutes from 5.45am to 9pm, half-hourly thereafter until 11pm, for the Gare d'Austerlitz and other métro connections (30F; train 35min, total journey around 50min). **Leaving Paris**, from Gare d'Austerlitz the train runs from 5.50am to 11.50pm. At 57F, **Orlyval** (every 5 to 7min from 6am to 10.30pm, from 7am on Sun and hols) is a more expensive option of fast *Val* train shuttle to RER station Anthony, where you can continue on to central Paris via RER line B, with métro connections at Denfert-Rochereau, St-Michel and Châtelet-les-Halles. It takes around thirty minutes to reach the centre. For 30F you can catch the **Orlybus** to Denfert-Rochereau RER/métro station in the 14e (every 12min from 6.30am to 11.30pm); journey time is 30 minutes. **Leaving Paris** the bus departs from place Denfert Rochereau (6am–11.30pm).

Air France buses (information in English ☎01.41.56.89.00) connect Orly with the Invalides Air France terminus via Montparnasse (also stopping at Porte d'Orléans and Duroc if requested in advance). The 35-minute services leave every 12 minutes from 5.50am to 11pm, and cost 45F one way, 75F return. **Leaving Paris** the bus can be caught from the Invalides Air France Terminal and from Montparnasse on rue du Commandant-René-Mouchotte in front of the *Méridien Hotel*. Alternatively, **Jetbus** runs to Villejuif-Louis Aragon métro, the terminus of line 7, every 12 to 15 minutes from 6am to 10.15pm. It takes 15 minutes and costs 24F (you will then need a métro ticket to get into the centre).

A **taxi** will take around 35 minutes to the centre of Paris and cost at least 130F. The **Airport Shuttle** door-to-door minibus service (see above) is also offered to and from Orly.

By rail

Each of Paris' six **main-line stations** is equipped with cafés, restaurants, tabacs, banks and bureaux de change (where you can expect lengthy waits in season). They are divided into *Grands Lignes* (main lines) and *Banlieue* (surburban lines), with separate ticket offices (*guichets*), and all are connected with the métro system.

The **Gare du Nord**, rue Dunkerque, 10e (trains from the north of France including Boulogne and Calais; the UK, including Eurostar – see below; Belgium, Holland and northern Germany, including Thalys; and Scandinavia) and **Gare de l'Est**, place du 11-Novembre-1918, 10e (serving eastern France, southern Germany, Switzerland and Austria) are side by side in the northeast of the city. The **Gare St-Lazare** (place du Havre, 8e; serving the Normandy coast, Dieppe) is the most central station, close to the Madeleine and the Opéra-Garnier. Still on the Right Bank but towards the southwest corner is the **Gare du Lyon** (place Louis-Armand, 12e), for trains from Italy and Switzerland and TGV lines from southeast France. South of the river, **Gare Montparnasse** (bd de Vaugirard, 15e) is the terminus for Chartres, Brittany, the Atlantic coast and TGV lines to southwest France; and **Gare d'Austerlitz** (bd de l'Hôpital, 13^e), for ordinary (not TGV) trains to southwest France, the Loire Valley, Spain and Portugal. The motorail station, Gare de Paris-Bercy, is down the tracks from the Gare du Lyon, on bd de Bercy, 12^e.

Gare du Nord and Gare du Lyon are the only two stations to have **tourist information** offices (same hours and accommodation booking; see opposite). The central phone number for **information in English** is ☎01.45.82.08.41 (for information on suburban lines call ☎01.40.52.75.75). For **reservations** in Île-de-France call ☎01.53.90.20.20, for the rest of France ☎08.36.35.35.35; you can book over the telephone but you have to actually buy your ticket in person within 48 hours at the relevant station. It's easiest to use the counter service for buying tickets, though the touch-screen computerized system available in most stations can be read in English and is a good way to check fares and times – simply press the red button to cancel the transaction.

At the time of writing, with the exception of Gare du Nord, **left-luggage** options are limited at train stations as a security precaution following a spate of bomb attacks in 1995; if you find there are no facilities at the station where you arrive, your best bet is to make your way to Gare du Nord.

Eurostar

Eurostar trains from Britain terminate at **Gare du Nord**, rue Dunkerque, 10e, a bustling convergence of international, long-distance and suburban trains, the métro and several bus routes. There are two **bureaux de change** at the station, which between them stay

open from 6.15am to 11pm daily, and a small **tourist office**
(Mon–Sat 8am–8pm), which can book accommodation for a rising-
scale fee of 20–55F (8F for a youth hostel), and sell museum passes.
On leaving the train, turn left for tourist information, the métro and
the RER, and right for taxis and heavy-security **left luggage**
(Mon–Fri 6.15am–11.15pm, Sat & Sun 6.45am–11.15pm), both
down the escalators opposite the Avis car rental desk. You can even
get a **shower** (21F for 20min) in the public toilets (daily 6am–9pm;
2.80F) at the bottom of the métro escalators.

By road

Eurolines (☎01.49.72.51.51) and almost all **buses** coming into
Paris – whether international or domestic – use the **main gare
routière** on the eastern edge of the city at 28 avenue du Général-du-
Gaulle, Bagnolet. The métro station here (M° Gallieni), the terminus
of line 3, provides a link to the centre.

If you're **driving** into Paris, don't try to go straight across the city
to your destination. Use the ring road – the **boulevard périphérique**
– to get to the **porte** nearest to your destination: it's much quicker,
except at rush hour, and easier to find your way at any time.

Once ensconced wherever you're staying, you'd be well advised to
park the car at your hotel and use public transport. **Parking** is a
major problem in the city centre (see p.60 for more details).

Information

The **main tourist office** is at 127 avenue des Champs-Elysées, 8^e
(April–Sept daily 9am–8pm, closed May 1; Oct–March Mon–Sat
9am–8pm, Sun 11am–6pm; ☎01.49.52.53.54, fax 01.49.52.53.00;
M° Charles-de-Gaulle-Étoile), where the efficient but overworked
staff will answer questions from the predictable to the bizarre. There
are **branch offices** at two of the main train stations, Gare du Lyon
(Mon–Sat 8am–8pm ☎01.43.43.33.24) and Gare du Nord (same
hours ☎01.45.26.94.82); and at the Eiffel Tower (daily April–Sept
11am–6pm ☎01.45.51.22.15). Each gives away large quantities of
glossy brochures and some useful fold-out leaflets detailing sights,
markets, shops, museums and excursions, as well as maps. Most of
the printed information is behind the counter and not all of it's free:
the tourist office's useful *Paris Map* costs 5F.

For recorded **tourist information in English**, phone
☎01.49.52.53.56. Alternative sources of information are the Hôtel
de Ville information office, **Bureau d'Accueil**, at 29 rue de Rivoli, 4^e
(Mon–Sat 9am–6pm ☎01.42.76.43.43; M° Hôtel de Ville), and **electronic billboards** dotted around town. Within the new Carrousel du
Louvre, 99 rue de Rivoli, 1er, underground below the triumphal arch
at the east end of the Tuilleries, you'll find the **Espace du Tourism**

d'Île de France (10am–7pm; closed Tues; ☎01.44.50.19.98) with stylishly presented information on attractions and activities in Paris and the surrounding area. For maps of the **métro**, see opposite.

Paris Le Journal, published by the mairie, is a free **monthly** detailing what's on, available at the Bureau d'Accueil as well as in museums and shops. Also good for the latest special exhibitions at museums and other cultural information are Paris' two listings magazines, *Pariscope* (with a small section in English) and *L'Officiel des Spectacles* (see p.32).

Getting around the city

Information on the forms of help available for disabled travellers on public transport is given on p.23.

Finding your way around is remarkably easy, as Paris proper, stripped of its suburbs, is compact and relatively small, with an integrated public transport system – the **RATP** (Régie Autonome des Transports Parisiens). The system is cheap, fast and meticulously signposted, comprising buses, underground métro and suburban express train lines of the RER (Réseau Express Régional). The whole network is divided into five **zones**, though the entire métro system fits into zones 1 and 2.

Fares and passes

Be sure to keep your ticket until the end of your journey: you'll be fined on the spot if you can't produce one.

For a short stay in the city, tickets can be bought in **carnets** of ten from any station or tabac showing a green métro ticket sign; the current cost is 48F, as opposed to 8F for a single ticket. Only one 8F carnet is ever needed per journey on the métro system, and within zones 1 and 2 for any RER or bus journey, but you cannot switch between buses or between bus and métro/RER on the same ticket. Night buses require separate tickets costing 30F each, unless you have a weekly or monthly travel pass (see below). For RER journeys beyond zones 1 and 2, you must buy an RER ticket; visitors often get caught out, for instance, when they take the RER instead of the métro to La Défense. **Children** under four travel free and from four to ten at half price.

If you've arrived early in the week and are staying three days or more, it may be more economical to obtain a **Carte Orange** (you'll need a passport photo – available from the booths in the main stations) – with a weekly coupon (*coupon hebdomadaire*; get one for zones 1 and 2 to cover the city and inner suburbs). Costing 75F, the zone 1 and 2 version is valid for an unlimited number of journeys from Monday morning to Sunday evening, and is on sale at all métro stations and tabacs. You can only buy a coupon for the current week until Wednesday; from Thursday you buy a coupon to begin the following Monday. There's also a monthly coupon (*mensuel*) for 255F for zones 1 and 2. You need to write your *Carte Orange* number on the coupon. A word of warning: the *Carte Orange* pass is technically for Île de France residents only, though most clerks will sell you one as a visitor.

Other options include the **Paris Visites**, 1-, 2-, 3- and 5-day visitors' passes at 50F, 80F, 120F and 170F for Paris and inner suburbs, or 100F, 175F, 245F and 300F to include the airports, Versailles and Disneyland Paris (make sure you buy this one when you arrive at Roissy Charles de Gaulle or Orly to get maximum value). A children's version is available at half price for 1, 2 or 3 days. The main advantage of *Paris Visites* passes is that, unlike the *coupon hebdomadaire* whose validity runs unalterably from Monday to Sunday, they can begin on any day. They also allow you discounts at certain monuments and museums.

Both the *Carte Orange* and the *Paris Visites* entitle you to **unlimited travel** (in the zones you have chosen) on bus, métro, RER, SNCF and the Montmartre funicular. On the métro you put the coupon through the turnstile slot, but make sure to return it to its plastic folder; it is reusable throughout the period of its validity. On the bus you show the whole *carte* to the driver as you board – don't put it into the punching machine.

A *mobilis* **day pass** is also available, taking in all forms of RATP transport (from 30F for the city, 70F to include the outer suburbs and airports).

Recorded information in English on all RATP services is available 24hr on the premium rate ☎ 08.36. 68.41.14

The métro and the RER

The **métro** (M°), providing the simplest way of moving around, runs from 5.30am to 12.30am; the RER from 5am to midnight. Stations are far more frequent than on most subway systems, though many entrances are a long way from the platforms and most interchanges involve long walks and lots of stairs. A choice of three free **maps** is available at most stations: the *Grand Plan de Paris* for the whole RATP system, which also usefully overlays the metro system onto a map of Paris' streets; the more at-a-glance *Petit Plan de Paris*; or the pocket-sized *Paris Plan de Poche*. In addition, every station has a big plan of the network outside the entrance and several inside, along with a large-scale map of the immediate neighbourhood.

The métro lines are colour-coded and numbered 1 to 14; the RER lines are designated by the letters A, B, C or D. Within the system, you find your way around by following signs bearing the name of the station at the end of the line in the direction in which you are travelling: *Direction Porte Dauphine, Direction Gallieni* and so on. The numerous interchanges, or **correspondances** (look for the orange signs), make it possible to travel anywhere in the city in a more or less straight line.

For RER journeys beyond the city, make sure that the station you want is illuminated on the platform display board.

A colour map of the Paris métro is at the back of the guide; see overleaf for the RER.

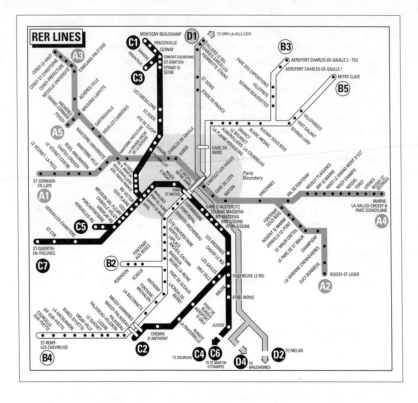

Buses

Don't, however, use the underground system to the exclusion of **buses**. These are easy to use and, of course, allow you to see much more. Free **route maps** are available at métro stations, bus terminals and the tourist office. The best bus map, showing the métro and RER as well, is the *Grand Plan de Paris* (see overleaf). Every bus stop displays the numbers of the buses that stop there, a map showing all the stops on the route, and the times of the first and last buses. Each bus has a map of its own route inside and some have a recorded announcement for each approaching stop; a red button should be pressed to request a stop and an *arrêt demandé* sign will then light up. Only the #20 bus (see opposite) is designed to be easily accessible for wheelchairs and prams. Generally speaking, buses run from around 6.30am to 8.30pm, with some services continuing to 12.30am. Many lines (nearly half of all routes) don't operate on Sundays and holidays or reduce their services at such times.

From mid-April to mid-September, a special **Balabus** service (not to be confused with Batobus, see p.60) passes all the major tourist

---

Touring Paris by public transport

A good way to take in the sights is to hop on a bus. **Bus #20** (wheelchair accessible) from Gare du Lyon follows the Grands Boulevards and does a loop through the 1er and 2e arrondissements. **Bus #24** between Porte de Bercy and Gare St-Lazare follows the left bank of the Seine. **Bus #29** has an open platform at the back, which makes it fun for sightseeing – it runs from Gare St Lazare past the Opéra Garnier, the Centre Pompidou, through the Marais and past the Bastille to the Gare du Lyon. For La Voie Triomphale, take a trip on **bus #73** between La Défense and the Musée d'Orsay. Many more bus journeys – outside rush hours – are worthwhile trips in themselves: get hold of the *Grand Plan de Paris* from a métro station and check out the routes of the #38, #48, #64, #67, #68, #69, #82, #87 and #95.

The **métro**, surprisingly, can also provide some scenery: the **overground** line on the southern route between Charles-de-Gaulle/Étoile and Nation (line 6) gives you views of the Eiffel Tower, the Île des Cygnes, the Invalides, the new National Library and the Finance Ministry.

---

sights between La Défense Grande Arche and Gare du Lyon, on Sundays and holidays between noon and 9pm; the entire route takes about 50min. Bus stops are marked "Balabus"; standard bus fares apply.

Night buses (Noctambus) ply eighteen routes every hour from 1am to 5.30am linking place du Châtelet (near the Hôtel de Ville) with the suburbs. Again, there is a reduced service on Sunday.

Taxis

If it's late at night or you feel like treating yourself, don't hesitate to use **taxis**, as charges are fairly reasonable – between 40F and 70F for a central daytime journey but considerably more if you call one out. Check that the meter shows the appropriate fare rate: you can see which of the three small indicator lights on its roof is switched on before you get into the taxi. "A" indicates the daytime rate (7am–7pm; around 3.45F/km) for Paris and the boulevard péripherique; "B" is the rate for Paris at night (7pm–7am), on Sundays and on public holidays, and for the suburbs during the day (around 5.45F/km); "C" is the night rate for the suburbs (around 7F/km). In addition, there's a pick-up charge of around 13F and a time charge (around 120F/hr) for when the car is stationary, an additional 5F charge if picked up from a main-line train station, and 6F per piece of luggage.

Taxis will often refuse to take more than three people (they don't like you to sit in the front seat); if they do take you, they'll charge extra for the fourth person (about 9F). **Tipping** is not mandatory, but ten percent will be expected. Finding one of Paris' 470 taxi ranks (*arrêt taxi*) is usually better than trying to hail one down in the street. The large white light means the taxi is free; the orange light below means it's engaged.

Boats

There remains one final mode of transport, **Batobus**, which operates
from May to September, stopping at six points along the Seine in the
following order: port de la Bourdonnais (Eiffel Tower–Trocadéro),
quai de Solférino (Musée d'Orsay), quai Malaquais (Saint Germain-
des-Prés), quai de Montebello (Notre-Dame), quai de l'Hôtel de Ville
(Hôtel-de-Ville–Centre-Pompidou) and quai du Louvre (Musée du
Louvre). Boats run every half-hour or so from 10am to 7pm: total
journey time is around twenty minutes, and tickets cost 20F for the
first stop, 10F for subsequent stops, which makes 60F for a day pass
the more reasonable option if you want to hop on and off.

Driving

Travelling around Paris by **car**, in the daytime at least, is hardly
worth it because of the difficulty of finding a **parking** space. You're
better off finding a motel-style place with parking on the edge of the
city and using the public transport system. If you're determined to
drive in and use the pay-and-display parking system, you must first
buy a **Paris Carte** from a tabac then look for the blue "P" signs
alongside grey parking meters. Feed the card into the meter; costs
are 10F an hour, with a two-hour maximum. Alternatively, covered
car parks cost up to 15F per hour. Whatever you do, don't park in a
bus lane or the *Axe Rouge* **express routes** (marked with a red
square).

*You have to be
18 to drive in
France,
regardless of
whether you
hold a licence
as a younger
driver.
Most rental
companies will
only deal with
people over 25.*

For **car rental**, the big international companies have offices at the
airports and at several locations in the city. Avis (☎01.46.10.60.60),
located at Gare du Nord, do good weekend prices: their "Parisien
weekend" car hire extends from noon on Thursday to noon on
Tuesday, with two days working out at 366F per day, to five days at
287F per day. Other big names are listed in the "Directory" of the
guide, p.368.

North Americans and Australians in particular should be fore-
warned that it's difficult to hire a car with automatic transmission in
France; if you can't drive a manual, try and book an automatic well
in advance, possibly before you leave home, and be prepared to pay
a much higher price for it.

Cycling

Since 1996 the Mairie de Paris has made great efforts to introduce
dedicated **cycle lanes** in Paris. You can pick up a free leaflet, *Paris
à Vélo*, outlining the routes, from town halls, the tourist office or
bike hire outlets. Unfortunately very few stretches are separate from
the roads and, given how Parisians park and drive, the new lanes are
very much a token gesture. The best road-free **cycle routes** are the
promenade plantée along the old railway line from Vincennes into
the 12e arrondissement, rue Vercingétorix from place de Catalogne

to Porte de Vanves in the 14e, and the quays of Canal St-Martin, the Bassin de la Villette and the Canal de l'Ourcq. The new bridge across the Seine, Pont Charles-de-Gaulle between the Gare du Lyon and Gare d'Austerlitz, has separate lanes, as do boulevard d'Auriol, rue Albert-Bayer, avenue Edison, and rues Baudricourt, Château-des-Rentiers and Nationale in the 13e. On Sundays cycling by the Seine is especially popular, when its central quais (and along the Canal St Martin) are closed to cars between 10am and 4pm. If you prefer cycling in a more natural environment, the Bois de Boulogne and the Bois de Vincennes have extensive bike tracks.

Air pollution is bad in Paris, and the occasional steep and cobbled street does not make for the smoothest of rides. The main hazard, however, is posed by drivers, though fortunately cycling is gaining popularity among Parisians.

For details of **bike rental** and guided cycling **tours**, see p.353 of "Daytime amusements and sports".

Museums and monuments

If you're planning to visit a great many museums in a short time, it's worth buying the **Carte Musées et Monuments** (1-day 80F, 3-day 160F, 5-day 240F), available from the tourist office, métro stations, museums, and the Eurostar terminals at London Waterloo and Ashford in Kent. Valid for seventy museums and monuments in and around Paris, the pass allows you to bypass ticket queues (though it doesn't provide entry to special exhibitions). **Reduced admission** is often available for those over 60 and under 18, for which you'll need your passport as proof of age, and for students under 26, for which you'll need the ISIC (International Student Identity Card). Many museums and monuments are free for children under twelve, and nearly always for kids under four. Under-26s can also get a free Youth Card, *Carte Jeune*, available in France from youth travel agencies like USIT and from main tourist offices (120F, valid one year), which entitles you to reductions throughout Europe. Some museums have free or half-price admission on Sunday; many are closed on Monday and Tuesday.

Below are some of the major museums and monuments covered in the guide, with bare-bones opening hours, entry fees, phone numbers and public transport. Refer to the relevant page number for more detailed accounts.

Arc de Triomphe Daily: April–Sept 9.30am–11pm; Oct–March 10am–10.30pm; 35F; ☎01.55.37.73.77; Mo Charles-de-Gaulle–Étoile; p.71.

Cité des Sciences et de l'Industrie Tues–Sat 10am–6pm, Sun 10am–7pm; closed Mon; 50F; ☎01.40.05.70.00; Mo Porte de la Villette; pp.195 & 364.

Conciergerie Daily: April–Sept 9.30am–6.30pm; Oct–March 10am–5pm; 32F; ☎01.53.73.78.50; Mo Cité; p.66.

Museums and monuments

Eiffel Tower Daily: Sept–June 9.30am–11pm; July & Aug 9am–midnight; 20–59F depending how high you go; ☎01.44.11.23.45; Mᵒ Bir-Hakeim/Trocadéro/Ecole-Militaire; RER Champ-de-Mars-Tour-Eiffel; p.139.

Galeries Nationale du Grand Palais Opening hours vary with exhibition; ☎01.44.13.17.17; Mᵒ Champs-Élysées-Clemenceau; p.74.

Grande Arche de la Défense Daily 10am–7pm; 40F; ☎01.49.07.27.57; Mᵒ/RER La-Défense-Grande Arche; p.226.

Institut du Monde Arabe Tues–Sun 10am–6pm; closed Mon; 25F; ☎01.40.51.39.53; Mᵒ Jussieu/Cardinal-Lemoine; p.121.

Jeu de Paume Tues noon–9.30pm, Wed–Fri noon–7pm, Sat & Sun 10am–7pm; closed Mon; 38F; ☎01.47.03.12.50; Mᵒ Concorde; p.75.

Musée de l'Armée Daily: April–Sept 10am–5.45pm; Oct–March 10am–5pm; 37F; ☎01.44.42.37.72; Mᵒ Invalides; p.142.

Musée des Arts Africains et Océaniens Mon, Wed–Fri & hols 10am–5.30pm, Sat & Sun till 6pm; closed Tues; 30F; ☎01.44.74.84.80; Mᵒ Porte-Dorée; p.214.

Musée des Arts Décoratifs Tues–Fri 11am–6pm, Wed until 9pm, Sat & Sun 10am–6pm; closed Mon; 30F (with Musée de la Mode et du Textile); ☎01.44.55.57.50; Mᵒ Palais-Royal/Musée-du-Louvre/Louvre-Rivoli; p.85.

Musée d'Art Moderne de la Ville de Paris Tues–Fri 10am–5.30pm, Sat & Sun 10am–6.45pm; closed Mon; 30F; ☎01.53.67.40.00; Mᵒ Iéna/Alma-Marceau; p.138.

Musée Carnavalet Tues–Sun 10am–5.40pm; closed Mon; 27F; ☎01.42.72.21.13; Mᵒ St-Paul; p.106

Musée Cognacq-Jay Tues–Sun 10am–5.40pm; closed Mon; 17F; ☎01.40.27.07.21; Mᵒ St-Paul/Chemin-Vert; p.107.

Musée Delacroix Wed–Mon 9.30am–6pm; closed Tues; 30F; ☎01.44.41.86.50; Mᵒ St-Germain-des-Prés; p.129.

Musée de l'Erotisme Daily 10am–2am; 40F; ☎01.42.58.28.73; Mᵒ Blanche; p.182.

Musée de l'Homme Daily 9.45am–5.15pm; closed Tues; 30F; ☎01.44.05.72.72; Mᵒ Trocadéro; p.138.

Musée Jacquemart-André Daily 10am–6pm; 45F; ☎01.42.89.04.91; Mᵒ Miromesnil/St-Philippe-du-Roule; p.225.

Musée du Louvre Main collection Mon & Wed–Sun 9am–6pm, till 9.45pm on Mon and Wed; closed Tues; 45F; ☎01.40.20.50.50; Mᵒ Palais-Royal/Musée-du-Louvre/Louvre-Rivoli; p.78.

Musée Maillol Daily except Tues 11am–6pm; 40F; ☎01.42.22.59.58; Mᵒ Rue-du-Bac; p.143.

Musée de la Mode et du Textile Tues–Fri 11am–6pm, Wed till 9pm, Sat & Sun 10am–6pm; closed Mon; 30F (with Musée des Arts Décoratifs); ☎01.44.55.57.50; Mᵒ Palais-Royal/Musée-du-Louvre/Louvre-Rivoli; p.85.

Musée National d'Art Moderne Due to reopen in 2000; ☎01.44.78.12.33; Mᵒ Hôtel-de-Ville/Rambuteau; p.102.

Musée National des Arts et Traditions Populaires Wed–Mon 9.45am–5.15pm; closed Tues; 25F; ☎01.44.17.60.00; Mᵒ Les Sablons /Porte-Maillot; p.222.

Musée Marmottan Tues–Sun 10am–5pm; closed Mon; 40F; ☎01.42.24.07.02; Mº Muette; p.219.

Musée de la Musique Tues–Thurs noon–6pm, Fri & Sat noon–7.30pm, Sun 10am–6pm; closed Mon; 35F; ☎01.44.84.46.00; Mº Porte-de-Pantin; p.197.

Musée National du Moyen-Age Wed–Mon 9.15am–5.45pm; closed Tues; 30F, 20F on Sun; ☎01.53.73.78.00; Mº Cluny-La Sorbonne/St-Michel; p.122.

Musée de l'Orangerie Open May–June 1999 then closed for renovation until 2001; ☎01.42.97.48.16; p.75.

Musée d'Orsay Tues, Wed, Fri & Sat 9/10am–6pm, Thurs till–9.45pm, Sun 9am–6pm; closed Mon; 40F; ☎01.40.49.48.48; Mº Solférino, RER Musée d'Orsay; p.144.

Musée Pasteur Daily 2–5.30pm; closed Aug; 15F; ☎01.45.68.82.83; Mº Pasteur; p.160.

Musée Picasso Wed–Mon 9.30am–6pm; closed Tues; 30F, 20F on Sun; ☎01.42.71.25.21; Mº Chemin Vert/St-Paul; p.107.

Musée Rodin Tues–Sun: April–Sept 9.30am–5.45pm; Oct–March 9.30am–5pm; closed Mon; 28F; ☎01.47.05.01.34; Mº Varenne; p.143.

Palais de la Découverte Tues–Sat 9.30am–6pm, Sun & hols 10am–7pm; 27F; ☎01.40.74.80.00; Mº Champs-Élysées-Clemenceau/Franklin-D-Roosevelt; p.74.

Panthéon Daily: April–Sept 9.30am–6.30pm; Oct–March 10am–5.30pm; 32F; ☎01.44.32.18.00; Mº Cardinal Lemoine, RER Luxembourg; p.125.

Père-Lachaise Cemetery Daily 7.30am–6pm; free; ☎01.43.70.70.33; Mº Gambetta/Père-Lachaise/Alexandre-Dumas; p.204.

**Museums
and
monuments**

Chapter 2

The Islands

Right in the heart of Paris, two river islands, the **Île de la Cité** and the **Île St-Louis**, are connected to the Left and Right Banks of the Seine by several bridges, and to each other by the Pont St Louis near the Île de la Cité's major monument, the cathedral of **Notre-Dame**. To the east, the smaller of the two islands, Île St-Louis is one of the most salubrious addresses in Paris.

Île de la Cité

The **Île de la Cité** is where Paris began. The earliest settlements were sited here, as was the small Gallic town of Lutetia, overrun by Julius Caesar's troops in 52 BC. A natural defensive site commanding a

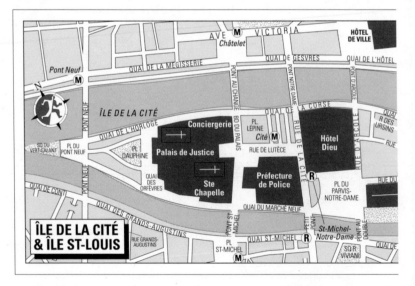

major east–west river trade route, it was an obvious candidate for a bright future. The Romans garrisoned it and laid out one of their standard military town plans, overlapping onto the Left Bank. While it never achieved any great political importance, they endowed it with an administrative centre that became the palace of the Merovingian kings in 508 AD, then of the counts of Paris, who in 987 became kings of France. Since these early days, the Île has been close to the administrative heart of France.

Today the lure of the island lies in the **square du Vert-Galant** and **the quais** in its tail end, in **place Dauphine** further east, and the **cathedral of Notre-Dame** itself, near its eastern extremity. Baron Haussmann's appointment as Napoleon III's *Préfet de la Seine* in 1853 led to the demolition of the central section of the island, displacing some 25,000 people and virtually breaking the island's back with the construction of four vast edifices in bland Baronial-Bureaucratik, largely given over to housing the law. He also perpetrated the now litter-blown space in front of Notre-Dame by razing the medieval houses that clustered close about – though that at least has the virtue of allowing a full-frontal view of the cathedral.

Île de la Cité

The Île de la Cité has its own métro station, Mᵒ Cité, and an exit for RER St-Michel-Notre-Dame.

Pont-Neuf and the quais

Arriving on the island by the **Pont-Neuf**, which despite its name is the city's oldest bridge (and the first to be constructed without the traditional medieval complement of houses on it), you'll see a statue of **Henri IV**, the king who commissioned it in 1607. It was during his reign that the first attempts were made to coordinate town planning in Paris.

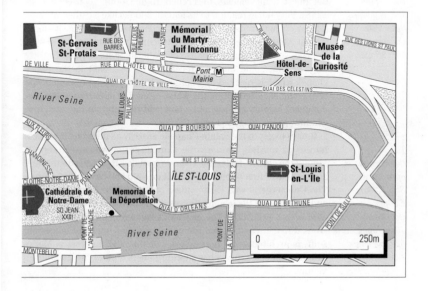

Île de la Cité

Behind his statue, a flight of steps goes down to the **quais** and the **square du Vert-Galant**, a small tree-lined green enclosed within the triangular stern of the island. The name *Vert-Galant*, meaning a "green" or "lusty" gentleman, allegedly celebrates Henri IV's success with women.

The prime spot to occupy is the extreme point by a weeping willow – haunt of lovers, sparrows and sunbathers. On the north quay is the dock for the tourist river boats, Bateaux-Vedettes du Pont-Neuf.

For details of the Bateaux-Vedettes du Pont-Neuf and other river boats, see p.345.

Sainte-Chapelle and the Conciergerie

On the eastern side of the bridge, across the street from the statue of **Henri IV**, seventeenth-century houses flank the entrance to the sanded, chestnut-shaded **place Dauphine**, one of the city's most secluded and exclusive squares, where the actress Simone Signoret lived until her death in 1985. The far end of the square is blocked by the dull mass of the **Palais de Justice**, which swallowed up the palace that was home to the French kings until Étienne Marcel's bloody revolt in 1358 frightened them off to the greater security of the Louvre. In earlier times it served as the Roman governors' residence.

The only part of the older complex that remains in its entirety is Louis IX's **Sainte-Chapelle**, built to house a collection of holy relics he had bought at extortionate rates from the bankrupt empire of Byzantium. It stands in a courtyard to the left of the main entrance (bd du Palais), looking somewhat squeezed by the proximity of the nineteenth-century law courts – which, incidentally, anyone is free to sit in on. Though much restored, the two-level chapel remains one of the finest achievements of French High Gothic (consecrated in 1248). Very tall in relation to its length, it looks like a cathedral choir lopped off and transformed into an independent building. Its most radical feature is the reduction of structural masonry to a minimum to make way for a huge expanse of exquisite **stained glass** (mostly original with some nineteenth-century restorations) in the upper chapel, which is reached by a spiral staircase. The impression inside is of being enclosed within the wings of myriad butterflies – the predominant colours are jewel-like blue and red, and, in the later rose window, grass-green and blue.

Ste-Chapelle is open daily April–Sept 9.30am–6.30pm, Oct–March 10am–5pm; 32F, combined ticket with Conciergerie 50F; M° Cité.

It pays to get to the Sainte-Chapelle as early as possible. It attracts hordes of tourists, as does the **Conciergerie**, whose entrance is around the corner, facing the river on quai de l'Horlage, where you'll also see Paris' first public clock, built in 1370 and now fully restored. The Conciergerie was Paris' oldest prison, where Marie-Antoinette and in their turn the leading figures of the Revolution were incarcerated before execution. The enormous vaulted late-Gothic **Salle des Gens d'Arme**, canteen and recreation room of the royal household staff, is architecturally impressive, but the chief interest is Marie-Antoinette's cell and various macabre mementos of the guillotine's victims.

The Conciergerie is open April–Sept 9.30am–6.30pm; Oct–March 10am–5pm; 32F, combined ticket with Ste-Chapelle 50F.

Henri IV

Henri IV was, first of all, king of Navarre in the Pyrénées, a bastion of Protestantism. On becoming king of France in 1589, he was obliged to convert to Catholicism out of deference to the sensibilities of the majority of his new subjects. "Paris is worth a Mass", he is reputed to have said, somewhat cynically.

Henri's great aim was to reconstruct and reconcile France, and it was he who guaranteed the civil rights of the Protestants in 1598. When they were abrogated a hundred years later by Louis XIV under the pressure of the Counter-Reformation, the Protestants scattered across the globe, from London's Spitalfields to the New World. Since many of them were highly skilled craftsmen, their departure was a blow to the Parisian economy – as was the death and exile of so many Communards two hundred years later, who in their turn were also largely the working-class élite.

For the loveliest view of what the whole ensemble once looked like, you need to get the postcard of the June illustration from the fifteenth-century Book of Hours **Les Très Riches Heures du Duc de Berry**, the most wonderful of medieval illuminated manuscripts. It shows the palace, with its towers and chimneys and trelliswork rose garden, with the Ste-Chapelle touching the sky in the right-hand corner. The Seine laps the curtain wall where now the quai des Orfèvres (goldsmiths) runs. In the foreground, pollarded willows line the Left Bank, while barefoot peasant girls rake hay into stooks and men scythe light-green swathes up the rue Dauphine. No sign of the square du Vert-Galant: it was just a swampy islet then, not to be joined to the rest of the Cité for another hundred years and more.

The original book of Les Très Riches Heures *is in the Musée Condé outside Paris – see p.392.*

Place Lépine and Pont d'Arcole

Continue along the north side of the island from the Conciergerie to reach **place Lépine**, named for the police boss who gave Paris' coppers their white truncheons and whistles. There's an exuberant **flower market** here Monday to Saturday, with birds and pets – cruelly caged – on Sunday.

Next bridge but one is the **Pont d'Arcole**, named after a young revolutionary killed in an attack on the Hôtel de Ville in the 1830 rising (see p.418), and beyond that the only bit of the Cité that survived Haussmann's attentions. In the streets hereabouts once flourished the cathedral school of Notre-Dame, forerunner of the Sorbonne.

Around the year 1200, one of the teachers was **Peter Abélard**, of Héloïse fame (see below). A philosophical whiz kid and cocker of snooks at the establishment intellectuals of his time, he was very popular with his students and not at all with the authorities, who thought they caught a distinct whiff of heresy. Forced to leave the cathedral school, he set up shop on the Left Bank with his disciples and, in effect, founded the University of Paris. Less successful, though much better known, is the story of his love life. While living

Abélard and Héloïse are buried in Père-Lachaise cemetery – see p.204.

near the rue Chanoinesse, behind the cathedral, he fell violently in love with his landlord's niece, Héloïse, and she with him. She had a baby, uncle had him castrated, and the story ended in convents, life-long separation and lengthy correspondence.

Notre-Dame

The cathedral can be visited Mon–Fri & Sun 8am–7pm, Sat 8am–12.30pm & 2–7pm (free); the towers open daily April–Sept 9.30am–7.30pm; Oct–March 10am–5pm; 32F, or 50F combined with the crypt; M° Cité or M° & RER St-Michel.

The **Cathédrale de Notre-Dame** itself is so much photographed, painted and sketched that, seeing it even for the first time, the edge of your response may be somewhat dulled by familiarity. Yet it is truly impressive, that great H-shaped west front, with its strong vertical divisions counterbalanced by the horizontal emphasis of gallery and frieze, all centred on the rose window – a solid, no-nonsense design that confesses its Romanesque ancestry. For a more fantastical kind of Gothic, look rather at the **north transept façade**, with its crocketed gables and huge fretted window-space. The cathedral's popularity is such that, especially at weekends and throughout the summer, there are long queues out onto the square. This is the real tourist heartland and can get uncomfortably crowded, while the immediate area is crammed with tacky souvenir shops.

Notre-Dame was begun in 1160 under the auspices of Bishop de Sully and completed around 1245. In the nineteenth century, Viollet-le-Duc carried out extensive renovation work, including remaking most of the statuary – the entire frieze of Old Testament kings, for instance, damaged during the Revolution by enthusiasts who took them for the kings of France – and adding the steeple and baleful-looking gargoyles, which you can see close-up if you brave the ascent of the towers. Ravaged by weather and pollution, the façade's beauty may still be partially masked by scaffolding put up for further restoration work.

Inside, the immediately striking feature is the dramatic contrast between the darkness of the nave and the light falling on the first great clustered pillars of the choir. It's the end walls of the transepts that admit all this light, nearly two-thirds glass, including two mag-

The cathedral's original statues are in the Musée National du Moyen-Âge, p.122.

nificent **rose windows** coloured in imperial purple. These, the vaulting, the soaring shafts reaching to the springs of the vaults, are all definite Gothic elements, yet, inside as out, there remains a strong sense of Romanesque in the stout round pillars of the nave and the general sense of four-squareness. Free **guided tours** (1hr–1hr 30min) take place in French every weekday at noon and Saturday at 2pm, and in English on Wednesday at noon. There are free organ recitals every Sunday at 5 or 5.30pm, plus four Masses on Sunday morning and one at 6.30pm. The **trésor** (daily 9.30am–6pm; 15F) is not really worth the entry fee.

Before you leave, walk round to the public garden at the east end for a view of the **flying buttresses** supporting the choir, and then along the riverside under the south transept, where you can sit – in springtime with the cherry blossom drifting down. And say a prayer of gratitude that the city authorities had the sense to throw out President "Paris-must-adapt-itself-to-the-automobile" Pompidou's scheme for extending the quayside expressway along here.

Out in front of the cathedral, in the square separating it from Haussmann's police HQ, is what appears to be (and smells like) the entrance to an underground toilet. It is, in fact, a very well-displayed and interesting museum, the **crypte archéologique**, in which are revealed the remains of the church that predated the cathedral, as well as streets and houses of the Cité dating as far back as the Roman era.

The crypte archéologique is open daily April–Sept 10am–6pm; Oct–March 10am–4.30pm; 32F, or 50F combined admission with the towers.

Kilomètre zéro and the Mémorial de la Déportation

On the pavement by the west door of Notre-Dame is a spot known as **kilomètre zéro**, from which all main road distances in France are calculated. For the Île de la Cité is the symbolic heart of the country, or at least of the France that in the school books fights wars, undergoes revolutions and launches space rockets.

It's fitting that the island should also be the symbolic tomb of the 200,000 French men and women who died in the Nazi concentration camps during World War II – Resistance fighters, Jews, forced labourers. Their moving memorial, **Le Mémorial de la Déportation**, is a kind of bunker-crypt, barely visible above ground, at the extreme eastern tip of the island. Stairs scarcely shoulder-wide descend into a space like a prison yard. A single aperture overlooks the Seine, barred by a grill whose spiky ends evoke the torments of the torture chamber. Above, nothing is visible but the sky and, dead centre, the spire of Notre-Dame. Inside, the walls of the tunnel-like crypt are studded with thousands of points of light representing the dead. Floor and ceiling are black and it ends in a black raw hole, with a single naked bulb hanging in the middle. Either side are empty barred cells. "They went to the other ends of the Earth and they have not returned. 200,000 French men and women swallowed up, exterminated, in the mists and darkness of the Nazi camps." Above the exit are the words "Forgive. Do not forget . . .".

The gates to the crypt of the Mémorial de la Déportation are open daily 10am–noon & 2–5pm; free.

The Île St-Louis

Often considered to be the most romantic part of Paris, the peaceful **Île St-Louis** is prime strolling territory. Unlike its larger neighbour, the Île la Cité, it has no monuments, or métro stations, and a single, small **museum** at 6 quai d'Orléans devoted to the Romantic Polish poet Adam Mickiewicz (Thurs 2–6pm or by appointment on ☎01.43.54.35.61; free). Instead, you'll find high houses on single-lane streets, tree-lined quais, a school, a church, assorted restaurants and cafés, and interesting little shops. For centuries it was swampy

Île St-Louis

The closest métro stops to Île St-Louis are M° Pont-Marie and M° Sully-Morland.

pastureland owned by Notre-Dame, until the seventeenth-century version of a real-estate developer, Christophe Marie, had the bright idea of filling it with elegant mansions, so that by 1660 the island was transformed. In the 1840s the island gained popularity as a Bohemian hang-out, much like the Île de Louviers (see p.114) a decade earlier. The Hashashins club met every month at the **Hôtel Lauzun**, 17 quai d'Anjou, where Baudelaire lived for a while in the attic and where he wrote *Les Fleurs du Mal*. The hôtel, built in 1657, has an intact interior, complete with splendid trompe l'oeil decorations; pre-arranged group visits are possible (☎01.42.76.57.99).

Nowadays, the island is the most covetable of the city's addresses – you only get to have your home here if you're the Aga Khan, the Pretender to the French throne, or an ex-grand duke of Russia.

For most visitors, the Île St-Louis is best remembered for its exceptional **sorbets**, chez *M. Berthillon*, at 31 rue St-Louis-en-l'Île (closed Mon & Tues). Nothing can rival the taste of iced passion or kiwi fruit, guava, melon or a number of other flavours; the taste of ripe, fresh-picked fruit is but a shadow in comparison.

A great stop on a window-shopping spree, Pylones, at 57 rue St-Louis-en-l'Île, has a big, playful display See p.338 for details.

A popular approach to the island to bring you right to Berthillon is to cross Pont Louis Phillipe just east of the Hôtel de Ville; you're then positioned to join the throngs strolling with their ice creams down rue St-Louis-en-l'Île for a spot of window shopping. If you're looking for absolute seclusion, head for the **southern quais**, clutching a triple-sorbet cornet as you descend the various steps, or climb over the low gate on the right of the garden across boulevard Henri-IV to reach the best sunbathing spot in Paris. Even when *Berthillon* and his six concessionaries are closed, the island and its quais have their own distinct charm – it's particularly atmospheric in the evening, and dinner here (see p.263 for restaurant recommendations), followed by an arm-in-arm wander along the quais, is a must in any lovers' itinerary.

Chapter 3

Along La Voie Triomphale

This chapter deals with the stretch of "Triumphal Way" from the Arc de Triomphe to the Louvre and Palais Royal, plus surrounding streets; for La Défense, see p.226.

T he city's most monumental axis, **La Voie Triomphale**, runs in a dead straight line from the **Louvre** palace along the central alley of the **Tuileries** gardens, across **place de la Concorde**, up the avenue des **Champs-Élysées**, and through the **Arc de Triomphe**. It then reaches along avenue de la Grande Armée to the city boundary at Porte Maillot and all the way out through the suburb of Neuilly to the business skyscrapers of La Défense. Its nine-kilometre length is punctuated by grandiose constructions erected over the centuries by kings and emperors, presidents and corporations, each a monumental gesture to promote French power and prestige.

The tradition of self-aggrandizement dies hard. President Mitterrand, whose *grands projets* for the city outdid even Napoléon's, stamped his mark at either end of La Voie Triomphale, with the glass pyramid entrance to the much-expanded Louvre and an immense marble-clad cubic arch at La Défense (see Chapter 10). Though plans exist for further extension westward, Mitterrand's *Grande Arche* and the Louvre effectively enclose the historic axis between them. The two great constructions echo each other in scale and geometry, with both aligned at the same slight angle away from the axis – a detail that, given the distance involved, has to be appreciated conceptually rather than visually.

For restaurants, cafés and bars in this area, see pp.263–265.

The Arc de Triomphe and the Champs-Élysées

The best view of this monumental yet simple geometry is from the top of the **Arc de Triomphe**, Napoléon's homage both to the armies of France and to himself. The emperor and his two royal successors spent ten million francs between them on this edifice, which victorious foreign armies would later use to humiliate the French. After the Prussians' triumphal march in 1871, the Parisians lit bonfires beneath the arch and down the Champs-Élysées to eradicate the

*The Arc de
Triomphe is
open daily
April–Sept
9.30am–11pm;
Oct–March
10am–
10.30pm; 35F;
M° Charles-de-
Gaulle & M°
Étoile.*

"stain" of German boots. In 1920, an **unknown soldier** killed in the
Great War was buried under the arch, his tomb marked by a contin-
ually burning flame – you can watch a ceremony conducted by war
veterans every evening at 6.30pm when the fire is stoked up.

Access to the Arc de Triomphe is gained from stairs on the north
corner of the Champs-Élysées. From the top of the arch, your attention is most likely to be caught, not by the view, but by the mesmer-
izing traffic movements below in place Charles-de-Gaulle, the
world's first organized roundabout – still better known as **place de
l'Étoile**. Of the twelve fat avenues making up the star (*étoile*), much
the busiest is the **avenue des Champs-Élysées**, which disgorges and
gobbles a phenomenal number of vehicles. (Recently, however, the
side lanes where cars used to prowl in search of parking spaces have
been removed, giving pedestrians an equal share of the avenue's
width.) This is where the fairy lights are draped at Christmas, and
where cars converge on December 31 to hoot in the New Year.
Bastille Day sees the president and an entourage of tanks, guns and
flags process down the avenue.

The glamour of the Champs-Élysées, particularly its upper end, may not be quite what it was, dominated as it is nowadays by airline offices, car showrooms, fast-food outlets and shopping arcades. But there's still the Lido cabaret, *Fouquet's* high-class bar and restaurant (which hosts the César film awards each year), and plenty of cinemas and outrageously priced cafés to bring the punters in. Further down, the perfumier Guerlain occupies an exquisite 1913 building at no. 68; the belle époque façade of the former *Claridge Hotel*, at no. 74, has been given a facelift; and the *Travellers Club* still glories in the mid-nineteenth-century opulence of the *Hôtel de la Païva*, at no. 25. Newer arrivals, mostly transatlantic, continue the avenue's connection with the entertainment industries: Virgin Megastore, a Disney shop and the *Planet Hollywood* restaurant. At the Renault showrooms (nos. 49–53; free) is a display of cars, bikes and vans from the earliest days.

The stretch between the **Rond-Point** roundabout, whose Lalique glass fountains disappeared during the German occupation, and **place de la Concorde** is bordered by chestnut trees and municipal flowerbeds, pleasant enough to stroll among, but not sufficiently dense to muffle the squeal of accelerating tyres. The gigantic building with overloaded Neoclassical exteriors, glass roofs and exuberant flying statuary rising above the greenery to the south is the Grand Palais, created with its neighbour, the Petit Palais, for the 1900 **Exposition Universelle**. Today, both the Grand Palais and Petit Palais contain permanent museums, as well as hosting good temporary exhibitions.

The best of the major art exhibitions at the **Grand Palais** draw queues that stretch down avenue Churchill. *Pariscope* and the like will have details, and you'll probably see plenty of posters around. Inside, the nave has been closed since 1993 awaiting restoration work. However, the **Galerie Nationale** space is still open for exhibitions, and fortunately the wing that houses the **Palais de la Découverte** has not been affected. The latter, the old science museum, has brightened itself up considerably since the Cité des Sciences came on the scene. It can't really compete, but it does have plenty of interactive exhibits, some very good temporary shows and an excellent planetarium.

*The Palais de
la Découverte
is open
Tues–Sat
9.30am–6pm,
Sun
10am–7pm;
27F, 40F with
planetarium;
Mº Champs-
Élysées-
Clemenceau &
Mº Franklin-D-
Roosevelt.*

As well as major, changing exhibitions in the **Petit Palais**, you'll find the **Musée des Beaux-Arts**, which at first sight seems to be a collection of leftovers, from every period from the Renaissance to the 1920s, after the other main galleries have taken their pick. It does, however, hold some real gems: Monet's *Sunset at Lavacourt* and Boudin's *Gust of Wind at Le Havre* stand out against some rather uninspiring Renoirs, Morisots, Cézannes and Manets. There's the seductive pose of actress Sarah Bernhardt, painted by Georges Clairin, and you'll also find a sculpture of her many years later, downstairs between galleries Zoubaloff and Dutuit. The latter gallery has a small collection of Dutch, Flemish and Italian Renaissance art, including an impressive selection of sixteenth-century ceramics. Other features of the collection include fantasy jewellery of the Art Nouveau period, effete eighteenth-century furniture, plaster models designed for the Madeleine church in the early nineteenth century, and vast canvases recording Paris' street battles during the 1830 and 1848 revolutions, trumpeting the victory of the Tricolour.

*The
permanent
collection of
the Petit Palais
is open
Tues–Sun
10am–5.40pm;
27F; Mº
Champs-
Élysées-
Clemenceau.*

A statue of Georges Clemenceau, French prime minister at the end of World War I, commands the aptly named **place Clemenceau**, between the Grand Palais and Petit Palais. From here the **avenue Winston-Churchill** leads down towards the Seine, culminating with a statue of Churchill, unveiled on November 11, 1998 on the eightieth anniversary of the Armistice. On the north side of the Champs-Élysées from the Grand and Petit palaces, combat police guard the high walls of the presidential **Élysée Palace** and the line of ministries and embassies ending with the US in prime position on the corner of place de la Concorde.

Place de la Concorde and the Tuileries

The graceful gradients of the Champs-Élysées, like a landing flight-path, finish up in the east at **place de la Concorde**, where more crazed traffic makes crossing over to the middle a death-defying task. As it happens, some 1300 people did die here between 1793 and 1795, beneath the Revolutionary guillotine: Louis XVI, Marie-Antoinette, Danton and Robespierre among them. The centrepiece of the *place*, chosen like its name to make no comment on these events, is an obelisk from the temple of Luxor, offered as a favour-currying gesture by the viceroy of Egypt in 1829. It serves merely as a pivotal point for more geometry: the alignment of the French parliament, the Assemblée Nationale, on the far side of the Seine, with the church of the Madeleine, at the end of rue Royale, to the north. The Neoclassical *Hôtel Crillon* – the ultimate luxury address for visitors to Paris – and its twin, the Hôtel de la Marine, housing the Ministry of the Navy, flank the entrance to rue Royale, which, needless to say, meets the Voie Triomphale at a precise right angle.

The symmetry of the Voie Triomphale continues into the formal layout of the **Tuileries gardens**, disrupted only by bodies lounging on the grass, kids chasing their boats round the ponds, and gays cruising on the terrace overlooking the river. The two buildings flanking the garden at the Concorde end are the Orangerie, by the river, and the Jeu de Paume, by rue de Rivoli.

Erstwhile home to the state's Impressionist collection before its relocation to the Musée d'Orsay, the **Jeu de Paume** is now a beautifully light space used for temporary shows of contemporary art, usually major retrospectives of established artists, but also, every autumn, more cutting-edge stuff by artists invited for the **Festival d'Automne**. Workers doing the refit claimed to have found an eighteenth-century tennis ball in the rafters – a wild shot from the building's earliest days as a royal tennis court.

The **Orangerie** houses a private art collection that's weighted heavily in favour of the Impressionists, including several of Monet's *Water Lilies*, inherited by the state with the stipulation that they should always stay together. The museum is closed as it undergoes a major transformation, which involves enlarging and restructuring the building, and converting many of the existing exterior walls to glass, in line with Monet's request that as much natural light as possible reach his masterpieces. If you're in Paris between May and July 1999, you'll have the opportunity to visit Monet's *Water Lilies* as part of an exhibition, after which the museum will close again until autumn 2001. After all the upheaval, the rest of the Orangerie's collection, containing works by Matisse, Cézanne, Utrillo, Modigliani, Renoir, Soutine and Sisley among others, will be rearranged and with luck, expanded drawing from the collection's reserves.

The Jeu de Paume is open Tues noon–9.30pm, Wed–Fri noon–7pm, Sat & Sun 10am–7pm; 38F; Mº Concorde.

The Tuileries

The first garden to take the place of the medieval warren of tilemak-
ers (*tuileries*) was that of Catherine de Médicis (her Palais des
Tuileries, which ran along what is now the underpass avenue du Gal-
Lemonnier, was burnt down by the Communards in 1870). She had
formal vegetable gardens, a labyrinth and a chequerboard of
flowerbeds laid out in the 1570s, to be admired by guests at her
sumptuous parties. A hundred years later, Le Nôtre created the
schema of the **Jardins des Tuileries**, of a central axis, *terrasses*, and
round and octagonal pools; the sculptures from Versailles and Marly
(Louis XIV's retreat from Versailles, no longer in existence),
appeared here under Louis XV. During the eighteenth century, the
gardens were where flash Parisians came to preen and party, and in
1783 the Montgolfier brothers, Joseph and Etienne, launched the
first successful hot air balloon here, the height and breadth of the
overgrown trees no doubt adding a certain frisson to the event. The
first serious replanting was carried out after the Revolution – a 200-
year-old plane tree with a three-metre circumference survives near
the octagonal pool. In the nineteenth century, rare species were
added to the garden, by this time dominated by chestnut trees.

The Tuileries have recently undergone another considerable renovation, necessary after decades of dryness, disease and parasites,
vandalism, lack of care and pollution had taken their toll on the trees.
The result of replanting some five hundred new trees, and of much
tree surgery, recasting of statues and relandscaping, is a Tuileries
that doesn't look much different but is at least fit for a new millennium. The original design by Le Nôtre remains the same and one can
still imagine generations of Parisian bourgeois families taking a
pleasant Sunday promenade. Nowadays, the chairs placed around
the water-features are normally occupied by tourists recovering from
the Champs-Élysées or the Louvre, the latter of which houses many
of the originals of the sculptures you can see in the Tuileries. More
modern sculpture can be found in the labyrinthine **Jardin du
Carrousel**, around the place du Carrousel, where Maillol's chunky
statues of female nudes repose as if under hypnosis.

The Palais du Louvre

When the Grand Louvre project was conceived in 1981 by newly
elected president Mitterrand, he was following in the footsteps of
François I, Catherine de Médicis, Louis XIV, Napoléon, and all the
other kings, queens and emperors who have added to and altered
Philippe-Auguste's original fortress, built to defend the city in 1200.
Charles V was the first French king to make the fortress his residence, but not until François I in the mid-sixteenth century were the
foundations of the palace laid and the original demolished. From

The Grand Louvre Project

The new **Grand Louvre**, finally inaugurated by President Mitterrand in spring 1989 and now nearing its completion, has admirably grappled with the enormity of what was a dusty dinosaur and created a truly modern museum.

The transformation began with the glass **Pyramid** – set to rival the Eiffel Tower, a hundred years its senior, as the symbol of the city. Next came the transformation of the **Richelieu wing** of the Musée du Louvre on the north side, former home of the Finance Ministry. Its two courtyards have been glassed over and are visible from windows in the passage Richelieu linking place du Palais-Royal and the cour Napoléon. You get a better view of Coustou's famous horses, the *Chevaux de Marly*, and Puget's monumental figures from this public passage than you do from within the museum itself.

The other major development of Mitterrand's project is underground – a vast space stretching from the **Hall Napoléon**, the entrance-hall to the Musée du Louvre, beneath the Pyramid, to beyond the Arc du Carrousel. Known as the **Carrousel du Louvre**, its central crossroads, place de la Pyramide Inversée, is fed with daylight through a smaller, inverted model of the Pyramid.

From the Hall Napoléon, shops and restaurants make up the cold, classy and commercial Carrousel du Louvre gallery. Beyond are several auditoriums and conference halls, car and bus parking areas, and new premises for the Louvre's research department, which boasts its own particle accelerator to examine sub-atomic bits of works of art and archeological finds. Before this subterranean complex was created, archeologists excavating here discovered Stone Age tools, remnants of an Iron Age farm that grew lentils, peas, fruit and cereals, a house dating from 300 BC and a fourteenth-century manor house complete with wall-paintings and garden.

The Grand Louvre project approaches completion at the time of writing, but there are still a few holes, notably the final leg of Italian and northern European painting sections, and the final part of the eastern Mediterranean circuit from the beginnings of Christianity. The information desk in the Hall Napoléon can give you an update.

then on, almost every sovereign added to it, with Catherine de Médicis, Henri II's widow, contributing the Palais des Tuileries extension, burnt to the ground during the Paris Commune (1871), across what is now the underpass avenue du Gal-Lemonnier. Twice in its history the Louvre has almost been razed to the ground. Its first close shave came when Bernini, hired by Louis XIV's minister, Colbert, to redesign the palace, favoured starting from scratch, but lost the commission. Then in the mid-eighteenth century, with the court firmly established at Versailles, the Louvre was taken over by artists and squatters, with a hundred different families living round the cour Carrée: Louis XV's immediate response to such impudence was to call for the building's destruction, but he was dissuaded by his officials, thereby allowing it to become the scene of his son's humiliation at the hands of revolutionaries in 1790.

The Palais du Louvre

Despite the alterations and additions over the centuries, the building remains surprisingly homogeneous, possessing a grandeur and symmetry entirely suited to this most historic of Parisian edifices. Then came the **Pyramid**, bang in the centre of the palace in the cour Napoléon, an extraordinary leap of daring and imagination. The creation of Chinese-born Ieoh Ming Pei (architect of the East Wing of Washington DC's National Gallery) it has no connection with its surroundings other than as a symbol of symmetry. Yet the sight of this huge glass pyramid, surrounded by a pool and fountains and three smaller pyramids, especially as you come out of the cour Carrée through the Pavillon de l'Horloge, is stunning. At night, illuminated, it's pure magic. Napoléon's pink marble **Arc du Carrousel** nearby, just east of place du Carrousel, which once served as a gateway to the former Tuileries Palace, has always looked a bit out of place (even though it sits precisely on the Voie Triomphale axis), but now it's definitively and forlornly upstaged by the Pyramid.

The **Palais du Louvre** itself houses **four museums**: the Musée du Louvre; the Musée de la Mode et du Textile; the Musée des Arts Décoratifs; and the Musée de la Publicité. Each has been revamped under the Grand Louvre project (the Musée de la Publicité has yet to re-open), and each is an important collection in its own right, but the most renowned by far – and *the* reason to come to Paris for many of its visitors – is the mighty Musée du Louvre.

The Musée du Louvre

The permanent collection of the Louvre is open Mon & Wed–Sun 9am–6pm, late opening till 9.45pm on Mon (selected rooms) and Wed; Histoire du Louvre rooms and Medieval Louvre Mon & Wed 9am–9.45pm, Thurs–Sun 10am–8.30pm; everything closed Tues; 45F, after 3pm & Sun 26F, free the first Sun of the month; same-day readmission allowed; tickets can also be bought in advance on ☎01.49.87.54.54, from branches of FNAC; Mᵒ Palais-Royal & Mᵒ Musée-du-Louvre & Mᵒ Louvre-Rivoli.

"You walked for a quarter of a mile through works of fine art; the very floors echoed the sounds of immortality . . . It was the crowning and consecration of art . . . These works instead of being taken from their respective countries were given to the world and to the mind and heart of man from whence they sprung . . ."

William Hazlitt, writing of the Louvre in 1802, goes on, in equally florid style, to proclaim this museum as the beginning of a new age when artistic masterpieces would be the inheritance of all, no longer the preserve of kings and nobility. Novel the Louvre certainly was. The palace, hung with the private collections of monarchs and their ministers, was first opened to the public in 1793, during the Revolution. Within a decade Napoléon had made it the largest art collection on earth with takings from his empire.

However inspiring it might have been then, the Louvre has been a bit of a nightmare over the last few decades, requiring heroic

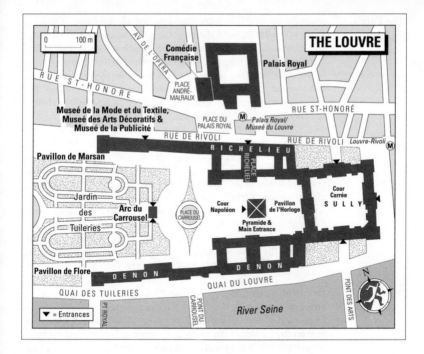

willpower and stamina to find one work of art that you want to see among the 25,000. The Grand Louvre project, however, has breathed new life into the building: exhibition floor-space has almost doubled, creating new departments such as the Medieval Louvre, and necessitating a complete redesign in order to display the thousands of works of art previously kept in the reserves. The number of visitors to the Louvre has gradually been increasing through the term of the project, and queues to get into the building and, once inside, queues for the facilities are a frustrating part of any visit.

Finding you way around the museum

The Pyramid now serves as main entrance and covers the **Hall Napoléon**, where you'll find a bookshop, cafés, information desk and the ticket office. Alternative **entrances** in the passage Richelieu (between place du Palais-Royal and cour Napoléon), at the Porte des Lions, or directly from the métro mean you can avoid the queue for the Pyramid, while buying your ticket in advance (see opposite) will save queueing at the ticket office once inside.

Lifts and escalators lead from the Hall Napoléon to each of the three wings of the building, each with four floors: the entresol (the level reached from the escalators in the Hall Napoléon), the rez-de-chaussée (ground floor), then the first and second floors. The three wings are **Sully** (around the cour Carrée), **Denon** (the south wing) and **Richelieu** (the north wing). These are subsequently divided into numbered rooms and colour-coded according to the main categories of the collection (see below). At first overwhelming and seemingly non-sensical, the layout of the museum is a delight to unravel. The indispensable **floor-plan**, available free from the information desk in the Hall Napoléon, highlights some of the more renowned master-pieces, such as the *Mona Lisa*, for those wishing to do a whistle-stop tour, although don't expect to be able to contemplate them peace-fully. If the crowds get too much, your ticket allows you to leave and re-enter as many times as you like throughout the day between reju-venating strolls in the Tuileries – there are entrances to the gardens via the passage Richelieu or on either side of the Arc du Carrousel.

The **eight basic categories** of the museum's collections are: Oriental Antiquities; Egyptian Antiquities; Greek, Etruscan and Roman Antiquities; Decorative Arts; Sculpture; Painting; Graphic Arts; and the Medieval Louvre. Each category, but for the last, spreads over more than one wing and several floors.

Oriental Antiquities

Oriental Antiquities – including the newly presented Islamic art col-lection – begin on the ground floor of the Richelieu wing with a sec-tion on the ancient civilizations of Mesopotamia. The rooms centred around the cour Khorsabad contain vestiges of Sumer and Akkad civ-ilizations, but the most important object belongs to the Babylonian period, the Code of Hammurabi, a basalt stele covered in Akkadian script revealing the code of conduct as pronounced by the king, who is pictured at the top praying to Shamash. The cour Khorsabad itself houses the immense winged bulls with human heads, found in the palace at Khorsabad built by Sargon II in the eighth century BC, which would have stood at the entrance to the palace as guardian spirits. Through into the Sully wing, the rooms of the Levant (A–D) contain the oldest item in the Louvre: the seemingly two-dimensional statue found at Aïn Ghazal is around 9000 years old. Downstairs, on the entresol level of the Richelieu wing, Islamic art starts with an introduction through text and photographs of Islamic architecture, before displaying the objects, retrieved from Spain, India and all points in between, by dynasty, with special sections devoted to ceramics and scientific instruments.

Egyptian Antiquities

One of the most publicized artistic events of 1997 was the opening of the **Egyptian Antiquities** collection, sparking off a whole year of exhibitions across the city on the Egyptian theme. The new layout re-creates the original 1827 design of the Egyptology collection's first curator, Jean-François Champollion (he who translated the hieroglyphics of the Rosetta Stone) – a thematic circuit followed by a chronological circuit, ranged across thirty rooms and two floors. The wealth of the collection makes it the biggest and most important Egyptian antiquities collection in the world after the Cairo museum. Starting on the ground floor of the Sully wing, the thematic circuit leads up from the atmospheric crypt of the Sphinx (room 1) to the Nile, source of all life in Egypt, and takes the visitor through the everyday life of pharaonic Egypt by way of cooking accessories, jewellery, the principles of hieroglyphics, musical instruments, sarcophagi and a host of mummified cats. Upstairs, on the first floor, the chronological circuit keeps the masterpieces on the right-hand side, while numerous pots and statuettes of more specialist interest are displayed to the left. Among landmarks in the development of Egyptian art are the studious *Seated Scribe* statue found at Saqqara, the bust of *Amenophis IV*, and the painted relief of *Goddess Hathor Protecting Seti I* found in Seti I's tomb in the Valley of the Kings.

Post-pharaonic Egypt between the fourth and twelfth centuries AD is exhibited on the entresol level of the Denon wing, and displays the links between the civilization of ancient Egypt and that of the Roman Empire. The legacy of the pharaohs is easily discernible in the funerary trappings of Roman Egypt, for example the Mummy of Pdijmenipet, while the Coptic section illustrates the presence of Christianity with a fine painting on wood of Christ Protecting Abbot Mena, displayed in a part reconstruction of the monastery church at Baouït, in middle Egypt.

Greek, Etruscan and Roman Antiquities

The **Greek, Etruscan and Roman Antiquities** section includes the Winged Victory of Samothrace (Denon, first floor, at the top of the great staircase) and the *Venus de Milo* (Sully, ground floor, room 12), two of the biggest crowd-pullers in the museum. Dating from the late second century BC, *Venus* strikes a classic pose glimpsed in some of her antecedents also on display, like the delightful Dame d'Auxerre (seventh century BC) on the entresol level. Also on the entresol, the Cycladic Idol dates to some time between 2700 BC and 2300 BC – its only discernible feature is a nose – while the gaze of the bronze *Apollo of Piombino* (room 5) has been fixed straight ahead since the fifth century BC. In room 7, there's a fragment of the *Panathenaic Frieze* from the Parthenon – the rest of the frieze is in the British Museum in London.

The Roman section boasts attractive mosaics from Asia Minor and luminous frescoes from Pompeii and Herculaneum. Works on the two lower levels are complemented by smaller groupings by medium on the first floor – here a daunting assemblage of Greek pottery (eight rooms worth) from the ninth to the second centuries BC, including an array of Black- and Red-Figured ware, comprise the bulk of the collection. There's also a section on Greek and Roman glass.

The Decorative Arts

The Decorative Arts collection (first floor, Richelieu and Sully wings, plus room 66 Denon wing) is heavily weighted on the side of imperial opulence. To modern eyes, these beautifully crafted pieces of furniture are less likely to incite the same aesthetic response they would have aroused at the time – just an appalled calculation of the cost. The same has to be said of the renowned cabinet-maker Boulle's work (active around 1700), immediately recognizable by the heavy square shapes and lavish use of inlays in copper, bronze and pewter, and such ecologically catastrophic exuberance as entire doors made of tortoiseshell. There is also tapestry after tapestry – all of the very first quality and workmanship – but of such acreage it can be a chore to work your way through the lot. Relief has to be sought in the smaller, less public items: the jewel-like enamelled *objets* from Limoges; the thirteenth-century Parisian ivories; or Marie-Antoinette's travelling case, fitted up with the intricacy of a jigsaw to take an array of bottles, vials and other queenly necessaries.

The final leg of the Decorative Arts circuit leads through the former Minister of State's apartments. Open to the public only since the Grand Louvre project ousted the Finance Ministry from the Richelieu wing, the renovated Second-Empire interior's overstated opulence is marked by immense chandeliers, gilded putti and caryatids, and dramatic ceiling frescoes in the Grand Salon that depict the linking of the Tuileries and the Louvre.

Further examples of extravagance await on the opposite side of the museum in the Apollon Gallery (Denon wing, first floor, room 66), where the crown jewels are displayed, including the mammoth Regent diamond sported by Charles X, Louis XV, Louis XVI and Napoléon.

Sculpture

The highlights of the Sculpture section can be previewed from the passage Richelieu, which looks onto the huge glass-covered courtyards of the Richelieu wing – the cour Marly with Coustou's horses, and the cour Puget with Puget's *Milo of Croton* as the centrepiece. The sculpture collection occupies the new Richelieu wing (ground floor and entresol overlooking the Marly and Puget courtyards), and exhibiting the development of the art form in France from the Romanesque period to the mid-nineteenth century. In addition, there's a separate section in the Denon wing devoted to Italian and northern European sculpture. You'll find copies of some of the most important sculptures from the entire collection in the Galerie d'Étude (Denon wing, entresol); these copies have been purposefully set aside to be touched, with texts written in Braille and French.

In room 1 of French sculpture, the Romanesque depiction of everyday, secular scenes, such as the grape-harvest, and the subtlety of expression in religious works like the *Christ of Lavaudieu*,

contrast starkly to the flamboyant movement out in the cour Marly.
As you move on, the earlier rigidity slowly gives way throughout the
Gothic period to more fluid movement and a greater understanding
of perspective, a transition notable in Colombe's early sixteenth-century relief of *St George Slaying the Dragon*. The seventeenth and
eighteenth centuries see French sculpture gaining momentum, with
rooms 15 to 19 brimming with pompous triumphal and funereal
monuments before you arrive at the impressive **Marly and Puget
courtyards**. Originally conceived for the parks of royal residences,
the sculptures are now protected from the harsh elements and grace-
fully lit by a glass roof that maximizes natural light. The final section
of the circuit takes you up to the mid-nineteenth century and through
Romanticism, with a playful marble *Neapolitan Fisherman* by
François Rude. Also represented in this section is Antoine-Louis
Barye, who made detailed studies of the animal world prior to sculpting his menagerie of bronze animals (room 33).

The highlights of the **Italian** sculpture section, over in the Denon
wing, are found on the ground floor (room 4): Michelangelo's
Slaves, designed for the tomb of Pope Julius II, and whose significance remains ambiguous, although they have been interpreted as
symbols of the Pope's earthly existence. In the same room is
Canova's delightfully delicate *Psyche and Cupid*, the edges of which
unfortunately bear the grubby marks left by admirer's hands.
Spanish and northern European sculpture are thinly represented,
tucked away on both the entresol and ground floor of the Denon
wing, but it's worth searching out Erhart's particularly natural wood-
en statue of *St Mary Magdalene* (Denon, entresol, room C), who
stands out among her more mannered peers.

Painting

The largest and most indigestible section of the Louvre by far is the
Painting section: French art from the fourteenth to mid-nineteenth
century predominates, with Italian, Dutch, German, Flemish, English
and Spanish painting represented, too. Among the multitude are
paintings so familiar from reproductions it takes you by surprise to
see them suddenly framed on the wall.

The **early Italians** (Denon, first floor, rooms 3–11) form the most
interesting part of the collection, with many of the big names represented – Giotto, Fra Angelico, Uccello, Mantegna, Botticelli, Filippo
Lippi, Raphael. If you want to get near Leonardo's *Mona Lisa*
(Denon, first floor, room 6), go first or last thing in the day. Few people, incidentally, pay the slightest bit of attention to the other
Leonardos round the corner in the 300-metre-long Grande Galerie,
including his *Virgin of the Rocks*.

A slightly more modest collection, in size as well as subject matter,
is that of the **northern European** schools, over on the second floor of
the Richelieu wing, whose subtle use of colour and smaller format is

The Palais du Louvre

less likely to overwhelm initially. That is until the Rubens explosion in the Médicis gallery (room 18), a whole room dedicated to the glory of Queen Marie de Médicis as commissioned by herself. The swirling colours and swaths of flapping cloth were to influence French painters from Fragonard to Delacroix. Rubens' more personal paintings are on view in room 21, where *The Village Fair* is just as busy but less pompous. A different approach altogether is apparent in the fine display of Rembrandts in the Dutch section. Again, the impeccable attention to light in Vermeer's *The Astronomer* and *The Lacemaker* (room 38), is the beauty of these calm domestic scenes.

French painting is obviously the most complete of the sections but, in comparison to the Italian and northern European collections, its overall impact suffers from being watered down, with minor works and masterpieces hung side by side. State pomp and ceremony feature prominently, but David's epic *Coronation of Napoleon I* (displayed with the large-format paintings on the first floor of the Denon wing, room 75) takes the biscuit: Napoleon is shown crowning himself, with a rather crestfallen clergy in the background.

The chronological circuit of French painting begins on the second floor of the Richelieu wing with the earliest known French portrait, *King John the Good*, in a style of portraiture still in evidence in the sixteenth century with the Clouet brothers' beautifully lit paintings of royalty and illustrious people of the day (room 7). Poussin dominates rooms 13–18 with his proliferation of classical scenes, and his outstanding *Four Seasons* in the octagonal room 16.

At this point, it's perhaps worthwhile saving your energy and moving on to the more compelling nineteenth-century schools, via a detour to the large-format rooms housed on the other side of the museum. Here, the first signs of Romanticism are visible in Géricault's dramatic display of human emotion, the *Raft of the Medusa* (Denon wing, first floor, room 77). Presented at the Salon in 1819, it's based on a shipwreck of 1816, its mere fifteen survivors depicted here, those still conscious in a state of extreme desperation. The same room hosts the famous icon of the nineteenth-century Revolution, *Liberty Leading the People* by Delacroix. To fully appreciate Delacroix's use of colour and ability to portray heightened emotion, however, find your way to room 62 on the second floor of the Sully wing, where Delacroix's *Women of Algiers* hangs with *The Taking of Constantinople by the Crusaders*. Room 60 showcases the work of Ingres, whose predilection for the female form can be seen in his sensuous *Turkish Bath*, oozing with languorous bodies. The final part of French painting takes in Corot and the Barbizon school of painters, the precursors of Impressionism.

The Louvre's collection of French painting stops at 1848, a date picked up by the Musée d'Orsay (see p.144).

Graphic Arts and the Medieval Louvre

Interspersed throughout the painting section are rooms dedicated to the Louvre's impressive collection of **Graphic Arts**, including prized sketches and preliminary drawings by Ingres and Rubens and some attributed to Leonardo. Because of their susceptibility to the light, however, they are exhibited by rotation.

An added bonus from all the recent building works has been the opportunity to excavate the remains of the **Medieval Louvre** – Philippe-Auguste's twelfth-century fortress and Charles V's fourteenth-century palace conversion – under the cour Carrée on the entresol level of the Sully wing. The foundations and archeological findings are now on show along with a permanent exhibition on the history of the Louvre, from the Middle Ages to contemporary transformations.

The other Palais du Louvre museums

Each of the three other museums housed in the Rohan wing of the Louvre palace (entrance at 107 rue de Rivoli) has been subject to recent reorganization. Two museums – the Musée de la Mode et du Textile and the Musée des Arts Décoratifs – are now up and running, though work is ongoing in the latter. The **Musée de la Publicité**, celebrating the art of advertising from nineteenth-century poster art to contemporary electronic publicity, is due to open by the year 2000.

The **Musée de la Mode et du Textile** houses an exquisite collection of fashion too unwieldy to be shown all at once – with individual items too fragile to be exposed for long periods. The result is a yearly rotation of garments and textiles based on changing themes.

The collection of religious artefacts and bourgeios *objets* in the **Musée des Arts Décoratifs** seems rather humble in comparison with the high art next door in the Musée du Louvre. But the craftsmanship is nonetheless apparent, and the thematic arrangement with two period mock-ups – a late-fourteenth-century castle bedroom and a fifteenth-century reception room – enlivens the objects. The museum starts on the third floor with a section devoted to the period from the Middle Ages to the Renaissance; the rest of the permanent collection may still be closed when you go, but comprises furnishings, fittings and everyday components of French interiors up to the present day, with works by French, Italian and Japanese designers. When it re-opens, the twentieth-century collection promises to be fascinating – a bedroom by Guimard, Jeanne Lanvin's Art Deco apartments, and a salon created by Georges Hoentschel for the 1900 Exposition Universelle.

The Musée de la Mode et du Textile and Musée des Arts Décoratifs are open Tues–Fri 11am–6pm, Wed until 9pm, Sat & Sun 10am–6pm; 30F.

The Palais Royal

With cars and coaches now banished to the Louvre's new underground car park, **place du Palais-Royal** has become a space for rollerbladers, pavement artists and performers. On the north side of the *place*, the **Palais Royal**, originally Richelieu's residence, houses various government and constitutional bodies as well as the **Comédie Française,** where the classics of French theatre are performed.

The palace gardens to the north were once the gastronomic, gambling and amusement hotspot of Paris. There was even a café mécanique, where you sat at a table, sent your order down one of its legs, and were served via the other. The prohibition on public gambling in 1838 put an end to the fun, but the flats above the empty cafés remained desirable lodgings for the likes of Cocteau and of Colette, who died here in 1954.

Folly has returned to the Palais itself, however, in the form of black and white pillars in different sizes standing above flowing water in the main courtyard. The artist responsible, Daniel Buren, was commissioned in 1982 by Jack Lang, the socialist Minister of Culture. His Chirac-ian successor's decision to let the work go ahead caused paroxysms among self-styled guardians of the city's heritage and set an interesting precedent. After a legal wrangle, the court ruled that artists had the right to complete their creations.

Kids use the monochrome Brighton Rock lookalikes as an adventure playground, the best game being to use magnets on strings to fish out coins thrown into the water. Grown-ups perch on the pillars eating their lunchtime sandwiches or reading the paper. Though Buren's work has had many detractors, it has turned what used to be a car park into a popular pedestrian space.

Chapter 4

Financial Paris, the Passages and Les Halles

In the narrow streets of the 1er and 2^e arrondissements, between the Louvre and the **Grands Boulevards**, the grandiose financial, cultural and political state institutions are surrounded by well-established commerce centred on the rag trade, newspapers, sex and well-heeled shopping. The most appealing features here are the nineteenth-century **passages** – shopping arcades long predating the concept of pedestrian precincts, with glass roofs, tiled floors and unobtrusive entrances. The next generation of indoor shopping, the major department stores, are next to the river and up in the 9e arrondissement, just north of the gaudy original opera house. For the seriously rich, the boutiques at the western end of the 1er and the streets to either side of the Champs-Élysées, display the wares of every top couturier, jeweller, art dealer and furnisher.

This is the area of Paris that has changed least in the last few decades: a mix of the monumental – the **Bourse, Banque de France, Bibliothèque Nationale**, the **Madeleine** and **Opéra**; the traditional, typified by the Grands Boulevards with their banks, brasseries and entertainment houses; and the intimate, represented by the passages. It is both very chic and seedy. The great exception is **Les Halles**, once the food market of Paris, which no former trader would recognize. Of all the changes to the city in the last 25 years, the transformation of Les Halles into an underground RER/métro station and shopping centre is the least inspired – though overground it does provide some much-needed greenery, and the shops attract the crowds.

The Grands Boulevards, the Opéra and Madeleine

The **Grands Boulevards** (boulevards de la Madeleine, des Capucines, des Italiens, Montmartre, Poissonnière, Bonne-Nouvelle, St-Denis and St-Martin) form one long, wide thoroughfare which

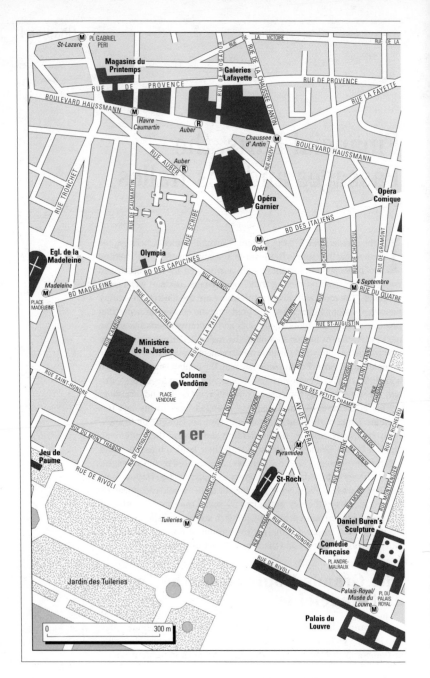

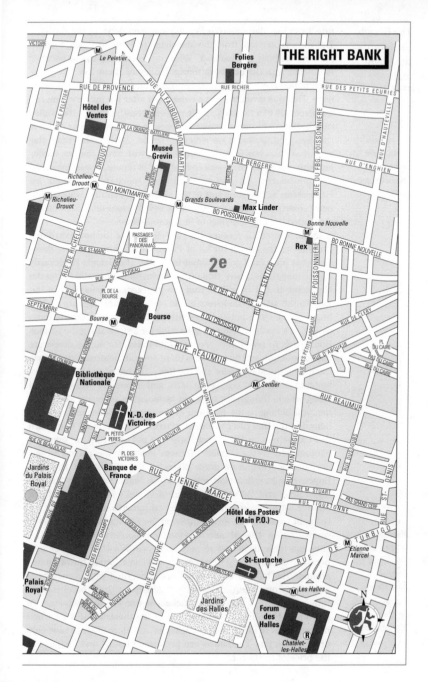

The Grands Boulevards, the Opéra and Madeleine

For restaurants, cafés and bars in this area, see p265.

runs from the **Madeleine** to République, then down to the Bastille. The western section, from the Madeleine to Porte St-Denis, follows the rampart built by Charles V. When its defensive purpose became redundant with the offensive foreign policy of Louis XIV, the walls were pulled down and the ditches filled in, leaving a wide promenade. This was given the name *boulevard* after the military term for the level part of a rampart. In the mid-eighteenth century, the boulevard became a fashionable place to be seen on horseback or in one's carriage, and gradually on which to reside. At the same time, the eastern section was far more entertaining, with street theatre, mime, juggling, puppets, waxworks and cafés of ill repute. It was known as the *boulevard du Crime*, and was inevitably targeted by Haussmann in the latter half of the nineteenth century, whose huge new crossroads – place de l'Opéra as well as place de la République – changed the physiognomy of the thoroughfare.

In the nineteenth century, the café clientele of the **boulevard des Italiens** set the trends for all of Paris, in terms of manners, dress and what one could gossip about in public. The Grands Boulevards were cobbled, and Paris' first horse-drawn omnibus rattled from the Madeleine to the Bastille. From the bourgeois intellectuals in the west to the artisan fun-lovers in the east, this thoroughfare had its finger on the city's pulse. As recently as the 1950s, a visitor to Paris would, as a matter of course, have gone for a stroll along the Grands Boulevards to see *"Paris vivant"*. And today, for all the desperate traffic pollution and burger bars, there are still theatres and cinemas (including the Max Linder and the Rex – the latter an extraordinary building inside and out, see p.315), and numerous brasseries and cafés, which, though not the most fashionable, innovative or amusing, still belong to the tradition of the Grands Boulevards, immortalized in the film *Les Enfants du Paradis*. It was at 14 **boulevard des Capucines**, in 1895, that Paris first put on a film, or animated photography, as the Lumière brothers' invention was called. An earlier artistic revolution took place at no. 35, where the first **Impressionist exhibition** was shown in Nadar's studio to an outraged art world. As one critic said of Monet's *Impression: Soleil Levant*, "it was worse than anyone had hitherto dared to paint". A remnant from the fun-loving times on the Grands Boulevards is the waxworks in the **Musée Grévin**, on boulevard Montmartre, although these days they're only really worth a visit if you're desperate to do something with the kids and can afford to throw money around. The bulk of the displays are concerned with scenes from French history, and the celebrities' gallery on the ground floor is rather exclusive, with a few politicians on one side and pop-stars on the other. Upstairs, a conjuring act in the theatre and a light and mirrors show in the "Palais des Mirages" are more likely to hold children's attention. The shows are performed hourly and included in the price of the ticket.

Musée Grévin is open daily 1–6.30pm (school hols 10am– 6.30pm); 55F; Mᵒ Rue Montmartre.

Nureyev and the Opéra Garnier

Rudolf Nureyev was director of the Paris Ballet here from 1983 to 1989,
and the Opéra presented his last production, *La Bayadère*, with the
Kirov, a few months before his death. At his funeral, in January 1993, the
steps of the opera house were strewn with white flowers as his coffin was
carried up to the foyer, and the orchestra played his favourite piece by
Bach. This was Nureyev's home, the venue for his first performance in the
West, and the place in which he took refuge after defecting from the Soviet
Union in 1961. He is buried in the Russian Orthodox cemetery outside
Paris in St-Geneviève-du-Bois.

Set back from the boulevard des Capucines is the Opéra de Paris,
the city's most preposterous building – known as the **Opéra Garnier**
since the new opera house was built at Bastille. The building's architect, Charles Garnier, looks suitably foolish in a golden statue on the
rue Auber side of his edifice, which so perfectly suited the by-then
defunct court of Napoléon III. Excessively ornate and covering three
acres, it provided ample space for aristocratic preening, ceremonial
pomp and the social intercourse of opera-goers, for whom the performance itself was very much a secondary matter. In order not to
mask the vista of the building, the avenue de l'Opéra, built at the
same time, was left deliberately bereft of trees.

*The Opéra
Garnier is
open for visits
daily
10am–5pm;
30F; Mº Opéra.*

By day you can visit the splendidly grand and gilded **interior**,
including the auditorium – as long as there are no rehearsals (best
chance between 1 & 2pm) – whose ceiling, depicting operatic and
balletic scenes, is the work of **Chagall**. Your entry ticket includes a
visit to the **Bibliothèque-Musée de l'Opéra**, containing model sets,
dreadful nineteenth-century paintings, and rather better temporary
exhibitions on operatic themes. The classic horror movie *The
Phantom of the Opera* was set, though never filmed, here; a real
underground stream lends credence to the tale.

To the north of the Opéra, on the barren boulevard du Haussmann,
you'll find two of the city's big department stores: **Magasins du
Printemps** and **Galeries Lafayette** (opposite the largest Paris
branch of Marks & Spencer). Though they still possess their proud,
fin-de-siècle glass domes, much of the beauty of their interiors has
been hacked away.

Southwest of the Opéra, the **church of the Madeleine** is an obese
Napoleonic structure on the classical temple model, ordered by the
emperor as yet another monument to the glory of his army. A popular venue for society weddings, it provides a perspective across place
de la Concorde and the Seine to the Assemblée Nationale. Along the
east side of the church, a **flower market** displays its blooms every
day except Sunday, and there's a luxurious **Art Nouveau loo** by the
métro at the junction of place and boulevard de la Madeleine. But it
is for rich gourmands and window-gazers that the place de la
Madeleine holds the most appeal. In the northeast corner, the shop

The Grands
Boulevards,
the Opéra
and
Madeleine

*Extensive list-
ings of
Parisian food
shops can be
found on
pp.334–337*

Fauchon tempts you in with among the best food displays in Paris, and, down the west side, you'll find the smaller Hédiard's, as well as caviar, truffle and spirit specialists.

Boulevard des Italiens, running south of boulevard Haussmann from the Opéra to Richelieu-Drouot, boasts a fine selection of banking façades. The Crédit Lyonnais (which broke records in 1994 for losing money) has its head branch at no. 19, with a huge gold clock surrounded by gigantic women in flowing disarray. Wrought-iron balconies and hunting friezes from the 1840s restaurant *Maison Dorée*, at no. 20, have been preserved by the Banque Nationale de Paris, and are on display next door to its sleek 1930s main building at no. 16.

The Passages, Palais-Royal garden and Bibliothèque Nationale

Conceived by town planners in the nineteenth century to give pedestrians protection from mud and horse-drawn vehicles, the **Passages** are enjoying a new lease of life as havens from today's far more dangerous traffic. For decades they were left to crumble and decay, but many have now been renovated and returned to their original chic and immaculate state – with mega-premiums on their leases. Their entrances, however, remain easy to miss, and where you emerge at the other end can be quite a surprise. Many are closed at night and on Sundays.

*For
restaurants,
cafés and bars
in this area,
see p266.*

The most homogeneous and aristocratic of the *passages*, with painted ceilings and panelled shop fronts divided by black marble columns, is **Galerie Véro-Dodat** (between rue Croix-des-Petits-Champs and rue Jean-Jacques Rousseau; Mº Palais-Royal & Mº Musée-du-Louvre), named after the two pork butchers who set it up in 1824. It's still a little dilapidated, with peeling paint on many of the shop fronts, and recent recession sealed the fate of several old businesses. But at no. 26, Monsieur Capia still keeps a collection of antique dolls in a shop piled high with miscellaneous curios.

The **Banque de France** lies a short way northwest of Galerie Véro-Dodat. Rather than negotiating its massive bulk to reach the *passages* further north, it's more pleasant to walk through the **garden of the Palais Royal** via place de Valois. **Galerie de Valois**, the arcade on the east side of the garden, has an exquisite purple-panelled parfumerie, Les Salons du Palais Royal Shiseido, at no. 142. Rue de Montpensier, running alongside the gardens to the west, is connected to rue de Richelieu by several tiny *passages*, of which Hulot brings you out at the statue of Molière on the junction of rues Richelieu and Molière. A certain charm also lurks about rue de Beaujolais, bordering the northern end of the gardens, with its corner café looking on the Théâtre du Palais-Royal, and with glimpses into *Le Grand Véfour* restaurant, plus more short arcades leading up to rue des Petits-Champs.

On the other side of rue des Petits-Champs, just to the left as you come from rue de Beaujolais, looms the forbidding wall of the **Bibliothèque Nationale**, part of whose enormous collection has been transferred to the new Bibiothèque Nationale Tolbiac in the 13e (see p.167). Visiting its temporary exhibitions (closed Mon) will give you access to some of the more beautiful parts of the building, the **Galerie Mazarin** in particular, and you can also pay to see a display of coins and ancient treasures in the **Cabinet des Monnaies, Médailles et Antiques**. There's no restriction on entering the library, nor on peering into the atmospheric reading rooms. Researchers take their cigarette and sandwich breaks in a courtyard on rue Vivienne, in a corner of which stands a pensive statue of Jean-Paul Sartre.

The library owns **Galerie Colbert**, one of two very upmarket *passages* linking rue Vivienne with rue des Petits-Champs. Gorgeously lit by bunches of bulbous lamps, Galerie Colbert hosts free temporary exhibitions of the library's treasures, and also contains an expensive 1830s-style brasserie, *Le Grand Colbert*, to which senior librarians and rich academics retire for lunch. The flamboyant decor of Grecian and marine motifs in the larger **Galerie Vivienne** establishes the perfect ambience in which to buy Jean-Paul Gaultier gear, or you can browse in the antiquarian bookshop, Librairie Jousseaume, which dates back to the *passage*'s earliest days.

Three blocks west of the Bibliothèque Nationale is a totally different style of *passage*. Just like a regular high street, the **passage Choiseul**, between rue des Petits-Champs and rue St-Augustin (and connected to rue Ste-Anne by passage Ste-Anne), has takeaway food, cheap clothes shops, stationers and bars, plus a few arty outlets along its chequerboard tiled length of almost 200m. It was here that the author Louis-Ferdinand Céline lived as a boy, a period and location vividly recounted in his novel *Death on Credit* (see "Books" on p.434).

For a combination of old-fashioned chic and workaday you need to explore the **passage des Panoramas**, the grid of arcades north of the Bibliothèque Nationale, beyond rue St-Marc, though they're still in need of a little repair and there are no fancy mosaics for your feet. Most of the eateries make no pretence at style, but one old brasserie, *L'Arbre à Cannelle*, has fantastic carved wood panelling, and there are still bric-a-brac shops, stamp dealers and an upper-crust printshop with its original 1867 fittings. It was around the Panoramas, in 1817, that the first Parisian gas lamps were tried out.

In **passage Jouffroy**, across boulevard Montmartre, a M. Segas sells walking canes and theatrical antiques opposite a shop displaying every conceivable fitting and furnishing for a doll's house. Near the romantic *Hôtel Chopin*, Paul Vulin spreads his second-hand

The Passages, Palais-Royal garden and Bibliothèque Nationale

The Cabinet des Monnaies, Médailles et Antiques is open Mon–Sat 1–5pm, Sun noon–6pm; 22F; M° Bourse.

The
Passages,
Palais-Royal
garden and
Bibliothèque
Nationale

books along the passageway, and Ciné-Doc serves cinephiles. Crossing rue de la Grange-Batelière, you enter **passage Verdeau**, where a few of the old postcard and camera dealers still trade alongside smart new art galleries and a designer Italian delicatessen.

At the top of rue Richelieu, the tiny **passage des Princes**, with its beautiful glass ceiling, stained-glass decoration and twirly lamps, has finally been restored, but its charm has been sapped by the fast-food chains and mundane shops. Its erstwhile neighbour, the passage de l'Opéra, described in surreal detail by Louis Aragon in *Paris Peasant*, was eaten up with the completion of Haussmann's boulevards – a project that demolished scores of old *passages*.

*Auctions are
announced in
the press,
under "Ventes
aux Enchères";
you'll find
details, includ-
ing photos of
pieces, in the
widely avail-
able weekly*
Gazette de
l'Hôtel Drouot.

While in this area, you could also take a look at what's up for auction at the Paris equivalent of Christie's and Sotheby's, the **Hôtel Drouot** (9 rue Drouot; Mº Le Peletier & Mº Richelieu-Drouot). To spare any fear of unintended hand movements landing you in the bankruptcy courts, you can simply wander round looking at the goods before the action starts (11am–6pm on the eve of the sale, 11am–noon on the day itself).

Back in the 2e arrondissement, close to Mº Étienne-Marcel, the three-storey **Grand-Cerf**, between rue St-Denis and rue Dessoubs, is stylistically the best of all the *passages*. The wrought-iron work, glass roof and plain-wood shop fronts have all been cleaned, attracting stylish arts, crafts and antique shops, but it lacks atmosphere and has yet to be discovered in the same way as the other *passages*. As you exit from the passage du Grand-Cerf at rue Dessoubs, you're faced with a mural entitled *The Imaginary City*, inspired by Robert Mallet-Stevens. Fortunately this urban vision is not what's intended for the Montorgueil-St-Denis quartier, which is now pedestrianized, its streets recobbled and fitted out with bollards and new street signs.

Clothes, sex, the stock exchange and news

Mass-produced clothing is the business of **place du Caire**, the centre of the rag-trade district. The frenetic trading and deliveries of cloth, the food market on **rue des Petits-Carreaux**, and the general toing and froing make a lively change from the office-bound quartiers further west. Beneath an extraordinary pseudo-Egyptian façade of grotesque Pharaonic heads (a celebration of Napoléon's conquest of Egypt), an archway opens onto a series of arcades, the **passage du Caire**. This, contrary to any visible evidence, is the oldest of all the *passages* and entirely monopolized by wholesale clothes shops.

*For
restaurants,
cafés and bars
in this area
see
pp.266–267.*

The garment business gets progressively more upmarket westwards from the trade area. The upper end of **rue Étienne-Marcel**, and Louis XIV's **place des Victoires**, adjoined to the north by the appealingly asymmetrical **place des Petits-Pères**, are centres for designer clothes, with extravagant window displays whose price tags deter all those without the necessary funds. The boutiques on **rue St-Honoré** and its Faubourg extension beyond rue Royale are home to the established names, matched only across the Champs-Élysées by those on **rue François-1er**, where Dior's empire spreads out on the corner with avenue Montaigne. Hermès, at 24 rue du Faubourg-St-Honoré, displays a small collection of its original saddlery items, while Pierre Marly, the optician's at 380 rue St-Honoré, contains a small museum dedicated to its craft, the **Musée des Lunettes et Lorgnettes**. The exhibits cover everything you could wish to know about the history of spectacle-wearing, from the first medieval corrective lenses to contemporary examples, taking in binoculars, spectacle cases and microscopes along the way. Many items are miniature masterpieces – bejewelled, inlaid, enamelled and embroidered. There are, for example, lenses set in the hinges of fans and the pommels of gentlemen's canes, and one lorgnette case pops open to reveal an eighteenth-century dame sitting on a swing above a waterfall. A special collection comprises pieces that have sat upon the bridges of the famous: Audrey Hepburn, the Dalai Lama, Sophia Loren and ex-president Giscard.

The **place Vendôme**, with Napoléon high on a column clad with recycled Austro-Russian cannons, also caters for a full wallet. Here you have all the fashionable accessories for haute couture – jewellery and perfumes – plus the original *Ritz*, various banks, and the Law and Order ministry.

After clothes, bodies are the most evident commodity on sale in the 1er and 2e arrondissements. **Rue St-Denis** has been the red-light district of Paris for centuries, and attempts by the 2e arrondissement mairie to rid the street of its pimps and prostitutes have been to no avail; despite pedestrianizing the area between rues Étienne-Marcel and Réaumur (to stop kerb-crawling) and encouraging cafés like the English *Frog and Rosbif* to move in among the porn outlets, weary women still wait in every doorway between peepshows, striptease joints and sex-video shops. Around rue Ste-Anne, business is gay, transvestite and under-age. It's also a notorious spot for heroin hustlers. Such are the libertarian delights of Paris streetlife.

In the centre of the 2^e stands the **Bourse**, the Paris stock exchange, which finally caught up with information technology in the late 1980s (long after the real financial sharks had decamped elsewhere to do their deals). Guided visits, which attempt to equate the business here with London, Tokyo or New York, are not worth the 30F admission fee. A far more convincing impression of efficiency and dynamism is given by the antennae-topped building of the French news agency, AFP, which overshadows the Bourse from the south. Rue Réaumur, running east from here, used to be the Fleet Street of Paris, but now only *Le Figaro*'s central offices remain, on the junction of rue Montmartre and rue du Louvre, alongside a mural of tulips laid across newspaper cuttings.

Clothes, sex, the stock exchange and news

The Musée des Lunettes et Lorgnettes is open Tues–Sat 10.30am–noon & 2.30– 5.30pm; free; M^o Place-de-la-Concorde & M^o Madeleine.

Clothes, sex,
the stock
exchange
and news

The emphasis along rues Montmartre, Montorgueil and Turbigo,
leading south from rue Réaumur, turns towards food as they
approach Les Halles. Strictly not for vegetarians, the shops and stalls
here feature wild boar, deer and feathered friends, alongside pâté de
foie gras and caviar. This is also where professional chefs come to
buy their equipment (see p.337).

Les Halles

In 1969, the main body of **Les Halles market** was moved out to the
suburbs after more than eight hundred years in the heart of the city.
There was widespread opposition to the destruction of Victor
Baltard's nineteenth-century pavilions, and considerable disquiet at
the changes renovation of the area might bring. The authorities'
excuse to proceed was the RER and métro interchange they had to
have below. Digging began in 1971, and the hole was only finally
filled at the end of the 1980s. Hardly any trace remains of the work-
For
restaurants, ing-class quarter, with its night bars and bistros for the market
cafés and bars traders. Nowadays, rents rival the 16ᵉ, and the all-night places serve
around Les and profit from a markedly different clientèle, such that Les Halles is
Halles, see constantly promoted as the hotspot of Paris, where the cool and
pp.267–269. famous congregate. In fact, anyone with any sense and money hangs
out in the traditional bourgeois quartiers to the west – many of the
people milling about here are up from the suburbs.

From Châtelet-Les Halles RER, you surface only after ascending
from levels -4 to 0 of the **Forum des Halles** centre, which stretches
underground from the Bourse du Commerce rotunda to rue Pierre-
Lescot. The overground section comprises aquarium-like arcades of

shops, encased by glass buttocks, with white steel creases sliding
down to an imprisoned patio. To temper all this commerce, the
Pavillon des Arts – a temporary art exhibition space – and poetry
and crafts pavilions top two sides, in a simple construction – save for
the mirrors – that just manages to be out of sync with the curves and
hollows below.

The gardens planted above the subterranean shopping area and
transport interchange have begun to outgrow their protective wire
cages and the green space is providing a welcome if crowded respite.
On the north side, in front of St-Eustache, the statue of a giant head

The Pavillon des Arts is open Tues–Sun 11.30am–6.30pm; 30F; Mº/RER Châtelet-Les Halles.

Music listings for the area around place du Châtelet can be found in Chapter 14.

and hand suggests the dislocation of this place. Beneath the garden, amidst the shops, there's scope for various diversions – swimming, games of billiards, discovering Paris through videos, movie-going, and photography exhibitions. The **Espace Photographique** de Paris (Weds–Fri 1–6pm, Sat & Sun 1–7pm; 10F), on level -3 of the Forum, has changing exhibitions of the greats – Cartier-Bresson, Brandt, Cameron and the like – as well as lesser known photographers.

After a spate of multi-levels, air-conditioning and artificial light, however, it's a relief to enter the high Gothic and Renaissance space of **St-Eustache**, on the north side of the gardens. From its pulpit, during the Commune, a woman "preached" the abolition of marriage; and in the Chapelle St-Joseph, a naïve relief, entitled *The Departure of Fruit and Vegetables from the Heart of Paris, 28 February 1969*, depicts the area's more recent history.

Alternatively, for an antidote to steel and glass troglodytism, you can join the throng around the **Fontaine des Innocents** to admire the water cascading down its perfect Renaissance proportions. Clowns imitating your movements for the amusement of everyone else are a regular hazard – or a delight, when you're not the victim.

There are always hundreds of people around the Forum, filling in time, hustling, or just loafing about. Pickpocketing and sexual harassment are pretty routine; the law, plus canine arm, are often in evidence, and at night it can be quite tense. The streets on the eastern side have plenty of cafés for breaks from the shoving crowds, while the area southwards to **place du Châtelet** teems with jazz bars, nightclubs and restaurants, and is far more crowded at 2am than 2pm.

South of Les Halles

There's a labyrinth of tiny streets to explore between the Fontaine des Innocents and place du Châtelet, once the site of a notorious fortress prison, now a maelstrom of Parisian traffic overlooked by two grand theatres, the **Théâtre Musicale de Paris** and the **Théâtre de la Ville**. On the quayside, whose name (*Mégisserie*) refers to the treatment of animal skins in medieval times when this was an area of abattoirs, there are now plants and miserable pets for sale. Further along the riverfront, towards the Louvre, the three blocks of **La Samaritaine** (Mon–Sat 9.30am–7pm, Thurs till 10pm) recall the days when aesthetics, not marketing psychology, determined the decoration of a department store. The building, now completely restored, was built in 1903 in pure Art Nouveau style, with gold, green, and glass exteriors, and, inside, brightly painted wrought-iron staircases and balconies against huge backdrops of ceramic floral patterns. Best of all is the view from the roof (take the lift to floor nine in Magasin 2 and then walk up two flights) – the most central high location in the city.

Beaubourg, the Marais and the Bastille

T he Centre Georges Pompidou – **Beaubourg** as it's known locally – lies a few blocks away from Les Halles across boulevard Sébastopol. A radical architectural breakthrough for its period – the 1970s – it's an enduring, popular focus for the Right Bank of the city. Currently, it's mostly closed for repairs and renovations, until a grand re-opening planned for the last day of 1999. Though the Pompidou Centre is no longer the focal point it once was, the surrounding **quartier Beaubourg**, full of art galleries and cafés, is still lively.

The **Marais**, to the east, is one of the loveliest areas of central Paris. The aristocratic mansions (many now housing museums and galleries), the medieval lanes, the Jewish quarter and a plethora of small, appealing restaurants, shops, cafés and gay bars have no major thoroughfares to disturb them.

The **Bastille** used to belong in spirit and in style to the working-class districts of eastern Paris. Since the building of the new opera house, however, it has become as fashionable a quartier as the Marais, and very much one of Paris' central hotspots.

Beaubourg

For years after its opening in 1977, the **Georges Pompidou National Art and Culture Centre** was notorious as Paris' most outrageous building. The novel concept of architects Renzo Piano and Richard Rogers was to put all the infrastructure on the outside, leaving maximum space for the interior. With brightly painted pipes and ducts, colour-coded according to their function, an escalator rising up within a glass tube on the outside, and lack of a monumental entrance – just a large, sloping plaza for buskers, magicians, clowns and anyone else to use as their stage – it was designed, in Rogers' words, as "horizontal streets in the air".

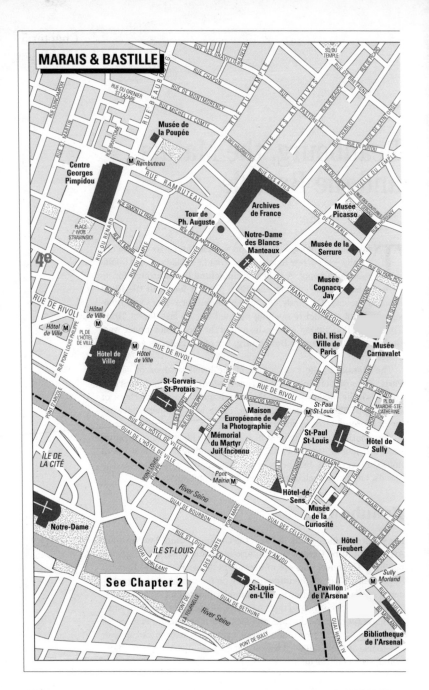

MARAIS & BASTILLE

Musée de la Poupée

Centre Georges Pimpidou

M Rambuteau

RUE RAMBUTEAU

PLACE IVOR STRAVINSKY

Tour de Ph. Auguste

Archives de France

Notre-Dame des Blancs-Manteaux

Musée Picasso

Musée de la Serrure

Musée Cognacq-Jay

4e

Hôtel de Ville

Hôtel de Ville M

RUE DE RIVOLI

PL DE L'HÔTEL DE VILLE

M

Hôtel de Ville

M Hôtel de Ville

RUE DE RIVOLI

Bibl. Hist. Ville de Paris

Musée Carnavalet

St-Gervais St-Protais

RUE DE RIVOLI

Maison Européenne de la Photographie

St-Paul M St-Louis

St-Paul St-Louis

Hôtel de Sully

Mémorial du Martyr Juif Inconnu

ÎLE DE LA CITÉ

QUAI DE L'HÔTEL DE VILLE

PL DU MARCHE-STE-CATHERINE

River Seine

Pont Marie M

Hôtel-de-Sens

Musée de la Curiosité

Notre-Dame

QUAI DE BOURBON

ÎLE ST-LOUIS

Hôtel Fieubert

RUE ST-LOUIS

QUAI D'ANJOU

Sully Morland M

See Chapter 2

St-Louis en-L'Ile

Pavillon de l'Arsenal'

River Seine

PONT DE SULLY

Bibliothèque de l'Arsenal

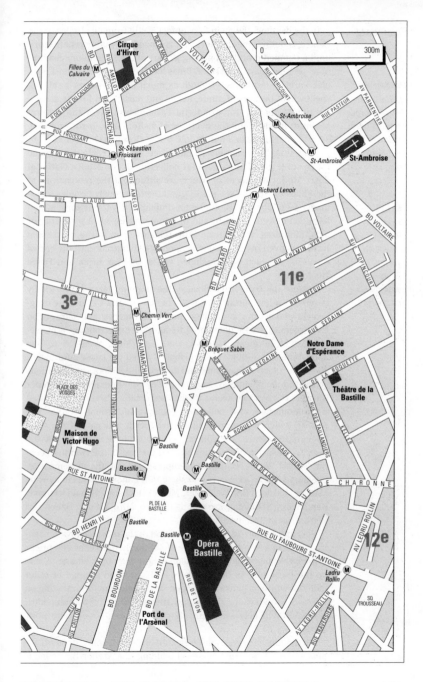

Beaubourg

The nearest métros to the Centre Georges Pompidou are M° Rambuteau & M° Hôtel-de-Ville.

The BPI Brantôme Library is detailed on p.348 of "Daytime amusements and sports".

In the daytime, the main flow of feet is still from Les Halles to the Centre, though three-quarters of it is **closed for major repair work** until a planned grand re-opening as part of the Millennium celebrations on New Years' Eve 1999. It has long been one of the most popular Parisian buildings – though as much for the piazza's shifting spectacle of buskers of mime, magic and music, and for the escalator ride to the top for wonderful Paris views, as for the cultural activities inside – and the overload of visitors and corrosion in the exterior steel have taken their toll. It was closed in October 1997 to provide time for necessary maintenance, and to create more space for the ever growing modern art collection **of the Musée National d'Art Moderne**, pieces of which are sitting out the renovations at the Palais de Tokyo (see p.138), and the ferociously popular multimedia **BPI Library** (Bibliothèque Publique d'Information), which has been moved to nearby rue Brantôme, at no. 11. A ground-floor exhibition area, the **Galerie Sud**, remains open in the centre and has been given over to major temporary exhibitions until the end of April 1999, which have included works by Max Ernst and David Hockney.

Despite the temporary closure, the sloping piazza is not totally deserted – a few portait artists still harass passers-by, and the drug-dealers who became another symptom of its success still hang out on its corners. It's now dominated by another extraordinary architectural sight, a gigantic tepee, the **Tipi** (Mon, Wed–Fri & Sun noon–6pm, Sat 2–6pm; free), inside of which the latest information about the future of the centre and its changing temporary exhibitions is relayed in a suitably high-tech way via interactive computer screens. You can also access images and details of some of the Musée d'Art Moderne's vast collection (comprising around 30,000 artworks), which formerly occupied the fourth and part of the third floors of the centre. The collection is second to none, with Fauvists, Cubists, Dadaists, Abstractionists and the rest of the twentieth century's First World art trends all represented. On the museum's re-opening, you can expect to see some of the most famous images by Matisse, Picasso, Braque, Léger, Marcel Duchamp, Sonia Delaunay, Kandindsky, Dali, Magritte and de Chirico, Miró, Calder, Bacon and Warhol, as well as Installation art.

We can't be sure of the configuration of the newly renovated centre, which will re-open during the life of this book. Times and prices will have changed, and in particular there may be a charge to ride up the escalator. As before, there is likely to be a range of other facilities within: a cinema, snack bar and restaurant (with seating on the roof), bookshop, dance and theatre space, cybercafé, kids' workshop and play areas, art shops for posters, books and postcards.

On the northern edge of the Beaubourg, down some steps off the piazza, a small separate one-level building, the **Atelier Brancusi**, is open as usual. Upon his death in 1956, the sculptor **Constantin Brancusi** bequeathed the contents of his 15^e arrondissement studio to the state, on the condition that it be reconstructed exactly as it was found. The artist became obsessed with the spatial relationship of the sculptures in his studio, going so far as to supplant each sold work with a plaster copy, and the four interlinked rooms of the studio faithfully adhere to his arrangements. Studios one and two are crowded with fluid sculptures of highly polished brass and marble, his trademark abstract bird and column shapes, stylized busts and objects poised as though they're about to take flight. Unfortunately, the rooms are behind glass, adding a feeling of sterility and distance. Perhaps the most satisfying rooms are ateliers 3 and 4, his private quarters – his tools are displayed on one wall almost like works of art themselves.

Beaubourg

The Atelier Brancusi is open Mon & Wed–Fri noon–8pm, Sat & Sun 10am–8pm; closed Tues & 1 May; 20F; M° Rambuteau.

Quartier Beaubourg and the Hôtel de Ville

The **visual entertainments** around **Beaubourg** are diverse. There's the clanking gold trompe l'oeil *Défenseur du Temps* clock in the Quartier de l'Horloge; a trompe l'œil as you look west along rue Aubry-le-Boucher from Beaubourg; a nine-digit timepiece counting down by milliseconds to the year 2000 on the side of the centre; and the **Fontaine Stravinsky**, colourful moving sculptures and fountains by Jean Tinguely and Niki de St-Phalle in the pool in front of **Église St-Merri** on place Igor Stravinsky. This squirting water-work pays homage to the composer and shows scant respect for passers-by; beneath it lies **IRCAM** (Intstitut de la Recherche et de la Coordination Acoustique/Musique), founded by the composer and conductor Pierre Boulez, a research centre for contemporary music, with an overground extension by Renzo Piano, one of the architects of the Beaubourg. IRCAM's activities are described on p.311.

Just north of the Beaubourg, a doll museum and a stash of art galleries provide some focus. Running off rue Beaborg, impasse Berthaud hides the **Musée de la Poupée**, where finely detailed tiny irons and sewing machines, furniture and pots and pans vie for attention with the dolls themselves. It's certain to appeal to small children.

The Musée de la Poupée is open Tues–Sun 10am–6pm; 30F; M° Rambuteau.

North of rue Aubry-le-Boucher on the narrow, picturesque **rue Quincampoix** is a concentration of small commercial art galleries, where you can browse to your heart's content for free – including Zabriskie, at no. 37 (Tues–Sat 2–7pm), which shows both classic and cutting-edge contemporary photography.

South of the Beaubourg, rue Renard runs down to **place de l'Hôtel de Ville**, where the oppressively gleaming and gargantuan mansion is the seat of the city's local government and one whole floor the private apartment of the mayor. An illustrated history of this edifice, always a prime target in riots and revolutions, is displayed along the platform of M° Châtelet on the Neuilly–Vincennes line.

Beaubourg

Those opposed to the establishments of kings and emperors created their alternative municipal governments at this building in 1789, 1848 and 1870. The poet Lamartine proclaimed the Second Republic here in 1848, and Gambetta the third in 1870. But, with the defeat of the Commune in 1871, the conservatives, in control once again, concluded that the Parisian municipal authority had to go, if order, property, morality and the suppression of the working class were to be maintained. For the next hundred years, Paris was ruled directly by the national government.

The next head of an independent municipality after the leaders of the Commune was **Jacques Chirac**, who became mayor in 1977. He ran Paris as his own fiefdom, with scant regard for other councillors. He even retained the mayorship while he was prime minister – a power base unequalled in French politics – and when he became president in 1995, he more or less nominated his successor, current mayor at the time of writing, **Jean Tiberi**.

The Marais

The **Marais** today comprises most of the 3^e and 4^e arrondissements. Yet until the thirteenth century, when the Knights Templar set up house in its northern section, now known as the **quartier du Temple**, and began to drain the land, it was an uninhabitable riverside swamp (*marais*). The grand and aristocratic character that has become its hallmark was not acquired until around 1600, when the area became the object of royal patronage, especially after the construction of the **place des Vosges** – or place Royale, as it then was – by Henri IV in 1605.

For eating and drinking options in the Marais, see pp.270–272.

Its apogee was relatively short-lived, for the aristocracy began to move away after the king took his court to Versailles in the latter part of the seventeenth century, leaving their mansions to the trading classes, who were in turn displaced during the Revolution. Thereafter, the masses moved in. The mansions were transformed into multi-occupied slum tenements. Their fabric decayed and the streets degenerated into unserviced squalor – and stayed that way until the 1960s.

Since then, however, gentrification has proceeded apace, and the quarter is now a sought-after enclave for arty and gay Parisians. Renovated mansions, their grandeur concealed by the narrow streets, have become museums, libraries, offices and chic flats, flanked by shops selling designer clothes, house and garden accoutrements, works of art and one-off trinkets. Nonetheless, having largely escaped the depredations of modern development as well as the heavy-handed attentions of Baron Haussmann, the Marais remains one of the most seductive districts of Paris – old, secluded, as unthreatening by night as it is by day, and with as many alluring shops, bars and places to eat as you could wish for.

Through the middle, dividing it in two, roughly north and south, runs the interminable **rue de Rivoli** and its continuation to Bastille, rue St-Antoine. South of this line is the quartier St-Paul-St-Gervais, the riverside, the Arsenal, and the Île St-Louis. To the north, more homogeneous as well as more fun to walk around, are most of the shops and museums, place des Vosges, the **Jewish quarter** and the quartier du Temple. Every street boasts an abundance of colour and detail: magnificent portes cochères (huge double carriage gates) with elaborate handles and knockers, stone and iron bollards that protected pedestrians from ruthless carriage drivers, cobbled courtyards, elegant iron railings and gates, sculpted house fronts, Chinese sweatshops, chichi boutiques, ethnic grocers – a wealth of interest.

Rue des Francs-Bourgeois

The main lateral street of the northern part of the Marais, which also forms the boundary between the 3^e and 4^e arrondissements, is the **rue des Francs-Bourgeois**. Beatnik Jack Kerouac translated it as "the street of the outspoken middle classes", which may be a fair description of the contemporary residents, though the name in fact means "people exempt from tax", in reference to the penurious inmates of a medieval almshouse that once stood on the site of no. 34.

At the western end of the street at no. 60, the eighteenth-century magnificence of the Palais Soubise houses the **Archives Nationales de France** and the **Musée de l'Histoire de France**, the latter of which hosts permanent and temporary exhibits of documents from the archives. Among authentic bits of paper that fill the archive's vaults are a medieval English monarch's challenge to his French counterpart to stake his kingdom on a duel, and Joan of Arc's trial proceedings with a doodled impression of her in the margin. A section on the Revolution includes the book of samples from which Marie-Antoinette chose her dress each morning, and a Republican children's alphabet where "J" stands for Jean-Jacques Rousseau and "L" for labourer. The museum also provides an opportunity to enter perhaps the Marais' most splendid mansion, with some fine Rococo interiors and paintings by the likes of Boucher.

Opposite the Palais Soubise, at the back of a driveway for the Crédit Municipal bank, stands a pepperpot tower that formed part of the **city walls**; these were built by King Philippe-Auguste early in the thirteenth century to link up with his new fortress, the Louvre. Further along, past several more imposing façades and the peculiarly public lycée classrooms at no. 28, you can enter the courtyard of the **Hôtel d'Albret** (no. 31). This eighteenth-century mansion is home to the cultural department of the mayor of Paris. The dignified façade is blocked by a revolting sculptural column, a 1989 Bicentennial work by Bernard Pagès, resembling thorns and red and blue sticky tape.

The Musée de l'Histoire de France is open Mon & Wed–Fri noon–5.45pm, Sat & Sun 1.45–5.45pm; closed Tues; 20F; M° Rambuteau & M° St-Paul.

The next landmarks on the street, at the junction with rues Payenne and Pavée, are two of the Marais' grandest hôtels, the sixteenth-century Carnavalet and Lamoignon, housing, respectively, the Musée Carnavalet (see below) and the **Bibliothèque Historique de la Ville de Paris**, the latter housing centuries' worth of texts and picture books about the city (see p.348 for opening times). Next to the Lamoignon, on rue Pavée – so called because it was among the first Paris streets to be paved, in 1450 – was the site of the **La Force prison**, where many of the Revolution's victims were incarcerated, including the Princesse de Lamballe, who was lynched in the massacres of September 1792. Her head was presented on a stake to her friend Marie-Antoinette.

Musée Carnavalet

The Musée Carnavalet is open Tues–Sun 10am–5.40pm; 27F, 35F with special exhibitions; M° St-Paul.

The **Musée Carnavalet**, its entrance at 23 rue de Sévigné, off rue des Francs-Bourgeois, follows the history of Paris from its origins until the early twentieth century in an extensive and beautifully presented collection. The museum focuses mainly on the era between François I and the belle époque, with a special emphasis on the French Revolution.

Paris's history is presented as viewed and lived by its people: the working class, bourgeoisie, aristocrats *and* royalty. The **ground floor** displays nineteenth- and early twentieth-century shop and inn signs, and fascinating models of Paris through the ages, along with maps and plans, show how much Haussmann's grand boulevards changed the face of the city.

On the **first floor**, decorative arts feature strongly, with numerous re-created salons and boudoirs from the time of Louis XII to Louis XVI from buildings that had to be destroyed for Haussmann's boulevards. One room is devoted to the famous letter-writer **Madame de Sévigné**, who lived in the Carnavalet mansion and wrote a series of letters to her daughter, which vividly portray her privileged lifestyle under the reign of Louis XIV. More modern settings include the Art Nouveau interior of the jeweller's shop Fouquet, and the hideously overblown decor of the ballroom of the Hôtel de Wendel of the same period.

The **second floor** has rooms full of sacred mementos of the **French Revolution**: models of the Bastille, original declarations of the Rights of Man and the Citizen, sculpted allegories of Reason, crockery with revolutionary slogans, glorious models of the guillotine and execution orders to make you shed a tear for the royalists as well.

Owing to limited funds, not all the rooms are open at the same time: the Second Empire to the twentieth century section is open only 10–11.50am, with that on the sixteenth to the eighteenth centuries open 1.10–5.40pm. Selections from the museum's impressive collection of photographs by Brassaï, Atget and Doisneau are periodically exhibited. If you want to see everything you should get here early, though the ticket lasts all day so you can return. After an exhausting trawl of the collection, you can rest in the peaceful, formally laid-out garden courtyards.

More Marais mansions

West of the Musée Carnavalet, three other Marais mansions now house museums. In a parallel street, rue Elzévir, one block west of rue Payenne, the **Musée Cognacq-Jay** occupies the Hôtel Donon at no. 8. The Cognacq-Jay family built up the Samaritaine department store – you can see a history of the family and their charitable works in a series of dioramas on the tenth-floor terrace of the store (see p.334 of "Shopping"). As well as being noted philanthropists, they were lovers of European art. Their collection of eighteenth-century pieces on show includes works by Canaletto, Fragonard, Tiepolo and Rembrandt, displayed in beautifully carved wood-panelled rooms filled with porcelain and furniture.

The Musée Cognacq-Jay is open Tues–Sun 10am–5.40pm; 17F; M° St-Paul & M° Chemin-Vert.

Heading north up rue Elzévir from the Musée Cognacq-Jay, at place de Thorigny, turn left into rue de la Perle, where at no. 1 you'll find the **Musée de la Serrure Bricard** in the cellars of the Hôtel Libéral-Bruand. This collection of locks throughout the ages includes the fittings for Napoléon's palace doors (the one for the Tuileries bashed in by revolutionaries), locks that trapped your hand or shot your head off if you tried a false key, and a seventeenth-century wonder made by a craftsman kept under lock and key for four years. The rest of the exhibits are pretty boring, though the Hôtel setting is some compensation.

The Musée de la Serrure Bricard is open Mon 2–5pm, Tues–Fri 10am–noon & 2–5pm; closed Aug; 30F; M° Chemin-Vert & M° St Paul.

Rue de la Perle's continuation, across rue Vielle du Temple, is rue des Quatre Fils. On its corner, at 60 rue des Archives, is the **Musée de la Chasse et de la Nature**, in the Hôtel Guénégaud. While hunt saboteurs, vegetarians and pacifists in general should certainly avoid this one – the nature element will be of most interest to taxidermists – this museum devoted to hunting is housed on three floors of a quite splendid mid-seventeenth-century mansion. Weapons range from prehistoric stone arrow-heads to highly decorative crossbows and guns, and there are many paintings by French artists romanticizing the chase.

The Musée de la Chasse et de la Nature is open 10am–12.30pm & 1.30–5.30pm; 30F; M° Rambuteau.

Musée Picasso

On the northern side of rue des Francs-Bourgeois, rue Payenne leads up to the lovely gardens and houses of **rue du Parc-Royal** and on to **rue de Thorigny**. Here, at no. 5, the magnificent classical façade of the seventeenth-century **Hôtel Salé**, built for a rich salt-tax collector, conceals the **Musée Picasso**. In the 1980s, the grandiloquent mansion was restored at a cost to the government of £3–4m to house the museum devoted to the Paris-based Spanish artist, and the French

*The Musée
Picasso is open
9.30am–6pm;
closed Tues;
30F, 20F on
Sun; M°
Chemin Vert &
St-Paul.*

are justly proud of the result. The spacious, yet undaunting interior is admirably suited to its contents: the largest collection of Picassos anywhere. A large proportion of the works belonged to Picasso at the time of his death in 1973, and the state had first option on them in lieu of taxes owed. They include the paintings he bought or was given by his contemporaries, his African masks and sculptures, photographs, letters and other personal memorabilia.

These are not Picasso's most enjoyable works – the museums of the Côte d'Azur and the Picasso gallery in Barcelona are more exciting. But the collection does leave you with a definite sense of the man partly because these were the works he chose to keep, including some portraits of his family members and lovers. The portrait of *Dora Maar*, like that of *Marie-Thérèse*, was painted in 1937, during the Spanish Civil War, when Picasso was going through his worst personal and political crises. This is the period when emotion and passion play hardest on his paintings and they are by far the best. A decade later, Picasso was a member of the Communist Party – his cards are on show along with a drawing entitled *Staline à la Santé* ("*Here's to Stalin*"). The *Massacre en Corée* (1951) demonstrates the lasting pacifist commitment in his work. Temporary exhibitions bring to the Hôtel Salé works from the periods least represented: the Pink Period, Cubism (despite some fine examples here, including a large collection of collages), the immediate postwar period and the 1950s and 1960s.

The modern museological accoutrements are all provided: audiovisuals and films in a special cinema, biographical and critical details displayed in each room, and a library. There's an outdoor café in the warmer months.

Place des Vosges and around

Continuing along rue des Francs-Bourgeois east of the Musée Carnavalet, you can't miss the **place des Vosges**, a masterpiece of aristocratic elegance and the first example of planned development in the history of Paris. It's a vast square of symmetrical brick and stone mansions built over arcades. Undertaken in 1605 at the inspiration of **Henri IV**, it was inaugurated in 1612 for the wedding of Louis XIII and Anne of Austria; it is Louis's statue – or, rather, a replica of it – that stands hidden by chestnut trees in the middle of the grass and gravel gardens. Originally called place Royale, it was renamed Vosges in 1800 in honour of the département, which was the first to pay its share of the expenses of the revolutionary wars.

Royal patronage of the area goes back to the days when a royal palace, the Hôtel des Tournelles, stood on the north side of what is now the place des Vosges. It remained in use until 1559, having served also as the residence of the Duke of Bedford when he governed northern France in the name of England in the 1420s.

In 1559, Henri II, whose queen was Catherine de Médicis, concluded the treaty of Cateau-Cambrésis, thereby ending his wars with the Holy Roman Empire. To cement the treaty he married his son to the Duke of Savoy and his daughter to Philip II of Spain in a double wedding whose celebrations took place near the place des Vosges. The finale was a jousting tournament, in which the king took part. He won two bouts, wearing the colours of his mistress, Diane de Poitiers, who watched, seated beside his wife. He then challenged the Duke of Montgomery, captain of his guards, who accidentally struck him in the eye. The king died in agony ten days later.

Montgomery fled to England but returned after some years to take part in the Wars of Religion on the Protestant side. He was captured and, in violation of the terms of his surrender, put to death by Catherine de Médicis. She also had the Hôtel des Tournelles demolished, and the space thus vacated became a huge **horse market**, trading between one and two thousand horses every Saturday. So it remained until Henri IV decided on the construction of his place Royale.

Since then, its name has changed many times, reflecting the fluctuating fortunes of different political tendencies. It stayed place Royale until 1792, when it became, first, Fédérés, then Indivisibilité, then Vosges in 1800. It was changed back to Royale with the Restoration of the monarchy in 1814, to Vosges in 1831, Royale again through the Second Empire up to the Third Republic in 1870, then back to republican Vosges, which it has remained.

Through all the vicissitudes of history, the *place* has never lost its cachet as a smart address. Today, well-heeled Parisians pause in the arcades at art, antique and fashion shops, and lunch alfresco at the restaurants while buskers play classical music. In the garden, toddlers, octogenarians, workers and schoolchildren on lunch breaks sit or play in the only green space of any size in the locality – unusually for Paris, you're allowed to sprawl on the grass.

Among the many celebrities who made their homes here was Victor Hugo; his house, at no. 6, where he wrote much of *Les Misérables*, is now a museum, the **Maison de Victor Hugo**, in which a whole room is devoted to posters of its various stage adaptations. Hugo was multi-talented: many of his ink drawings are exhibited, and there's an extraordinary Japanese dining room he put together. That apart, the usual portraits, manuscripts and memorabilia shed sparse light on the man and his work, particularly if you don't read French.

The Maison de Victor Hugo is open Tues–Sun 10am–5.40pm; Mᵒ Chemin-Vert & Mᵒ Bastille.

From the southwest corner of the *place*, a door leads through to the formal château garden, orangerie and exquisite Renaissance façade of the **Hôtel de Sully**. The garden, with its park benches, makes for a peaceful rest-stop, or you can pass through the building, nodding at the sphinxes on the stairs, as a pleasing short cut to rue St-Antoine. Temporary photographic exhibitions, usually with social, historical or anthropological themes, are mounted in the hôtel by the

Mission du Patrimoine Photographique (Tues–Sun 10am–6.30pm; 25F). You can also browse in the history-focused bookshop (Tues–Sun 10am–7pm).

A short distance back to the west along rue St-Antoine, almost opposite the sixteenth-century **church of St-Paul**, which was inaugurated by Cardinal Richelieu, you'll find another square. A complete contrast to the imposing formality of the place des Vosges, the tiny **place du Marché-Ste-Catherine** is a perfect example of that other great French architectural talent: an unerring eye for the intimate, the small-scale, the apparently accidental, and the irresistibly charming.

The Jewish quarter: rue des Rosiers

As the tide of chichification seeps remorselessly northwards up the Marais, the only remaining islet of genuine local, community life is in the city's main Jewish quarter, still centred around **rue des Rosiers**, just as it was in the twelfth century. Although the *hammam* is now a trendy café, and many of the little grocers, bakers, bookshops and original cafés are under pressure to follow suit (for a long time local flats were kept empty, not for property speculation but to try to stem the middle-class invasion), the area manages to retain its Jewish identity. There's also a distinctly Mediterranean flavour to the quartier, testimony to the influence of the **North African Sephardim**, who, since the end of the World War II, have sought refuge here from the uncertainties of life in the French ex-colonies. They have replenished Paris' Jewish population, depleted when its Ashkenazim, having escaped the pogroms of Eastern Europe, were rounded up by the Nazis and the French police and transported back east to concentration camps.

The Centre de Documentation Juive Contemporaine is open Mon–Thurs & Sun 10am–1pm & 2–6pm, Fri 2–5pm; 15F; M° St-Paul & M° Pont-Marie.

Don't leave the area without wandering the surrounding streets: rue du Roi-de-Sicile, the minute **place Bourg-Tibourg** off rue de Rivoli, **rue des Écouffes**, **rue Ste-Croix-de-la-Bretonnerie** (with its lively gay bars), **rue Vieille-du-Temple** (full of contemporary art galleries), and **rue des Archives**, where a medieval cloister, the Cloître des Billettes, at nos. 22–26, hosts free exhibitions of art and crafts (daily 10am–8pm). On the other side of rue de Rivoli, at 17 rue Geoffroy l'Asnier, the **Centre de Documentation Juive Contemporaine** mounts exhibitions concerned with all genocides and oppression of peoples, and guards the sombre **Mémorial du Martyr Juif Inconnu** (Memorial to the Unknown Jewish Martyr).

The Quartier du Temple

The northern part of the Marais is ethnic, local, old-fashioned, working-class, and gradually being "discovered" by those who wax lyrical and nostalgic about the little workshops and traditional cafés and the "realness" of the people. As you get beyond the cluster of art galleries and brasseries that have sprung up around the

Picasso museum, or, over to the west, across rue Michel-le-Comte, the aristocratic stone façades of the southern Marais give way to the more humble, though no less attractive, stucco, paint and thick-slatted shutters of seventeenth- and eighteenth-century streets. Some bear the names of old rural French provinces: **Beauce**, **Perche**, **Saintonge**, **Picardie**. Ordinary cafés and shops occupy the ground floors, while rag-trade leather workshops and printers – though these are getting fewer – operate in the interior of the cobbled courtyards.

Robespierre lived in the **rue de Saintonge**, at no. 64, demolished in 1834. In the adjacent **rue Charlot**, at no.9, yet another Marais mansion, the Hôtel de Retz, has been colonized by artists. It now houses the **Passage de Retz**, with changing exhibitions of fine art and design from young artists; arty events are also sometimes staged. Opposite, in the dead-end **ruelle de Sourdis**, one section of street has remained unchanged since its construction in 1626. Further along, on the corner of **rue du Perche**, a little classical façade on a leafy courtyard hides the Armenian church of Ste-Croix, testimony to the many Armenians who sought refuge here from the **Turkish pogroms** of World War I. Further still, on the left and almost to the busy rue de Bretagne, is the easily missed entrance to the **Marché des Enfants-Rouges**, one of the smallest and least-known food markets in Paris, which was being renovated at the time of writing. Across rue de Bretagne, rue de Picardie leads up to the **Carreau du Temple**.

The Marais

The Passage de Retz is open daily 10am–7pm; 30F; M° Filles-du-Calvaire.

Opposite the Carreau du Temple is Paris' best cybercafé, the Web Bar *(see p.272 for this and other places to eat and drink nearby).*

The Knights Templar

The military order of the **Knights Templar** was established in Jerusalem at the time of the Crusades to protect pilgrims to the Holy Land. Its members quickly became exceedingly rich and powerful, with some nine thousand commanderies spread across Europe. They acquired land in the marais in Paris around 1140, and began to build. After the loss of Palestine in 1291, this fortress property, which covered the area now bounded by rues du Temple, Bretagne, Picardie and Béranger and constituted a separate town without the city walls, became their international headquarters, as the seat of their Grand Master.

They came to a sticky end, however, early in the fourteenth century, when King Philippe le Bel, alarmed at their power and in alliance with Pope Clement V, had them tried for sacrilege, blasphemy and sodomy. Fifty-four of them were burnt, including, in 1314, the Grand Master himself, in the presence of the king. Thereafter the order was abolished.

The Temple buildings continued to exist until the Revolution, with about four thousand inhabitants: a mixed population, consisting of artisans not subject to the city's trade regulations, debtors seeking freedom from prosecution, and some rich residents of private hôtels. Louis XVI and the royal family were imprisoned in the keep in 1792 (see box overleaf). It was finally demolished in 1808 by Napoléon, determined to eradicate any possible focus for royalist nostalgia.

The Marais

More information about the Marché des Enfants-Rouges, the Carreau du Temple and other Parisian markets is given in Chapter 16.

Nothing remains of the **Knights Templar**'s installations beyond the name of "Temple", although some of the fortifications survived until the Revolution, notably the keep. Now the only direct heirs of the old traditions are the markets and workshops; for the Temple was always a tax-free zone for non-guild craftsmen and a prosecution-free zone for debtors. The **Carreau** itself, which is a fine *halles*-like structure, shelters a clothes market (Tues–Sun mornings) with a heavy preponderance of leather gear. **Rue de la Corderie**, a pretty little street on the north side, opening into an otherworldly *place*, has a couple of pleasant cafés under the trees.

These streets have a genteel and somewhat provincial air about them, but a couple of blocks to the west it is a different story. **Rue du Temple**, itself lined with many beautiful houses dating back to the seventeenth century (no. 41, for instance, the Hôtel Aigle d'Or, is the last surviving coaching inn of the period), is the dividing line, full of fascinating little businesses trading in fashion accessories: chains, buckles, bangles and beads – everything you can think of. At no. 71, the Hôtel de Saint-Aignan is now home to the **Musée d'Art et d'Historie du Judaisme**, which opened in late 1998 and has swallowed up the collection of the now closed Musée d'Art Juif in Montmartre. The new museum has a much larger collection, which includes items of worship, models of synagogues and works by Chagall. Consult *Pariscope* for opening times.

The Temple and Louis XVI

Louis XVI, Marie-Antoinette, their two children and immediate family were imprisoned in the keep of the Knights Templar's ancient fortress in August 1792 by the revolutionary government. By the end of 1794, when all the adults had been executed, the two children – a teenage girl and the nine- or ten-year-old dauphin, now, in the eyes of royalists, Louis XVII – remained there alone, in the charge of a family called Simon. Louis XVII was literally walled up, allowed no communication with other human beings, not even his sister, who was living on the floor above. He died in 1795, a half-crazed imbecile, and was buried in a public grave.

At least that is what appeared to be his fate. A number of clues, however, point to hocus-pocus. The doctor who certified the child's death kept a lock of his hair, but it was later found not to correspond with the colour of the young Louis XVII's hair, as remembered by his sister. Mme Simon confessed on her deathbed that she had substituted another child for Louis XVII. And a sympathetic sexton admitted that he had exhumed the body of this imbecile child and reburied it in the cloister of the Église Ste-Marguerite in the Faubourg St-Antoine (see p.207), but when this body was dug up it was found to be that of an eighteen-year-old.

A plausible theory is that the real Louis XVII died early in 1794. But since Robespierre needed the heir to the throne as a hostage with which to menace internal and foreign royalist enemies, he had Louis disposed of in secret and substituted the idiot. Taking advantage of this atmosphere of uncertainty, 43 different people subsequently claimed to be Louis XVII.

The streets to the west of rue du Temple are narrow, dark, and riddled with passages, the houses half-timbered and bulging with age. Practically every house is a Chinese wholesale business, many of them trading leather – and, on the face of it at least, not very friendly. This was Paris' **original Chinatown**, fed by thousands of immigrant workers brought in to fill the factories while French men were being sent off to the trenches of World War I.

West of rue Volta is the **Musée des Arts et Métiers,** at 292 rue St-Martin. Interminable works – renovations and archeological excavations – have kept this museum of technology semi-closed for years; 1998 was the current projected completion date but at the time of writing it was still closed. The museum is part of the Conservatoire des Arts et Métiers, itself incorporating the former Benedictine priory of St-Martin-des-Champs, its original chapel dating from the fourth century. Its most important exhibit is Foucault's pendulum, normally suspended from the ceiling of the ground floor former church. In 1997 it was loaned to the Panthéon, where Foucault's successful experiment to prove the rotation of the earth was conducted in 1851 – now a working model of the bronze pendulum has been permanently installed there. Other exhibits include the laboratory of Lavoisier, the French chemist who first showed that water is a combination of oxygen and hydrogen. Consult *Pariscope, L'Officiel des Spectacles* or the tourist office for details of the opening hours.

South: the Quartier St-Paul-St-Gervais and the Pavillon de l'Arsenal

In the southern section of the Marais, below rues de Rivoli and St-Antoine, the crooked steps and lanterns of rue Cloche-Perce, the tottering timbered houses of rue François-Miron, the medieval buildings behind the church of St-Gervais-St-Protais, and the smell of flowers and incense on rue des Barres, all provide the opportunity to indulge in Paris picturesque. The late Gothic St-Gervais-St-Protais, somewhat battered on the outside due to a direct hit from a shell fired from Big Bertha in 1918, is more pleasing inside, with some lovely stained glass and a seventeenth-century organ, Paris' oldest. Between rues Fourcy and François-Miron, a gorgeous Marais mansion, the early eighteenth-century Hôtel Hénault de Cantobre, has been turned into a vast and serene space dedicated to the art of contemporary photography, the **Maison Européenne de la Photographie** (entrance at 4 rue de Fourcy). Temporary shows combine with a revolving exhibition of the Maison's permanent collection; young photographers and news photographers get a look in, as well as artists using photography in multi-media creations or installation art. A library and videothèque can be freely consulted, and there's a stylish café designed by architect Nestor Perkal.

The Maison Européenne de la Photographie is open Wed–Sun 11am–8pm; 30F, free Wed after 5pm; Mᵒ St-Paul & Mᵒ Pont Marie.

Shift eastwards to the next tangle of streets and you'll find modern, chichi flats in the **"Village St-Paul"**, with clusters of expensive

The Marais

The Musée de
la Curiosité et
de la Magie is
open Wed, Sat
& Sun 2–7pm;
45F; M° St-
Paul & M°
Sully-Morland.

The Pavillon
de l'Arsenal is
open Tues–Sat
10.30am–
6.30pm, Sun
11am–7pm;
free; disabled
access; M°
Sully-Morland.

antique shops in the courtyards off **rue St-Paul**. This part of the Marais suffered a postwar hatchet job, and, although seventeenth- and eighteenth-century magnificence is still in evidence (there's even a stretch of the city's defensive wall dating from the early thirteenth century in the lycée playground on rue des Jardins St-Paul), it lacks the architectural cohesion of the Marais to the north. The fifteenth-century **Hôtel de Sens**, on the rue de Figuier, looks bizarre in its isolation. The public library it now houses, the **Bibliothèque Forney**, filled with volumes on fine and applied arts, makes a good excuse to explore this outstanding medieval building. See pp.347–348 for the library's opening hours.

Rue St-Paul itself has some good addresses, including the **Musée de la Curiosité et de la Magie** at no. 11, a delightful museum dealing with magic and illusion. A few tricks are explained, but don't expect to glean all the answers. Automatas, distorting mirrors and optical illusions, things that float on thin air, a box for sawing people in half – they're all on view with examples from the eighteenth and nineteenth centuries, as well as contemporary magicians' tools. The best fun is a live demonstration of the art (every 30min from 2.30–6pm) by a skilled magician. The museum shop sells books on conjuring and magic cards, wands, boxes, scarves and the like. Groups of schoolchildren tend to visit on Wednesday, so it's better to visit at weekends.

On rue du Petit-Musc, there's an entertaining combination of 1930s' modernism and nineteenth-century exuberance in the *Hôtel Fieubert* (now a school). Diagonally opposite, at 21 bd Morland, the **Pavillon de l'Arsenal** is an excellent addition to the city's art of self-promotion, signalled by a sculpture of Rimbaud with his feet in front of his head, entitled *The Man With His Soles In Front*. The aim of the pavilion is to present the city's current **architectural projects** to the public and show how past and present developments have evolved as part and parcel of Parisian history. To this end they have a permanent exhibition of photographs, plans and models, including one of the whole city, with a spotlight to highlight a touch-screen choice of 30,000 images. The temporary exhibitions are equally impressive, and the best thing about the whole display is to see schools, industrial units and hospitals treated with the same respect as La Villette and La Grande Arche.

The **southeast corner of the 4ᵉ arrondissement**, jutting out into the Seine, has its own distinct character. It's been taken up since the last century by the Célestins barracks and previously by the Arsenal, which used to overlook a third island in the Seine. Boulevard Morland was built in 1843, covering over the arm of the river that formed the Île de Louviers. The mad poet Gérard de Nerval escaped here as a boy and lived for days in a log cabin he made with wood scavenged from the island's timberyards. In the 1830s, his more extrovert contemporaries – Victor Hugo, Liszt, Delacroix, Alexandre

Dumas and co – were using the library of the former residence of Louis XIV's artillery chief as a meeting place. While the literati discussed turning art to a revolutionary form, the locals were on the streets giving the authorities reason to build more barracks.

The Bastille

The column surmounted by the gilded "Spirit of Liberty" on **place de la Bastille** was erected to commemorate not the surrender of the **prison** with its last seven occupants in 1789, but the July Revolution of 1830, which saw the autocratic Charles X replaced with the "Citizen King" Louis-Philippe. When he in turn fled in the more significant 1848 Revolution, his throne was burnt beside the column and a new inscription added. Four months after the birth of the Second Republic in that year, the workers took to the streets. All of eastern Paris was barricaded, with the fiercest fighting on rue du Faubourg-St-Antoine. The rebellion was quelled with the usual massacres and deportation of survivors, and it is of course the 1789 Bastille Day, symbol of the end of feudalism in Europe, that France celebrates every year on July 14. The importance of place de la Bastille as a rallying point for political protestors remains even today.

The only visible remains of the Bastille prison were transported to square Henri-Galli, at the end of bd Henri-IV.

The Bicentennial of the French Revolution in 1989 was marked by the inauguration of a new opera house on place de la Bastille, the **Opéra Bastille**. François Mitterrand's pet project was the subject of the most virulent sequence of rows and resignations, and the finished building is proving inordinately expensive to run. Filling almost the entire block between rues de Lyon, Charenton and Moreau, it has shifted the focus of place de la Bastille, so that the column is no longer the pivotal point; in fact, it's easy to miss it altogether when dazzled by the night-time glare of lights emanating from the Opéra. One critic described it as a "hippopotamus in a bathtub", and you can see his point. The architect, Carlos Ott, was concerned that his design should not bring an overbearing monumentalism to place de la Bastille. The different depths and layers of the semicircular façade do give a certain sense of the building stepping back, but self-effacing it is not. Time, use and familiarity have more or less reconciled it to its surroundings, and people happily sit on its steps, wander into its shops and libraries, and camp out all night for the free performance on July 14. When a giant condom was pulled over the Spirit of Liberty column for AIDS awareness, old traditions and contemporary styles were truly wedded.

For details of performances given at the Opéra Bastille, see p.310. Its shop, FNAC Musique, is detailed on p.339.

The opera's construction destroyed no small amount of low-rent housing, but as with most speculative developments, the pace of change is uneven: old tool shops and ironmongers still survive alongside cocktail haunts and sushi bars; and laundries and cobblers flank electronic notebook outlets. You'll find art galleries clustered around

The Bastille

For moving beyond the Bastille further into the 11ᵉ and 12ᵉ arrondissements, see Chapter 10.

rue Keller and the adjoining stretch of rue de Charonne; indie music shops and gay, lesbian and hippie outfits on rues Keller and des Taillandiers; and, on rue de Lappe, one survivor of that very Parisian tradition of bals musettes, or dance halls of 1930s "*gai Paris*" – frequented between the wars by Piaf, Jean Gabin and Rita Hayworth. The most famous, *Balajo*, was founded by one Jo de France, who introduced glitter and spectacle into what were then seedy gangster dives, enticing Parisians from the other side of the city to savour the rue de Lappe lowlife. Today, the rue de Lappe is one of the liveliest night-time spots in Paris, crammed with animated, young bars. People promenade from the place de la Bastille up rue de la Roquette and into rue de Lappe, stopping in the bars here before heading onto trendier rue de Charonne which harbours another slew of drinking places.

Chapter 6

The Left Bank

T he **Left Bank** (*rive gauche*) has become synonymous with all
things Bohemian, dissident, intellectual – with the radical-stu-
dent type, whether eighteen years of age or eighty. As a topo-
graphical term, it refers particularly to their traditional haunts, the
warren of medieval lanes round the **boulevards St-Michel** and **St-
Germain**, known as the **Quartier Latin** because, until the
Revolution, that was the language of the university sited there. In
modern times the area's reputation for turbulence and innovation
has been renewed by the activities of painters and writers like
Picasso, Apollinaire, Breton, Henry Miller, Anaïs Nin and
Hemingway after World War I; Camus, Sartre, Juliette Greco and the
Existentialists after World War II; and the political turmoil of 1968,
which escalated from student demonstrations and barricades to factory occupations, massive strikes and the near-overthrow of de
Gaulle's presidency. This is not to say that the whole of Paris south
of the Seine is the exclusive territory of revolutionaries and avant-
gardists. It does, however, have a different and distinctive feel and
appearance, noticeable as soon as you cross the river. And it's here,
still, that the city's myth-makers principally gather: the writers,
painters, philosophers, politicians, journalists, designers – the people who tell Paris what it is.

Quartier Latin

The pivotal point of the **Quartier Latin** is **place St-Michel**, where the
tree-lined boulevard St-Michel begins. The *place* has long lost its
radical penniless chic, preferring harder commercial values. The
cafés and shops are jammed with people, mainly young and (in summer) largely foreign; the fountain in the *place* is a favourite meeting
spot. **Rue de la Huchette** – the mecca of beats and bums in the post-
World War II years, with its Théatre de la Huchette still showing
Ionesco's *Cantatrice Chauve* more than fifty years on – is given
over to Greek restaurants of indifferent quality and inflated prices, as

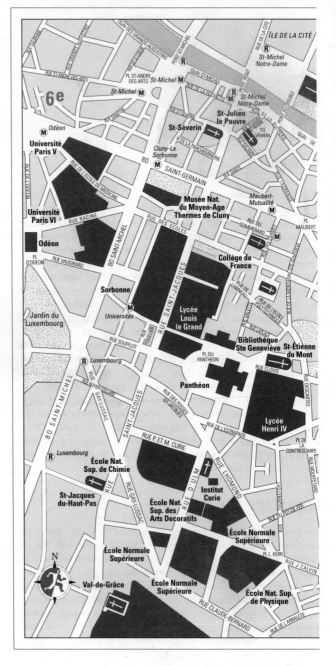

Quartier
Latin

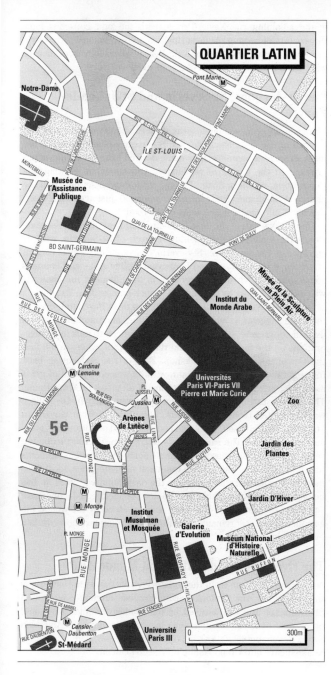

QUARTIER LATIN

Notre-Dame

Pont Marie Ⓜ

RUE REGARD EN L'ÎLE

ÎLE ST-LOUIS

RUE DES DEUX PONTS

RUE BUDÉ EN L'ÎLE

PONT MARIE

MONTEBELLO

Musée de
l'Assistance
Publique

RUE DE BIÈVRE

PONT DE L'ARCHEVÊCHÉ

RUE ST-VICTOR

PONT DE LA TOURNELLE

QUAI DE LA TOURNELLE

PONT DE SULLY

BD SAINT-GERMAIN

RUE DES FOSSÉS ST-BERNARD

RUE DE CARDINAL LEMOINE

RUE AUX FERS

RUE DE PONTOISE

RUE ST-VICTOR

RUE DES ÉCOLES

RUE MONGE

Institut du
Monde Arabe

Musée de la Sculpture
en Plein Air

QUAI SAINT-BERNARD

Cardinal Ⓜ
Lemoine

RUE DES
BOULANGERS

PL
JUSSIEU

Jussieu Ⓜ

Universités
Paris VI-Paris VII
Pierre et Marie Curie

RUE JUSSIEU

Zoo

RUE DU CARDINAL LEMOINE

5e

RUE ROLLIN

Arènes
de Lutèce

ARÈNES

RUE LINNÉ

RUE CUVIER

Jardin des
Plantes

RUE LACÉPÈDE

RUE MONGE

RUE NAVARRE

RUE LACÉPÈDE

Ⓜ

Ⓜ Monge

Ⓜ

Institut
Musulman
et Mosquée

Jardin D'Hiver

PL MONGE

RUE MONGE

Galerie
d'Evolution

RUE GEOFFROY ST-HILAIRE

Muséum National
d'Histoire
Naturelle

RUE BUFFON

RUE DE MIRBEL

RUE CENSIER

RUE DAUBENTON

Ⓜ Censier-
Daubenton

St-Médard

Université
Paris III

0   300m

*Eating and
drinking
options in the
Quartier Latin
are detailed on
pp.274–278.*

is the adjoining rue Xavier-Privas, with the odd couscous joint thrown in. Connecting rue de la Huchette to the riverside is the city's narrowest street, **rue du Chat-qui-Pêche**, alarmingly evocative of what Paris must have looked like at its medieval worst.

Rue St-Jacques, St-Séverin and St-Julien-le-Pauvre

Things improve as you move away from the boulevard St-Michel. At the end of rue de la Huchette, **rue St-Jacques** is aligned along the main street of Roman Paris, its name derived from the medieval pilgrimage to the shrine of St Jacques (St James) in Santiago de Compostela, northern Spain. For the millions who set out from the church of St-Jacques (only the tower remains), just across the river, this bit of hill was their first taste of the road.

One block south of rue de la Huchette, and west of rue St Jacques, stands the mainly fifteenth-century **church of St-Séverin**, with its entrance on rue des Prêtres St-Séverin. One of the city's most elegant churches, it was built in the Flamboyant Gothic style, and contains some splendidly virtuoso chiselwork in the pillars of the choir, as well as stained glass by the modern French painter Jean Bazaine.

One block to the south of the church, **rue de la Parcheminerie**, as the name suggests, is where medieval scribes and parchment sellers used to congregate. It's worth cricking your neck to look at the decorations on the façades, including that of no. 29, where you'll find the Canadian-run Abbey Bookshop. East of rue St-Jacques, back towards the river, **square Viviani**, with its welcome patch of grass and trees, provides the most flattering of all views of Notre-Dame. The ancient, listing tree propped on a concrete pillar by the church wall is reputed to be Paris' oldest, brought over from Guyana in 1680. The church itself, mutilated and disfigured on the ouside, is **St-Julien-le-Pauvre**. The same age as Notre-Dame, it used to be the venue for university assemblies until some rumbustious students tore it apart in the 1500s. It's a quiet and intimate place, ideal for a moment's soulful reflection. For the last hundred years it has belonged to a Greek Catholic sect, hence the unexpected iconostasis screening the sanctuary. The hefty slabs of stone by the well at the entrance are all that remain of the Roman thoroughfare now overlain by rue St-Jacques.

The river bank and Institut du Monde Arabe

Across rue Lagrange from the square Viviani, rue de la Bûcherie is the home of the American-run English-language bookshop **Shakespeare and Co**, haunted by the shades of James Joyce and other great expatriate literati. Only by proxy though – the American Sylvia Beach, publisher in 1922 of Joyce's *Ulysses*, had her original **Shakespeare and Co** bookshop on rue de l'Odéon.

St-Séverin is open to visitors Mon–Fri 11am–7.30pm, Sat 11am–8pm, Sun 9am–9pm; Mᵒ St-Michel & Mᵒ Cluny-La-Sorbonne.

St-Julien-le-Pauvre is open for visitors daily 10am–7.30pm; Mᵒ St-Michel & Mᵒ Maubert-Mutualité.

The Abbey Bookshop, Shakespeare & Co. and other English-language bookshops are detailed on pp.325–326.

More books, postcards, prints, sheet music, records and assorted goods are on sale from the **bouquinistes**, who display their wares in green, padlocked boxes hooked onto the parapet of the **riverside quais** – which, in spite of their romantic reputation, are not much fun to walk along because of the ceaseless traffic.

Continuing upstream to quai de la Tournelle, you can stop en-route at the Hôtel de Miramion (at no. 47) where the **Musée de l'Assistance Publique-Hopitaux de Paris** (Wed–Sat 10am–5pm; closed Aug; 20F) recounts the history of Paris' hospitals through paintings, sculptures, pharmaceutical containers, surgical instruments – though it's for cast-iron stomachs only. Better to press on as far as the tip of the Île St-Louis and the **Pont de Sully**, from which there's a dramatic view of the apse and steeple of Notre-Dame, and the beginning of a riverside garden dotted with pieces of modern sculpture, known as the **Musée de Sculpture en Plein Air**.

At the end of the Pont de Sully, in the angle between quai St-Bernard and rue des Fossés-St-Bernard, shaming the hideous factory-like building of the Paris-VI university next door, stands the **Institut du Monde Arabe**. Another of Mitterand's *Grands Projets*, it opened in 1987 as a cultural centre whose aim is to further French understanding of the Arab world. Designed principally by Jean Nouvel, the architect later responsible for the equally ambitious Fondation Cartier building (see p.152), its elegant glass and aluminium mass is cleft in two, the riverfront half bowed and tapering to a knife-like prow, while the broad southern façade, comprising thousands of tiny light-sensitive shutters, employs hi-tech ingenuity to mimic the *moucharabiyah* – the traditional Arab latticework balcony. Spread over seven spacious floors, the museum of the Institute has something of the atmosphere of a mosque – a rarefied place where you can talk and walk or think and study, at ease in the gracefulness of the building. There's abundant information, in the form of interactive videos and information sheets (in both French and English) which you can take with you, and a choice of impressive exhibits.

Weights and measures, celestial globes, astrolabes, compasses and sundials, along with the grinding and mixing implements for medicines, illustrate Arab scientific research between 750 and 1258 AD. There are coins from an even earlier era, and illuminated manuscripts. Among the half-dozen or so exquisite silk carpets, one, of sixteenth-century Persian origin, has arabesques of flowers and birds with a swirling movement far removed from the static geometries usually associated with oriental carpet design. Ceramics and the tools of calligraphy and cookery are also represented.

On the ground floor are **contemporary paintings and sculpture from the Arab world**. Many of these have an emotional charge lacking in most Western contemporary art. Perhaps it's the political context that makes, for example, the brilliant bands of colour denoting sea,

The Musée de Sculpture en Plein Air is open Tues–Sun 10am–5pm; free; M° Jussieu & M° Gare de l'Austerlitz.

The Institut du Monde Arabe is open Tues–Sun 10am–6pm; museum entry 25F, special exhibitions extra; M° Jussieu & M° Cardinal-Lemoine.

sand and city in Saliba Douaihy's *Beirut-Mediterranean*, painted during the Civil War in Beirut, such a powerful statement. Sami Mohamed Al-Saleh's bronze sculpture *Sabra and Chatila* would represent profound agony in any context. Not all the paintings, by any means, address political issues. They represent a wonderful diversity of the main artistic movements currently being explored in the Arab world.

Also housed within the institute is a space for temporary exhibitions, a library, facilities for research, debate and publishing, and an audiovisual centre. This last, the Espace Image et Son (Tues–Sat 10am–6pm; free), is located in the basement and stores thousands of slides, photographs, films and recordings, which you can access yourself. There is also a specialist library (Tues–Sat 1–8pm; free). Film previews are shown, and in the Salle d'Actualités you can watch current news broadcasts from around the Arab world. When you need a rest, take lifts up to the ninth floor for expensive Lebanese eats, and enjoy a brilliant view over the Seine that stretches from La Grande Arche to Buttes-Chaumont. In summer drink mint tea and nibble on cakes at the outdoor café downstairs, marvelling at the aperture action of the windows; the downstairs café, the lifts and terrace restaurant, the library and the media centre can be visited without paying for the museum.

The Musée Nationale du Moyen-Age (Thermes-de-Cluny)

The Pontoise-Quartier Latin pool is detailed on p.351.

Walking back west along boulevard St-Germain towards bd St-Michel, past rue de Pontoise with its Art-Deco swimming pool and primary school, you come to **place Maubert** (good market Tues, Thurs and Sat am), at the foot of the **Montagne Ste-Geneviève**, the hill on which the Panthéon stands and the best strolling area this side of boulevard St-Michel. The best way in is either from the *place* or from the crossroads of boulevards St-Michel and St-Germain, where the walls of the third-century **Roman baths** are visible in the garden of the **Hôtel de Cluny**. A sixteenth-century mansion resembling an Oxford or Cambridge college, the *hôtel* was built on top of the ruined baths by the abbots of the powerful Cluny monastery, as their Parisian pied-à-terre. It now houses the very beautiful **Musée Nationale du Moyen-Age**, entered at no. 6 place Paul-Painlevé, off rue des Écoles. There is no charge for entry to the quiet shady courtyard or to the grounds running along boulevard St-Germain, the latter of which harbour lawns and flowers, benches and a children's playground.

The Musée Nationale du Moyen-Age is open 9.15am–5.45pm; closed Tues; 30F, 20F on Sun, guided tours 35F; Mº Cluny-La-Sorbonne & Mº St-Michel.

The two-level museum is a treasure house of medieval art and tapestries, its masterpiece being the wonderful tapestry series of *The Lady with the Unicorn*. The building provides a perfect setting for the art – from the huge carved-stone medieval fireplaces and its perfect little vaulted chapel hung with tapestries, to the cool, intricately bricked Gallo-Roman baths filled with sculptural fragments. A pamphlet in English provides a plan of the museum, and while you're wandering around look out for the laminated information sheets in English provided in some rooms – these are few and far between and you usually have to wait a while to get your hands on them.

The tapestries

The **tapestry rooms** – tapestries, fabrics and embroidery are located mainly in rooms 2–4 and 12–14 – are purposefully kept fairly dim to halt the fading of the pieces, though the subtle high-tech lighting system enhances the colours and textures. The numerous beauties include a marvellous depiction of the grape harvest in room 2. In room 3, there's a Resurrection scene embroidered in gold and silver thread, with sleeping guards in medieval armour, and a fourteenth-century embroidery of two leopards in red and gold. Some Coptic textile fragments, woven around the fourth to the sixth centuries, are a revelation, such bright colours having managed to survive so long. Scenes of manorial life are hung in room 4: these sixteenth-century Dutch tapestries are full of flowers and birds, and include scenes of a woman spinning while her servant patiently holds the threads for her, a lover making advances, a woman in her bath which is overflowing into a duck pond, a hunting party leaving for the chase.

But the greatest wonder of all is the late fifteenth-century **Lady with the Unicorn**, displayed in a special round room (**room 13**) on the first floor. It's quite simply the most stunning piece of tapestry you are ever likely to see. Six richly coloured and detailed allegoric scenes, five relating to each of the senses, each show a beautiful though rather sorrowful-looking young woman flanked by a lion and a unicorn. Dating from the late fifteenth century, the series was perhaps made in Brussels for the Le Viste family, merchants from Lyon. Their family coat of arms – three crescents on a diagonal blue stripe – is shown on the flags floating in various scenes. Almost Oriental in the level of decorativeness, the ground of each panel is a delicate red worked with a myriad of tiny flowers, birds and animals. In the centre, on a green island, equally flowery and framed by stylized trees and the lion and the unicorn, the young woman plays a portable organ (hearing); takes a sweet from a proffered box (taste); makes a necklace of carnations, while a pet monkey, perched on the rim of a basket of flowers, holds one to his nose (smell); holds a mirror up to the unicorn who whimsically admires his reflection with his front hooves perched uncomfortably on her lap (sight); and strokes the unicorn's horn with one hand (touch). The final panel, entitled *A Mon Seul Désir* ("To My Only Desire") remains ambiguous, a scene of the woman putting away her necklace into a jewellery box held out by her servant. Two popular interpretations are that it represents the rejection of sensual pleasure or the doctrine of free choice – but that's for you to ponder.

The vaulted chapel (**room 20**) provides a perfect setting for another wall hanging, while more textile art can be found in rooms 12, 14, 18, 19 and 21.

Regular concerts of medieval music are held in the Roman Baths. Concert tickets (around 60F) also provide after-hours access to the museum. Information on ☎01.53.73. 78.00.

Ste-Chapelle, on the Île de la Cité, is detailed on p.66.

Other highlights

A vast array of medieval sculptures include fascinating fragments such as the twenty-one heads of the thirteenth-century **Kings of Judea** (room 8) from the cathedral of Notre-Dame, lopped off during the French Revolution in the rather too general anti-royal frenzy, and only discovered in a 1977 excavation near the Opéra Garnier. The great crowned heads of these Old Testament kings, with blurred, eroded faces, their noses rudely detached, are displayed in rows, next to a stage of headless robed figures. Nearby, the **Gallo-Roman baths** consist of three chambers, the frigidarium (cold bath room), caldarium (hot bath room) and tepidarium (tepid bath room), and contain Romanesque sculpture and architectural remnants from various French churches.

Other remnants from churches provide a fascinating opportunity to view things in fine detail that would normally be part of the big picture. **Room 5** holds wood and alabaster altarpiece carvings produced in England by the **Nottingham workshops**, which found homes in churches all over Europe. **Room 6** is full of stained-glass panels from Ste-Chapelle, removed here during the chapel's mid-nineteenth-century renovation. Some particularly grisly scenes in glass include one of a man getting his eye gouged out.

In **room 18** are fifteenth-century church stalls, and pages from **Books of Hours** complete with zodiac signs – these are behind glass but you can mechanically turn the pages. The most precious item among a fine collection of jewellery and **metalwork** is the delicate, long-stemmed **Golden Rose of Basel**, dating from 1330, in **room 16**.

The Sorbonne, the Panthéon and St-Étienne-du-Mont

The Musée de la Préfecture de Police is open Mon–Fri 9am–5pm, Sat 10am–5pm; closed Sun & hols; free; Mᵒ Maubert-Mutualité.

Four blocks east of the Musée Nationale du Moyen-Age, just north of rue des Écoles, is the **Musée de la Préfecture de Police**, at 1bis rue des Carmes. The history of the Paris police force, as presented in this collection of uniforms, arms and papers, stops at 1944 and is, as you might expect, all of the "legendary criminals" variety. The grim-looking buildings to the south of rue des Écoles are the **Sorbonne**, the **Collège de France** – where Michel Foucault taught – and the **Lycée Louis-le-Grand**, which numbers Molière, Robespierre, Pompidou and Victor Hugo among its graduates, and Sartre among its teachers. All these institutions are major constituents of the brilliant and mandarin world of French intellectual activity. You can have a look around the Sorbonne courtyard without anyone objecting. The **Richelieu chapel**, dominating the uphill end and containing the tomb of the great cardinal, was the first Roman-influenced building in seventeenth-century Paris and set the trend for subsequent developments. Nearby, the traffic-free **place de la Sorbonne**, with its lime trees, cafés and student habitués, is a lovely place to sit.

Further up the hill, the broad rue Soufflot provides an appropriately grand perspective on the domed and porticoed **Panthéon**. Louis XV's thank-you to Sainte Geneviève, patron saint of Paris, for curing him of illness, it was transformed by the Revolution into a mausoleum for the great, with the ashes of Voltaire, Rousseau, Hugo and Zola in the vast barrel-vaulted crypt below. The interior is worth a visit for sheer understanding of the French "grand design" – and, if you've ever read Umberto Eco, to see a working model of **Foucault's Pendulum** swinging from the dome (the original is owned by the Musée des Arts et Métiers; see p.113). The French physicist Léon Foucault devised the experiment, conducted at the Panthéon in 1851, to vividly demonstate the rotation of the earth: while the pendulum appeared to rotate over a 24-hour period, it was in fact the earth beneath it turning. The demonstration wowed the scientific establishment and the public alike, with huge crowds turning up to watch the ground move beneath their feet. A video with headphones in English tells the whole story.

Opposite, at 10 place du Panthéon, pop your head into the entry hall of the **Bibliothèque Ste-Geneviève** (for details about which, see p.348) and peek at its muralled ceiling. The wrought-iron decorated nineteenth-century reading room – which you have to apply to use – is even more impressive. Immediately east of the Panthéon, on the corner of rue Clovis, is the mainly sixteenth-century church of **St-Étienne-du-Mont**, whose beautifully carved façade combines Gothic, Renaissance and Baroque elements. The interior, if not exactly beautiful, is highly unexpected, its space divided into three aisles by free-standing pillars connected by a narrow catwalk, and flooded with light by an exceptionally tall clerestory. Again, unusually – for they mainly fell victim to the destructive anti-clericalism of the Revolution – the church still possesses its rood screen, a broad low arch supporting a gallery reached by twining spiral stairs. There is also some good seventeenth-century glass in the cloister. Further down rue Clovis, a huge piece of Philippe-Auguste's **twelfth-century city walls** emerges from among the houses.

South of place du Panthéon, between rues Gay-Lussac and Lhomond, are further academic institutions: the École Normale Supérieure, a *grande école* that trains teachers and theorists and bred structuralism in the 1970s; the Curie and oceanographic institutes; and the *grandes écoles* for chemistry, physics and decorative arts. Entry to the *grandes écoles* is by exam following two years of preparation after the equivalent of A-levels or a high-school diploma, the *baccalauréat*. Started by Napoléon to provide professionally trained engineers and technicians, they represent the élite of French educational establishments.

There's not much point in going further south on rue St-Jacques. The area is dull and lifeless once you're over the Gay-Lussac intersection, though Baroque enthusiasts might like to take a look at the

Quartier Latin

The Panthéon is open April–Sept 9.30am–6.30pm, Oct–March 10am–5.30pm; closed hols; 32F; RER Luxembourg & Mº Cardinal-Lemoine.

Head towards the Luxembourg gardens from the Panthéon to find several cafés, including the beer specialist La Gueuze (see p.275).

St-Étienne-du-Mont is open to visitors daily 8am–noon & 2–7.30pm; RER Luxembourg & Mº Cardinal-Lemoine.

Quartier
Latin

*Val-de-Grâce is
open for visi-
tors daily
9am–5pm;
RER Port-
Royal.*

seventeenth-century church of **Val-de-Grâce** on place Alphonse-Laveran, with its pedimented front and ornate cupola copied from St Peter's in Rome. Round the corner, on boulevard de Port-Royal, there are several brasseries and another big **market** (for more on which see p.344).

East of the Panthéon: Mouffetard and Contrescarpe

More enticing wandering is to be had in the villagey streets east of the Panthéon. **Rue de la Montagne-Ste-Geneviève** climbs up from place Maubert across rue des Écoles to the gates of what used to be the **École Polytechnique**, the grandest of the *grandes écoles* (see overleaf) for entry to the top echelons of state power. The school has decamped to the suburbs, leaving its buildings to become the Ministry of Research and Technology – a trip down memory lane for many of its staff, no doubt. There's a sunny little café outside the gate and several restaurants in rue de l'École-Polytechnique, facing the Ministry.

From here, **rue Descartes** runs south into the tiny **place de la Contrescarpe**. An erstwhile arty hang-out, where Hemingway wrote – in the café *La Chope* – and Georges Brassens sang, it's now a tourist hotspot. Just to the east, on rue Lacépède, is a municipal crèche, built in 1985, whose lovely curved frontage was inspired by the shape of a pregnant woman's belly.

The medieval **rue Mouffetard** begins just off place de la Contrescarpe. A cobbled lane, it winds downhill to the church of **St-Médard**, which was once a country parish beside the now-covered River Bièvre. On the façade of no. 12 is a curious painted-glass sign from a less PC era, depicting a Negro in striped trousers waiting on his mistress, with the unconvincing legend, "*Au Nègre Joyeux*". At no. 64, a shoe shop run by Georges the Armenian sells genuine espadrilles from the southwest of France, and the last of the French wooden clogs (or *sabots*). But most of the upper half of the street is given over to eating places, mainly Greek – there's not much local colour, but they're not bad value. Like any place devoted to the entertainment of tourists, it has become a bit tacky, though the bottom half, with its sumptuous fruit and veg stalls – among lots of clothes and shoe shops and cafés – still maintains an authentic local ambience. On place des Patriarches, one block east, an old market hall has been replaced by a beautiful 1980s construction, containing low-cost flats and a gym, harking back to the style of its predecessor while being unashamedly modern.

The Paris mosque and Jardin des Plantes

A little further east of rue Mouffetard, across rue Monge, are some of the city's most agreeable surprises. Down rue Daubenton, past a delightful Arab shop selling sweets, spices and gaudy tea-glasses, you come to the crenellated walls of the **Paris mosque**, topped by greenery and a great square minaret. You can visit the sunken garden and patios with their polychrome tiles and carved ceilings on a guided tour, but not the prayer room (unless you're worshipping, of course). There's also a **hammam**, open to all (though with different days for the two sexes; see pp.351–352 for details), a **tearoom** and restaurant (see p.274), and a shop selling clothes, birdcages and souvenirs.

Opposite the mosque, the **Jardin des Plantes** was founded as a medicinal herb garden in 1626. It gradually evolved as Paris' botanical gardens, with hothouses, shady avenues of trees, lawns to sprawl on, a brace of museums and a zoo. There's an entrance at the corner of rues Geoffroy-St-Hilaire and Buffon, alongside the museum shop selling wonderful books and postcards; other entrances are further north on the corner with rue Cuvier, the main gate on rue Cuvier itself, and on quai St-Bernard.

Magnificent, varied floral beds make a fine approach to the collection of buildings that forms the **Muséum National d'Histoire Naturelle**. The four musty old museums of paleontology, mineralogy, entomology and paleobotany (all open Mon & Wed–Sun 10am–5pm; 15–30F) were upstaged by the opening of the **Grande Galerie de l'Évolution** in 1994, in a dramatic transformation of the old nineteenth-century Galerie de Zoologie, overlooking rue Geoffroy-St-Hilaire (with its entrance off rue Buffon). Behind the scrubbed stone façade, you'll be wowed by the sheer scale of the magnificent interior, supported by iron columns and roofed with glass. It has been adapted to tell the story of evolution and the relations between human beings and nature, with a cast of stuffed animals (rescued from the dusty old zoology museum and restored to such spruceness that they look alive) near enough to touch, a combination of clever lighting effects, ambient music and birdsong, videos and touch-screen databases. If you really want to do something as old-fashioned as reading, there are wooden lecture boards in English, which you can pull out to accompany the aurals and visuals. On the lower level, submarine light suffuses the space where the murkiest deep ocean creatures are displayed. Above, glass lifts rise silently from the savannah – where a closely packed line of huge African animals, headed by an elephant, look as if they are stepping onto Noah's ark. It's all great fun for children, and there's even a small interactive centre for kids on the first floor (see "Kids' Paris", p.364).

In a contrastingly small space, real animals can be seen in the small **Ménagerie** across the park to the northeast near rue Cuvier. This is France's oldest zoo, operating here since the Revolution. Despite its scale, the Ménagerie is home to a surprising assortment of creatures, from big cats to snakes, possible because of their unacceptably cramped conditions.

Tours of the mosque are offered 9am–noon & 2–6pm; 15F; no tours Fri & Muslim hols; M° Censier-Daubenton.

The Grande Galerie de l'Évolution is open 10am–6pm, Thurs till 10pm; closed Tues & 1 May; 40F.

The Ménagerie is open summer Mon–Sat 9am–6pm, Sun till 6.30pm; winter Mon–Sat 9am–5pm, Sun till 6.30pm; 30F.

Quartier Latin

The Jardin des Plantes is open daily: summer 7.30am–7.45pm; winter 8am–dusk; M° Austerlitz & M° Jussieu & M° Monge.

The **gardens** are a pleasant space to while away the middle of a day. Near the rue Cuvier entrance stands a fine Cedar of Lebanon, planted in 1734 and raised from seed sent over from the Botanical Gardens in Oxford, plus a slice of an American sequoia more than 2000 years old, with the birth of Christ and other historical events marked on its rings. In the nearby physics labs, Henri Becquerel discovered radioactivity in 1896, and two years later the Curies discovered radium (Pierre ended his days under the wheels of a brewer's dray on rue Dauphine).

A short distance away to the northwest, with entrances on rue de Navarre, rue des Arènes and through a passage on rue Monge, is Paris' other Roman remain, the **Arènes de Lutèce**, an unexpected and peaceful backwater hidden from the street. This partly restored amphitheatre has a boules pitch in the centre, benches, gardens and a kids' playground behind.

St-Germain

The northern half of the 6e arrondissement, asymmetrically centred on **place St-Germain-des-Près**, is the most picturesque, animated and stimulating square kilometre in the entire city. It's got the money, elegance and sophistication, but also an easy-going tolerance and simplicity that comes from a long association with mould-breakers and trend-setters in the arts, philosophy, politics and sciences. However, increasingly, the fashion business is taking over from the literary world, with many names more associated with the Right Bank opening up shop here, pushing out booksellers and the like who cannot afford the spiralling rents.

Across Pont des Arts

The most dramatic approach to St-Germain is to cross the river from the Louvre by the **Pont des Arts** footbridge, taking in the classic upstream view of the Île de la Cité, with barges moored at the quai de Conti, and the Tour St-Jacques and Hôtel de Ville breaking the skyline of the Right Bank.

The Musée de la Monnaie is open Tues–Fri 11am–5.30pm, Sat & Sun noon–5.30pm; 20F, free on Sun; M° Pont-Neuf, M° St-Michel & M° Odéon.

The dome and pediment at the end of the bridge belong to the **Institut de France**, seat of the Académie Française, an august body of writers and scholars whose mission is to safeguard the purity of the French language. Recent creations include the excellent word *baladeur* for "Walkman", but rearguard actions against Anglo-Saxon terms in the sciences, information technology and management have been hopelessly ineffective.

This is the grandiose bit of the Left Bank riverfront. Next door to the Institut, at 11 quai de Conti, is the **Hôtel des Monnaies**, redesigned as the Mint in the late eighteenth century. It now houses the **Musée de la Monnaie**, which has an interesting free display in the foyer on the **Euro**, the new European Monetary Union currency that will replace the franc sometime in the year 2002. From early 1999, businesses will begin to show prices in Euros as well as Francs, part of a plan to familiarize the public with the idea and worth of the new money well in advance. To the west of the Institut lies the **École des Beaux-Arts**, the School of Fine Art, whose students throng the quais on sunny days, sketch pads on knee; it's sometimes open for exhibitons of students' work.

The riverside

The riverside part of the quartier is cut lengthways by **rue St-André-des-Arts** and **rue Jacob**, and is full of bookshops, commercial art galleries, antique shops, cafés and restaurants. Poke your nose into courtyards and side streets. The houses are four- to six-storeys high, seventeenth- and eighteenth-century, some noble, some stiff, some bulging and askew, all painted in infinite gradations of grey, pearl and off-white. Broadly speaking, the further west, the posher they get.

Historical associations are legion. Picasso painted *Guernica* in rue des Grands-Augustins. Molière started his career in rue Mazarine. Robespierre et al. split ideological hairs at the *Le Procope* in rue de l'Ancienne-Comédie. In rue Visconti, Racine died, Delacroix painted, and Balzac's printing business went bust. In the parallel rue des Beaux-Arts, Oscar Wilde died, Corot and Ampère – father of amps – lived, and crazy poet Gérard de Nerval walked a lobster on a lead.

If you're looking for lunch, **place** and **rue St-André-des-Arts** both offer numerous places to snack, but this is still very much tourist territory, and you would do better to look further afield. There is, for instance, a brilliant **food market** in rue de Buci, up towards boulevard St-Germain (see p.344). Before you get to it, there's a little *passage* on the left, **Cour du Commerce St André**, between a crêperie and *Le Mazet* café. Marat had his printing press here, and Dr Guillotin perfected his machine by lopping off sheep's heads in a loft next door. Since *Le Procope* – Paris' first coffeehouse, opening its doors in 1686 – was done up for the Bicentennial in 1989, with portraits of famous frequenters, Voltaire and Robespierre, outside, a revolutionary theme has enveloped the *passage*. A couple of smaller courtyards open off it, revealing a stretch of Philippe-Auguste's twelfth-century wall.

An alternative corner for midday food or quiet is around rue de l'Abbaye and rue de Furstemberg, where Delacroix's old studio, at no. 6 rue de Furstemberg, overlooks a secret garden and has been converted into the **Musée Delacroix**. The artist lived and worked here from 1857 until his death in 1863. Some attractive watercolours, illustrations from *Hamlet*, and a couple of versions of a lion hunt hang in the painter's old apartment and the studio, with its

Le Mazet *and* Le Procope *are detailed on pp.278 & 281 with other local eating and drinking options.*

The Musée Delacroix is open 9.30am–6pm, closed Tues; 30F; Mº St-Germain-des-Prés.

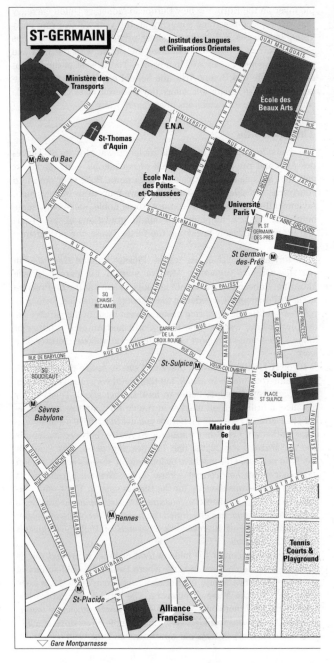

ST-GERMAIN

Institut des Langues
et Civilisations Orientales

QUAI MALAQUAIS

Ministère des
Transports

RUE

DE

École des
Beaux Arts

RUE

L'UNIVERSITÉ

E.N.A.

RUE JACOB

BONAPARTE

RUE

St-Thomas
d'Aquin

RUE DES SAINTS PÈRES

RUE

M Rue du Bac

R DE LILLE

RUE JACOB

RUE JACOB

ST-BENOIT

École Nat.
des Ponts-
et-Chaussées

Université
Paris V

R DE L'ABBE-GREGOIRE

BD SAINT-GERMAIN

PL ST
GERMAIN-
DES-PRÉS

BD RASPAIL

RUE DE GRENELLE

St Germain-
des-Prés M

RUE DES SAINTS-PÈRES

RUE DU DRAGON

RUE B PALISSY

FOUR

RUE PRINCESSE

SQ
CHAISE-
RECAMIER

RUE DE RENNES

DU

RUE DES CANETTES

CARREF
DE LA
CROIX ROUGE

RUE

RUE MADAME

RUE DE BABYLONE

RUE DE SÈVRES

RUE DU

St-Sulpice M

VIEUX-COLOMBIER

St-Sulpice

SQ
BOUCICAUT

RUE DU CHERCHE-MIDI

RUE BONAPARTE

PLACE
ST SULPICE

M Sèvres
Babylone

RUE SERVANDONI

RUE FÉROU

Mairie du
6e

RUE

R DUPIN

RUE DU CHERCHE-MIDI

RENNES

RUE D'ASSAS

RUE DE VAUGIRARD

RUE SAINT-PLACIDE

RUE DU REGARD

BD

M Rennes

RUE DE VAUGIRARD

RUE GUYNEMER

RUE MADAME

Tennis
Courts &
Playground

RUE DE VAUGIRARD

RASPAIL

M
St-Placide

RUE D'ASSAS

Alliance
Française

▽ Gare Montparnasse

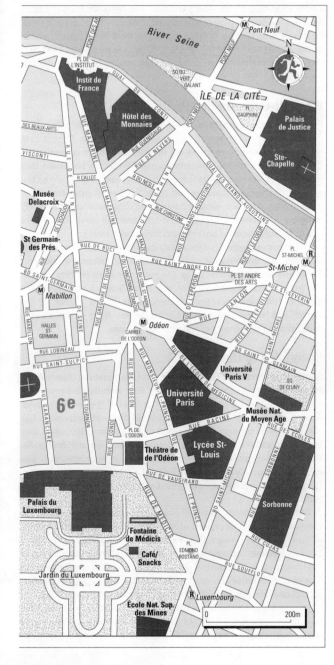

See pp.278–281 for eating and drinking options in St-Germain.

attractive garden on the courtyard side. The renovated and enlarged museum holds changing temporary exhibitions of Delacroix's work (consult *Pariscope* for details); his major work is exhibited permanently at the Louvre and the Musée d'Orsay (see pp.84 and 145), and you can see the murals he painted at the nearby St-Sulpice church (see below).

Place St-Germain-des-Près

Deux Magots, Le Flore *and* Brasserie Lipp are *detailed on pp.278 & 280.*

Place St-Germain-des-Prés, the hub of the quartier, is only a two-minute walk from the Musée Delacroix, with the *Deux Magots* café on the corner, and *Flore* just down the street. Both are renowned for the number of philosophico-politico-poetico-literary backsides that have shined their seats, as is the snootier *Brasserie Lipp*, across the boulevard, longtime haunt of the more successful practitioners of these trades. All these establishments are expensive and extremely crowded in summer. A place on the *terrasse* will inevitably involve you in the attentions of buskers and street performers.

The tower opposite *Les Deux Magots* belongs to the **church of St-Germain**, all that remains of an enormous Benedictine monastery. There has been a church on the site since the sixth century. Inside, the pure Romanesque lines are still clear beneath the deforming paint of nineteenth-century frescoes, while in the corner of the churchyard by rue Bonaparte, a little Picasso head of a woman is dedicated to the memory of the poet Apollinaire.

St-Sulpice to the Odéon

Aux Charpentiers *is detailed on p.280, along with other local eating and drinking options.*

South of boulevard St-Germain, the streets around the church of St-Sulpice (see below) are calm and classy. **Rue Mabillon** is pretty, with a row of old houses set back below the level of the modern street. Among its two or three restaurants is the old-fashioned *Aux Charpentiers*, property of the Guild of Carpenters, decorated with models of rafters and roof-trees. On the left are the **halles St-Germain**, incorporating a swimming pool, gym, auditorium and commercial complex, built on the site of a fifteenth-century market. Rue Lobineau, which runs along its south side, has a tempting pâtisserie at no. 2.

Rue Mabillon abuts on rue St-Sulpice, which leads through to the

The church of St-Sulpice is open daily 7.30am– 7.30pm; Mº St-Sulpice.

front of the enormous **church of St-Sulpice**. Erected around the turn of the eighteenth century, this is an austerely classical edifice, with a Doric colonnade surmounted by an Ionic, and Corinthian pilasters in the towers – the only finished one serves as a nesting site for kestrels. The gloomy interior, containing three Delacroix murals in the first chapel on the right, including one of St-Michael slaying a dragon, is not to everyone's taste. But, softened by the chestnut trees and fountain of the square, the ensemble is peaceful and harmonious. To the south, rue Férou – where a gentleman called Pottier composed the revolutionary anthem, the *Internationale*, in 1776 – connects with rue de Vaugirard, Paris' longest street, and the **Luxembourg gardens** (see below).

On the sunny north side of the **place St-Sulpice** is the popular *Café de la Marie*, but the main attraction here are the fashion boutiques, like Agnés B and Christian Lacroix, and the very elegant **Yves Saint Laurent Rive Gauche** on the corner of the ancient **rue des Canettes**. Further along the same side of the *place*, there's Saint Laurent for men, and then it's consume, consume all the way, with your triple-gilt uranium-plated credit card, down rues Bonaparte, Madame, de Sèvres, de Grenelle, du Four, des Saints-Pères . . .

Hard to believe now, but smack in the middle of all this, at the carrefour de la Croix Rouge, there was a major barricade in 1871, fiercely defended by Eugène Varlin, one of the **Commune**'s leading lights. He was later betrayed by a priest, half-beaten to death and shot by government troops on Montmartre hill. These days you're more likely to be suffering from till-shock than shell-shock. You may feel safer in rue Princesse at the small, friendly and well-stocked American bookshop, The Village Voice, where you can browse through the latest literature and journals. Or you could retreat to the less stylish eastern edge of the quartier, around boulevard St-Michel, where the university is firmly implanted, its attendant bookshops displaying scientific and medical tomes, as well as skeletons and instruments of torture. But there is really no escape from elegance in these parts, as you'll see in rue de Tournon and rue de l'Odéon, both leading up towards the Luxembourg gardens, the latter taking in the Doric portico of the **Théâtre de l'Odéon** en route.

For more on the Commune, see pp.176 & 419 .

The Luxembourg palace and around

It was Marie de Médicis, Henri IV's widow, who had the **Jardin** and **Palais du Luxembourg** built to remind her of the Palazzo Pitti and Giardino di Boboli of her native Florence. The palace forms yet another familiar Parisian backdrop, behind which the members of the French senate have their seat. Opposite the gates, scarcely noticeable on the end wall of the colonnade of no. 36 rue de Vaugirard, is a metre rule, set up during the Revolution to guide the people in the introduction of the new metric system.

The **gardens** are the chief lung and recreation ground of the Left Bank, with tennis courts, pony rides, a children's playground, boules pitch, yachts to rent on the pond and, in the wilder southeast corner, a miniature orchard of elaborately espaliered pear trees. With its strollers and garish parterres, it has a distinctly Mediterranean air on summer days, when the most contested spot, particularly for lovers, is the shady, seventeenth-century **Fontaine de Médicis**, in the northeast corner. There are many other sculptural works in the park, including an 1890 monument to the painter Delacroix by Jules Dalou.

The nearest stations to the Luxembourg Gardens are Mº Odéon & RER Luxembourg.

St-Germain

Annually in the last week of September, an "Expo-Automne" takes place in the **Orangerie** (entrance from 19 rue de Vaugirard, opposite rue Férou) where fruits – including the Luxembourg's own wonderful pears – and floral decorations are sold.

Just west of the Jardins du Luxembourg is another of Paris' obscure museums, the **Musée Branly** (Mon–Fri 9am–noon & 2–5pm; closed July & Aug; by appointment only; ☎01.49.54.52.00), at 21 rue d'Assas. In the 1890s Marconi used Branly's invention of an electric wave detector – the first coherer – to set up a startling system of communication that didn't need wires. The coherer in question is exhibited along with other pieces from the physicist's experiments.

Chapter 7

Trocadéro, Eiffel Tower and Les Invalides

F rom the terrace of the **Palais de Chaillot** on place du Trocadéro, as you look out across the river to the **Tour Eiffel** and **École Militaire**, or let your gaze run from the ornate 1900 Pont Alexandre III along the grassy Esplanade to the **Hôtel des Invalides**, the vistas are absolutely splendid. This is town planning on a grand scale, taking little account of the small-scale interests and details of everyday lives.

The **7ᵉ arrondissement**, to which the Left Bank sections of these nineteenth- and twentieth-century urban landscapings belong, has the greatest concentration of ministries, embassies and official residences in Paris. The **Assemblée Nationale** is here, in the Palais Bourbon facing place de la Concorde across the river. But corners of more amenable life do exist – in **rue Babylone**, and in the streets between the Invalides and the Champs de Mars. There's also the world's best-used decommissioned railway station, the unmissable **Musée d'Orsay**, bridging the gap between the Louvre and Beaubourg collections, on the river bank towards St-Germain.

For restaurants, cafés and bars in the area, see pp.281–282.

Of all the mega-monuments of this area, the best is, undoubtedly, the Eiffel Tower. No matter how many pictures, photos, models or glimpses from elsewhere in the city you may have seen, it is still, when you get up close, an amazing structure.

The Palais de Chaillot

The **Palais de Chaillot** was built in 1937 for the Exposition Universelle on a site that has been a ruler's favourite since Catherine de Médicis constructed one of her playpens there in the early sixteenth century. Today's monster is home to the enormous Théâtre National de Chaillot, which stages diverse but usually radical productions in the northern wing, and to a brace of interesting museums in the southern wing. Damage from a fire in 1996 closed the **Musée**

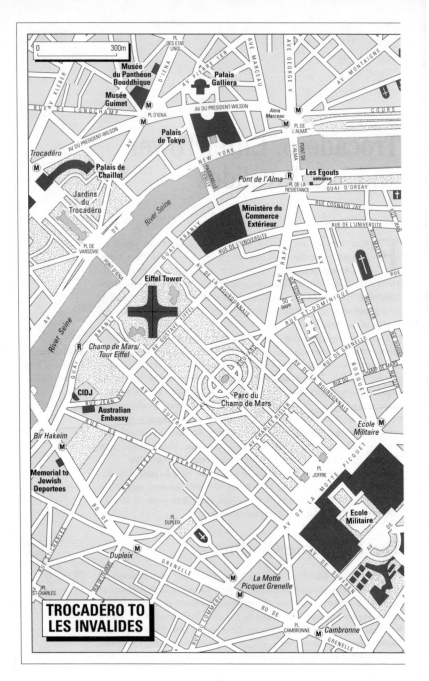

TROCADÉRO TO
LES INVALIDES

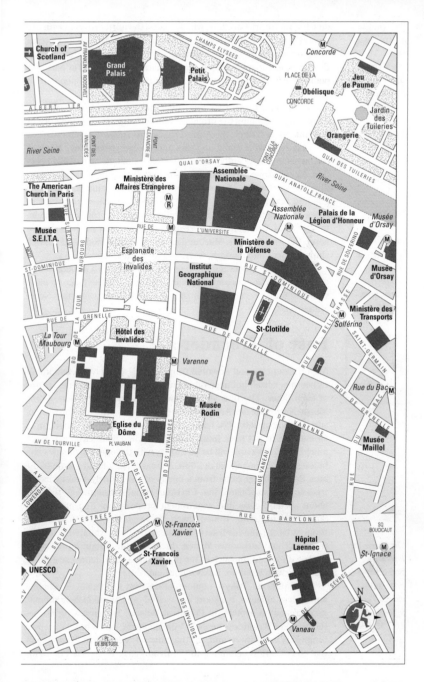

du Cinéma Henri-Langlois, which shared the northern wing with the theatre and now waits to be re-housed in the new Maison du Cinéma being built at Bercy. A further museum, the **Musée des Monuments Français**, is currently closed for renovation, and will form part of a planned "Cité de l'Architecture et du Patrimoine" due to open here in 2001.

The larger of the two remaining museums is the **Musée de l'Homme**, examining the origins, cultures, languages and genetics of humans, from "Lucy", the *Australopithecus afarensis* who roamed Ethiopia roughly 3.2 million years ago, to the present day. Much of the museum has recently been renovated, to include an excellent section on the Americas, and its often high-tech, interactive displays now reflect the best of contemporary French museum design. It's a gigantic place, and you'll have to be selective unless you want to camp overnight among the mummified Incas, Menton Man's skeleton, hosts of African masks or Descartes' skull. Sharing the southern wing, the **Musée de la Marine** displays beautiful models of French ships, ancient and modern, warring and commercial.

The *terrasse* extending between the two wings is a popular hangout for in-line skaters and souvenir vendors – and the place to plant yourself for the view across to the Eiffel Tower and the École Militaire.

East of Trocadéro

As you head east and downhill from Trocadéro, there's a handful of rather specialized but accessible museums all within a stone's throw of each other. The first you'll come across, on place d'Iéna, is the **Musée Nationale des Arts Asiatiques – Guimet**, which before its closure for renovation work featured a huge and exquisite collection of Oriental art from China, India, Japan, Tibet and Southeast Asia. Much more of the collection will be on display with the opening of new exhibition space in the middle of 2000. A great collector and patron of the arts, Émile Guimet came from a family of enormously wealthy industrialists and espoused the Christian-socialist-egalitarian theories about society, class and government proposed by Fournier, Saint-Simon and, in Britain, Robert Owen. His original collection, which he brought back from his travels in Asia in 1876, is exhibited nearby in the small and attractive **Musée du Panthéon Bouddhique**, at 19 avenue d'Iéna. At the back of the museum is a small Japanese garden, complete with bamboo, pussywillow and water.

The **Palais de Tokyo**, contemporary with the Palais de Chaillot and no less hideous, is a short way east of the Panthéon Bouddhique, its entrance on avenue du Président Wilson. The east wing houses the **Musée d'Art Moderne de la Ville de Paris**, which hosts excellent temporary exhibitions and, for the moment, a selection from the displaced collection belonging to the Beaubourg. While the Pompidou

Centre exhibit takes centre stage, most of the museum's outstanding permanent collection of twentieth-century art – which includes pieces by Vlaminck, Zadkine, Picasso, Braque, Gris, Valadon, Matisse, Dufy, Utrillo, both Delaunays, Chagall, Modigliani, Léger – is in storage until the end of 1999.

You can still see Robert and Sonia Delaunay's huge whirling wheels and cogs of rainbow colour in the ground-floor corridor, or the pale leaping figures of Matisse's *The Dance*. Don't miss Dufy's enormous mural *The Electricity Fairy* (*La Fée Électricité*), which fills an entire, curved room with 250 lyrical, colourful panels recounting the story of electricity from Aristotle to the then-modern power station – a reminder of the building's beginnings as the Electricity Pavilion in the 1937 Exposition Universelle. The upper floors of the gallery are reserved for all sorts of contemporary and experimental work, including music and photography.

The west wing of the Palais de Tokyo has been the subject of several projects, the last of which, a Palais du Cinéma, was abandoned halfway through construction, and relocated to Bercy, leaving the space once again neglected.

Opposite the Palais de Tokyo, set in small gardens at 10 avenue Pierre 1er de Serbie, stands the grandiose Palais Galliera, home to the **Musée de la Mode et du Costume**. The museum's collection of clothes and fashion accessories from the eighteenth century to present day is exhibited in temporary, themed shows. There are two or three per year – during changeovers the museum is closed.

Avenue du Président Wilson leads down from place du Trocadéro, past the grounds of the Musée de la Mode et du Costume, to **place de l'Alma**, where there's a replica of the flame from the Statue of Liberty, given to France by the USA in 1987 as a symbol of Franco-American relations. Adopted by mourners from all over the world, the golden flame is covered in messages and flowers deposited since Princess Diana's fatal car crash in the underpass on the other side of the junction.

From here, if you head back downstream, you can reach the Eiffel Tower via the Passerelle Debilly footbridge (in front of the Palais de Tokyo) and quai Branly.

East of Trocadéro

The Musée d'Art Moderne is open Tues–Fri 10am–5.30pm, Sat & Sun 10am–6.45pm; 30F; M^o Iéna & M^o Alma-Marceau.

The Musée de la Mode et du Costume is open during exhibitions only, Tues–Sun 10am–6pm; 45F; M^o Iéna & M^o Alma-Marceau.

The Eiffel Tower

On its completion in 1889, the **Eiffel Tower** was, at 300m, the tallest building in the world. At the time, it incited some violent reactions:

> *[We] protest with all our force, with all our indignation, in the name of unappreciated French taste, in the name of menaced French art and history, against the erection, in the very heart of our capital, of the useless and monstrous Eiffel Tower . . . Is Paris going to be associated with the grotesque, mercantile imaginings of a constructor of machines?*

The Eiffel Tower

The Eiffel Tower is open Sept–June 9.30am–11pm; July & Aug 9am–midnight; M° Bir-Hakeim, M° Trocadéro & M° Ecole-Militaire.

Eiffel himself thought it was beautiful. "The first principle of architectural aesthetics," he said, "prescribes that the basic lines of a structure must correspond precisely to its specified use . . . To a certain extent the tower was formed by the wind itself." Needless to say, it stole the show at the 1889 Exposition Universelle, for which it had been constructed.

Lit from within in 1986 by a complex system of illumination, the tower's superstructure looks at its magical best after dark, as light and fanciful as a filigree minaret. By day, it's only really worth the expense of going to the top if the weather is absolutely clear. **Tickets** cost 59F to the top (by lift) or 31F (first two levels by stairs and the final level by lift); you can go part way for 20F and 42F respectively for the first two levels by lift, or 14F if you take the stairs. All tickets allow free entry to the audiovisual show about the Tower on the first level.

Around the École Militaire

Stretching back from the legs of the Tower, the long rectangular gardens of the **Champ de Mars** lead to the eighteenth-century buildings of the **École Militaire**, founded in 1751 by Louis XV for the training of aristocratic army officers. No prizes for guessing who the most famous graduate was. A less illustrious but better loved French soldier, Cambronne, has his name remembered in a neighbouring street and square. He commanded the last surviving unit of Napoléon's Imperial Guard at Waterloo. Surrounded and reduced to a bare handful of men, Cambronne was called on to surrender by the English. He shouted back into the darkness one word – "*Merde*" – the most common French swear word, known euphemistically ever since as *le mot de Cambronne*.

The surrounding quartier may be expensive and sought after as an address, but physically it's uninspiring – a case in point is the exterior of the **UNESCO building** at the back of the École Militaire. Controversial at the time of its construction in 1958, these days it looks somewhat pedestrian, and badly weathered. Open to the public (Mon–Fri 9.30am–5.30pm), it does have some interesting internal spaces, as well as a number of artworks, both inside and in the garden, the most noticeable being an enormous mobile by Alexander Calder. The finest feature is a quiet Japanese garden, to which you can repair on a summer's day to read a paper bought from the well-stocked kiosk in the foyer.

Most unexpected, therefore, in this rather austere quartier is the wedge of early nineteenth-century streets between avenue Bosquet and the Invalides. Chief among them is the market street **rue Cler**, whose cross-streets, rue de Grenelle and rue St-Dominique, are full of classy little shops, including a couple of boulangeries with their original painted glass panels.

Down by the quai: the American Church, the sewers and SEITA

Out on the river bank at quai d'Orsay, the Gothic Revival **American Church in Paris**, together with the American College in nearby avenue Bosquet (no. 31), provides a focus for the life of the city's large American community. The notice board is plastered with job and accommodation offers and requests, and the people here are welcoming and helpful.

Other quayside attractions include the **Musée des Égouts** – in celebration of the city's sewers – the entrance to which is 50m east of the Pont de l'Alma and quai d'Orsay junction. Your nose will tell you all you need to know, if not the cadaverous pallor of the superannuated sewermen who wait on you. A visit consists of an unilluminating slide-show, a selection of short videos on the maintenance of the sewers, and a small museum set in some tunnels with a lot of smelly water swirling about. Victor Hugo's description in *Les Misérables* is far more satisfying to interested parties: twenty pages on the value of human excrement as manure (25 million francs' worth down the plughole in the 1860s), and the history of the sewer system, including the sewage flood of 1802 and the first perilous survey of the system in 1805, whose findings included a piece of Marat's winding sheet and the skeleton of an orang-utan.

The sewers are open Mon–Wed, Sat & Sun: May–Oct 11am–5pm; Nov–April 11am–4pm; 25F; Mᵒ Alma-Marceau.

Serious students of urban planning can find some interesting items in the museum, among other things an appropriate memorial to Louis Napoléon: an inscription beginning, "In the reign of His Majesty Napoléon III, Emperor of the French, the sewer of the rue de Rivoli . . .". However, everything considered, the museum lacks the atmosphere expected from such a historic place and finishes up being more of a publicity exercise.

Back at street level, just off the quai d'Orsay, the state tobacco company, **SEITA**, at 12 rue Surcouf, has a small **museum** in its

SEITA is open Tues–Sun 11am–7pm; free; Mᵒ Invalides.

Notable buildings in the 7ᵉ arrondissement

29 avenue Rapp (RER Pont de l'Alma). An over-the-top Art Nouveau number with bulls' heads, turbaned women and revolting colour changes. Designed by Lavirotte, 1901.

Square Rapp, off avenue Rapp (RER Pont de l'Alma). A bizarre ensemble: more Lavirotte at no. 43, a trellis trompe l'oeil and the Société Théosophique de France.

12 rue Sédillot (RER Pont de l'Alma). Art Nouveau and Art Deco elements in superb dormers and wrought-iron grills and balconies, again by Lavirotte, 1899.

Conservatoire de Musique, 7 rue Jean-Nicot (Mᵒ Invalides). Christian Portzamparc playing with a half-peeled tube of a tower.

---

offices, presenting the pleasures of smoking, and none of the dangers, with pipes and pouches from every continent – early Gauloises packets, painted tabac signs and all kinds of smoking paraphernalia. SEITA also hosts excellent contemporary art exhibitions – prices vary according to the show.

Newspapers reporting on French foreign policy use "the quai d'Orsay" to refer to the Ministère des Affaires Étrangères (Ministry of Foreign Affairs), which sits between the Esplanade des Invalides and the Palais Bourbon, home of the **Assemblée Nationale**. Napoléon, never a great one for democracy, had the riverfront façade of the Palais Bourbon done to match the pseudo-Greek of the Madeleine. The result is an entrance that suggests very little illumination within.

Les Invalides

The **Esplanade des Invalides**, striking due south from **Pont Alexandre III**, is a more attractive vista than Chaillot–École Militaire. The wide façade of the **Hôtel des Invalides,** topped by its distinctive dome, resplendent with gilding to celebrate the Bicentenary of the Revolution, fills the whole of the further end of the Esplanade. It was built on the orders of Louis XIV as a home for invalided soldiers. Under the dome are two churches: one for the soldiers, the other intended as a mausoleum for the king but now containing the mortal remains of Napoléon.

Both churches are cold and dreary inside. The **Église du Dôme**, in particular, is a supreme example of architectural pomposity. Corinthian columns and pilasters abound. The dome – pleasing enough from the outside – is covered with paintings and flanked by four round chapels displaying the tombs of various luminaries. Napoléon's sarcophagus, of smooth red porphyry, is sunk into the floor and enclosed within a gallery whose friezes, displaying execrable taste and grovelling piety, are captioned with quotations of awesome conceit from the great man himself: "Co-operate with the plans I have laid for the welfare of peoples"; "By its simplicity my code of law has done more good in France than all the laws which have preceded me"; "Wherever the shadow of my rule has fallen, it has left lasting traces of its value."

The Hôtel also houses the **Musée de l'Armée**, France's vast national war museum, occupying two wings on either side of the central courtyard. The ground floor of the west wing displays ancient weapons and armoury with row upon row of suits of armour, including that of Francois Ier, and some beautifully decorated oriental war outfits. Upstairs, seek out the section devoted to the two world wars, with deportation and resistance covered in addition to the battles. Secret Service sabotage devices number among some of the oddest exhibits – for instance, a rat, and a lump of coal stuffed with explosives. Over in the east wing, the largest section is devoted to the uni-

The Musée de l'Armée is open daily: April–Sept 10am–5.45pm; Oct–March 10am–5pm; 37F, ticket includes entry to Napoléon's tomb (open till 7pm June 15–Sept 15); M° Invalides.

forms and weaponry of Napoléon's armies. Napoléon's personal effects include his campaign tent and bed, and even his dog, stuffed. Later French wars are represented, too, through paintings, maps and engravings.

The fourth floor of the east wing houses the newly opened **Musée des Plans-reliefs** (included in the ticket for the Musée de l'Armée), an important collection of models of strategic and fortified towns once indispensable for military reconnaissance and planning manoeuvres. The collection was begun in 1668 by Louvois, Louis XIV's war minister, and was classed a historic monument in 1927 – their usefulness superseded by technical advances.

The Rodin Museum to rue de Babylone

Immediately east of the Invalides is the **Musée Rodin**, at no. 77 rue de Varenne, housed in a beautiful eighteenth-century mansion which the sculptor leased from the state in return for the gift of all his work at his death. In the garden you'll find major projects like *The Burghers of Calais*, *Balzac*, *The Gates to Hell* and *Ugolini and Sons*, this last forming the centrepiece of the ornamental pond. Indoors, and somewhat obscured by the crowds, are works in marble like *The Kiss*, *The Hand of God* and *The Cathedral*. Don't miss the room devoted to Camille Claudel, Rodin's pupil, model and lover, among whose works is a bust of Rodin himself. Claudel's perception of her teacher was so akin to Rodin's own that he considered it as his self-portrait.

The Musée Rodin is open Tues–Sun: April–Sept 9.30am–5.45pm; Oct–March 9.30am–5pm; 28F, 18F on Sun, garden only 5F; Mº Varenne.

The rest of rue de Varenne is lined with aristocratic mansions, including the **Hôtel Matignon**, the prime minister's residence. On the equally elegant, parallel rue de Grenelle, at no. 61, an eighteenth-century house has been turned into the **Musée Maillol**. The exhibits inside belong to Dina Vierny, former model and inspiration to the sculptor Aristide Maillol, whose work adorns the Jardin du Carrousel by the Louvre. It's a peculiar, far-reaching collection: huge numbers of Maillol's female nudes, which, sculpted or painted, can be overbearing en masse; some not particularly wonderful drawings by Matisse, Dufy and Bonnard, for whom Dina also modelled; hideous naïve paintings by Seraphine and Bombois; the odd Picasso, Degas, Gauguin and Kandinsky; Duchamp urinals and bike wheels; a happy spider by Redon (in the furthest corner of the top floor); and a selection of Soviet installation art of the 1970s. Perhaps the most interesting works fall into this last category: Ilya Kabakov's *Communal Kitchen*, based on the rows and grumblings of Soviet families sharing a tiny eating and cooking space; and Vladimir Yankilevski's *The Door*, in which the shape of a downtrodden man returning to his flat provides the outline, on the other side of the door, for a vision of sky and sea.

The Musée Maillol is open daily except Tues 11am–6pm; 40F; Mº Rue-du-Bac.

The Rodin Museum to rue de Babylone

From the Musée Maillol, rue du Bac leads into rue de Sèvres, cutting across **rue de Babylone**, another of the 7e arrondissement's livelier streets, which begins with the city's oldest department store, **Au Bon Marché**, renowned for its food halls, and ends with the crazy, rich man's folly **La Pagode**, the city's most exotic cinema, now closed indefinitely due to financial problems.

The Musée d'Orsay

The Musée d'Orsay is open summer Tues, Wed & Fri–Sun 9am–6pm, Thurs till 9.45pm; winter opens at 10am; 40F; M° Solférino & RER Musée-d'Orsay.

The same could almost be said of the stone façade that disguises the huge vault of steel and glass that is the **Musée d'Orsay**, a few blocks east of the Assemblée Nationale, on the riverfront at 1 rue de Solférino. Once inside, however, illumination is all-pervasive. The building was inaugurated as a railway station in time for the 1900 World Fair, and continued to serve the stations of southwest France until 1939. The theatre troupe Reynaud-Barrault, in their squatting phase, staged several productions here. Orson Welles used it as the setting for his film of Kafka's *The Trial*, filling the high, narrow corridors with filing cabinets to create a nightmarishly claustrophobic setting. De Gaulle used it to announce his coup d'état of May 19, 1958 – his messianic return to power to save the patrie from disintegration over the Algerian liberation war.

Notwithstanding this illustrious history, it was only saved from a hotel developer's bulldozer by the colossal wave of public indignation and remorse at the destruction of Les Halles. The job of redesigning the interior as a museum was given, in 1986, to Milanese Gae Aulenti, the fashionable architect who had transformed Venice's flashy Palazzo Grassi two years earlier.

The conversion of the disused Gare d'Orsay into the Musée d'Orsay marked a major advance in the reorganization of the capital's art collections. Three floors of painting and sculpture of the immediately pre-modern period, 1848–1914, attempt to bridge the gap between the Louvre and the Pompidou collections. The focus is the electrifying collection of **Impressionists** rescued from the cramped corridors of the Jeu de Paume – though not, unavoidably, from the coach parties and school outings – though the works of the **Post-Impressionists** brought in from the Palais de Tokyo are no less exciting.

The design of the museum is, without doubt, very clever, and the artworks have been given the best lighting you could wish for. But for some the space is overdesigned, the sequences of galleries on the upper floors too intense, and the ground floor so marbled it feels like a tomb. There's also an enormous amount of indigestible nineteenth-century establishment work, admired at the time but of limited general interest nowadays.

The collection

The **collection** is ranged across a cavernous central space and on three storeys of two facing sides of the building, one overlooking the Seine, the other the rue de Lille. The **general layout** follows a more or less chronological thread, beginning on the ground floor, continuing up to the upper floor and finishing on the middle level.

Romantic and Neoclassical artists are exhibited on the ground floor, where chief among the **mid-nineteenth-century sculptors** in the central aisle is Carpeaux, whose controversial *The Dance* shocked contemporary audiences with its nude dancers. Also occupying the centre gallery you'll find casts of naturalistic bronze animals by Barye. The far left corner of the building displays **furniture** and **architectural models** from Viollet-le-Duc right up to Frank Lloyd Wright; while the far end of the ground floor features models and drawings of the **Opéra Garnier**, completed in 1875.

To the right of the central gallery, rooms dedicated to Ingres and Delacroix (a greater number of whose works are in the Louvre) are highlights of the **early nineteenth century**. Puvis de Chavannes, Gustave Moreau and early Degas follow, while over in the galleries to the left, Daumier, Corot, Millet and the **Realist school** depart from the academic parameters of an often moralizing subject matter and idealization of the past. Enter the ground-breaking works that were to inspire the early Impressionists: among these, Manet's *Olympia* (1863) is a fine example, as controversial in its day for its colour contrasts and sensual surfaces, as for the portrayal of Olympia as a high-class whore. Courbet's *Origin of the World* (room 7) has a power to shock even contemporary audiences. The explicit, nude female torso was recently acquired from psychoanalyst Jacques Lacan, who had had it screened behind a curtain in his consulting rooms.

The Café des Hauteurs on the upper level of the museum, and a restaurant and tearoom in gilded spaces on the middle level, are good spots to recuperate.

To continue chronologically, proceed to the top level by taking the lift at the back of the ground-floor space. Here you'll pass first through the private collection donated by Moreau-Nélaton, in room 29. An assiduous collector and art historian, he accrued some of the most famous Impressionist images – Monet's *Poppies*, as well as Manet's more controversial *Déjeuner sur l'Herbe*, which sent the critics into apoplexies of rage and disgust when it appeared in 1863, and was refused from that year's Salon. The next few rooms serve up **Impressionism**'s most identifiable masterpieces: Degas' ballet dancers, caught backstage and arranged in Japanese-influenced compositions; and numerous landscapes and outdoor scenes by Renoir, Sisley, Pissarro and Monet. *The Cradle*, by Berthe Morisot, the only woman in the group of early Impressionists, synthesizes the classic techniques of the movement with complex human emotion. A very different touch, all shimmering light and wide brush strokes, is to be seen in Renoir's depiction of a good time being had by all in *Dancing at the Moulin de la Galette* (room 32) – a favourite Sunday afternoon out on the Butte Montmartre.

The Musée d'Orsay

The development of Monet's obsession with light continues with five of his Rouen cathedral series (room 34), each painted at different times of day, along with one from his *Water Lilies* series painted around fifteen years later. The **Post-Impressionists** begin their move away from the mainstream Impressionists' preoccupations in room 35, full of the blinding colours and disturbing rhythms of Van Gogh, while Cézanne is wonderfully represented in room 36.

The rest of the top level is given over to the various offspring of Impressionism. Among a number of **Pointilliste** works by Seurat, Signac and others, is Rousseau's dream-like *Snake Charmer* of 1907. There's Gauguin, post- and pre-Tahiti, as well as plenty of Toulouse-Lautrec at his caricaturial nightclubbing best – one large canvas including a rear view of Oscar Wilde at his grossest.

The middle level takes in Rodin and other **late nineteenth-century sculptors**, several rooms of superb **Art Nouveau** and **Jugendstil** furniture and *objets*, and the original sumptuous reception room (room 51) of the station hotel. The **Nabis** painters, Vuillard and Bonnard are tucked away here (rooms 71–72), while Klimt and Munch feature in room 60 overlooking the Seine.

Chapter 8

Montparnasse and the southern arrondissements

Montparnasse serves to divide the lands of the well-heeled opinion-formers and power-brokers of St-Germain and the 7ᵉ from the amorphous populations of the three **southern arrondissements**. Overscale developments from the 1950s to the present day have scarred some parts of this southern side of the city, but new spaces have also opened up, and some of the contemporary smaller scale developments are delightful. Here are pockets of Paris that have been allowed to evolve in a happily patchy way – **Pernety** and **Plaisance** in the 14ᵉ, the **rue du Commerce** in the 15ᵉ, and the **Butte-aux-Cailles** quartier in the 13ᵉ. These are genuinely pleasant places to explore, and well off the beaten tourist tracks.

Montparnasse

In the eighteenth century, the pile of spoil from the Denfert-Rochereau quarries, on what is now the corner of boulevard du Montparnasse and boulevard Raspail, was named Mont Parnasse (Mount Parnassus) by drunken students who liked to declaim poetry from the top of it. The area, today **Montparnasse**, stretching from the railway station to the Paris Observatory, was to keep its associations with art, bohemia and left-leaning intellectuals, attracting the likes of Verlaine and Baudelaire in the nineteenth century, and Trotsky, Picasso, Man Ray, Chagall, Hemingway, Sartre and Simone de Beauvoir in the twentieth.

Boulevard du Montparnasse runs southeast from rue de Sèvres to Port Royal, passing through the area around the station – a mix of workers' barracks and old-fashioned streets dominated by the gigantic **Tour Montparnasse**. Most of the celebrated **literary cafés** are on the stretch of the boulevard between place du 18-Juin-1940 and boulevard Raspail, and many of their habitués are buried in **Montparnasse cemetery**, between the station and Denfert-

For restaurants, bars and cafés in the area, see pp.282–283.

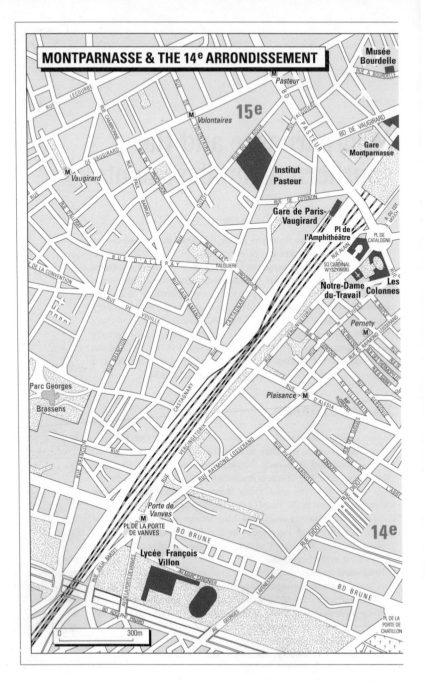

MONTPARNASSE & THE 14ᵉ ARRONDISSEMENT

Musée
Bourdelle

RUE A. BOURDELLE

Pasteur

15ᵉ

Volontaires

BD DE VAUGIRARD

Gare
Montparnasse

Vaugirard

Institut
Pasteur

RUE DE COTENTIN

Gare de Paris-
Vaugirard

PL DE
CATALOGNE

Pl de
l'Amphithéâtre

SQ CARDINAL
WYSZYNSKI

RUE ALAIN

RUE D'ALLERAY

PL
FALGUIÈRE

Notre-Dame
du-Travail

Les
Colonnes

RUE DE VOUILLÉ

Pernety

RUE RAYMOND LOSSERAND

DE LA CONVENTION

Parc Georges

Brassens

Plaisance

RUE
D'ALÉSIA

RUE PIERRE LAROUSSE

RUE RAYMOND LOSSERAND

Porte de
Vanves

PL DE LA PORTE
DE VANVES

BD BRUNE

14ᵉ

Lycée François
Villon

AV MARC SANGNIER

BD BRUNE

AV JULIA BARTET

AV GEORGES

BD ADOLPHE CHÉRIOUX

PL DE LA
PORTE DE
CHÂTILLON

0   300m

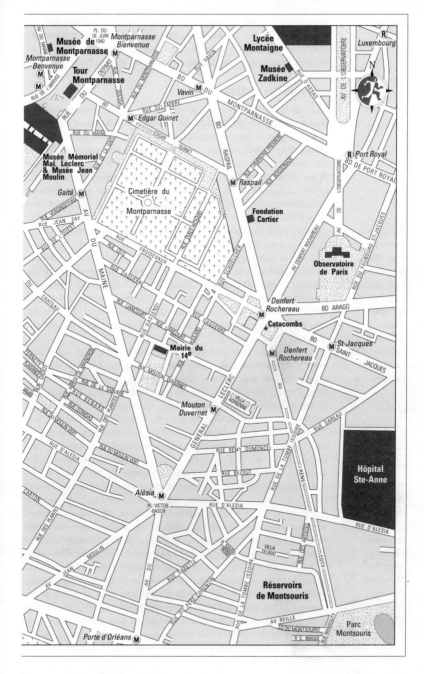

Rochereau. To the east of the cemetery is the **Paris Observatory**, connected to the Jardin du Luxembourg by the avenue de l'Observatoire, which crosses the eastern end of boulevard de Montparnasse and the beginning of boulevard de Port-Royal en route.

Around the station

Montparnasse was once the great arrival and departure point for boat travellers across the Atlantic, whether impoverished emigrants or passengers on luxury cruises, and for Bretons seeking work in the capital. The Breton influence is still evident in the names of some of the nearby restaurants, and the Atlantic connection is remembered in the Jardin Atlantique. Yet, as a dramatic introduction or farewell to the capital, the scene is hardly auspicious. Despite a new fishbowl glass frontage with curved bits of blue and grey steel, the station fails to impose, mainly because its prospect of the city is blocked by the colossal **Tour Montparnasse**. This has become one of the city's principal and least-liked landmarks – most tolerable at night, when the red corner lights give it a certain elegance. At 200m, it held the record as Europe's tallest office building until it was overtaken by the tower at London Docklands' Canary Wharf. You can take a tour for less than it costs to go to the top of the Eiffel Tower, or you could spend the same amount on a drink in the 56th-storey bar – the lift ride is free – where you get a tremendous view westwards over the city, especially at sunset.

The viewing platform of the Tour Montparnasse is open summer 9.30am–11.30pm; winter 9.30am–10.30pm; 48F; entrance on the north side.

In front of the tower, on **place du 18-Juin-1940**, is an enormous, largely subterranean shopping complex, on the front of which a plaque records that this was the spot where General Leclerc of the Free French forces received the surrender of von Choltitz, the German general commanding Paris, on August 25, 1944. Under orders from Hitler to destroy the city before abandoning it, von Choltitz luckily disobeyed. The name of the *place* commemorates the date (June 18, 1940), when de Gaulle broadcast from London, calling on the people of France to continue the struggle in spite of the armistice signed with the Germans by Marshal Pétain.

The Musée Jean Moulin and the Mémorial du Maréchal Leclerc are open Tues–Sun 10am–5.40pm; 17.50F; Mᵒ Montparnasse-Bienvenue.

A **memorial** to Leclerc, combined with a **museum** dedicated to the Resistance leader Jean Moulin, has been opened overlooking the newly created and soulless **Jardin Atlantique**, all built on a raised platform over the railway lines behind the station, surrounded by hideous high-rise offices. Very much an official interpretation of events, the museum's highlight is a panoramic slide show of the summer of 1944. The museum gives rather short shrift to US involvement in the proceedings, a stance echoed in the fortieth anniversary celebrations, when American visitors to Paris were shocked at the absence of the Stars and Stripes from the tanks parading the streets.

On the other side of boulevard Vaugirard, next to the post office, is the **Musée de la Poste**. Not just stamps, though there are plenty of those, the museum covers the history of sending messages, from the earliest times to the present. Currently being refurbished, it's due to re-open at the end of 1999.

Only a short distance away, at 21 avenue du Maine, a piece of Montparnasse's illustrious artistic heritage has been saved from demolition. A rambling, ivy-clad alley leads to what was once Marie Vassilieff's studio, now converted into the **Musée du Montparnasse**, hosting temporary exhibitions based on the Montparnasse artists past and present. Vassilieff lived here between 1912 and 1929, during which time many leading contemporary artists (Picasso, Léger, Modigliani, Chagall, Braque, among others) visited to wine, dine and dance with her. Artists still occupy many of the studios nearby, and there's a flower shop whose beautiful blooms in unusual arrangements spill out into the alley.

On rue Antoine-Bourdelle, opposite 21 avenue du Maine, a garden of sculptures invites you into the **Bourdelle museum**, the artist's old atelier. The work of the early twentieth-century sculptor is reminiscent of his tutor Rodin's, and includes casts, drawings and tools, in his studio-house, and an extension in which you can see studies for the great works such as the homage to Mickiewicz. At the end of the street and to the right on rue Falguière are the stunning offices of the Île de France urban-planning department. The building veers up and away from the line of the street in the smoothest of curves, like the hull of a fantasy spaceship.

To the east of the station, the **market** on boulevard Edgar-Quinet provides down-to-earth clientèle for cafés in the surrounding streets, in marked contrast to renowned establishments a stone's throw away on boulevard du Montparnasse. On Sundays, the market is dedicated to the arts (10.30am–dusk), with all the stalls run by the artists or craftworkers themselves.

Rue de la Gaité, the street where Trotsky lived, is a slice of turn-of-the-century theatreland, with the Théâtre Montparnasse facing the Théâtre Gaité-Montparnasse, and a fair share of porn outlets and junkies. At no. 17, **La Comedia Italienne** has cupids and commedia della'arte characters on its black exterior, while the **Rive Gauche**, at no. 6, has an equally spectacular frontage. The street is featured in a mural that's visible as you look south from boulevard Edgar-Quinet.

The boulevard du Montparnasse

Most of the life of the Montparnasse quartier is concentrated around place du 18-Juin-1940 and along the immediate eastern stretch of the boulevard du Montparnasse. Like other Left Bank quartiers, Montparnasse still trades on its association with the wild characters of the interwar artistic and literary boom. Many were habitués of the cafés *Select, Coupole, Dôme, Rotonde* and *Closerie des Lilas*, all still going strong on the boulevard along with six multi-screen cinemas and several more in the neighbouring streets. It stays up late,

The Musée du Montparnasse is open Wed–Sun 1–7pm; 20F; M° Montparnasse-Bienvenue & M° Falguière.

The Bourdelle museum is open daily except Mon 10am–5.40pm; 18F, 27F with temporary exhibition; M° Montparnasse-Bienvenue & M° Falguière.

and negotiating the pavements, never mind the road, requires careful concentration at all times.

The animated part of the boulevard ends at **boulevard Raspail**, where Rodin's *Balzac* broods over the traffic, though literary curiosity might take you down as far as the rather swanky brasserie **Closerie des Lilas**, on the corner of the tree-lined avenue connecting the Observatory and Luxembourg Gardens in a classic grand Parisian vista. Hemingway used to come here to write, and Marshal Ney, one of Napoléon's most glamorous generals, was killed by a royalist firing squad on the pavement outside in 1815. He's still there, waving his sword, immortalized in stone. Close by, dwarfed by apartment buildings at 100 bis rue d'Assas, is the **Musée Zadkine** occupying the Russian sculptor **Ossip Zadkine**'s house and garden, the latter of which lies hidden away among tall apartment blocks. His angular, Cubist bronzes shelter among the trees or emerge from a clump of bamboos. The rustic cottage, like the garden, is full of his sculptures and invites contemplative lingering.

The Musée Zadkine is open Tues–Sun 10am–5.30pm; 27F; Mᵒ Vavin & RER Port-Royal.

South along boulevard Raspail at no. 261, about 500m from boulevard du Montparnasse, is the **Fondation Cartier pour l'Art Contemporain**, a stunning glass and steel construction designed by Jean Nouvel in 1994. A glass wall following the line of the street is attached by steel tubes to the building behind, leaving a space for trees to grow. All kinds of contemporary art – installations, videos, multi-media – often by American artists little known in France, are shown in temporary exhibitions that use the light and the very generous spaces to maximum advantage.

The Fondation Cartier pour l'Art Contemporain is open daily except Mon noon–8pm; 30F; Mᵒ Raspail.

Montparnasse cemetery and the catacombs

Just off to the southern side of boulevard Edgar-Quinet is the main entrance to the **Montparnasse cemetery**, a suitably gloomy spot containing ranks of miniature temples, dreary and bizarre, and plenty of illustrious names. To the right of the entrance, by the wall, is the unembellished joint grave of Jean-Paul Sartre and Simone de Beauvoir. Sartre lived out the last few decades of his life just a few metres away on boulevard Raspail.

Montparnasse cemetery is open April–Oct Mon–Fri 8am–6pm, Sat from 8.30am, Sun from 9am; Nov–March closes at 5.30pm; Mᵒ Edgar-Quinet & Mᵒ Raspail.

Down avenue de l'Ouest, which follows the western wall of the cemetery, you'll find the **tombs** of Baudelaire (who has a more impressive cenotaph by rue Émile-Richard, on avenue Transversale), the painter Soutine, Dadaist Tristan Tzara, sculptor Zadkine, and the Fascist Pierre Laval, a member of Pétain's government who, after the war, was executed for treason, not long after an unsuccessful suicide attempt. As an antidote, you can pay homage to Proudhon, the anarchist who coined the phrase "Property is theft!"; he lies in Division 1, by the Carrefour du Rond-Point.

In the southwest corner of the cemetery is an old windmill, one of the seventeenth-century taverns frequented by the carousing, versifying students who gave the Montparnasse district its name.

Notable buildings around boulevard Montparnasse and the Montparnasse cemetery

26 rue Vavin, 6ᵉ. Mᵒ Vavin. A block of flats decked in white and blue tiles, with terraced balconies filled with exuberant gardens in the air. Built by Henri Sauvage in 1912.

Rue Schoelcher and rue Froidevaux, 14ᵉ, Mᵒ Raspail & Mᵒ Denfert-Rochereau. An excellent selection of nineteenth- and twentieth-century styles, of particular note being 5, 5bis and 11 rue Schoelcher, 11 and 23 rue Froidevaux, this last a 1930s block of artists' studios, with huge windows for northern light and fabulous ceramic mosaics.

266 boulevard Raspail, 14ᵉ. Mᵒ Raspail & Mᵒ Denfert-Rochereau. An interior design school with a marked Beaubourg influence: external stairs and blue pipe columns in front, plus the 1990s delight of glass and metal shuttering.

31 rue Campagne-Première, 14ᵉ. Mᵒ Raspail. A myriad of earthernware tiles cover the concrete structure of these desirable 1912 *appartements* with huge windows.

Across rue Émile-Richard, in the eastern section of the cemetery, lie car-maker André Citroën, Guy de Maupassant, César Frank, and the celebrated victim of turn-of-the-century French anti-Semitism, Captain Dreyfus. Right in the northern corner is a tomb with a sculpture by Brancusi – *The Kiss* – which makes a far sadder statement than the dramatic and passionate scenes of grief adorning so many of the graves here. And, for the bizarre, by the wall along avenue du Boulevard (parallel to boulevard Raspail) you can see the inventor of a safe gas lamp, Charles Pigeon, in bed next to his sleeping wife, reading a book by the light of his invention.

If you're determined to spend your time among the deceased, you can descend into **the catacombs** in nearby **place Denfert-Rochereau**, formerly place d'Enfer or "Hell Square". (The entrance is on the east side of avenue Général-Leclerc; don't go down in fancy new shoes – it's wet and gungy underfoot.) These are abandoned quarries stacked with millions of bones cleared from the old charnel houses in 1785, claustrophobic in the extreme, and cold to boot. Some years ago a group of punks and art students developed a macabre taste for this as the ultimate party location, but the overseeing authorities soon put an end to that.

The catacombs are open Tues–Fri 2–4pm, Sat & Sun 9–11am & 2–4pm; 27F; Mᵒ Denfert-Rochereau.

As well as interesting architecture around the cemetery (see box above), there are quiet little streets to the south, between avenue du Maine and place Denfert-Rochereau, plus clothes and craft shops and a busy food market on rue Daguerre. Before and during the war, Sartre and Simone de Beauvoir kept separate rooms in the hotel at no. 24 rue Cels; a plaque gives a quote from each on the subject of their togetherness.

Not far away, to the northeast of Denfert-Rochereau, the Paris meridian line originated in the **Observatoire de Paris**, entrance on rue Cassini. From the 1660s, when the Observatory was constructed, to 1884, all French maps had the zero meridian running through the middle of this building. After that date, they reluctantly agreed that 0° longitude should pass through a village in Normandy, which happens to be due south of Greenwich. Visiting the Observatoire is a complicated procedure and all you'll see are old maps and instruments. The original line is visible in the garden behind on boulevard Arago.

Commerce and convention: the 15ᵉ

Between the Montparnasse train tracks and the river lies Paris' largest, most populated and characterless arrondissement, the 15ᵉ. It was in **rue du Commerce** that George Orwell worked as a dishwasher in a White Russian restaurant in the late 1920s, described in his *Down and Out in Paris and London*. Although there are still run-down and poor areas, an ever-widening stretch back from **the river front** is plush high-rise with underground parking, serviced lifts and electronic security. A **new park** has appeared on the site of the old Citroën works down in the southwest corner, while over towards the rail lines the **Parc Georges-Brassens** is now well established on the former abattoir site.

The riverbank section

The western edge of the 15ᵉ arrondissement fronts the Seine from the Eiffel Tower to beyond Pont du Garigliano. Its transformation is such that to anyone returning from a thirty-year absence, it would be almost totally unrecognizable. The most recent addition to the riverfront skyline is the glass **Maison de la Culture du Japon á Paris**, at 101 quai Branly. A symbol of prosperous Franco-Japanese relations, the building contains a cinema, exhibition-space and the opportunity to take part in a Japanese tea ceremony, for which reservations are necessary (☎01.44.37.95.95; 50F). Just off Pont de Bir-Hakeim, at the beginning of boulevard de Grenelle, in a rather undignified enclosure sandwiched by high-rise buildings, a plaque commemorates the notorious **rafle du Vel d'Hiv**, the Nazi and French-aided round-up of 13,152 Parisian Jews in July 1942. Nine thousand of them, including four thousand children, were interned here at the now-vanished cycle track for a week before being carted off to Auschwitz. Only thirty adults were to survive.

The quaysides are pretty inaccessible, but one place to walk is the **Allée des Cygnes**, a narrow island in midstream joining the Pont de Grenelle and the double-decker road and rail bridge, Pont de Bir-Hakeim. It's a strange place – one of Samuel Beckett's favourites – with just birds, trees and a path to walk along, and, at the downstream end, a scaled-down version of the **Statue of Liberty**. This was one of the four preliminary models constructed between 1874 and 1884 by sculptor Auguste Bartholdi, with the help of Gustave Eiffel, before the finished article (originally intended for Alexandria in Egypt) was presented to New York. Contemporary photos show the final version, assembled in Bartholdi's rue de Chazelles workshop, towering over the houses of the 17e like a bizarre female King Kong.

The river bank down to Pont Mirabeau is marred by a sort of mini-Défense development of half-cocked futuristic towers bearing pretentious galactic names like Castor and Pollux, Vega and Orion, rising out of a litter-blown pedestrian platform some 10m above ground level.

Three major streets fan into the arrondissement from Rond-Point du Pont-Mirabeau. Between rue Émile-Zola (demarcation line for the expensive tower block sector) and the long rue de la Convention lie the buildings of the **Imprimerie Nationale**, the national printworks. Their shop (Mon–Thurs 10am–6pm, Fri 10am–5pm) on rue Paul-Hervieu displays some of their publications – beautifully bound art books, musical scores, the *Rights of Man* on vellum, and current tax regulations. Two blocks east on rue St-Charles is a pocket of street life – rare for this side of the 15e – with small food shops, cafés and an excellent boulangerie on the corner with rue Javel.

Where the yuppie apartment blocks end at Rond-Point du Pont-Mirabeau, yuppie offices begin, notably the gleaming white, smooth hulk of the TV company Canal +. At this point, the quayside road diverts underground – to the fury of Parisian cyclists who now have to make a two-kilometre detour. The reason for this was the creation of the new Parc André-Citroën, on the site of the old car factory.

The Parc André-Citroën and Citroën-Cévennes quartier

The **Parc André-Citroën**, on the banks of the Seine, between Pont du Garigliano and Pont Mirabeau, seems to have achieved mythical status: every Parisian has heard of it, most of them have an opinion on it, but few have actually been there. The initial overriding opinion, when landscaped in 1993, was one of disapproval, but as the plants have grown, the park has come into its own, and its popularity has grown. The landscaping of the park is truly a breakaway from other Parisian parks – this is somewhere designed for everyone's pleasure. There's a sound garden with bubbling water on one side and a gushing cascade on the other; a blue garden, pink garden, black garden present a new colourful display with every season; there are secluded gardens in which you can sit or lounge, and public stretches of grass for playing games, hothouses with mimosa, fish-tailed palms and other sweet-smelling shrubbery, and a capricious set of fountain jets, which on a hot day tempts children and occasionally adults to run through. The down side is that there's rather too much concrete here, including the absurdist extravagance of an arch over the RER lines by the river, which is not a bridge, just a decorative device.

The Parc André-Citroën is open summer Mon–Fri 7.30am–8.30pm, Sat & Sun 9am–8.30pm; winter closes at 7pm; Mo Javel & Mo Balard.

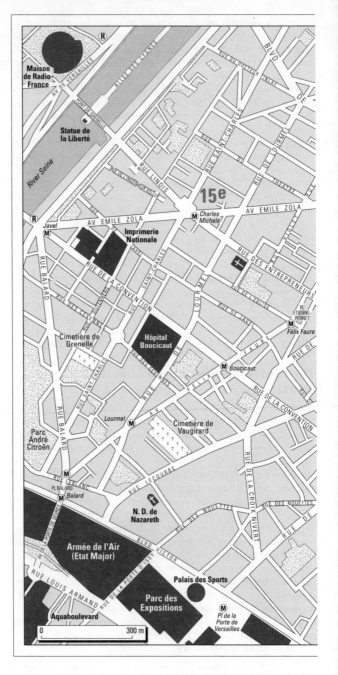

Maison de Radio-France

Statue de la Liberté

River Seine

R

Javel

15e

AV DE VERSAILLES

ALLÉE DES CYGNES

PONT DE GRENELLE

RUE LINOIS

RUE DE L'INGÉNIEUR KELLER

RUE SAINT-CHARLES

BLVD DU DOCTEUR INLAY

RUE DU THÉATRE

RUE DE LOURMEL

AV EMILE ZOLA

AV EMILE ZOLA

Charles Michels

Imprimerie Nationale

RUE DES ENTREPRENEURS

RUE DE LA CONVENTION

RUE DES ÉPINETTES

RUE SAINT-CHARLES

RUE DE LAVE

RUE DE L'ÉGLISE

PL ETIENNE-PERNET

Félix Faure

Cimetière de Grenelle

Hôpital Boucicaut

RUE DE LA

RUE FÉLIX FAURE

RUE DE

Boucicaut

RUE DES MORILLONS

RUE SAINT-CHARLES

RUE BALARD

Lourmel

AV FÉLIX

Cimetière de Vaugirard

RUE DE LA CONVENTION

Parc André Citroën

RUE DE LA CROIX NIVERT

RUE LECOURBE

RUE LEBLANC

PL BALARD

Balard

N. D. de Nazareth

RUE DES NOUETTES

RUE DES NOUETTES

RUE DE

Armée de l'Air (Etat Major)

BLVD VICTOR

AV DE LA PORTE DE SÈVRES

RUE LOUIS ARMAND

RUE DE LA PORTE D'ISSY

Palais des Sports

Aquaboulevard

Parc des Expositions

Pl de la Porte de Versailles

0   300 m

Montparnasse

For restaurants, cafés and bars in the 15e, see pp.283–286.

*For transport
through the
15e, 14e and
13^e
arrondisse-
ments, bus
#62 plies a
useful route
along rues
Convention,
Alésia and
Tolbiac.*

Across rue Balard, which runs down the eastern side of the park, is the totally new **quartier du Citroën-Cévennes**, with pedestrian streets, sports centres, youth clubs and the **Bibliothèque St-Charles**, a children's library on rue de la Montagne-d'Aulas. The peculiar black building, with slanting metallic bands, was built in 1990 and designed by Franck Hammoutene. It has windows on only one side and inside around a circular courtyard in which a cherry tree struggles up towards the light.

From the École Militaire to Parc Georges-Brassens

If you start walking down **avenue de la Motte-Picquet**, by the École Militaire, you'll get the full flavour of the **quartier du Commerce**. That's the staid end, where brasseries throng with officers from the École, and 150 expensive antique shops in the rather dreary **Village Suisse** (all open Thurs–Mon) display Louis Quinze and Second Empire furnishings. The nature of the quartier changes at **boulevard de Grenelle**, where the métro runs on iron piers above the street. Seedy hotels rent rooms by the month, and the corner cafés offer cheap *plats du jour*. **Rue du Commerce** begins here, a lively, old-fashioned high street – once you're past the *McDonald's* and Monoprix – full of small shops and peeling, shuttered houses. Scale and architecture give it a sunny, friendly atmosphere. The best-known cheap eating establishment is *Le Commerce*, at no. 51, and there are other restaurants and interesting shops in the surrounding streets.

Towards the end of the street is **place du Commerce**, with trees and a bandstand in the middle – a model of old-fashioned, petit-bourgeois respectability. Cafés and pâtisseries proliferate as rue du Commerce ends at place Étienne-Pernet, where quaint, two-storey houses still exist on the west side of the *place*. If you follow rue des Entrepreneurs east, past a beautiful apartment building at no. 109, you come to the surprisingly generous green space of **square Lambert**, with fountains and lawns overlooked by the prison-like premises of a lycée, or top-stream secondary school.

If you carry on south, rue de la Croix-Nivert brings you to the **Porte de Versailles**, where, at an informer's signal, government troops first entered the city in their final assault on the Commune on May 21, 1871. Today it's the site of several large **exhibition halls** that host the foires – the Agricultural Show, Ideal Home Exhibition and the like. To the west, along boulevard Victor, are good discount clothes shops and the wonderful 1930s École Nationale Supérieure de Techniques Avancées, decorated with reliefs depicting "advanced technologies". Behind the headquarters of the French Air Force, to which the school is attached, is Aquaboulevard, the city's largest **leisure centre**, whose main attraction is an artificial tropical lagoon complete with beaches, exotic plants and giant water chutes (see p.351).

More traditional relaxation – and for free – is on hand at **Parc Georges-Brassens**, whose main entrance, on rue des Morillons, is flanked by two bronze bulls. The old Vaugirard abattoir was transformed into this park in the 1980s, and the original clock tower remains, surrounded by a pond. It's a delight, especially for children – attractions include puppets and rocks and merry-go-rounds for the kids, a mountain stream with pine and birch trees, beehives and a tiny terraced vineyard, and a garden of scented herbs and shrubs designed principally for the blind (best in late spring). The corrugated pyramid with a helter-skelter-like spiral is a theatre, the Silvia-Montfort (see pp.319–320).

On Saturday and Sunday mornings, take a look in the sheds of the old horse market between the park and rue Brançion where dozens of **book dealers** set out their genuinely interesting stock. The success of the park has rubbed off on **rue des Morillons** and **rue Brançion** – new restaurants and tearooms have opened, and old cafés have livened up.

On the west side of the park, in a secluded garden in passage Dantzig, off rue Dantzig, stands an unusual polygonal building known as **La Ruche**. It was designed by Eiffel and started life as the wine pavilion for the 1900 trade fair (see box below).

Commerce and convention: the 15^e

Discount clothes shops are reviewed on p.331.

La Ruche

After the World Fair ended, the wine pavilion was bought by Alfred Boucher, sculptor of public monuments and friend of Rodin, and re-erected in passage Dantzig in an altruistic gesture of help for struggling artists. Very soon **La Ruche**, or the Beehive, became home to Fernand Léger, Modigliani (briefly), Chagall, Soutine, Ossip Zadkine and many others, mainly Jewish refugees from pogroms in Poland and Russia. Boucher, somewhat overwhelmed by the unconventional work and behaviour of his protégés, commented good-naturedly: "I'm like a hen who finds she has laid ducks' eggs."

Léger, evoking the poverty, recalls how he was invited to lunch one day by four Russian residents who had just made a few francs selling cat pelts. The meal was the cats, dismembered and fricasséed in vodka. "It burnt your mouth and it stank," he noted, "but it was better than nothing."

The writer Blaise Centrars was a regular visitor, as were Apollinaire and Max Jacob, who provided a link with the Picasso gang across the river in Montmartre, and there was much cross-fertilization going on in the cafés, too, especially *La Rotonde*, at 105 boulevard du Montparnasse (see p.283). But at La Ruche itself, the French were in a minority – you were much more likely to hear Yiddish, Polish, Russian or Italian spoken.

It's still something of a Tower of Babel these days, with Irish, American, Italian and Japanese artists in residence, although, as an Italian mosaicist who has been there since the 1950s said, there's no longer the Bohemian camaraderie and festivity of the old days. The buildings were saved from the bulldozers in 1970 by a campaign led by Marc Chagall, since which time physical conditions have improved.

---

*The Musée
Pasteur is
open daily
2–5.30pm,
closed Aug;
15F; Mᵒ
Pasteur.*

If you're heading towards Montparnasse from Parc Georges-Brassens, take bus #89 rather than slogging it on foot. Not a lot happens in this eastern stretch of the 15ᵉ. To the north, between rue du Docteur-Roux and rue Falguière, is the **Pasteur Institute**, renowned for its founder Louis, and for its research into AIDS. A pass obtained from the office opposite allows you to enter the building, where guided tours (English version available) take you through the great nineteenth-century chemist-biologist's apartment, laboratory and Byzantine-style mausoleum. Of non-scientific, but equal, interest in the museum is the sombre interior decoration (plus innovative plumbing) of a nineteenth-century Parisian middle-class home.

The 14ᵉ below Montparnasse

The 14ᵉ is one of the most characterful of the outer arrondissements. While the area beside the train tracks immediately south of Gare Montparnasse has changed dramatically, old-fashioned networks of streets still exist in the **Pernety** and **Plaisance** quartiers, and between avenues Réné-Coty and Général-Leclerc. In the early years of the twentieth century, so many outlawed Russian revolutionaries lived in the 14ᵉ that the Tsarist police ran a special Paris section to keep tabs on them. The 14ᵉ was also a favourite address for artists, who could live in seclusion in its many *villas* (mews) built in the 1920s and 1930s. There's still a thriving artistic community here, though only the very successful can afford the *villas* these days. Down in the southeast corner you'll find plenty of green space, in the **Parc Montsouris** and in the **Cité Universitaire**, erstwhile home to more revolutionaries in their student days.

*For
restaurants,
cafés and bars
in the 14ᵉ, see
pp.286–287.*

Pernety, Plaisance and down to the perimeter

Had it not been for the efforts of the local campaign group "Vivre dans le 14ᵉ", there might have been an expressway flanked by tower blocks all the way down the western edge of the arrondissement to the boulevard péripherique. Instead, the old **rue Vercingétorix**, running down the western side of the Pernety and Plaisance quarters, has become a walkway and cycle track past gardens, kids' play areas, boules pitches and tennis courts.

This is not at all what you'd expect if you approach from **place de Catalogne**, where the Catalan architect Ricardo Bofill has created one of his gargantuan Wagnerian complexes of amphitheatres and colonnades bedecked with classical features stripped of any structural purpose. They're an improvement, however, on the supremely gross office blocks that bridge the train lines between boulevard Pasteur and place de Catalogne. The large disc fountain in the *place* looks rather derelict and runs dry these days – not only does it cost a fortune to run, but local power-cuts tended to coincide with an operational fountain.

It's a relief to find yourself in front of **Notre-Dame du Travail**, designed for humans rather than imaginary giants. The church was built at the end of the nineteenth century to cater for a congregation swollen by the men employed in building the Eiffel Tower and the surrounding exhibition palaces for the Exposition Universelle. The stone came from the Cloth Pavilion and the slender metal columns of the interior from the Palace of Industry, while the bell hails from Sebastopol – a present to the local people from Napoléon III.

The 14e below Montparnasse

No trace remains of the flats where these skilled builders would have lived on rue Vercingétorix or rue de l'Ouest (birthplace of comic actor/director Jacques Tati); nor of the working-class population that would have outnumbered the present residents of Pernety and Plaisance by two to one. But wander westwards through the streets between rue Raymond-Losserand and rue des Plantes, and you'll find pockets where the physical fabric, if not the social make-up, hasn't changed since Notre-Dame du Travail was built. And artists still choose to live in this part of town.

Cité Bauer, the road that runs between rue Boyer-Barret and rue Didot, has adorable little houses with gardens; neighbouring rue des Thermopyles has its secluded courtyards; and below rue d'Alésia, more quiet *villas* lead off from rue Didot. Giacometti's old ramshackle studio and home still stands on the corner of rue du Moulin Vert and rue Hippolyte-Maindron. At the end of Impasse Floriment, behind a petrol station on rue d'Alésia and holding out against development threats, a bronze relief of Georges Brassens, smoking his pipe – created by a contemporary local artist – adorns the tiny house where Brassens lived and wrote his songs from 1944–66.

At 3 rue Jonquoy, running west off rue Didot, the **Musée Adzak** is a showcase for the work of British army artist Roy Adzak. He built the studio with his own hands in the 1980s, as well as a living and working space for artists from all round the world, who are given lodgings in the rabbit warren of rooms behind the studio. It's much less formal than most Parisian art galleries. Temporary exhibitions – of painting, drawing, sculpture, prints – are organized by artists belonging to the Association du Musée Roy Adzak (to which anyone can belong).

The Musée Adzak opens during exhibitions only – check the local press or ring ☎01.45.43. 06.98 for details; free; M° Plaisance.

Cinema has one of its best Parisian venues at *L'Entrepôt*, 7–9 rue Francis-de-Pressensé, with spaces for talks, meals and drinks, and even a garden where they sometimes light incense in the trees on summer nights (see p.315). **Rue Raymond-Losserand**, the main street of Pernety and Plaisance, is lines with crowded bars, though new smart hotels are edging in. A mural of books faces north at the junction with avenue Villemain, while a Chagallesque painting of horses, doves, elephants and hunters adorns the garden wall on the corner with rue d'Alésia. Further down rue Raymond-Losserand, the superbly proud and ugly building at no. 168 is the ancient Plaisance electricity substation.

Rue d'Alésia, the main east–west route through the 14e, has a small **food market** every Thursday and Sunday between the Plaisance métro and rue Didot, but is best known for its good-value **clothes shops**, many selling discounted couturier creations. These congregate towards place Victor & Hélène Basch, where there's another delightful example of an old-style mews, the Villa d'Alésia.

At the weekend it's worth heading out to the southern edge of the arrondissement, past the characterless flats on boulevard Brune, for one of the city's best **flea markets**. Starting at daybreak (see p.341), it spreads along the pavements of avenues Marc-Sangnier and Georges-Lafenestre, petering out at its western end in place de la Porte-de-Vanves, where the city fortifications used to run until the 1920s.

South from Denfert-Rochereau

From Denfert-Rochereau to Parc Montsouris, most of the space is taken up by RER lines, reservoirs and **Ste-Anne's psychiatric hospital**, where the great political philosopher Louis Althusser was incarcerated after murdering his wife. His autobiography, which was written in Ste-Anne's but came out posthumously in 1992 because as a patient he had no right to publish, suggests that he would have preferred to have been tried and sent to prison. The plea of madness was, under French law, not a mitigating circumstance, but a total denial that a crime had taken place. His wife, Hélène, had supported him through fits of severe mental illness for more than thirty years, and some say she had had enough and threatened to leave him – a tragic story that was mercilessly exploited by the right-wing French press.

At the junction of rue d'Alésia and avenue Réné-Coty, steep steps lead up into rue des Artistes and one of the most isolated spots in the city. At the end of the street, brambles grow over the fencing round the Montsouris reservoir. Dali, Lurgat, Miller, Durrell and other artists found homes around here in the cobbled cul-de-sac of **Villa Seurat**, off rue de la Tombe-Issoire. Lenin and his wife, Krupskaya, lived across the street at 4 rue Marie-Rose.

South of the reservoir nestle more secluded cobbled streets and mews. The **square du Montsouris** leads off avenue Reille, close by one of Corbusier's earliest Parisian commissions, the studio at no. 53 for his friend Ozenfant, the painter who styled the Hispano-Suiza cars of the 1920s. The roof has been altered, but not the Corbusier trademark of horizontal slices of windows. All manner of styles – even a mock Norman farmhouse – can be spied along the verdant and secretive square du Montsouris, whose other entrance is on rue Nansouty. There are more *villas* off this street: Georges Braque lived at no. 6 in the one named after him.

Parc Montsouris, at the other end of the square du Montsouris, was a favourite walking place of Lenin's, and no doubt of all the local artists, too. Its peculiarities include a meteorological office, a marker of the old meridian line, near boulevard Jourdan, and, by the southwest entrance, a kiosk run by the French Astronomy Association. Alas, the most surprising structure, a beautiful reproduction of the Bardo palace in Tunis, built for the 1867 Exposition Universelle, burnt down in half an hour in the early 1990s, just after restoration work had finished. But the park is nonetheless a good place to stroll, with its unlikely contours, winding paths and the cascade above the lake – even the RER tracks cutting right through it fail to dent its charm.

The 14e below Mont-parnasse

On the other side of boulevard Jourdan, several thousand students from more than one hundred different countries live in the curious array of buildings of the **Cité Universitaire**. The central Maison Internationale resembles the Marlinspike of *Tintin* books, while the diverse styles of the others reflect the variety of nations and peoples who study here. Armenia, Cuba, Indo-China and Monaco are neighbours at the western end; Japan, Brazil, Italy, India and Morocco gather together at the other; Cambodia is guarded by startling stone creatures next to the boulevard péripherique; Switzerland (designed by Le Corbusier during his stilts phase) and the USA are the most popular for their relatively luxurious rooms, while the Collège Franco-Britannique is a red-brick monster.

A stroll in the pleasant grounds and sports facilities round the back reveals the multitude of nations living there. The Cité puts on films, shows and other events (check the notice boards in the Maison Internationale), and you can eat cheaply in the cafeterias if you have a student card.

The 13^e

To the tight-knit community who lived in the crowded, rat-ridden and ramshackle slums around **rue Nationale** in the postwar years, Paris was another place, rarely ventured into. Come the 1950s and 1960s, however, the city planners, here as elsewhere, came up with their usual solution to the housing problem – getting rid of the slums to make way for tower blocks. Today's community lives in flats that are hygienic, secure and costly to run, the nextdoor neighbour is a stranger, and only a couple of cafés remain on rue Nationale. The architectural gloom of the southeastern half of the arrondissement is only alleviated by the culinary delights of the **Chinese quarter**, the admirable **Dunois jazz venue** (see p.308), and one or two clever new buildings.

For restaurants, cafés and bars in the 13e, see pp.287–288.

West of avenue d'Italie and avenue des Gobelins – site of the famous tapestry works – there remains the almost untouched quartier of the **Butte-aux-Cailles**, and little streets and cul-de-sacs of prewar houses and studios. The eastern edge of the 13e, meanwhile, along the riverfront, is in the throes of mammoth development centred around the new **Bibliothèque de France** (see p.167). Eventually everything from the Gare d'Austerlitz out

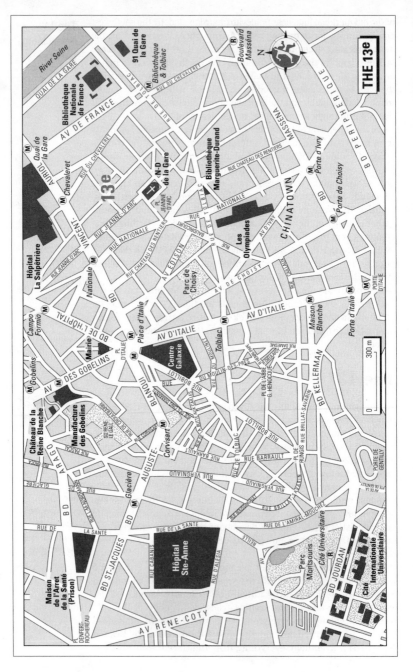

to the périphérique will be transformed and known as "Paris Rive Gauche".

The 13e

Butte-aux-Cailles and the old quartiers

Between rue de Tolbiac and the stretch of boulevard Auguste-Blanqui where the food market is held, from place d'Italie to beyond Corvisart métro, rises a hill – the *butte* – on which the quails – *cailles* – of the quartier's name must once have roamed. The five-storey houses on rue **Butte-aux-Cailles** are typical of pre-1960s Paris, and though many of the flats have shared loos and no bathrooms, the rents are not cheap. It's a pleasantly animated street, recently recobbled and furnished with lampposts, where you can find book, wine and food shops, a newsagents, a community action centre, and one of the green Art Nouveau municipal drinking fountains donated to the city by the nineteenth-century British art collector Sir Richard Wallace. New bars and restaurants have opened up without putting old ones out of business: there's a co-operative jazz bar, *La Folie en Tête*, at no. 33, and a restaurant, *Le Temps des Cerise*, at nos. 18–20, plus plenty of other places to eat and drink, most of which stay open till the early hours. In addition to these are the establishments on the streets between rue Butte-aux-Cailles and boulevard Auguste-Blanqui, to which there's a short cut by a path and steps from rue des Cinq-Diamants.

South of rue de Tolbiac, small houses with fancy brickwork, decorative tiles and timbers, crazy-paving walls and near-vertical roofs have remained intact: especially between rues Boussingault and Brillat-Savarin, near place de Rungis, and on place de l'Abbé-G-Henocque, rue Dieulafoy and rue Henri-Pape.

Place d'Italie, the Gobelins workshops and La Salpêtrière

Place d'Italie, the central junction of the 13e, is one of those Parisian roundabouts that takes half an hour to cross. On its north side is the ornate mairie of the arrondissement, while to the south the huge white edifice with a tangled coloured wire appendage houses a new cinema. In the 1848 Revolution, the *place* was barricaded and the scene of one short-lived victory of the Left. A government general and his officers were allowed through the barricades, only to be surrounded and dragged off to the police station, where the commander was persuaded to write an order of retreat and a letter promising three million francs for the poor of Paris. Needless to say, neither was honoured and reprisals were heavy. Many of those involved in the uprising were tanners, laundry-workers or dye-makers, with their workplace the banks of the River Bièvre. This area was deemed a health hazard and covered over in 1910 (creating rues Berbier-du-Mets and Croulebarbe) – the main source of pollution being the dyes from the **Gobelins tapestry workshops**, at 42 avenue des Gobelins, which had operated here for some four hundred years. Tapestries are still being made by the same, painfully slow methods, now featuring cartoons by contemporary painters.

Hidden just north of Gobelins is an exquisite fairy-tale octagonal tower and gateway hemmed in by workshops and lockups. This is all that remains of the **Château de la Reine Blanche**, where the young Charles VI of France supposedly went mad after a riotous party in 1393 when he was nearly burnt alive. The château was rebuilt in the sixteenth century, from which the remaining structures date. You can take a look through a gateway on rue des Gobelins or through the courtyard at 4 rue Gustave-Geffroy. A stone's throw away, between rues Berbier and Corvisart, is a big public garden – although nothing very special, it's handy for a snooze or picnic if you're out this way.

The ornate, bourgeois buildings between boulevards St-Marcel and Vincent-Auriol are dominated by the immense **Hôpital de la Salpêtrière**, built under Louis XIV to dispose of the dispossessed, and later used as a psychiatric hospital – today it's a general hospital. Jean Charcot, who believed that susceptibility to hypnosis proved hysteria, staged his theatrical demonstrations here, with Freud one of his fascinated witnesses. If you ask very nicely in the Bibliothèque Charcot (block 6, red route), the librarian may show you a book of photographs of the desperate female victims of these experiments. A more positive statement on women is provided by the building at 5 rue Jules-Breton, on the other side of boulevard de l'Hôpital, which declares in large letters on its façade, "In humanity, woman has the same duties as man. She must have the same rights in the family and in society."

Chinatown and around

The area between rue de Tolbiac, avenue de Choisy and boulevard Masséna is what is known as the **Chinatown** of Paris, with no concessions to organic matter unless it's to be ingested. From rue de Tolbiac, just east of rue Baudricourt, steps and escalators lead up to a concrete platform known as "Les Olympiades", where the tower blocks hide a clutch of brilliant Asiatic restaurants and sundry arcades with east Asian high-street businesses – travel agents, video libraries, hairdressers and bowling alleys – where few transactions are carried out in French. As you step out into avenue d'Ivry, you'll find the **Tang-Frères supermarket** and a larger **covered market**, where birds circle above the mind- and stomach-boggling goods. Chinese, Laotian, Cambodian, Thai and Vietnamese shops and restaurants fill avenue d'Ivry and avenue de Choisy all the way down to the city limits, many of them in shopping mazes on the ground floors of tower blocks.

If this is all too materialistic for you, head into the underground service road, rue du Disque, just by the escalators up to Les

Olympiades at 66 avenue d'Ivry. Red and gold lanterns announce the entrance to a Buddhist temple. Community activities as well as worship go on here, and no-one will mind your presence.

Back on rue de Tolbiac, on the corner with rue Nationale, there's a wonderful municipal library in a steel-framed, curved building with a giant, semi-transparent photograph on the rue Nationale side. It houses the **Bibliothèque Marguerite Durand**, the first official feminist library in France (see p.38), and has newspapers and a video auditorium.

Alternatively, you can relax outside in the **parc de Choisy**, on the north side of rue de Tolbiac, with outdoor ping-pong tables with concrete nets, archery targets, and shady trees. There are more good modern buildings near here: Christian de Portzamparc's public housing estate on rue des Hautes-Formes, and, at 106 rue du Château-des-Rentiers, a ten-storey block of public flats whose façade, on rue Jean-Colly, has a map of the quartier in coloured tiles, with pipes to show the métro lines.

Serious Le Corbusier fans could make the long slog down rue Cantagrel, where his Salvation Army building, blackened by traffic fumes, stands at no. 12. Alternatively take bus #62 east along rue de Tolbiac towards the Seine, and you'll come to the most recent monumental construction of the city, the new national library, part of the last of Mitterrand's *grands projets*, Paris Rive Gauche.

Paris Rive Gauche

After a few teething troubles, the grand plans for the three new quartiers that make up **Paris Rive Gauche** – Austerlitz (from the station to boulevard Vincent-Auriol), Tolbiac (around the library), and Masséna (out to the perimeter) – are finally taking root. Tolbiac is the most developed area so far of the three: the first stage in its revivification was the construction of the library, which opened in December 1996. The Austerlitz and Masséna quartiers are due to be completed in the second decade of the twenty-first century, with an estimated 15,000–20,000 people to become smart Paris Rive Gauche residents, and a further 60,000 working here.

The Bibliothèque Nationale de France

The four enormous L-shaped glass towers of the **Bibliothèque Nationale de France**, house a general public library as well as some of the more specialist collections moved from the original Bibliothèque Nationale (see p.348). The towers, overlooking the Seine between Pont de Bercy and Pont de Tolbiac, looked lovely in the original models. Unfortunately, Dominique Perrault's design failed to take into account the effect of light on printed matter, so blinds had to be added, lending an orange hue and an office block appearance to what was supposed to suggest open books and accessibility of knowledge. In addition, the scale is so vast that when

The Bibliothèque Nationale de France is open Tues–Sat 10am–7pm, Sun noon–6pm; day-pass 20F.

Visiting the library

Admission to the complex is via all sides except that facing the railway and is a short walk from either the newly inaugurated M° Bibliothèque & Av-de-France or M° Quai-de-la-Gare, with entrances to the building itself between the towers at either end. Access to the library on the garden level is only granted to bona fide researchers (you can make an appointment with a librarian on the spot to state your case). The library above, where less rare books can be consulted from open shelves, can be used by any-one aged over eighteen. There are still shops and restaurants to open, though the latter may be exclusively for pass-holders. The wood is off lim-its to everyone.

viewed from the river the towers bear no obvious relation to each other. But once you mount the wooden steps surrounding the library, the perspective changes. Now you're looking down into a sunken pine wood with glass walls that filter light into the floors below your feet, and the towers seem somehow closer than the 250m length and 130m width that separate their corners. This vast space, though open on all sides, feels enclosed, cut off from everything beyond, like being at the edge of a volcano crater. It's a startlingly original concept.

The sense of isolation deepens as you descend into the library (all the public spaces are below ground). Even with all the building works going on nearby, not a whisper of external sound penetrates; that goes for the birds in the wood as well. To reach the lower levels, where researchers can access every book, periodical and audio-visual material ever published or produced in France, you travel down steep escalators beneath the towers whose walls are hung with a metal mesh like chain mail. From what seems like a dungeon in the bowels of the earth you pass into daylight – at ground level in rela-tion to the trees. A rich russet carpet muffles footfalls; metallic lamps, air-conditioning cylinders and more fireproof mesh shine sil-ver while the desks, chairs and shelves are made of pale, warm, com-forting wood. Mezzanines divide but don't partition off this study space that occupies the entire building's length. It feels strangely cosy, like a luxuriously converted monastery.

Around the library

There's something very disconcerting about the attempt to create a new, and enormous, district from scratch; eradicating all past traces of the area, so that every park, street and building belongs to just one period of approximately twenty years. However, fears of a sterile, bureaucratic quartier the likes of La Défense, were unfounded. Green spaces are a priority, and interesting cultural events are springing up in their own right. The barge *Guinguette Pirate*, moored along the quay, in front of the library, is an excellent place to hear live music and have a drink, while cutting-edge art galleries have sprung up on rue Louise Weiss, behind the library, and a massive thirteen-screen MK2 cinema complex is planned for 2001, complete with film studios. The stylish métro station, part of the new, ultra-modern meteor-line, opened in October 1998. The offices that are ready are nearly all sold, and there are signs of life behind the strange decor – butterflies, plants and words painted on glass – of the new apartment blocks next to the library. However, avenue de France, the thirty-hectare platform over the railway lines, is progressing very slowly and could slow the whole project down.

It's not all new, though: the gigantic old **mills** and warehouses just south of Pont de Tolbiac, occupied by musicians, anarchists, oddballs and artists, are, thankfully, set to stay. At 91 quai de la Gare, the old SNCF building is due to be renovated, and the artists' studios, flats and exhibition spaces inside will remain, while the vieux moulins de Paris (the old Paris mills) recall the history of this long-ignored industrial corner of the city – those nearer boulevard Masséna, have been earmarked to host several university faculties.

Chapter 9

Montmartre and northern Paris

Montmartre lies in the middle of the largely petit-bourgeois and working-class 18e arrondissement, respectable round the slopes of the hill (or Butte Montmartre), distinctly less so around **Pigalle** on the northern edge of the 9^e arrondissement and towards the **Gare du Nord** and **Gare de l'Est** into the 10^e arrondissement, where the colourful bazaar-like shops and depressing slums of the **Goutte d'Or** crowd along the rail lines. On its northern edge, across the so-called "plain of Montmartre", lies the extensive **St-Ouen flea market**. To the west, between avenue de **Clichy** and the St-Lazare train lines, is the little-explored **Batignolles** quartier.

Montmartre

At 130m, the **Butte Montmartre** is the highest point in Paris. The various theories as to the origin of its name all have a Roman connection: it could be a corruption of *Mons Martyrum* – "the Martyrs' hill" – the martyrs being St Denis and his companions; on the other hand, it might have been named *Mons Mercurii*, in honour of a Roman shrine to Mercury; or possibly *Mons Martis*, after a shrine to Mars.

In spite of being one of the city's chief tourist attractions, the Butte manages to retain the quiet, almost secretive, air of its rural origins. Incorporated into the city only in the mid-nineteenth century, it received its first major influx of population from the poor displaced by Haussmann's rebuilding programme. Its heyday was from the last years of the century to World War I, when its rustic charms and low rents attracted crowds of artists. Although that traditional community of workers and artists has largely been supplanted by a more chic and prosperous class of Bohemians, the quartier's physical appearance has changed little, thanks largely to the warren of **plaster-of-Paris quarries** that perforate its bowels and render the ground too unstable for new building.

For restaurants, cafés and bars around Montmartre, see pp.288–290.

THE CITY: CHAPTER 9

The most popular **access** route is via the rue de Steinkerque and the steps below the **Sacré-Cœur**, Montmartre's hill-top church and most famous landmark (the funicular railway from place Suzanne-Valadon is covered by the *Carte Orange*). But for a quieter approach, head up via place des Abbesses or rue Lepic, where you'll still have the streets to yourself.

Place des Abbesses to the Butte

Place des Abbesses is postcard-pretty, with one of the few complete surviving Guimard Art Nouveau métro entrances (transferred from the Hôtel de Ville), with glass porch as well as original railings and the slightly obscene orange-tongued lanterns. The bizarre-looking church of St-Jean de Montmartre, on the downhill side of the *place*, had the distinction of being the first concrete church in France (1904), its internal structure remarkably pleasing despite the questionable taste of the decoration.

East from the *place*, at the Chapelle des Auxiliatrices in rue Yvonne-Le-Tac, Ignatius Loyola founded the **Jesuit** movement in 1534. This is also supposed to be the spot where **Saint Denis**, the first Bishop of Paris, had his head chopped off by the Romans around 250 AD. He's said to have carried it until he dropped, on the site of the cathedral of St-Denis, in what is now a traditionally Communist suburb north of the city (see p.383). Just beyond the end of rue Yvonne-Le-Tac, in the beautiful little **place Charles-Dullin**, the Théâtre de l'Atelier is still going strong after nearly two centuries. Heading west from the place Charles-Dullin, you'll return to the place des Abbesses, from where there's a choice of two quiet and attractive routes to the top of the Butte. You can either climb up **rue de la Vieuville** and the stairs in rue Drevet to the minuscule **place du Calvaire**, which has a lovely view back over the city, or go up **rue Tholozé**, then right below the **Moulin de la Galette** – the last survivor of Montmartre's forty-odd windmills, immortalized by Renoir – into rue des Norvins; stopping at the corner of rues Lepic and d'Orchampt on the way up offers the best view of the Moulin de la Galette.

Rue Poulbot, at the beginning of rue des Norvins, leads round to the underground **Espace Montmartre – Salvador Dalí**, at no. 9–11. Black walls and atmospheric sound effects set off the less well-known, yet still very familiar, Dali works: watercolour illustrations for books – *Alice in Wonderland*, the Bible, Boccaccio's *Decameron* – and small sculptures of soft watches, the spatial elephant and other phantasms from the incomprehensible mind of the self-promoting master. Unfortunately, the commercial side of the gallery takes up more room than the exhibition, with a large space downstairs displaying copies of his work for sale, and a souvenir shop upstairs.

The Espace Montmartre – Salvador Dalí is open daily 10am–6pm; 35F; Mᵒ Abbesses.

Artistic associations abound hereabouts. Zola, Berlioz, Turgenev, Seurat, Degas and Van Gogh lived in the area. Picasso, Braque and

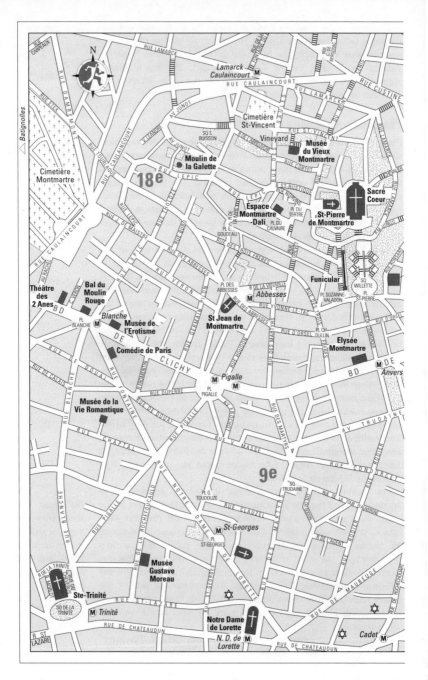

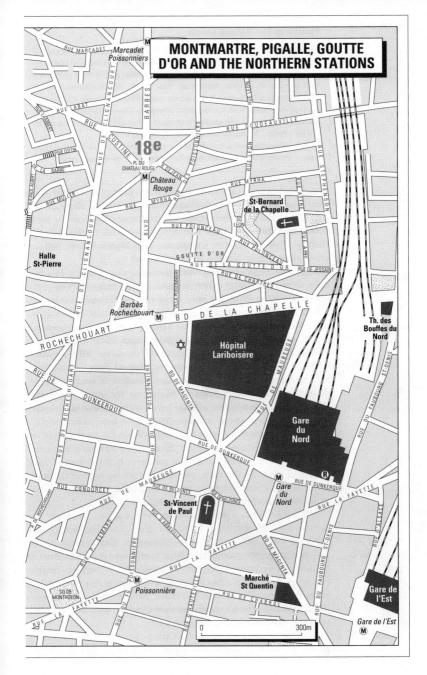

Montmartre

Juan Gris invented Cubism in an old piano factory in the tiny place Émile-Goudeau, known as the **Bateau-Lavoir** (see box above); it still provides studio space for artists, though the original building burnt down some years ago. At the corner of boulevard de Clichy and place Blanche, Toulouse-Lautrec's inspiration, the **Moulin Rouge**, still survives, albeit a mere shadow of its former self.

Rue Lepic begins here, its winding contours recalling the lane that once served the plaster quarry wagons. A busy market occupies the lower part of the street, but once above rue des Abbesses it reverts to a mixture of tranquil and furtive elegance. Round the corner above rue Tourlaque, a flight of steps and a muddy path sneak between gardens to **avenue Junot**, where the actress Anouk Aimée has her home. To the left is the secluded and exclusive cul-de-sac **Villa Léandre**, while to the right, the Cubist house of Dadaist poet Tristan Tzara stands on the corner of another exclusive enclave of houses and gardens, the **Hameau des Artistes**. Higher up the street the **square Suzanne-Buisson** provides a gentle haven, with a sunken boules pitch overlooked by a statue of St Denis clutching his head to his breast.

Further on, **rue des Saules** tips steeply down the north side of the Butte past the terraces of the tiny **Montmartre vineyard**; its annual harvest of about 1500kg of grapes produces in the region of 1500 bottles of wine. To the right, **rue Cortot** cuts through to the water tower, whose distinctive form, together with that of the Sacré-Cœur, is one of the landmarks of the city's skyline.

At 12 rue Cortot, a pretty old house with a grassy courtyard was occupied at different times by Renoir, Dufy, Suzanne Valadon and her mad son, Utrillo. It's now the **Musée de Montmartre,** whose mainly disappointing exhibits attempt to re-create the atmosphere of Montmartre's pioneering heyday, via a selection of Toulouse-Lautrec posters, a mock-up of a bar complete with original zinc, and various painted impressions of how the Butte once looked. The museum does, however, offer a magnificent view from the back over the vineyard and the northern reaches of the city.

The Musée de Montmartre is open Tues–Sun 11am–6pm; 25F; M° Lamarck-Caulaincourt.

Next to the vineyard on **rue St-Vincent** is a patch of totally overgrown ground that looks like a vacant building lot. It is, in fact, the garden belonging to the museum, officially left wild since 1985, to allow a space for the natural development of Paris' native flora and fauna (April–Oct Mon 4–6pm, except during school and public hols, Sat 2–6pm; free; further information from Paris Espace Nature; ☎01.43.28.47.63). Berlioz lived just beyond it with his English wife, in the corner house on the steps of rue du Mont-Cenis, whence there is a breathtaking view northwards along the canyon of the steps, as well as back up towards place du Calvaire. The steps are perfect sepia-romantic Montmartre: a double handrail runs down the centre, with the lampposts between. The streets below are among the quietest and least touristy in Montmartre.

Place du Tertre and the Sacré-Cœur

The heart of Montmartre, the place du Tertre, photogenic but total-ly bogus, is jammed with tourists, overpriced restaurants and "artists" doing quick while-u-wait portraits. Its trees, until recently under threat of destruction for safety reasons by overzealous offi-cialdom, have been saved by the well-orchestrated protests of its influential residents.

Between place du Tertre and the Sacré-Cœur, the church of St-Pierre – the oldest in Paris, along with St-Germain-des-Prés – is all that remains of a Benedictine convent that occupied the Butte Montmartre from the twelfth century onwards. Though much altered, it still retains its Romanesque and early Gothic feel. The four ancient columns inside the church, two by the door and two in the choir, are leftovers from the Roman shrine that stood on the hill, while the cemetery dates from Merovingian times.

Crowning the Butte is the Sacré-Cœur, a romantic and graceful pastiche, whose white pimply domes are an essential part of the Paris skyline. Construction was started in the 1870s on the initiative of the Catholic Church to atone for the "crimes" of the Commune (see box overleaf). The thwarted opposition, which included Clemenceau, eventually got its revenge by naming the space at the foot of the mon-umental staircase square Willette, after the local artist who turned out on inauguration day to shout, "Long live the devil!"

The best thing about the Sacré-Cœur is the view from the top. It's almost as high as the Eiffel Tower, and you can see the layout of the whole city – a wide, flat basin ringed by low hills, with stands of high-rise blocks in the southeastern corner, on the heights of Belleville, and at La Défense in the west. In the hazy distance, the tall flat faces of the suburban workers' barracks rise like slabs of tombstone.

To the south and east of the Sacré-Cœur, the slopes of the Butte drop much more steeply down towards boulevard Barbès and the Goutte d'Or (see p.184). Directly below are the gardens of square Willette, milling with tourists. To avoid the crowds, opt instead for the stepped rue Utrillo and rue Paul Albert, which joins rue Ronsard

The dome of the Sacré-Cœur is open daily: summer 9am–7pm; winter 9am–6pm; 15F; M° Abbesses & M° Anvers.

*The Halle St-
Pierre is open
daily
10am–6pm;
closed Aug;
museum free,
admission to
temporary
shows varies;
Mᵒ Anvers.*

along the edge of the gardens. The circular **Halle St-Pierre**, at the bottom of rue Ronsard, hosts excellent changing exhibitions of *art brut* and *art naïf*, as well as the **Musée d'Art Naïf Max Fourny**, with works from all over the world. There's also an auditorium for film, theatre, music and dance, a bookshop and a cheap cafeteria with the day's papers to read. It's a great place, totally ignored by the tourists being disgorged from their coaches only metres away.

Outside, in **rue Ronsard**, masked by overhanging greenery, are the now-sealed entrances to the quarries where plaster of Paris was extracted, and which were used as refuges by the revolutionaries of 1848.

The Paris Commune

On March 18, 1871, in the **place du Tertre**, Montmartre's most illustrious mayor and future prime minister of France, **Georges Clemenceau**, flapped about trying to prevent the bloodshed that gave birth to the **Paris Commune** and the ensuing civil war with the national government.

On that day, Adolphe Thiers' government dispatched a body of troops under General Lecomte to take possession of 170 guns, which had been assembled at Montmartre by the National Guard in order to prevent them falling into German hands. Although the troops seized the guns easily in the dark before dawn, they had forgotten to bring any horses to tow them away. That gave Louise Michel, the great woman revolutionary, time to raise the alarm.

A large and angry crowd gathered, fearing another restoration of empire or monarchy such as had happened after the 1848 Revolution. They persuaded the troops to take no action and arrested General Lecomte, along with another general, Clément Thomas, whose part in the brutal repression of the 1848 republican uprising had won him no friends among the people. The two generals were shot and mutilated in the garden of **no. 36 rue du Chevalier-de-la-Barre**, behind the Sacré-Cœur. By the following morning, the government had decamped to Versailles, leaving the Hôtel de Ville and the whole of the city in the hands of the National Guard, who then proclaimed the Commune.

Divided among themselves and isolated from the rest of France, the Communards only finally succumbed to government assault after a week's bloody street-fighting between May 21 and 28. No-one knows how many of them died – certainly no fewer than 20,000, with another 10,000 executed or deported. By way of government revenge, Eugène Varlin, one of the founder-members of the First International and a leading light in the Commune, was shot on the selfsame spot where the two generals had been killed just a few weeks before.

It was a working-class revolt, as the particulars of those involved clearly demonstrate, but it hardly had time to be as socialist as subsequent mythologizing would have it. The terrible cost of repression had long-term effects on the French working-class movement, both in terms of numbers lost and psychologically. For, thereafter, not to be revolutionary seemed like a betrayal of the dead.

For more details on the German siege of Paris and on the Commune, see p.419.

The Montmartre cemetery

West of the Butte, near the beginning of rue Caulaincourt in place Clichy, lies the **Montmartre cemetery** (March 16–Nov 5 Mon–Fri 8am–6pm, Sat from 8.30am, Sun from 9am; Nov 6–March 15 Mon–Fri 8am–5.30pm, Sat & Sun opens as March–Nov; M° Blanche & M° Place-de-Clichy). Tucked down below street level in the hollow of an old quarry, it's a tangle of trees and funerary pomposity, more intimate and less melancholy than Père-Lachaise or Montparnasse (see pp. 000 and 000).

The illustrious dead at rest here include Zola, Stendhal, Berlioz, Degas, Feydeau, Offenbach, Dalida and François Truffaut. There's also a large Jewish section by the east wall. The entrance is on avenue Rachel under rue Caulaincourt, next to an antique cast-iron poor-box (*Tronc pour les Pauvres*).

Batignolles to Clichy

West of Montmartre cemetery, in a district bounded by the St-Lazare train lines, marshalling yards and avenue de Clichy, lies the "village" of **Batignolles** – sufficiently conscious of its uniqueness to have formed an association for the preservation of its *caractère villageois*. Its heart is rue des Batignolles. The poet Verlaine was brought up here, while Stéphane Mallarmé lived on boulevard des Batignolles, at the end of rue des Batignolles. At the northern end of the street, the attractive semicircular **place du Dr F. Lobligeois** frames the colonnaded church of **Ste-Marie-des-Batignolles**, its entrance modelled on the Madeleine; behind the church, the tired and trampled greenery of **square Batignolles** stretches back to the big rail marshalling yards. On the corner of the *place*, the modern *L'Endroit* bar attracts the bourgeois youth of the neighbourhood until 2am.

From rue des Batignolles, rue Legendre and rue des Dames lead southeast across the train lines to **rue de Lévis** and one of the city's most flamboyant and appetizing food and clothes markets, held every day except Monday.

To the northeast, the long **rue des Moines** leads towards Guy-Môquet, with a covered market on the corner of rue Lemercier. This is the working-class Paris of the movies: all small, animated, friendly shops, four- or five-storey houses in shades of peeling grey, and brown-stained bars, where locals stand and drink at the "zinc".

Across avenue de Clichy, round **rue de la Jonquière**, the quiet streets are redolent of petit-bourgeois North African respectability, interspersed with decidedly upper-crust enclaves. The latter are typified by the film-set perfection of the **Cité des Fleurs**, a residential lane of magnificent private houses and gardens.

From Guy-Môquet, it's a short walk to rue Lamarck, which will take you up to Montmartre, or back along avenue de St-Ouen to rue

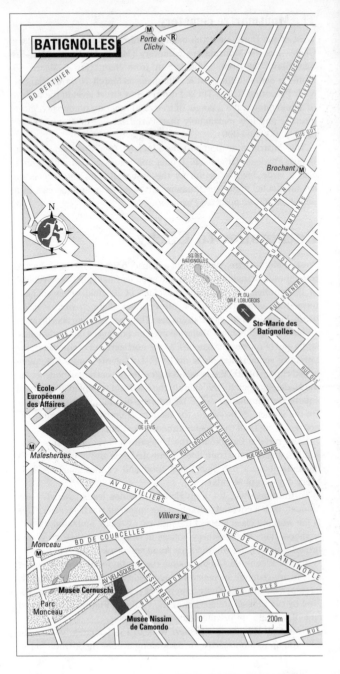

THE CITY: CHAPTER 9

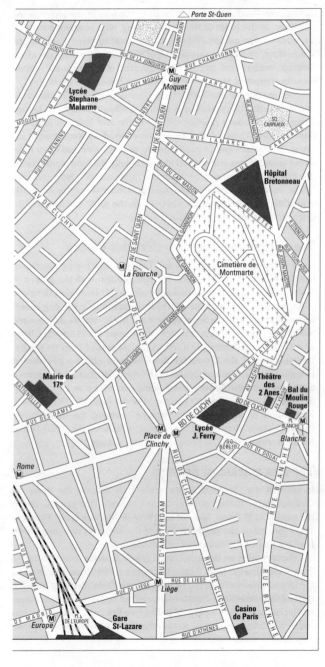

For restaurants, bars and cafés around Batignolles, see p.290.

du Capitaine-Madon, leading through to the wall of the Montmartre cemetery. In the heart of this cobbled alley, with washing strung at the windows, the ancient *Hôtel Beau-Lieu* still survives. Ramshackle and peeling, on a tiny courtyard full of plants, it epitomizes the kind-hearted, instinctively arty, sepia Paris that every romantic visitor secretly cherishes. Most of the guests have been there years.

From avenue de St-Ouen, the so-called *plaine* of Montmartre stretches respectably eastwards until it reaches the slummy district lining the rail tracks heading north to Lille and Belgium from the Gare du Nord. There's little of note to see, besides a long street market at the western end of **rue Ordener**, an attractive and lively little sector round the mairie of the 18^e – especially the food shops round the rue du Poteau and rue Duhesme junction. It's here that the "Mont" in Montmartre begins to make particular sense, for the north side of the Butte is very much steeper than the south and looms quite dramatically above the contrasting *plaine*.

The Batignolles and Cimetière des Chiens

Right at the frontier of the 17e and Clichy, under the péripherique, lies the little-visited **Cimetière des Batignolles**, with the graves of André Breton, Verlaine and Blaise Cendrars (M^o Porte-de-Clichy).

Asnières' dog cemetery is open mid-March to mid-Oct 10am–7pm, mid-Oct to mid-March 10am–5pm, closed Tues & hols; M^o Mairie-de-Clichy.

A great deal more curious, and more lugubrious, is the **dog cemetery** on the banks of the Seine at Asnières. It's accessible on the same métro line, about fifteen minutes' walk from M^o Mairie-de-Clichy along boulevard Jaurès, then left at the far end of Pont de Clichy. Privately owned, the **Cimetière des Chiens** occupies a tree-shaded ridgelet that was once an island in the river. Most of its tiny graves decked with plastic flowers, some going back as far as 1900, belong to dogs and cats, many with epigraphs of the kind: "To Fifi, the only consolation of my wretched existence". Among the more exotic cadavers are a Muscovite bear, a wolf, a lioness, the 1920 Grand National winner, and the French Rintintin, vintage 1933.

The flea market of St-Ouen

In spite of the "St-Ouen" in its name, it is actually the **Porte de Clignancourt** – the old gateway to the Channel – that gives access to the market of St-Ouen, and not the Porte de St-Ouen itself. The market is located on the northern edge of the 18e arrondissement, now hard up against the boulevard péripherique.

Officially open on Saturday, Sunday and Monday from 7.30am to 7pm – unofficially, from 5am – the **puces de St-Ouen** claims to be the largest flea market in the world, the name "flea" deriving from the state of the second-hand mattresses, clothes and other junk sold here when the market first operated in the free-fire zone outside the city walls. Nowadays, however, it's predominantly a proper – and very expensive – **antiques** market, selling mainly furniture but also such

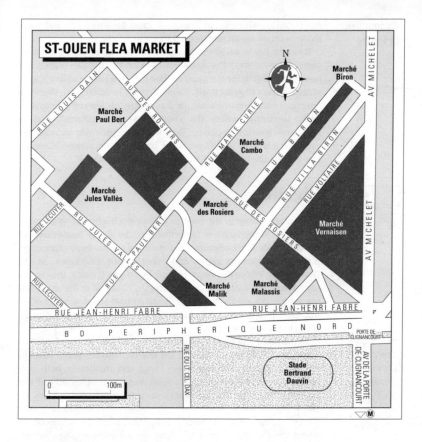

trendy "junk" as old café counters, telephones, traffic lights, posters, juke-boxes and petrol pumps, with what is left of the rag-and-bone element confined to the further reaches of **rue Fabre** and **rue Lécuyer**.

First impressions as you arrive from the métro are that there's nothing for sale but jeans and leather jackets. There are, however, ten official markets within the complex: Marché **Biron**, Marché **Cambo** and Marché **Malassis** selling serious and expensive antique furniture; Marché **Vernaison** – the oldest – which has the most diverse collection of old and new furniture and knick-knacks; Marché **Paul-Bert**, offering all kinds of furniture, china, and the like; Marché **Serpette** specializing in items from the period 1900–1940; Marché **des Rosiers** concentrating on twentieth-century decorative pieces; Marché **Malik**, with mostly clothes, some high-class couturier stuff, and a lot of uninteresting new items; Marché **Michelet**, with new jeans, trainers and leather goods; and Marché

Jules-Vallès, which is the cheapest, most junk-like . . . and most likely to throw up an unexpected treasure.

It can be fun to wander around, but it's foolish to expect any bargains. In some ways the streets of St-Ouen beyond the market are just as interesting for the glimpse they give of a tempo of living long vanished from the city itself. Should hunger overtake you, there's a touristy *restaurant-buvette* in the centre of Marché Vernaison, *Chez Louisette*, where the great gypsy jazz guitarist, Django Reinhardt, sometimes played. But for more dependable and cheaper eating, it's best to go to one of the brasseries on avenue Michelet, just outside the market, or back on boulevard Ornano.

Pigalle

From place Clichy in the west to Barbès-Rochechouart in the east, the hill of Montmartre is underlined by the sleazy **boulevards of Clichy** and **de Rochechouart**, the centre of the roadway often occupied by bumper-car pistes and other funfair sideshows. At the **Barbès** end, where the métro clatters by on iron trestles, the crowds teem round the Tati department store, the cheapest in the city, while the pavements are thick with Arab and African street vendors offering watches, trinkets and textiles. The best place to watch is from the stairs to the Barbès métro.

For restaurants, bars and cafés around Pigalle, see p.290.

At the **place Clichy** end, tour buses from all over Europe feed their contents into massive hotels. In the middle, between **place Blanche** and **place Pigalle**, sex shows, sex shops and prostitutes, both male and female, vie for the custom of *solitaires* and couples alike. It's an area in which respectability and sleaze rub very close shoulders. On **place Pigalle** itself, huge anatomical blow-ups (unveiled only after dark in deference to residents' sensibilities) assail the senses on the very corner of one of the city's most elegant private *villas*, **avenue Frochot**. In the adjacent streets – **rues de Douai, Victor-Massé** and **Houdon** – specialist music shops (this is *the* area for instruments and sound systems) and grey house façades are interspersed with tiny ill-lit bars where "hostesses" lurk in complicated tackle.

The Musée de l'Erotisme is open daily 10am–2am; 40F; M° Blanche.

Perfectly placed among the sex shops and shows, the new **Musée de l'Erotisme** endeavours to explore different cultures' approaches to sex. The ground and first floors are dedicated to sacred and ethnographic art, in which depictions of proud phalluses and intertwining positions in the art from Asia, Africa and pre-Columbian Latin America expose a strong link between the spiritual and the erotic. European art, on the other hand, as a rule – the exception being the copies of Ancient Greek vases, where there's no beating about the bush – uses sex to satirize and ridicule religion, with lots of naughty nuns and priests caught in compromising situations. There's an interactive element to the displays in the basement, where you can trace the metal outline of a naked women with a metal ring and baton

Cabarets and sex around Pigalle

For many foreigners, Paris is still synonymous with a use of the stage perpetuated by those mythical names the Moulin Rouge, Folies Bergères and Lido. These **cabarets**, which flash their presence from the Champs-Élysées to boulevard Montmartre, predate the film industry, though it appears as if the glittering Hollywood musicals of the 1930s were their inspiration rather than their offspring. They define an area of pornography that would have trouble titillating a prudish Anglo-Saxon, and, though the audience is mainly male, the whole event is to live sex shows what glossy fashion reviews are to "girlie" mags. Apart from seeing a lot of bare breasts, your average coached-in tourist may well feel they have not got what they paid (rather excessively) for – making some all the more easy prey for the pimps of Pigalle.

The *Lido*, for example, takes breaks from multi-coloured plumage and illuminated distant flesh to bring on a conjuror to play tricks with the clothes and possessions of the audience. Then back come the computer-choreographed "Bluebell Girls", in a technical tour de force of light show, music and a moving stage transporting the thighs and breasts to more faraway exotica – the sea, a volcano, arctic plain or Pacific island.

The *Moulin Rouge* is of the same ilk with its "Doriss Girls", and still trades on its Toulouse-Lautrec painted fame as the place for "the most celebrated can-can in the world". The oldest cabaret, the *Folies Bergères*, re-opened in 1993 after a brief closure, with a new pastiche show starring a drag artist as the lead chorus "girl".

At the *Crazy Horse*, the theatrical experience convinces the audience that they are watching art as well as the prettiest girls in Paris. In the ranks of defences for using images of female bits to promote, sell, lure and exploit, Frenchmen are particular in putting "art and beauty" in the front line. In upholding the body suspendered and pouting, weak and whimpering, usually nude and always immaculate, they claim to protect the femininity, beauty and desirability of the Frenchwoman as she would wish it herself.

Moving from the glamour cabarets to the **"Live Sex"** and **"Ultra-Hard Live Sex"** venues is to leave the world of elegant gloss and exportable Frenchness for a world of sealed-cover porn that knows no cultural borders.

attached – the aim is to get the ring from one end to the other without it touching the filament. The longer you succeed, the more she moans – be warned, it's quite loud. The rest of the floors upstairs are devoted to temporary exhibitions, which change every three months.

South of Pigalle

The rest of the 9e arrondissement, which stretches south of Pigalle, boasts an illustrious artistic past to which its two fine museums, the **Musée Gustave Moreau** and **Musée de la Vie Romantique**, pay testimony. However, these days it's a rather quiet quarter and a tad dull, with the exception of some blocks of streets round **place St-Georges**, where Thiers, president of the Third Republic, lived in a house that's now a library (rebuilt after being burnt by the

The Musée de la Vie Romantique is open Tues–Sun 10am–5.40pm, closed public hols; 17.50F; M° St-Georges, M° Blanche & M° Pigalle.

The Musée Gustave Moreau is open Mon & Wed 11am–5.15pm, Thurs–Sun 10am–12.45pm & 2–5.15pm; 22F; M° St-Georges, M° Blanche & M° Pigalle.

Commune). In the centre of the *place* stands a statue of the nineteenth-century cartoonist Gavarni, who made a speciality of lampooning the mistresses that were de rigueur for bourgeois males of the time. This was the mistresses' quartier – they were known as *lorettes*, after the nearby church of Notre-Dame-de-Lorette.

The cheap rents hereabouts also attracted musicians, painters and writers in the nineteenth century – Chopin, Dumas, Delacroix and George Sand all lived in the area. A **museum** at 16 rue Chaptal sets out to evoke the Romantic period in what was once the portrait painter Ary Scheffer's abode. The house itself is a delightful surprise: a shuttered provincial house on a cobbled courtyard at the end of a private alley behind an imposing street front. George Sand used to visit here, and the collection consists mainly of bits and pieces (jewels, lockets of hair) associated with her. Scheffer's studio is also open to the public, though it's of less interest.

Further east, **place Toudouze** and **rues Clauzel**, **Milton** and **Rodier** are worth a look. Renovation has revealed some beautiful and elegantly ornamented façades. **Rue St-Lazare**, between the St-Lazare station and the hideous church of Ste-Trinité, is a welcome swath of activity amid the residential calm. Opposite rue de la Tour-des-Dames, where two or three gracious mansions and gardens recall the days when this was the very edge of the city, you'll find the bizarre and little-visited **museum** dedicated to the works of **Gustave Moreau**. There's an overcrowded collection of cluttered, joyless paintings by the Symbolist painter within, and you can also visit the stuffy apartments – tiny in comparison to the amount of space given over to his studio – where he lived with his parents. If you know you like Moreau's works, go along; otherwise, give it a miss.

The Goutte d'Or and the northern stations

Continuing east from Pigalle, boulevard Rochechouart becomes boulevard de la Chapelle, along the north side of which, between **boulevard Barbès** and the **Gare du Nord** rail lines, stretches the poetically named, crumbling and squalid quartier of the **Goutte d'Or**. Its name – the "Drop of Gold" – derives from the vineyard that occupied this site in medieval times. Since World War I, however, when large numbers of North Africans were imported to replenish the ranks of Frenchmen dying in the trenches, it has gradually become an immigrant ghetto.

In the late 1950s and early 1960s, during the Algerian war, few middle-class Parisians would have dreamt of entering the quartier, not just for its reputation for score-settling, prostitution and drugs, but because of the clandestine activity of the Algerian National Liberation Front (FLN). In fact, the new residents of the quartier had far better reason to fear the respectable "law-abiding" French.

Many of the buildings in the area remain in a lamentable state of decay. While artists, writers and others have moved in, attracted by the only affordable property left in the city, a major programme of pulling down, rebuilding and cleaning up is underway. As the physical backdrop changes, so inevitably does the character of the quartier. Much of **rue de la Goutte-d'Or** itself is new, including a lovely nursery school on the corner with rue Islettes. For the moment, however, rue de la Goutte-d'Or and its tributary lanes, especially to the north – rue Myrha, rue Léon, the Marché Dejean, rue Polonceau (with its basement mosque at no. 55) – and the cobbled alley and gardens of **Villa Poissonnière** remain distinctly North African and poor.

Washing hangs from every balcony and tiny shops sell snazzy cloth and jewellery as well as traditional *djellabas*. The windows of the pâtisseries are stacked with trays of equally brightly coloured cakes and pastries. Sheeps' heads grin from the slabs of the halal butchers. The grocers shovel their wares from barrels and sacks, and the plangent sounds of Arab music echo evocatively from the record shops. In the playground of square Léon, just to the north of the rue de la Goutte d'Or, you'll find authorized graffiti and three brilliant murals. It's an interesting place to sit (although women on their own can attract unwanted attention), as all sectors of the community come here for recreation. The cafés and bars of the Goutte d'Or tend to be too small and intimate to appeal to outsiders, but you'd certainly be able to find a good mint tea.

The stations and faubourgs

On the south side of boulevard de la Chapelle lie the big northern stations, the **Gare du Nord** (serving the Channel ports and places north) and **Gare de l'Est** (serving northeastern and eastern France and Eastern Europe), with the major traffic thoroughfares, boulevard de Magenta and boulevard de Strasbourg, both bustling, noisy and not in themselves of much interest.

For restaurants, bars and cafés around the stations and faubourgs, see p.291.

To the right of the Gare de l'Est as you face the station, a high wall encloses the gardens of **square Villemin**, which once belonged to the Couvent des Récollets – the near wreck of a building along rue du Faubourg-St-Martin. The same campaign groups that saved the gardens for public use (entrance on rue des Récollets), including a 200-day occupation to stop the bulldozers, are now focusing on the convent. Various projects are in the air and local people fear the building will deteriorate beyond the point of repair as decisions are postponed. Given their success with the gardens, however, the campaigners may well win this one, too.

The liveliest part of the quarter is the **rue du Faubourg-St-Denis**, full, especially towards the lower end, of charcuteries, butchers,

Brasserie
Julien *and*
Brasserie Flo
are reviewed
on p.291.

greengrocers and foreign delicatessens, as well as a number of restaurants, including *Brasserie Julien* and *Brasserie Flo*, the latter in an old stableyard, the cour des Petites-Écuries. A number of immigrant communities are now well established in the streets running off rue du Faubourg-St-Denis. **Passage Brady** is the hub of Paris' "Little India", with shops and restaurants that will transport you to the subcontinent. Rues d'Enghien and de l'Echiquier are quieter but have several restaurants, cafés and shops serving the area's Turkish community.

Spanning the end of rue du Faubourg-St-Denis is the **Porte St-Denis**, a triumphal arch built in 1672 on the Roman model to celebrate the victories of Louis XIV. Feeling secure behind Vauban's extensive frontier fortifications, Louis demolished Charles V's city walls and created a swath of leafy promenades, where the Grands Boulevards now run. In place of the city gates he planned a series of triumphal arches, of which this and the neighbouring **Porte St-Martin**, at the end of rue du Faubourg-St-Martin, were the first.

The whole area between the two faubourgs ("suburbs") through to the provincial **rue du Faubourg-Poissonnière** is honeycombed with *passages* and courtyards. China and glass enthusiasts should take a walk along **rue de Paradis**, whose shops specialize in such wares, with the Baccarat firm's collection of exquisite crystal, the **Musée du Cristal** at no. 30, tucked away with the shop behind the classical façade bearing the names of the Baccarat and St Louis cristallerie. Close by, at no. 18, is the magnificent mosaic and tiled façade of Monsieur Boulenger's Choisy-le-Roi tileworks shop, now closed to the general public, but you can peer through the gate and admire more exuberant ceramics featuring peacock tails and flamingoes on the stairs and floors.

*The Musée du
Cristal is open
Mon–Fri
9am–6.30pm
& Sat
10am–6pm;
15F; M°
Poissonière &
M° Gare-de-
l'Est.*

Across boulevard Bonne-Nouvelle, the southern limit of the 10e arrondissement, are the *passages* of place du Caire and rue St-Denis leading down to Les Halles.

Chapter 10

Eastern Paris

Paris east of the **Canal St-Martin** has long been a working-class area, from the establishment of the **Faubourg St-Antoine** as the workshop of the city in the fifteenth century, to the colonization of the old villages of **Belleville**, **Ménilmontant** and **Charonne** by the French rural poor during the Industrial Revolution in the mid-nineteenth century. These were the populations that supplied the people-power for the latter century's great **rebellions**: the insurrections of 1830, 1832, 1848 and 1851, and the short-lived Commune of 1871, which divided the city in two, with the centre and west battling to preserve the status quo against the oppressed and radical east. Even during the 1789 Revolution, when Belleville, Ménilmontant and Charonne were still just villages the most progressive demands came from the artisans of the Faubourg St-Antoine.

Until quite recently, nothing was to be more feared than the "descente de Belleville", the descent from the heights of Belleville of the revolutionary mob. It was in order to contain this threat that so much of the Canal St-Martin, a natural line of defence, was covered over by **Baron Haussmann** in 1860.

Today, precious little stands in remembrance of these events. The *Mur des Fédérés* in **Père-Lachaise cemetery** records the death of 147 Communards; the Bastille column (see p.115) and its inscription commemorate 1830 and 1848; a few streets bear the names of the people's leaders. But nothing you now see in the 11e, for instance, suggests its history as the most fought-over arrondissement in the city.

Indeed, the physical backdrop itself is also slowly being transformed. Narrow streets and artisans' houses still survive in Belleville, Ménilmontant and off the Canal St-Martin, but many of the crumbling, dank, damp and insanitary houses have now been demolished. Rebuilding in the 1960s and 1970s produced shelving-unit apartment blocks, but in recent years the new constructions have shown far more imagination and aesthetic sensitivity.

Though some of the new is public housing to accommodate resident populations, redevelopments have inevitably shifted old popu-

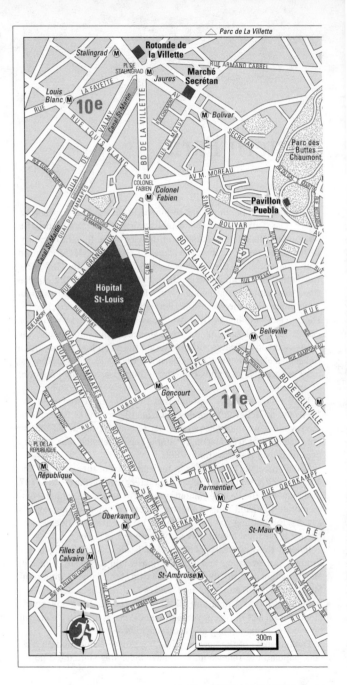

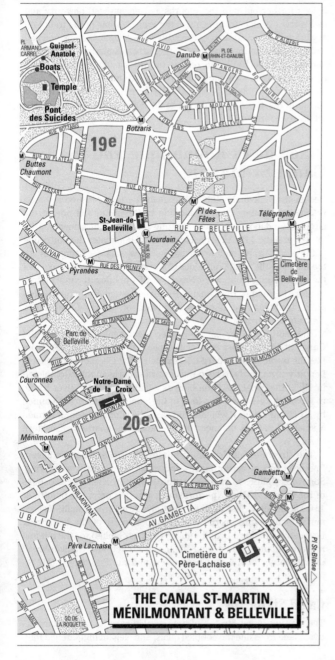

For eating and
drinking
options in the
area, see pp.
292–297.

THE CANAL ST-MARTIN, MÉNILMONTANT & BELLEVILLE

lations further out into the suburbs and encouraged new arty and media intelligentsia in, effacing in the process some of the traditional working-class character of area. If you look hard, though, you can still find some of the most fascinating urban landscapes in the city here. And while **Belleville** retains the most extraordinary mix of races and cultures, **rue du Faubourg-St-Antoine** is still full of cabinet-makers and joiners. Only **La Villette**, up in the city's northeast corner in the 19ᵉ, and **Bercy**, along the Seine in the 12ᵉ, have been totally transformed.

Place de la République and the Canal St-Martin

Designed as a pivotal point in Haussmann's counter-insurgency road scheme, the grimly barren **place de la République** is one of the largest roundabouts in Paris, abutting three arrondissements – the 3ᵉ, 10ᵉ and the 11ᵉ. An army barracks still dominates the north side of the *place*, from which seven major streets radiate, cutting through the then-volatile neighbourhoods of working-class Paris to make this the most blatant example of Napoléon III's political town-planning. In order to build it, Haussmann destroyed a number of popular theatres, including the famed Funambules of Marcel Carné's *Les Enfants du Paradis*.

The motivation for covering over a substantial section of the **Canal St-Martin** (just east of the place de la République), from Bastille to rue du Faubourg-du-Temple with the boulevard Richard-Lenoir was similarly to keep the eastern suburbs in line. Completed in 1825, the canal had been built as a short cut for the river traffic to lop off the great western loop of the Seine around Paris. Spanned by six swing-bridges, which could easily be jammed open, it formed a splendid natural defence for the rebellious quarters of eastern Paris.

The streets to either side of **boulevard Richard-Lenoir** have a fine selection of eating places and make for pleasant wandering. Some possibilities to incorporate into a walk are the iced-cake looks of the **Cirque d'Hiver** (performances Oct–Jan only; see p.363), at 110 rue Amelot, just by Filles-du-Calvaire métro; a multi-layered mural of literature on rue Nicolas-Appert (east of the boulevard, between Mᵒ Richard-Lenoir and Mᵒ Bréguet-Sabins); or the gilt and mirrored boulangerie selling Viennese, French and English bread on the corner of rue du Chemin-Vert and rue Popincourt (Mᵒ St-Ambroise).

Le Clown Bar, 14 rue Amelot, is a popular place for a drink or meal; for details of this and other nearby eating and drinking options, see p.292.

Canal St-Martin

The **southernmost stretch** of the revealed canal is the most attractive. Plane trees line the cobbled quais, and elegant high-arched footbridges punctuate the spaces between the locks, from where you can still watch the odd barge slowly rising or sinking to the next level. The canalside houses are solid bourgeois-looking residences of the mid-nineteenth century. The potential of the canal frontage has clearly caught developers' eyes, and modernization and gentrification here is well advanced. Be thankful at least it hasn't been turned into the motorway envisaged by President Pompidou.

Down side streets and back streets, ancient corners do still exist, harbouring a handful of resilient small businesses and workshops. Take the steps down to **rue des Vinaigriers**, where a Second Empire shopfront bears fluted wooden pilasters crowned with capitals of grapes and a gilded Bacchus. Across the street, the surely geriatric Cercle National des Garibaldiens still has a meeting place, and at no. 35 Poursin has been making brass buckles since 1830.

On Sundays the quais along the Canal St-Martin are closed to cars between 10am and 4pm.

On the other side of the canal, in the **rue de la Grange-aux-Belles** (see box below), the name of *Le Pont-Tournant* (The Swing-Bridge) café recalls the canal's more vigorous youth. Traditionally, the barges that once plied the canal came from the north, whence the name of the **Hôtel du Nord**, at 102 quai de Jemmapes, made famous by Marcel Carné's film starring Arletty and Jean Gabin. For a long time, there was talk of transforming the venue into a movie museum, but now, with its façade restored, it thrives as a bar and bistro, incorporated into a block of modern apartments.

Local residents are very active in the preservation of their neighbourhood – the **square Villemin** gardens abutting the canal just above rue des Récollets (see p.185) being one successful instance. A neighbourhood magazine, *La Gazette du Canal*, publicizes local campaigns and gives addresses of cafés, restaurants and events in the area.

Just across the canal from the gardens is one of the finest buildings in Paris, the early seventeenth-century **Hôpital St-Louis**, built in the same style as the **place des Vosges** (see p.104). Although it still functions as a hospital, you can walk into its quiet central courtyard and admire the elegant brick and stone façades and steep-pitched

---

The Montfaucon gallows

Long ago, **rue de la Grange-aux-Belles** was a dusty track leading uphill, past fields, en route to Germany. Where no. 53 now stands, a path led to the top of a small hillock. Here, in 1325, on the king's orders, an enormous **gallows** was built, consisting of a plinth 6m high, on which stood sixteen stone pillars each 10m high. These were joined by chains, from which malefactors were hanged in clusters. They were left there until they disintegrated, by way of example, and they stank so badly that when the wind blew from the northeast they infected the nostrils of the still far-off city. The practice continued until the seventeenth century. Bones and other remains from the pit into which they were thrown were found during the building of a garage in 1954.

roofs that once sheltered Paris' plague victims – its horrific original purpose.

Place de la Bataille de Stalingrad and Bassin de la Villette

A cycle path runs almost continuously from the Bassin de la Villette (south side) on quai de Loire to the Parc de la Villette. The ride to the Cité des Sciences is 2km.

Both banks of the canal along the northern section to La Villette were thoroughly sanitized in the late 1980s. The one major improvement is the restoration of the **place de la Bataille de Stalingrad**, now sanded and grassed.

The square is dominated by the Neoclassical **Rotonde de la Villette**, with portico and pediments surmounted by a rotunda, its stonework freshly scrubbed. This was one of the toll houses designed by the architect Ledoux as part of Louis XVI's scheme to tax all goods entering the city. At that time, every road out of the city had a customs post, or *barrière*, linked by a six-metre-high wall, known as "Le Mur des Fermiers-Généraux" – a major irritant in the run-up to the French Revolution.

The general clean-up has extended to the elegant aerial stretch of métro, supported by Neoclassical iron and stone pillars, which backs the toll house. Looking back from further up the **Bassin de la Villette**, it provides a focus for an impressive new monumental vista. The recobbled docks area today bears few traces of its days as France's premier port, its dockside buildings now offering **canal boat trips**, and boasting a multiplex cinema with a popular waterfront brasserie, *Le Rendez-Vous des Quais*. The old portside restaurant *Au Rendez-Vous de la Marine* is still going, however. On Sundays and holidays people stroll along the quais, play boules, fish or take a rowboat out in the dock, but despite the clean-up, the area retains a slightly seedy feel.

Full details of Le Rendez-Vous des Quais and Au Rendez-Vous de la Marine can be found on p.292, along with other local eating options.

At rue de Crimée, a **hydraulic bridge** dating to 1885 marks the end of the dock and the beginning of the **Canal de l'Ourcq**. To the east, the slums of the rue de Flandres have given over to new housing developments, and it's all a bit of a wasteland scenically from here up to the junction with the Canal St-Denis, where across the water lies the architectural cacophony of Paris' most extravagant high-tech park, the Parc de la Villette.

Parc de la Villette

All the meat for Paris used to come from **La Villette**. Slaughtering and butchering, and industries based on the meat markets' by-products, provided plenty of jobs for its dense population, whose recreation time was spent betting on cockfights, skating or swimming, and eating in the numerous local restaurants famed for their fresh meat. In the 1960s, vast sums of money were spent modernizing La Villette, including the building of a gigantic new abattoir. Yet, just as

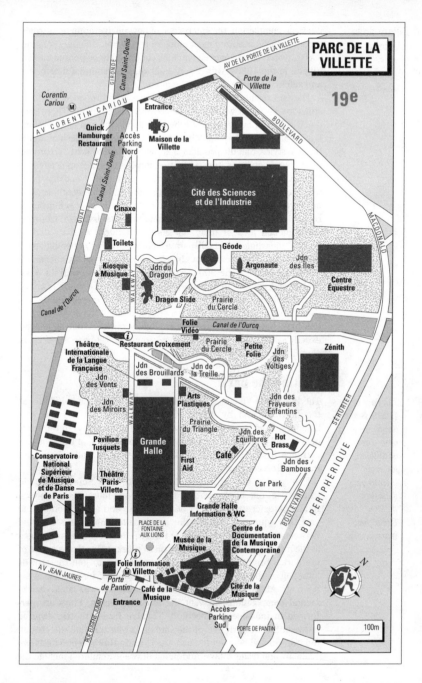

it neared completion, the emergence of new refrigeration techniques rendered the centralized meat industry redundant. The only solution was to switch course entirely: billions continued to be poured into La Villette in the 1980s, with the revised aim of creating a **music, art and science complex** to blow the mind.

The end result, the **Parc de la Villette**, which opened in 1986, stuns not so much with brilliance as with brain fatigue. There's so much going on here, most of it highly stimulating and entertaining, but it's all so disparate and disconnected, with such a clash of architectural styles, that the problem is knowing where to start. According to the park's creators, this is all intentional, and philosophically justified. Conceived by Bernard Tschumi as a futuristic "activity" park that would dispense with the eighteenth- and nineteenth-century notion of parks and gardens as places of gentle and well-ordered relaxation. Instead, we're offered a landscape that backs off from the old-fashioned idea of unity, meaning and purpose, that "deconstructs" the whole into its disparate elements, thereby opening up all possible interpretations. Yet there's something vaguely menacing about the setting. The 900-metre straight **walkway**, with its wavy shelter and complicated metal bridge across the Canal de l'Ourcq, seems to insist that you cover the park from end to end, and there's something too dogmatic about the arrangement of the bright red **follies** like chopped-off cranes, each slightly different but all spaced exactly 120m apart. The park's focal point, the Cité des Sciences, is alarming for its sheer bulk.

Visiting the park

*The Parc de la
Villette is open
daily
6am–1am;
admission fee
for some
themed gardens. See
p.359 of "Kids'
Paris" for
more details.*

The Parc de la Villette is **accessible** from M° Porte-de-la-Villette, at the northern end by avenue Corentin-Cariou and the Cité des Sciences; from the Canal de l'Ourcq's quai de la Marne to the west; or from M° Porte-de-Pantin, on avenue Jean-Jaurès, at the southern entrance by the Cité de la Musique and Grande Halle. There are **information centres** at all three entrances.

The park's key attraction is the **Cité des Sciences et de l'Industrie**, one of the world's finest science museums. High-tech film experiences are on offer at the **Cinaxe** and at the **Géode**, and you can squeeze through the *Argonaute* submarine beached between the Cité and the Canal de l'Ourcq. Rock concerts are staged at the inflatable **Zenith** venue, and there's jazz at **Hot Brass** in one of the park's bright red follies. Or you might opt to join the crowds lounging on the acres of grass known as "prairies" for a movie in the open air. At the **Cité de la Musique** you can hear the latest experimental compositions, or visit the **music museum**. Plays are performed in the nineteenth-century **Théatre Paris-Villette**, dwarfed between the western half of the Cité de la Musique and the elegant old iron-framed beef market hall, the **Grande Halle**, venue for large-scale art and trade shows. Additional draws for children include the dragon slide of recycled drums and pipes; **gardens** of "mirrors", "mists", "winds and dunes" and "islands"; other areas with trampolines, sounds, bamboos and vines; and a prairie where a giant bicycle appears half buried in the ground.

The Cité des Sciences et de l'Industrie

The park's dominant building is the enormous **Cité des Sciences et de l'Industrie**, an abandoned abattoir redesigned by architect Adrien Fainsilber into a high-tech museum. Four times the size of the Georges Pompidou Centre, from the outside it appears fortress-like, despite the transparency of its giant glass walls hanging beneath a dark blue lattice of steel, reinforced by walkways that accelerate out towards the Géode across a moat that is level with the underground floors. Once you are inside, however, the **three themes** of water (around the building), vegetation (in three greenhouses) and light (with which the building is flooded, from vast skylights as well as the glass façade), totally reverse the solidity of first impressions.

The Cité des Sciences et de l'Industrie is open Tues–Sat 10am–6pm, Sun 10am–7pm; closed Mon; 50F day-pass includes entry to Explora, temporary exhibitions, the planetarium, the Louis-Lumière Cinema and the submarine.

This is the science museum to end all science museums, and worth visiting for the interior of the building alone: all glass and stainless steel, crow's-nests and cantilevered platforms, bridges and suspended walkways, the different levels linked by lifts and escalators around a huge central space open to the full 40m height of the roof. It may be colossal, but you are more likely to lose yourself mentally rather than physically, and come out after several hours reeling with images and ideas, while possibly none the wiser (unless you read French well) about DNA, quasars, bacteria reproduction, curved space or rocket launching. Entry to the building itself is free, as are some of the facilities within – the cafés, aquarium, médiathèques, and viewing of documentaries (in French) in the Salle Jean-Bertin and the Salle Jean-Painlevé. The ticket for Explora (the permanent exhibition), with its magnetic strip, is valid throughout the day, but be careful how many times you pop in and out, as it's valid for four entries only.

An **audioguide in English** is available at the counter in the main hall (25F), and includes details about the architecture, explanations for Explora and the soundtrack for some of the planetarium shows (2pm, 3pm, 4pm & 5pm). It's recommended if you want to make the most of the museum, unless your French is very good.

For details of the Cité des Enfants, temporary exhibitions geared to kids, and the Médiathèque des Enfants (for all of which you have to be accompanied by a child), plus the Techno Cité designed for teenagers, see p.364.

The exhibition space, **Explora**, is ranged across the top two floors (pick up a detailed plan in English from the welcome desk on *niveau* 1) and includes both temporary shows and a permanent exhibition divided into twenty units. These cover a variety of subjects, among them sound, robots, computer science, expression and behaviour, oceans, energy, light, the environment, mathematics, medicine, space and language. As the name suggests, the emphasis is on exploring, and the means used are interactive computers, multimedia displays, videos, holograms, animated models and games.

On **level 1**, a classic example of chaos theory introduces the **maths section**: La Fontaine Turbulente is a wheel of glasses rotating below a stream of water in which the switch between clockwise and anticlockwise motion is unpredictable beyond two minutes. An "inertial carousel" – a revolving drum (2–6pm only) – provides a four-minute insight into the strange transformations of objects in motion. In **Les Sons** (sounds), you can watch a video of an x-rayed jaw and throat talking or sit in a cubicle and feel your body tingle with physical sensations as a rainstorm crashes around you. In **Expressions et Comportements**, you can take part in interactive videos, changing the behaviour of the characters to engineer a different outcome, and you can watch an "Odorama" video. In **Computers**, you can steer robots through mazes, make music by your own movements, try out a flight simulation, or watch computer-guided puppet shows and holograms of different eras' visions of the universe.

On **level 2**, in the **biology section**, you can examine microbes magnified millions of times. In the **medicine section**, smell the herbs used by different cultures as alternative remedies. In **Etoiles et Galaxies**, explore large-scale models of space rockets and space stations and a real Mirage jet fighter. The **Jeux de Lumière** is a whole series of experiments to do with colour, optical illusions, refraction and the like. You can have your head spun further by a session in the **planetarium** (shows 11am, noon, 2pm, 3pm, 4pm & 5pm; 35min; audioguide in English is 25F and does not translate the first two showings); to be sure of a seat you can book a place when buying your ticket.

There are always several **temporary exhibitions** within Explora (and in other spaces throughout the building), plus a major one each year based on an inter-disciplinary theme to which all the natural and social sciences, plus art and literature, can be brought into play.

Back on the ground floor, the **Cinéma Louis-Lumière** shows short stereoscopic (3D) films every half hour or so, for which you'll have to queue. General documentaries in French only are shown in the **Salle Jean-Bertin** (programmes at 10.15am, 2.15pm & 4.15pm; free), and more serious scientific documentaries in the **Salle Jean-Painlevé** (*niveau* S1; Sat & Sun 4pm & 5.30pm; free). In the **Médiathèque** (S1 & S2; noon–8pm; free), a multi-media library, you can select from over 4000 films at individual consoles, as well as consulting educational software, books and magazines. Information on current French and international scientific research is displayed in the **Salle Science Actualités** (S1), next door to the new **Cité des Métiers** (noon–8pm; free), the latter of which provides free access to information on finding work, changing careers, training, creating your own employment, and working conditions in different countries. It even offers an on-the-spot consultancy with a careers advisor. Finally, on the lowest floor (S2), you can eat and drink beside an **aquarium** filled with Mediterranean sea life.

Parc de la Villette

The Géode, the Cinaxe and the Argonaute
In front of the museum complex balances the **Géode**, a bubble of reflecting steel dropped from an intergalactic boules game into a pool of water that ripples with the mirrored image of the Cité. Inside, the sphere holds a screen for Omnimax 180° films, not noted for their plots but a great visual experience. Or there's the **Cinaxe**, between the Cité and the Canal St-Denis (screenings every 15min 11am–6pm, closed Mon; 34F, or 29F with day-pass) combining 70mm film shot at thirty frames a second with seats that move, so that a bobsleigh ride down the Cresta Run, for example, not only looks unbelievably real, but feels it, too. You can clamber around a real 1957 French military **submarine** beside the Géode, the *Argonaute* (Tues–Fri 10.30am–5.30pm, Sat & Sun 10.30am–6pm; 25F, or free with day-pass), and view the park through its periscope.

The Géode has hourly shows (57F) 10am–9pm; closed Mon.

The Cité de la Musique
Crossing the Canal de L'Ourcq south of the Géode, a walkway leads past Grande Salle to the **Cité de la Musique**, in two complexes either side of the Porte-de-Pantin entrance. To the west the waves and funnels, irregular polygons and non-parallel lines of the avenue Conservatoire de Paris, the city's music school, make abstract sense: windows in sequences like musical notation; the wavy roof, which, according to the architect, **Christian de Portzamparc**, is like a Gregorian chant, but could equally suggest the movement of a dancer or a conductor's baton; and the crescendo of the rising curves of the façade.

The wedge-shaped complex to the east contains the public spaces, which include the brand-new Musée de la Musique, the chic *Café de la Musique*, a music and dance information centre, and a concert hall whose ovoid dome rises like a perfect soufflé from the roof line. The harsh semi-exterior element of a girdered "arrow" pointing down to the entrance arch pretending to be another red folly hides an unexpectedly sensual interior. A glass-roofed arcade surrounds the auditorium with pale blue sloping walls that give out deep relaxation sounds. Other walls are coloured and textured like abstract paintings.

The Café de la Musique *is detailed on p.293, along with the popular Lebanese* Au Saveurs du Liban.

The Musée de la Musique
The **Musée de la Musique** presents the history of music from the end of the Renaissance to the present day, both visually, exhibiting some 4500 instruments, and aurally, via headsets (available in English;

*The Musée de
la Musique is
open Tues–
Thurs
noon–6pm, Fri
& Sat noon–
7.30pm, Sun
10am–6pm;
35F; M° Porte-
de-Pantin.*

free) and interactive displays. Glass case after glass case hold gleaming, beautiful instruments – bejewelled crystal flutes and a fabulous lyre-guitar, all made in Paris in the early 1800s, are some impressive examples – with a minimum of written word. The instruments are presented in the context of a key work in the history of Western music: as you step past each case, the headphones are programmed to emit a short scholarly narration, followed by a delightful concert. It's truly a transporting – and educational – experience to gaze at the grouping of harps, made in Paris between 1760 and 1900, which are as heavenly looking as the music you're hearing. It seems an oversight that there is not a single seat from which to listen to the music in comfort.

The museum also includes an **auditorium**, where regular concerts are held, in addition to a huge musical documentation centre, and spaces for workshops, films and audiovisuals.

Belleville, Ménilmontant and Charonne

The old villages of **Belleville**, **Ménilmontant** and **Charonne**, only incorporated into the city in 1860, are strung out along the western slopes of a ridge that rises steadily from the Seine at Bercy to an altitude of 128m near Belleville's place des Fêtes, the highest point in Paris after Montmartre. The area is popular with the young and arty – Ménilmontant in particular hosts quite an alternative scene with some good bars. The quickest and easiest way to get out here is to take a trip on the #26 **bus** from the Gare du Nord, getting on and off at strategic points along the **avenue de Simon-Bolivar** and **rue des Pyrénées**, which between them run the whole length of the ridge to Porte de Vincennes.

At the northern end of the Belleville heights, the sculpted **Parc des Buttes-Chaumont** looks like something from a fairy tale, with its lake overlooked by a temple-crowned promontory. It was constructed under the guidance of Haussmann in the 1860s to camouflage what until then had been a desolate warren of disused quarries, rubbish dumps and shacks. The park stays open all night and, equally rarely for Paris, you're not cautioned off the grass.

At its centre, a huge rock upholds a delicate Corinthian temple. You can cross the lake that surrounds it, via a suspension bridge, or take the shorter **Pont des Suicides**. This, according to Louis Aragon, the literary grand old man of the French Communist Party, "before metal grills were erected along its sides, claimed victims even from passersby who had had no intention whatsoever of killing themselves but were suddenly tempted by the abyss . . ." (*Le Paysan de Paris*).

Most striking, however, is the unlikeliness of this park – that it exists in this erstwhile working-class corner of the city, with its views of the Sacré-Cœur and beyond, its grotto of stalactites, and the concrete fences moulded to imitate wood.

Belleville

East of the parc des Buttes-Chaumont, between rue de Crimée and **place de Rhin-et-Danube**, dozens of cobbled and gardened *villas* lead off from rue Miguel-Hidalgo, rue du Général-Brunet, rue de la Liberté, rue de l'Égalité and rue de Mouzaïa. It is so light and airy here, you wonder why places like Auteuil and Passy should ever have seemed so much more desirable. Heading south, the first main street you meet is the **rue de Belleville**. Close to its highest point is the **place des Fêtes**, still with a market, though no longer so festive. Once the village green, it's now surrounded by concrete tower blocks and shopping parades, a terrible monument to the unimaginative redevelopment of the 1960s and 1970s. However, the little *place* is green nonetheless, containing a small park with a rotunda, lawns and trees, its benches filled with locals on a pleasant day. As you descend the steepening gradient of rue Belleville, round the church of St-Jean-Baptiste-de-Belleville, among the boulangeries and charcuteries, you could be in the busy main street of any French provincial town. Continuing down rue de Belleville past rue des Pyrénées, at the corner of **rue Julien-Lacroix**, you come to a square that has been created from an empty lot. On the side of one of the exposed apartment building walls, there's a large mural of a detective and nearby the neo-realist artist Ben has sculpted a trompe-l'œil sculpture of a sign being erected which says "*Il faut se mélier des mots*" ("Words must be mistrusted").

The nearest métro to place des Fêtes is M° Place-des-Fêtes; nearest to the church of St-Jean-Baptiste-de-Belleville is M° Jourdain; and nearest to rue Julien-Lacroix is M° Pyrénées.

Below rue des Pyrénées, bits of old Belleville remain – dilapidated – alongside the new. On the wall of no. 72 rue de Belleville, a plaque commemorates the birth of the legendary chanteuse, **Édith Piaf**, although she was in fact found abandoned as a baby on the steps here.

The Musée Édith Piaf is detailed on p.202.

A little lower off rue de Belleville, the cobbled **rue Piat** climbs past the beautiful wrought-iron gate of the jungly **Villa Otoz** to the **Parc**

Claude Chappe and the rue du Télégraphe

The **rue du Télégraphe**, running south off the eastern end of rue de Belleville alongside the **Cimetière de Belleville**, is named in memory of Claude Chappe's invention of the optical telegraph. Chappe first tested his device here in September 1792, in a corner of the cemetery. When word of his activities got out, he was nearly lynched by a mob that assumed he was trying to signal to the king, who was at that time imprisoned in the Temple (see p.112). Eventually, two lines were set up, from Belleville to Strasbourg and the east, and from Montmartre to Lille and the north. By 1840, it was possible to send a message to Calais in three minutes, via 27 relays, and to Strasbourg in seven minutes, using 46 relays.

Belleville,
Ménilmon-
tant and
Charonne

*The
restaurants of
Belleville are
detailed on
pp.292–295.*

de Belleville, created in the mid-1990s. From the terrace at the junction with rue des Envierges, there's a fantastic view across the city, especially at sunset. At your feet, the small park descends in a series of more terraces and waterfalls – a total success compared to the nondescript development of the previous decade. Inevitably, this has brought the establishment of one or two rather chic eating and drinking places in the surrounding area.

Continuing straight ahead, a path crosses the top of the park past a minuscule vineyard and turns into steps that drop down to **rue des Couronnes**. Some of the adjacent streets are worth a wander for a feel of the changing times – rue de la Mare, rue des Envierges, rue des Cascades – with two or three beautiful old houses in overgrown gardens, alongside new housing that follows the height and curves of the streets and *passages* between them.

Between the bottom of the park and boulevard de Belleville, original housing and a teeming street life have been almost erased, despite the concerted efforts of the local organization for the preservation of Belleville. They fought hard for restoration rather than demolition and for saving the little cafés, restaurants and shops that gave the quartier its animation. Rue Ramponeau, running west from the Parc de Belleville, has a historic record of resistance: at the junction with rue de Tourtille, the very last barricade of the Commune was defended single-handedly for fifteen minutes by the last fighting Communard, before he melted away – to write a book about it all.

It's also in these streets and on the boulevard that the strong ethnic diversity of Belleville becomes apparent. Rue Ramponeau, for example, is still full of kosher shops, belonging to Sephardic Jews from Tunisia. Around the crossroads of rue du Faubourg-du-Temple and boulevard de Belleville, there are dozens of Chinese restaurants and a scattering of eateries owned by Turks, Greeks and East European descendants of refugees from nineteenth-century pogroms in Russia and Poland, and from the twentieth-century atrocities of the Nazis. On the boulevard, especially during the Tuesday and Friday morning market, you see women from Mali, Gambia and

---

La descente de la Courtille

The name *Courtille* comes from *courti*, "garden" in the Picard dialect. The heights of Belleville were known as **La Haute Courtille** in the nineteenth century, while the lower part around rue du Faubourg-du-Temple and rue de la Fontaine-au-Roi was **La Basse Courtille**. Both were full of boozers and dance halls, where people flocked from the city on high days and holidays.

The wildest revels of the year took place on the night of Mardi Gras, when thousands of masked people turned out to celebrate the end of the *carnaval*. Next morning – Ash Wednesday – they descended in drunken procession from Belleville to the city, in up to a thousand horse-drawn vehicles: *la descente de la Courtille*.

Zaire, often wearing local dress, and men in burnouses. All this diversity is reflected in the produce on sale.

The boulevard is now lined with dramatic new architecture, employing jutting triangles, curves, and the occasional reference to the roof lines of nineteenth-century Parisian blocks. The combination of old and new continues in **Basse Belleville**, in the large triangle of streets below boulevard de Belleville, bounded by rue du Faubourg-du-Temple (the most lively) and avenue de la République. The area retains a blend of French and immigrant workshops, small businesses, and traditional houses built with *passages* burrowing into courtyards. Here, *La Java*, at 105 rue du Faubourg-du-Temple, was a favourite hang-out of Piaf's in its *bal musette* days; the original dance hall interior is still intact, but the dancing and music now distinctly Latino. Zany high-tech metal and glass at no. 117 on the same street co-exists with small unchanged business premises in the Cour des Bretons. Goods still cost around half the price that they do in shops in the centre of the city, despite a number of increasingly fashionable restaurants.

Belleville, Ménilmontant and Charonne

For details about entertainment at La Java, see p.302 of "Music and nightlife".

Ménilmontant

Like Belleville, **Ménilmontant** aligns itself along one straight, steep, long street, the rue de Ménilmontant. It has always been less dilapidated than Belleville, and although it has its black spots, it somehow seems more respectable.

The bygone eastern villages

Before redevelopment, the superb hillside location combined with cobbled lanes, individual gardens, numerous stairways, and local shops and cafés perfectly integrated with human-scale housing, gave the area around Belleville and Ménilmontant a unique charm – quite the equal of Montmartre, but without the touristy commercialism.

For a picture of what it was like, there's no more evocative record than Willy Ronis's atmospheric photographs in *Belleville Ménilmontant*. But there's still on-the-ground evidence, in addition to the little cul-de-sacs of terraced houses and gardens east of rue des Pyrénées. There are alleys so narrow that nothing but the knife-grinder's tricycle could fit down them, like **passage de la Duée**, 17 rue de la Duée, and little detached houses, like 97 rue Villiers-de-l'Îsle-Adam. You can also see the less romantic side of life in the grim neo-Gothic fortress housing estates of 140 rue de Ménilmontant, built in 1925 for the influx of rural populations after World War I, and the 1913 Villa Stendhal, off rue Stendhal. In marked contrast is the housing right over to the east, near the Porte de Bagnolet, provided for workers in 1908 and almost unmatched in the city. From place Octave-Chanute, wide stone steps bordered by lanterns lead up to a miraculous little sequence of streets of terraced houses and gardens, some with Art Nouveau glass porches, fancy brickwork and the shade of lilac and cherry trees.

Café Charbon,
in a renovated
dance hall, is
among the
hippest places
in rue
Oberkampf's
unique bar
scene; for
more of the
like, see p.293.

For half its length, the **rue de Ménilmontant** is a busy, multi-racial shopping street, full of traditional, small shops and snack bars, the continuation of the equally busy rue Oberkampf. The upper reaches, above rue Sorbier, are quieter. Looking back from here, you find yourself dead in line with the rooftop of the Centre Beaubourg, a measure of how high you are above the rest of the city.

Like Belleville itself, the area closest to boulevard Belleville has been almost completely demolished and rebuilt – on a small scale, around courtyards with open spaces for kids to play. Centred around rue des Amandiers, this part of Ménilmontant is all a bit squeaky-clean and unweathered as yet, and the café count has dropped to near zero. **Rue Elisa-Borey** turns into steps alongside the extraordinary France Telecom building, which is topped with great bunches of masts and faces a lovely small park on rue Sorbier.

Cross the park, take a right, then a left into rue Boyer, and you'll find the splendid mosaic and sculpted constructivist façade of **La Bellevilloise** at no. 25, built for the PCF in 1925 to celebrate fifty years of work and science. Saved from demolition by a preservation order, it is now home to a theatre school.

A short way before it, a delightful lane of village houses and gardens, **rue Laurence-Savart**, climbs up to rue du Retrait. The latter street ends on rue des Pyrénées opposite the poetically named alley of sighs, the *"passage des Soupirs"*. **Rue des Pyrénées**, the main cross-route through this quartier, is itself redolent of the provinces, getting busier as it approaches place Gambetta. The post office at no. 248 has a big ceramic wall-piece by the sculptor Zadkine. Close by place Gambetta, on rue Malte-Brun, is the big glass frontage of the **Théâtre National de la Colline**, built in 1987 to replace the dingy old cinema that used to house the theatre. You can snack in its **cafeteria** and pick up brochures on current productions.

Just 200m west of the place Gambetta is the Père-Lachaise cemetery (see p.204). There is more melancholy to be found near the northeast corner of the cemetery, where the the **street names** echo the long-vanished orchards and rustic pursuits of the villagers: Amandiers (almond trees), Pruniers (plum trees), Mûriers (mulberry trees), Pressoir (wine press). Further west, across boulevard de Ménilmontant, another era is captured in the **Musée Édith Piaf**, at 5 rue Créspin-du-Gast. Piaf was not an acquisitive person: the few clothes (yes, a little black dress), letters, toys, paintings and photographs that she left are almost all here, along with every one of her recordings. The venue is a small flat lived in by her devoted friend Bernard Marchois, and the "Amis d'Édith Piaf" will show you around and tell you stories about her.

The Musée
Édith Piaf is
open
Mon–Thurs
1–6pm; closed
Sept; admis-
sion by
appointment
only on
☎01.43.55.52.
72 (donation);
M° Ménil-
montant & M°
St-Maur.

Charonne

With it's perfect little Romanesque church, St-Germain-de-Charonne, and the cobbled street of rue St-Blaise, Charonne retains

its village-like atmosphere. To get to this unexpected and little visited corner of the city, take the southwest radial, avenue du Père-
Lachaise from place Gambetta, and then turn left along rue des
Rondeaux, the street that follows the Père-Lachaise cemetery wall,
past some very desirable residences. Cross rue des Pyrénées by the
bridge in rue Renouvier, turn right on rue Stendhal (Villa Stendhal
is opposite – see box on p.201serves as a gigantic header tank for
the stopcocks that wash the city's gutters, and go down the steps at
the end to rue de Bagnolet. Alternatively, take rue Lisfranc off rue
Stendhal and right on rue des Prairies then straight on to rue de
Bagnolet. It's a longer way round, but **rue des Prairies** has excellent
examples of sensitive and imaginative housing developments. The
new buildings have a pleasing variety of designs and colours, with
bright tiling and ochre shades of cladding.

In place St-Blaise stands **St-Germain-de-Charonne**, which
has changed little, and its Romanesque belfry not at all, since the
thirteenth century. It's one of only two Paris churches to have its
own graveyard (the other is St-Pierre in Montmartre) – several
hundred murdered Communards were buried after being accidentally disinterred during the construction of a reservoir in
1897. Elsewhere in Paris, charnel houses were the norm, with
the bones emptied into the catacombs as more space was
required. It was not until the nineteenth century that public
cemeteries appeared on the scene, the most famous being **Père-
Lachaise** (see overleaf).

Opposite the church, the old cobbled village high street, **rue St-
Blaise**, pedestrianized to place des Grés, was one of the most picturesque in Paris, until it was prettified further, the face-lift remov-
ing much of its charm. Beyond place des Grès, everything has been
rebuilt, and though an avenue of green trees has softened the hard
new edges of the modern housing development, the line of shops
(including a supermarket) are characterless as are the few cafés.
Rue de Vitruve, however, which crosses rue St-Blaise at place des
Grès, has a great modern swimming pool and the colourfully modern *Artignan* youth hostel just to the north (see p.248 for details);
and to the south, at no. 39, a school, built in 1982. Designed by
Jacques Bardet, the school's rectangular mass is broken up by
open-air segments, enclosed only by the structural steel lattice of
the building over which plants spread. But the best thing is hidden
round the corner, visible as you approach from rue des Pyrénées –
a huge sculptured **salamander** and its footprints mounted on the
windowless side of a building on rue R-A-Marquet. Engraved above
the street sign are the words: "A legend is told that a salamander,
after passing by the square where it would have left a long trail, set
off towards rue R-A-Marquet and stopped to rest on a corner of rue
Vitruve."

Belleville,
Ménilmon-
tant and
Charonne

*A great place
for a drink
amid some
wild decor is*
La Fleche d'Or,
*at 102 bis rue
Bagnolet; for
details on this
and other eat-
ing & drinking
options, see
p.293.*

*The nearest
métros to the
church of St-
Germain-de-
Charonne are
M° Porte de
Bagnolet & M°
Gambetta.*

Père-Lachaise cemetery

The **cimetière Père-Lachaise** is like a miniature city devastated by a neutron bomb: a great number of dead, empty houses and temples of every size and style, and exhausted survivors, some congregating aimlessly, some searching persistently for their favourite famous dead in an arrangement of numbered divisions that is neither entirely haphazard nor strictly systematic.

The cemetery is open daily 7.30am–6pm; free; Mᵒ Gambetta & Mᵒ Père-Lachaise & Mᵒ Alexandre-Dumas.

The cemetery was opened in 1804 and was an incredibly successful piece of land speculation. Nicolas Frochot, the urban planner who bought the land, persuaded the civil authorities to have **Molière**, **La Fontaine**, **Abélard** and **Héloïse** reburied in his new cemetery. To be interred in Père-Lachaise quickly became the ultimate status symbol for the rich and successful. Ironically, Frochot even sold a plot to the original owner for considerably more money than the price he had paid for the entire site. Even today, the rates are still extremely high.

Pick up a free map at the rue des Rondeaux entrance by av du Père-Lachaise; 10F buys a more detailed map from the newsagents and florists on av Père-Lachaise, or near bd de Ménilmontant entrance.

Some of the most celebrated dead have unremarkable tombs, while those whose fame died with them have the most expressive monuments. Swarms flock to ex-Doors lead singer **Jim Morrison**'s tomb in Division 6. Once graffiti-covered and wreathed in marijuana fumes, it has been completely refurbished, its neighbours scrubbed clean as well, and put under police guard to ensure it stays that way. Femme fatale **Colette**'s tomb, close to the main entrance in Division 4, is very plain, though always covered in flowers. The same holds true for the divine **Sarah Bernhardt**'s (Division 44) and the great chanteuse **Édith Piaf**'s (Division 97). **Marcel Proust** lies in his family's conventional tomb (Division 85), which honours the medical fame of his father.

In contrast, one **Jean Pezon**, a lion-tamer, is shown riding the pet lion that ate him (Division 86). In Division 92, nineteenth-century journalist **Victor Noir** – shot for daring to criticize a relative of Napoléon III – lies flat on his back, fully clothed, his top hat fallen by his feet. His prostrate figure has been a magnet, not for anti-censorship campaigners, but for infertile women rubbing themselves against him as a sexual charm. Close by, a forgotten French diplomat must turn in his grave with envy – he provided himself with an enormous tapering phallus, admirably higher than the trees around it, in Division 48. In Division 71, two men lie together hand in hand – a pair of balloonists who went so high they died from lack of oxygen.

Other bed scenes include **Félix Faure** (Division 4), French president, who died in the arms of his mistress in the Élysée palace in 1899. Draped in a French flag like a sheet, his head is raised and his hand seems to be groping the flagpole as if it might be his lover. **Géricault** reclines on cushions of stone (Division 12), paint palette in hand, his neck and bony face taut with concentration. Close by is

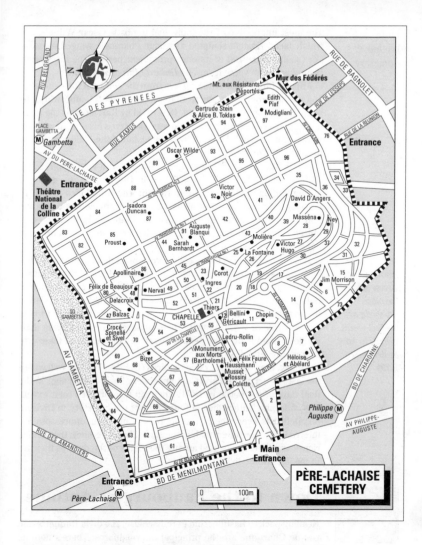

PÈRE-LACHAISE CEMETERY

Mur des Fédérés

Mt. aux Résistants Déportés

Edith Piaf

Gertrude Stein & Alice B. Toklas · 94

Modigliani · 97

Entrance

Oscar Wilde · 93

Gambetta

AV. DU PÈRE-LACHAISE

RUE DES PYRÉNÉES

RUE BELGRAND

RUE RAMUS

RUE DE BAGNOLET

RUE DE LESSEPS

RUE DE LA RÉUNION

PLACE GAMBETTA

Entrance

Théâtre National de la Colline

Isadora Duncan · 87

Proust ·

Victor Noir ·

David D'Angers

Masséna · Ney

Auguste Blanqui · 91

Sarah Bernhardt

Molière

La Fontaine

Victor Hugo

Apollinaire · 86

Corot

Ingres

Jim Morrison

Félix de Beaujour · 80

Nerval ·

Delacroix

Balzac · 47

Thiers

Bellini · Chopin

Géricault

CHAPELLE

Crocé-Spinelli et Sivel · 71

Ledru-Rollin

Bizet

Monument aux Morts (Bartholomé)

Félix Faure

Haussmann

Héloïse et Abélard

Musset

Rossini

Colette

Philippe Auguste

AV PHILIPPE-AUGUSTE

RUE DES AMANDIERS

AV GAMBETTA

BD DE CHARONNE

Main Entrance

Entrance

BD DE MÉNILMONTANT

Père-Lachaise

0   100m

the relaxed figure of **Jean Carriès**, a model-maker, in felt hat and overalls, holding one of his figures in the palm of his hand. For a more fearsome view of death, there's the tomb of a French judge, **Raphaël Roger**, in Division 94, where a figure, cowled from head to foot, stands sentinel beneath a pointed arch; or the poet in Division 6, bursting out of his granite block.

Painter **Corot** (Division 24) and novelist **Balzac** (Division 48) both have superb busts, Balzac looking particularly satisfied with his life. **Chopin** (Division 11) has a willowy muse weeping for his loss.

The most impressive of the individual tombs is **Oscar Wilde's**, for which Jacob Epstein sculpted a strange Pharaonic winged messenger (sadly vandalized of its once prominent penis). The inscription behind is a grim verse from *The Ballad of Reading Gaol*.

Approaching Oscar Wilde's grave from the centre of the cemetery, you pass the tomb of **Auguste Blanqui** (Division 91), after whom so many French streets are named. Described by Karl Marx as the nineteenth century's greatest revolutionary, he served his time in jail – 33 years in all – for political activities that spanned the 1830 Revolution to the Paris Commune.

Below Blanqui's and Wilde's graves – along with Victor Noir, Édith Piaf and Raphaël Roger – you'll find in Division 96 the grave of **Modigliani** and his lover **Jeanne Herbuterne**, who killed herself in crazed grief a few days after he died in agony from meningitis. **Laura Marx**, Karl's daughter, and her husband **Paul Lafargue**, who committed suicide together in 1911, also lie in this southeast corner of the cemetery (Division 76).

The rue de la Réunion and streets around the place Gambetta are the best places nearby to eat or drink. See p.294.

It is the monuments to the collective, violent deaths, however, that have the power to change a sunny outing to Père-Lachaise into a much more sombre experience. In Division 97, you'll find the memorials to the **victims of the Nazi concentration camps**, to executed **Resistance fighters** and to those who were never accounted for in the genocide of World War II. The sculptures are relentless in their images of inhumanity, of people forced to collaborate in their own degradation and death.

Finally, there is the **Mur des Fedérés** (Division 76), the wall where the last troops of the Paris Commune were lined up and shot in the final days of the battle in 1871. The man who ordered their execution, **Adolphe Thiers**, lies in the centre of the cemetery in Division 55. Defeat is everywhere: the oppressed and their oppressors are interred with the same ritual, in the same illustrious spot; the relative riches and fame as unequal among the tombs of the dead as they are in the lives of the living.

Down to the Faubourg St-Antoine

Heading back to Bastille from Père-Lachaise, **rue de la Roquette** and **rue de Charonne** are the principal thoroughfares. There's nothing particularly special about the numerous passages and ragged streets that lead off into the lower 11e arrondissement, except that they are utterly Parisian, with the odd detail of a building, the obscurity of a shop's speciality, the display of vegetables in a simple greengrocer's, the sunlight on a café table, or the graffiti on a Second Empire street fountain to charm an aimless wanderer. And the occasional reminder of the sheer political toughness of French working-class tradition, as in the plaque on some flats in **rue de la Folie-Regnault** commemorating the first FTP (Francs-Tireurs Partisans) Resistance group, which used to meet here until it was betrayed and its members executed in 1941. Further north, **square de la Roquette** was the site of an old prison, where 4000 members of the Resistance were incarcerated in 1944. The low, foreboding gateway on rue de la Roquette has been preserved in their memory.

South of rue de Charonne, between rue St-Bernard and impasse Charrière, stands the rustic-looking **church of Ste-Marguerite**, with a garden beside it dedicated to the memory of Raoul Nordling, the Swedish consul who persuaded the retreating Germans not to blow up Paris in 1944. The church itself was built in 1624 to accommodate the growing population of the faubourg, which was about 40,000 in 1710 and 100,000 in 1900. The sculptures on the transept pediments were made by its first full-blown parish priest. The inside of the church is wide-bodied, low and quiet, with an un-urban feel, as if it were still out in the fields. The stained-glass windows record a very local history: the visit in 1802 of Pope Pius VII, who was in Paris for Napoléon's coronation; the miraculous cure of a Madame Delafosse in the rue de Charonne on May 31, 1725; the fatal wounding of Monseigneur Affre, the archbishop of Paris, in the course of a street battle in the faubourg on June 25, 1848; the murder of sixteen Carmelite nuns at the Barrière du Trône in 1794 (presumably, more revolutionary anti-clericalism); and the quartier's dead of World War I.

In the now disused cemetery of Ste-Marguerite, the story goes – though no-one has been able to prove it – lies the body of Louis XVII, the 10-year-old heir of the guillotined Louis XVI, who died in the Temple prison (see box on p.112). The cemetery also received the dead from the Bastille prison.

From square R-Nordling, rue de la Forge-Royale – with the *Casbah* nightclub magnificently decorated in North African style at no. 18 – takes you down to rue du Faubourg-St-Antoine. Or you can continue down rue de Charonne and hit the stretch of Faubourg-St-Antoine that has a series of courtyards, villas and alleyways, providing quiet havens from the the the Bastille traffic. At no. 56, ivy and roses curtain the building, with window boxes on every storey, and lemon trees in tubs tilted on the cobbles.

After Louis XI licensed the establishment of craftsmen in the fifteenth century, the faubourg became the principal working-class quartier of Paris, cradle of revolutions and mother of street-fighters. From its beginnings, the principal trade associated with it has been **furniture-making**, and this was where the classic styles of French furniture – Louis Quatorze, Louis Quinze, Second Empire – were developed. The maze of interconnecting yards and *passages* are still full of the workshops of the related trades: stainers, polishers, inlayers and the like, many of whom are still producing those styles.

To the east, rue du Faubourg-St-Antoine ends at **place de la Nation**, along with boulevard Voltaire which cuts diagonally right across the 11e arrondissement and the continuation of boulevard de Ménilmontant.

Down to the Faubourg St-Antoine

The nearest métro to rue de la Folie-Regnault and square de la Roquette is M⁰ Phillipe-Auguste.

Ste-Marguerite is open Mon–Sat 8am–noon & 3–7.30pm, Sun 8.30am–noon & 5–7.30pm; M⁰ Charonne.

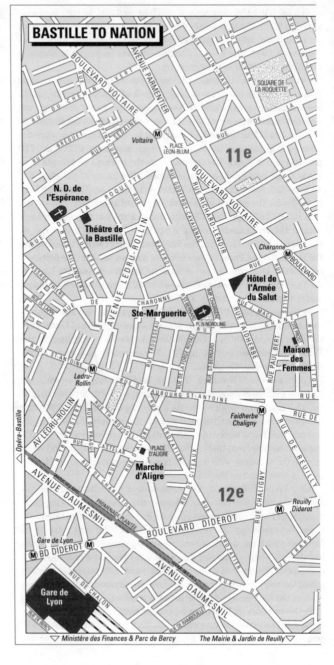

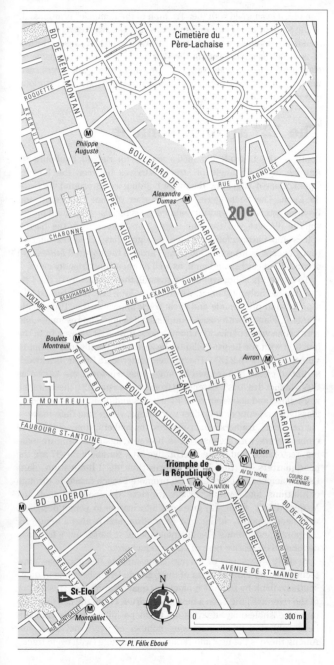

Down to the Faubourg St-Antoine

For eating and drinking options in the rue du Faubourg-St-Antoine area, see p.295.

The *place* is adorned with the "Triumph of the Republic" bronze, and, at the start of the Cours de Vincennes, the bizarre ensemble of two medieval monarchs, looking very small and sheepish in pens on the top of two high columns. During the Revolution, when the old name of place du Trône became place du Trône-Renversé, ("the overturned throne"), more people were guillotined here than on the more notorious execution site of place de la Concorde.

The 12ᵉ arrondissement

South of the Ledru-Rollin métro station on rue du Faubourg-St-Antoine, a small tangle of streets survives between the Bastille Opera, place d'Aligre and the major building works around the **Gare du Lyon**. The boulangerie on the corner of rues Charenton and Emilio-Castelar has beautiful painted glass panels – and good bread. On rue d'Aligre you can buy tagine pots, olives from the barrel, spices and cheap clothes. **Place d'Aligre**, has a raucous market (daily except Mon) with food in and around the covered *halles* and second-hand clothes and junk, as well as cheap and friendly cafés.

The place d'Aligre and other food markets are detailed on p.344.

To the south, along avenue **Daumesnil**, the main artery of the 12ᵉ, runs the old railway viaduct, which has, at long last, been turned into a pedestrian promenade and cycle track known as the "Promenade Plantée". Planted with roses, camellias, viburnum and rosemary, and with prime views of chaotic chimneypots, it runs all the way from the junction with rue Ledru-Rollin to the Jardin de Reuilly and on out to Vincennes (see p.213). The arches underneath, their brickwork scrubbed clean, and fronted by huge glass windows, are known as the "Viaduct des Arts". Extending from no. 9 to no. 129, these are the workshops and showrooms of 45 artisans and designers – including glassblowers, copper and silver workshops, violin- and flute-makers, hat designers, framers, paper-makers, toy-makers, stone-cutters and embroiderers, with the main focus, however, again on furniture-making, restoration and related decorative arts. Numbers 29–37 are the headquarters of the VIA (Valorisation de l'Innovation dans l'Ameublement), whose task is to promote French furniture through exhibitions and events. SEMA (Societé d'Encouragement aux Métiers d'Art), at no. 23, gives out information to young designers who need support, advice and promotion, and is also a venue for temporary exhibitions of indigenous talent. It hands out a free map detailing the creative bent of each viaduct arch.

The VIA is open Mon–Sat 10.30am–7pm, Sun 11am–6pm; free; ☎01.46.28.11. 11 for exhibition details; SEMA is open Tues–Fri 1–5pm, plus weekends (same hours) during exhibitions; ☎01.55.78.85. 85; Mᵒ Gare de Lyon & Mᵒ Bastille.

A short way south of avenue Daumesnil is the gorgeous nineteenth-century extravaganza of the **Gare de Lyon**, hemmed in on its southern flank by the office blocks of quai de la Rapée. This stretch of the river has long been a business quarter, but in the last ten years or so the whole quayside right out to the périphérique has gradually been subjected to an increasing number of major developments. Among these is the new and rather elegant bridge (with cycle track),

Pont Charles de Gaulle, between Pont d'Austerlitz and Pont de Bercy.

Just downstream of the **Pont de Bercy** is the **Ministère des Finances**, built in 1988 after the treasury staff had finally agreed to move out of the Richelieu wing of the Louvre. It stretches like a giant loading bridge from above the river (where higher bureaucrats and ministers arrive by boat) to rue de Bercy, a distance of some 400m. Kafka would have loved it, and contemporary Czechs would probably imagine the hand of Stalin on it. The best view of the monster is from the Charles-de-Gaulle–Nation métro line as it crosses the Pont de Bercy.

From the métro – which also gives good views of the new national library, the Bibliothèque Nationale de France François Mitterand, on the opposite bank – you can see, on the east side of boulevard de Bercy, the **Palais Omnisports de Bercy**. Built in 1983, its concrete bunker frame, clad with sloping lawns, covers a vast arena used for sporting and cultural events. Beyond it used to be the old Bercy warehouses, where for centuries the capital's wine supplies were unloaded from river barges. This has now been turned into a very welcome green space, the **Parc de Bercy**, with various sculptural oddities, neat flowerbeds with box hedges, an *orangerie*, a "Pavillon" for contemporary art expos (Wed–Sun, noon–6pm; free), and a single house preserved from the old days. In the course of demolition and excavation, archeologists unearthed the remains of Neolithic dug-out boats, dwellings and other bits and pieces dating back to around 4000 BC, adding an extra dimension to the city's history.

There are still wine vendors on avenue **des-Terroirs-de-France**, beyond the southern edge of the park, selling wholesale and to the public from gleaming modern offices, and the privately owned funfair museum, the **Musée des Arts Forains** at no. 53, is housed in one of Bercy's old stone wine warehouses. At the time of writing, it offers tours to groups only, though this may change, and at any rate, there's no stopping you peeking into the entrance at the traditional architecture.

New constructions surround the park, from the ugly megahotels rearing up beside the Palais Omnisports to the line of steel and reflecting glass offices at the eastern end, and a new 18-screen multiplex cinema, Ciné Cité. On the north side, on rue Paul-Belmondo, is the now-closed **American Centre**, designed by the architect Frank O. Gehry. Constructed from zinc, glass and limestone, it resembles a falling pack of cards – according to Gehry, the inspiration was Matisse's collages, done "with a simple pair of scissors".

Bercy's grand-scale new development is to complement the emerging "Seine Rive Gauche" (see p.167) on the opposite bank. Planners have envisaged the whole of eastern Paris as the new ultramodern, high-tech zone of the city, between the two "poles" of La

The 12e arrondissement

The Palais Omnisports de Bercy (Mo Bercy) is the place for spectator sports; see p.356 for details.

Villette and the Seine Rive Gauche. For the moment, however, Bercy is cut off from the rest of the 12ᵉ arrondissement by the rail tracks of the Gare de Lyon and the Gare de Paris-Bercy (the motorail station). You can walk under the lines along boulevard de Bercy or rue Proudhon, but it's not much fun. The only bus is the #62 from Pont de Tolbiac and place Lachambeaudie to place Félix-Eboué, and all the new building works may disrupt its route.

North of the tracks, on the eastern intersection of avenue Daumensil and rue de Charenton, stands the ebullient mairie of the 12ᵉ, with a particularly splendid rear side on rue Bignon. A short way down rue Charenton, at nos. 119–120, a block built in 1911 has sculpted figures of a tired miner, sailor, industrial worker and farm labourer holding up the heavy weight of the window bays.

The traditional work in this area used to be at the freight station of Reuilly to the north of the mairie. This has now become the **Jardin de Reuilly**, a large circle of grass that you can walk, sleep or play on, with water gardens, a kids' playground, and statues baring their rears to avenue Daumesnil. There's a sundial with the hours marked on the ground (and, in typical French fashion, details of the calculation methods, the movements of the earth, the history of sundials and so on engraved on it), and a lovely wooden footbridge that crosses over the park to the pedestrian **allée Vivaldi**. Though not very exciting architecturally, this leads on, through a tunnel beneath rue de Reuilly, to the continuation of the Promenade Plantée, now running below the level of the surrounding streets, in the old railway cutting.

The nearest métro to the Jardin de Reuilly is Mᵒ Montgallet or Mᵒ Dugommier.

Rue de Reuilly meets avenue Daumesnil at place Félix-Eboué, graced with some very smug lions. A short way east along avenue Daumesnil, an extremely narrow brickwork façade, topped by the tallest bell tower in Paris, conceals the vast cupola – filling the whole block behind the street – of the **Église du Saint-Esprit**. It was built in 1931 in memory of the colonial missionaries. The Roman Catholic Church was worried by the possible reaction of the anticlerical, communist sympathies of the local residents, hence the disguise of its enormous dimensions. Between rues Tourneux and Fecamp, one block down from the church, one of the city's grim 1920s housing estates has been cleaned up and restored.

The nearest métro to Saint-Esprit is Mᵒ Daumesnil.

Another peculiar church, **St-Éloi**, built in 1968, lies north of the Jardin de Reuilly on place M. de Fontenay, off rue de Reuilly. Its ground-plan is a right-angled triangle with the altar positioned at one of the non-right-angled corners. It feels more like an industrial building: both outside and inside are clad with lacquered aluminium leaves, in honour of St Éloi, patron saint of jewellers and iron-workers who lived in this area in the seventh century.

The nearest métro to St-Éloi is Mᵒ Montgallet.

Close by the church of St-Éloi, on the other side of rue de Reuilly, is one of the most perfect *villas* in Paris, the **impasse Mousset**. Roses, clematis, wisteria and honeysuckle wind across telegraph lines and up the whitewashed walls of its tiny houses. A rusted hotel sign advertising wines and liqueurs as well as beds still hangs from one of the houses. You can hear children playing in hidden gardens; there are no designer offices here, just homes, the odd artist's studio and a small, still busy, printworks.

Vincennes

Beyond the 12e arrondissement, across the boulevard péripherique, lies the **Bois de Vincennes**. Besides the Bois de Boulogne, this is the only large green space that the city has to offer, and hence a favourite family Sunday retreat. Unfortunately, it's so crisscrossed with roads that countryside sensations don't stand much of a chance, but it has some pleasant corners: the Parc Floral, the Château de Vincennes on the northern edge, the arboretum and the two lakes.

To reach the Bois de Vincennes from the 12^e, you can take bus #86 from rue du Faubourg-St-Antoine, or more directly bus #46, which runs along rue de Reuilly and the last stretch of avenue

Vincennes

The Musée des Arts Africains et Océaniens is open Mon, Wed–Fri 10am–5.30pm, Sat & Sun till 6pm; 30F.

The Parc Zoologique is open April–Sept Mon–Sat 9am–6pm, Sun 9am–6.30pm; Oct–March Mon–Sat 9am–5pm, Sun 9am–5.30pm; 40F.

Daumesnil. On the other side of Porte Dorée, bus #46 passes the **Musée des Arts Africains et Océaniens**, at 293 avenue Daumesnil, with its 1930s colonial façade of jungles, hard-working natives and the place names of the French Empire representing the "overseas contribution to the capital". Inside this strange museum – one of the least crowded in the city – you can see an African gold brooch of curled-up sleeping crocodiles on one floor and, in the basement, five live crocodiles in a tiny pit surrounded by tanks of tropical fish. Imperialism is much in evidence in a gathering of culture and creatures from the old French colonies: hardly any of the black African artefacts are dated, as the collection predates European acknowledgement of history on that continent, and the captions are a bit suspicious, too. These masks and statues, furniture, adornments and tools should be exhibited with paintings by Expressionists, Cubists and Surrealists to see in which direction inspiration went. Picasso and friends certainly came here often.

The #46 bus next stops at the **Parc Zoologique**, which was one of the first zoos to replace cages with trenches and use landscaping to give the animals room to exercise. The entrance is at 53 avenue de St-Maurice.

You can spend an afternoon **boating** on Lac Daumesnil (just by the zoo), or rent a bike from the same place and take some stale baguette over to the ducks on Lac des Minimes, on the other side of the wood. In the southeast corner off route de la Pyramide you can wander among 2000 trees of over 800 different species that have been cultivated in the **Arboretum** (Mon–Fri 9.30am–6.30pm; free).

The fenced enclave on the southern side of Lac Daumesnil harbours a **Buddhist centre**, with Tibetan temple, Vietnamese chapel and international pagoda, and all occasionally visitable (information on ☎01.40.04.98.06). As far as real woods go, the *bois* comes into its own once you're east of avenue de St-Maurice. Boules competitions are popular – there's usually a collection of devotees between route de la Tourelle and avenue du Polygone.

For children's entertainments in the park, see p.360.

The **Parc Floral** (summer 9.30am–8pm; winter 9.30am–dusk; 10F; Mᵒ Château de Vincennes, then bus #112 or a short walk), just behind the fort, is one of the best gardens in Paris. Flowers are always in bloom in the Jardin des Quatres Saisons; you can picnic beneath pines while the kids play on slides, flying foxes and climbing frames, then wander through concentrations of camellias, cacti, ferns, irises and bonsai trees. Between April and September, there are art and horticultural exhibitions in several pavilions, free jazz and classical music concerts, and numerous activities for children including a mini-golf of Parisian monuments. A brasserie in the centre of the Parc Floral has decent *plats* for 56F and a children's menu at 30F.

To the east of the Parc Floral is the **Cartoucherie de Vincennes**, an old ammunitions factory, now home to four theatre companies, including the radical Théâtre du Soleil (see p.317).

On the northern edge of the *bois*, the **Château de Vincennes** – erstwhile royal medieval residence, then state prison, porcelain factory, weapons dump and military training school – is still undergoing restoration work started by Napoléon III. Guided tours on a choice of two different circuits are available (daily 10am–noon & 1.15–6pm; 1hr 15min guided tours at 11am, 2.15pm, 3pm & 4.30pm, 32F, 40min tours at 10.15am, 11.45am, 1.30pm & 5.15pm, 25F), though the fourteenth-century keep is currently closed for a five-year repair job; what you can visit (on both circuits) is the Flamboyant-Gothic **Chapelle Royale**, completed in the mid-sixteenth century and decorated with superb Renaissance stained-glass windows around the choir.

Chapter 11

Western Paris

For eating and drinking options in the Beaux Quartiers, see pp.297–298.

T he so-called **Beaux Quartiers** of western Paris are essentially the 16ᵉ and 17ᵉ arrondissements. The 16ᵉ is aristocratic and rich; the 17ᵉ, or at least the southern part of it, bourgeois and rich, embodying the staid, cautious values of the nineteenth-century manufacturing and trading classes. The northern half of the 16ᵉ, towards place Victor-Hugo and place de l'Étoile, is leafy and distinctly metropolitan in feel. The southern part, round the old villages of **Auteuil** and **Passy**, has an almost provincial air, and is full of pleasant surprises for the walker. One good focus for a walk is the **Musée Marmottan**, in avenue Raphael, which has a marvellous collection of late Monets. The district also boasts a number of interesting examples of turn-of-the-century and early **twentieth-century architecture**, especially those pieces by Hector Guimard, designer of the swirly green Art Nouveau métro stations, and by Le Corbusier and Mallet-Stevens, architects of the first "Cubist" buildings.

Auteuil

The ideal place to start an architectural exploration of the Beaux Quartiers is the **Église d'Auteuil** métro station. Around this area are several of Hector Guimard's **Art Nouveau** buildings: at 34 rue Boileau, 8 avenue de la Villa-de-la-Réunion, 41 rue Chardon-Lagache, 142 avenue de Versailles, and 39 boulevard Exelmans.

The house at no. 34 **rue Boileau** was one of Guimard's first commissions, in 1891. To reach it from Église d'Auteuil métro, head directly west along rue d'Auteuil for 200m, then turn left (south) into Boileau. A high fence, creepers and a huge satellite dish obscure much of the view, but you can see some of the decorative tile-work under the eaves and around the doors and windows. Further down the street, just before you reach boulevard Exelmans, the house at no. 62 successfully combines 1970s Western architecture with the traditional Vietnamese elements of a pagoda roof and earthenware tiles. Continue south for half a kilometre along rue Boileau beyond

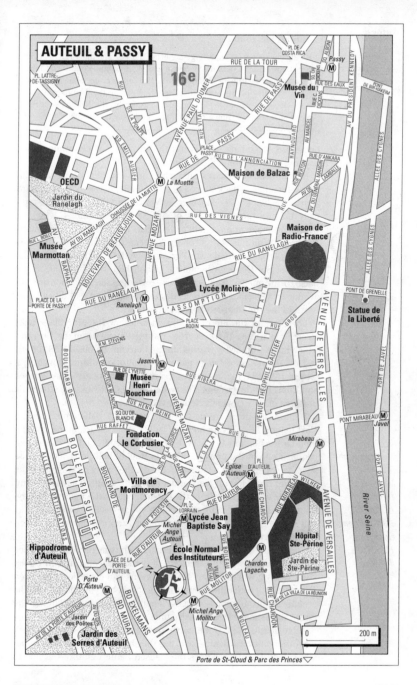

AUTEUIL & PASSY

16e

PL DE COSTA RICA

Passy Ⓜ

RUE DE LA TOUR

PL. LATTRE-DE-TASSIGNY

PONT DE BIR-HAKEIM

RUE DES EAUX

Musée du Vin

RUE RAYNOUARD

AV. DU PRESIDENT KENNEDY

ALLÉE DES CYGNES

AVENUE PAUL DOUMER

RUE VITAL

BD EMILE AUGIER

PLACE DE PASSY

RUE DE PASSY

RUE DE L'ANNONCIATION

RUE D'ANKARA

RUE BRETON

AV. DU GENERAL MANGIN

OECD

Ⓜ *La Muette*

Maison de Balzac

Jardin du Ranelagh

CHAUSSÉE DE LA MUETTE

RUE DES VIGNES

RAPHAEL

RUE L. BOILLY

AV DU RANELAGH

BOULEVARD DE BEAUSEJOUR

AVENUE MOZART

Maison de Radio-France

ALLÉE DES CYGNES

Musée Marmottan

RUE DU RANELAGH

PONT DE GRENELLE

PLACE DE LA PORTE DE PASSY

RUE DU RANELAGH

Ranelagh Ⓜ

Lycée Molière

RUE DE L'ASSOMPTION

Statue de la Liberté

BOULEVARD DE

PLACE RODIN

AVENUE DE VERSAILLES

PORT DE JAVEL

R. M. STEVENS

RUE DU DOCTEUR BLANCHE

Jasmin Ⓜ

RUE DE L'YVETTE

RUE RIBERA

AVENUE THEOPHILE GAUTIER

RUE GROS

Musée Henri Bouchard

RUE HENRI HEINE

AVENUE MOZART

SQ DU DR. BLANCHE

RUE RAFFET

PONT MIRABEAU Ⓜ *Javel*

Fondation le Corbusier

RUE G.

Mirabeau Ⓜ

PORT DE JAVEL

Villa de Montmorency

RUE RAFFET

Église d'Auteuil Ⓜ

PL. D'AUTEUIL

RUE D'AUTEUIL

River Seine

BOULEVARD SUCHET

ALLÉE DES FORTIFICATIONS

BOULEVARD DE

PL. DE LORRAIN

RUE POUSSIN

Ⓜ **Lycée Jean Baptiste Say**

RUE CHARDON

RUE MIRABEAU WILHEM

AVENUE DE VERSAILLES

Hippodrome d'Auteuil

Michel Ange Auteuil Ⓜ

École Normal des Instituteurs

RUE BOILEAU

Ⓜ

Hôpital Ste-Périne

PLACE DE LA PORTE D'AUTEUIL

Porte D'Auteuil

RUE D'AUTEUIL

Chardon Lagache

Jardin de Ste-Périne

VILLA DE LA VILLA DE LA RÉUNION

AV DE LA PORTE D'AUTEUIL

BD MURAT

RUE MOLITOR

RUE CHARDON

Jardin des Poètes

BD EXELMANS

Michel Ange Molitor Ⓜ

Jardin des Serres d'Auteuil

RUE BOILEAU

0 ————— 200 m

Porte de St-Cloud & Parc des Princes ▽

Auteuil

Auteuil bus routes

Handy bus routes for exploring Auteuil are the #52 and the #72. The #52 runs between M° Opéra in the centre and M° Boulogne-Pont-de-St-Cloud near the Parc de Princes, stopping at rue Poisson en route, while the #72's route extends between métro Hôtel de Ville in the Marais and M° Boulogne-Pont-de-St-Cloud, stopping en route by the Exelmans crossroads near some of Guimard's buildings on avenue de Versailles.

boulevard Exelmans, and you'll find a series of charming *villas* backing onto the Auteuil cemetery.

Rue Boileau terminates on avenue de Versailles, where you can turn left and head back to the Église d'Auteuil métro via the Guimard apartment block at 142 avenue de Versailles (1905), with the typically bulging, heaving effect of Art Nouveau buildings, which at worst can make you feel almost seasick. It's just by the Exelmans crossroads (on bus #72's route). You can then cut across the surprisingly large **Jardin de Ste-Périne**, once the rural residence of the monks of Ste Geneviève's abbey, established here in 1109, to get back to the métro. The entrances to the garden are opposite 135 avenue de Versailles and alongside the hospital on rue Mirabeau, just north of the rue Chardon-Lagache junction.

For more of the life of the quartier, follow the old village high street, **rue d'Auteuil**, west from the métro exit to **place Lorrain**, which hosts a Saturday market. In rue Poussin (on bus #52's route), just off the *place*, carriage gates open onto **Villa Montmorency**, a typical 16ᵉ *villa*, in the sense of a sort of private village of leafy lanes and English-style gardens. The writer André Gide, and the Goncourt brothers of Prix Goncourt fame, lived in this one.

Behind it, in a cul-de-sac off rue du Dr-Blanche, are **Le Corbusier**'s first private houses (1923), the Villa Jeanneret and the Villa La Roche, now in the care of the Fondation Le Corbusier. You can visit one of the houses, the **Villa Roche**, built in strictly Cubist style, very plain, with windows in bands, the only extravagances the raising of one wing on piers and a curved frontage. They look commonplace enough now from the outside, but what a contrast to anything that had gone before, and once you're inside, the spatial play still seems groundbreaking. The interior is appropriately decorated with Cubist paintings.

Further north along rue du Dr-Blanche, the tiny rue Mallet-Stevens was built entirely by the architect of the same name, also in Cubist style. No. 12, where Robert Mallet-Stevens had his offices, has been altered, along with other houses in the street, but you can still see the architectural intention – familiar enough today – of sculpting the entire street space as a cohesive unit.

After taking a left at the northern end of rue du Dr-Blanche, then right on boulevard Beauséjour, use the short cut immediately opposite rue du Ranelagh across the disused Petite Ceinture rail line to

The Villa Roche is open Mon–Fri 10am–12.30pm & 1.30–6.30pm, closed Aug; 15F; M° Jasmine.

reach avenue Raphaël, followed by a pleasant walk along the shady trees of the pretty **Jardin de Ranelagh** (with a rather engaging sculpture of La Fontaine with the eagle and fox) and on to the **Musée Marmottan**, 2 rue Louis-Boilly. Inside, there are some splendid examples of First Empire pomposity: chairs with golden sphinxes for armrests, candelabra of complicated headdresses and twining serpents, and a small and beautiful collection of thirteenth- to sixteenth-century manuscript illuminations. But the star of the show is the collection of **Monet paintings** bequeathed to the museum by the artist's son. Among them is *Impression Soleil Levant (Impression, Sunrise)*, a canvas from 1872 of a misty Le Havre morning, and whose title the critics usurped to give the Impressionist movement its name. The painting was stolen from the gallery in October 1985, along with eight other paintings. After a police operation lasting five years which extended as far afield as Japan, the paintings were discovered in a villa in southern Corsica – they're now back on show with greatly tightened security. There's also a dazzling selection of works from Monet's last years at Giverny, which includes several *Waterlilies*, where rich colours are laid on in thick, excited whorls and lines. Some paintings **by Renoir**, Monet's contemporary, and **Berthe Morisot** also feature in the collection.

Returning to place Lorrain, **rue de la Fontaine**, running northeast from the *place* to the Radio-France building, has Guimard buildings at nos. 14, 17, 19, 21 and 60. Among these, no. 14 is the most famous: the "Castel Béranger" (1898), with exuberant Art Nouveau decoration and shapes in the bay windows, the roofline and the chimney. At no. 65 there's a huge block of artists' studios by Henri Sauvage (1926) with a fascinating colour scheme, again bearing signs of a Cubist influence. **Radio-France**, its entrance at 116 avenue du Président Kennedy, is the national radio headquarters; you can visit here for free concerts or take a guided tour through the **Musée de Radio-France**, which illustrates the history of broadcasting through a wide collection of equipment including some early Marconi radios.

Auteuil

The Musée Marmottan is open daily except Mon 10am–5pm; 40F; M° Muette.

The Musée de Radio-France offers guided tours only, Mon–Sat at 10.30am, 11.30am, 2.30pm, 3.30pm & 4.30pm; RER Av-du-Pres-Kennedy–Maison-de-Radio-France & M° Mirabeau. For details about concerts, see the box on p.309.

Poets, greenhouses and gardens

West of place de la Porte d'Auteuil are two gardens: the **Jardin des Poètes**, with its entrance on avenue du Général Sarrail, and the **Jardin des Serres d'Auteuil**, its main entrance at 3 avenue de la Porte d'Auteuil, (or you can enter from the Jardin des Poètes). You can't escape the traffic noise completely, but the Jardin des Poètes is extremely tranquil. Famous French poets are each remembered by a verse (of a mostly pastoral nature) engraved on small stones surrounded by little flowerbeds. A statue of Victor Hugo by Rodin, almost obscured by a laurel bush, stands in the middle of this very informal garden. Approaching the Auteuil garden and its green-

**Poets,
greenhouses
and gardens**

*The Jardin des
Poètes is open
daily 9am–
6pm (free)
and the Jardin
des Serres
d'Auteuil daily
10am–5/6pm
(5F); M° Porte
d'Auteuil.*

*The Musée du
Sport Français
is open
Mon–Fri
9.30am–
12.30pm &
2–5pm, Sun
10.30am–
12.30pm &
2–6pm; 20F;
M° Porte-de-St-
Cloud.*

houses (*serres*) from the Jardin des Poètes, you pass the delightful potting sheds with rickety wooden blinds. Then you're into a formal garden, beautifully laid out around the big old-fashioned metal-frame greenhouses. There may be a special exhibition on – azaleas in April, for example – in which case there'll be an extra entrance fee for the greenhouses.

Directly beyond the Jardin des Serres d'Auteuil is the **Stade Roland Garros**, venue for the French tennis championships (see p.356 for information about watching a tournament). To the south is the main rugby and domestic football stadium, the **Parc des Princes**, at 24 rue du Commandant-Guilbaud, where apart from seeing a match (for more on which see p.355), you can visit the **Musée du Sport Français**. Here books, posters, paintings and sculptures tell the history of French sport, along with trophies and boots, caps, rackets and gloves worn by the famous, and the vanity case of the greatest French Wimbledon champion, Suzanne Lenglen.

The **Jardins Albert Kahn**, (Tues–Sun 11am–6/7pm; garden & museum entry 22F; M° Boulogne-Pont-de-St-Cloud & M° Marcel-Semblat) at 14 rue du Port, in the neighbouring suburb of Boulogne-Billancourt to the south, consists of a very pretty garden and a small museum dedicated to temporary exhibitions of "*Les Archives de la Planète*" – photographs and films collected by banker and philanthropist Albert Kahn between 1909 and 1931 to record human activities and ways of life that he knew would soon disappear for ever. His aim in the design of the garden was to combine English, French, Japanese and other styles to demonstrate the possibility of a harmonious, peaceful world. It's an enchanting place, with rhododendrons and camellias under blue cedars, a rose garden and an espaliered orchard, a forest of Moroccan pines and streams with Japanese bridges beside pagoda tea houses, Buddhas and pyramids of pebbles. A palm hothouse has been turned into a very chic *salon de thé*, serving such delights as pear liqueur and *marrons glacés* sorbet.

Passy

Northeast of Auteuil, the area around the old village of **Passy**, too, offers scope for a good meandering walk, from La Muette métro, through old characterful streets like rue de l'Annonciation, to Balzac's house, and through more cobbled streets to the Seine and Pont de Bir-Hakeim near Passy métro.

From La Muette métro, head east along the old high street, **rue de Passy**, past an eye-catching parade of boutiques, until you reach **place de Passy** and the crowded but leisurely terrace of *Le Paris Passy* café. From the *place*, stroll southeast along cobbled, pedestrianized **rue de l'Annonciation**, a pleasant blend of down-to-earth and genteel well-heeled which gives more of the flavour of old Passy. You may no longer be able to have your Bechstein repaired here or your furniture lacquered, but the food shops that now dominate the street have delectable displays – there'll be no holding back the salivary glands.

Passy

From métro La Muette, Chaussée-de-la-Muette leads into the Jardins du Ranelagh and the Musée Marmottan – see p.219.

When you hit rue Raynouard, cross the road and veer to your right, where at no. 47 you'll discover a delightful, summery little house with pale-green shutters and a decorative iron entrance porch, tucked away down some steps among a tree-filled garden. Balzac moved here in 1840 to outrun his debts and stayed for seven years. In fact the deceptively tiny *place* extends down the hillside for three storeys, enabling an easy backdoor exit for Balzac as necessary. The **Maison de Balzac** repays a visit even if you've never read the writer's works. You can contemplate the study where Balzac famously stayed up all night writing, fuelled by coffee. One room is devoted to the development of ideas for the creation of a monument to Balzac, resulting in the famously blobby Rodin sculpture of the writer: caricatures of the sculpture by cartoonists of the time are on display here. Another room is devoted to the many adaptations, both filmic and theatrical, of Balzac's novel *Le Colonel Charbert*, the most recent being the 1994 film starring Gerard Depardieu. There's also a research library which you can apply to use. Outside, the shady garden is a delightful place to dally on wrought-iron seats, surrounded by busts of the writer.

The Maison de Balzac is open Tues–Sun 10am–5.40pm; 17.50F; Mᵒ Av-du-Pres-Kennedy–Maison-de-Radio-France & Mᵒ Passy.

Behind Balzac's house, and reached via some steps descending from rue Raynouard, **rue Berton** is a cobbled path with gas lights still in place, blocked off by the heavy security of the Turkish embassy. The building, an eighteenth-century château shrouded by greenery and screened by a high wall and guards, was once a clinic where the pioneering Dr Blanche tried to treat the mad Maupassant and Gérard de Nerval, among others; before that it was the home of Marie-Antoinette's friend, the Princesse de Lamballe. You can get a better view of the building from cobbled **rue d'Ankara**, reached by heading down avenue de Lamballe and then right into avenue du Général-Mangin.

From here, head northeast along avenue Marcel-Proust, from where you can take some steps back to rue Raynouard. If you turn right here you'll find another set of steps, the passage des Eaux, leading down to the **rue des Eaux**, where fashionable Parisians used to come in the eighteenth century for the therapeutic benefits of the once-famous ferruginous and sulphuric Passy waters. Today, the street is enclosed by a canyon of moneyed apartments, which dwarf the eighteenth-century houses of **square Charles-Dickens**. In one of them, burrowing back into the cellars of a vanished monastery, which produced wine until it was finished by the Revolution, the **Musée du Vin** puts on a disappointing display of viticultural bits and bobs and the visit includes a *dégustation*. While the exhibition, which includes some awful waxworks, will leave you yawning, the extensive stone vaulted cellars, however, are worth seeing, connect-

The Musée du Vin is open daily 10am–6pm; 35F admission includes a glass of wine.

The nearby Cimetière de Passy, just west of the place du Trocadéro, holds the graves of Édouard Manet and Berthe Morisot; Mᵒ Trocadéro.

ing to the ancient quarry tunnels – not visitable – from which the stone for Notre-Dame was hewn. You can also see a well where people used to come to take the waters. The place also acts as a restaurant, and you can just come in for a glass of wine (from 19F a glass) and some cheese (29F for three types) between 3pm and 5pm – enjoy the cellars and skip the museum.

Back on rue Raynouard, head northeast to place de Costa-Rica, take the first right into rue de l'Alboni and go down the steps into square Alboni, a patch of garden enclosed by tall apartment buildings as solid as banks. Here the métro line emerges from what used to be a vine-covered hillside for the Passy stop – more like a country station – before rumbling out across the river by the **Pont de Bir-Hakeim**, the distinctive bridge famously featured in the racy Bertolucci film *Last Tango in Paris*, starring Marlon Brando. From here you're well placed to hop back onto the metro, or cross the bridge and head north along the water to the Eiffel Tower about 500m along.

Bois de Boulogne

The **Bois de Boulogne**, running all the way down the west side of the 16ᵉ, was designed by Baron Haussmann and supposedly modelled on London's Hyde Park – though it's a very French interpretation. The "bois" of the name is somewhat deceptive, though the extensive parklands (just under 900 hectares) do contain some remnants of the once great Fôret de Rouvray. When it opened in the eighteenth century, it was popularly said that *"Les mariages du bois de Boulogne ne se font pas devant Monsieur le Curé"*– "Unions cemented in the Bois de Boulogne do not take place in the presence of a priest." Today's after-dark unions are no less disreputable – the woods are a favoured haunt for prostitutes and accompanying kerb-crawlers, so don't be tempted to go in at night.

More information about the Jardin d'Acclimatation and activities for kids in the Bois de Boulogne is given on p.359. For details on sporting and leisure activities, see Chatper 17.

While entry to the overall park is free and unrestricted at any time day or night, there are several attractions within it that have separate opening times or entry fees: the **Jardin d'Acclimatation**, which is aimed at kids; the excellent **Musée National des Arts et Traditions Populaires**; the beautiful floral displays of the **Parc de Bagatelle**; and the **racecourses** at Longchamp and Auteuil. You can also partake of a wealth of activities: there's a **riding** school, a bowling alley, **bike rental** at the entrance to the Jardin d'Acclimatation and 14km of cycling routes; and **boating** on the Lac Inférieur. The best, and wildest, part for **walking** is towards the southwest corner.The fascinating **Musée National des Arts et Traditions Populaires** lies on the northern edge of the park, at 6 avenue du Mahatma Gandhi, beside the main entrance to the Jardin d'Acclimatation and signposted from Mᵒ Les Sablons (from where it's about a fifteen-minute walk). It celebrates the highly specialized skills and techniques behind beautiful artefacts in the run-up to industrialization, standardization and mass production – boat-building, shepherding, farm-

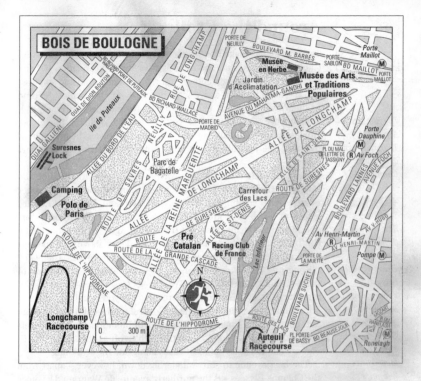

ing, weaving, blacksmithing, pottery, stone-cutting and games are all beautifully illustrated. Downstairs, there's a study section with casefuls of various implements, and cubicles where you can call up explanatory slide shows (explanations in French).

Southwest of the folk art museum, between the route de la Marguerite and the Seine, spreads the **Parc de Bagatelle**, (open daily April–Oct 9am–8pm, Nov–March 9am–5.30pm; M° Porte-Maillot, then bus #244) comprising a range of garden styles from French and English to Japanese. Its most famous feature is the stunning **rose garden** of the charming Chateau de Bagatelle. The château was designed and built in just over sixty days in 1775 as a wager between Comte d'Artois, the owner, and his sister-in-law Marie Antoinette, who said it could not be achieved in less than three months. The best time for the roses is June, while in other parts of the garden there are beautiful displays of tulips, hyacinths and daffodils in early April, irises in May, and waterlilies in early August.

Bang in the middle of the Bois de Boulogne, the Pré Catalan park is famous for its huge beech tree and, outside an open-air theatre, its **Jardin Shakespeare**, where you can study the herbs, trees and flowers referred to in his plays.

The Musée is open daily except Tues 9.45am–5.15pm; 25F, 32F with special exhibitions; M° Les Sablons & M° Porte-Maillot.

Around the Étoile

Twelve avenues make up the star of the **Étoile**, or place Charles-de-Gaulle, with the Arc de Triomphe at its centre. The northern 16e and eastern 17e arrondissements are for the most part cold and soulless, and the huge fortified apartments here are empty much of the time as their owners – royal, exiled royal, ex-royal or just extremely rich – move between their other residences dotted about the globe. However, one such building, the Hôtel André, houses the highlight of the area, the magnificent art collection of the **Musée Jacquemart André**.

The Étoile and Arc de Triomphe are detailed in Chapter 3.

Avenue Foch runs southwest from the Étoile to the Bois de Boulogne through the 16e with one museum en route and another nearby. The combined **Musée Arménien** and **Musée d'Ennery** stands at no.59. The ground floor displays Armenian artefacts, art and historical documents from the Middle Ages to the genocide by the Turks at the start of this century. The floors above hold the personal acquisitions of nineteenth-century popular novelist Clémence d'Ennery: Chinese and Japanese objects including thousands of painted and sculpted buttons. Two blocks west of here is the beginning of rue de la Faisanderie, where at no. 16 you'll find one of Paris' oddest museums, the **Musée de la Contrefaçon**, set up to deliver an anti-counterfeiting message. Examples of imitation products, labels and brand marks trying to pass themselves off as the "genuine article" are all on display, in most cases alongside the real thing.

The Musées Arménien & d'Ennery are open Sun, Thurs & public hols only 2–6pm; closed Aug; free. The Musée de la Contrefaçon opens Mon–Thurs 2–5pm, Fri 9.30am–noon, Sun 2–6pm; closed Sun in Aug; 15F. M^o Porte-Dauphine.

The best avenue to start wandering down, however – apart from the Champs-Élysées – is the northerly **avenue de Wagram**. Devotees of Art Nouveau can stop in front of no. 34, Jules Lavirotte's design of 1904, to see if they can honestly persist in saying the style is beautiful. Less taxing aesthetic judgements are called for in front of the flower market and cafés of **place des Ternes**, the first big junction on avenue de Wagram, where rue du Faubourg-St-Honoré begins, heading southeast. You can take this street and then the second left – you're in the 8e arrondissement now – to admire the five gold onion domes of the Cathédrale Alexandre-Nevski, at 6 rue Daru, before turning right on rue de Courcelles, which brings you to the enormous gilded gates of the avenue Hoche entrance to **Parc de Monceau** (M^o Monceau). The park has a roller-skating rink and kids' play facilities, but is otherwise a formal garden with antique colonnades and artificial grottoes. Half the people who command the heights of the French economy spent their infancy there, promenaded in prams by their nannies.

The Musée Cernuschi is open Tues–Sun 10am–5.40pm; 30F.

On avenue Velasquez, by the east gate of Parc de Monceau, at no. 7, the **Musée Cernuschi** houses a small collection of ancient Chinese art bequeathed to the state by the banker Cernuschi, who nearly lost his life for giving money to the Commune. There are some exquisite pieces here, but of fairly specialized interest. Right beside the

Cernuschi, with its entrance at no. 63 rue de Monceau, is the **Musée Nissim de Camondo**, named after Count Camondo's son, who was killed while flying missions for France in World War I. It's worth forking out for this museum if you share the count's taste for eighteenth-century French aristocratic luxuries: tapestries, paintings, gilded furniture, and tableware of the porcelain and solid silver variety.

Around the Étoile

The Musée Camondo opens Wed–Sun 10am–5pm; 27F. M° Monceau & M° Villiers.

Musée Jacquemart-André

More interesting, and just a few blocks to the south of the Parc de Monceau, at 158 boulevard Haussmann, is the lavishly ornamented palace of the nineteenth-century banker and art-lover Édouard André and his wife, former society portraitist Niélie Jacquemart. Built in 1870 to grace Baron Haussmann's grand new boulevard, the Hôtel André functions today as the **Musée Jacquemart-André**, housing their impressive private collection and a fabulous *salon de thé* – the meeting place of the elegant and discreet. Bequeathed to the Institut de France by Édouard's widow, the Hôtel André deploys the couple's art collection exactly as they ordained. Edouard's widow painted his portrait in 1872 – on display in what were their private apartments on the ground floor – and nine years later they were to wed, after which Niélie gave up her painting career and the pair devoted their spare time to collecting art, travelling around Europe searching for pieces. They loved Italian art above all, and a stunning collection of fifteenth- and sixteenth-century Italian genius, including the works of Botticelli, Donatello, Mantegna, Bellini and Uccello, forms the core of their collection. Almost as compelling as the splendid interior and art collection is the insight gleaned into an extraordinary marriage and grand nineteenth-century lifestyle, brought to life by the fascinating narration on the free audio headphones (available in English). You can choose to keep the information simple, or go into more scholarly detail about various works of art, using the hand held keypad.

The Musée Jacquemart-André is open daily 10am–6pm; 45F; M° Miromesnil & M° St-Philippe-du-Roule.

In Room 1, mostly eighteenth-century French paintings are displayed, including several portraits by **Boucher**, in addition to two lively paintings of Venice by Canaletto. Room 2, the reception area, has specially constructed folding doors which when opened transformed the space into a ballroom large enough to contain a thousand guests. Room 3 contains three huge tapestries depicting Russian scenes which capture the fashion for Slav exoticism of the mid-eighteenth century. Room 6, formerly the library, focuses on Dutch and Flemish paintings, including two by **Rembrandt** – *The Portrait of Dr A. Tholinx* and *The Pilgrims of Emmais* – and three by **Van Dyck**. Room 7 is the Salon de Musique (and the other half of the ballroom), whose dramatic high ceiling is decorated with a mural by Pierre Victor Galant; the musicians would play from the gallery, and you're treated to a mini-concert on the audiotape as you gaze at the

Around the Étoile

You can enter the fabulous salon de thé (11am–6pm) without a museum ticket (see p.298).

ceiling art. In Room 8, a Tiepolo fresco, rescued from a villa near Venice, graces the extraordinary marble, bronze and wrought-iron double spiral staircase that leads from an interior garden of palm trees up to the musician's gallery. Room 9, once the smoking retreat, is hung with the work of eighteenth-century English portraitists, among them a painting by **Joshua Reynolds**.

Leading off the music gallery are the intimate rooms in which the couple displayed their **early Renaissance Italian collection**. The rooms have a peaceful, contemplative air. The first was intended as Niélie's studio, but she instead decorated it as a sculpture gallery – including two pieces by **Donatello** – its walls covered in friezes. The dimly lit Florentine room next door includes a wonderful, brightly coloured depiction by **Paolo Uccello** of *Saint George Slaying the Dragon* (1440), a **Botticelli** *Virgin and Child* (1470) and an exquisite sixteeenth-century inlaid choir stall. Adjacent is the Venetian room, with paintings by **Bellini** and **Mantegna** among those on show.

La Défense

La Défense, accessible by RER line A and métro line 1, has been elevated to one of the top places of pilgrimage for visitors to Paris by the construction of **La Grande Arche**. This beautiful and astounding structure, a 112-metre hollow cube clad in white marble, is positioned 6km out from the Arc de Triomphe at the far end of the Voie Triomphale, completing the western axis of the monumental east–west vista. Suspended within its hollow, large enough to enclose Notre-Dame with ease, are open lift shafts and a "cloud" canopy. Designed by the Danish architect Johann Otto von Spreckelsen, who died before its completion, La Grande Arche is a pure and graceful example of design wedded to innovative engineering, on a par with the Eiffel Tower and in marked contrast to other recent Parisian monuments. The building was intended to coincide with the 1989 Bicentennial, but squabbles between Chirac and Mitterrand over its use delayed the project. It now houses a government ministry, international businesses, an information centre on the European Union ("Sources d'Europe"; Mon–Fri 10am–6pm) and, in the roof section, the Fondation Internationale des Droits de l'Homme, which stages exhibitions and conferences on issues related to human rights.

The closest stations to La Défense are M° and RER Grande-Arche-de-la-Défense.

A ride to the top of the arch (daily 10am–7pm) costs 40F.

Transparent lift shafts make for a thrilling ride to the rooftop, from where as well as having access to the exhibitions, you can admire Jean-Pierre Raynaud's "Map of the Heavens" marble patios. The lift, however, is pricey, and the views no more impressive than from the series of steps that lead up to the base of the arch, itself a popular meeting and viewing point – on a clear day, you can scan from the marble path on the *parvis* below you to the Arc de Triomphe, and beyond to the Louvre.

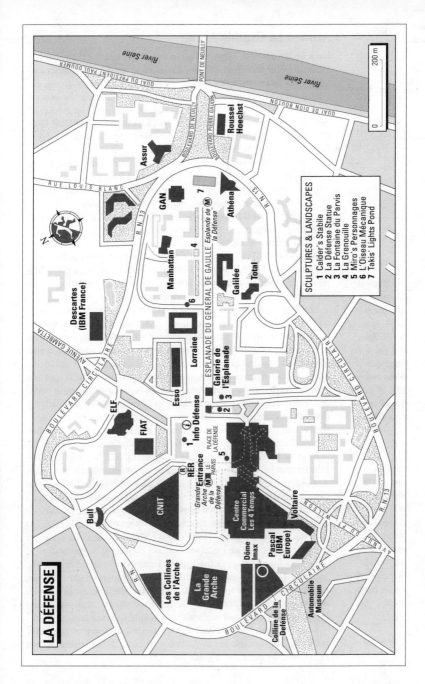

LA DÉFENSE

SCULPTURES & LANDSCAPES
1 Calder's Stabile
2 La Défense Statue
3 La Fontaine du Parvis
4 La Grenouille
5 Miro's Personnages
6 L'Oiseau Mécanique
7 Takis' Lights Pond

River Seine

River Seine

QUAI DU PRÉSIDENT PAUL DOUMER

QUAI DE DION BOUTON

PONT DE NEUILLY

BOULEVARD DE NEUILLY

BOULEVARD PIERRE GAUDIN

Roussel
Hoechst

Assur

RUE LOUIS BLANC

R.N. 13

GAN

Manhattan

Esplanade de
la Défense

Athéna

Galilée

Total

Descartes
(IBM France)

AVENUE GAMBETTA

Lorraine

ESPLANADE DU GÉNÉRAL DE GAULLE

Galerie de
l'Esplanade

Esso

BOULEVARD CIRCULAIRE

ELF

FIAT

Info Défense

PLACE DE
LA DÉFENSE

RER

Grande Entrance
Arche de la
Défense

LE
PARVIS

Bull

CNIT

Centre
Commercial
Les 4 Temps

Voltaire

Pascal (IBM
Europe)

AVENUE DU PRÉSIDENT WILSON

R.N. 13

Les Collines
de l'Arche

R.N. 13

La Grande
Arche

Dôme
Imax

BOULEVARD CIRCULAIRE

Automobile
Museum

Colline de la
Défense

BOULEVARD CIRCULAIRE

N

0   200 m

Around La Grande Arche

Back on the ground, between La Grande Arche and the river extends Paris' prestige **business district**, La Défense, an extraordinary monument to late-twentieth-century capitalism, stretching along the pedestrianized, sculpture and fountain-strewn Esplanade du Général de Gaulle. In front of you, along the axis of the Voie Triomphale, an assortment of towers – token apartment blocks, offices of ELF, Gan, Fiat, banks and other businesses – compete for size and dazzle of surface. Finance made flesh, they are worth the trip out in themselves. Over ten thousand people come here to work during the week, but as thousands live in the apartment blocks on the edge of the district, and with cinemas, tourist attractions, art and a huge shopping centre, it's a popular and animated place on weekends, too.

Looking down the Esplanade from beneath the arch, you can't miss on your right the **Dôme-Imax**, another galactic boule lobbed from the realms of higher technology, come to displace La Villette's Géode (see p.197) as the world's largest cinema screen. In the same building complex, named the "Colline de la Défense", you'll find the **Musée de l'Automobile**, with 100 models proudly exhibiting developments from the advent of motoring history to the present day.

The Musée de l'Automobile is open daily 12.30–7pm, Sat till 8pm; 35F, combined ticket with Dôme-Imax 60F; Mº & RER Grande-Arche-de-la-Défense.

The **bizarre artworks** scattered around the Esplanade provide welcome relief from the corporate skyscrapers. **Joan Miró**'s giant wobbly creatures bemoan their misfit status beneath the biting edges and curveless heights of the buildings. Opposite is **Alexander Calder**'s red iron offering – a stabile rather than a mobile – while in between the two, a black marble metronome shape releases a goal-less line across the *parvis*. **Torricini**'s huge fat frog screams to escape to a nice quiet pond. A statue commemorating the **defence of Paris** in 1870 (for which the district is named) perches on a concrete plinth in front of a coloured plastic waterfall and fountain pool, while nearer the river, disembodied people clutch each other round endlessly repeated concrete flowerbeds.

Get off a stop early, at Mº Esplanade-de-la-Défense, for the most dramatic approach to the Grande Arche and to see the sculptures.

Next to La Grande Arche, the triangular CNIT building was the first intimation of the area's modernist architectural future when it was erected in the 1950s as a trade exhibition centre. It looks a bit like a covered stadium with businesses instead of seats. The pitch, all gleaming granite, is softened by slender bamboo trees; all the serious activity takes place beyond the far goal, where every major computer company has an office. There's also a FNAC store, and a selection of overpriced cafés and brasseries. Less damaging to the pocket, if unhealthy for the soul, is the Quatre-Temps commercial centre, the biggest of its ilk in Europe with some 250 shops on three levels, across the *parvis*, opposite. To minimize the encounter (if you should so wish), enter from the left-hand doors, and you'll find crêperies, pizzerias and cafés without having to leave ground level.

Info Défense (daily 10am–6pm), located in front of the CNIT building, displays models and photographs of the artworks, with a map to locate them and a guide for 15F.

Île de la Jatte and Île de Chatou

Above La Défense, to the northeast, the **Île de la Jatte** floats in the Seine just off rich and leafy Neuilly, an ideal venue for a romantic riverside walk. From the Pont de Levallois, near the métro of the same name, a flight of steps descends to the tip of the island. Formerly an industrial site, it's now part public garden (Mon–Fri 8.30am–6pm, Sat & Sun 10am–8pm) and part stylish new housing development. On the right of the development, a former *manège* (riding-school) has become the smart *Café de la Jatte*, while beside the bridge the pricey *Guinguette de Neuilly* restaurant still flourishes.

A long narrow island in a loop of the Seine further downstream, the **Île de Chatou** was once a rustic spot where Parisians came on the newly opened rail line to row, dine and flirt at the riverside *guinguettes* (eating and dancing establishments). The one *guinguette* to survive, just below the Pont de Chatou bridge, is the **Maison Fournaise**. This was a favourite haunt of Renoir, Monet, Manet, Van Gogh, Seurat, Sisley and Courbet, half of whom were in love with the proprietor's daughter, Alphonsine. One of Renoir's best-known canvases, *Le Déjeuner des Canotiers*, shows his friends lunching on the balcony. Vlaminck and his fellow-Fauves, Derain and Matisse, were also habitués.

It was from the Île de Chatou that Vlaminck set off for the 1905 Salon des Indépendents with the truckload of paintings that led critics to coin the term "Fauvism".

Though derelict for many years, the *Maison Fournaise* (for more on which see p.298) re-opened a few years ago, restored and refurbished, as a very agreeable **restaurant**. The outbuildings have been renovated, too, and house a small **museum** of memorabilia from this artistic past, in addition to temporary exhibitions. It's a great site, with a huge plane tree shading the river bank and a view of the barges being carried past by the current.

Access to the island is from the Rueil-Malmaison RER stop. Take the Sortie avenue Albert-1er, go left out of the station and right along the dual carriageway onto the bridge – a ten-minute walk. Bizarrely, there's a twice-yearly **ham and antiques fair** on the island, which is fun to check out (March and Sept).

The Musée is open Thurs & Fri 11am–5pm, Sat & Sun 11am–6pm; 25F.

Gustave Flourens

One of the boldest and most colourful of the Commune's commanders – **Gustave Flourens**, commander of the Red Belleville battalions – met his death on the Île de Chatou. Although far from being a proletarian himself, Flourens was a flamboyant champion of freedom, who had already taken part in Crete's attempts to throw off the Turkish yoke in the 1860s – whence his preferred uniform and arm, a Grecian kilt and *yataghan*. Impatient with the inertia of his colleagues, he led an attack on the government forces at Versailles. He continued, when others fell back. Surrounded and outnumbered, he was ultimately captured and had his head split in two.

i

Listings

Chapter 12

Accommodation

The hotels and hostels of Paris are often heavily booked, so it's wise to reserve a place well in advance, if you can. If not, there are two agencies to turn to for help: the tourist board's Bureaux d'Accueil, and the youth-oriented Accueil des Jeunes en France (AJF). The former charges a small commission (20–55F for a hotel room depending on how many stars it has, 8F for a hostel): its function is to bale you out of last-minute difficulty rather than find the most economical deal. The AJF guarantees to find you a room – in a hostel (around 120F B&B) if you arrive early enough, or in a hotel (240F upwards). You pay for the accommodation, plus a 10F fee, and receive vouchers to take to the establishment. The best area for budget priced hotels is the 11^e. There are bargains in the 17^e as well, but they're a lot further from the centre, where cheapies fill up quickly and need reserving well in advance. Not all hotels accept credit cards – you may have to send an international money order with your reservation.

Each year, the Paris hoteliers' organization publishes a list of the most heavily booked periods for accommodation, which is available from French Government Tourist Offices (see p.24). The list is based on the dates of the salons or trade fairs; September and October are invariably the worst months to find somewhere to stay, otherwise dates vary slightly from year to year. It's worth checking them out when planning a trip.

Bureaux d'Accueil

Office du Tourisme, 127 av des Champs-Élysées, 8e; ☎01.49.52.53.54, fax 01.49.52.53.00 (M° Charles-de-Gaulle-Étoile). May–Sept daily 9am–8pm, closed May 1; Oct–April Mon–Sat 9am–8pm, Sun & hols 11am–6pm.

Gare de Lyon, exit from main-line platforms, 20 bd Diderot, 12e; ☎01.43.43.33.24. Mon–Sat 8am–8pm; closed hols.

Gare du Nord, arrival point for international trains, 18 rue de Dunkerque, 10e; ☎01.45.26.94.82. Mon–Sat 8am–8pm; closed hols.

Tour Eiffel, Champ de Mars, 7^e; ☎01.45.51.22.15 (RER Champs-de-Mars/Tour Eiffel). April–Sept daily 11am–6pm.

Information in English (24hr): ☎01.49.52.53.56.

Accueil des Jeunes en France (AJF)

OTU Voyages Beauborg, 119 rue St-Martin, opposite Pompidou Centre, 4^e; ☎01.40.29.12.12 (M° Châtelet-Les-Halles). Mon–Fri 10am–6.45pm, Sat 10am–5.30pm.

Gare du Nord, Banlieue section, 10e; ☎01.42.85.86.19. June–Sept daily 10am–6.30pm.

Accommodation

Bed and breakfast

Accommodation on a **bed and breakfast** basis in private houses is a reasonably priced option in Paris. Two organizations to contact are:

Accueil France Famille, 5 rue François-Copée, 15ᵉ; ☎01.45.54.22.39, fax 01.45.58.43.25 (Mº Boucicaut). From 200F, plus 300F annual membership. Minimum stay one week.

France Lodge, 41 rue La Fayette, 9ᵉ; ☎01.53.20.02.54, fax 01.53.20.01.25 (Mº Le-Peletier). From 120F, plus 85F annual membership. Essential to arrange in advance. They can also organize accommodation in furnished apartments by the week or month (☎01.53.20.09.09).

Hotels

If you value your independence and have a preferred location, there's obviously more scope in booking a hotel yourself than using the official reservation services.

There are a great many in all price categories, with a still considerable, if dwindling, number of small **family-run hotels** with budget-priced rooms.

The hotels listed in this section have been arranged by arrondissement and divided into the following **eight price categories**:

①   up to 160F
②   160–220F
③   220–300F
④   300–400F
⑤   400–500F
⑥   500–600F
⑦   600–700F
⑧   over 700F

The prices given are for the **cheapest double rooms** normally available in **high season**. Most hotels have a selection of rooms at different prices; where there are very few rooms in the lower category or where the range in any one establishment is particularly large, we have used more than one symbol; eg ①–② or ②–⑤. In addition to the quoted prices, a **visitors' tax** (*taxe de séjour*) is also payable, from 1F to 7F a night per person.

Price seems to relate chiefly to location, condition of paintwork, glitziness of the reception area, and the presence or absence of a lift. Most small Paris hotels are in converted old buildings, with faded decor, dark stairs, cramped rooms and views onto an internal courtyard. Where we think conditions are at the limit of what most people will accept, we say **"basic"**. These are perfectly viable for hardened budget-travellers, but we would not recommend them to people who are at all fastidious about their comforts.

All hotels are obliged to display **room prices** somewhere prominent – usually in the entrance or by the reception desk. Certain **standard terms** recur: *Eau courante* (EC) means a room with washbasin (*lavabo*) only, *cabinet de toilette* (CT) means basin and bidet with a partition for privacy. In both cases there will be communal toilets on the landing and probably a communal shower as well. *Douche/WC* and *Bain/WC* mean that you have a shower or bath as well as toilet in the room. A room with a *grand lit* (double bed) is invariably cheaper than one with *deux lits* (two separate beds). Out of season, it's possible to "negotiate" a reduction of up to 10 percent of the advertised rate, perhaps more, depending on your length of stay. You should at least be able to haggle away the charge for a shower on the landing in the cheaper places.

Breakfast (*petit déjeuner*, or PD) is sometimes included (*compris*) in the room price but is normally extra (*en sus*) – the amount varies between about 30F and 45F per person. Though it isn't supposed to be obligatory, you may get a sour-faced look if you decline to take it: always make it clear whether you want breakfast or not when you take the room. It's usually a fairly indifferent continental affair, and you'll get a fresher, cheaper one at the local café.

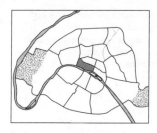

Accommodation

1er arrondissement

Hôtel Henri IV, 25 place Dauphine;
☎01.43.54.44.53 (M° Pont-Neuf/Cité).
An ancient and well-known cheapie in
the beautiful place Dauphine at the
sharp end of the Île de la Cité. Nothing
more luxurious than a *cabinet de toilette*
and now very run-down. Essential to
book. ②.

Hôtel de la Vallée, 84 rue St-Denis;
☎01.42.36.46.99, fax 01.42.36.16.66
(M° Étienne-Marcel/Châtelet). Great
location, absolutely smack in the middle
of Les Halles. Perfectly adequate rooms.
②.

Vauvilliers, 6 rue Vauvilliers;
☎01.42.36.89.08 (M° Châtelet-Les
Halles/Louvre). Book far in advance for
this well-established cheapie. ②.

Hôtel de Lille, 8 rue du Pélican;
☎01.42.33.33.42 (M° Louvre/Palais-
Royal). Small, gloomy, but clean and in
a good central location. ③.

Hôtel du Palais, 2 Quai de la
Mégisserie; ☎01.42.36.98.25, fax
01.42.21.41.67 (M° Châtelet). The
rooms at the top are basic and cheap;
alternatively pay 100F more for a view
over the Seine and a shower in your
room. Location and views at this price
are hard to beat. ③.

Hôtel Lion d'Or, 5 rue de la Sourdière;
☎01.42.60.79.04, fax 01.42.60.09.14 (M°
Tuileries). Poky and busily decorated, but
clean, friendly and very central. ④.

Hôtel St-Honoré, 85 rue St-Honoré;
☎01.42.36.20.38, fax 01.42.21.44.08 (M°
Châtelet/Les Halles/Louvre). Conveniently
close to the heart of things and stylishly
renovated. ④.

Agora, 7 rue Cossonerie;
☎01.42.33.46.02, fax 01.42.33.80.99 (M°
Châtelet-Les-Halles). Charming, peaceful
hotel with individually styled rooms. ⑥.

Ducs d'Anjou, 1 rue Ste-Opportune;
☎01.42.36.92.24, fax 01.42.36.16.63 (M°
Châtelet). A carefully renovated old building overlooking the endlessly crowded
place Ste-Opportune, the focus for Les
Halles nightlife. ⑦.

Tonic Hôtel du Louvre, 12–14 rue du
Roule; ☎01.42.33.00.71, fax
01.40.26.06.86 (M° Louvre/Rivoli).
Expensive for a two-star hotel but not
for the location nor for the steam
baths and jacuzzis in each
bathroom. ⑦.

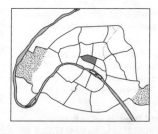

2e arrondissement

Hôtel Tiquetonne, 6 rue Tiquetonne;
☎01.42.36.94.58 (M° Étienne-Marcel).
Old-fashioned, well-maintained cheapie
on a pedestrian street, but close to the
red-light stretch of rue St-Denis. ②.

Hôtel Vivienne, 40 rue Vivienne;
☎01.42.33.13.26, fax 01.40.41.98.19
(M° Grands-Boulevards). Traditional
comfort and wooden floors. Ideal location for the Opéra Garnier, Grands
Boulevards and adjacent nightlife.
④–⑤.

Les Noailles, 9 rue Michodière;
☎01.47.42.92.90, fax 01.49.24.92.71 (M°
Opéra/Quatre-Septembre). Although part
of an international chain, it hasn't lost it's
own identity. Contemporary styling with
traditional pleasures of garden and *terrasse*. ⑦.

Accommodation

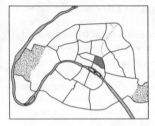

3e arrondissement

Hôtel du Marais, 16 rue de Beauce; ☎01.42.72.30.26 (M° Arts-et-Métiers/Filles-du-Calvaire/Temple). The genuine article: a prewar Paris cheapie, complete with brown spiral stairs, iron handrail, tiled floors and Turkish loos. Primitive but clean, with very nice *patron* who runs a similarly old-fashioned bar downstairs. Quiet street. ②.

Paris France Hôtel, 72 rue de Turbigo; ☎01.42.78.64.92, fax 01.42.71.99.43 (M° Temple/République). On a noisy road but in an animated quartier off the beaten track. ③–④.

Hôtel Picard, 26 rue de Picardie; ☎01.48.87.53.82, fax 01.48.87.02.56 (M° Temple/République). Clean and comfortable establishment, run by a very accommodating Pole, set in a great location overlooking the Carreau du Temple and next door to Paris' best Internet café (see p.272). Popular with young American backpackers. Ten percent reduction if you produce your *Rough Guide*. ③.

Hôtel du Séjour, 36 rue du Grenier-St-Lazare; ☎01.48.87.40.36 (M° Rambuteau/Étienne-Marcel). A very clean, modest establishment run by a nice couple, and only a short walk from the Pompidou Centre . ③.

Hôtel de Saintonge, 16 rue de Saintonge; ☎01.42.77.91.13, fax 01.48.87.76.41 (M° Filles-du-Calvaire). In a sixteenth-century house on the edge of the Marais, near the Picasso Museum, though only the stone-vaulted cellar,

where breakfast is taken, retains much original character. A soothing place to stay, with all mod cons, including cable TV and safes in every room, while all the bathrooms have tubs to soak in. ⑥.

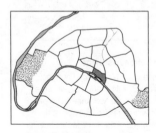

4^e arrondissement

Hôtel Moderne, 3 rue Caron; ☎01.48.87.97.05 (M° St-Paul/Bastille). Much better than a first impression of the staircase would suggest, and the price is amazing for this area. ②.

Grand Hôtel du Loiret, 8 rue des Mauvais-Garçons; ☎01.48.87.77.00, fax 01.48.04.96.56 (M° Hôtel-de-Ville). Simple small rooms, but very good value for the price. ②.

Castex Hôtel, 5 rue Castex; ☎01.42.72.31.52, fax 01.42.72.57.91 (M° Bastille/Sully-Morland). Renovated building in a quiet street on the edge of the Marais run by a friendly, helpful family. Book well in advance. ③–④.

Grand Hôtel Jeanne d'Arc, 3 rue de Jarente; ☎01.48.87.62.11, fax 01.48.87.37.31 (M° St-Paul). Clean, quiet and attractive. Rooms have all mod cons including cable TV. Booking essential. ④.

Hôtel Sévigné, 2 rue Mahler; ☎01.42.72.76.17 (M° St-Paul). Very comfortable, pleasant hotel frequented by foreigners, and consequently essential to book in advance. ④.

Hôtel de Nice, 42bis rue de Rivoli; ☎01.42.78.55.29, fax 01.42.78.36.07 (M° Hôtel-de-Ville). Very pretty rooms, and a *salon* where guests can mingle – no TVs in the rooms. ⑤.

Hôtel du Septième Art, 20 rue St-Paul; ☎01.42.77.04.03, fax 01.42.77.69.10 (M° St-Paul/Sully Morland). Pleasant, comfortable place decorated with posters and photos from old movies; a similarly themed *salon de thé* downstairs. The stairs and bathrooms live up to the black-and-white-movie style. Every room equipped with a safe. ⑤.

Hôtel Central Marais, 33 rue Vieille-du-Temple; ☎01.48.87.56.08, fax 01.42.77.06.27 (M° Hôtel-de-Ville). The only gay hotel in Paris, with a relaxed bar downstairs. Shared bathrooms. ⑥.

Grand Hôtel Mahler, 5 rue Mahler; ☎01.42.72.60.92, fax 01.42.72.25.37 (M° St-Paul). Right in the heart of the Marais; breakfast in a recently renovated seventeenth-century vaulted wine cellar. ⑥.

Hôtel St-Louis Marais, 1 rue Charles-V; ☎01.48.87.87.04, fax 01.48.87.33.26 (M° Sully-Morland). A very comfortable restored seventeenth-century mansion. ⑦.

Hôtel de Lutèce, 65 rue St-Louis-en-l'Île; ☎01.43.26.23.52, fax 01.43.29.60.25 (M° Pont-Marie). Small but exquisite rooms on the most desirable island in France. ⑧.

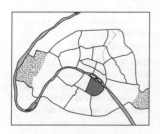

5ᵉ arrondissement

Hôtel du Commerce, 14 rue de la Montagne-Ste-Geneviève; ☎01.43.54.89.69 (M° Maubert-Mutualité). Only for those on the tightest of budgets, this somewhat gloomy hotel is extremely economical for the heart of the Latin Quarter. Communal washing and toilets. No reservations, so arrive before 10am and be brave – a potentially surly greeting awaits. ①.

Hôtel Médicis, 214 rue St-Jacques; ☎01.43.54.14.66 (RER Luxembourg). Very primitive, but the prices are unbeatable. It's popular with hard-up backpackers, and the owners are charming. ①–②.

Hôtel Port-Royal, 8 bd Port-Royal; ☎01.43.31.70.06 (M° Gobelins). A real bargain – clean, attractive and friendly. It's at the rue Mouffetard end of the boulevard, close to the métro. ②–④.

Hôtel Le Central, 6 rue Descartes; ☎01.46.33.57.93 (M° Maubert-Mutualité/Cardinal-Lemoine). Clean, decent but dowdy rooms in a typically Parisian house atop the Montagne Ste-Geneviève, overlooking the gates of the former École Polytechnique and surrounded by popular brasseries; all rooms come with a shower. One of a dying breed. ③.

Hôtel Marignan, 13 rue du Sommerard; ☎01.43.54.63.81 (M° Maubert-Mutualité). One of the best bargains in town, with breakfast included in the price. Totally sympathetic to the needs of rucksack-toting foreigners, with free laundry and ironing facilities, plus a room to eat your own food in – plates, fridge, microwave and kettle provided. Rooms for 2, 3 and 4–5 people; no reservations for single rooms, though you need to turn up early. ③.

Hôtel des Alliés, 20 rue Berthollet; ☎01.43.31.47.52, fax 01.45.35.13.92 (M° Censier-Daubenton). Simple, clean and well run, with bargain prices. Rooms with bathroom are very spacious. No lift. ③–④.

Hôtel Gay-Lussac, 29 rue Gay-Lussac; ☎01.43.54.23.96, fax 01.40.51.79.49 (RER Luxembourg). Friendly, no-frills establishment with an adjoining café-bar. Excellent value for the area – close to Luxembourg gardens. No credit cards. Book at least a week in advance. ③–④.

Hôtel du Progrès, 50 rue Gay-Lussac; ☎01.43.54.53.18 (RER Luxembourg/Port-Royal). No frills and old-fashioned, but

Accommodation

Hotels are listed in order of price category:
① up to 160F
② 160–220F
③ 220–300F
④ 300–400F
⑤ 400–500F
⑥ 500–600F
⑦ 600–700F
⑧ over 700F
For a fuller explanation, see p.234.

well-situated and fine for a cheap stay. Free showers for rooms without them. ③–④.

Hôtel Esmeralda, 4 rue St-Julien-le-Pauvre; ☎01.43.54.19.20, fax 01.40.51.00.68 (M° St-Michel/Maubert-Mutualité). A discreet and ancient house on square Viviani, with a superb view of Notre-Dame. Most rooms are doubles with shower and toilet, but there are some much cheaper singles (②), with wash basin only. ④–⑤.

Familia Hôtel, 11 rue des Écoles; ☎01.43.54.55.27, fax 01.45.29.61.77 (M° Cardinal-Lemoine/Maubert-Mutualité/Jussieu). Friendly hotel in the heart of the quartier. Rooms are small but characterful, decorated with pretty wall murals; all are en suite with cable TV, and some have their own balcony complete with table and chairs. ⑤.

Hôtel du Mont-Blanc, 28 rue de la Huchette; ☎01.43.54.22.29, fax 01.46.34.14.56 (M° St-Michel). Refurbished hotel in a great location a stone's throw from Notre-Dame. The lively, restaurant-filled street can be noisy, though all the windows have double glazing – not much use in summer, though. ⑤.

Hôtel de la Sorbonne, 6 rue Victor-Cousin; ☎01.43.54.58.08, fax 01.40.51.05.18 (RER Luxembourg/M° Maubert-Mutualité). An attractive old building in the heart of things, but quiet; comfortable and close to the Luxembourg gardens. ⑤.

Hôtel St-Jacques, 35 rue des Écoles; ☎01.44.07.45.45, fax 01.43.25.65.50 (M° Maubert-Mutualité/Odéon). Completely refurbished in 1997, this very pretty hotel in the heart of the district combines original nineteenth-century features, including a wrought-iron staircase and decorative ceiling mouldings, with modern comforts. Rooms, all en suite, are spacious. Murals feature throughout and some rooms have balconies with great views of the Panthéon. Helpful staff. ⑤–⑥.

Hôtel des Grandes Écoles, 75 rue du Cardinal-Lemoine; ☎01.43.26.79.23,

fax 01.43.25.28.15 (Mo Cardinal-Lemoine). A beautiful, recently decorated hotel in old buildings in the heart of the Latin Quarter, enclosing a lovely court-yard garden. Book well ahead. A few cheaper singles, but most ⑤–⑦.

Hôtel des Carmes, 5 rue des Carmes; ☎01.43.29.78.40, fax 01.43.29.57.17 (M° Maubert-Mutualité). Long-established but recently refurbished tourist hotel; modern and clean with colourful en-suite rooms and an excellent view of the nearby Panthéon. ⑥.

Hôtel des Trois Collèges, 16 rue Cujas; ☎01.43.54.67.30, fax 01.46.34.02.99 (RER Luxembourg). Light, airy rooms and young, helpful staff in this classy, modernized hotel; breakfast is served in the attached *salon de thé*. ⑦.

Grand Hôtel St-Michel, 19 rue Cujas; ☎01.46.33.33.02 (M° Odéon/Cluny). The lap of luxury in a great location in a great location between the Panthéon and the Luxembourg gardens. ⑧.

Libertal Quartier Latin, 9 rue des Écoles; ☎01.44.27.06.45, fax 01.43.25.36.70 (M° Cardinal-Lemoine/Maubert-Mutualité). Part of the Libertal group focusing on small charming hotels in Paris. The individual rooms come straight from a style mag, with air-conditioning, double-glazing and a kettle to ensure you're entirely comfortable, plus luxuriously spacious en-suite bathrooms. ⑧.

Agora St-Germain, 42 rue des Bernardins; ☎01.46.34.13.00, fax 01.46.34.75.05 (M° Maubert-Mutualité). A very comfortable and well-appointed hotel with all the creature comforts from satellite TV to mini-bar. ⑧.

6e arrondissement

Hôtel St-Michel, 17 rue Gît-le-Coeur; ☎01.43.26.98.70, fax 01.40.46.95.69 (M° St-Michel). Simple, but perfectly acceptable and friendly. Great location in a very attractive old street close to the river and opposite a little art-house cinema. Breakfast included in the price. ③.

Hôtel de Nesle, 7 rue de Nesle; ☎01.43.54.62.41 (M° St-Michel). Characterful former hippie-haven, small and friendly. No reservations, so get there before 10am. ③–④.

Hôtel Delhy's, 22 rue de l'Hirondelle; ☎01.43.26.58.25, fax 01.43.26.51.06 (M° St-Michel). Just off place St-Michel. An old house in a tiny street – spotlessly maintained, if a little overpriced. ④–⑤.

Hôtel du Dragon, 36 rue du Dragon; ☎01.45.48.51.05, fax 01.42.22.51.62 (M° St-Germain-des-Prés/Sèvres-Babylone). Fairly basic, but clean, friendly and in a great location. Closed Aug. ④–⑤.

Hôtel Récamier, 3bis place St-Sulpice; ☎01.43.26.04.89, fax 01.46.33.27.73 (M° St-Sulpice/St-Germain-des-Prés). Comfortable, old-fashioned, superbly situated, and solidly bourgeois hotel offering few concessions to modernity or fashion. ④–⑦.

Grand Hôtel des Balcons, 3 rue Casimir-Delavigne; ☎01.46.34.78.50, fax 01.46.34.06.27 (M° Odéon). An attractive and comfortable hotel, complete with Art Deco entrance, in a lovely location near the Odéon and Luxembourg gardens. ⑤.

Welcome Hotel, 66 rue de Seine; ☎01.46.34.24.80, fax 01.40.46.81.59 (M° Odéon). Adequate rooms in a great but rather noisy location by the rue de Buci street market and its speciality food shops. ⑥.

Hôtel des Marronniers, 21 rue Jacob; ☎01.43.25.30.60, fax 01.40.46 83.56 (M° St-Germain-des-Prés). Relatively pricey, but a delightful place with a dining room overlooking a secret garden. Good for a special occasion. ⑦.

Hôtel de l'Angleterre, 44 rue Jacob; ☎01.42.60.34.72, fax 01.42.60.16.93 (M° St-Germain-des-Prés). Classy and elegant, this was once the British Embassy. Later, Hemingway lived in room 14, though back then he paid only three francs a night, not the 980F you'll be surrendering. ⑧.

Hôtel de l'Odéon, 13 rue St-Sulpice, ☎01.43.25.70.11, fax 01.43.29.97.34 (M° St-Sulpice/Odéon). Old-fashioned luxury for more than 1000F a room – flowers, twin beds, antique furniture. ⑧.

Accommodation

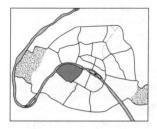

7e arrondissement

Hôtel du Champs-de-Mars, 7 rue du Champs-de-Mars; ☎01.45.51.52.30, fax 01.45.51.64.34 (M° École-Militaire). Completely refurbished. Comfortable but slightly small rooms in a very attractive neighbourhood. ④.

Hôtel Eiffel Rive-Gauche, 6 rue du Gros-Caillou; ☎01.45.51.24.56, fax 01.45.51.11.77 (M° École-Militaire). A great little hotel practically underneath the Eiffel Tower. ④.

Hôtel de la Paix, 19 rue du Gros-Caillou; ☎01.45.51.86.17 (M° École-Militaire). Recent renovations have inflated prices, but this is still the best bargain within proximity of the Eiffel Tower. ④.

Grand Hôtel Lévêque, 29 rue Cler; ☎01.47.05.49.15, fax 01.45.50.49.36 (M° École-Militaire/Latour-Maubourg). Recently renovated, clean hotel run by nice people, who speak some English. Good location smack in the middle of the rue Cler market. Book a month ahead. ④.

Hôtel Malar, 29 rue Malar; ☎01.45.51.38.46, fax 01.45.55.20.19

Hotels are listed in order of price category:
① up to 160F
② 160–220F
③ 220–300F
④ 300–400F
⑤ 400–500F
⑥ 500–600F
⑦ 600–700F
⑧ over 700F
For a fuller explanation, see p.234.

Accommodation

(Mo Latour-Maubourg/Invalides). Small, with slightly poky rooms, but in a very attractive street close to the river. ④.

Hôtel Rapp, 8 av Rapp; ☎01.45.51.42.28, fax 01.43.59.50.70 (M°Alma-Marceau/RER Pont-de-l'Alma). A little dingy and charmless, but close to the Seine and the Palais Chaillot. Some singles at ③; doubles ④.

Hôtel la Serre, 24bis rue Cler; ☎01.47.05.52.33, fax 01.40.62.95.66 (M° École-Militaire). An old-fashioned, no-frills establishment on a lively street in a posh and attractive neighbourhood. Reserve a fortnight in advance. ④.

Royal Phare Hôtel, 40 av de la Motte-Picquet; ☎01.47.05.57.30, fax 01.45.51.64.41 (M°École-Militaire). A bit impersonal, but very convenient and with some good views. Close to rue Cler and its sumptuous market. ④. M°

Hôtel Muguet, 11 rue Chevert; ☎01.47.05.05.93, fax 01.45.50.25.37 (M° École-Militaire/Latour-Maubourg). A pleasantly renovated oldie in a quiet street between the Eiffel Tower and Invalides. ⑤–⑥.

Le Pavillon, 54 rue St-Dominique; ☎01.45.51.42.87, fax 01.45.51.32.79 (M° Invalides/Latour-Maubourg). A tiny former convent set back from the tempting shops of the rue St-Dominique in a leafy courtyard. A lovely setting, but the rooms are a little poky for the price. ⑤–⑥.

Hôtel de Beaune, 29 rue de Beaune; ☎01.42.61.24.89, fax 01.49.27.02.12 (M° Rue-du-Bac). A very pretty hotel in an ideal location close to St-Germain and the Musée d'Orsay. ⑥.

Hôtel du Palais Bourbon, 49 rue de Bourgogne; ☎01.45.51.63.32, fax 01.45.55.20.21 (M° Varenne). A handsome old building in a sunny street by the Musée Rodin. Rooms are spacious and light. Book in advance for the two cheaper doubles (③). Otherwise ⑥.

Hôtel Solférino, 91 rue de Lille; ☎01.47.05.85.54, fax 01.45.55.51.16 (M° Solférino/RER Musée-d'Orsay). Attractive place near the Musée d'Orsay and river, featuring an old-fashioned cage-lift. A few cheaper rooms available. ⑥.

Hôtel de la Tulipe, 33 rue Malar; ☎01.45.51.67.21, fax 01.47.53.96.37 (M° Latour-Maubourg). Patio for summer breakfast and drinks; beamy and cottagey. But, as with all hotels in this area, you are paying for the location rather than great luxury. ⑥.

Hôtel de Varenne, 44 rue de Bourgogne; ☎01.45.51.45.55, fax 01.45.51.86.63 (M° Varenne). Set back from the road in a small courtyard where breakfast is served in the summer. A relaxed atmosphere in a smart area. ⑥–⑦.

Hôtel Bersoly's St-Germain, 28 rue de Lille; ☎01.42.60.73.79, fax 01.49.27.05.55 (M° Rue-du-Bac). Small but exquisite rooms, each named after an artist. Impeccable service. ⑦.

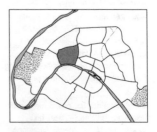

8ᵉ arrondissement

Hôtel d'Artois, 94 rue la Boétie; ☎01.43.59.84.12, fax 01.43.59.50.70 (M° St-Philippe-du-Roule). One of the cheapest in this smartest part of town, with unusually gracious and spacious rooms. A bargain. ③.

Hôtel de la Paix, 22 rue Roquépine; ☎ and fax 01.42.65.14.36 (M° St-Augustin). A bit gloomy, but in a very Parisian fashion. ④.

Hôtel des Champs-Élysées, 2 rue Artois; ☎01.43.59.11.42, fax 01.45.61.00.61 (M° Franklin-D-Roosevelt/St-Philippe-du-Roule). Old-fashioned hospitality and excellent value for the area. ⑤.

Hôtel de l'Élysée, 12 rue des Saussaies; ☎01.42.65.29.25, fax 01.42.65.64.28 (M° St-Philippe-du-Roule). Chandeliers and four-posters – classic luxury. ⑦.

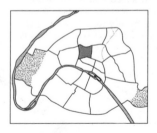

9ᵉ arrondissement

Perfect Hôtel, 39 rue Rodier; ☎01.42.81.18.86, fax 01.42.85.01.38 (M° Anvers). Popular hotel on a lively street lined with restaurants. Simple, clean rooms and a warm welcome. ②.

Hôtel des Arts, 7 Cité-Bergère; ☎01.42.46.73.30, fax 01.48.00.94.42 (M° Grands-Boulevards). A charming and friendly hotel and one of the cheaper ones in this quiet alley close to the Grands Boulevards. ④.

Hôtel Imperial, 45 rue de la Victoire; ☎01.48.74.10.47, fax 01.44.63.02.47 (M° Le Peletier/Chaussée-d'Antin). Young, efficient manager speaking excellent English. Fairly nondescript but adequate rooms. ④.

Modial Hôtel, 21 rue Notre-Dame-de-Lorette; ☎01.48.78.60.47, fax 01.42.81.95.58 (M° St-Georges). Acceptable, if uninspired, by the lovely place St-Georges. Rooms for four, 660F. ④.

Hôtel de Beauharnais, 51 rue de la Victoire; ☎01.48.74.71.13 (M° Le Peletier/Trinité). Louis Quinze, First Empire . . . every room decorated in a different period-style. At the cheaper end of this price bracket with reasonable discounts outside the high season. ⑤.

Hôtel des Croisés, 63 rue St-Lazare; ☎01.48.74.78.24, fax 01.49.95.04.43 (M° Trinité). Low on mod cons but great on style: a hotchpotch of different periods. Good value. ⑤.

Hôtel Chopin, 46 passage Jouffroy; ☎01.47.70.58.10, fax 01.42.47.00.70 (M° Grands-Boulevards). Entrance on bd Montmartre, near rue du Faubourg-Montmartre. A splendid, characterful period building in the old *passage*. Rooms are acceptable. ⑤.

Hôtel Riboutté Lafayette, 5 rue Riboutté; ☎01.47.70.62.36, fax 01.48.00.91.50 (M° Cadet). In a pleasantly quiet area but well placed for the Grands Boulevards, Gare du Nord and Pigalle. Warmly decorated and welcoming. ⑤.

Hôtel du Léman, 20 rue Trévise; ☎01.42.46.50.66, fax 01.48.24.27.59 (M° Grands-Boulevards). Tiny rooms, but a delightful address. ⑥.

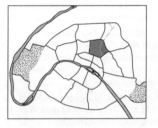

10ᵉ arrondissement

Hôtel Moderne du Temple, 3 rue d'Aix; ☎01.42.08.09.04, fax 01.42.41.72.17 (M° République/Goncourt). Bargain cheapie, Czech-run, just the job for a low budget. ①–②.

Hôtel Palace, 9 rue Bouchardon; ☎01.40.40.09.45 or 01.42.06.59.32, fax 01.42.06.16.90 (M° Strasbourg-St-Denis). Gloomy corridors but acceptable rooms in a busy, colourful and central district near the Porte St-Martin. Popular with backpackers. Nice, helpful owners. A good deal. ①–③.

Hôtel du Jura, 6 rue de Jarry; ☎01.47.70.06.66 (M° Gare-de-l'Est/Château-d'Eau). Primitive, but friendly and decent. ②.

Accommodation

Hotels are listed in order of price category:
① *up to 160F*
② *160–220F*
③ *220–300F*
④ *300–400F*
⑤ *400–500F*
⑥ *500–600F*
⑦ *600–700F*
⑧ *over 700F*
For a fuller explanation, see p.234.

Accommodation

Hôtel du Brabant, 18 rue des Petits-Hôtels; ☎01.47.70.12.32, fax 01.47.70.20.32 (M° Poissonnière/Gare-du-Nord/Gare-de-l'Est). Six floors of gloomy but manageable rooms in an ancient, liftless building. ②–③.

Grand Hôtel d'Amiens, 88 rue du Faubourg-Poissonnière (nr junction with rue La-Fayette); ☎01.48.78.71.18, fax 01.48.74.89.41 (M° Poissonnière). Worn stairs and no frills, but clean and reasonably spacious rooms. ②–③.

Hôtel Jarry, 4 rue Jarry, ☎01.47.70.70.38 (M° Gare-de-l'Est/Château-d'Eau). First impression is rather sterile, but the rooms are perfectly acceptable and fresher than other cheapies in this street. Breakfast is only 18F. ②–③.

Hôtel Parisiana, 21 rue de Chabrol; ☎01.47.70.68.33, fax 01.48.00.00.67 (M° Gare-de-l'Est). Unimaginative decor but clean, and staff are helpful. ③.

Hôtel Mazagran, 4 rue Mazagran; ☎01.48.24.25.26, fax 01.42.47.17.96 (M° Bonne-Nouvelle). Agreeable accommodation in a quiet but central street close to the Turkish quarter. ③–④.

Nord-Est Hôtel, 12 rue des Petits-Hôtels; ☎01.47.70.07.18, fax 01.42.46.73.50 (M° Poissonnière/Gare-du-Nord/Gare-de-l'Est). Rooms are clean and modern, though characterless, which comes as a bit of a disappointment after the exquisite garden in front of the hotel ④.

Hôtel-Résidence Magenta, 35 rue Yves-Toudic; ☎01.42.40.17.72, fax 01.42.02.59.66 (M° République/Jacques-Bonsergent). Friendly, clean, attractive hotel with patio breakfast area. The top two rooms, 61 and 62, are particularly nice. ④–⑤.

Adix Hôtel, 30 rue Lucien-Sampaix, ☎01.42.08.19.74, fax 01.42.08.27.28 (M° Jacques-Bonsergent). In a pleasant street close to the St-Martin canal. Reasonable value for money: all rooms with TV, radio and bathroom. ⑤.

Belta Hôtel Résidence, 46 rue Lucien-Sampaix; ☎01.46.07.23.87, fax 01.42.09.87.27 (M° Gare-de-l'Est). Good location on the St-Martin canal bank. Totally renovated in bland airport style, but comfortable. ⑥.

Hôtel St-Louis, 8 rue Buisson-St-Louis; ☎01.46.34.04.80, fax 01.46.34.02.13 (M° Belleville). Very pleasant, modern building; all rooms are en suite with cable TV and other conveniences. ⑦.

11e arrondissement

Hôtel de la Nouvelle France, 31 rue Keller, ☎01.47.00.40.74 (M° Brèguet-Sabin). A basic, rough-and-ready hotel in an excellent location, highly suitable for those more interested in the surrounding Bastille nightlife than where they stay. Make sure you look at a room upstairs, not in the seedier section out back. Free showers. No bookings. ①.

Hôtel de Nevers, 53 rue de Malte; ☎01.47.00.56.18, fax 01.43.57.77.39 (M° Oberkampf/République). You couldn't find better value than this clean, decent hotel run by a very sympathetic proprietor. Excellent breakfasts. ②.

Hôtel de Vienne, 43 rue de Malte; ☎01.48.05.44.42 (M° Oberkampf/République). Very pleasant, clean, good-value cheapie, with nicely decorated rooms (none with toilet, though some have showers), run by a charming older couple. No lift. No credit cards. Closed Aug. ②, with some cheaper singles.

Cosmo's Hotel, 35 rue Jean-Pierre Timbaud; ☎ & fax 01.43.57.25.88 (M° Parmentier). Clean and decent, with good restaurants nearby. ②–③.

Mary's Hotel, 15 rue de Malte; ☎01.47.00.81.70, fax 01.47.00.58.06 (M° Oberkampf/République). Comfortable and clean hotel on the edge of the Marais, run by courteous people. The cheaper rooms are good value for money, the en-suite rooms less so. ②–③.

Hôtel des Arts, 2 rue Godefroy-Cavaignac; ☎01.43.79.72.57 (M° Voltaire). Pretty foyer and well-furnished rooms, but overall not much charm, and a tad fusty. Hospitable, however, and acceptable at the price. No lift. ③.

Pax Hotel, 12 rue de Charonne; ☎01.47.00.40.98, fax 01.42.28.57.81 (M° Ledru-Rollin/Bastille). A reasonable establishment if you want to be in the centre of the Bastille's nightlife. Can be noisy. No lift. ③.

Grand Hôtel Amelot, 54 rue Amelot; ☎01.48.06.15.19, fax 01.48.06.69.77 (M° St-Sébastien-Froissart). Recently renovated, well-run establishment in a good location on the edge of the Marais and close to the Cirque en Hiver where there are several good bars. Rooms very spacious and nicely decorated. Excellent value: except for a few bargain 150F singles, all rooms have bathrooms – lovely and modern, some with bathtubs – and cable TV. ③–⑤.

Garden Hôtel, 1 rue du Général-Blaise; ☎01.47.00.57.93, fax 01.47.00.45.29 (M° St-Ambroise). Comfortable, renovated hotel located on the pleasant square Parmentier. ④.

Hôtel du Nord et de l'Est, 49 rue de Malte; ☎01.47.00.71.70, fax 01.43.57.51.16 (M° Oberkampf/République). Clean and comfortable, all rooms en suite with direct phone, TV and bathroom; popular with business travellers. ④.

Plessis-Hôtel, 25 rue du Grand-Prieuré; ☎01.47.00.13.38, fax 01.43.57.97.87 (M° République/Oberkampf). Comfortable mid-range hotel in a good location. ④.

Hôtel St-Martin, 12 rue Léon-Frot; ☎01.43.71.09.14, fax 01.43.71.88.44 (M° Boulets-Montreuil). Dull neighbour-hood, but a nice, friendly hotel with all mod cons. ④.

Hôtel Beaumarchais, 3 rue Oberkampf; ☎01.43.38.16.16, fax 01.43.38.32.86 (M° Filles-du-Calvaire/Oberkampf). Fashionable, gay-friendly hotel with personal service and colourful Fifties-inspired decor; all rooms en suite with air conditioning, safes and cable TV. ⑤.

Hôtel-Résidence Trousseau, 13 rue Trousseau; ☎01.48.05.55.55, fax 01.48.05.83.97, email *tr@hroy.com* (M° Bastille/Ledru-Rollin). Modern, serviced studio apartments, which can sleep from two to six people, and come with fully equipped kitchens – perfectly positioned for food shopping in the nearby place d'Aligre market – plus satellite TV. Car parking available for 80F per day. ⑤.

Méridional, 36 bd Richard-Lenoir; ☎01.48.05.75.00, fax 01.43.57.42.85 (M° Brèguet-Sabin/Bastille). Attractive, with light rooms and a decorative courtyard garden. ⑥.

Accommodation

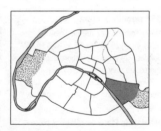

12ᵉ arrondissement

Hôtel de Reims, 26 rue Hector-Malot; ☎01.43.07.46.18 (M° Gare-de-Lyon/Ledru-Rollin). Old-fashioned hotel on a quiet street with access to the Promenade Plantée, and close to the place d'Aligre market. Closed Aug. ②.

Grand Hôtel Doré, 201 av Daumesnil; ☎01.43.43.66.89, fax 01.43.43.65.20 (M° Daumesnil). Not very central, but smart for the price. ③.

Hôtel du Midi, 31 rue Traversière; ☎01.43.07.88.68, fax 01.43.07.37.77 (M°

Accommodation

Ledru-Rollin). Clean, pleasant accommodation close to the Gare du Lyon and the Viaduc des Arts; most rooms have shower, toilet and TV. ③–④.

Hôtel des Pyrénées, 204 rue du Faubourg-St-Antoine; ☎01.43.72.07.46, fax 01.43.72.98.45 (M° Faidherbe-Chaligny). Comfortable and quiet behind its posh reception area. ④.

Hôtel Saphir, 35 rue de Citeaux; ☎01.43.07.77.28, fax 01.43.46.67.45 (M° Faidherbe-Chaligny). On a quiet street off Faubourg St-Antoine. No special charms, but comfortable. ⑤.

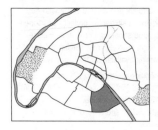

13ᵉ arrondissement

Hotels are listed in order of price category:
① up to 160F
② 160–220F
③ 220–300F
④ 300–400F
⑤ 400–500F
⑥ 500–600F
⑦ 600–700F
⑧ over 700F
For a fuller explanation, see p.234.

Hôtel Tolbiac, 122 rue de Tolbiac; ☎01.44.24.25.54, fax 01.45.85.43.47 (M° Tolbiac). On a noisy junction, but all rooms are very pleasant, with loos and showers; breakfast is only 15F. In July and Aug you can rent small studios by the week. ②.

Hôtel de la Place des Alpes, 2 place des Alpes; ☎01.42.16.92.93, fax 01.45.86.30.06 (M° Place-d'Italie). Agreeable enough for the price. ③.

Résidence Les Gobelins, 9 rue des Gobelins; ☎01.47.07.26.90, fax 01.43.31.44.05 (M° Les-Gobelins). Delightful, popular establishment that must be booked well in advance. ④–⑤.

Hôtel du Vert-Galant, 41 rue Croulebarbe; ☎01.44.08.83.50, fax 01.44.08.83.69 (M° Les-Gobelins). In a quiet, verdant backwater, with a vine climbing up the wall from the garden, above a renowned Basque restaurant. Cosy rooms, some with kitchenette. ⑤.

14ᵉ arrondissement

Ouest Hotel, 27 rue de Gergovie; ☎01.45.42.64.99, fax 01.45.42.46.65 (M° Pernety). Basic but perfectly acceptable, in a very pleasant part of town. ②.

Hôtel Le Lionceau, 22 rue Daguerre; ☎01.42.22.53.43, fax 01.44.10.72.49 (M° Denfert-Rochereau). Decent-sized rooms and decorated with murals throughout. On the pedestrian market street. ③.

Hôtel de la Loire, 39bis rue du Moulin-Vert; ☎01.45.40.66.88, fax 01.45.40.89.07 (M° Alésia/Plaisance). Attractive hotel on a very quiet street, with breakfast served in a little garden. ④.

Hôtel du Parc Montsouris, 4 rue du Parc-Montsouris; ☎01.45.89.09.72, fax 01.45.80.92.72 (M° Porte-d'Orléans/RER Cité-Universitaire). Modern, a bit impersonal, but in a lovely tiny street right by the park. ④.

Virginia Hotel, 66 rue du Père-Corentin; ☎01.45.40.70.90, fax 01.45.40.95.21 (M° Porte-d'Orléans). Quiet part of town some way from the centre, but close to the périphérique: parking available. ④.

Hôtel Istria, 29 rue Campagne-Première; ☎01.43.20.91.82, fax 01.43.22.48.45 (M° Raspail). Beautifully decorated, with legendary artistic associations: Duchamp, Man Ray, Aragon, Mayakovsky and Rilke all stayed here. ⑤.

Comfort Hotel Losserand, 76 rue Raymond-Losserand; ☎01.40.52.12.40, fax 01.40.52.12.41 (M° Pernety). Part of a chain and business-oriented, but with stylish rooms and a dependable level of service and comfort. ⑥.

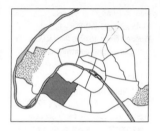

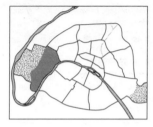

Accommodation

15e arrondissement

Mondial Hôtel, 136 bd de Grenelle;
☎01.45.79.73.57, fax 01.45.79.58.65 (M°
La Motte-Picquet). Despite its rather grim
appearance, this hotel is friendly and
decent, with large rooms and good views.
Right opposite the raised métro. ③.

Hôtel Fondary, 30 rue Fondary;
☎01.45.75.14.75, fax 01.45.75.84.42 (M°
Émile-Zola). Quiet and agreeable location
in one of the more animated areas of
the 15e. ④.

Hôtel King, 1 rue de Chambéry;
☎01.45.33.99.06, fax 01.42.50.02.34 (M°
Porte-de-Vanves/Convention). Quiet and
pleasant, conveniently close to parc
Georges-Brassens. ④.

Hôtel Pasteur, 33 rue du Docteur-Roux;
☎01.47.83.53.17, fax 01.45.66.62.39 (M°
Pasteur). A small garden, and rooms that
are comfortable and well-equipped for
the price. ④.

Hôtel Tour Eiffel Dupleix, 11 rue Juge;
☎01.45.78.29.29, fax 01.45.78.60.00 (M°
Dupleix). Recently renovated, with tasteful rooms and a tiny garden in which to
breakfast. ⑤–⑥.

Hôtel Wallace, 89 rue Fondary;
☎01.45.78.83.30, fax 01.40.58.19.43 (M°
Émile-Zola). Unpretentious and charming
place with a pretty garden in the courtyard. ⑦.

16e arrondissement

Hôtel Keppler, 12 rue Keppler;
☎01.47.20.65.05, fax 01.47.23.02.29 (M°
George-V/Kléber). Rooms a little small,
but spotless, quite comfortable, and just
a few steps from the Champs-Élysées.
⑤.

Hameau de Passy, 48 rue Passy;
☎01.42.88.47.55, fax 01.42.30.83.72 (M°
Muette). Tucked away in a *villas* – utterly
peaceful and with faultless service. ⑥.

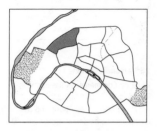

17e arrondissement

Hôtel Savoy, 21 rue des Dames;
☎01.42.93.13.47 (M° Place-
Clichy/Rome). Typical unmodernized Paris
cheapie; basic, but decent. ①.

Hôtel Avenir-Jonquière, 23 rue de la
Jonquière; ☎01.46.27.83.41, fax
01.46.27.88.08 (M° Guy-
Môquet/Brochant). Clean, friendly establishment offering bargain accommodation and particularly reasonable single
rates. Close to the tempting food stores
on av de St-Ouen. ②.

Hôtel des Batignolles, 26–28 rue des
Batignolles; ☎01.43.87.70.40, fax
01.44.70.01.04 (M° Rome/Place-Clichy).
A quiet and very reasonable establishment in a neighbourhood that prides
itself on its village character. Triples for
385F. ②–④.

Jouffroy, 28 passage Cardinet;
☎01.47.54.06.00, fax 01.47.63.83.12 (M°
Malesherbes). Charming owners and
pastel-coloured floral wallpaper in a

Accommodation

Hotels are listed in order of price category:
① *up to 160F*
② *160–220F*
③ *220–300F*
④ *300–400F*
⑤ *400–500F*
⑥ *500–600F*
⑦ *600–700F*
⑧ *over 700F*
For a fuller explanation, see p.234.

quiet *passage* between rue Jouffroy and rue Cardinet. ④.

Hôtel du Roi René, 72 place Félix-Lobligeois; ☎01.42.26.72.73, fax 01.42.63.74.99 (M° Rome/Villiers). A mid-priced hotel in a very nice location by a mini-Greek temple and public garden. ⑤.

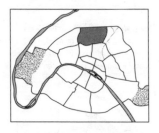

18ᵉ arrondissement

Hôtel du Commerce, 34 rue des Trois-Frères; ☎01.42.64.81.69 (M° Abbesses/Anvers). Very basic and dirt-cheap; for the hardened dosser only. ①.

Hôtel Caulaincourt, 2 square Caulaincourt (by 63 rue Caulaincourt); ☎01.46.06.42.99, fax 01.46.06.48.67 (M° Lamarck-Caulaincourt). One of the nicest, cleanest and friendliest of the cheaper hotels – magnificent view from room 16. ①–③.

Hôtel Versigny, 31 rue Letort; ☎01.42.59.20.90, fax 01.42.59.32.66 (M° Jules-Joffrin). Unmodernized and basic – but fine if you're tough and want a cheap sleep. ②.

Hôtel du Puy de Dôme, 180 rue Ordener (av St-Ouen end); ☎01.46.27.78.55, fax 01.42.29.13.67 (M° Guy-Môquet). On the north side of Montmartre, close to a big street market and the métro. A pleasant, cheap and friendly hotel, recently reno-vated. ②.

Idéal Hôtel, 3 rue des Trois-Frères; ☎01.46.06.63.63, fax 01.42.64.97.01 (M° Abbesses). Marvellous location on the slopes of Montmartre. Basic, but clean, friendly and used to backpackers. ②–③.

Style Hôtel, 8 rue Ganneron (av Clichy

end); ☎01.45.22.37.59, fax 01.45.22.81.03 (M° Place-Clichy). Wooden floors, marble fireplaces, a secluded internal courtyard, and nice people – great value. No lift and no credit cards. ②–③.

Hôtel André Gill, 4 rue André-Gill; ☎01.42.62.48.48, fax 01.42.62.77.92 (M° Pigalle/Abbesses). Perfectly adequate, quiet rooms in a great location on the slopes of Montmartre, in a cul-de-sac off rue des Martyrs. ③–④.

Hôtel le Bouquet de Montmartre, 1 rue Durantin; ☎01.46.06.87.54, fax 01.46.06.09.09 (M° Abbesses). The decor a rather uninspiring marriage of browns and florals, but the location, on the cor-ner of place des Abbesses, unbeatable for Montmartre views and choice of lively bars. ④.

Ermitage, 24 rue Lamarck; ☎01.42.64.79.22 (M° Lamarck-Caulaincourt/Château-Rouge). Discreet hotel only a stone's throw from Sacré Cœur yet completely undisturbed by the throngs of tourists. Decorated in deep, dark colours with plenty of rugs and paintings. Approach via M° Anvers and the funicular to avoid the steep climb. ⑤.

Timotel, 11 place Émile-Goudeau; ☎01.42.55.05.06, fax 01.42.55.00.95 (M° Abbesses/Blanche). Rooms are modern, comfortable and freshly decorated in a nondescript chain-hotel way. The loca-tion, however, is unbeatable, on the beautiful shady square where Picasso had his studio in 1900, with views across the whole city. ⑤.

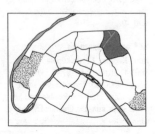

19^e arrondissement

Ibis Paris La Villette, 31 Quai de L'Oise; ☎01.40.38.04.04, fax 01.40.38.90 (M° Corentin Cariou/Ourcq). Situated right on the canal facing the Parc de la Villette, this good-value modern chain hotel is a great spot to stay if you want to spend a few days exploring the park or attending concerts at the Cité de la Musique. It's also a wise choice for car drivers, as it's easily reached from the boulevard périphérique exiting at the Porte de la Villette; free parking for guests. ③.

Hôtel Rhin et Danube, 3 place Rhin-et-Danube, ☎01.42.45.10.13, fax 01.42.06.88.82 (M° Danube). Way out of the centre on the airy heights of Belleville, and geared to self-catering. Good value. ④.

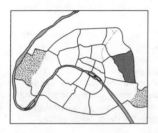

20e arrondissement

Ermitage Hôtel, 42bis rue de l'Ermitage; ☎01.46.36.23.44 (M° Jourdain). A clean and decent cheapie, close to the leafy rue des Pyrénées with its provincial feel. ②.

Hôtel Tamaris, 14 rue des Maraîchers; ☎01.43.72.85.48, fax 01.43.56.81.75 (M° Porte-de-Vincennes). Simple, clean, attractive, and run by nice people. Extremely good value. Close to the métro and terminus of bus route #26 from Gare du Nord. ②.

Mary's, 118 rue Orfila (at the rue Pelleport end); ☎01.43.61.51.68 (M° Pelleport). A little far out, but simple, clean, friendly and good value. ②–③.

Hôtel Nadaud, 8 rue de la Bidassoa; ☎01.46.36.87.79 (M° Gambetta, exit Place Martin-Nadaud). A great little place

close to Père-Lachaise cemetery. No luxury, but comfortable and clean, attentive and friendly. Closed Aug. ②–③.

Hôtel Pyrénées-Gambetta, 12 av du Père-Lachaise; ☎01.47.97.76.57, fax 01.47.97.17.61 (M° Gambetta). Perfect for anyone passionate about Père-Lachaise cemetery. Unpretentious and very pleasant. All rooms with cable TV. ④.

Accommodation

Hostels, foyers, student accommodation and campsites

The cheapest **hostel** accommodation is to be found in those run by the **French Youth Hostel Association (FUAJ)**, for which you need Hostelling International (HI) membership, and those connected with the **MIJE** (*Maison Internationale de la Jeunesse et des Étudiants*), **UCRIF** (*Union des Centres de Rencontres Internationaux de France*) and **CISP** (*Centre International de Séjour a Paris*). There's also a handful of privately run **independent hostels**, and church-, state- or charity-operated **foyers** – residential hostels aimed at students during term time and young workers new to Paris (including a couple of women-only options), which also welcome travellers. Except where indicated, there is no effective age limit at these places.

Current **costs** per person for dorm bed and (usually) breakfast are: youth hostels from 120F, MIJE hostels from 125F, and UCRIF hostels between 120F and 130F. **Independent hostels** are even cheaper, around 98F for a dorm room off-season, rising to about 110F in summer, but they tend to be noisier party places. Some hostels have double rooms, costing around 130–140F per person, which at 260–280F, means you'd often be better off in a cheap hotel. That said, the MIJE hostels, most of which are centrally situated in historic Marais buildings, are very pleasant places to stay. They have a seven-night limit to how long you can stay; other hostels' maximum **length of stay** varies, but it's normally less generous.

Accommodation

Bear in mind, too, that there is occasionally a **curfew** of around 11pm, though some hostels will loan you a key. Most do not take advance bookings – we have indicated when they do – and you need to turn up in the morning to guarantee a room.

Several, suburban hostels exist on the outskirts of Paris; the tourist office has a list of these and can provide directions.

Another budget alternative is **student accommodation**, made available to travellers during university vacation time. The organization to contact is **CROUS**, Académie de Paris, 39 av Georges-Bernanos, 5e; ☎01.40.51.36.00 (M° Port-Royal).

Your cheapest option is of course **camping**, with three sites on the outskirts of Paris.

HI (FUAJ) hostels

There are three HI (FUAJ) **youth hostels** in or very close to Paris proper – *D'Artagan, Jules Ferry* and *Cité des Sciences*. It's advisable to book ahead in summer – this can be done anywhere in the world via their computerized International Booking Network, **IBN** (contact your nearest Hostelling International office before leaving home or look up details on the Internet: *www.fuaj.fr*). In Paris itself, the central FUAJ office is near the Pompidou Centre at at 9 rue Brantôme, 3e (☎01.48.04.70.40).

Several hostels also exist on the outskirts of Paris, often in rather inconvenient locations. All **charge** 120F including breakfast. They are ranged by proximity to the centre.

Jules Ferry, 8 bd Jules-Ferry, 11e; ☎01.43.57.55.60, fax 01.40.21.79.92 (M° République). Smaller and more central than *D'Artagan*, in a lively area at the foot of the Belleville hill. Very difficult to get a place but when full, they will help you find a bed elsewhere.

D'Artagnan, 80 rue Vitruve, 20e; ☎01.40.32.34.53, fax 01.42.32.34.55 (M° Porte-de-Bagnolet). Colourful, funky modern hostel, with a fun atmosphere and lots of facilities including a video cinema,

restaurant and bar, and with a local swimming pool nearby. On the eastern edge of the city near the village-like Charonne with some good bars, and handy for the Père-Lachaise cemetery. Very popular so try to arrive early – reservations by fax or from other HI hostels only. Doubles 129F per person; both dorms and doubles.

Léo Lagrange, 107 rue Martre, Clichy; ☎01.41.27.26.90, fax 01.42.70.52.53 (M° Mairie-de-Clichy). Some way out of centre in a huge and impersonal building (338 beds); suffers, too, from a lack of services nearby. Some double rooms available (130F per person).

Cité des Sciences, 24 rue des Sept-Arpents 93310, Le Pré-St-Gervais; ☎01.48.43.24.11, fax 01.48.43.26.82 (M° Hoche). Modern 125-bed hostel just northeast of the city. Family rooms available.

Arpajon, 3 rue Marcel-Duhamel, Arpajon 91290; ☎01.64.90.28.85 (RER line C4 to Arpajon). Southwest of Paris. Make sure you get on one of the first four carriages of the RER when coming out from the city, otherwise you'll have to get off and change. Once you get there, though, it's particularly cheap: 46F per person.

MIJE hostels

MIJE's hostels are superbly and very centrally situated, occupying historic buildings in the Marais. They cannot be booked in advance, and the maximum length of stay is seven nights.

Le Fauconnier, 11 rue du Fauconnier, 4e; ☎01.42.74.23.45 (M° St-Paul/Pont-Marie). A superbly renovated, seventeenth-century building with a courtyard. Dorms sleep four to eight people. Breakfast included.

Le Fourcy, 6 rue de Fourcy, 4e; ☎01.42.74.23.45 (M° St-Paul). Another beautiful mansion, this one boasting a small garden and a restaurant with menus from 50F. Dorms only, sleeping 4–8.

Maubuisson, 12 rue des Barres, 4e; ☎01.42.74.23.45 (M° Pont-Marie/Hôtel-de-Ville). Magnificent medieval building in a quiet street. Restaurant has menus from 32F. Dorms only, sleeping 4. Breakfast included.

UCRIF hostels

UCRIF has at its disposal a few hostels in or close to Paris, for which there is no advance booking. UCRIF advises you either to phone individual hostels on arrival in Paris or to go along to the **main office** at 27 rue de Turbigo, 2e; ☎01.40.26.57.64, fax 01.40.26.58.20; Mon–Fri 10am–6pm. All the following provide canteen meals for around 62F.

(BVJ) Centre International de Paris/Louvre, 20 rue Jean-Jacques-Rousseau, 1er; ☎01.53.00.90.90, fax 01.53.00.90.91 (M° Louvre/Châtelet-Les Halles).

(BVJ) Centre International de Paris/Quartier Latin, 44 rue des Bernardins, 5e; ☎01.43.29.34.80 (M° Maubert-Mutualité).

Maison des Clubs UNESCO de Paris, 43 rue de la Glacière, 13e; ☎01.43.36.00.63, fax 01.45.35.05.96 (M° Glacière).

CISP hostels

There are two **CISP** (Centre International de Séjour de Paris) hostels in Paris, both of which have singles (186F) and doubles (156F per person) available. Price includes breakfast, and reservations are taken.

Kellermann, 17 bd Kellermann, 13e; ☎01.44.16.37.38 (M° Porte-d'Italie).

Maurice Ravel, 6 av Maurice-Ravel, 12e; ☎01.44.75.60.00, fax 01.43.44.45.30 (M° Porte-de-Vincennes).

Independent hostels

Aloha Hostel, 1 rue Borromé, 15e; ☎01.42.73.03.03, fax 01.42.73.14.14 (M° Volontaires). Same management as *Three Ducks Hostel*, below. Nov–June 90F, July–Oct 107F. Book in advance by credit card or arrive by 9am.

Association des Étudiants Protestants de Paris (Protestant Student Association), 46 rue de Vaugirard, 6e; ☎01.43.33.23.30, fax 01.46.34.27.09 (M° Mabillon/St-Sulpice/RER Luxembourg). Friendly but pretty basic, for people aged 18–26 of all nationalities and creeds. No advance booking; turn up or phone on the day – early. Maximum stay five weeks. Current cost is 10F membership (valid for subsequent visits) and 77–95F, depending on size of dormitory, for B&B, plus 200F deposit.

Auberge International des Jeunes Ste-Marguérite, 10 rue Trousseau, 11e; ☎01.47.00.62.00, fax 01.47.00.33.16 (M° Bastille/Ledru-Rollin). Despite the official-sounding name, a laid-back independent (though noisy) hostel in a great location 5min walk from the Bastille. Clean and professionally run with 24-hour reception, generous breakfast and free luggage storage. Under 100F, including breakfast.

Maison Internationale des Jeunes, 4 rue Titon, 11e; ☎01.43.71.99.21, fax 01.43.71.78.58 (M° Faidherbe-Chaligny). For 18- to 30-year-olds. Operates like a youth hostel, but does not require YHA membership. Dorms and doubles, both 110F B&B per person.

Three Ducks Hostel, 6 place Étienne-Pernet, 15e; ☎01.48.42.04.05, fax 01.48.42.99.99 (M° Émile-Zola). A private youth hostel with no age limit, though guests are mainly young and noisy. The place has been totally renovated, and offers kitchen facilities as well as a bar with the cheapest beer in town. Essential to book ahead between May and Oct: send the price of the first night. Lock-out noon–5pm, curfew at 2am. 87F Oct–May, 127F June–Sept; some rooms for couples at 147F per person.

Woodstock Hostel, 48 rue Rodier, 9e; ☎01.48.78.87.76 (M° Anvers/St-Georges). Another hostel in the *Three Ducks* stable, with its own bar. A great location in a pretty untouristy street near Montmartre. 97F for a dormitory bed, 107F per person for a double; price includes breakfast.

Accommodation

Accommodation

For other women-only addresses visit the CIDJ office at 101 quai Branly, 15ᵉ (Mᵒ Bir-Hakeim).

Young and Happy Hostel, 80 rue Mouffetard, 5ᵉ; ☎01.45.35.09.53, fax 01.47.07.22.24 (Mᵒ Monge/Censier-Daubenton). Noisy, basic and studenty hostel in a lively, if a tad touristy, spot. Dorms, with shower, sleep 4–8, and there are a few doubles (127F each). You can book in advance, but turn up early, between 8am and 11am, to keep the room. Dorms 107F, cheaper in winter.

Foyers

Maison des Étudiants, 18 rue Jean-Jacques-Rousseau, 1ᵉʳ; ☎01.45.08.02.10, fax 01.40.28.11.43 (Mᵒ Palais-Royal). Available to travellers July & Aug; minimum stay four nights. B&B in double room costs 140F per night if staying less than a week, 130F per night if longer; 160F and 140F respectively in a single.

Résidence Bastille, 151 av Ledru-Rollin, 11ᵉ; ☎01.43.79.53.86, fax 01.43.79.35.63 (Mᵒ Ledru-Rollin/Bastille/Voltaire). Under-35s only. Dorms 120F, singles 160F; breakfast included.

Foyer des Jeunes Filles, 234 rue Tolbiac, 13ᵉ; ☎01.44.16.22.22, fax 01.45.71.78.58 (Mᵒ Glacière). Caters to 18–30s women only. Excellent facilities. 120F.

Cité Universitaire, bd Jourdan, 14ᵉ; ☎01.44.16.64.41 (RER Cité-Universitaire). Mon–Fri 9am–5pm. The student campus can provide a list of the different *maisons* or *fondations* that let out rooms during the summer holidays, some April–Sept. These include the *Maison des États-Unis* (☎01.45.89.35.79) and the *Collège Franco-Britannique* (☎01.44.16.24.00). Costs vary from around 100F to 170F a night. Sometimes there's a minimum length of stay, around five nights.

Foyer International d'Accueil de Paris Jean Monnet, 30 rue Cabanis, 14ᵉ; ☎01.45.89.89.15, fax 01.45.81.63.91 (Mᵒ Glacière). A huge, efficiently run foyer in a fairly sedate area. Facilities include meeting-rooms and a disco; ideal for groups. 281F for a single, 131F in a dormitory.

Centre d'Accueil et d'Animation Paris 20e, 46 rue Louis-Lumière, 20ᵉ; ☎01.43.61.24.51 (Mᵒ Porte-de-Bagnolet/Porte-de-Montreuil). Maximum 8-day stay. 120F including breakfast.

Camping

With the exception of the one in the Bois de Boulogne, most of Paris' **campsites** are some way out of town. Below is a selected list: for other possibilities, contact the tourist office.

Camping du Bois de Boulogne, Allée du Bord-de-l'Eau, 16ᵉ; ☎01.45.24.30.00, fax 01.42.24.42.95 (Mᵒ Porte-Maillot/bus #244 to Route des Moulins 6am–8.30pm). Open all year; camping shuttle bus runs April–Oct from 8.30am to 1am. Much the most central campsite, next to the River Seine in the Bois de Boulogne, and usually booked out in summer. The ground is pebbly, but the site is well-equipped with plenty of toilet blocks, a shop, bar, games room, cafeteria/restaurant, and a useful information office. Costs are 70–95F for a tent with two people; and there are also mobile homes from 250F per night.

Camping du Parc de la Colline (east of Paris near Disneyland), Route de Lagny, 77200 Torcy; ☎01.60.05.42.32 (RER line A4 to Torcy, then phone from the station to be collected, or take bus #421 to stop Le Clos). Open all year.

Camping du Parc-Étang (southwest of Paris), Base de Loisirs, 78180 Montigny-le-Bretonneux; ☎01.30.58.56.20 (RER line C St-Quentin-en-Yvelines; Métro connections for RER line C at Mᵒ Invalides/St-Michel/Gare-d'Austerlitz). Open all year.

Chapter 13

Eating and drinking

As in the rest of France, Parisian cooking has art status, the top chefs are stars, and dining out is a national pastime, whether it's at the bistro on the corner or at a famed house of haute cuisine. In recent years, prices at the top end of the market have come down – with some superb-value midday menus on offer – while the quality at the bottom end, particularly in the tourist hotspots, has sunk. Our advice to gourmets is to snack it out for a few days, then go for a blowout (but don't forget that wine with a 220F menu can easily send the bill to 400F).

Paris is also renowned for its foreign cuisine. There are numerous excellent Thai, Chinese and Vietnamese establishments, and you will find restaurants of Caribbean, Middle Eastern, North African, Central African and Western and Eastern European origin, along with Kurdish, Afghan, Japanese and even Tibetan.

Like other Latin Europeans, the French seldom separate the major pleasures of eating and drinking. **Drinking** is never an end in itself, as it so often is for Anglo-Saxons, and drink other than wine falls into the categories of *apéritifs* and *digestifs*. There are in consequence thousands of establishments in Paris where you can both eat and drink. In order to simplify matters, we have divided them into two broad categories: **Restaurants** and **Cafés and bars**. The former is fairly unambiguous. "Cafés and bars", on the other hand, includes places that offer anything from a sandwich to a

full-blown meal, or no food at all – even where food is served, however, as a general rule you can comfortably sit and have a coffee or other drink without choosing to eat.

The listings below are arranged in alphabetical order under the same geographical headings as are used in Chapters 1 to 11. By way of an introduction, we have included a description of the kinds of food and drink you might expect to find in the various kinds of establishment, as well as some indication of the conventions which surround eating and drinking in France.

Following that list are boxes on vegetarian (p.257), ethnic (p.284) and late-night (p.296) restaurants in Paris.

Cafés and bars

In our "Cafés and bars" category in the listings that follow, we've included cafés, café-bars, café-brasseries, *salons de thé*, *bistrots à vin*, cocktail-type bars, and beer cellars/pubs. Of these, the last two are the only ones where you may not find anything to eat.

Some **brasseries** are more restaurant than café (see p.255), and have little to distinguish them from cafés and café-bars. The principal difference is that anything with "brasserie" in the title will serve proper meals in addition to the usual range of sandwiches, snacks, alcoholic and non-alcoholic drinks. **Salons de thé** and **bistrots à vin**, on the other hand, do have a distinctive identity,

Eating and drinking

Choosing a café

The most enjoyable cafés in Paris are often ordinary, local places, but there are particular areas which café-lizards head for. Boulevards Montparnasse and St-Germain on the Left Bank are especially favoured. There you'll find the *Select*, *Coupole*, *Closerie des Lilas*, *Deux Magots* and *Flore* – the erstwhile hang-outs of Apollinaire, Picasso, Hemingway, Sartre, de Beauvoir and most other literary/intellectual figures of the last seven decades. Most are still frequented by the big, though not yet legendary, names in the Parisian world of arts and letters, cinema, fashion, politics and thought, as well as by their hangers-on and other lesser mortals.

The location of other lively Left Bank café concentrations is determined by the geography of the university. Science students gravitate towards the cafés in rue Linné, by the Jardin des Plantes. The humanities gather in the place de la Sorbonne and rue Soufflot. And all the world – especially non-Parisians – finds its way to the place St-André-des-Arts and the downhill end of boulevard St-Michel.

But the more contemporary, up-and-coming gay, arty and hip café culture is found on the Right Bank around the Marais, and the Bastille and eastern Paris, where the new concept of the culture café goes beyond the literary scene

and intellectual discussions into art exhibitions, live music and Internet access in places like the *Web Bar* (see p.272) and the *Fleche d'Or* (p.293), or a focus on playing pool at *Le Blue Billard* (p.293) and *Lou Pescalou* (p.294). The opening of the landmark Bastille Opéra in 1989 saw a growth in new cafés, art galleries, restaurants and bars in the immediate area and the influence stretched east into traditional working class areas of Belleville, Ménilmontant and Charonne. As the young and the trendy have moved in, they've kept the old charm of premises like the *Café Charbon* while giving them a very Nineties energy. You can leisurely drink coffee in a plethora of gay bars in the Marais by day before they transform into spots for night-time revelry. Nearby, Les Halles, once fashionable, now finds its trade is principally transient out-of-towners up for the bright lights.

As to cost, obviously, addresses in the smarter or more touristy arrondissements set prices soaring. The Champs-Élysées and rue de Rivoli, for instance, are best avoided, at double or triple the price of a café in Belleville, La Villette or the lower 14e. As a rule of thumb, if you are watching your budget, avoid the main squares and boulevards. Cafés a little removed from the main thoroughfares are invariably cheaper.

---

which is not adequately conveyed by the standard English translations, tearoom and wine bar; for details, see p.254.

There's really no difference between **cafés** and **bars**. Although the number of them in Paris is said to be decreasing rapidly, you still see them everywhere: big ones, small ones, scruffy ones, stylish ones, snobby ones, arty ones. They line the streets and cluster around crossroads and squares. **Cybercafés** have also arrived on the scene, charging from 15F for a 15min connection to the Internet, to 40–50F for an hour (the cheapest,

with the best ambience, is the *Web Bar* see p.272).

Many bars and cafés advertise **les snacks** or *un casse-croûte* (a bite) with pictures of omelettes, fried eggs, hot dogs or various sandwiches displayed on the pavement outside. But, even when they don't, they will usually make you a half or a third of a baguette (French bread stick), buttered or filled with cheese or meat (*une tartine/au beurre/au jambon*, etc). This, or a croissant, with hot chocolate or coffee, is generally the best way to eat **breakfast** – and cheaper than the rate charged by most hotels. (Brasseries also are possibilities for cups of coffee, eggs, snacks and other breakfast- or brunch-type food.)

If you **stand at the counter**, which is always cheaper than sitting down, you may see a **basket of croissants** or some hard-boiled eggs (they're usually gone by 9.30am or 10am). The drill is to help yourself – the waiter will keep an eye on how many you've eaten and bill you accordingly.

Many cafés, you will find, also offer reasonably priced **lunches**. These usually consist of salads, the more substantial kind of snack such as *croque-monsieurs* or *croque-madames* (both of which are variations on the grilled-cheese sandwich), a **plat du jour** (chef's daily special), or a **formule**, which is a limited or no-choice set menu.

Full price lists have to be displayed in every bar or café by law, usually without the fifteen percent service charge added, but detailing separately the prices for consuming at the bar (*au comptoir*), sitting down (*la salle*), or on the terrace (*la terrasse*) – all progressively more expensive. You pay when you leave, unless your waiter is just going off shift, and you can sit for hours over just one cup of coffee.

Alcoholic and soft drinks

All cafés and bars serve a full range of alcoholic and non-alcoholic drinks throughout the day. Although on the whole there is much less drunkenness than in Britain, it's still common to see people starting their day with a beer, cognac or *coup de rouge* (glass of red wine). A *café cogna* is the popular combination of a cup of espresso and a glass of cognac.

On the **soft drink** front, bottled fruit juices and the universal standard canned 7-Up-style lemonades (*limonade*), Cokes (*Coca*) and clones are available. You can also get freshly squeezed orange and lemon juice (*orange/citron pressé*), the latter of which is a refreshing choice on a hot day – the lemon juice is served in the bottom of a long ice-filled glass, with a jug of water and a sugar bowl so you

can sweeten it to your taste. Particularly French are the various **sirops**, diluted with water to make cool, eye-catching drinks with traffic-light colours, such as *menthe* (peppermint) and *grenadine* (pomegranate). Bottles of **mineral water** (*eau minérale*) are widely drunk, from the best-selling Badoit to the most obscure spa product. Ask for *gazeuse* for sparkling, *plate* for still. That said, there's not much wrong with the tap water (*l'eau de robinet*), which will always be brought free to your table if you ask for it.

Characteristically French **apéritifs** are the aniseed drinks – *pastis*, in French – Pernod and Ricard. Like Greek *ouzo*, they turn cloudy when diluted with water and ice cubes (*glaçons*) – very refreshing and inexpensive. Two other drinks designed to stimulate the appetite are *Pineau* (cognac and grape juice) and *kir* (white wine with a dash of *cassis* – blackcurrant syrup – or champagne instead of wine for a *kir royal*).

Beers are the familiar Belgian and German brands, plus home-grown ones from Alsace. Draught (*à la pression*, usually Kronenbourg) is the cheapest drink you can have next to coffee and wine. Ask for *un demi* (one-third of a litre). A light, summertime option is shandy (*une panachée*). For a wider choice of draughts and bottles you need to go to the special beer-drinking establishments, or English- and Irish-style pubs found in abundance in Paris. A small bottle at one of these places will cost at least twice as much as a *demi* in a café. In supermarkets, however, bottled or canned beer is exceptionally cheap.

As for the harder stuff, there are dozens of **eaux de vie** (brandies distilled from fruit) and **liqueurs**, in addition to the classic cognacs or Armagnac. Among less familiar names, you could try Poire William (pear brandy), Marc (a spirit distilled from grape pulp) or the grappa-like Basque Izarra. Measures are generous, but they don't come cheap: the same applies for imported spirits like whisky, often called *scotch*.

Eating and drinking

Eating and drinking

Wine

Wine – *vin* – is drunk at just about every meal or social occasion. Red is *rouge*, white *blanc*, or there's *rosé*. *Vin de table* or **vin ordinaire** – table wine – is always cheap and generally drinkable.

AC – **Appellation d'Origine Contrôlée** – wines are another matter. They can be excellent value at the lower end of the price scale, where favourable French taxes keep prices down to 15–25F a bottle, but move much above it and you're soon paying serious prices for serious bottles. This said, you can buy a very decent bottle of wine for 20F or 30F; 60F and over will buy you something really nice.

Restaurant mark-ups of AC wines can be outrageous. Popular AC wines found on most restaurant lists include Côtes du Rhône (from the Rhône valley), St-Émilion and Médoc (from Bordeaux), Beaujolais (the release of the 'new' Beaujolais – 'le Beaujolais Nouveau est arrivé' – is a much heralded event on November 15 of every year) and very upmarket Burgundy.

The **basic wine terms** are *brut*, very dry; *sec*, dry; *demi-sec*, sweet; *doux*, very sweet; *mousseux*, sparkling; *méthode champenoise*, mature and sparkling. There are grape varieties as well, but the complexities of the subject take up volumes.

A **glass of wine** at a bar is simply *un verre de rouge, de blanc* or *de rosé*. If it is an AC wine you may have the choice of *un ballon* (a large round glass). *Un pichet* (a pitcher) is normally a quarter-litre of the house wine if available.

Salons de thé

Salons de thé are a relatively new-fangled invention, cropping up characteristically in both established upper-class haunts and newly gentrified parts of town. As bars are still characteristically more popular with men, *salons de thé* often have a more feminine ambience and attract a female clientele. More refined than anything suggested by the translation "tea room", they serve everything from light midday meals, brunches, salads and quiches to rich confections of cake and ice-cream. The oldest *salon de thé* is *Angélina's* (see p.263), with its marble cake-frosting exterior. More exotic and relaxed is *La Mosquée de Paris* (p.274), in one of the least Parisian of the city's buildings.

Bistrots à vins

Bistrots à vins, unlike *salons de thé*, are an ancient institution, traditionally working-class sawdust-on-the-floor drinking haunts.

Coffee and tea

Coffee is invariably made with an espresso machine and is very strong. *Un café* or *un express* is black; *une noisette* has a touch of milk; *un crème* is milky; and *un grand café* or *un grand crème* is a large cup. In the morning you could also ask for *un café au lait* – espresso in a large cup or bowl filled up with hot milk. *Un déca*, decaffeinated coffee, is very widely available. **Hot chocolate** (*chocolat chaud*) can also be had in any café.

Drinkers of **tea** (*thé*), nine times out of ten, have to settle for *Lipton's* tea-bags. Tea is served black, and you can usually have a slice of lemon (*limon*) with it if you want; in order to have milk with it, ask for *un peu de lait frais* (some fresh milk). *Tisanes* or *infusions* are the generic terms for **herb teas**. Every café serves them. They're particularly soothing after overeating or overdrinking, as well as for stomach upsets. The more common ones are *verveine* (verbena), *tilleul* (lime blossom), *menthe* (mint) and *camomille*.

Snacks and picnics

For those occasions when you don't want – or can't face – a full meal, Paris offers numerous **street stalls** and stand-up **sandwich bars.** In addition to the indigenous *frites* (French fries), *crêpes, galettes* (wholewheat pancakes), *gauffres* (waffles) and fresh sandwiches, there are Tunisian snacks like *brik à l'oeuf* (a fried pastry with an egg inside), *merguez* (spicy North African sausage), Greek *souvlaki* (kebabs), Middle Eastern *falafel* (deep-fried chickpea balls with salad), Japanese titbits, and all manner of good things from eastern European delicatessens.

For **picnics** and takeaway food, head for either a **charcuterie** proper or the delicatessen counter in a good supermarket. Although specializing in pork-based preparations like salami and ham, most charcuteries also stock a wide range of cold cuts, pâtés, terrines, ready-made salads and fully prepared main courses. These are not exclusively meaty, either: artichokes *à la grecque*, stuffed tomatoes and *paellas* are common. You buy by weight, by the slice (*tranche*) or by the carton (*barquette*). See pp.334–337 of the Shopping chapter for listings of charcuteries and other specialist food outlets.

Some genuine *bistrots* still exist, such as *La Tartine* (p.271), *Le Rubis* (p.267) and *Le Baron Rouge* (p.296), unpretentious and catering for everyone. The newer generation, however, who ironically owe their existence in large part to the English influence, have a distinctly yuppified flavour, and are far from cheap. Most serve at least a limited range of dishes or *plats*, often deriving from a particular regional cuisine, and specialize in the less usual and less commercial wines, again often from a particular region. Some, like *Le Baron Rouge*, sell good, inexpensive wine from the barrel if you bring your own containers. The basic idea is to enable you to try wines by the glass.

Restaurants

In terms of both quality and price, there's nothing to choose between restaurants (*auberges* or *relais*, as they sometimes call themselves) and brasseries. The distinction is that **brasseries**, which often resemble cafés, serve quicker meals and at most hours of the day, while restaurants tend to stick to the **traditional mealtimes** of noon until 2pm, and 7pm until 9.30pm or 10.30pm.

The **latest time** at which you can walk into a restaurant and order is usually about 9.30pm or 10pm, although

once ensconced you can often remain well into the night. (Hours – last orders – are stated in the listings below, and unusually or specifically **late-night places** are included in the box on p.296.) After 9pm or so, some restaurants serve only *à la carte* meals, which invariably work out more expensive than eating the set menu. For the more upmarket places, it's wise to make **reservations** – easily done on the same day. When hunting, avoid places that are half-empty at peak time, and treat the business of sizing up different menus as an enjoyable appetizer in itself.

Prices

You should find a display of prices and what you get for them posted outside every restaurant. There is usually a choice between one or more **menus fixes**, where the number of courses for the stated price is fixed and the choice accordingly limited. There are numerous fixed-price menus **under 80F**, particularly at lunchtime.

At that price, menus will be three courses with a choice of four to six entrées, three main courses, and three or four desserts. They will be fairly standard dishes, such as steak and chips (*steak frites*), chicken and chips (*poulet frites*), or various preparations of offal. Look for the *plat du jour*, which may be a regional

Eating and drinking

dish and more appealing. You will also find **formules**, usually choices of a main dish plus starter or dessert.

The more you pay, the greater the choice. Menus **between 150F and 200F** offer a significantly more interesting range of dishes, including, probably, some regional and other specialities, and once **over 200F** you should get some serious gourmet satisfaction. Eating **à la carte**, of course, gives you access to everything on offer, plus complete freedom to construct your meal as you choose. But it will cost a great deal more. The *à la carte* prices we give are for an average three-course meal with half a bottle of wine. One simple and perfectly legitimate ploy is to have just one course instead of the expected three or more. There is no minimum charge.

Wine (*vin*) or a drink (*boisson*) may be included, though it's unlikely on menus less than 100F. When ordering house wine (*vin ordinaire*), ask for *un pichet* (a small jug); they come in quar-

Paris for vegetarians

Vegetarians will find that for the most part French chefs have yet to grasp the idea that tasty and nutritious meals do not need to be based on meat or fish. Consequently, the chances of finding vegetarian main dishes on the menus of regular restaurants are slim. However, it's possible to have a vegetarian meal at even the most meat-oriented brasserie by choosing dishes from among the starters (*crudités*, for example, are nearly always available) and soups, or by asking for an omelette. Useful French phrases to help you along are "*Je suis végétarien(ne)*" (I'm a vegetarian) and "*Il y a quelques plats sans viande?*" (Are there any non-meat dishes?).

You'll be much better off going to an ethnic restaurant – Middle Eastern or Indian make good choices – or a proper **vegetarian restaurant**. There are not many of the latter, but the numbers are slowly increasing as ideas of health and vegetarian diet catch on (the moral/ecological motive is very rare among Parisians). All the establishments listed below are reviewed in the pages that follow.

Eating and drinking

Aquarius 1, 54 rue Ste-Croix-de-la-Bretonnerie, 4e; p.271.
Aquarius 2, 40 rue Gergovie, 14e; p.286.
Bol en Bois, 35 rue Pascal, 13e; p.287.
Country Life, 6 rue Daunou, 2e; p.265.
Au Grain de Folie, 24 rue de La Vieuville, 18e; p.289.
Grand Appetit, 9 rue de la Cerisaie, 4e; p.273.
Le Grenier de Notre-Dame, 18 rue de la Bûcherie, 5e; p.277.

Joy in Food, 2 rue Truffaut, 17e; p.290.
Pemathang, 13 rue de la Montagne-St-Geneviève, 5e; p.277.
La Petite Légume, 36 rue Boulangers, 5e; p.277.
Piccolo Teatro, 6 rue des Écouffes, 4e; p.272.
Les Quatre et Une Saveurs, 72 rue du Cardinal-Lemoine, 5e; p.277.
La Ville de Jagannath, 10 rue St Maur, 11e; p.294.

---

ter-litre (*un quart*) or half-litre (*un demi*) sizes. A bottle of wine can easily add 80F to the bill.

Service compris (or *s.c.*) means the **service charge** is included in the price of the fixed menu. *Service non compris* (*s.n.c.*) or *service en sus* means it isn't, and you need to calculate an additional fifteen percent. The bill for a fixed-price menu will always include the service charge, so there is no need to leave a tip.

Student restaurants

Students of any age are eligible to apply for tickets for the **university restaurants** under the direction of *CROUS de Paris*. A list of addresses, which includes numerous cafeterias and brasseries, is available from their offices at 39 av Georges-Bernanos, 5e (☎01.40.51.36.00; Mon–Fri 9am–5pm; RER Port-Royal). The tickets, however, have to be obtained from the particular restaurant of your choice

(opening hours generally 11.30am–2pm & 6–8pm). Not all serve both midday and evening meals, and times change with each term. Though the food is less than wonderful, it's certainly filling, and you can't complain for the **price**. Some are less fussy than others about student credentials, and will sell tickets to anyone for 28.20F. They will cost you 13.70F if you're studying at a French university, 23F if you can produce an International Student Card.

Chapter 2: The Islands

Île de la Cité

CAFÉS AND BARS

Taverne Henri IV, 13 place du Pont-Neuf, Île de la Cité, 1er (M° Pont-Neuf). One of the good older wine bars, opposite Henri IV's statue. Yves Montand used to come

Eating and drinking

FOODS AND DISHES

Basics

Pain	Bread	*Sel*	Salt	*Couteau*	Knife
Beurre	Butter	*Sucre*	Sugar	*Cuillère*	Spoon
Oeufs	Eggs	*Vinaigre*	Vinegar	*Table*	Table
Lait	Milk	*Bouteille*	Bottle	*L'addition*	The bill
Huile	Oil	*Verre*	Glass		
Poivre	Pepper	*Fourchette*	Fork		

Snacks

Crêpe	Pancake (sweet)	*Omelette*	Omelette
au sucre	with sugar	*nature*	plain
au citron	with lemon	*aux fines herbes*	with herbs
au miel	with honey	*au fromage*	with cheese
à la confiture	with jam	*Salade de*	Salad of
aux oeufs	with eggs	*tomates*	tomatoes
à la crème	with chestnut	*betteraves*	beetroot
de marrons	purée	*concombres*	cucumber
Galette	Buckwheat (savoury) pancake	*carottes rapées*	grated carrots

Un sandwich/ une baguette ...	A sandwich ...	**Other fillings/salads**	
		Anchois	Anchovy
jambon	with ham	*Andouillette*	Tripe sausage
fromage	with cheese	*Boudin*	Black pudding
saucisson	with sausage	*Coeurs de palmiers*	Palm hearts
rillettes	with coarse pâté	*Fonds d'artichauts*	Artichoke hearts
à l'ail	with garlic	*Hareng*	Herring
au poivre	with pepper	*Langue*	Tongue
pâté	with pâté	*Poulet*	Chicken
(de campagne)	(country-style)	*Thon*	Tuna
croque-monsieur	Grilled cheese & ham sandwich		
croque-madame	Grilled cheese & bacon, sausage, chicken or an egg	**Related terms**	
		Chauffé	Heated
		Cuit	Cooked
		Cru	Raw
panini	Flat toasted Italian sandwich	*Emballé*	Wrapped
		A emporter	Takeaway
Oeufs	Eggs	*Fumé*	Smoked
au plat	fried	*Salé*	Salted/spicy
à la coque	boiled	*Sucré*	Sweet
durs	hard-boiled		
brouillés	scrambled		

Soups (soupes)

Bisque	Shellfish soup	*Potage*	Thick vegetable soup
Bouillabaisse	Marseillais fish soup	*Rouille*	Red pepper, garlic &
Bouillon	Broth or stock		saffron mayonnaise
Bourride	Thick fish soup		with fish soup
Consommé	Clear soup	*Velouté*	Thick soup, usually
Pistou	Parmesan, basil & garlic paste added to soup		made with fish or poultry

Starters (hors d'oeuvres)

Assiette anglaise	Plate of cold meats	*Hors d'oeuvres*	Combination of the
Crudités	Raw vegetables with	*variés*	above, plus smoked
	dressings		or marinated fish

Eating and drinking

Fish (poisson), seafood (fruits de mer) and shellfish (crustaces or coquillages)

Anchois	Anchovies	*Moules*	Mussels (with shallots
Anguilles	Eels	*(marinière)*	in white wine sauce)
Barbue	Brill	*Oursin*	Sea urchin
Bigourneau	Periwinkle	*Palourdes*	Clams
Brème	Bream	*Praires*	Small clams
Cabillaud	Cod	*Raie*	Skate
Calmar	Squid	*Rouget*	Red mullet
Carrelet	Plaice	*Saumon*	Salmon
Claire	Type of oyster	*Sole*	Sole
Colin	Hake	*Thon*	Tuna
Congre	Conger eel	*Truite*	Trout
Coques	Cockles	*Turbot*	Turbot
Coquilles St-Jacques	Scallops		
		Fish: dishes and related terms	
Crabe	Crab	*Aïoli*	Garlic mayonnaise
Crevettes grises	Shrimps		served with salt cod
Crevettes roses	Prawns		& other fish
Daurade	Sea bream	*Béarnaise*	Sauce made with egg
Eperlan	Smelt or whitebait		yolks, white wine,
Escargots	Snails		shallots & vinegar
Flétan	Halibut	*Beignets*	Fritters
Friture	Assorted fried fish	*Darne*	Fillet or steak
Gambas	King prawns	*La douzaine*	A dozen
Hareng	Herring	*Frit*	Fried
Homard	Lobster	*Fumé*	Smoked
Huîtres	Oysters	*Fumet*	Fish stock
Langouste	Spiny lobster	*Gigot de mer*	Large fish baked
Langoustines	Saltwater crayfish		whole
	(scampi)	*Grillé*	Grilled
Limande	Lemon sole	*Hollandaise*	Butter & vinegar
Lotte	Burbot		sauce
Lotte de mer	Monkfish	*A la meunière*	In a butter, lemon &
Loup de mer	Sea bass		parsley sauce
Louvine, loubine	Similar to sea bass	*Mousse/*	Mousse
Maquereau	Mackerel	*mousseline*	
Merlan	Whiting	*Quenelles*	Light dumplings

Meat (viande) and poultry (volaille)

Agneau	Lamb (grazed on salt	*Boudin blanc*	Sausage of white meats
(de pré-salé)	marshes)	*Boudin noir*	Black pudding
Andouille,	Tripe sausage	*Caille*	Quail
andouillette		*Canard*	Duck
Boeuf	Beef	*Caneton*	Duckling
Bifteck	Steak		

Continues. . .

Eating and drinking

Contrefilet	Sirloin roast	Mouton	Mutton
Coquelet	Cockerel	Museau de veau	Calf's muzzle
Dinde, dindon	Turkey	Oie	Goose
Entrecôte	Ribsteak	Onglet	Cut of beef
Faux filet	Sirloin steak	Os	Bone
Foie	Liver	Porc	Pork
Foie gras	Fattened	Poulet	Chicken
	(duck/goose) liver	Poussin	Baby chicken
Gigot (d'agneau)	Leg (of lamb)	Ris	Sweetbreads
Grillade	Grilled meat	Rognons	Kidneys
Hâchis	Chopped meat or	Rognons blancs	Testicles
	mince hamburger	Sanglier	Wild boar
Langue	Tongue	Tête de veau	Calf's head (in jelly)
Lapin, lapereau	Rabbit, young rabbit	Tournedos	Thick slices of fillet
Lard, lardons	Bacon, diced bacon	Tripes	Tripe
Lièvre	Hare	Veau	Veal
Merguez	Spicy, red sausage	Venaison	Venison

Meat and poultry: dishes and related terms

Aile	Wing	Au feu de bois	Cooked over wood fire
Blanquette	Veal in cream	Au four	Baked
de veau	& mushroom sauce	Garni	With vegetables
Boeuf	Beef stew with burgundy,	Gésier	Gizzard
bourguignon	onions & mushrooms	Grillé	Grilled
Canard à	Roast duck with an	Magret de	Duck breast
l'orange	orange-and-wine	canard	
	sauce	Marmite	Casserole
Carré	Best end of neck,	Médaillon	Round piece
	chop or cutlet	Mijoté	Stewed
Cassoulet	A casserole of beans	Museau	Muzzle
	& meat	Pavé	Thick slice
Choucroute	Sauerkraut served with	Rôti	Roast
garnie	sausages or cured	Sauté	Lightly cooked in butter
	ham	Steak au	Steak in a black
Civit	Game stew	poivre	(green/red)
Confit	Meat preserve	(vert/rouge)	peppercorn sauce
Coq au vin	Chicken with wine,	Steak tartare	Raw chopped beef,
	onions & mushrooms,		topped with a raw egg
	cooked till it falls off		yolk
	the bone		
Côte	Chop, cutlet or rib	**For steaks**	
Cou	Neck	Bleu	Almost raw
Cuisse	Thigh or leg	Saignant	Rare
Daube,	All are types of stew	A point	Medium
estouffade,		Bien cuit	Well done
hochepôt,		Très bien cuit	Very well cooked
navarin and		Brochette	Kebab
ragoût			
En croûte	In pastry	**Garnishes and sauces**	
Épaule	Shoulder	Beurre blanc	Sauce of white wine &
Farci	Stuffed		shallots, with butter

Chasseur	White wine, mushrooms & shallots	Mornay	Cheese sauce
Diable	Strong mustard seasoning	Pays d'Auge	Cream & cider
Forestière	With bacon & mushroom	Piquante	Gherkins or capers, vinegar & shallots
Fricassée	Rich, creamy sauce	Provençale	Tomatoes, garlic, olive oil & herbs

Vegetables (légumes), herbs (herbes) and spices (épices)

Ail	Garlic	Persil	Parsley
Algue	Seaweed	Petits pois	Peas
Anis	Aniseed	Piment	Pimento
Artichaut	Artichoke	Pois chiche	Chickpeas
Asperges	Asparagus	Pois mange-tout	Snow peas
Avocat	Avocado	Pignons	Pine nuts
Basilic	Basil	Poireau	Leek
Betterave	Beetroot	Poivron	Sweet pepper
Carotte	Carrot	(vert, rouge)	(green, red)
Céleri	Celery	Pommes (de terre)	Potatoes
Champignons, cèpes, chanterelles	Mushrooms of various kinds	Primeurs	Spring vegetables
		Radis	Radishes
		Riz	Rice
Chou (rouge)	(Red) cabbage	Safran	Saffron
Chou-fleur	Cauliflower	Salade verte	Green salad
Ciboulettes	Chives	Sarrasin	Buckwheat
Concombre	Cucumber	Tomate	Tomato
Cornichon	Gherkin	Truffes	Truffles
Échalotes	Shallots		
Endive	Chicory	**Vegetables: dishes and related terms**	
Épinards	Spinach	Beignet	Fritter
Estragon	Tarragon	Farci	Stuffed
Fenouil	Fennel	Gratiné/au gratin/ gratin de	Browned with cheese or butter
Flageolet	White beans		
Gingembre	Ginger	Forestière	With mushrooms
Haricots verts rouges beurres	Beans string (French) kidney butter	À la parisienne	Sautéed in butter (potatoes); with white wine sauce & shallots
Laurier	Bay leaf	Parmentier	With potatoes
Lentilles	Lentils	Jardinière	With mixed diced vegetables
Maïs	Corn		
Menthe	Mint	Sauté	Lightly fried in butter
Moutarde	Mustard		
Oignon	Onion	À la vapeur	Steamed
Pâte	Pasta or pastry		

Fruits (fruits) and nuts (noix)

Abricot	Apricot	Brugnon, nectarine	Nectarine
Amandes	Almonds	Cacahouète	Peanut
Ananas	Pineapple	Cassis	Blackcurrants
Banane	Banana		Continues...

Eating and drinking

Cérises	Cherries	*Pamplemousse*	Grapefruit
Citron	Lemon	*Pêche (blanche)*	(White) peach
Citron vert	Lime	*Pistache*	Pistachio
Figues	Figs	*Poire*	Pear
Fraises (de bois)	Strawberries (wild)	*Pomme*	Apple
Framboises	Raspberries	*Prune*	Plum
Fruit de la passion	Passion fruit	*Pruneau*	Prune
Groseilles	Redcurrants & gooseberries	*Raisins*	Grapes
Mangue	Mango	**Fruit: related terms**	
Marrons	Chestnuts	*Beignets*	Fritters
Melon	Melon	*Compôte de . . .*	Stewed . . .
Myrtilles	Bilberries	*Coulis*	Sauce
Noisette	Hazelnut	*Flambé*	Set aflame in alcohol
Noix	Nuts	*Frappé*	Iced
Orange	Orange		

Desserts (desserts or entremets) and pastries (pâtisserie)

Barquette	Small boat-shaped flan	*Macarons*	Macaroons
Bavarois	Refers to the mould, could be mousse or custard	*Madeleine*	Small sponge cake
		Marrons Mont Blanc	Chestnut purée & cream on a rum-soaked sponge cake
Bombe	A moulded ice cream dessert	*Mousse au chocolat*	Chocolate mousse
Brioche	Sweet, high yeast breakfast roll	*Palmiers*	Caramelized puff pastries
Charlotte	Custard & fruit in lining of almond fingers	*Parfait*	Frozen mousse, sometimes ice cream
Coupe	A serving of ice cream	*Petit Suisse*	A smooth mixture of cream & curds
Crème Chantilly	Vanilla-flavoured & sweetened whipped cream	*Petits fours*	Bite-sized cakes/pastries
Crème fraîche	Sour cream	*Poires Belle Hélène*	Pears & ice cream in chocolate sauce
Crème pâtissière	Thick eggy pastry-filling	*Sablé*	Shortbread biscuit
Crêpe	Pancake	*Savarin*	A filled, ring-shaped cake
Crêpe suzette	Thin pancake with orange juice & liqueur		
Fromage blanc	Cream cheese	*Tarte*	Tart
Galette	Buckwheat pancake	*Tartelette*	Small tart
Gênoise	Rich sponge cake	*Truffes*	Truffles, chocolate or liqueur variety
Glace	Ice cream		
Île flottante/ oeufs à la neige	Soft meringues floating on custard	*Yaourt, yogourt*	Yoghurt

Cheese (fromage)

There are over 400 types of French cheese, most of them named after their place of origin. *Chèvre* is goat's cheese and *brebis* is cheese made from sheep's milk. *Le plateau de fromages* is the cheeseboard, and bread – but not butter – is served with it.

Addressing the waiter or waitress

Always call the waiter or waitress *Monsieur* or *Madame* (*Mademoiselle* if a young woman), never *garçon*, no matter what you've been taught in school.

here when Simone Signoret lived in the adjacent place Dauphine. Today it's full of lawyers from the Palais de Justice. The food is good if a bit pricey for a full meal. Plates of meats and cheeses around 70F, sandwiches 30F, wine from 20F a glass. Mon–Fri noon–10pm, Sat noon–4pm; closed Sun & Aug.

RESTAURANTS

Au Rendez-vous des Camionneurs, 72 quai des Orfèvres, Île de la Cité, 1er; ☎01.43.54.88.74 (M° St-Michel). Crowded, traditional establishment serving snails, steaks and scallops. Midday *menus* under 100F; evening *menu* 130F, *á la carte* around 175F. Daily noon–2pm, 7–11.30pm.

Île St-Louis

CAFÉS AND BARS

Berthillon, 31 rue St-Louis-en-l'Île, Île St-Louis, 4e (M° Pont-Marie). Long queues onto the street for their excellent, home-made ice creams and sorbets (22F a triple *cornet*). Takeaway Wed–Sun 10am–8pm; eat-in Wed–Fri 1–8pm, Sat & Sun 2–8pm The same ice creams are also sold at *Lady Jane* and *Le Flore-en-l'Île*, both on quai d'Orléans also on the Île St-Louis, and at four other island sites listed on the door.

Les Fous de l'Île, 33 rue des Deux-Ponts, 4e (M° Pont-Marie). Light lunches in bookish surroundings for around 75F, tea and cakes till 7pm and dinner until 11pm; closed Mon.

Le St-Régis, 92 rue St-Louis-en-l'Île, 4e (M° Pont-Marie). An unpretentious brasserie opposite the Pont St-Louis, with views of Notre-Dame. *Plats du jour* from 62F; menu 90F.

RESTAURANTS

Le Castafiore, 51 rue St-Louis-en-l'Île, 4e; ☎01.43.54.78.62 (M° Pont-Marie). Italian specialities. Very pleasant *patron*. Pasta from 56F, meat dishes from 78F. Menu 90F before 8pm, 158F after. Daily till 10.30pm.

Le Gourmet de l'Île, 42 rue St-Louis-en-l'Île, 4e; ☎01.43.26.79.27 (M° Pont-Marie). A bargain four-course *menu* for 140F, including wonderful monkfish with crab sauce, in this down-to-earth restaurant. Wed–Sun noon–2pm & 7–10pm; closed Aug.

Chapter 3: Along la Voie Triomphale

CAFÉS AND BARS

Angélina, 226 rue de Rivoli, 1er (M° Tuileries). A long-established gilded cage, where the well-coiffed sip the best hot chocolate in town. Pâtisseries and other desserts of the same high quality. Not cheap. Daily 9am–7pm; closed Tues in July & Aug.

Barry's, 9 rue Duras, 8e (M° Champs-Élysées-Clemenceau). Salads, snacks and sandwiches for under 30F in a tiny street behind the Élysée palace. Mon–Sat 11am–3pm.

Café de la Comédie, 153 rue St-Honoré, 1er (M° Palais-Royal-Musée-du-Louvre). Small café opposite the Comédie Française, complete with a mirror painted with theatrical scenes at the back. Tues–Sun 10am–midnight.

Café Marly, Cour Napoléon du Louvre, 93 rue de Rivoli, 1er (M° Palais-Royal-Musée-du-Louvre). Inside the Louvre, with tables beneath the colonnade overlooking the Pyramid; very chic, very classy and very expensive. Daily to 2am.

Café Véry (also known as *Dame Tartine*), Jardin des Tuileries, 1er (M° Concorde). The best of an ever-increasing number of snack bars in the gardens. Ice creams, sandwiches, cold beers. Daily noon–11pm.

E. Fahy Patissier, 165 rue du Faubourg-St-Honoré, 8e (M° St-Philippe-du-Roule/George-V). A boulangerie selling sandwiches, tarts, quiches, ready-made salads to take away or eat in a corner at the back. Mon–Sat 7am–7.30pm.

Fauchon, 30 place de la Madeleine, 8e (M° Madeleine). Head for the café downstairs where you can gobble deli-

Eating and drinking

Eating and drinking

See p.257 for a list of vegetarian restaurants in Paris.

cious pâtisseries, *plats du jour* and sandwiches – at a price. Mon–Sat 9.45am–7pm.

Le Fouquet's, 99 av des Champs-Élysées, 8ᵉ (Mᵒ George-V). Such a well-established watering hole for stars of the stage and screen, politicians, newspaper editors and advertising barons, that it's now been classified as a *Monument Historique*. You pay dearly to sit in the deep leather armchairs and, as for the restaurant, don't expect any change from 300F. Daily till 1.30am.

Le Griffonier, 6 rue des Saussaies, 8ᵉ (Mᵒ Champs-Élysées). Well-paid office types frequent this small wine bar with a good selection of Loire wines at 23–30F a glass. Mon–Fri 8am–9pm, Thurs open till 10.30pm.

Osaka, 163 rue St-Honoré, 1ᵉʳ (Mᵒ Palais-Royal). Japanese snack bar with meals for 60F. More expensive sushi, sashimi and tempura bar on the left. Daily noon–9pm, except Tues when closes at 6pm.

Restorama, Le Carrousel du Louvre, 1ᵉʳ (Mᵒ Louvre). One vast underground fast-food eating hall served by more than a dozen different outlets: rôtisseries, hamburgers, pizzas, Tex-Mex, Chinese, Lebanese, Japanese, crêperies, salad bars. Easy to eat for under 40F. Access from place du Carrousel or the Louvre Pyramid. Daily 9am–9pm.

Torréfaction Marbeuf, 25 rue Marbeuf, 8ᵉ (Mᵒ Franklin-D-Roosevelt). Principally a coffee shop where they roast their own beans, but a couple of tables outside and standing room in the shop allow for tasting. 7F for an espresso. Mon–Fri 9am–7pm; July & Aug closed 2–4pm.

RESTAURANTS

Aux Amis du Beaujolais, 28 rue d'Artois, 8ᵉ; ☎01.45.63.92.21 (Mᵒ George-V/St-Philippe-du-Roule). If you can fathom the hand-written menu, you'll find good traditional French dishes of stews and sautéed steaks, and of course Beaujolais. Around 150F. Mon–Sat

noon–3pm & 6.30–9pm; closed middle two weeks of July.

L'Appart', 9 rue du Colisée, 8ᵉ; ☎01.53.75.16.34 (Mᵒ St-Philippe-du-Roule). A modern restaurant done out to look like an apartment. Inventive dishes on a 175F *menu*, and brunch for 110F on a Sunday. Daily noon–midnight.

Cité St-Honoré (formerly *Relais du Sud-Ouest*), 154 rue St-Honoré, 1ᵉʳ; ☎01.42.60.62.01 (Mᵒ Palais-Royal-Musée-du-Louvre). An ancient map of the southwest of France on the wall, an old kitchen range, candlelit tables and traditional southwest specialities. Good-value 85F *menu*. Mon–Sat till 10.30pm.

Le Dauphin, 167 rue St-Honoré, 1ᵉʳ; ☎01.42.60.40.11 (Mᵒ Palais-Royal-Musée-du-Louvre). A genuine *bistrot* with *menus* at 95F and 150F. Seafood platter during oyster season (Sept–April) for 167F. Excellent *lapereau* (young rabbit) *à la grand-mère* and *magret de canard*. Daily noon–2.30pm & 7–11.30pm; June–Oct till 12.30am.

Dragons Élysées, 11 rue de Berri, 8ᵉ; ☎01.42.89.85.10 (Mᵒ George-V). The Chinese-Thai cuisine includes dim sum, curried seafood and baked mussels, but the overriding attraction here is the extraordinary decor. Beneath a floor of glass tiles water runs from pool to pool inhabited by exotic fish. Water even pours down part of one wall, and on the ceiling pinpoints of light imitate stars. And all this amid the usual chinoiserie of red lanterns and black furniture. 80F *menu*, 200F Thai seafood *menu*, *carte* 250F. Daily 11am–3pm & 7–11pm.

La Fermette Marbeuf 1900, 5 rue Marbeuf, 8ᵉ; ☎01.53.23.08.00 (Mᵒ Franklin-D-Roosevelt). Try to eat in the tiled and domed inner room, where the original Art Nouveau decor has been restored. A rather well-heeled clientele, foreign as well as French, but not stuffy. A good inclusive *menu* for 175F; *carte* up to 350F. Sun–Thurs noon–3pm & 7–11.30pm, Fri & Sat closes at 12.30am.

Le Jardin du Royal Monceau, *Hôtel Royal Monceau*, 35 av Hoche, 8ᵉ (Mᵒ

Charles-de-Gaulle/Étoile). Seriously good food in a luxury hotel. À la carte will set you back 500F or more, but there's a midday menu for 290F. Mon–Fri noon–2.30pm & 7–10.30pm.

Planet Hollywood, 78 av Champs-Élysées, 8ᵉ; ☎01.53.83.78.27 (Mᵒ George-V). Parisians adore this Californian import. The entrance is a marketing franchise; you descend to the bar and restaurant, where models of filmstars and props plus soundtracks provide a Hollywood ambience. Expensive American and French food; bar drinks 35F. Daily 11.30am–1am.

Restaurant au Café St-Honoré, 95 rue St-Honoré, 1ᵉʳ; ☎01.42.86.08.72 (Mᵒ Louvre-Rivoli). Small, old-style restaurant serving traditional French food. Menus at 160F and 200F. Mon–Sat till 9.30pm, closed Sat lunch & Sun.

La Table de Margot, 40 rue de Ponthieu, 8ᵉ; 01.53.96.06.88 (Mᵒ Franklin-D-Roosevelt). Good traditional food and amazingly cheap prices for this part of town: 49F midday menu, 85F and 99F evening menus. Open Mon & Tues 11am–4pm & 6–10.30pm, Wed 11am–4pm, Thurs–Sat 2–4pm & 6–10.30pm.

Yvan, 1bis rue J-Mermoz, 8ᵉ; ☎01.43.59.18.40 (Mᵒ Franklin-D-Roosevelt). Fish specialities and pigeon with polenta attract a stylish clientele. Extremely good food and menus from 168F. Mon–Fri noon–2.30pm & 7pm–midnight, Sat 7pm–midnight, closed Sat lunchtime & Sun.

Chapter 4: Financial Paris, the Passages and Les Halles

Grands Boulevards, the Opéra and Madeleine

CAFÉS AND BARS

Le Grand Café Capucines, 4 bd des Capucines, 9ᵉ (Mᵒ Opéra). A favourite all-nighter with over-the-top, belle époque

decor and excellent seafood. Boulevard prices mean 20F for an espresso.

Kitty O'Shea's, 10 rue des Capucines, 2ᵉ (Mᵒ Opéra). An Irish pub with excellent Guinness and Smithwicks – a favourite haunt of Irish expats. The *John Jameson* restaurant upstairs serves high-quality, pricey, Gaelic food, including seafood flown in from Galway. Daily noon–1.30am.

La Taverne Kronenbourg, 24 bd des Italiens, 9ᵉ (Mᵒ Opéra). Silver chandeliers, clocks, bells and old shop signs decorate this otherwise typical boulevard brasserie. *Plats du jour* from 76F, menu 150F. Daily 11–1am.

RESTAURANTS

Chartier, 7 rue du Faubourg-Montmartre, 9ᵉ; ☎01.47.70.86.29 (Mᵒ Grands-Boulevards). Brown linoleum floor, dark-stained woodwork, brass hat-racks, clusters of white globes suspended from the high ceiling, mirrors, waiters in long aprons – the original decor of a turn-of-the-century soup kitchen. Worth seeing and, though crowded and rushed, the food is not bad at all. Under 100F. See box on p.269. Daily 11.30am–3pm & 6–10pm.

Country Life, 6 rue Daunou, 2ᵉ; ☎01.42.97.48.51 (Mᵒ Opéra). Vegetarian soup, hors d'oeuvres, lasagne and salad for less than 70F. Menu details gluten and soya contents. No alcohol, no smoking. Mon–Thurs 11.30am–2.30pm & 6.30–10pm, Fri 11.30am–2.30pm.

Drouot, 103 rue de Richelieu, 2ᵉ; ☎01.42.96.68.23 (Mᵒ Richelieu-Drouot). Same management as *Chartier*. Admirably cheap food served at a frantic pace, in Art Deco surroundings. *Menu* around 80F. Daily noon–3pm & 6.30–10pm.

Au Petit Riche, 25 rue Le Peletier, 9ᵉ; ☎01.47.70.68.68 (Mᵒ Richelieu-Drouot). A long-established restaurant with a mirrored, early-1900s interior. Prompt and attentive service, good food. Very much a business hang-out. *Menu* at 140F. Mon–Sat noon–2pm & 7pm–12.15am.

Eating and drinking

Our glossary of French food and dishes begins on p.258.

Eating and drinking

Some of Paris' top gourmet restaurants are listed on p.256.

Passages, Palais-Royal Garden & Bibliothéque Nationale

CAFÉS AND BARS

L'Arbre à Cannelle, 57 passage des Panoramas, 2e (Mº Grands-Boulevards). Exquisite wooden panelling, frescoes and painted ceilings; puddings, flans and *assiettes gourmandes* for 60–75F. Mon–Sat till 6.30pm.

Le Bar de l'Entracte, on the corner of rue Montpensier and rue Beaujolais, 1er (Mº Palais-Royal-Musée-du-Louvre). Theatre people, bankers and journalists come for quick snacks of *gratin de pomme de terre* and Auvergnat ham in this almost traffic-free spot. Fills up to bursting during the intervals at the Palais-Royal theatre just down the road. Daily 10am–2am, except Mon when closes at 9pm.

Aux Bons Crus, 7 rue des Petits-Champs, 1er (Mº Palais-Royal). A relaxed workaday place that has been serving good wines and cheese, sausage and ham for more than eighty years. Wine from 10F a glass; plate of cold meats from 55F. Mon–Sat 11am–midnight, closed Mon evening & Sun.

Juveniles, 47 rue de Richelieu, 2e (Mº Palais-Royal). Very popular, tiny wine bar run by a Brit. Wine from 68F a bottle; *plats du jour* around 68F. Mon–Sat noon–midnight.

La Muscade, Galerie de Montpensier, 1er (Mº Palais-Royal-Musée-du-Louvre). Smart café in the Palais Royal gardens where the hot chocolates, fruit and herb teas and cakes are superb (afternoon tea served 3–6.15pm). Open daily 12.15–10.30pm.

A Priori Thé, 35 Galerie-Vivienne, 2e (Mº Pyramides/Sentier). Classy little *salon de thé* in a charming nineteenth-century gallery. Tea and cakes, but more substantial dishes also available. Mon–Fri 9am–6pm, Sat noon–6.30pm, Sun 12.30–6.30pm.

RESTAURANTS

Le Grand Colbert, passage Colbert, rue Vivienne, 2e; ☎01.42.86.87.88 (Mº Bourse). In the same high style as the *passage* in which it's situated. Solid French cooking – *canard confit* and *andouillette* – and a 155F *menu* including wine. Daily noon–3pm & 7.30pm–1am; closed mid-July to mid-Aug.

Le Grand Véfour, 17 rue de Beaujolais, 1er; ☎01.42.96.56.27 (Mº Pyramides/Bourse). The carved wooden ceilings, frescoes, velvet hangings and late eighteenth-century chairs haven't changed since Napoléon brought Josephine here. Considering the luxuriance of the cuisine, the lunchtime *menu* for 345F is a cinch. Go *à la carte* and the bill could top 800F. Mon–Fri 12.30–2pm & 7.30–10pm.

L'Incroyable, 26 rue de Richelieu, 1er; ☎01.42.96.24.64 (Mº Palais-Royal). Hidden in a tiny *passage*, this very pleasant restaurant serves decent meals for 80F at midday and 110F in the evening. Tues–Fri lunchtime & 6.30–9pm, Sat & Mon lunch only; closed Sun.

Le Vaudeville, 29 rue Vivienne, 2e; ☎01.40.20.04.62 (Mº Bourse). A lively, late-night brasserie, often with a queue to get a table. Good food, attractive marble-and-mosaic interior. *À la carte* from 150F; 115F *menu* after 10pm. Open daily till 2am.

Clothes, sex, the stock exchange and news

CAFÉS AND BARS

Le Café, 62 rue Tiquetonne, 2e (Mº Les Halles/Étienne-Marcel). On the junction with rue Étienne-Marcel; quiet and secluded with people playing chess and old maps adorning the walls. *Plats du jour* 45–55F. Daily 10am–2am.

La Champmeslé, 4 rue Chabanais, 2e (Mº Pyramides). Lesbian bar, with the back room reserved for women, and the front rooms for mixed company. Cocktails (from 45F), painting/photo exhibitions, and Thurs night cabaret. Open Mon–Wed 7pm–2am, Thurs–Sat till 4am.

Du Croissant, cnr rue du Croissant and rue Montmartre, 2e (Mº Montmartre). On

July 31, 1914, the Socialist and pacifist leader Jean Jaurès was assassinated in this café for his anti-war activities. The table he was sitting at still remains.

Lina's Sandwiches, 8 rue Marbeuf, 8ᵉ (Mᵒ Alma-Marceau); also at 50 rue Étienne-Marcel, 2ᵉ (Mᵒ Étienne-Marcel), 27 rue St-Sulpice, 6ᵉ (Mᵒ St-Sulpice), 7 av de l'Opéra, 1ᵉʳ (Mᵒ Pyramides), 30 bd des Italiens, 9ᵉ (Mᵒ Opéra), 105 rue du Faubourg-St-Honoré, 8ᵉ (Mᵒ St-Philippe-du-Roule). Excellent sandwiches, plus salads, soups, brownies and breakfasts – ideal for a window-shopping break. Mon–Sat 9am–6pm; the bd des Italiens branch is open Mon–Sat 9am–11pm, Sun 11am–6pm.

Le Rubis, 10 rue du Marché-St-Honoré, 1ᵉʳ (Mᵒ Pyramides). One of the oldest wine bars, with a reputation for excellent wines, snacks and *plats du jour*. Very small and very crowded. Glasses of wine from 5.50F. Mon–Fri 7am–10pm, Sat 8am–4pm; closed mid-Aug.

Le Tambour, 41 rue Montmartre, 2ᵉ (Mᵒ Sentier). A local habitués' café, with photos above the bar of old Les Halles traders. Coffee not brilliant. Open 24hr daily.

RESTAURANTS

Dilan, 13 rue Mandar, 2ᵉ; ☎01.42.21.14.88 (Mᵒ Les Halles/Sentier). An excellent-value Kurdish restaurant. Beautiful starters, stuffed aubergines (*babaqunuc*), fish with yoghurt and courgettes (*kanarya*). Midday *menu* 62F. Mon–Sat noon–2pm & 7.30–11pm.

Foujita, 41 rue St-Roche, 1ᵉʳ; ☎01.42.61.42.93 (Mᵒ Tuileries/Pyramides). One of the cheaper but best Japanese restaurants, as proved by the numbers of Japanese eating here. Quick and crowded; soup, sushis, rice and tea for 72F at lunchtime; plate of sushi or sashimi for under 110F. Mon–Sat noon–2.15pm & 7.30–10pm; closed mid-Aug.

Higuma, 32bis rue Ste Anne, 1ᵉʳ; ☎01.47.03.38.59 (Mᵒ Pyramides). Authentic Japanese canteen with cheap,

filling ramen dishes and a variety of set *menus* starting at 63F. Daily 11.30am–10pm.

Al Mina, 9 rue du Nil; ☎01.42.33.11.70 (Mᵒ Sentier). Very good Lebanese food – delicious lamb kebabs and meze. Lunchtime *menus* from 60F, evening *menus* from 95F. Open Mon–Fri lunch & evening till 10pm, closed Sat lunch & Sun.

Les Halles

CAFÉS AND BARS

L'Arbre á Palabres, 44 rue St-Honoré, 1ᵉʳ (Mᵒ Louvre-Rivoli/Châtelet). Light and attractive *salon de thé*, decorated with South American "palaver" (*palabre*). Soup and savoury *tarte* for 50F. Daily 8am–2am.

A la Cloche des Halles, 28 rue Coquillière, 1ᵉʳ (Mᵒ Châtelet-Les Halles/Louvre). The bell hanging over this little wine bar is the one that used to mark the end of trading in the market halls. Though today's noise is from traffic on this busy corner, you are assured of some very fine wines. Open till 8.30pm, closed Sat eve & Sun.

Le Cochon à l'Oreille, 15 rue Montmartre, 1ᵉʳ (Mᵒ Châtelet-Les Halles/Étienne-Marcel). This classic little café, with raffia chairs outside and scenes of the old market in ceramic tiles inside, opens early for the local fishmongers and meat traders. Mon–Sat 7am–5pm.

L'Eustache, 37 rue Berger, 1ᵉʳ (Mᵒ Les Halles). A traditional brasserie, in marked contrast to the trendy *Le Comptoir* next door, with line jazz on Thursday evening. *Plats du jours* 70–80F. Daily till 2am.

Au Père Tranquille, cnr rues Pierre-Lescot and des Pécheurs, 1ᵉʳ (Mᵒ Châtelet-Les Halles). One of the big Les Halles cafés, overlooking the favoured stage where clowns make fools of passers-by against the backdrop of the horrid mirror structures. Expensive. Daily till 2am.

La Rose des Halles, 19 rue du Roule, 1ᵉʳ (Mᵒ Louvre-Rivoli). Tiny, old-fashioned bar with a low zinc counter and newspapers on wooden batons. Daily 9am–midnight.

Eating and drinking

RESTAURANTS

1 Le Béarn
2 La Fresque
3 Le Gros Minet
4 L'Ostrea
5 Au Pied du Cochon
6 La Tour de Montlhéry
(Chez Denise)

CAFÉS AND BARS

7 L'Arbre á Palabres
8 A la Cloche des Halles
9 Le Cochon à l'Oreille
10 L'Eustache
11 Au Père Tranquille
12 La Rose des Halles
13 Self-Service de la Samaritaine
14 Le Sous-Bock
15 Au Trappiste

See p.284 for a list of various ethnic restaurants in Paris.

Self-Service de la Samaritaine, Magasin 2, rue de la Monnaie, 1er (M° Pont-Neuf). In the number two *magasin*. The view over the Seine is probably more of an attraction than the food, though that isn't bad for the price (55F *plat du jour*). Open May–Oct Mon–Sat 9.30am–7pm, Thurs 9.30am–9pm.

Le Sous-Bock, 49 rue St-Honoré, 1er (M° Châtelet-Les Halles). Hundreds of bottled beers (around 40F a pint) and whiskies to sample, plus simple, inexpensive food. Mussels a speciality (60–75F). Frequented by night owls. Happy hour 3–7pm. Open daily 11am–5am.

Au Trappiste, 4 rue St-Denis, 1er (M° Châtelet). Numerous draught beers include Jenlain, France's best-known *bière de garde*, Belgian Blanche Riva and

Kriek from the Mort Subite (Sudden Death) brewery – plus mussels and *frites* for 69F and various *tartines*. Daily 11am–2am.

RESTAURANTS

Le Béarn, 2 place Ste-Opportune, 1er; ☎01.42.36.93.35 (M°Châtelet). Watch the various Halles characters pass by from an outside table on this lively square. Traditional cooking à la carte for under 100F. Mon–Sat noon–10pm.

La Fresque, 100 rue Rambuteau, 1er; ☎01.42.33.17.56 (M° Étienne-Marcel/Les Halles). Nicely dingy with the old decor of a snail merchant's hall appearing through the gloom. 68F midday *menu* with wine. *Carte* 120F. Daily till midnight; closed Sun midday.

Chartier

One hundred years old in March 1996, *Chartier* was first opened in 1896 by Camille and Frédéric Chartier. Their idea was to provide affordable meals for those who could not manage regular restaurant prices. It was a roaring success, coinciding as it did with the arrival in Paris of tens of thousands of people escaping the poverty and hardship of life in the hills of the Massif Central: the *bougnats*, as they were called, in imitation of their accents and the fact that so many of them were involved in the charcoal industry – *charbougna*. It spawned some thirty similar establishments, but the original *Chartier* is the only one to have survived. And little changes at *Chartier*: same staff and same customers for years and years.

Le Gros Minet, 1 rue des Prouvaires, 1er; ☎01.42.33.02.62 (M° Châtelet-Les Halles). Relaxed, small restaurant with distinct charm. The menu centres on duck, including *carpaccio de canard* (very thin slices of raw duck), but there are plenty of alternatives on offer. *Formule* at 95F, *à la carte* around 110F. Mon–Sat noon–2pm & 7.30–11.30pm.

L'Ostrea, 4 rue Sauval, 1er; ☎01.40.26.08.07 (M° Louvre-Rivoli/Châtelet). Charming fish and seafood restaurant. *Plateau de fruits de mer* for two 350F; *moules* from 65F. Noon–2pm & 7–11pm; closed Sat lunchtime, Sun & Aug.

Au Pied de Cochon, 6 rue Coquillière, 1er; ☎01.42.36.11.75 (M° Châtelet-Les Halles). For extravagant middle-of-the-night pork chops and oysters. Seafood platter 198F, *carte* up to 300F. Open 24hr.

La Tour de Montlhéry (Chez Denise), 5 rue des Prouvaires, 1er; ☎01.42.36.21.82 (M° Louvre-Rivoli/Châtelet). An old-style Les Halles *bistrot* serving substantial food; always crowded and smoky; *carte* from 200F. Open till midnight; closed Sat evening & Sun.

Chapter 5: Beaubourg, the Marais and the Bastille

Beaubourg and Hôtel de Ville

CAFÉS AND BARS

Café Beaubourg, 43 rue St-Merri, 4e (M° Rambuteau/Hôtel-de-Ville). An intellectuals' haunt designed by Christian de Partzamparc and overlooking the Pompidou Centre's piazza. Expensive, rather sour service. And very stylish loos. Mon–Thurs & Sun 8am–1am, Sat 8am–2am.

Dame Tartine, 2 rue Brisemiche, 4e (M° Rambuteau/Hôtel-de-Ville). Overlooking the Stravinsky fountain, this is a friendly and affordable place with mellow yellow walls to match the relaxed atmosphere. Particularly delicious open toasted sandwiches from 30F, and a kids *menu* at 49F. Daily noon–11.30pm.

Le Petit Marcel, 63 rue Rambuteau, 3e (M° Rambuteau). Speckled tabletops, mirrors and Art Nouveau tiles, cracked and faded ceiling and about eight square metres of drinking space. Friendly bar staff and "local" atmosphere. Mon–Sat till midnight.

RESTAURANTS

Les Fous d'en Face, 3 rue du Bourg-Tibourg, 4e; ☎01.48.87.03.75 (M° Hôtel-de-Ville). Delightful little restaurant and wine bar serving wonderful marinated salmon and scallops. Midday *menu* under 90F, otherwise *carte* 140F upwards. Daily 11.30am–3pm & 7pm–midnight.

Le Grizli, 7 rue St-Martin, 4e; ☎01.48.87.77.56 (M° Châtelet). Turn-of-the-century *bistrot* serving superb food with specialities from the Pyrénées. 115F midday *menu*, 155F evening. Mon–Sat till 11pm.

Le Quincampe, 78 rue Quincampoix, 3e; ☎01.40.27.01.45 (M° Étienne-Marcel/Rambuteau/RER Châtelet).

Eating and drinking

See p.257 for a list of vegetarian restaurants in Paris.

See p.296 for a list of cafés and restaurants that stay open late.

Moroccan restaurant and *salon de thé*. Eat high-quality food – including the recommended *tagines* – or simply take a delicious mint tea. In winter a real fire in the room at the back enhances the already pleasant atmosphere. *Plat du jour* at 80F. Noon–11pm, closed Mon pm, Sat lunch & Sun.

The Marais

CAFÉS AND BARS

L'Apparement Café, 18 rue des Coutures-St-Servais, 3e (Mº St-Sébastien-Froissart). Chic but cosy café resembling a series of comfortable sitting rooms, with quiet corners and deep sofas. Popular Sunday brunch until 4pm costs 90F. Open Mon–Fri noon–2am, Sat 4pm–2am, Sun 12.30pm–midnight.

Bar Central, 33 rue Vieille-du-Temple, cnr rue Ste-Croix-de-la-Bretonnerie, 4e (Mº St-Paul). One of the most enduring gay bars in the Marais, attracting a quieter, non-scene clientele. Mon–Thurs 4pm–1am, Fri–Sun 2pm–2am.

Bar de Jarente, 5 rue de Jarente, 4e (Mº St-Paul). A lovely old-fashioned café-bar off the pretty place du Marché Ste-Catherine, which remains nonchalantly indifferent to the shifting trends around it. Closed Sun & Mon.

Le Bouchon du Marais, 15 rue François-Miron, 4e; ☎01.48.87.44.13 (Mº St-Paul). A small relaxed wine *bistrot* serving the patron's own wines from Touraine. Sandwiches as well as meals. *Menu* 115F. Mon–Sat 10am–2.30pm & 7.30–11pm; closed Sun & July & Aug.

Café Martini, 11 rue du Pas-de-la-Mule (Mº St-Paul). Just off place du Vosges but much more down-to-earth, this airy and relaxing little place offers low prices, a wood-beamed ceiling and taped jazz in the background. Toasted Italian sandwiches from 20F, good cappuccino, and a *demi* (small draught beer) is only 13F. Hard to squeeze into, but you can always take the sandwiches away and picnic on the grass of the nearby *place*. Daily 8.30am–2am.

Café des Psaumes, 14–16 rue des Rosiers, 4e; ☎01.42.77.63.98 (Mº St-Paul). Bustling little place on two levels – wonderful wooden interior – serves up kosher falafel for 35F (takeaway 25F) and *plats du jour* from 70F. Noon–midnight; closed Sat.

Au Caprice du Diane, 22 rue des Francs-Bourgeois, 3e (Mº St-Paul). Amid all the expensive, too-trendy cafés around here, this relaxed, inexpensive place, with windows at the back looking onto a refreshing green courtyard, is a godsend. Wonderful sandwiches from 17–28F (including warm goat's cheese with salad), but the speciality of the house are the home-made tarts (48F), displayed at the counter. Mon–Fri 7.30am–8pm, Sat 11.30am–7pm, Sun noon–7pm.

Le Coude Fou, 12 rue du Bourg-Tibourg, 4e (Mº Hôtel-de-Ville). A popular, rather pricey wine bar, which serves some good and unusual wines, charcuterie, and cheese from 32F; *plats* 88–95F. Daily noon–3pm & 8pm–midnight.

L'Ébouillanté, 6 rue des Barres, 4e (Mº Hôtel-de-Ville). Tiny *salon de thé* in a picturesque, cobbled, pedestrian-only street behind the church of St-Gervais, serving chocolate cakes and pâtisseries as well as generous salads and savoury simple fare, at reasonable prices. *Plats du jour* for 67F, savoury Tunisian crepes for 45F. Tues–Sun noon–10pm, till 9pm in winter.

L'Enoteca, 25 rue Charles-V, 4e; ☎01.42.78.91.44 (Mº St-Paul). A very pleasant and fashionable Italian *bistrot à vins*. *Plats* between 60F and 75F; two-course lunchtime *menu* for 75F including a glass of wine. Open daily until 2am.

Épices et Délices, 53 rue Vieille-du-Temple, 4e (Mº St-Paul). Restaurant and *salon de thé* with very pleasant service and fantastic food; salads from 60F, 90F evening *menu*. Daily till midnight.

The Hairy Lemon, 4 rue Caron, 4e (Mº St-Paul). A small, modern bar, run by a rugby and Guinness fan, and attracting a young, fun expat crowd who revel in silly theme nights. Mon–Sat 11am–2am (happy hour 6–8pm), Sun 8.30am–6pm.

The Lizard Lounge, 18 rue du Bourg-Tibourg, 4e (Mo Hôtel-de-Ville). Loud and lively, attractive, stone-walled bar on two levels; American-run, popular with young expats. Especially busy for Sunday brunch, featuring 25F Bloody Marys. Daily noon–2am.

Ma Bourgogne, 19 place des Vosges, 3e (Mo St-Paul). A quiet and pleasant arty café with tables under the arcades on the northwest corner of the square. Best in the morning when the sun hits this side of the square. Serves somewhat pricey meals, too – lunch and dinner menu 195F, à la carte around 220F. Daily until 12.30am or 1am in summer.

La Perla, 26 rue François-Miron, cnr rue du Pont-Louis-Philippe, 4e (Mo St-Paul). A spacious, trendy corner café specializing in things Mexican. The tequila cocktails are especially good (average price 45F). Daily noon–2am.

Le Petit Fer à Cheval, 30 rue Vieille-du-Temple, 4e (Mo St-Paul). This very attractive, small *bistrot*/bar with trad decor – including a huge zinc bar – is a popular drinking spot, with tables outside. Agreeable wine, good-value *plats*, and sandwiches from 35F. Mon–Fri 9am–2am, Sat & Sun 11am–2am; food served noon–midnight.

Le Pick-Clops, 16 rue Vieille-du-Temple, cnr rue du Roi-de-Sicile, 4e (Mo Hôtel-de-Ville). An attractive, easy-going bar, popular with the youngish and hippish. Mon–Sat 8am–2am, Sun 2pm–2am. Happy hour 8–9pm.

Le Quetzal, 10 rue de la Verrerie, cnr rue Moussy, 4e (Mo St-Paul). A fashionable and stylish gay bar, with space for dancing. Mon–Thurs 2pm–4am, Fri–Sun 5pm–5am.

Le Rouge Gorge, 8 rue St-Paul, 4e (Mo St-Paul). A young, enthusiastic clientele sip familiar wines and snack on *chèvre chaud* and smoked salmon salad, or tuck into more substantial fare (*plats du jour* around 60F) while listening to jazz or classical music. Mon–Sat 11am–2am, Sun 11am–8pm.

La Tartine, 24 rue de Rivoli, 4e (Mo St-Paul). The genuine 1900s article, which still cuts across class boundaries in its clientele. A good selection of affordable wines, plus excellent cheese and *saucisson* with *pain de campagne*. Mon & Wed–Sun till 10pm; closed Tues & Aug.

Le Trumilou, 84 quai Hôtel-de-Ville 4e; ☎01.42.77.63.98 (Mo Pont-Marie). The Parisian equivalent of a diner. Pigs' trotters, Lyonnais sausage, and wonderful sweet chestnut *charlotte*. 65F and 80F *menus*. Daily till 11pm.

Au Volcan de Sicile, 62 rue du Roi-de-Sicile, 4e (Mo Hôtel-de-Ville). Flooded with sunshine at midday, this is a good café to sit and sip on the corner of the exquisite and minuscule place Tibourg.

RESTAURANTS

L'Ambroisie, 9 place des Vosges, 4e; ☎01.42.78.51.45 (Mo Chemin-Vert/St-Paul). Scoring 18 out of 20 in the gourmet's bible *Gault et Millau*, this offers exquisite food in an exquisite location, with main dishes starting from 380F and cheese at 140F – it will put a serious dent in your budget. Booking imperative. Daily till 10.30pm; closed first three weeks in Aug plus Sun & Mon during school hols.

Aquarius 1, 54 rue Ste-Croix-de-la-Bretonnerie, 4e; ☎01.48.87.48.71 (Mo St-Paul/Rambuteau). Vegetarian restaurant established in 1974, though now serving alcohol and not the austere and penitential place it once was. A health food store and New Age bookshop to boot. Lunch *menu* at 62F, evening 62F and 92F. Hot dishes from 22–64F. Strictly no smoking. Mon–Sat noon–10pm; closed last fortnight in Aug.

Auberge de Jarente, 7 rue Jarente, 4e; ☎01.42.77.49.35 (Mo St-Paul). A hospitable and friendly Basque restaurant, serving first-class food: *cassoulet*, hare stew, *magret de canard*, and *piperade* – the Basque omelette. *Menus* at 117F and 132F; 185F with wine. Tues–Sat noon–2.30pm & 7.30–10.30pm; closed Aug.

Eating and drinking

Our glossary of French food and dishes begins on p.258.

A marvellous delicatessen on rue des Rosiers for takeaway Eastern European/Jewish snacks is Sacha Finkelsztajn. See "Shopping", p.335.

Eating and drinking

See p.284 for a selection of Paris' many ethnic restaurants.

L'Excuse, 14 rue Charles-V, 4ᵉ; ☎01.42.77.98.97 (Mᵉ St-Paul). The cuisine is *nouvelle*-ish, as refined and elegant as the very pretty decor. A good place for a quiet but stylish date. Midday weekday *menu* at 120F, evening 185F, *carte* from 290F. Noon–2pm & 7.30–11pm; closed Sun & mid-Aug.

Goldenberg's, 7 rue des Rosiers, 4ᵉ; ☎01.48.87.20.16 (Mᵉ St-Paul). The best-known Jewish restaurant in the capital, though success has made service pretty surly. Its *borscht, blinis*, potato strudels, *zakouski* and other central European dishes are nonetheless a treat. Daily changing *plat du jour* 80F, *carte* around 200F. Daily until 2am.

Piccolo Teatro, 6 rue des Écouffes, 4ᵉ; ☎01.42.72.17.79 (Mᵉ St-Paul). Great vegetarian restaurant, with among the best lunch menus at 45F and 55F, evening at 85F and 110F. Tues–Sun noon–3pm & 7–11pm; closed Aug.

Pitchi-Poï, 7 rue Caron, cnr place du Marché-Ste-Catherine, 4ᵉ; ☎01.42.77.46.15 (Mᵉ St-Paul). Excellent Polish/Jewish cuisine in a lovely location with sympathetic ambience. Lunch and dinner *menu* 150F, kids' *menu* 73F, choice of delicious hors d'oeuvres from 43F. Daily noon–3pm & 7.30–11pm.

Le Ravaillac, 10 rue du Roi-de-Sicile, 4ᵉ; ☎01.42.72.85.85 (Mᵉ St-Paul). Long-established Polish restaurant. Specialities include meat *perushkis*, beef stroganoff, and *choucroute*. Excellent quality for the price – around 120F *à la carte*. Noon–3pm & 7–10.30pm; closed Sun & Aug.

Thanksgiving, 20 rue St-Paul, cnr rue Charles-V, 4ᵉ (Mᵉ St-Paul). Highly regarded restaurant serving Cajun and Louisiana cuisine, plus some regular American favourites. It made it into the *Gault et Millau*, the French gourmet's bible, in 1997. You can get it all here: gumbo, jambalaya, crabcakes, even spare ribs and bagels and lox. Lipsmacking 145–165F *menus*. Weekends brunch only. Tues–Fri noon–2.30pm & 7.30–10.30pm, Sat & Sun 11am–4pm.

Quartier du Temple

CAFÉS AND BARS

Le Taxi Jaune, 13 rue Chapon, 3ᵉ (Mᵉ Arts-et-Métiers). An ordinary café made special by the odd poster, good taped rock and new wave music, as well as interesting food. Lunchtime *menu* at 68F with wine, evening *menu* 89F, cocktails 35F. Offers the occasional concert. Mon–Sat until 11pm; closed Sat lunch & Sun.

Web Bar, 32 rue de Picardie, 3ᵉ (Mᵉ République/Filles-du-Calvaire). Paris' best cybercafé, on three levels in a converted industrial space, with fifteen terminals on a gallery level – 25F for 30min, 40F for an hour. A real culture zone: pick up a printed programme of the art exhibitions, short film screenings and other arty events or consult their Web site: *www.webbar.fr*. Comfy couches to loll on and a resident DJ make it a good place to chill, and simple healthy food comes in generous portions (37F for delicious quiche with loads of salad; lunch *menu* 51F or 61F). Mon–Fri 8.30am–2am, Sat 11am–2am, Sun 11am–midnight.

RESTAURANTS

Chez Jenny, 39 bd du Temple, 3ᵉ; ☎01.42.74.75.75 (Mᵉ République). Thirties Alsatian brasserie serving superb *choucroute*. Weekday *formules* 58F and 65F, *menus* 139F and 169F, kids' *menu* 49F, *carte* around 200F. Daily 11.30am–1am.

Chez Nénesse, 17 rue Saintonge, 3ᵉ; ☎01.42.78.46.49 (Mᵉ Arts-et-Métiers). Steak in bilberry sauce and figs stuffed with cream of almonds are two of the unique delights of this restaurant, along with home-made chips on Thursday lunchtimes. *À la carte* around 160F. Mon–Fri noon–2pm & 7.45–10pm; closed Aug.

Chez Omar, 47 Rue de Bretagne, 3ᵉ (Mᵉ Arts-et-Metiers). Very popular North African restaurant in a nice old brasserie set with mirrors. Attracts a young crowd. Couscous 60–98F. Closed Sun.

Le Marais-Cage, 8 rue de Beauce, 3ᵉ; ☎01.48.87.44.51 (Mᵒ Arts-et-Métiers/Filles-du-Calvaire). Friendly, popular West Indian restaurant, serving good food, especially seafood. Midday *menu* 130F; 160F and 199F evening, wine included with each. Mon–Fri noon–2.15pm & 7–10.30pm, Sat evenings only; closed Sun & Aug.

Bastille

CAFÉS AND BARS

Bar des Ferrailleurs, 18 rue de Lappe, 11ᵉ (Mᵒ Bastille). Dark and stylishly sinister, with rusting metal decor, an eccentric owner and fun wig-wearing bar staff. Crowd relaxed and friendly. Daily 5pm–2am.

Boca Chica, 58 rue de Charonne, 11ᵉ (Mᵒ Ledru-Rollin). Popular tapas bar/bodega, heaving by night, and restful in the morning when you can get coffee and a croissant for 10F, and a newspaper for an extra 5F. Colourful arty decor. Daily 8am–2am.

Café de l'Industrie, 16 rue St-Sabin, 11ᵉ (Mᵒ Bastille). Rugs on the floor around solid old wooden tables, miscellaneous objects on the walls, and a young, unpretentious crowd enjoying the lack of chrome, minimalism or Philippe Starck. One of the best Bastille addresses. *Plats du jour* from 48F. Noon–2am, closed Sat.

Café des Phares, 7 place de la Bastille (west side), 4ᵉ (Mᵒ Bastille). Every Sunday at 11am a public philosophy debate is held in the back room here, run by Nietzsche specialist Marc Sautet, who also offers private philosophical consultations. Some academic colleagues say he's incapable of coherence; others see these sessions as the first revolutionary move since May 1968. Either way, it's good theatre. Daily 7am–4am.

La Fontaine, 1 rue de Charonne, 11ᵉ (Mᵒ Bastille). Gentrified, as are all the cafés hereabouts, but not too self-conscious or expensive. On the corner of rue du Faubourg-St-Antoine, by the fountain. Daily 8.30am–2am.

Fouquet's, 130 rue de Lyon, 12ᵉ (Mᵒ Bastille). A smart and expensive café-restaurant underneath the Opéra Bastille, sister establishment to the Champs-Élysées *Fouquet's*. With perfect French courtesy they will leave you undisturbed for hours with a 15F coffee. *Menu*, including wine, at 170F. Mon–Fri till midnight; closed Sat & Sun midday.

Grand Appetit, 9 rue de la Cerisaie, 4ᵉ (Mᵒ Bastille). Vegetarian meals served by dedicated eco-veggies at the back of a shop. Mon–Thurs noon–7pm, Fri & Sun noon–2pm; closed Sat.

Havanita Café, 11 rue de Lappe, 11ᵉ (Mᵒ Bastille). Large, comfortable Cuban-style bar with battered old leather sofa. Cocktails from 48F; happy hour till 8pm. Open daily 5pm–2am.

Iguana, 15 rue de la Roquette, cnr rue Daval, 11ᵉ (Mᵒ Bastille). A place to be seen in. Decor of trellises, colonial fans, and a brushed bronze bar. The clientele studies *récherché* art reviews, and the coffee is excellent. Daily 10am–2am.

Pause Café, 41 rue de Charonne, cnr rue Keller, 11ᵉ (Mᵒ Ledru-Rollin). A fashionable Bastille café, down among the galleries, with popular sidewalk seating. *Plats* 52F. Tues–Sat 8am–2am, Sun till 9pm.

SanZSanS, 49 rue du Faubourg-St-Antoine, 11ᵉ (Mᵒ Bastille). Gothic decor of red velvet, oil paintings and chandeliers, with a young clientele in the evening. Drinks reasonably priced; main courses for around 48–65F, and there's always a vegetarian dish on offer. Daily 9am–2am.

Le Temps des Cerises, 31 rue de la Cerisaie, 4ᵉ (Mᵒ Bastille). It's hard to say what's so appealing about this café, with its dirty yellow decor, old posters and prints of *vieux Paris*, save that the *patronne* knows most of the clientele, who are young, relaxed and not the dreaded *branchés*. 68F *menu*. Mon–Fri until 8pm; food at midday only; closed Aug.

Eating and drinking

See p.257 for a list of vegetarian restaurants in Paris.

Eating and drinking

The cafés and restaurants of the Quartier Latin are keyed on the map on p.276.

There is another branch of Café Oz at 18 rue St-Denis, 1er.

RESTAURANTS

Blue Elephant, 43–45 rue de la Roquette, 11e; ☎01.47.00.42.00 (Mº Bastille/Richard-Lenoir). Superb Thai restaurant with tropical forest decor. Worth every centime. 150F midday *menu*; otherwise over 270F. Daily till midnight; closed Sat midday.

Bofinger, 7 rue de la Bastille, 3e; ☎01.42.72.87.82 (Mº Bastille). A well-established and popular turn-of-the-century brasserie, with stunning original decor, serving classic brasserie fare from oysters to perfectly cooked fish and lamb. Weekday lunchtime *menu* at 119F, evening 169F, both including wine, otherwise over 200F. Open daily until 1am. *Le Petit Bofinger* (☎01.42.72.05.23; noon–3pm & 7pm-midnight), opposite at no.6, is under the same management, and serves lighter dishes, with *plats du jour* from 76F.

La Canaille, 4 rue Crillon, 4e; ☎01.42.78.09.71 (Mº Sully-Morland/Bastille). Bar in front, restaurant behind, decorated with revolutionary posters invoking rather more durable old-fashioned values than the usual contemporary fast-buck stuff. The food is simple, traditional and well cooked. Delightful, friendly atmosphere. Offers 79F and 89F lunch *menus* – 130F in the evening – and *à la carte* at around 140F. Daily till midnight, closed Sat & Sun lunch.

Chez Paul, 13 rue de Charonne, cnr rue de Lappe, 11e; ☎01.47.00.34.57 (Mº Bastille). Wonky corner building housing a small restaurant which preserves the faded colours and furnishings of an older Bastille, with details right down to the black-and-white tiles on the floor still intact. The young customers who pack the place out have their own very contemporary style. Food is traditional and affordable, the ambience very congenial. Mains from 62F. Daily noon–2.30pm & 7.30pm–12.30am.

Le Petit Keller, 13 rue Keller, 11e; ☎01.47.00.12.97 (Mº Ledru-Rollin). Colourful restaurant, with decorative tiled floor and art exhibitions on the walls, serving surprisingly affordable food. While the scenery is very 1990s, the food is traditional home-cooking – dishes like rabbit with prunes, and very fresh vegetable-oriented starters. Mon–Sat 8am–2.30pm & 7.30–11pm.

Chapter 6: The Left Bank

Quartier Latin

CAFÉS AND BARS

Le Bâteau Ivre, 40 rue Descartes, 5e (Mº Cardinal-Lemoine). Happy hour is 5–9pm at this small bar just clear of the Mouffetard tourist hotspot. Daily 5pm–2am.

Café des Arts, cnr place Contrescarpe and rue Lacépède, 5e (Mº Monge). Prettier cups, cheaper coffee and a younger crowd than its touristy neighbour *La Chope* in this café-packed square.

Café de la Mosquée, 39 rue Geoffroy-St-Hilaire, 5e (Mº Monge). In fine weather you can drink mint tea and eat sweet cakes beside a fountain and assorted fig trees in the courtyard of this Paris mosque – a delightful haven of calm. The interior of the *salon* is beautifully Arabic. Meals are served in the adjoining restaurant: couscous from 55F, tagines from 70F. Daily 8am–midnight.

Café Notre-Dame, cnr quai St-Michel and rue St-Jacques, 5e (Mº St-Michel). With a view right across to the cathedral. Lenin used to drink here.

Café Oz, 184 rue St-Jacques, 5e (RER Luxembourg). Friendly, Australian-run pub, complete with Aboriginal cave paintings, kitsch souvenirs and a range of antipodean wines and brews. Can get very crowded. Daily 4pm–2am.

Connolly's Corner, cnr rues Patriarches and de Mirbel, 5e (Mº Monge/Censier-Daubenton). An Irish bar with darts, Kilkenny and not a lot of space, but plenty of atmosphere. Very smoky. Daily 4pm–2am.

Cyber Café Latino, 13 rue de l'École-Polytechnique, 5e (M° Maubert-Mutualité). Small friendly bar with a Venezuelan owner, Latino sounds and fruit smoothies and tapas on the menu. Six computers out the back to surf the net. Mon–Sat 11.30am–2am.

Les Fontaines, 9 rue Soufflot, 5e (RER Luxembourg). A brasserie serving huge seafood salads (38F) and traditional meat and fish dishes – the menu changes daily. Main courses 68–98F. Mon–Sat noon–3pm & 7.30–10.30pm.

La Fourmi Ailée, 8 rue du Fouarre (M° Maubert-Mutualité). Simple, light fare – including weekend brunch – served in this newly transformed *salon de thé* – the book-filled wall is a reminder of its days as a feminist bookshop. A high ceiling painted with a lovely mural adds to the rarefied atmosphere. Around 69F for a *plat*. Daily noon–midnight.

La Gueuze, 19 rue Soufflot, 5e (RER Luxembourg). Comfy surroundings – lots of wood and stained glass. Kitchen specials are *pierrades*: dishes cooked on hot stones. Numerous bottles and several draught Belgian beers, including cherry beer. Close to the university, hence lots of student habitués. Mon–Sat noon–2am.

Le Piano Vache, 8 rue Laplace, 5e (M° Cardinal-Lemoine). Venerable student bar with canned music and relaxed atmosphere. Daily noon–2am.

Les Pipos, 2 rue de l'École-Polytechnique, 5e (M° Maubert-Mutualité/Cardinal-Lemoine). Old carved wooden bar and sculpted chimney piece, its own wines, and a long-established position opposite the gates of the former *grande école*. Wine at 14–25F a glass; *plats* for 50–75F. Mon–Sat 8am–2am; closed Sun & three weeks in Aug.

Polly Magoo, 11 rue St-Jacques, 5e (M° St-Michel/Maubert-Mutualité). A scruffy all-nighter – closes 4–5am – frequented by chess addicts.

Le Verre à Pied, 118bis rue Mouffetard, 5e (M° Monge). An old-fashioned café-bar with cheap drinks. Lunchtime menu 50F. Closed Sun afternoon & Mon.

Le Violon Dingue, 46 rue de la Montagne-Ste-Geneviève, 5e (M° Maubert-Mutualité). A long, dark, student pub that's also popular with young travellers. Noisy and friendly, with English-speaking bar staff and cheap drinks. Happy hour 6–10pm. Daily 6pm–1.30am.

RESTAURANTS

Bistro de la Sorbonne, 4 rue Toullier, 5e; ☎01.43.54.41.49 (RER Luxembourg). Traditional French and delicious North African food served in copious portions at reasonable prices. Crowded and attractive student/local ambience. 69F lunchtime *menu*; 95F and 140F in the evening. Closed Sun.

Brasserie Balzar, 49 rue des Écoles, 5e; ☎01.43.54.13.67 (M° Maubert-Mutualité). A traditional literary-bourgeois brasserie, frequented by the intelligentsia of the Latin Quarter. About 180F *à la carte*. Daily until 1am; closed Aug.

Au Buisson Ardent, 25 rue Jussieu, 5e; ☎01.43.54.93.02 (M° Jussieu). Generous helpings of first-class traditional cooking: mussels, duck, warm goat cheese salad, lamb and more. Lunchtime *menu* 70F, 145F in the evening. Reservations recommended. Closed Sat, Sun and two weeks in Aug.

Chez Léna et Mimile, 32 rue Tournefort, 5e; ☎01.47.07.72.47 (M° Censier-Daubenton). The south-facing high *terrasse* is the main attraction, overlooking a shady little square, and the 185F *menu* (wine and coffee included) is excellent. 98F *menu* at lunchtime on weekdays. Until 11pm; closed Sat noon and Sun.

Chez René, 14 bd St-Germain, cnr rue du Cardinal-Lemoine, 5e; ☎01.43.54.30.23 (M° Maubert-Mutualité). A grand old *bistrot* serving the old favourites: coq au vin, boeuf bourguignon. Not cheap: around 150F without wine, except at lunchtime, when the 150F *menu* includes wine. Closed Sat & Sun.

Eating and drinking

See p.296 for a list of cafés and restaurants that stay open late.

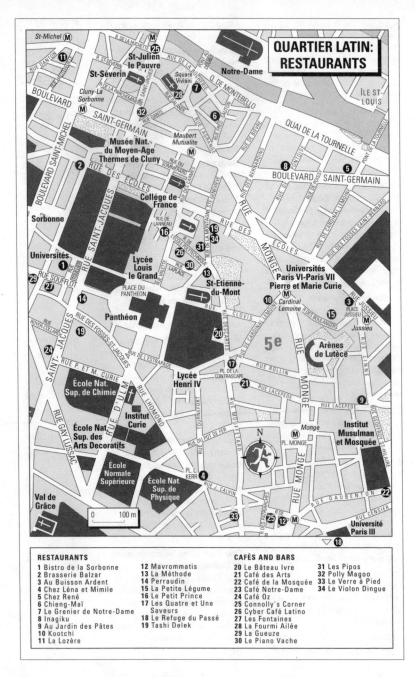

QUARTIER LATIN: RESTAURANTS

RESTAURANTS

1 Bistro de la Sorbonne
2 Brasserie Balzar
3 Au Buisson Ardent
4 Chez Léna et Mimile
5 Chez René
6 Chieng-Maï
7 Le Grenier de Notre-Dame
8 Inagiku
9 Au Jardin des Pâtes
10 Kootchi
11 La Lozère
12 Mavrommatis
13 La Méthode
14 Perraudin
15 La Petite Légume
16 Le Petit Prince
17 Les Quatre et Une Saveurs
18 Le Refuge du Passé
19 Tashi Delek

CAFÉS AND BARS

20 Le Bâteau Ivre
21 Café des Arts
22 Café de la Mosquée
23 Café Notre-Dame
24 Café Oz
25 Connolly's Corner
26 Cyber Café Latino
27 Les Fontaines
28 La Fourmi Ailée
29 La Gueuze
30 Le Piano Vache
31 Les Pipos
32 Polly Magoo
33 Le Verre à Pied
34 Le Violon Dingue

Chieng-Maï, 12 rue Frédéric-Sauton, 5e; ☎01.43.25.45.45 (M° Maubert-Mutualité). Excellent Thai dishes; 69F at lunchtime, otherwise 122 and 173F *menus*. Closed Sun.

Foyer du Vietnam, 80 rue Monge, 5e; ☎01.45.35.32.54 (M° Monge). Casual, authentic Vietnamese with dishes from 30F and *menus* for 56F and 67F. Mon–Sat till 10pm.

Le Grenier de Notre-Dame, 18 rue de la Bûcherie, 5e (M° Maubert-Mutualité). See for yourself: some veggies love this tiny place, which has been operating since 1978; others hate its posh candle-lit atmosphere, cramped tables and cheesy music. Substantial fare, including cous-cous, fried tofu, cauliflower cheese. *Menus* at 75F and 105F. Daily noon–11.30pm.

Inagiku, 14 rue Pontoise, 5e; ☎01.43.54.70.07 (M° Maubert-Mutualité). Authentic Japanese: four pieces sushi 65F; 88F midday *menu*. Mon–Sat noon–2.15pm & 7–10.45pm.

Au Jardin des Pâtes, 4 rue Lacépède, 5e; ☎01.43.31.50.71 (M° Jussieu). Delicious home-made pasta only, but with all manner of flourishes and garnishings. Around 100F for a full meal. Closed Mon.

Kootchi, 40 rue du Cardinal-Lemoine, 5e; ☎01.44.07.20.56 (M° Cardinal-Lemoine). Afghan restaurant, with pretty good prices: 55F *menu* at lunchtime; 98F in the evening. Closed Sun.

Mavrommatis, 42 rue Daubenton, 5e; ☎01.43.31.17.17 (M° Censier-Daubenton). A sophisticated Greek restaurant, whose cooking has been favourably influenced by French attention to detail. Quite expensive – even the lunchtime *menu* is 120F – but you are definitely tasting Greek food at its best. Closed Mon.

La Méthode, 2 rue Descartes, 5e; ☎01.43.54.22.43 (M° Cardinal-Lemoine). Very friendly, family-run resto in a late-sixteenth-century building. Enormous snail starter, duck and home-made dessert on 145F *menu*. Daily 7–11.30pm.

Pemathang, 13 rue de la Montagne-St-Geneviève, 5e; ☎01.43.54.34.34 (M° Maubert-Mutualité). Tibetan restaurant with a vegetarian menu for 107F and a range of Tibetan vegetarian specialities from 60F, as well as more meat-oriented dishes. Closed all Sun, Mon lunch & Aug.

Perraudin, 157 rue St-Jacques, 5e (RER Luxembourg). One of the classic *bistrots* of the Left Bank, with lots of atmosphere and solid home cooking. A midday *menu* at 63F; *carte* around 120–130F. No reservations, but you can wait at the bar for a place. Service until 10.15pm; closed Sun, midday on Sat & Mon, last fortnight in Aug.

Le Petit Prince, 12 rue Lanneau, 5e; ☎01.43.54.77.26 (M° Maubert-Mutualité). Good food in a restaurant full of Latin Quarter charm in one of the quartier's old-est lanes. Value for money with generous servings. *Menus* at 76F, 118F and 142F. Evenings only, until 12.30am.

La Petite Légume, 36 rue Boulangers, 5e (M° Jussieu). This is a health-food grocery store that doubles as a restaurant, serv-ing quality ingredients in a variety of *plats* for around 58F. Mon–Sat noon–2.30pm & 7.30–10pm.

Les Quatre et Une Saveurs, 72 rue du Cardinal-Lemoine, 5e; ☎01.43.26.88.80 (M° Cardinal-Lemoine). Inventive, high-class macrobiotic vegetarian food. 120F or 130F *menu* includes coffee. Tues–Sat till 10pm.

Le Refuge du Passé, 32 rue du Fer-à-Moulin, 5e; ☎01.47.07.29.91 (M° Les Gobelins). Stuffed full of bric-a-brac and musical instruments, this is a rare home for French *chansons*. Also dishes out decent food from southwest France. 119F midday *menu* with wine; 150F evening *menu*. Open till midnight; closed Sun & midday Mon & Sat.

Student restaurants at 8bis rue Cuvier, 5e (M° Jussieu); 31 av G-Bernanos, 5e (RER Port-Royal); 31 rue Geoffroy-St-Hilaire, 5e (M° Censier-Daubenton); rue de Santeuil (M° Censier-Daubenton) & 12 place du Panthéon (M° Cardinal-Lemoine). See box p.257 for details.

Eating and drinking

See p.284 for a list of various ethnic restaurants in Paris.

Eating and drinking

See p.296 for a list of cafés and restaurants that stay open late.

Tashi Delek, 4 rue des Fossés-St-Jacques, 5ᵉ; ☎01.43.26.55.55 (RER Luxembourg). An enjoyable Tibetan restaurant – run by refugees – where you can eat for as little as 52F at lunchtime and 64F in the evening. There is even yak bitter tea for those immune to altitude sickness. Closed Sun & Aug.

St-Germain

CAFÉS AND BARS

L'Alsace à Paris, 9 place St-André-des-Arts, 6ᵉ; ☎01.43.26.21.48 (Mº St-Michel). A very busy and well-worn brasserie, with *menus* at 119F and 169F – but also delicious and cheap *tartes flambées* like thin pizzas that you can take away.

L'Assignat, 7 rue Guénégaud, 6ᵉ (Mº Pont-Neuf). Zinc counter, bar stools, bar football and young regulars from the nearby art school in an untouristy café close to quai des Augustins. Sandwich and a glass of wine for 27F. Mon–Sat 7.30am–8.30pm; food served noon–3.30pm; closed July.

Le Bonaparte, cnr rue Bonaparte and place St-Germain, 6ᵉ (Mº St-Germain-des-Prés). Meeting place for the quartier's intellectuals, quieter and less touristy than *Les Deux Magots* or *Le Flore*. Hot and cold snacks and crêpes served at reasonable prices.

Café de la Mairie, place St-Sulpice, 6ᵉ (Mº St-Sulpice). A peaceful, pleasant café on the sunny north side of the square, opposite the church of St-Sulpice. Mon–Sat 7am–2am.

Chez Georges, 11 rue des Canettes, 6ᵉ (Mº Mabillon). An attractive wine bar in the spit-on-the-floor mode, with its old shop front still intact in a narrow street leading off place St-Sulpice. Can get very crowded. Tues–Sat noon–2am; closed July 14–Aug 15.

À la Cour de Rohan, cour du Commerce, off rues St-André-des-Arts and Ancienne-Comédie, 6ᵉ (Mº Odéon). A genteel, chintzy drawing-room atmosphere down a picturesque eighteenth-century alleyway close to bd St-Germain. Cakes,

tartes, poached eggs, etc. No smoking. *Plats du jour* 60–67F. Daily noon–7.30pm; closed mid-July–mid-Aug.

Les Deux Magots, 170 bd St-Germain, 6ᵉ (Mº St-Germain-des-Près). Right on the corner of place St-Germain-des-Prés, it too owes its reputation to the intellectuals of the Left Bank, past and present. In summertime it picks up a lot of foreigners seeking the exact location of the spirit of French culture, and buskers galore play to the packed terrace. Come early for an expensive but satisfying 75F breakfast. Daily 6.30am–1.30am; closed one week in Jan.

Le 10, 10 rue de l'Odéon, 6ᵉ (Mº Odéon). The beer here is very cheap, hence its youthful and foreign clientele. Small dark bar with old posters, a jukebox, and a lot of chatting-up. Daily 6.30pm–2am.

L'Écluse, 15 quai des Grands-Augustins, 6ᵉ (Mº St-Michel). Forerunner of the new generation of wine bars, with decor and atmosphere in authentic traditional style – just lacking the workmen to spit on the floor. Small and intimate: a very agreeable place to sit and sip. It has spawned several offspring, none of which is as pleasant. Daily 11.30am–2am.

Le Flore, 172 bd St-Germain, 6ᵉ (Mº St-Germain-des-Près). The great rival and immediate neighbour of *Les Deux Magots*, with a similar clientele. Sartre, De Beauvoir, Camus and Marcel Carné used to hang out here. Daily 7am–1.30am.

Le Mazet, 60 rue St-André-des-Arts, 6ᵉ (Mº Odéon). A well-known hang-out for buskers (with a lock-up for their instruments), and heavy drinkers. For an evil concoction, try a *bière brûlée* – it's flambéed with gin. Small glass beer 20F, cocktails 49F. Mon–Thurs 10am–2am, Fri & Sat until 3.30am. Happy hour 5–8pm.

La Paillote, 45 rue Monsieur-le-Prince, 6ᵉ (RER Luxembourg/Mº Odéon). *The* late-night bar for jazz fans, with one of the best collections of recorded jazz in the city. Drinks start from 30F. Mon–Sat 9pm till dawn; closed Aug.

ST-GERMAIN: RESTAURANTS

0   100 m

Université
Paris V

6e

St-Germain-
des-Prés

Mabillon

St-
Sulpice

St-Sulpice

N

PLACE
ST-SULPICE

Université
Paris

RESTAURANTS

1 Aux Charpentiers
2 Jacques Cagna
3 Lipp
4 La Lozére
5 La Maroussia
6 Le Muniche
7 Orestias
8 Le Petit Mabillon
9 Le Petit St-Benoît
10 Le Petit Vatel
11 Le Petit Zinc
12 Polidor
13 Le Procope
14 Restaurant des Beaux-Arts
15 La Rôtisserie d'en Face

CAFÉS AND BARS

16 L'Alsace à Paris
17 L'Assignat
18 Le Bonaparte
19 Café de la Mairie
20 Chez Georges
21 À la Cour de Rohan
22 Les Deux Magots
23 Le 10
24 L'Écluse
25 Le Flore
26 Le Mazet
27 La Paillote
28 La Palette
29 La Pinte
30 Pub St-Germain

31 La Table d'Italie
32 La Taverne de Nesle
33 Au Vieux Colombier

La Palette, 43 rue de Seine, 6ᵉ (Mᵒ Odéon). Once-famous Beaux-Arts student hang-out, now more for art dealers and their customers. The service can be uncivil and the bill rather expensive, but the *terrasse*, murals and every detail of the decor are superb, including, of course, a large selection of colourful used palettes. Mon–Sat 8am–2am.

La Pinte, 13 carrefour de l'Odéon, 6ᵉ (Mᵒ Odéon). Boozy, crowded beer cellar, with

Eating and drinking

live piano and jazz. Daily 6.30pm–2am; closed Aug.

Pub St-Germain, 17 rue de l'Ancienne-Comédie, 6ᵉ (Mᵒ Odéon). Twenty-six draught beers and hundreds of bottles. Huge, crowded and expensive. Hot food at mealtimes, otherwise cold snacks. For a taste of "real" French beer try ch'ti (patois for "northerner"), a *bière de garde* from the Pas-de-Calais. Live music nightly from 10pm. Open daily 24hr.

La Table d'Italie, 69 rue de Seine, 6ᵉ (Mᵒ Mabillon/St-Germain-des-Près). Pasta, Italian snacks, etc, at the counter, plus a grocery selling pasta and other Italian delicatessen products. 88F *menu*.

La Taverne de Nesle, 32 rue Dauphine, 6ᵉ (Mᵒ Odéon). Vast selection of beers. Full of local night owls. Cocktails from 45F. Mon–Thurs & Sun 9pm–4am, Fri & Sat till 5am.

Au Vieux Colombier, 65 rue des Rennes, 6ᵉ (Mᵒ St-Sulpice). An Art Deco café on the corner of rue du Vieux-Colombier, with enamelled dove medallions, ice cream cone lights and stained green wooden window frames.

RESTAURANTS

Aux Charpentiers, 10 rue Mabillon, 6ᵉ; ☎01.43.26.30.05 (Mᵒ Mabillon). A friendly, old-fashioned place belonging to the Compagnons des Charpentiers (Carpenters' Guild), with appropriate decor of roof-trees and tie beams. Traditional *plats du jour* are their forte, for about 75F. Around 200F *à la carte*. Lunchtime *menu* at 120F. Daily until 11pm; closed hols.

Jacques Cagna, 14 rue des Grands-Augustins, 6ᵉ; ☎01.43.26.49.39 (Mᵒ Odéon/St-Michel). Classy surroundings for very classy food – beef with Périgord truffles and the like for 350F a dish upwards, though there is a midday *menu* for 260F. Till 10.30pm; closed Sat lunchtime, all Sun & three weeks in Aug.

Lipp, 151 bd St-Germain, 6ᵉ (Mᵒ St-Germain-des-Près). A 1900s brasserie, and one of the best-known establishments on the Left Bank; haunt of the

very successful and very famous. *Plat du jour* 100–115F, *carte* 200–250F; no reservations, so be prepared to wait. Daily until 12.30am; closed mid-July to mid-Aug.

La Lozère, 4 rue Hautefeuille, 6ᵉ; ☎01.43.54.26.64 (Mᵒ St-Michel). A scrubbed-wood restaurant serving up the cuisine, cheeses, etc, of the Lozère *département*. *Menus* at 94F (lunchtime only during the week, wine included), 128F and 159F. Closed Sun & Mon, mid-July to mid-Aug & the last week in Dec.

La Maroussia, 9 rue de l'Éperon, 6ᵉ; ☎01.43.54.87.50 (Mᵒ Odéon). Polish and Ukrainian dishes – *bigos* (sausage and cabbage stew), *shashlik* (kebabs), salmon *kulibiak* (soup) and *zakouskis* (cold hors d'oeuvres). *Menus* at 150F 170F, *carte* 250F – and carafes of vodka to go with them. Music Sat & Wed eves. Closed Sun, Mon & two weeks each in May & Aug.

Le Muniche, 7 rue St-Benoît, 6ᵉ; ☎01.42.61.12.70 (Mᵒ St-Germain-des-Prés). A crowded old-style brasserie with an oyster bar, mirrors and theatre posters on the walls, and classic French brasserie fare on the menu: seafood, *choucroute*, leg of lamb. *Menus* at 98F and 149F; *carte* 180F. Daily noon–2am.

Orestias, 4 rue Grégoire-de-Tours, 6ᵉ; ☎01.43.54.62.01 (Mᵒ Odéon). A mixture of Greek and French cuisine. Good helpings and very cheap – with a *menu* at 46F (weekdays only until 8pm). Mon–Sat lunchtime & eve until 11.30pm.

Le Petit Mabillon, 6 rue Mabillon, 6ᵉ; ☎01.43.54.08.41 (Mᵒ Mabillon). A little Italian restaurant, justly popular for its good food and reasonable prices. Three-course menu at 77F. Closed Sun & lunch Mon.

Le Petit St-Benoît, 4 rue St-Benoît, 6ᵉ; ☎01.42.60.27.92 (Mᵒ St-Germain-des-Prés). A simple, genuine and very appealing local for the neighbourhood's chattering classes. Another of the St-Germain institutions, serving solid traditional fare. *Menu* at 130F. Mon–Fri noon–2.30pm & 7–10.30pm.

Le Petit Vatel, 5 rue Lobineau, 6ᵉ; ☎01.43.54.28.49 (Mᵒ Mabillon). A tiny, matey atmospheric place nicely done out with bright yellow walls, old train posters and quirky colourful cutlery. Popular with students. Good, plain home cooking, including a vegetarian *plat* – for around 50–55F. A three-course meal will set you back 100F. Mon–Sat lunchtime & 7pm–midnight, Sun eve only.

Le Petit Zinc, 11 rue St-Benoît, 6ᵉ; ☎01.42.61.20.60 (Mᵒ St-Germain-des-Prés). Excellent traditional dishes, especially seafood, in stunning Art Nouveau-style premises (built thirty years ago). Popular pavement tables. Not cheap – *menu* 169F, seafood platter 450F for two. Daily noon–2am.

Polidor, 41 rue Monsieur-le-Prince, 6ᵉ; ☎01.43.26.95.34 (Mᵒ Odéon). A traditional *bistrot*, open since 1845, whose visitors' book, they say, boasts more of history's big names than all the glittering palaces put together. Not as cheap as it was in James Joyce's day, but good food and great atmosphere. Lunches at 55F during the week, and an excellent 100F evening *menu*. Mon–Sat until 12.30am, Sun until 11pm.

Le Procope, 13 rue de l'Ancienne-Comédie, 6ᵉ; ☎01.40.46.79.00 (Mᵒ Odéon). Since opening in 1686 as the first establishment to serve coffee in Paris, it has retained its reputation as the place for powerful intellectuals. It's popular with tourists, too, which is not surprising as it still offers a good 109F *menu* (up to 8pm) and 123F *menu* with wine included after 11pm. At other times you won't see any change out of 200F. Daily noon–1am.

Restaurant des Beaux-Arts, 11 rue Bonaparte, 6ᵉ; ☎01.43.26.92.64 (Mᵒ St-Germain-des-Prés). The traditional hangout of the art students from the Beaux-Arts across the way. The choice is wide, portions are generous and queues are long in high season. The atmosphere is generally good, though the service can be tetchy. *Menu* at 79F including wine.

Daily lunchtime & evening until 10.45pm.

Le Rôtisserie d'en Face, 2 rue Christine, 6ᵉ; ☎01.43.26.40.98 (Mᵒ Odéon/St-Michel). An annexe to *Jacques Cagna* (see opposite). Excellent grilled meats (210F) or a midday *menu* at 100F or 160F in a rather too businesslike atmosphere.

Student restaurants at 8 bis rue de l'Eperon, 6ᵉ (Mᵒ Odéon); 46 rue de Vaugirard, 6ᵉ (RER Luxembourg/Mᵒ Mabillon); and 21 rue d'Assas, 6ᵉ (RER Port-Royal/Mᵒ Notre-Dame-des-Champs).

Chapter 7: Trocadéro, Eiffel Tower and Les Invalides

CAFÉS AND BARS

Café du Musée d'Orsay, 1 rue Bellechasse, 7ᵉ (RER Musée-d'Orsay/Mᵒ Solférino). Superb views over the Seine in the museum's magnificent rooftop café. Snacks and drinks, quick and friendly service. Tues–Sun 11am–5pm, Thurs till 9pm.

Le Poch'tron, 25 rue de Bellechasse (Mᵒ Solférino). With a fine selection of wines by the glass, this is an excellent place to revive yourself after visiting the arrondissement's museums. Also serves lunch and dinner, with main dishes around 70F. Mon–Fri 9am–10.30pm.

Sancerre, 22 av Rapp, 7ᵉ (Mᵒ Alma-Marceau). Wine shop and bar serving glasses of Sancerre from 22F and sandwiches from 16F. Try the rosé and other Loire wines. Mon–Sat 8.30am–7.30pm.

Le Suffren, cnr avs Motte-Piquet and Suffren, 15ᵉ (Mᵒ École-Militaire/La Motte-Piquet). Big café-brasserie distinguished by serving dark Swiss chocolate with its *café crème*, and being the only obvious place to sit down after walking the length of the École-Militaire. Daily noon–midnight.

Totem, southern wing of the Palais de Chaillot, place du Trocadéro, 16ᵉ (Mᵒ Trocadéro). Native-American themed

Eating and drinking

Some of Paris' top gourmet restaurants are listed on p.256.

Tea and Tattered Pages, *at 24 rue Mayet, 6ᵉ, is an American-run bookshop/ salon de thé where you can indulge cravings for cheesecake and brownies; popular Sunday brunch, too. See p.283.*

Eating and drinking

Some of Paris' top gourmet restaurants are listed on p.256.

restaurant, but with some French traditional dishes thrown in; the 129F lunch menu isn't bad, but the views of the Eiffel Tower from the terrace are magnificent. Daily noon–2am.

Veggie, 38 rue de Verneuil, 7ᵉ (Mᵒ Solférino). Organic takeaway from health-food shop near the Musée d'Orsay. Mon–Fri 10.30am–2.30pm & 4.30–7.30pm.

RESTAURANTS

L'Ami Jean, 27 rue Malar, 7ᵉ; ☎01.47.05.86.89 (Mᵒ Latour-Maubourg). Pleasant ambience, if rather hurried, and good Basque food (*paella, pipérade, poulet basquaise*) for around 130–150F. Mon–Sat lunchtime & 7–10.30pm; closed Sun & Aug.

Au Babylone, 13 rue de Babylone, 7ᵉ; ☎01.45.48.72.13 (Mᵒ Sèvres-Babylone). Lots of old-fashioned charm and culinary basics like *rôti de veau* and steak, plus wine on the 90F *menu*. Mon–Sat lunchtime only; closed Aug.

Le Basilic, 2 rue Casimir-Périer, 7ᵉ; ☎01.44.18.94.64 (Mᵒ Solférino). Very classy with lots of polished brass and a terrace overlooking the apse of Ste-Clotilde church. Specialities such as lamb from Sisteron in thyme sauce will set you back 102F. Count on 250F for a full meal. Daily noon–2.30pm & 7.30–10.30pm.

Le Bourdonnais, 113 av La Bourdonnais, 7ᵉ; ☎01.47.05.47.06 (Mᵒ École-Militaire). A gem of a restaurant and a high-class one at that. *À la carte* costs upwards of 400F, but there's a superb midday *menu* including wine for 240F, and an evening *menu* at 320F. Daily noon–2.30pm & 8–11pm.

Café de Mars, 11 rue Augereau, 7ᵉ; ☎01.47.05.05.91 (Mᵒ École-Militaire). A fashionable American-style café close to the Eiffel Tower and frequented by students from the American College nearby. *Plats du jour* at 50F and a 70F *menu* at lunchtime. Brunch on Sat & Sun for around 130F. Open daily lunchtime and Tues–Sat 8–11.30pm.

Chez Germaine, 30 rue Pierre-Leroux, 7ᵉ; ☎01.42.73.28.34 (Mᵒ Duroc/Vaneau). A simple, tiny and unbelievably cheap restaurant, with a midday 49F *menu* and evening 60F *menu*, including wine. The *carte* costs up to about 90F. Noon–2.30pm & 7–9.30pm; closed Sun, Sat eve & Aug.

Au Pied de Fouet, 45 rue de Babylone, 7ᵉ (Mᵒ St-François-Xavier/Sèvres-Babylone). Good food and a great little place. Little is the operative word: there are just four tables and no reservations. Around 80–90F. Mon–Fri noon–2pm & 7–9.30pm, Sat noon–2pm; closed Sun & Aug.

Thoumieux, 79 rue St-Dominique, 7ᵉ; ☎01.47.05.49.75 (Mᵒ Latour-Maubourg). A large and popular establishment in this rather smart district, with traditional brasserie service. A *menu* at 67F, usually offal, another at 160F, otherwise you have to be careful to get away with spending less than 180F. Daily lunchtime & 6.30pm–midnight, Sun non-stop service.

La Varangue, 27 rue Augereau, 7ᵉ; ☎01.47.05.51.22 (Mᵒ École-Militaire). A simple and relaxed sort of place with the emphasis on salads, greens and desserts. *Menu* at 96F or a two-course *formule* for 77F including wine or cider. Closed Sat & Sun.

Chapter 8: Montparnasse and the southern arrondissements

Montparnasse

CAFÉS AND BARS

La Closerie des Lilas, 171 bd du Montparnasse, 6ᵉ (Mᵒ Port-Royal). The smartest, artiest, classiest one of all, with excellent cocktails for around 60F in the bar. The tables are name-plated after celebrated habitués (Verlaine, Mallarmé, Lenin, Modigliani, Léger, Strindberg). The restaurant is very expensive, but you can eat at the brasserie for under 140F, and there's a resident pianist. Daily noon–1.30am.

Le Dôme, 108 bd du Montparnasse, 6ᵉ (Mᵉ Vavin). Next door to *La Coupole* (see below), and another of Sartre's haunts. Cinema pics decorate each alcove. Beautiful and expensive. Daily noon–12.30am.

Mustangs, 84 bd du Montparnasse, 14ᵉ (M° Montparnasse-Bienvenue). Young crowd and happy atmosphere. A good place to finish up the evening after nightclubbing in St-Germain. Tex-Mex food, cocktails and beers. Happy hour Mon–Fri 4–7pm; frozen margaritas recommended. Open daily 9am–5am.

La Pause Gourmande, 27 rue Campagne-Première, 14ᵉ (M° Raspail). Delicious salads and savoury and sweet *tartes* from 28F. Mon–Fri 8.30am–7pm, Sat 8.30am–3pm.

Le Rosebud, 11bis rue Delambre, 14ᵉ (M° Vavin). A slightly more exclusive bar just off the bd Montparnasse. The clientele usually makes an amusing spectacle. Cocktails around 62F. Daily till 3am.

La Rotonde, 105 bd du Montparnasse, 6ᵉ (M° Vavin). Another of the grand old Montparnasse establishments frequented by Lenin and Trotsky in their time. Daily till 2am.

Le Select, 99 bd du Montparnasse, 6ᵉ (M° Vavin). The least spoilt and most traditional of the Montparnasse cafés. Daily until 3am.

Tea and Tattered Pages, 24 rue Mayet, 6ᵉ (M° Duroc). Rather a long way from anywhere, and looks like a shop from the outside, but inside you can have tea and cakes, speak English and browse through a very good selection of cheap second-hand English books. Daily 11am–7pm.

RESTAURANTS

Chez Maria, 16 rue du Maine, 14ᵉ; ☎01.43.20.84.61 (M° Montparnasse). Zinc bar and candlelight, posters and paper tablecloths – an intimate gloom that appeals to arty theatre creatures after hours. Very pleasant. Around 170F. Mon–Sat 8.30pm–1.30am.

La Coupole, 102 bd du Montparnasse, 14ᵉ; ☎01.43.20.14.20 (M° Vavin). The largest and perhaps the most famous and enduring arty-chic Parisian hang-out for dining, dancing and debate. It has been lavishly renovated by the prince of Paris' turn-of-the-century brasseries, Jean-Paul Bucher of *Flo* and *Julien* fame . . . but it ain't the same, say the old habitués. Some complain that the lighting is now too bright, that the intimacy has gone and the food has deteriorated; others say the opposite. Either way its future is assured, even if it's for who has eaten there rather than who's to be seen tonight. One definite improvement is an after 11pm *menu* at 119F including wine. *Carte* and coffee 170–310F. Dancing 3–7pm weekends (Sat 60F, Sun 80F) and 9.30pm–4am Fri & Sat (90F). Daily 7.30–10.30am for breakfast, then noon–2am.

La Mamma, 46 rue Vavin, 6ᵉ; ☎01.46.33.17.92 (M° Vavin). Affordable and good Italian restaurant. 69F *menu*; pizzas from 38F. Daily noon–2.30pm & 7pm–midnight.

L'Ostréade, 11 bd Vaugirard, 15ᵉ; ☎01.43.21.87.41 (M° Montparnasse). A seafood brasserie with tapas on a 89F *formule*, and excellent oysters. Around 175F for a full whack. Daily 11.30am–5pm & 7–11pm.

The 15ᵉ arrondissement

CAFÉS AND BARS

Au Roi du Café, 59 rue Lecourbe, 15ᵉ (M° Volontaires/Sèvres-Lecourbe). An oasis in the midst of the 15ᵉ arrondissement. Traditional café with decor that has changed little this century, and with a pleasant terrace albeit on a busy road. Daily till 2am.

RESTAURANTS

Da Attilio, 21 rue Cronstadt, 15ᵉ; ☎01.40.43.91.90 (M° Convention/Porte-de-Vanves). Close to the Parc Georges Brassens. Unprepossessing decor, but friendly service and great atmosphere.

Eating and drinking

See p.257 for a list of vegetarian restaurants in Paris.

See p.296 for a list of cafés and restaurants that stay open late.

Eating and drinking

See p.257 for a list of vegetarian restaurants.

Ethnic restaurants in Paris

Our selection of Paris' **ethnic restaurants** can only scratch the surface of what's available. **North African** places can be found throughout the city; apart from rue Xavier-Privas in the Latin Quarter, where the trade is chiefly tourists, the heaviest concentration is the Little Maghreb district along bd de Belleville. **Indo-Chinese** restaurants are also widely scattered, with notable concentrations around av de la Porte-de-Choisy in the 13ᵉ and in the Belleville Chinatown. **Indian** restaurants abound in and around the passage Brady in the 10ᵉ. The **Greeks** are tightly corralled, in rue de la Huchette, rue Xavier-Privas and along rue Mouffetard, all in the 5ᵉ and, for the most part, a bit of a rip-off.

AFGHAN

Kootchi, 40 rue du Cardinal-Lemoine, 5ᵉ; p.277.

AFRICAN AND NORTH AFRICAN

Le Berbère, 50 rue de Gergovie, 14ᵉ. North African; p.286.

Bistro de la Sorbonne, 4 rue Toullier, 5ᵉ. North African and French; p.275.

Café de la Mosquée, 39 rue Geoffroy-St-Hilaire, 5ᵉ. North African; p.274.

Entoto, 143–145 rue Léon-Maurice-Nordmann, 13ᵉ. Ethiopian; p.287.

Fouta Toro, 3 rue du Nord, 18ᵉ. Senegalese; p.289.

L'Homme Bleu, 57 rue Jean-Pierre-Timbaud, 11ᵉ. Berber; p.292.

La Mansouria, 11 rue Faidherbe-Chaligny, 11ᵉ. Moroccan; p.295.

N'Zadette M'Foua, 152 rue du Château, 14ᵉ. Congolese; p.287.

Au Port de Pidjiguiti, 28 rue Étex, 18ᵉ. Co-operative run by a village in Guinea-Bissau; p.289.

Le Quincampe, 78 rue Quincampoix, 3ᵉ; Moroccan; p.269.

CAJUN

Thanksgiving, 20 rue St-Paul, cnr rue Charles-V, 4ᵉ; p.272.

CARIBBEAN

Le Marais-Cage, 8 rue de Beauce, 3ᵉ; p.273.

EAST EUROPEAN AND JEWISH

Goldenberg's, 7 rue des Rosiers, 4ᵉ. Jewish; p.272.

La Maroussia, 9 rue de l'Éperon, 6ᵉ. Polish and Ukrainian; p.280.

Pitchi-Poï, 7 rue Caron, 4ᵉ. Polish/Jewish; p.272.

Le Polonia, 3 rue de Chaumont, 19ᵉ. Polish; p.294.

Le Ravaillac, 10 rue du Roi-de-Sicile, 4ᵉ. Polish; p.272.

GREEK

Égée, 19 rue de Ménilmontant, 20ᵉ; p.294.

Mavrommatis, 42 rue Daubenton, 5ᵉ; p.277.

Orestias, 4 rue Grégoire-de-Tours, 6ᵉ; p.280.

ITALIAN

Da Attilio, 21 rue Cronstadt, 15ᵉ; p.283.

Le Castafiore, 51 rue St-Louis-en-L'Île, 4ᵉ; p.263.

L'Enoteca, 25 rue Charles-V, 4ᵉ; p.270.

Au Jardin des Pâtes, 4 rue Lacépède, 5ᵉ; p.277.

Different Italian specialities each day; *plats du jour* 50F. Mon–Sat till 9.30pm.

Le Bistrot d'André, 232 rue St-Charles, 15ᵉ; ☎01.45.57.89.14 (Mº Balard). A reminder of the old Citroën works before the Parc André-Citroën was created, with pictures and models of the classic French car. Great puds; midday *menu* 63F, otherwise around 140F. Mon–Sat noon–2.45pm & 7.45–10.30pm, closed Sun.

RESTAURANTS

Le Clos Morillons, 50 rue Morillons, 15ᵉ; ☎01.48.28.04.37 (Mº Porte-de-Vanves). Rabbit stuffed with aubergines, veal in

La Mamma, 46 rue Vavin, 6ᵉ; p.283.
Le Petit Mabillon, 6 rue Mabillon, 6ᵉ; p.280.
Rittal & Courts, 1 rue des Envierges, 20ᵉ; p.295.
La Table d'Italie, 69 rue de Seine, 6ᵉ; p.280.

INDIAN
Pooja, 91 passage Brady, 10ᵉ; p.291

INDO-CHINESE
Blue Elephant, 43–45 rue de la Roquette, 11ᵉ. Thai; p.274.

Chieng-Maï, 12 rue Fréderic-Santa, 5ᵉ. Thai; p.277.

Dragons Élysées, 11 rue de Berri, 8ᵉ. Chinese-Thai; p.264.

Foyer du Vietnam, 80 Rue Monge, 5ᵉ. Vietnamese; p.277.

Lao Siam, 49 rue de Belleville, 19ᵉ. Thai and Laotian; p.294.

Lao-Thai, 128 rue de Tolbiac, 13ᵉ. Thai and Laotian; p.287.

Le Pacifique, 35 rue de Belleville, 20ᵉ. Chinese; p.294.

Pho-Dong-Huong, 14 rue Louis-Bonnet, 11ᵉ. Vietnamese; p.294.

Phuong Hoang, Terrasse des Olympiades, 52 rue du Javelot, 13ᵉ. Vietnamese, Thai and Singaporean; p.288.

Le Royal Belleville and Le Président, 19 rue Louis-Bonnet, 11ᵉ. Chinese; p.295.

Taï Yen, 5 rue de Belleville, 20ᵉ. Chinese; p.295.

Thuy Huong, Kiosque de Choisy, 15 av de Choisy, 13ᵉ. Chinese and Cambodian; p.288.

JAPANESE
Foujita, 41 rue St-Roch, 1ᵉʳ; p.267.

Higuma, 32bis rue Ste-Anne. 1ᵉʳ; p.267.

Inagiku, 14 rue Pontoise, 5ᵉ; p.277.

Osaka, 163 rue St-Honoré, 1ᵉʳ; p.264.

KURDISH
Dilan, 13 rue Mandar, 2ᵉ; p.267.

LEBANESE
Baalbeck, 16 rue Mazagran, 10ᵉ; p.291.

Al Mina, 9 rue du Nil, 2ᵉ; p.267.

Au Saveurs du Liban, 11 rue Eugène-Jumin, 19ᵉ; p.293.

MEXICAN
La Perla, 26 rue François-Miron, cnr rue du Pont-Louis-Philippe, 4ᵉ; p.271.

SPANISH
Boca Chica, 58 rue de Charonne, 11ᵉ. Tapas; p.273.

Au Pavillon Puebla, Parc Des Buttes-Chaumont, 19ᵉ. Catalan; p.294.

TIBETAN
Pemathang, 13 rue de la Montagne-St-Geneviève, 5ᵉ; p.277.

Tashi Delek, 4 rue des Fossés-St-Jacques, 5ᵉ; p.278.

TURKISH
Égée, 19 rue de Ménilmontant, 20ᵉ; p.294.

Eating and drinking

---

lemon and almond purée, alluring fish dishes and some vegetarian choices. *Menus* at 175F and 285F. Mon–Fri 12.15–2.15pm & 8–10.15pm, Sat 8–10.30pm.

Le Commerce, 51 rue du Commerce, 15ᵉ; ☎01.45.75.03.27 (Mᵒ Émile-Zola). A two-storey restaurant that has been

catering for *le petit peuple* for more than a hundred years. Still varied, nourishing and cheap. Midday *menu* 100F; *plats du jour* 55–65F; 82F and 117F *formules*; *carte* around 145F. Daily noon–midnight.

Sampieru Corsu, 12 rue de l'Amiral-Roussin, 15ᵉ (Mᵒ Cambronne). Decorated with posters and passionate declara-

Eating and drinking

tions of international socialism, this restaurant has as its purpose the provision of meals for the homeless, the unemployed, the low-paid. The principle is that you pay what you can and it's left to your conscience how you settle the bill. The minimum requested is 45F for a three-course meal with wine. However poor you might feel, as a tourist in Paris you should be able to pay more. The restaurant only survives on the generosity of its supporters, and it's a wonderful place. Mon–Fri lunchtimes & 7–9.30pm.

Student restaurant at 156 rue Vaugirard, 15e (Mo Pasteur). See p257 for details.

The 14e arrondissement

CAFÉS AND BARS

L'Entrepôt, 7–9 rue Francis-de-Pressensé, 14e (Mo Pernety). Cinema with a spacious café. Midday *menu* 77F; 150F *à la carte* in the evening. Mon–Sat 2–11.30pm.

Le Rallye, 6 rue Daguerre, 14e (Mo Denfert-Rochereau). A good place to recover from the catacombs or Montparnasse cemetery. The patron offers a bottle for tasting; gulping the lot would be considered bad form. Good cheese and *saucisson*. Tues–Sat until 8pm; closed Aug.

RESTAURANTS

Aquarius 2, 40 rue Gergovie, 14e; ☎01.45.41.36.88 (Mo Pernety). Imaginative vegetarian meals served with proper Parisian bustle; 60F *menu* midday. Mon–Sat noon–2.15pm & 7–10.30pm.

Le Berbère, 50 rue de Gergovie, 14e; ☎01.45.42.10.29 (Mo Pernety). A very unprepossessing place decor-wise, but serves wholesome, unfussy and cheap North African food. Couscous from 60F. Daily, lunchtime & evening until 10pm.

Bergamote, 1 rue Niepce, 14e; ☎01.43.22.79.47 (Mo Pernety). A small and sympathetic *bistrot* in a quiet, ungentrified street off rue de l'Ouest.

Only about ten tables; you'll need to book weekends. *Formule* for 98F at lunchtime; 125F in the evening; *carte* around 160F. Tues–Sat lunchtime & evening until 11pm; closed Aug.

Pavillon Montsouris, 20 rue Gazan, 14e; ☎01.45.88.38.52 (RER Cité-Universitaire). A special treat for summer days. Sit on the terrace overlooking the park, and choose from a menu featuring truffles, *foie gras* and the divine *pêche blanche rôtie à la glace vanille*. Menus at 198F and 298F. Daily 12.15–2.30pm & 7.45–10.30pm.

Phineas, 99 rue de l'Ouest, 14e; ☎01.45.41.33.50 (Mo Pernety). A gallery-restaurant specializing in plates of food arranged into funny faces. Several veggie dishes and a friendly atmosphere. A good one for kids, and it's easy to eat for less than 100F. Mon–Sat 9am–11.30pm; closed Mon midday.

La Régalade, 49 av Jean-Moulin, 14e; ☎01.45.45.68.58 (Mo Alésia). You need to book several days in advance for this very high-class and good-value restaurant. Around 170F. Till midnight; closed Sat lunchtime, Sun, Mon & mid-July to last week of Aug.

Au Rendez-vous des Camioneurs, 34 rue des Plantes, 14e; ☎01.45.40.43.36 (Mo Alésia). No lorry drivers any more, but good food for under 100F; *menu* at 72F and a quart of wine for less than 15F. Wise to book. Mon–Fri lunchtime & 6–9.30pm; closed Aug.

La Route du Château, 123 rue du Château, 14e; ☎01.43.20.09.59 (Mo Pernety). An old-fashioned *bistrot* atmosphere, with linen tablecloths and a rose on each table. The food is beautifully prepared and cooked – try the thin slice of rump steak (well over 150F). *Menus* at 85F and 148F. Mon lunchtime only, Tues–Sat lunchtime & evening until 12.30am; closed Aug.

Student restaurants at 13/17 rue Dareau (Mo St-Jacques) and in the Cité-Universitaire (RER Cité-Universitaire). See p.257 for details.

L'Univers, 73 rue d'Alésia (cnr rue Marguerin), 14ᵉ; ☎01.43.27.17.71 (Mᵒ Alésia). Solid cooking under 100F. Excellent-value Sancerre rosé.

N'Zadette M'Foua, 152 rue du Château, 14ᵉ; ☎01.43.22.00.16 (Mᵒ Pernety). Small Congolese restaurant serving such tasty dishes as *maboké* (meat or fish baked in banana leaves). Reservations required at weekends. *Menu* at 85F, *à la carte* around 120F. Daily 7pm–2am.

The 13ᵉ arrondissement

CAFÉS AND BARS

Le Diapason, 15 rue Butte-aux-Cailles, 13ᵉ (Mᵒ Place d'Italie/Corvisart). A more staid alternative to *Le Merle Moqueur*. Happy hour 6–8pm. Open daily till 1am.

La Folie en Tête, 33 rue Butte-aux-Cailles, 13ᵉ (Mᵒ Place-d'Italie/Corvisart). Cheap beer, sandwiches and occasional concerts and solidarity events from some of the people who used to run *Le Merle Moqueur* and *Le Temps des Cerises*. A very warm and laid-back address. Mon–Sat 5pm–2am.

Le Merle Moqueur, 11 rue Butte-aux-Cailles, 13ᵉ (Mᵒ Place-d'Italie/Corvisart). Still going strong and still popular, with live rock some nights. Daily 9pm–1am.

RESTAURANTS

Auberge Etchegorry, 41 rue Croulebarbe, 13ᵉ; ☎01.44.08.83.51 (Mᵒ Gobelins). A former *guinguette* on the banks of the Biévre, this Basque restaurant preserves an old-fashioned atmosphere of relaxed conviviality. The food's good, too. *Menus* from 130F. Mon–Sat till 10.30pm.

Bistrot du Viaduc, 12 rue du Tolbiac, 13ᵉ; ☎01.45.83.74.66 (Mᵒ Bibliothèque-Tolbiac). Situated near the new library in the redevelopment area of the 13ᵉ, though you won't even notice the building works once ensconced in these pleasant and simple surroundings. Lunch *menu* at 89F, evening at 148F. Mon–Sat till 10.30pm.

Bol en Bois, 35 rue Pascal, 13ᵉ; ☎01.47.07.27.24 (Mᵒ Gobelins). Macrobiotic, organic veg tempura and

fish. They have a shop opposite at no. 40. "Zen" *menu* for 129F. Generous portions. Mon–Wed & Fri noon–2.30pm & 7–10pm, Thurs & Sat closes at 10.30pm.

Chez Gladines, 30 rue des Cinq-Diamants, 13ᵉ; ☎01.45.80.70.10 (Mᵒ Corvisart). This small corner *bistrot* is always welcoming. Excellent wines and dishes from the southwest. The mashed/fried potato is a must and goes best with *magret de canard*. Around 120F for a full meal. Daily 9am–2am.

Chez Grand-Mère, 92 rue Broca, 13ᵉ; ☎01.47.07.13.65 (Mᵒ Gobelins). Excellent terrines, rabbit in mustard sauce, and stuffed trout. Midday *menu* 79F; evening *menu* at 119F. Open Mon–Sat noon–2.15pm & 7.15–10.15pm.

Chez Paul, 22 rue Butte-aux-Cailles, 13ᵉ; ☎01.45.89.22.11 (Mᵒ Place-d'Italie/Corvisart). Elegant *bistrot* serving traditional French country food. From 150F. Daily till midnight.

Entoto, 143–145 rue Léon-Maurice-Nordmann, 13ᵉ; ☎01.45.87.08.51 (Mᵒ Glacière). An Ethiopian restaurant where you can share plates, using *indjera* (bread) rather than knives and forks. Veggie and meat dishes, some of them spiced with very hot pepper called *mit-mita*. Around 160F. Tues–Sat lunchtime & 7.30–10pm.

Le Jean-Baptiste-Clément, 11 rue Butte-aux-Cailles, 13ᵉ; ☎01.45.80.27.22 (Mᵒ Place d'Italie/Corvisart). Kebabs chargrilled at your table. 85F *menu* before 10pm. Tues–Sun till 1am.

Le Languedoc, 64 bd Port-Royal, 5ᵉ; ☎01.47.07.24.47 (Mᵒ Gobelins). Just in the 5ᵉ, but closer to the Gobelins than the Latin Quarter. A traditional checked tablecloth *bistrot* with an illegible menu on which you might decipher frogs' legs, snails, *museau de boeuf* and the like. Good value 105F *menu* including wine. Thurs–Mon noon–2pm & 7–10pm; closed Aug.

Lao-Thai, 128 rue de Tolbiac, 13ᵉ; ☎01.44.24.28.10 (Mᵒ Tolbiac). Big glass-fronted resto on a busy interchange. Finely spiced Thai and Laotian food, with

Eating and drinking

See p.296 for a list of cafés and restaurants that stay open late.

A glossary of French food and dishes begins on p.258.

Eating and drinking

See p.296 for a list of cafés and restaurants that stay open late.

coconut, ginger and lemongrass flavours. Around 120F. Mon & Tues, Thurs–Sun 11.30am–2.30pm & 7–11pm.

Phuong Hoang, Terrasse des Olympiades, 52 rue du Javelot, 13e; ☎01.45.84.75.07 (Mº Tolbiac: take the escalator up from rue Tolbiac). Like most of its neighbours, this is a family business and the quality varies depending on which uncle, nephew or niece is at the stove that day. Vietnamese, Thai and Singapore specialities on lunch *menus* at 50F and 70F; *carte* 100–150F. If it's full or doesn't take your fancy, try *Le Lai* or *New Chinatown* nearby. Mon–Fri noon–3pm & 7–11.30pm.

Student restaurant 105 bd de l'Hôpital, 13e (Mº St-Marcel). See p.257.

Le Temps des Cerises, 18–20 rue Butteaux-Cailles, 13e; ☎01.45.89.69.48 (Mº Place-d'Italie/Corvisart). A well-established workers' co-op with elbow-to-elbow seating and a different daily choice of imaginative dishes. 58F lunch *menu*, and evening *menus* starting at 78F. Mon–Fri noon–2pm & 7.30–11pm, Sat 7.30–11pm.

Thuy Huong and **Tricotin**, Kiosque de Choisy, 15 av de Choisy, 13e; ☎01.45.86.87.07 and 01.45.84.74.44 (Mº Porte-de-Choisy). *Thuy Huong* is in the inner courtyard of this Chinese shopping centre and is more of a café. *Tricotin* has two restaurants, visible from the avenue; no. 1 specializes in Thai dishes, no. 2 in the other Asiatic cuisines. Not easy to work out what's on the menu (*méduse*, by the way, is jellyfish), but you can depend on the *dim sum*, the duck dishes and the Vietnamese rice pancakes. Around 100F, or 80F at *Thuy Huong*. Noon–2.30pm & 7–10.30pm; closed Thurs.

Chapter 9: Montmartre and northern Paris

Montmartre

CAFÉS AND BARS

Aux Négociants, 27 rue Lambert (cnr rue Custine), 18e; ☎01.46.06.15.11 (Mº

Château-Rouge). An intimate and friendly *bistrot à vins* with a selection of well-cooked *plats* and good wines: around 140F for a full meal. The clientele is arty-intellectual. Wise to book. Lunchtime Mon–Fri & eve till 10pm on Tues, Wed & Thurs; closed Sat, Sun, public hols & Aug.

La Petite Charlotte, 24 rue des Abbesses, 18e (Mº Abbesses). Crêpes, pâtisseries and 58F *formule* on sunny tables. Tues–Sun till 8pm.

Le Refuge, cnr rue Lamarck and the steps of rue de la Fontaine-du-But, 18e (Mº Lamarck-Caulaincourt). A gentle café stop with a long view west down rue Lamarck to the country beyond. Mon–Sat till 8.30pm.

Le Sancerre, 35 rue des Abbesses, 18e (Mº Abbesses). As the southern slopes of Montmartre have become cleaner and more gentrified, this café and its neighbours have become a fashionable hangout for the young and trendy of all nationalities. Daily 7am–2am.

RESTAURANTS

L'Assiette, 78 rue Labat, 18e; ☎01.42.59.06.63 (Mº Château-Rouge). A bit out of the way, but very friendly, with an extraordinarily good-value 98F *menu*, delicious *champignons forestières*, chocolate charlotte, and a surprising beetroot sorbet starter. Closed Wed evening & Sun.

La Casserole, 17 rue Boinod, 18e; ☎01.42.54.50.97 (Mº Simplon/Marcadet-Poissonniers). Good and copious helpings, a wide variety of game in season, and a jolly atmosphere. The place is festooned with knick-knacks. *Menu* at 120F; 70F at lunchtime in the week. Closed Sun, Mon & Aug.

Chez Ginette, 101 rue Caulaincourt, 18e; ☎01.46.06.01.49 (Mº Lamarck-Caulaincourt). Good, uncomplicated food (*blanquette de veau, boeufgros sel*) in a traditional Parisian environment, with live piano and dancing: noisy and fun. *Carte* around 130F. Wise to book, especially at weekends. Mon–Sat lunchtime & eve until 2am; closed Sun & Aug.

Chez Paula, 26 rue Letort, 18ᵉ; ☎01.42.23.86.41 (Mᵒ Joffrin/Porte-de-Clignancourt). A genuine local, with straightforward home cooking. Lunchtime *menu* at 55F, evening 72F. Rather out of the way unless you're staying in the neighbourhood – close to the colourful rue du Poteau market. Mon–Fri till 10pm.

Fouta Toro, 3 rue du Nord, 18ᵉ; ☎01.42.55.42.73 (Mᵒ Marcadet-Poissonniers). A tiny, crowded, welcoming Senegalese diner in a very scruffy alley northeast of Montmartre. No more than 70F all in. Be prepared for a wait unless you come at the 7.30pm opening time, or after about 10.30pm. Open 7.30pm–1am; closed Tues.

Au Grain de Folie, 24 rue La Vieuville, 18ᵉ; ☎01.42.58.15.57 (Mᵒ Abbesses). Tiny, simple, cheap and friendly vegetarian place, with just the sort of traditional atmosphere that you would hope for from Montmartre. Soup and tart 60F, *menu* 100F. Daily 12.30–2.30pm & 7–11.30pm.

L'Homme Tranquille, 81 rue des Martyrs, 18ᵉ; ☎01.42.54.56.28 (Mᵒ Abbesses). Simple and pleasant *bistrot* ambience, with posters and nicotine-coloured paint. Imaginative French dishes include chicken in honey, coriander and lemon. *Menu* at 118F. Eve only, 7–11.30pm; closed Sun, Mon & Aug.

Le Maquis, 69 rue Caulaincourt, 18ᵉ; ☎01.42.59.76.07 (Mᵒ Lamarck-Caulaincourt). Menus at 100F or 155F (with wine, but no dessert); *carte* around 180F. Courteous place with a hint of elegance. Mon–Sat lunchtime & eve until 10pm.

Marie-Louise, 52 rue Championnet, 18ᵉ; ☎01.46.06.86.55 (Mᵒ Simplon). A place with a well-deserved reputation. A bit of a trek north, but very much worth the journey for the excellent traditional French cuisine. *Menu* at 130F, otherwise around 180F. Lunchtime & eve until 10pm; closed Sun, Mon & Aug.

Le Moulin à Vins, 6 rue Burq, 18ᵉ; ☎01.42.52.81.27 (Mᵒ Abbesses). Wine bar with interesting selection of wines to accompany the cheese, charcuteries or *plats* such as *coq au vin* – around 140F. Open 6pm–12.30am (bar till 2am), plus lunchtime Wed & Thurs only; closed Sun, Mon & three weeks in Aug.

A la Pomponnette, 42 rue Lepic, 18ᵉ; ☎01.46.06.08.36 (Mᵒ Blanche/ Abbesses). A genuine old Montmartre *bistrot*, with posters, drawings, zinc-top bar, nicotine stains, etc. The food is excellent, but will cost you 200–250F *à la carte*; good *menu* including coffee at 150F. Lunchtime, and eve until 9.30pm; closed all Sun, Mon lunchtime & Aug.

Au Port de Pidjiguiti, 28 rue Étex, 18ᵉ; ☎01.42.26.71.77 (Mᵒ Guy-Môquet). Very pleasant atmosphere and excellent African food for about 120F; *menu* at 100F. It's run by a village in Guinea-Bissau, whose inhabitants take turns in staffing the restaurant; the proceeds go to the village. Good-value wine list. Lunchtime, and eve till 11pm; closed Mon & Jan.

Le Relais de la Butte, 12 rue Ravignan, 18ᵉ; ☎01.42.23.94.64 (Mᵒ Abbesses). A quaint building in a beautiful spot on the corner of the little square where Picasso's Bateau-Lavoir studio used to be. *Menus* at 105F and 150F (*carte* only at lunchtime) – there's a touch of cheese in practically everything, but it's very good. Extremely crowded on summer evenings. Daily until 11.30pm.

Le Rendez-vous des Chauffeurs, 11 rue des Portes-Blanches, ; ☎01.42.64.04.17 (Mᵒ Marcadet-Poissonniers). The 63F *menu*, including wine, offers a large range of excellent quality traditional French fare. Of course, that means this little restaurant is always packed – you'll usually have to share a table. Arrive early or reserve. Noon–2.30pm & 7.30–11pm; closed Wed.

Le Restaurant, 32 rue Véron, 18ᵉ; ☎01.42.23.06.22 (Mᵒ Abbesses). An attractive corner restaurant offering unexpected tastes. A good value *formule* for 75F at lunchtime and a 120F *menu* for dinner. Noon–2.30pm & 7–11pm; closed Sun.

Eating and drinking

Eating and drinking

Au Virage Lepic, 61 rue Lepic, 18ᵉ; ☎01.42.52.46.79 (Mᵒ Blanche/Abbesses). Simple traditional fare in a noisy, friendly atmosphere enhanced by singers. A small, claustra-phobic and smoky space, but it's very enjoyable. Around 100F. Evening only, 7pm–2am; closed Tues.

Batignolles

CAFÉS AND BARS

Bar Belge, 75 av de St-Ouen, 17ᵉ (Mᵒ Guy-Môquet). Belgian beers and *moules frites* for 65F, *coq au vin* 70F and *poulet aux cèpes* 65F. Tues–Sun 3.30pm–1am.

L'Endroit, 67 place Félix-Lobligeois, 17ᵉ; ☎01.42.29.50.00 (Mᵒ Rome/La Fourche). A smartish late-night bar serving the local youth. Drinks from about 60F as well as a copious Sunday brunch. Daily noon–2am.

RESTAURANTS

Joy in Food, 2 rue Truffaut, 17ᵉ; ☎01.43.87.96.79 (Mᵒ Place-Clichy). Minuscule veggie, with open meditation sessions at 8pm Mon–Sat. Good, inex-pensive food, and attractive atmosphere. *Menus* 71–100F. Mon–Sat noon–2.30pm.

Pigalle

CAFÉS AND BARS

Le Dépanneur, 27 rue Fontaine, 9ᵉ; ☎01.40.16.40.20 (Mᵒ Pigalle). A relaxed and fashionable all-night bar, in black and chrome, just off place Pigalle. Open 24hr.

RESTAURANTS

L'Alsaco, 10 rue Condorcet (at the extreme eastern end), 9ᵉ; ☎01.45.26.44.31 (Mᵒ Poissonnière). Closed Sat lunchtime, Sun & Aug. A real Alsatian *winstub* serving the traditional dishes and wines of Alsace. Lunch *menu* 87F, 95F in the eve, and a massive one at 168F; *carte* 100–140F. Noon–2.15pm & 7pm–midnight.

Auberge Bourbonnaise, 45 rue St-Georges, 9ᵉ; ☎01.48.78.40.30 (Mᵒ St-Georges). *Menus* at 78F and 120F will give you a good, if not terribly exciting, meal at this pretty corner restaurant with lace curtains at its windows and 100-year-old paintings on its walls. Closed Sat lunchtime, Sun, Mon eve and three weeks in Aug.

Aux Deux-Théâtres, 18 rue Blanche (cnr rue Pigalle), 9ᵉ; ☎01.45.26.41.43 (Mᵒ Trinité). A distinctly bourgeois but wel-coming and friendly place serving partic-ularly good food; 169F *menu* includes coffee and wine – a bottle for two. And it's open on Sun. Daily till 12.30am.

Haynes, 3 rue Clauzel (cnr rue des Martyrs), 9ᵉ; ☎01.48.78.40.63 (Mᵒ St-Georges). A black-American restaurant serving generous quantities of rich and heavy dishes from the southern states. It's been going since the 1940s and is now run by widow Haynes. Despite the grotto-like decor, the atmosphere is warm, and there's jazz on Fri & Sat from 9pm (piano and singer, guitar and bass). It's certainly something different in Paris. *À la carte* only, at around 160F, with wine. Tues–Sat 7.30pm–12.30am.

Le Relais Savoyard, 13 rue Rodier (cnr rue Agent-Bailly), 9ᵉ; ☎01.45.26.17.18 (Mᵒ Notre-Dame-de-Lorette/ Anvers/Cadet). You enter what looks like a very ordinary local bar. At the back is the dining room, where you can get a very good three-course meal for 72F. The *carte* is around 130–140F, and there's a more sophisticated *menu* at 115F. Noon–2.30pm & 7.30–9.30pm; closed Sun & Aug.

La Table d'Anvers, 2 place d'Anvers, 9ᵉ; ☎01.48.78.35.21 (Mᵒ Anvers). This is one of the city's really top restaurants, whose chef is renowned for his creativ-ity, daring to combine the most improba-ble elements. Lunchtime *menus* at 190F and 450F give a good taste of his skills. Evening *menus* at 250F and 550F; *à la carte* will cost more than 600F. Closed Sat lunchtime and Sun.

Velly, 52 rue Lamartine, 9ᵉ;
☎01.48.78.60.05 (Mº Notre-Dame-de-
Lorette). Excellent modern French cooking in an intimate setting. Plenty of good
wines for less than 100F and a *menu* at
160F. Noon–2.30pm & 7.30–10.45pm;
closed Sat lunch & Sun.

The stations and feaubourgs

CAFÉS AND BARS

L'Atmosphère, 49 rue Lucien-Sampaix,
10ᵉ (Mº Gare-de-l'Est). Lively bar with
food and occasional live music, next to
the canal St-Martin. The *Hôtel du Nord*
on the opposite bank was the setting for
the eponymous film of 1938 and for the
famous quote that inspired the title of
this bar. Tues–Fri 11am–2am, Sat & Sun
5.30pm–2am.

China Express Nord, 3 bd Denain, 10ᵉ
(Mº Gare-du-Nord). A good place to fill
up on chicken and noodles, near the
Gare du Nord. Dish of the day and can-
tonese rice 30F. Daily 11am–10pm;
closed Sun in winter.

Quasre Shireen, 14 rue Faubourg-St-
Denis, 10ᵉ (Mº Strasbourg-St-Denis). Fast-
food Indian cheapie, with rice and curry
for 25F. Daily till midnight.

Le Réveil du Dixième, 35 rue du
Château-d'Eau, 10ᵉ; ☎01.42.41.77.59
(Mº Château-d'Eau). A welcoming, unpretentious wine bar, serving wine by the
glass, and regional *plats* or a *menu* at
150F including wine. Mon–Sat
7.15am–9pm.

RESTAURANTS

Baalbeck, 16 rue de Mazagran, 10ᵉ;
☎01.47.70.70.02 (Mº Bonne-Nouvelle).
Much liked by the moneyed refugees,
this Lebanese restaurant has dozens of
appetizers. For 595F you can have a representative selection for four, with *arak*
to drink. Belly-dancing and sticky
Levantine/Turkish cakes, too. Very busy,
so reserve or go early. Mon–Sat
lunchtime & 8pm–midnight.

Chez Arthur, 25 rue du Faubourg-St-
Martin, 10ᵉ; ☎01.42.08.34.33 (Mº

Strasbourg-St-Denis). An easy-going,
attractive restaurant, popular with the-
atre-goers and actors. Good classic
French cuisine; *menu* at 120F. Lunchtime
Mon–Fri, eve Tues–Sat till 11.30pm.

L'Enchotte, 11 rue de Chabrol, 10ᵉ;
☎01.48.00.05.25 (Mº Gare-de-l'Est). A
relaxed, friendly wine bar opposite the
St-Quentin market, with cheese and
charcuteries at around 50–70F.
Lunchtime *menu* at 65F, evening *menu*
at 100F. Open 12.30–2.30pm &
7.30–10.30pm. Closed Sat & Sun and
second half of Aug.

Flo, 7 cours des Petites-Écuries, 10ᵉ;
☎01.47.70.13.59 (Mº Château-d'Eau).
Handsome old brasserie, all dark-stained
wood, mirrors and glass partitions, in
attractive courtyard off rue du Faubourg-
St-Denis. You eat elbow-to-elbow at long
tables, served by waiters in ankle-length
aprons. Excellent food and atmosphere.
Fish, *choucroute* and seafood (platter for
198F) are among the specialities. From
around 200F; really good-value *menus*
at 123F midday, 169F evenings, with a
128F *formule* after 10pm. Wine is included in the price of all *menus*. Daily until
1.30am.

Julien, 16 rue du Faubourg-St-Denis, 10ᵉ;
☎01.47.70.12.06 (Mº Strasbourg-St-
Denis). Part of the same enterprise as
Flo, with an even more splendid decor.
Same good Alsatian – vaguely Germanic
– cuisine; same prices and similarly
crowded. Daily until 1.30am.

Pooja, 91 passage Brady, 10ᵉ.
☎01.48.24.00.83 (Mº Strasbourg-St-
Denis/Château-d'Eau). Located in a passage that is Paris' own slice of the Indian
subcontinent. Authentic, good-value
Indian cuisine. *Formules* at 45F lunch
and 85F evening. Daily noon–2.30pm &
5–11pm; closed Mon lunchtime.

Terminus Nord, 23 rue de Dunkerque,
10ᵉ; ☎01.42.85.05.15 (Mº Gare-du-
Nord). A magnificent 1920s brasserie,
with same management and prices as
Flo and *Julien* above. A full meal costs
around 250F, but you could easily satisfy
your hunger with just a main course –

Eating and
drinking

*At the south
end of rue du
Faubourg-St-
Denis, there
are numerous
good, ethnic
snack bars
and restau-
rants – mainly
Turkish and
Kurdish in rue
d'Enghien and
rue de
l'Échiquier,
Indian and
Pakistani
around pas-
sage Brady.*

Eating and drinking

an excellent steak, for example – and still enjoy the decor for considerably less money. Daily until 1am.

Chapter 10: Eastern Paris

République and the Canal St-Martin

CAFÉS AND BARS

Chez Imogéne, cnr rue Jean-Pierre-Timbaud and rue du Grand-Prieuré, 11e (M° Oberkampf). Cheap and cheerful crêperie with 53F midday *menu* including drink. The 87F dinner *menu* includes a *kir breton* (cassis with cider instead of champagne) and three courses. There's also a kids' *menu* at 45F. Mon–Sat till 10.30pm.

Le Clown Bar, 114 rue Amelot, 11e; ☎01.43.55.87.35 (M° Filles-du-Calvaire). An attractive and increasingly popular wine bar near the Cirque d'Hiver with a circus clientele come the colder months; the beautifully tiled interior shows the antics of clowns, of course. *Plats du jour* from 60F. Closed Sat lunchtime, Sun & Aug.

La Divette de Valmy, 71 quai de Valmy, 10e (M° Jacques-Bonsergent). An ordinary café-brasserie at the foot of one of the arching canal bridges but lovely in the afternoon sun.

L'Opus, 167 quai de Valmy, 10e; ☎01.40.34.70.00 (M° Louis-Blanc). A stylish modern-chintzy atmosphere in a barn-like space used as British officers' mess during World War I. Live music every evening: chansons, gospel, blues, salsa, African – no longer the classical only of the early days. Drinks 60–80F average, plus 60F entry for the music. Mon–Sat 8pm–4am.

RESTAURANTS

Anjou-Normandie, 13 rue de la Foli-Méricault, 11e; ☎01.47.00.30.59 (M° St-Ambroise). Fresh ingredients, and renowned for its patés and *andouillettes*. Lunchtime two-course *formule* for 68F; *menus* at 137F and, with fish, 169F. Best

Fans of The Fabulous Furry Freak Brothers will love Thé-Troc at 52 rue Jean-Pierre-Timbaud, 11e, a quirky combination salon de thé and comic-book shop; details on pp.327–328.

to book ahead. Till 9pm; closed Sat, Sun & Aug.

Astier, 44 rue Jean-Pierre-Timbaud, 11e; ☎01.43.57.16.35 (M° Parmentier). Very successful and popular. Simple decor, unstuffy atmosphere, and food renowned for its freshness and refinement. Essential to book. *Menu* at 135F. Mon–Fri until 10pm; closed Aug, fortnight each in May & at Christmas.

Au Gigot Fin, 56 rue de Lancry, close to the Canal St-Martin, 10e; ☎01.42.08.38.81 (M° Jacques-Bonsergent). Another very Parisian old-timer, like the *Bourgogne*, with solid country fare, and specializing in lamb. Midday *menu* at 60F and 80F, evening *menus* 110F and 175F. Lunchtime & eves until 10.30pm; closed Sat lunchtime & Sun.

L'Homme Bleu, 57 rue Jean-Pierre-Timbaud, 11e (M° Parmentier). Very affordable and pleasant Berber restaurant. Popular with students. Mon–Sat evenings only till 10pm.

Au Rendez-Vous de la Marine, 14 quai de la Loire, 19e; ☎01.42.49.33.40 (M° Jaurès). A busy, successful old-time restaurant on the east bank of the Bassin de la Villette – but no water view – renowned for its meats and desserts. A really good meal for around 140F; fish dishes from 59F. Need to book. Lunchtime & eves until 10pm; closed Sun & Mon.

Le Rendez-Vous des Quais, 10 quai de la Seine, 19e; ☎01.40.37.02.81 (M° Jaurès). Part of the MK2 cinema complex on the west bank of the Bassin de la Villette, this is a great spot for a coffee before taking a canal cruise (the office is opposite; see p.346). With tables overlooking the water. *Plats* 70–78F. Daily 10am–2am.

Restaurant de Bourgogne, 26 rue des Vinaigriers, 10e; ☎01.46.07.07.91 (M° Jacques-Bonsergent). Homely old-fashioned restaurant with midday *menu* at 55F and evening *menu* at 65F including a drink. Still has a strong local character despite the changing nature of the area.

Lunchtime & eve until 10pm; closed Sat eve, Sun & last week July to third week Aug.

Au Trou Normand, 9 rue Jean-Pierre-Timbaud, 11ᵉ; ☎01.48.05.80.23 (Mᵒ Filles-du-Calvaire/Oberkampf/République). A small, totally unpretentious local *bistrot* serving good traditional food at knockdown prices. *Plat du jour* from 30F. Mon–Fri lunchtime & eve until 9.30pm, Sat eve only; closed Aug.

Au Val de Loire, 149 rue Amelot, 11ᵉ; ☎01.47.00.34.11 (Mᵒ République). Simple, good food in a rather dingy street. Lunch *menu* at 46F and 50F, evening at 59F and 105F; *plat du jour* 40F. A real bargain. Noon–2.30pm & 6.30–9.45pm; closed Sun & Aug.

La Villette

CAFÉS AND BARS

Café de la Musique, 213 av Jean-Jaurès, 19ᵉ (Mᵒ Porte-de-Pantin). Part of the new Cité de la Musique; a typical subtle space by Cité-architect Portzamparc, exuding sophistication, discretion and comfort. Popular outdoor terrace overlooking a fountain. Weekday *plats* from 60F. Daily till 2am.

RESTAURANTS

Aux Saveurs du Liban, 11 rue Eugène-Jumin, 19ᵉ (Mᵒ Porte-de-Pantin). Excellent authentic Lebanese food at this tiny restaurant in a lively local street not far from the Parc de la Villette. Very good value, with *plats* for 30F and wine at 9F a glass; sandwiches from 18F to take away; 40F lunchtime *formule*. Mon–Sat 11am–11pm.

Belleville, Ménilmontant, Charonne and Père-Lachaise

CAFÉS AND BARS

Le Baratin, 3 rue Jouye-Rouve, 20ᵉ (Mᵒ Pyrénées). Friendly, unpretentious *bistrot à vins* in a run-down area with a good mix of people. Fine selection of lesser-known wines and whiskies. Midday

menu 65F. Tues–Fri 11am–1am, Sat 6pm–1am.

Bistrot-Cave des Envierges, 11 rue des Envierges, 20ᵉ (Mᵒ Pyrénées). Another *bistrot à vins*, purveying good-quality, lesser-known wines to connoisseurs. An attractive bar – though more a place to taste and buy wine than eat – in a great location above the Parc de Belleville. Wed–Sat noon–2am, Sun noon–9pm; closed two weeks Aug.

Le Blue Billard, 111–113 rue St-Maur, 11ᵉ (Mᵒ St-Maur/Parmentier). Young and arty, featuring blue-carpeted bar and billiard tables, in a glass-roofed ex-factory. Daily 11am–2am.

Café Charbon, 109 rue Oberkampf, 11ᵉ (Mᵒ St-Maur/Parmentier). A very successful and attractive resuscitation of a turn-of-the-century café. Particularly popular with the younger, fashionable crowd who are moving into these old working-class districts. Nice *plats du jour* 50–60F at lunchtime: lots of salads and vegetarian dishes. DJ Fri & Sat eves 10pm–2am and live music on Sun from 8.30pm. Daily 9am–2am.

Cithea, 114 rue Oberkampf, 11ᵉ (Mᵒ Parmentier). Bar and music venue next door to the *Café Charbon* for Afro funk, funk reggae, world beat, jazz fusion, etc on Thurs, Fri & Sat nights. Cocktails 45F. No admission charge for the music, but busy. Daily 5pm–2am.

La Flèche d'Or, 102bis rue de Bagnolet, cnr rue des Pyrénées, 20ᵉ; ☎01.43.72.04.23 (Mᵒ Porte-de-Bagnolet/Alexandre-Dumas – a 15min walk in either case). A large, lively café attracting the biker, arty, post-punkish Parisian young. The decor is *très destroy* (railway sleepers and a sawn-off bus front hanging from the ceiling), and the building itself is the old Bagnolet station on the *petite ceinture* railway that encircled the city until around thirty years ago. It's a nightly venue for live World Music, pop, punk, ska, fusion and chanson, and the reasonably priced food (lunch *menu* 69F) also has a multicultural slant, with West African, Moroccan and

Eating and drinking

Eating and drinking

See p.296 for a list of cafés and restaurants that stay open late.

Some of Paris' top gourmet restaurants are listed on p.256.

South American *menus* at 115–135F. Daily 10am–2am.

Lou Pescalou, 14 rue des Panoyaux, 20ᵉ (M° Ménilmontant). Trendy but friendly bar with a popular pool table. Daily 9am–2am.

Le Vieux Belleville, 12 rue des Envierges, 20ᵉ; ☎01.44.62.92.66 (M° Pyrénées). An old-fashioned café, simple and attractive. Lunchtime *menu* 65F. 7am–11pm; closed Sun.

La Ville de Jagannath, 10 rue St Maur, 11ᵉ (M° St-Maur). Authentic vegetarian Indian food served in thalis. Lunch *menu* 50F. For a small corkage fee you can bring your own wine. Closed Mon lunch & Sun.

RESTAURANTS

Aucune Idée, 2 place St-Blaise, 20ᵉ; ☎01.40.09.70.67 (M° Porte-de-Bagnolet/Gambetta). Opposite the Charonne parish church, on the corner of the very pretty rue St-Blaise. Modern, chi-chi place where the food is adventurous – they have grilled kangaroo steak – as well as copious, and the atmosphere very pleasant. *Menu* 62F and 135F at lunch; 165F eves. Closed Sun eve, Mon & two weeks in Aug.

Chez Jean, 38 rue Boyer (near cnr with rue de Ménilmontant), 20ᵉ; ☎01.47.97.44.58 (M° Gambetta/Ménilmontant). A charming, friendly, intimate place, with a small but carefully chosen menu. 66F midday *menu*; 130F *à la carte*. Mon–Fri lunchtime & eves till 10.30pm; closed Sat midday, Sun & first half of Aug.

Égée, 19 rue de Ménilmontant, 20ᵉ; ☎01.43.58.70.26 (M° Ménilmontant). Greek and Turkish specialities served with home-made bread. *Plats* 47–66F; *à la carte* more like 120F. Noon–2.30pm & 7.30–11.30pm.

La Fontaine aux Roses, 27 av Gambetta, 20ᵉ; ☎01.46.36.74.75 (M° Père-Lachaise). Small, beautiful restaurant with first-rate *menus*: midday 120F and eves 170F, both including *kir royale*, wine and coffee. Tues–Sat till 10pm, closed Sun evening, Mon & Aug.

Lao Siam, 49 rue de Belleville, 19ᵉ; ☎01.40.40.09.68 (M° Belleville). Extremely good Thai and Laotian food, popular with locals. Dishes 42–60F. Daily till 11pm.

Louis Valy, 49 rue Orfila, 20ᵉ; ☎01.46.36.73.60 (M° Gambetta/Pelleport). Generous helpings of good terrines, meat dishes and cheeses, and a very convivial, down to earth atmosphere. *Menu* at 140F. Lunchtime only; closed Sun & Aug.

Le Pacifique, 35 rue de Belleville, 20ᵉ; ☎01.42.49.66.80 (M° Belleville). A huge Chinese eating house with variable culinary standards, but low prices. Mains from 50F; 85F or 100F *menu*. Daily 11am–1am.

Au Pavillon Puebla, Parc des Buttes-Chaumont, 19ᵉ; ☎01.42.08.92.62 (M° Buttes-Chaumont). Luxury cuisine in an old hunting lodge (enter by the rue Botzaris/av Bolivar gate to the park). Poached lobster, stuffed baby squid, duck with *foie gras*, and spicy oyster raviolis are some *à la carte* delights. There's also a very fishy 180F Catalan *menu*. Around 450F *à la carte*; midday *menus* at 180F; evening *menus* 240F. Tues–Sat noon–10pm.

Pho-Dong-Huong, 14 rue Louis-Bonnet, 11ᵉ; ☎01.43.57.42.81 (M° Belleville). Spotlessly clean Vietnamese resto, where all dishes are under 50F and come with piles of fresh green leaves. Spicy soups, crispy pancakes, but service can be slow. Daily except Tues noon–10.30pm.

Le Polonia, 3 rue de Chaumont, 19ᵉ; ☎01.42.49.87.15 (M° Jaurès). Don't be put off by the grubby exterior, underneath a hotel of the same name. Inside there's a jovial Polish welcome and good Polish dishes for as little as 50F; lunchtime *menus* at 50F and 75F. Food lunchtime & eves until 10.30pm, bar 8am–2am; closed Sun & Aug.

Aux Rendez-Vous des Amis, 10 av Père-Lachaise, 20ᵉ; ☎01.47.97.72.16 (M° Gambetta). Unprepossessing surroundings for very good, simple and satisfying family cooking. Mains 45–78F; *menu* at 65F. Mon–Sat noon–2.30pm; closed last week July to mid-Aug.

Rittal & Courts, 1 rue des Envierges, 20e; ☎01.47.97.08.40 (Mo Pyrénées). Café, wine bar and trattoria (food served noon–2.30pm & 8–11.30pm) in contemporary surroundings in an unbeatable situation overlooking the delightful Parc de Belleville. Get a pavement table on a summer evening, and you'll have the best restaurant view in Paris. The Italian food is tasty and affordable, with a large pasta selection, including loads of vegetarian options, for 50–90F. Short films (*courts metrages*) are shown daily 6–7pm & midnight–1am. Daily 10.30am–2am.

Le Royal Belleville, 19 rue Louis-Bonnet, 11e (☎01.43.38.22.72), and **Le Président** (☎01.47.00.17.18), the floor above – entrance on rue du Faubourg-du-Temple (Mo Belleville). A dramatic blood-red double staircase leads up to *Le Président*, the more expensive of these two cavernous Chinese restaurants. You go for the atmosphere and decor rather than the food, though the spring rolls and rum banana fritters are acceptable. The Thai dishes also on offer at *Le Président* are not very special. Dishes from 45F, average dish 65F. Daily noon–3pm & 7am–2am.

Taï Yen, 5 rue de Belleville, 20e; ☎01.42.41.44.16 (Mo Belleville). You can admire the koi carps like embroidered satin cushions idling round their aquarium while you wait for the copious Chinese soups and steamed specialities. 65F *menu*, dishes from 49F. Daily 10am–2am.

Le Zéphyr, 1 rue Jourdain, 20e; ☎01.46.36.65.81 (Mo Jourdain). A rather trendy but relaxed 1930s-style *bistrot* with *menus* at 69F and 130F including wine and coffee. Mon–Sat till 11.30pm.

To the Faubourg St-Antoine

CAFÉS AND BARS

Jacques-Mélac, 42 rue Léon-Frot, 11e; ☎01.43.70.59.27 (Mo Charonne). Some way off the beaten track (between Père-Lachaise and place Léon-Blum) but a highly respected and very popular *bistrot à vins*, whose patron makes his own wine – the solitary vine winds round the front of the shop (harvest celebrations in the second half of Sept). The food (*plats* around 70F, *menu* 130F), wines and atmosphere are great, but you can't book, so it pays to get there early. Mon–Fri 9am–10.30pm; closed weekends & Aug.

Eating and drinking

RESTAURANTS

Les Amognes, 243 rue du Faubourg-St-Antoine, 11e; ☎01.43.72.73.05 (Mo Faidherbe-Chaligny). Excellent, interesting food in a very popular place – you need to book. A *menu* at 190F; otherwise well over 250F. Noon–2.30pm & 7.30–10.30pm; closed Mon lunch, Sun & two weeks in Aug.

Le Bistrot du Peintre, 116 av Ledru-Rollin, 11e; ☎01.47.00.34.39 (Mo Faidherbe-Chaligny). Small tables jammed together beneath Art Nouveau frescoes and wood panelling. Traditional Parisian *bistrot* food with *plats du jour* at 62F. Mon–Sat 7am–2am, Sun 10am–8pm.

Chardenoux, 1 rue Jules-Vallès, 11e; ☎01.43.71.49.52 (Mo Faidherbe-Chaligny). An authentic oldie, with engraved mirrors dating to 1900. Still serving solid meaty fare like calves' kidneys grilled in mustard. Upwards of 160F *à la carte*. Noon–2pm & 8–10pm; closed Sat lunch, Sun & Aug.

Les Cinq Points Cardinaux, 14 rue Jean-Macé, 11e; ☎01.43.71.47.22 (Mo Faidherbe-Chaligny/Charonne). An excellent, simple, old-time *bistrot*, still mainly frequented by locals and decorated with the old tools of their trades. Prices under 60F for lunch; around 100F in the evening. The snails in basil and the profiteroles are well worth trying. Mon–Fri noon–2pm & 7–10pm; closed Aug.

La Mansouria, 11 rue Faidherbe-Chaligny, 11e; ☎01.43.71.00.16 (Mo Faidherbe-Chaligny). An excellent and elegant Moroccan restaurant. Superb couscous and tagines. *Menus* 135F (lunch) and 168F. *Carte* around 240F.

Eating and drinking

Late-night Paris

Late-opening bars and brasseries are not unusual in Paris. The list below comprises cafés and bars open after 2am, and restaurants open until midnight and beyond.

CAFÉS AND BARS

Café des Phares, 7 place de la Bastille, west side, 4ᵉ. Daily 7am–4am; p.273.

La Champmeslé, 4 rue Chabanais, 2ᵉ. Open till 4am Thurs–Sat; p.266.

Le Dépanneur, 27 rue Fontaine, 9ᵉ. All-nighter; p.290.

Le Grand Café Capucines, 4 bd des Capucines, 9ᵉ. All-nighter; p.265.

Le Mazet, 60 rue St-André-des-Arts, 6ᵉ. Mon–Thurs until 2am, Fri & Sat until 3.30am; p.278.

Mustangs, 84 bd Montparnasse, 14ᵉ. Daily till 5am; p.283.

L'Opus, 167 quai de Valmy, 10ᵉ. Until 4am; p.292.

La Paillote, 45 Monsieur-Le-Prince, 6ᵉ. Mon–Sat until dawn; p.278.

Polly Magoo, 11 rue St-Jacques, 5ᵉ. Until 4–5am; p.275.

Pub St-Germain, 17 rue de l'Ancienne-Comédie, 6ᵉ. 24 hours; p.280.

Le Quetzal, 10 rue de la Verrerie, 4ᵉ. Mon–Thurs 2pm–4am, Fri–Sun 5pm–5am; p.271.

Le Rosebud, 11bis rue Delambre, 14ᵉ. Until 3am; p.283.

Le Select, 99 bd du Montparnasse, 6ᵉ. Until 3am; p.283.

Le Sous-Bock, 49 rue St-Honoré, 1ᵉʳ. Until 5am; p.268.

Le Tambour, 41 rue Montmartre, 2ᵉ. 24 hours; p.267.

La Taverne de Nesle, 32 rue Dauphine, 6ᵉ. Mon–Thurs & Sun until 4am, Fri & Sat till 5am; p.280.

Le Viaduc Café, 43 av Daumesnil, 12ᵉ. Until 4am; p.297.

RESTAURANTS

Aux Deux-Théâtres, 18 rue Blanche, 9ᵉ. Till 12.30am; p.290.

Blue Elephant, 43–45 rue de la Roquette, 11ᵉ. Until midnight; p.274.

Bofinger, 7 rue de la Bastille, 3ᵉ. Until 1am; p.274.

Brasserie Balzar, 49 rue des Écoles, 5ᵉ. Until 1am; p.275.

Chez Ginette, 101 rue Caulaincourt, 18ᵉ. Mon–Sat until 2am; p.288.

Chez Gladines, 30 rue des Cinq-Diamants, 13ᵉ. Until 2am; p.287.

Lunchtimes and eves until 11.30pm; closed Sun, Mon lunchtime, and a fortnight in Aug.

Palais de la Femme, 94 rue de Charonne, 11ᵉ; ☎01.43.71.40.37 (Mᵒ Charonne/Faidherbe-Chaligny). A good self-service restaurant in the women's hostel, run separately and open to all. Solid meals for less than 60F. 11.30am–2pm & 6.30–8pm; closed Sat.

The 12ᵉ arrondissement

CAFÉS AND BARS

Le Baron Rouge, 1 rue Théophile-Roussel, cnr place d'Aligre market, 12ᵉ (Mᵒ Ledru-Rollin). Another popular local bar, as close as you'll find to the spit-on-the-floor stereotype of the old movies. As well as the wines – you can fill your own containers from the barrel for around 16F per litre – it serves a few snacks of cheese, *foie gras*, and charcuterie to the shoppers and workers of the Aligre market. Tues–Sat 10am–2pm & 5–9.30pm, Sun 10am–2pm only.

Le Penty Bar, cnr place d'Aligre and rue Emilio-Castellar, 12ᵉ (Mᵒ Ledru-Rollin). Small, old-fashioned café making no concessions to modern plumbing and still charging only 7F for a sit-down cup of coffee.

Chez Jenny, 39 bd du Temple, 3ᵉ. Until 1am; p.272.

Chez Maria, 16 rue du Maine, 14ᵉ. Mon–Sat 1.30am; p.283.

Chez Paul, 13 rue de Charonne, 11ᵉ. Until 12.30am; p.274.

La Coupole, 102 bd du Montparnasse, 14ᵉ. Until 2am; p.283.

L'Enoteca, 25 rue Charles-V, 4ᵉ. Till 2am; p.270.

Flo, 7 cours des Petites-Écuries, l0ᵉ. Until 1.30am; p.291.

Les Fous d'en Face, 3 rue du Bourg-Tibourg, 4ᵉ. Until midnight; p.269.

Fouta Toro, 3 rue du Nord, 18ᵉ. Until 1am except Tues; p.289.

Goldenberg's, 7 rue des Rosiers, 4ᵉ. Until 2am; p.272.

Le Grand Colbert, passage Colbert, rue Vivienne, 2ᵉ. Until 1am; p.266.

Haynes, 3 rue Clauzel, 9ᵉ. Tues–Sat till 12.30am; p.290.

Le Jean-Baptiste-Clément, 11 rue Butte-aux-Cailles, 13ᵉ. Tues–Sun till 1am; p.287.

Julien, 16 rue du Faubourg-St-Denis, l0ᵉ. Until 1.30am; p.291.

Lipp, 151 bd St-Germain, 6ᵉ. Until 12.30am; p.280.

Le Moulin à Vins, 6 rue Burq, 18ᵉ. Mon–Sat till 12.30am; p.289.

Le Muniche, 22 rue Guillaume-Apollinaire, 6ᵉ. Until 2am; p.280.

N'Zadette M'Foua, 152 rue du Château, 14ᵉ. Daily till 2am; p.287.

Le Pacifique, 35 rue de Belleville, 20ᵉ. Until 1am; p.294.

Le Petit Prince, 12 rue Lanneau, 5ᵉ. Until 12.30am; p.277.

Le Petit Zinc, 11 rue St-Benoît, 6ᵉ. Until 2am; p.281.

Au Pied de Cochon, 6 rue Coquillière, 1ᵉʳ. 24 hours; p.269.

Planet Hollywood, 78 av des Champs-Élysées, 8ᵉ. Until 1am; p.265.

Polidor, 41 rue Monsieur-le-Prince, 6ᵉ. Mon–Sat until 12.30am; p.281.

Le Procope, 13 rue de l'Ancienne-Comédie, 6ᵉ. Until 1am; p.281.

La Route du Château, 123 rue du Château, 14ᵉ. Tues–Sat till 12.30am; p.286.

Le Royal Belleville/Le Président, 19 rue Louis-Bonnet, 11ᵉ. Until 2am; p.295.

Taï Yen, 5 rue de Belleville, 20ᵉ. Until 2am; p.295.

Terminus Nord, 23 rue de Dunkerque, 10ᵉ. Until 1am; p.291.

Le Vaudeville, 29 rue Vivienne, 2ᵉ. Until 2am; p.266.

Au Virage Lepic, 61 rue Lepic, 18ᵉ. Daily except Tues till 2am; p.290.

Eating and drinking

Le Viaduc Café, 43 av Daumesnil, 12ᵉ (Mᵒ Gare-de-Lyon). In one of the Viaduc des Arts' converted railway arches, with a crowded (and traffic-fumey) terrace, where you might see some of the artisans who display their work in the surrounding showrooms sipping a coffee. Sunday brunch from noon–4pm is popular, costing around 125F for several courses. Daily noon–4am.

RESTAURANTS

L'Ébauchoir, 43–45 rue de Cîteaux, 12ᵉ; ☎01.43.42.49.31 (Mᵒ Faidherbe-Chaligny). Good *bistrot* fare in a sympathetic atmosphere; midday *menu* for 66F;

carte 150F upwards. Best to book for the evening. Mon–Sat until 11pm.

La Gourmandise, 271 av Daumesnil, 12ᵉ; ☎01.43.43.94.41 (Mᵒ Porte-Dorée). Superb and original food, with a good *menu* at 165F. Till 10.30pm; closed Mon midday, Sun & first half Aug.

Chapter 11: Western Paris

Auteuil and Passy

RESTAURANTS

Aéro-Club de France, 6 rue Galilée, 16ᵉ; ☎01.47.20.42.51 (Mᵒ Boissière). Open to all, this massive upmarket canteen serves

See p.285 for a list of the various ethnic restaurants in the Guide.

Eating and drinking

very nourishing and tasty fillers at 75F, 90F and 105F; you get an extra course with each increase in price. Pretty good value. Lunchtime only; closed Sat, Sun & Aug.

Les Chauffeurs, 8 chaussée de la Muette, 16e; ☎01.42.88.50.05 (M° Muette). A relaxed, easy-going brasserie-café that takes its food seriously. You can't beat the 65F *menu* (not available on Sun) for this part of the world. Daily noon–2.30pm & 7.30–10pm.

The 17e arrondissement

CAFÉS AND BARS

Musée Jacquemart-André, 158 bd Haussmann, 8e; ☎01.45.62.11.59 (M° St-Philippe-du-Roule/Miromesnil). Sumptuously appointed *salon de thé* in a nineteenth-century *palazzo*, with salads at 57–85F, a lunchtime *formule* at 86F, and a popular weekend brunch for 130F. You do not need a museum ticket to use it. Daily 11am–6pm.

RESTAURANTS

Natacha, 35 rue Guersant, 17e; ☎01.45.74.23.86 (M° Porte-Maillot). A bit out of the way, beyond the place des Ternes, but a great bargain. For 85F at midday or 110F in the evening, you can help yourself to hors d'oeuvres and wine, with three other very respectable

courses to follow. Not surprisingly, it pulls in the crowds. Best to be early. Lunchtime & eves until 10.30pm (11pm on Sat); closed Sat lunch, Sun & two weeks in Aug.

Sangria, 13bis rue Vernier, 17e; ☎01.45.74.78.74 (M° Porte-de-Champerret). As at *Natacha*, for 85F at midday and 110F in the evening you can help yourself to starters and wine in addition to enjoying three other courses. Also very popular and crowded – and just has the edge over *Natacha*.

Île de Chatou

RESTAURANTS

Restaurant Fournaise, Île de Chatou; ☎01.30.71.41.91 (RER line A2 to Rueil-Malmaison, then a 10min walk along the dual carriageway to the bridge). The food is good, but the location is the real attraction (see p.229). The restaurant, now beautifully restored, was a favourite haunt of the Impressionists and is the subject of Renoir's painting *Le Déjeuner des Canotiers*. The veranda, which features in the painting, is still here, shaded by a magnificent riverside plane tree. A real treat for a lunchtime in spring, or dinner on a warm summer night. There is a *menu* at 159F; the *carte* is more like 200–220F. Lunchtime & eves until 10pm; closed Sun eve in winter.

Chapter 14

Music and nightlife

The strength of the Paris music scene is its diversity – a reputation for which has been gained mainly from its absorption of immigrant and exile populations. The city has no rivals in Europe for the variety of world music to be discovered: West and Central African, Caribbean and Latin American sounds are represented in force both by city-based groups and touring bands.

You can spend any number of nights sampling mixtures of salsa, calypso, reggae and African sounds from Zaire, Congo, Senegal and Nigeria. Algerian raï has come out from the immigrant ghettos, and the French language has been discovered to be a great vehicle for rap and hip-hop or the ragamuffin combination.

Jazz fans, too, are in for a treat. Paris has long been home to new styles and old-time musicians. The *Caveau de la Huchette* and *Le Petit Journal*, both in the Latin Quarter and both associated with traditional jazz, are two of the oldest clubs in the city. The *New Morning*, doyen of the modern clubs, hosts big names from all over the world. It's not hard to fill the late hours passing from one club to another in St-Germain or Les Halles – assuming your wallet can take it. Standards are high and the line-ups varied, and the ancient cellars housing many of the clubs make for great acoustics and atmosphere.

One variety of home-grown popular music is the tradition of **chansons**, epito-

mized by Édith Piaf and developed to its greatest heights by Georges Brassens and the Belgian Jacques Brel. This music has been undergoing something of a revival since the 1950s star, Juliette Greco, performed again in 1991 at the temple of French music, L'Olympia. Another retrospective experience is **ballroom dancing** at the old music halls or surburban eating and drinking venues known as *guinguettes*.

Recent successes of the band Daftpunk and DJ Laurent Garnier – who performed at L'Olympia in 1998 – have given French **techno** music greater credibility both nationally and internationally, and the unusual blend of psychedelic rock and techno of Air has attracted fresh attention to the newest French sounds.

On the whole, however, commercial French **popular music** is best avoided. Although most singers – like Patrick Bruel, idol of depressed adolescents – lay claim to the *chansonniers* tradition, few have genuine roots in it, with the notable exception of Patricia Kaas. Vanessa Paradis went so far as to switch to English in order to pursue an international career. Two bands whose music is worth listening to for its fascinating mix of all kinds of styles are Mano Negra and Les Négresses Vertes.

Classical music, as you might expect in this Neoclassical city, is alive and well and takes up twice the space of "jazz-pop-folk-rock" in the listings magazines. The **Paris Opéra**, with its two homes –

Music and nightlife

the Opéra Garnier and Opéra Bastille – puts on a fine selection of ballet as well as opera. **Le Chatelet Théâtre Musical de Paris** also puts on interesting productions. For **concerts**, the choice is enormous. The two main orchestras are the Orchestre de Paris, based at the Salle Pleyel, and the Orchestre Nationale. Many concerts are put on in the city's churches – at very reasonable prices – but the need for advance reservations is a major inhibiting factor. If you're interested in the **contemporary** scene of Systems composition and the like, check out the state-sponsored experiments of Laurent Bayle at Beaubourg (Centre Pompidou), L'Ensemble Intercontemporain at La Villette's Cité de la Musique, and Iannis Xenakis out at Issy-Les-Moulineaux.

In the listings in this chapter, **nightlife** recommendations – for **dance clubs and discos** – are to some extent incorporated in those for rock, world music and jazz, with which they merge. Separate sections, however, detail places that are mainly disco, and those that cater for a gay or lesbian clientele.

The chapter's final section details all the **big venues**, where major concerts – from heavy metal to opera – are promoted.

Tickets and information

The best place to get **tickets** for concerts, whether rock, jazz, *chansons* or classical, is FNAC Forum des Halles, 1–5 rue Pierre-Lescot, 1ᵉʳ, ☎01.40.41.40.00 (Mᵒ Chatelet-Les Halles), which takes more than fifty percent of sales. Or try the FNAC Musique branches at 4 place de la Bastille, 12ᵉ (Mᵒ Bastille; Mon, Tues, Thurs & Sat 10am–8pm, Wed & Fri 10am–10pm), and 24 bd des Italiens, 9ᵉ (Mᵒ Richelieu-Drouot/Quatre-Septembre/Chaussée-d'Antin; Mon–Sat 10am–midnight); the FNAC bookshops (see p.326); and the Virgin Megastore, at 56–60 av des Champs-Élysées, 8ᵉ (Mᵒ Franklin-D-Roosevelt), and at the Carrousel du Louvre, beneath the Louvre, 1ᵉʳ (Mᵒ Palais-Royal/Musée-du-Louvre); both open Mon–Sat 10am–midnight, Sun noon–midnight.

For **information**, *Pariscope* and *Officiel des Spectacles* both list a fair selection of concerts, clubs and so on, and you'll see posters around town (particularly in the Latin Quarter). *Les Inrockuptibles* is the serious magazine with in-depth analysis and interviews on the independent music scene. Keep an eye out also for *Lylo*, published every three weeks, the most compre-

---

Music on TV and radio

The private **TV** channel Canal Plus broadcasts big European concerts (Michael Jackson, Dire Straits, the Rolling Stones and the like) and was responsible for initiating presenter Antoine de Caunes' *Rapido* to bring new popular sounds to a wider audience. M6 has some late-night music programmes as well as numerous video clips during the day, while Arte, the fifth channel (after 7pm), shows contemporary opera productions and documentaries on all types of music.

Of the **local radio stations**, Radio Nova (101.5 MHz) plays a good cross-section of what's new from rap to funk; Radio France-Mahgreb (99.5 MHz) does raï; FIP (105.1 MHz) has plenty of jazz; Africa Numero 1 (107.5 MHz) has African music; AYP FM (106.7 MHz) plays exclusively Armenian music; Radio Latina (99.0 MHz) is the Latin American music station; Oui (102.3 MHz) is the all-day rock radio; and techno and house can be heard on the gay radio station Radio FG (98.2 MHz). The **national station** Europe 1 (104.7 MHz) has some imaginative music programming, and France-Musique (91.7 and 92.1 MHz) carries classical, contemporary, jazz, opera and anything really big. Under strict new language laws, forty percent of pop music played by any radio station has to be French, and there's now a dire Parisian radio station playing nothing but French music, Chante France (90.9 MHz).

---

hensive listings magazine for rock, world, jazz and *chansons*, which can be picked up free from many bars and other venues. The best way to find out about the latest club-nights is by picking up flyers at Parallèles, 47 rue St-Honoré, 1er (M° Châtelet-les-Halles), or in the trendy shops and cafés of the Marais and Bastille. For information about African music gigs, good places to go are the record shops Afric'Music, 3 rue Plantes, 14e, ☎01.45.42.43.52 (Mon–Sat 10am–7pm; M° Mouton-Duvernet); and Crocodisc, 42 rue des Écoles, 5e (Tues–Sat 11am–7pm; M° Maubert-Mutualité); for reggae, try Blue Moon, 84 rue Quincampoix, 3e, ☎01.40.29.45.60 (Mon–Sat 11am–7pm; M° Rambuteau).

World music and rock

The last few years have seen considerable diversification in the Paris clubs and rock venues, which now concentrate more on international sounds, leaving the big Western rock bands to play the major arenas. Almost every club features **Latin and African** dance music, and big names from these worlds – in particular **zouk** musicians from the French Caribbean, for whom Paris is a second home – are almost always in town. The divisions between world sounds are blurring more and more, too. Even "ethnically French" Parisians have produced their own rewarding hybrids, best exemplified in the Pogue-like chaos of Les Négresses Vertes, who successfully survived the death in 1993 of their lead singer, Helno. One brilliant vocalist to look out for at the moment is Angélique Kidjo, from Benin. The group Zebda is the latest generation of hybrid rock with a strong Magrebian influence and an admirable social conscience. Profits from some of their records have been donated to suburban regeneration projects, and by subsidizing the price of their own concert tickets, many more of their fans can afford to see them.

France's only rock'n'roll megastar still rocks on, now in his mid-fifties and packing out stadiums, most recently the Stade de France. But fortunately **Johnny Halliday** does not represent contemporary French rock. Until their recent break-up, the best "alternative" rock band has been the Franco-Spanish **Mano Negra**, whose music, heavily influenced by their Latin American tours, combines rap, reggae, rock and salsa sounds. A former member of the band, Manu Chau, has pursued a successful solo career continuing in the tradition of the band but in his own inimitable way. Other quality rock musicians worth their salt are the soloist **Miossec**, the chart-topping **Louise Attaque** and **Kat Onoma**. All that said, half of all albums bought in France are still recorded by British and American bands.

There are numerous **heavy metal** bands with English names like "Megadeath". Then there's **trashpop**, an amalgam of funk, punk and splashes of bebop, heavy metal and psychedelia.

Algerian **raï** continues to flourish, with singers like Cheb Khaled and Cheb Mami enjoying megastar status. But the rage is increasingly for professionally produced **techno** raves and the "marginale" culture of the *banlieue*, the dispossessed immigrant suburbs, depicted so powerfully in the movie *La Haine*, and finding musical expression in **rap** and **hip-hop**. Names to look out for are NTM, IAM and MC Solaar, who moves beyond traditional rap to something a good deal more melodic and musical, with superb words that you need to be pretty fluent to appreciate.

Music venues

Most of the venues listed below are clubs. A few of them will have live music all week, but the majority host bands on just a couple of nights, usually Friday and Saturday, when admission prices are also hiked up. *La Locomotive, Le Saint* and the two barges moored to the banks of the Seine, *La Guingette Pirate* and *La Péniche Makara*, are your best bets for a not-too-expensive good night out.

Music and nightlife

Music and nightlife

MAINLY ROCK

Chapelle des Lombards, 19 rue de Lappe, 11e; ☎01.43.57.24.24 (M° Bastille). See opposite, under "Bals musettes and guinguettes".

La Cigale, 120 bd de Rochechouart, 18e; ☎01.42.23.15.15 (M° Pigalle). Music from 8.30pm. Punk, indie, etc; an eclectic programming policy in an old-fashioned converted theatre, long a fixture on the Pigalle scene.

Le Divan du Monde, 75 rue des Martyrs, 18e; ☎01.44.92.77.66 (M° Pigalle). Daily 7pm–5am. A youthful venue in a café whose regulars included Toulouse-Lautrec. An eclectic and exciting programming policy. Admission for concerts 50–80F.

Élysée Montmartre, 72 bd de Rochechouart, 18e; ☎01.44.92.45.45 (M° Anvers). An historic Montmartre nightspot, now dedicated to rock. Inexpensive and fun, it pulls in a young and excitable crowd. Around 80F.

Le Gibus, 18 rue du Faubourg-du-Temple, 11e; ☎01.47.00.78.88 (M° République). For twenty years English rock bands on their way up have played their first Paris gig at *Le Gibus* – the Clash and Police among them. Fourteen nights of dross will turn up perhaps one decent band, but it's always hot, loud, energetic, and crowded with young Parisians heavily committed to the rock scene. Tues–Sat 11pm–5am; Sat only in Aug; admission 70F, 80F with drink.

La Guinguette Pirate, quai de la Gare, 13e; ☎01.44.24.89.89 (M° Quai-de-la-Gare). Beautiful Chinese barge, moored alongside the quay in front of the Bibliothèque Nationale, hosting funk, reggae, rock and folk concerts. Tues–Sat 9pm–2am; 30F.

La Locomotive, 90 bd de Clichy, 18e; ☎01.42.57.37.37 (M° Blanche). Enormous high-tech nightclub boasting three dance floors: one for techno; one for rock, heavy metal and concerts; and one for rap and funk. Also one of the most crowded, popular and democratic clubs in the city, and you're sure of a good time. Concerts start at 1am. Closed Mon; 60F weekdays; 100F weekends, including one drink.

New Riverside, 7 rue Grégoire-de-Tours, 6e; ☎01.43.54.46.33 (M° Odéon). Good, friendly club playing rock and pop music in a sixteenth-century cellar. Daily 11pm–dawn. At weekends, breakfast included in admission price; and free admission for women weekdays and before midnight Fri and Sat. Otherwise, Mon–Thurs 70F; Fri, Sat & Sun 100F.

Péniche Makara, quai de la Gare, 13e; ☎01.44.24.09.00 (M° Quai-de-la-Gare/Bibliothèque-Tolbiac). Another barge moored to the banks of the Seine with a varied entertainments programme. Mainly reggae, rock and world concerts, but also theatre performances. Tues–Sun 6pm–2am; admission 30F.

Le Rex Club, 5 bd Poissonnière, 2e; ☎01.42.36.83.98 (M° Montmartre). Separate rooms for the club (drum'n'bass and house) and the live music venue – rock, funk, soul, raï and rap. Tues–Sun 11pm–6am; sometimes closed Sun & Mon. Concerts start around 8pm; 60–100F. Club from 11pm; 60–90F.

Le Saint, 7 rue St-Séverin, 5e; ☎01.43.25.50.04 (M° St-Michel). Good value, varied music played in an ancient cellar; popular with students. Tues–Sun 11am–dawn. 50F including one drink Tues–Thurs; 80F weekends.

MAINLY LATIN AND CARIBBEAN

L'Escale, 15 rue Monsieur-le-Prince, 6e; ☎01.43.54.63.47 (M° Odéon). More Latin American musicians must have passed through here than any other club. The dancing sounds, salsa mostly, are in the basement (disco on Wed), while on the ground floor every variety of South American music is given an outlet. Daily 11pm–4am. Drinks around 80F.

La Java, 105 rue du Faubourg-du-Temple, 10e; ☎01.42.02.20.52 (M° Goncourt/Belleville). The oldest disco in town has welcomed Édith Piaf in its time. These days it's renowned for its

Cuban jam sessions featuring live bands and DJs. Thurs & Fri 11pm–dawn. Admission 80F Thurs, 100F Fri. Reasonably priced drinks.

Mambo Club, 20 rue Cujas, 5e; ☎01.43.54.89.21 (M° St-Michel/Odéon). Afro-Cuban and Antillais music in a seedy dive attracting people of all ages and nationalities. Wed–Sat 11pm–dawn, Sunday 4pm–dawn for "themed soirées". Entrance 80F by day, 110F by night.

BALS MUSETTES AND GUINGUETTES

Balajo, 9 rue de Lappe, 11e; ☎01.47.00.07.87 (M° Bastille). The last and greatest survivor of the old-style dance halls of working-class and slightly louche Paris. The *Balajo* dates from the 1930s and has kept its extravagant contemporary decor, with a balcony for the orchestra above the vast dance floor. The clientele is all sorts now, and all ages, though recently the bouncers have started to show a preference for a younger generation. The music encompasses everything from mazurka to tango, cha-cha, twist, and the slurpy *chansons* of between the wars. There are disco and modern hits as well, but that's on Mon nights when the kids from across town come and all the popular nostalgia disappears. Mon, Fri & Sat 10pm–4.30am. Admission around 100F. Mon, free for women between 11.30pm and 1am.

Chapelle des Lombards, 19 rue de Lappe, 11e; ☎01.43.57.24.24 (M° Bastille). This erstwhile *bal musette* of the rue de Lappe still plays the occasional waltz and tango, but for the most part the music is salsa, reggae, steel drums, gwo-kâ, zouk, raï and the blues. Today it's better renowned as a pick-up joint. Tues–Sat and the eve of public hols 10.30pm–dawn; closed Sun. Tues–Thurs 100F admission and first drink, 120F Fri & Sat; 50F upwards for the next drinks.

Chez Gégène, 162bis quai de Polangis, Joinville-le-Pont; ☎01.48.83.29.43 (RER Joinville-le-Pont). Just the other side of the Bois de Vincennes, this is a genuine

Music and nightlife

guinguette established in the 1900s. You don't have to dine to dance (around 70F entrance for non-diners). Open mid-March to mid-Oct only, Fri & Sat 9.30pm–2am, Sun 3–7pm.

Le Petit Robinson, 164 quai de Polangis, Joinville-le-Pont; ☎01.48.89.04.39 (RER Joinville-le-Pont). Fifty metres along from *Chez Gégène* and a bit more upmarket, this is the place where serious dancers go to show off their immaculate waltzes, foxtrots and tangos. Like its neighbour, it has a huge dance floor, but it also boasts a live orchestra and is open year-round. Fri–Sat 8pm–2am, Sun–Mon 3–7pm. Admission and drink 80F; 60F Mon afternoon, ladies free Fri evening.

Le Tango, 13 rue au-Maire, 3e; ☎01.42.72.17.78 (M° Arts-et-Métiers). No vetting here. People wear whatever clothes they happen to be in and dance with abandon to please themselves, not the adjudicators of style. The music is jazzy Latin American: salsa, calypso and reggae. It is, however, a prime pick-up joint, and women are likely to be propositioned in no uncertain terms the moment they've agreed to a dance. Best to go with friends. Fri, Sat & the eve of public hols only, 11pm–dawn. Admission 60F Sat; 40F Fri. Drinks from 30F; obligatory cloakroom fee.

Nightclubs and discos

Clubs listed below are essentially **discos**, though a few have the odd live group. They're also prone to sudden closure – often due to court proceedings over complaints of noise and behaviour – but

Music and nightlife

it seems to be business as usual once the court case is over. Also listed below are venues, like the *Moloko* and *What's Up Bar*, which are officially bars with DJs and dancing, and charge little or no entrance fee but have the fussy bouncers and often pricey drinks better associated with nightclubs.

In any case, as a customer, you contribute on a financial level – and in many places your ornamentation potential is equally important. Being sized up by a leather-clad American bouncer acting as the ultimate arbiter of style and prosperity can be a very demeaning experience. Men generally have a harder time than women. English-speakers are at an advantage, blacks are not. The one place that doesn't discriminate and should be at the top of any disco list is *Le Palace*.

Arapaho, 30 av de l'Italie, 13e; ☎01.45.89.65.05 (M° Place-de-l'Italie). Famous Asia Folly theme night, with extravagant decoration and costumes, on Friday. Changing themes on Saturdays and occasional live bands during the week. Fri & Sat 11pm–3am. Admission 80F.

Les Bains, 7 rue du Bourg-l'Abbé, 3e; ☎01.48.87.01.80 (M° Étienne-Marcel). Midnight–dawn every day (Sun, rock; Mon, "Disturbance of the peace"; Wed, "Disco inferno"). This is as posey as they come – an old Turkish bathhouse where the Stones filmed part of their *Under Cover of the Night* video, now redone in the anti-perspirant, passionless style pioneered for the *Café Costes*. The music is house, rap and funk, with occasional live (usually dross) bands. It's not a place where a 500F note has much life expectancy. The decor features a plunging pool by the dance floor in which the punters are wont to ruin their non-colour-fast designer creations. Whether you can watch this spectacle depends on the bouncers, who have fixed ideas. If you're turned away, be thankful and head down the road to *Le Tango* (see overleaf). 100F admission, drinks expensive.

La Casbah, 18–20 rue de la Forge-Royale, 11^e; ☎01.43.71.71.89. (M° Bastille). The outstanding feature of this rather fancy and exclusive place is the decor: beautiful and authentic stuff from Morocco – doors, furniture, plasterwork – matched by the *zouave* costumes of the waiters and waitresses. Bar upstairs, dancing down. North African food served. Thurs–Sat 9pm–5am. Admission around 100F; 150F for a table.

Duplex, 2bis av Foch, 16e; ☎01.45.00.45.00 (M° Charles-de-Gaulle-Étoile). Model types and starlets are the norm in this upmarket, fashionable nightspot. Tues–Sun 11.30pm–dawn; 100F with first drink. Restaurant, too: same days 9pm–1am; around 300F.

El Globo, 8 bd Strasbourg, 10e; ☎01.42.41.55.70 (M° Strasbourg-St-Denis). Currently very popular with Beaux Quartiers rebels, 10e arrondissement punks and all sorts. Lots of room to dance to international hits past and present. Drinks 50F; 25F between 11pm and midnight. 1970s disco on Saturday night. Sat, Sun & public hols 10pm–dawn; entry 100F.

Flash Back, 37 rue Grégoire-de-Tours, 6e; ☎01.43.25.56.70 (M° Mabillon). Techno and commercial rock in a futuristic decor. Tues–Sun 11am–dawn; 70F entry.

Le Moloko, 26 rue Fontaine, 9e; ☎01.48.74.50.26 (M° Blanche). A fashionable and successful addition to the night scene, frequented by the young and gorgeous, the trendy and posey, all sorts. Jukebox instead of DJs, occasionally live music in the early evening. Drinks from 50F. Daily 9pm–6am; admission on Wed & Sat only 20F/40F.

Niel's, 27 av des Ternes, 17^e; ☎01.47.66.45.00 (M° Ternes). Like the *Duplex*, this place attracts the stars, but there's always the restaurant-booking technique to guarantee entry. Daily: disco 12.30am–dawn; restaurant 9pm–midnight (around 350F). Admission Fri & Sat 100F with drink; weekdays 95F.

Le Palace, 8 rue du Faubourg-Montmartre, 9ᵉ; ☎01.47.70.75.02 (Mᵒ Montmartre). Time was when everyone went to the *Palace*; it's still packed nightly with revellers, whether they've scraped together their week's savings or are just out to exercise their credit cards, and they all don their best party gear. Some nights it's thematic fancy dress, some nights the music is all African, other times the place is booked for TV dance shows. It's big, the bopping is good, and the clientele are an exuberant spectacle in themselves. Weekends are mainly techno and attract a gay crowd. Daily 11pm–dawn. Entry 100F Mon–Thurs; 120F weekends; drinks from 50F.

Le Shéhérazade, 3 rue de Liège, 9ᵉ; ☎01.40.40.16.18 (Mᵒ Liège). Exotic decor in a former Russian cabaret; vodka 80–90F a shot. Popular with a youthful, mixed, dancing crowd. House music, with occasional variant evenings. Mon–Thurs 11pm–dawn, weekends midnight–dawn; 100F admission plus drink.

What's Up, 15 rue Daval, 11ᵉ; ☎01.48.05.88.33 (Mᵒ Bastille). Fashionable bar hosting house record-label nights and other trendy events. Mon–Thurs & Sun 7pm–3am, Fri & Sat till 5am. Admission free, or 30–50F depending on the event.

Zed Club, 2 rue des Anglais, 5ᵉ; ☎01.43.54.93.78 (Mᵒ Maubert-Mutualité). *The* rock 'n' roll club. Wed–Sat 10.30pm–3.30am; admission 50F Wed; 50F plus drink Thurs; 100F plus drink Fri & Sat.

Lesbian and gay bars, clubs and discos

Lesbian clubs in Paris find it hard to be exclusively female, and you may find that none of the varied atmospheres is agreeable. The pleasures of **gay men** are far better catered for, though some Marais bars have been forced to close and others prosecuted for noise, contravention of drinking laws, and even for allowing plants to spread over the pavement. It seems that the residents of the Marais have become a good deal less tolerant.

While the selection of gay male-oriented establishments below only scratches the surface, for gay women our listings more or less cover all that's available. Lesbians, however, are welcome in some of the predominantly male clubs. For a complete rundown, consult *Paris Scene* (Gay Men's Press, £5.99), or Gai Pied's *Guide Gai*, published annually. Alternatively, tune into Paris' gay radio station RadioFG (98.2 FM).

WOMEN

La Champmeslé, 4 rue Chabanais, 2ᵉ; ☎01.42.96.85.20 (Mᵒ Opéra/Pyramides). Intimate, relaxed bar with back room reserved for women, front rooms for mixed company. Cabaret on Thurs. Drinks 30–50F. Mon–Wed 7pm–2am, Thurs–Sat 7pm–4am. Closed Sun.

Chez Moune, 54 rue Pigalle, 18ᵉ; ☎01.45.26.64.64 (Mᵒ Pigalle). In the red-light heart of Paris, this mixed but predominantly women's cabaret and disco may shock or delight. The evening includes a striptease (by women) without the standard audience for such shows (any man causing the slightest fuss is kicked out). Sunday afternoon tea dances (4.30–8pm) are strictly women-only. Otherwise daily 11pm–dawn.

Entre Nous, 17 rue Laferrière, 9ᵉ; ☎01.48.78.11.67 (Mᵒ St-Georges). A small, women-only club with intimate atmosphere and catholic taste in music. Fri & Sat only, 11pm–dawn.

Le Pulp, 25 bd Poissonnière, 2ᵉ; ☎01.40.26.01.93 (Mᵒ Montmartre). Diverse music – from techno to Madonna. Thurs–Sun from 11.30pm; Sat & Sun 50F entrance from midnight. Happy hour 11pm–1.30am. Drinks 40F.

Les Scandaleuses, 8 rue des Ecouffes, 4ᵉ; ☎01.48.87.39.26 (Mᵒ Hôtel-de-Ville). Trendy and lively women-only bar in the Marais. Nightly 5pm–2am.

Unity Bar, 176–178 rue St-Martin, 3ᵉ; ☎01.42.72.70.59 (Mᵒ Rambuteau/Les-Halles). Popular women-only bar with billiards and a happy hour 4–8pm. Open daily 4pm–2am.

Music and nightlife

For gay and lesbian information, see Basics, p.39.

Music and nightlife

L'Utopia, 15 rue Michel le Comte, 3ᵉ; ☎01.42.71.63.43 (Mᵒ Rambuteau). Bar on two levels, with billiards and chess downstairs. Themed nights, varied music and friendly atmosphere. Predominantly women. Mon–Sat 7pm–2pm.

MEN

Banana Café, 13 rue de la Ferronnerie, 1ᵉʳ; ☎01.42.33.35.31 (Mᵒ Chatelet-Les Halles). Popular, expensive and very trendy. Try and catch the cabaret and go-go dancing. Daily 4.30pm–dawn.

Le Bar Central, 33 rue Vieille-du-Temple, 4ᵉ; ☎01.48.87.99.33 (Mᵒ Hôtel-de-Ville). Small, crowded and friendly bar. Daily 2pm–2am. Drinks 20–60F.

La Luna, 28 rue Keller, 11ᵉ; ☎01.40.21.09.91 (Mᵒ Bastille). The latest high-tech rendezvous for the gay Bastille, complete with mirrors to dance in front of. Wed–Sun 11pm–6am. Weekend entry 50F; drinks from 45F.

Mixer Bar, 23 rue Ste-Croix de la Bretonnerie, 4ᵉ; ☎01.42.78.26.20 (Mᵒ Hôtel-de-Ville). Another popular and crowded Marais bar, which the law has been particularly heavy with in the past. Women also welcome. Daily 4pm–2am.

Open Bar, end of rue Vieille-du-Temple & rue des Archives, 4ᵉ (Mᵒ Hôtel-de-Ville). The first gay bar/café to have tables out on the pavement. Daily 10am–2am.

Le Piano Zinc, 49 rue des Blancs-Manteaux, 4ᵉ; ☎01.42.74.32.42 (Mᵒ Rambuteau/Hôtel-de-Ville). From 10pm, when the piano-playing starts, this bar becomes a happy riot of songs, music-hall acts, and dance, which may be hard to appreciate if you don't follow French

very well. Tues–Sun 6pm–2am. Drinks 36–47F.

Le Queen, 102 av des Champs-Élysées, 8ᵉ; ☎01.53.89.08.90 (Mᵒ George-V). Women welcome except Thurs. Drag queens and model types mostly. "Disco inferno" on Mon, otherwise mainly house. Nightly 11pm–dawn. Admission free Tues–Thurs; weekends 100F including drink.

Le Quetzal, 10 rue de la Verrerie, 4ᵉ; ☎01.48.87.99.07 (Mᵒ Hôtel-de-Ville). Lots of beautiful bodies cram into this popular nightspot. Mon–Thurs 2pm–4am, Fri–Sun 5pm–5am.

Le Skeud, 35 rue Ste-Croix de la Bretonnerie, 4ᵉ; ☎01.40.29.44.40 (Mᵒ Rambuteau/Hôtel-de-Ville). One of the newest and most popular bars in the Marais, with house and garage most nights; Eighties night on Thurs. Nightly 9pm–2am.

Jazz, blues and chansons

Jazz has long enjoyed an appreciative audience in France, most especially since the end of World War II, when the intellectual rigour and agonized musings of bebop struck an immediate chord of sympathy in the existentialist hearts of the *après-guerre*. Charlie Parker, Dizzy Gillespie, Miles Davis – all were being listened to in the 1950s, when in Britain their names were known only to a tiny coterie of fans.

Gypsy guitarist Django Reinhardt and his partner, violinist Stéphane Grappelli, whose work represents the distinctive and undisputed French contribution to the jazz canon, had much to do with the music's popularity. But it was also greatly enhanced by the presence of many

---

A note on prices

For virtually all of the **jazz clubs** listed, expense is a real drawback to enjoyment – the *Théâtre Dunois*, *L'Eustache* and *Utopia* are the cheaper ones. Admission charges are generally high and, when they're not levied, there's usually a whacking charge for your first drink. Subsequent drinks, too, are absurdly priced – about twice what you'd pay in a similar club in London, and more than double what you'd pay in New York.

---

front-rank black American musicians, for whom Paris was a haven of freedom and culture after the racial prejudice and philistinism of the States. Among them were the soprano sax player Sidney Bechet, who set up in legendary partnership with French clarinettist Claude Luter, and Bud Powell, whose turbulent exile partly inspired the tenor man played by Dexter Gordon (himself a veteran of the *Montana* club) in the film *Round Midnight.*

Jazz is still alive and well in the city, with new venues opening all the time, where you can hear all styles from New Orleans to current experimental. Some **local names** to look out for are saxophonists François Jeanneau, Barney Willen, Didier Malherbe, André Jaume and Steve Lacey; violinist Didier Lockwood; British-born but long Paris-resident guitarist John McLaughlin; pianist Alain Jeanmarie; accordionist Richard Galliano; and bass player Jean-Jacques Avenel. All of them can be found playing small gigs, regardless of the size of their reputations.

MAINLY JAZZ

All Jazz Club, 7–11 rue St-Benoît, 6ᵉ; ☎01.42.61.87.02 (Mᵒ St-Germain-des-Près). Formerly the *Latitudes Jazz Club*, now lavishly redecorated and rechristened, though its programme remains traditional-style jazz. Nightly 10.30pm–2am. Entrance 120–160F, includes free first drink.

Le Baiser Salé, 58 rue des Lombards, 1ᵉʳ; ☎01.42.33.37.71 (Mᵒ Châtelet). A bar downstairs and a small, crowded upstairs room with live music every night from 11pm – usually jazz, rhythm & blues, Latino-rock, reggae or Brazilian. Open daily 8am–5am. 123F for first drink includes charge for music.

Le Bilboquet, 13 rue St-Benoît, 6ᵉ; ☎01.45.48.81.84 (Mᵒ St-Germain). A rather smart, comfortable bar/restaurant with live jazz every night, featuring local and international stars. Food served until 1am. The music starts at 10.45pm. Mon–Sat 9pm–dawn; no admission, but pricey drinks (120F).

Caveau de la Huchette, 5 rue de la Huchette, 5ᵉ; ☎01.43.26.65.05 (Mᵒ St-Michel). A wonderful slice of old Parisian life in an otherwise horribly touristy area. Live jazz, usually trad, to dance to on a floor surrounded by tiers of benches, and a bar decorated with caricatures of the barman drawn on any material to hand. Nightly 9.30pm–2am or later. Sun–Thurs 60F (students 55F); Fri & Sat 70F; drinks from 20F. Fri–Sun 5–9pm, swing during happy hour, free entrance.

La Cithéa, 114 rue Oberkampf, 11ᵉ; ☎01.40.21.70.95 (Mᵒ Parmentier). Live funk and afro-jazz Thursday to Saturday nights attracting a young, fashionable crowd. Reasonably priced drinks. Get there early if you want to get in the door. Nightly 8.30pm–2am.

Au Duc des Lombards, 42 rue des Lombards, 1ᵉʳ; ☎01.42.33.22.88 (Mᵒ Châtelet-Les Halles). Small, unpretentious bar with performances every night from 10pm – jazz piano, blues, ballads, fusion. Sometimes big names. Daily until 3am. Drinks from 58F or 78F.

L'Eustache, 37 rue Berger, 1ᵉʳ; ☎01.40.26.23.20 (Mᵒ Châtelet-Les Halles). Young and friendly Les Halles café, the cheapest place to hear good jazz in the capital. Live jazz 10.30pm–2am on Thurs. Daily 11am–4am.

Instants Chavirés, 7 rue Richard-Lenoir, Montreuil; ☎01.42.87.25.91 (Mᵒ Robespierre). Avant-garde jazz joint – no comforts – on the eastern edge of the city, close to the Porte de Montreuil. A place where musicians go to hear each other play, its reputation has attracted subsidies from both state and local authorities. Tues–Sat 8pm–1am; concerts at 9.30pm. Admission 35–80F, depending on the celebrity of the band; drinks from 15F.

Lionel Hampton Bar, *Hôtel Méridien*, 81 bd Gouvion-St-Cyr, 17ᵉ; ☎01.40.68.30.42 (Mᵒ Porte-Maillot). First-rate jazz venue, with big-name musicians. Inaugurated by Himself, but other-

Music and nightlife

The tradition of jazz clubs in rue St-Benoît, 6ᵉ, goes back to the 1950s, when Dexter Gordon, Miles Davis, Bud Powell among others hung out here.

Music and nightlife

wise the great man is only an irregular visitor. Mon–Sat 10pm–2am. Drinks from 130F.

New Morning, 7–9 rue des Petites-Écuries, 10ᵉ; ☎01.45.23.51.41 (M° Château-d'Eau). This is the place where the big international names in jazz come to play. Blues and Latin, too. Daily 9pm–1.30am (concerts start around 10pm); admission around 110F.

Le Petit Journal, 71 bd St-Michel, 5ᵉ; ☎01.43.26.28.59 (M° Luxembourg). Small, smoky bar, long frequented by Left Bank student-types, with good, mainly French, traditional and mainstream sounds. First drink 100–150F. These days rather middle-aged and tourist-prone. Mon–Sat 10pm–2am; closed Aug.

Le Petit Journal Montparnasse, 13 rue du Commandant-Mouchotte, 14ᵉ; ☎01.43.21.56.70 (M° Montparnasse). Under the *Hôtel Montparnasse*, and sister establishment to the above, with bigger visiting names, both French and international. Mon–Sat 9pm–2am. First drink 100F.

Le Petit Opportun, 15 rue des Lavandières-Ste-Opportune, 1ᵉʳ; ☎01.42.36.01.36 (M° Châtelet-Les Halles). It's worth arriving early to get a seat for the live music in the dungeon-like cellar, where the acoustics play strange tricks and you can't always see the musicians. Fairly eclectic policy and a crowd of genuine connoisseurs. Tues–Sat 9pm–3am. Music from 11pm. First drink 100F.

Quai des Blues, 17 bd Vital-Bouhot, Île de la Jatte, Neuilly; ☎01.46.24.06.00 (M° Pont-de-Levallois, then down the steps from the bridge). Not the easiest of places to get to. Mainly blues, R&B, gospel – American musicians. Thurs–Sat, music at 10.45pm & midnight; 80F.

Les 7 Lézards, 10 rue des Rosiers, 4ᵉ; ☎01.48.87.08.97 (M° St-Paul). This new jazz club is already making a name for itself, attracting local and international acts alike. There's also a restaurant. Wed–Sat 10pm–2am. Admission 60F.

Slow Club, 130 rue de Rivoli, 1ᵉʳ; ☎01.42.33.84.30 (M° Châtelet/Pont-Neuf). A jazz club where you can bop the night away to the sounds of Claude Luter's sextet and visiting New Orleans musicians. Tues & Thurs–Sat 10pm–4am. Admission 60F; Fri & Sat 75F.

Le Sunset, 60 rue des Lombards, 1ᵉʳ; ☎01.40.26.46.20 (M° Châtelet-Les Halles). Restaurant upstairs, jazz club in the basement, featuring the best musicians – the likes of Alain Jeanmarie and Turk Mauro – and frequented by musicians in the wee small hours. Mon–Sat 8pm–4am. Admission and first drink 50–100F.

Théâtre Dunois, 108 rue du Chevaleret, 13ᵉ; ☎01.45.70.81.16 (M° Chevaleret). A new location for the *Dunois*, more modern, no stage, and a bigger bar. The musical policy still gives consistent support to free and experimental jazz. One of the few places in Paris to hear improvised music, as opposed to free jazz. Daily from 7pm; closed July & Aug. 70F admission; 50F students. Concerts Mon–Fri & Sun 8.30–11.30pm.

Utopia, 1 rue de l'Ouest, 14ᵉ; ☎01.43.22.79.66 (M° Pernety). No genius here, but good French blues singers interspersed with jazz and blues tapes, and a mostly young and studentish crowd. Generally very pleasant atmosphere. Drinks from 50F. Mon–Sat 10.30pm–dawn; closed Aug.

La Villa, 29 rue Jacob, 6ᵉ; ☎01.43.26.60.00 (M° St-Germain-des-Près). Popular joint with a good atmosphere and usually well-established musicians. Mon–Sat 10pm–3am. Admission 120F with first drink.

MAINLY CHANSONS

Casino de Paris, 19 rue de Clichy, 9ᵉ; ☎01.49.95.99.99 (M° Trinité). This decaying, once-plush casino in one of the seediest streets in Paris is a venue for all sorts of performances – *chansons*, poetry combined with flamenco guitar, cabaret. Check the listings magazines under "*Variétés*". Tickets from 120F to 180F.

Caveau des Oubliettes, 11 rue St-Julien-le-Pauvre, 5ᵉ; ☎01.43.54.94.97 (Mº St-Michel). French popular music of bygone times – Piaf and earlier – sung with exquisite nostalgia in the ancient prisons of Châtelet. Fri & Sat only 9pm–2am; admission 70F; drinks from 20F.

Le Lapin Agile, 22 rue des Saules, 18ᵉ; ☎01.46.06.85.87 (Mº Lamarck-Caulaincourt). Old haunt of Apollinaire, Utrillo and other Montmartre artists, some of whose pictures adorn the walls. Cabaret, poetry and *chansons*; you may be lucky enough to catch singer-composer Arlette Denis, who carries Jacques Brel's flame. Tues–Sun 9pm–2am. 130F including drink, students 90F.

Classical and contemporary music

Paris is a stimulating environment for **classical music**, both established and contemporary. The former is well represented with a choice of ten to twenty concerts every day of the week, with numerous performances making the most of churches' fine acoustics, often for free or relatively little. There are also excellent concerts, usually of chamber music, performed at the Musée du Louvre and Musée d'Orsay.
Contemporary and experimental computer-based work flourishes, too; leading exponents are Paul Mefano and Pierre Boulez, founder of Beaubourg's

IRCAM centre and himself one of the first pupils of Olivier Messiaen, the grand old man of modern French music, who died in 1992.

The new **Cité de la Musique**, at La Villette in the 19ᵉ, is an important venue, with regular concerts in the Conservatoire (the Academy), in the museum amphitheatre and in the fabulously designed "modular" Salle des Concerts. Ancient music, contemporary works, jazz, *chansons* and music from all over the world are featured.

The city hosts a good number of **music festivals**, which vary from year to year. For details, pick up the current year's festival schedule from the tourist office or the Hôtel de Ville.

Two **periodicals** devoted to the music scene are *La Semaine*, published weekly by the Maison de la Radio; and the tri-monthly *Résonance*, published by IRCAM at the Beaubourg and specializing in contemporary music.

Regular concert venues

Tickets for classical concerts are best bought at the box offices, though for big names you may find overnight queues, and a large number of seats are always booked by subscribers. The price range is very reasonable. The listings magazines and daily newspapers will have details of concerts in these venues, in the churches and in the suburbs. Look out for posters as well.

Music and
nightlife

Radio-France free concerts

Squeezed by the all-too-familiar business reasoning of the age, the state radio's music station, France-Musique, has adopted a more commercial programming policy, aimed at wider public taste and better audience ratings, to the dismay, inevitably, of purists. However, a major advantage has been a significant increase in the number of **admission-free concerts** at the Maison de la Radio, 166 av du Président-Kennedy, 16ᵉ; ☎01.42.30.15.16 or 01.42.30.22.22 (Mº Passy). All you have to do is turn up half an hour in advance at Studio 106, the main auditorium, renamed Salle Olivier Messiaen in memory of the composer, to secure a yellow *carton d'invitation*.

Another interesting opportunity is the daily programme **Les démons de Midi**, which goes out live at 12.30pm from Studio 101. It consists of recitals of all kinds of music from medieval to modern, with discussions and interventions by young musicians who turn up to take part. Again, all you have to do to attend is turn up half an hour early, at noon, and collect your *carton*.

Music and nightlife

AUDITORIUMS AND THEATRES

Cité de la Musique, 221 av Jean-Jaurés, 19e; ☎01.44.84.44.84 for the Salle des Concerts and ☎01.40.40.46.46 for the Conservatoire (M° Porte-de-Pantin).

Conservatoire National Supérieur de Musique et de Danse de Paris, 209 av Jean Jaurés, 19e; ☎01.40.40.46.46 (M° Porte-de-Pantin).

Salle Gaveau, 45 rue de la Boétie; ☎01.49.53.05.07 (M° Miromesnil).

Salle Pleyel, 252 rue du Faubourg-St-Honoré, 8e; ☎01.45.61.53.00 (M° Ternes). Home of the Orchestre de Paris, the Paris symphony orchestra.

Théâtre des Champs-Élysées, 15 av Montaigne, 8e; ☎01.49.52.50.50 (M° Alma-Marceau).

Théâtre Musical de Paris, Théâtre du Châtelet, 1 place du Châtelet, 1er; ☎01.40.28.28.40 (M° Châtelet). Closed for renovations at the time of writing, but due to re-open mid-1999.

CHURCHES AND MUSEUMS

Musée du Louvre, palais du Louvre, 1er; ☎01.40.20.84.00 (M° Louvre-Rivoli/Palais-Royal-Musée-du-Louvre). Midday and evening concerts of chamber music in the auditorium. 40–135F.

Musée d'Orsay, 1 rue de Bellechasse, 7e; ☎01.40.49.47.17 (M° Solférino/RER Musée d'Orsay). Varied programme of midday and evening concerts in the auditorium. 40–80F.

St-Julien-le-Pauvre, 23 quai de Montebello, 5e; ☎01.42.08.49.00 (M° St-Michel). Varied programmes. 80–150F.

St-Séverin, 1 rue des Prêtres St-Séverin, 5e (M° St-Michel). Varied programmes. Entrance free.

Ste-Chapelle, 4 bd du Palais, 1er; ☎01.42.77.65.65 (M° Cité). Mainly chamber music. 90–150F.

Opera

Opera would seem to have had its rewards in President Mitterrand's millennial endowments. The **Opéra Bastille** (see

p.115) was his most extravagant legacy to the city. It opened, with all due pomp, in 1989. Its first production – a six-hour performance of Berlioz's *Les Troyens* – cast something of a shadow on the project's proclaimed commitment to popularizing the art. "We are audacious", was the defence of the president, Pierre Bergé, who got his job after a lot of acrimonious political wrangling, which included the dismissal of Daniel Barenboim as musical director. This was shortly followed by the dismissal of Rudolph Nureyev from the same post. Resignations and a severe loss of morale followed the company's accident at the Seville Expo 92, when a chorus singer was killed and many others injured. The relatively unknown South Korean, Myung Whun Chung, was a controversial but popular musical director until he was sacked by the new chief, Hughes Gall, who has decided to take smaller productions back to the lavishly refurbished old **Opéra Garnier**, place de l'Opéra, 9e; ☎08.36.69.78.68 (M° Opéra; tickets 60–750F).

Opera in Paris creams off almost two-thirds of the whole annual state budget for music. Potentially, the Bastille orchestra is one of the best, and though people disagree about the acoustics, the place manages to be packed every night. To judge for yourself: **tickets** (60–650F) can be booked Monday to Saturday 9am to 7pm on ☎08.36.69.78.68 or at the ticket offices (Mon–Sat 9am–7pm within two weeks of the performance). The cheapest seats are only available to personal callers; unfilled seats are sold at discount to students five minutes before the curtain goes up. For programme details, phone ☎08.36.69.78.68.

More large-scale opera productions are staged at the **Théâtre Musical de Paris**, part of the **Théâtre du Châtelet** (see p.322). Rather less grand opera is performed at the **Opéra-Comique** (Salle Favard, 5 rue Favart, 2e; ☎01.42.44.45.40; M° Richelieu-Drouot). Occasional operas and concerts by solo singers are hosted by the **Théâtre des Champs Elysées** (see p.321). Both opera and recitals are also staged at the multipurpose performance halls (see below).

Contemporary music

One of the few disadvantages of the high esteem in which the French hold their intellectual and artistic life is that it encourages, at the extremes, a tendency to sterile *intellectualisme*, as the French themselves call it. In the eyes of many music lovers, and musicians, this has been nowhere more evident than in music, where the avant-garde is split into post-serialist and spectral music factions. Doyen of the former is composer Pierre Boulez; of the latter, it is Paul Mefano, director of the 2E2M ensemble.

Boulez's experiments for many years received massive public funding in the form of a vast laboratory of acoustics and "digital signal processing" – a complex known as **IRCAM** – housed next to the Beaubourg arts centre, on place Igor-Stravinsky. Boulez's Ensemble Intercontemporain is now based in the Cité de la Musique, but IRCAM occasionally opens its doors to the public.

The IRCAM building has recently been extended, creating new teaching areas and a mediathèque, which is open for public consultation Mon, Wed & Fri 10am–7pm, Thurs noon–7pm & Sat 1–7pm (closed second half July & first half Aug; 20F). Concerts are advertised in *Pariscope* and the like.

Other Paris-based practitioners of contemporary and experimental music include Philippe Manoury, Jean-Claude Eloy, Pascal Dusapin, Luc Ferrarie, and the English composer George Benjamin. Among the younger generation of less sectarian composers, some names to look out for are Nicos Papadimitriou, Thierry Pécourt, François Leclere, Marc Dalbavie, Yan Mharesz, and Georges Aperghis, whose speciality is musical theatre.

The big performance halls

Events at any of the performance spaces listed below will be well advertised on billboards and posters throughout the city. Tickets can be obtained at the halls themselves, though it's easier to get them through agents like FNAC or Virgin Megastore (see p.340).

Le Bataclan, 50 bd Voltaire, 11ᵉ; ☎01.47.00.39.12 (Mᵒ Oberkampf). One of the best places for visiting and native rock bands.

Forum des Halles, *niveau* 3, Porte Rambuteau, 15 rue de l'Équerre-d'Argent, 1ᵉʳ; ☎01.42.03.11.11 (Mᵒ Châtelet). Varied functions – theatre, performance art, rock – often with foreign touring groups.

Maison des Cultures du Monde, 101 bd Raspail, 6ᵉ; ☎01.45.44.72.30 (Mᵒ Rennes). All the arts from all over the world, for once not dominated by Europeans.

Olympia, 28 bd des Capucines, 9ᵉ; ☎01.47.42.25.49 (Mᵒ Madeleine/Opéra). An old, recently refurbished, music hall hosting occasional well-known rock groups and large popular concert performers.

Palais des Congrès, place de la Porte-Maillot, 17ᵉ; ☎01.40.68.22.22 (Mᵒ Porte-Maillot). Opera, ballet, orchestral music, trade fairs, and the superstars of US and British rock.

Palais Omnisports de Bercy, 8 bd de Bercy, 12ᵉ; ☎01.43.46.12.21 (Mᵒ Bercy). Opera, cycle racing, Bruce Springsteen, ice hockey, and Citroën launches – the newest multi-purpose stadium with seats to give vertigo to the most level-headed, but an excellent space when used in the round.

Palais des Sports, Porte de Versailles, 15ᵉ; ☎01.48.28.40.48 (Mᵒ Porte-de-Versailles). Another vast-scale auditorium, ideal if you want to see your favourite rock star in miniature a kilometre away.

Zenith, Parc de la Villette, 211 av Jean-Jaurès, 20ᵉ; ☎01.42.08.60.00 or 01.42.40.60.00 (Mᵒ Porte-de-Pantin). Seating for 6500 people in an inflatable stadium designed exclusively for rock and pop concerts. Head for the concrete column with a descending red aeroplane.

Music and nightlife

Chapter 15

Film, theatre and dance

Movie-goers have a choice of around 300 films showing in Paris in any one week, which puts moving visuals on an equal footing with the still visuals of the art museums and galleries. And they cover every place and period, with new works (with the exception of British movies) arriving here long before they reach London and New York.

If your French is good enough to cope with subtitles, go and see a Senegalese, Taiwanese, Brazilian or Finnish **film** that might never be seen in Britain or the USA at all, except perhaps on television at 4am a year or two later.

The language barrier makes **theatre** less accessible to non-natives, too, although the Théâtre National de Chaillot has a subtitling facility. There is stimulation in the cult of the director, however: Paris is home to Peter Brook, Ariane Mnouchkine and other exiles, as well as its own French talent. Also, transcending language barriers, there are exciting developments in **dance**, much of it incorporating mime, which, alas, no longer seems to have a separate status.

Tipping

It is common practice in Parisian theatres and occasionally in independent cinemas for the ushers to expect a small tip from each customer (5F or so). They may ask for the money if it's not immediately forthcoming.

As for **sex shows** and **soft porn cabarets**, with names that conjure up the classic connotations of the sinful city – *Les Folies Bergères* or the *Moulin Rouge* – they thrive and will no doubt continue for as long as Frenchmen's culture excuses anything on the grounds of appreciation of female beauty.

Listings for all films and stage productions are detailed in *Pariscope* and other weeklies, with brief résumés or reviews. Venues with wheelchair access will say "*accessible aux handicapés*".

Film

In recent years several of the tiny little *salles* in obscure corners of the city, where you could find yourself the sole audience for an afternoon showing of *Hiroshima Mon Amour* or *The Maltese Falcon*, have closed. The big cinema chains, UGC and Gaumont, have opened new multi-screen cinemas equipped with escalators and popcorn carton holders by each seat. But there are more special film festivals these days, and Paris remains one of the few cities in the world in which it's possible to get not only serious entertainment but a serious film education from the programmes of regular – never mind the specialist – cinemas.

In a typical week it might be possible – not counting new and recent releases of American and other films – to catch **retrospective seasons** of films

French cinema

The French have treated cinema as an art form, deserving of state subsidy, ever since its origination with the Lumière brothers in 1895. The state invests huge amounts in film production and appreciation. Tickets are heavily subsidized by the state, who are also injecting funds into the new Maison du Cinéma project at Bercy, which will include a cinémathèque, museum, library and teaching resources. The medium has (as yet) never had to bow down to TV as has happened elsewhere, the seat of judgement stays in Cannes, and Paris remains the cinema capital of Europe.

Film, theatre and dance

The **Cinémathèque Française**, currently based at the Palais de Chaillot and the Salle Grands Boulevards, though due to be housed in the new Maison du Cinéma at Bercy in 2000, possesses the largest collection of silent and early talkie movies in the world. All the pre-1960 stock, whose celluloid nitrate is dissolving, is in process of being transferred onto acetate.

While the old is treasured and preserved, the new in French cinema for a while revolved around the Nureyev of moviedom, **Gérard Depardieu**. Jean-Paul Rappeneau's 1990 screening of the late nineteenth-century play *Cyrano de Bergerac*, starring Depardieu and with rhyming couplets throughout, was at the time the most expensive French film ever made (it has since been outdone in terms of the budget several times over) and exceeded all box-office expectations in America and Britain. Depardieu went on to act in English in the American film *Green Card*, then played Columbus in the American-French co-production *1492: Conquest of Paradise* before returning to French cinema as the collier Maheu in the movie version of Zola's *Germinal*.

Contemporary politics and cinematographic innovation made a dramatic comeback to French cinema with the 1996 winner of the French Césars award for best film, *La Haine* by Mathieu Kassovitz. A brilliant and strikingly original portrayal of exclusion and racism in the Paris *banlieue*, *La Haine* is worlds away from the early 1980s style of movies that used Paris as a backdrop, such as *Diva* and *Subway*. But *La Haine* would seem to be a one-off, with glossy star-vehicle "heritage" movies like *Beaumarchais l'Insolent* (a French equivalent of *The Madness of King George*) and *Le Hussard sur le Toit*, which broke budget records and flopped, lapping up funds. There is still no current force in French movie-making to touch on the prolific New Wave period of the Sixties, pioneered by **Jean-Luc Godard** and others. Luc Besson, Alain René, Maurice Pialat, Bernard Tavernier and Patrice Chereau (also well known as a theatre director) are some of the stalwarts. Many foreign directors have benefited from public subsidies with or without making their films in France – Wajda and Kieslowski both worked in France, but Kurosawa made all his films in Japan and Kiarostami remains in Iran.

There are plenty of new names in the world of French cinema keeping the tradition alive: watch out for actors Elodie Bouchez and Natacha Regnier, both of whom won the *Prix d'interpretation féminine* at Cannes in 1998 for Eric Zonca's tragicomic *La Vie Rêvée des Anges*. Look out, too, for the directors Arnaud Desplechin and Laurence Ferreira-Barboza, the latter one of many women representing this new wave of directors, whose themes often deal with the lost hopes of the younger generation.

The row over cultural subsidies in the mid-1990s GATT negotiations revealed just how threatened France feels by American **movie imports**. The top box-office hits in Paris tend to be transatlantic imports, and a quick scan down the listings for any week shows a dominance of foreign films. Nonetheless, the city remains the perfect place to see movies, from the latest blockbuster to the least-known works of the earliest directors.

Film, theatre and dance

Film festivals

Paris plays host to an **International Festival of Women's Films**, which takes place annually at the end of March or beginning of April. It's organized by the Maison des Arts in Créteil, a southeastern suburb at the end of the Balard–Créteil métro line. As the festival enters its third decade, its influence in promoting and encouraging works by women continues to strengthen, particularly in France. Chinese, Indian, Russian, American, Japanese and European films compete for the eight awards, six of which are voted for by the audiences. Programme details are available from mid-March onwards, from the Maison des Arts, place Salvador-Allende, 94000 Créteil; ☎01.43.99.22.11 (Mº Créteil-Préfecture) or on the Internet at *www.coproductions.com/AFIFF/*.

At the same time of year and also in the suburbs, in Bobigny to the northeast of the city, the Magic Cinéma (rue du Chemin-Vert, 9300 Bobigny; ☎01.41.60.12.34) runs a **Festival au Théâtre Cinéma**, which concentrates on the links between literature and the cinema.

During the summer, the Parc de la Villette (Mº Porte-de-Pantin) organizes the **Festival du Cinéma en Plein Air** (☎01.40.03.75.00; free). Films based on changing themes are shown every night at 10pm to an audience of picnickers on the grass; deckchairs (20F) are available for hire, too.

by Fassbinder, Antonioni, Almodovar, David Lynch, Peter Greenaway, Polanski, and Serge Gainsbourg, a festival of contemporary Irish cinema, Vietnamese films, and any number of historically significant movies such as Fritz Lang's *Metropolis*, Oshima's *Empire of the Senses*, Kubrick's *A Clockwork Orange*, Orson Welles' *Citizen Kane*, Sergio Leone's *Once Upon a Time in the West*, Visconti's *Death in Venice*, Louis Malle's *Zazie dans le Métro*, Carné's *Hôtel du Nord*, Rossellini's *Rome Open City* and Bresson's *Pickpocket*.

Among cinemas that run **seasons** of the work of a particular director or actor/actress, such as those outlined above, are the Action chain, the Escurial, the Entrepôt and Le Studio 28. In addition, some of the **foreign institutes** in the city have occasional screenings, so if your favourite director is a Hungarian, a Swede or a Korean, for example, check what's on at those countries' cultural centres. These will be listed along with other cinema-clubs and museum screenings under "*Séances exceptionnelles*" or "*Ciné-clubs*", and are usually cheaper than ordinary cinemas.

Almost all of the huge selection of **foreign films** will be shown at some cinemas in the original language – *version originale* or *v.o.* in the listings – as opposed to *version française* or *v.f.*, which means it's dubbed into French. *Version anglaise* or *v.a.* means it's the English version of an international co-production.

Times and prices

Movie-going is not exclusively an evening occupation: the *séances* (programmes) start between 1 and 3pm at many places, sometimes as early as 11am, and usually continue through to the early hours.

Cinema **tickets** rarely need to be purchased in advance, and they're cheap by European standards. The average price is 40–45F; and most cinemas have lower rates on Monday or Wednesday, as well as reductions for students from Monday to Thursday. Some matinée *séances* also have discounts. UGC and Gaumont sell booklets of tickets, which work out at around 30F a seat, and some independents offer a *carte de fidélité*, giving you a free sixth entry.

For three days at the end of June during the **Fête du Cinéma**, a film ticket to any of a host of Paris cinemas gives you a "passport" to see as many other films as you like for 10F a go. In February, there's a week of **18 hrs 18F**, whereby 6pm screenings cost 18F.

All Paris' cinemas are non-smoking, and in some cases the ushers are unwaged and so positively *have* to be tipped (see box on p.312).

Cinemas

L'Arlequin, 76 rue des Rennes, 6e (Mo St-Sulpice). Owned by Jacques Tati in the 1950s, then by the Soviet Union as the cosmos cinema until 1990, L'Arlequin has now been renovated and is once again *the* cinephile's palace in the Latin Quarter. There are special screenings of classics every Sunday at 11pm, followed by debates in the café opposite.

L'Entrepôt, 7–9 rue Francis-de-Pressensé, 14e (Mo Pernety). One of the best alternative Paris movie houses, which has been keeping ciné-addicts happy for years with its three screens dedicated to the obscure, the subversive and the brilliant – among those categories many Arab and African films. It also shows videos, satellite and cable TV, and has a bookshop (Mon–Sat 2–8pm) and a restaurant (daily noon–midnight).

L'Escurial Panorama, 11 bd de Port-Royal, 13e (Mo Gobelins). Combining plush seats, big screen, and more art than commerce in its programming policy, this cinema is likely to be showing something like *Eraserhead* on the small screen and the latest offering from a big-name director – French, Japanese or American – on the panoramic screen (never dubbed).

Gaumont Grand Écran Italie, 30 place d'Italie, 13e (Mo Place-d'Italie). Three screens, including the 24-metre-wide *grand écran*. Big-draw movies inevitably, with all foreign titles dubbed.

Grand Action & Action Écoles, 5 & 23 rue des Écoles, 5e (Mo Cardinal-Lemoine/Maubert-Mutualité); **Action Christine Odéon**, 4 rue Christine, 6e (Mo Odéon/St-Michel). The Action chain spe-

cializes in new prints of ancient classics and screens collections of contemporary films from different countries.

Le Grand Rex, 1 bd Poissonnière, 2e (Mo Bonne-Nouvelle). Just as outrageous as La Pagode (see below) but in the kitsch line, with a *Metropolis*-style tower blazing its neon name, 2750 seats and a ceiling of stars and a Spanish city skyline. This is the ultimate Thirties public movie-seeing experience, though you're most likely to be watching a blockbuster and, if foreign, it'll be dubbed.

Le Latina, 20 rue du Temple, 4e (Mo Hôtel-de-Ville). Specializes in Latin American, Portuguese and Spanish films, as well as food and art in its restaurant and gallery.

Lucernaire Forum, 53 rue Notre-Dame-des-Champs, 6e (Mo Notre-Dame-des-Champs/Vavin). An art complex with three screening rooms, two theatres, an art gallery, bar and restaurant, showing old arty movies and undubbed current films from all round the world.

Max Linder Panorama, 24 bd Poissonnière, 9e (Mo Bonne-Nouvelle). Opposite Le Grand Rex, this always shows films in the original, and has almost as big a screen, state-of-the-art sound, and Art Deco decor.

MK2 Quai de la Seine, 14 quai de la Seine, 19e (Mo Jaurès/Stalingrad). Part of the MK2 chain but distinctive in style – covered in famous cinematic quotes and on the banks of the Bassin de la Villette – and with a varied art-house repertoire.

La Pagode, 57bis rue de Babylone, 7e (Mo François-Xavier). The most beautiful of all the capital's cinemas, originally transplanted from Japan at the turn of the century to be a rich Parisienne's party place. The wall panels of the Grande Salle are embroidered in silk; golden dragons and elephants hold up the candelabra; and a battle between Japanese and Chinese warriors rages on the ceiling. Unfortunately, recent financial problems could mean that this unique cinema is closed; check *Pariscope* before you turn up.

Film, theatre and dance

Film,
theatre and
dance

Le Studio des Ursulines, 10 rue des Ursulines, 5ᵉ (M° Censier-Daubenton). This was where *The Blue Angel* had its world première. Avant-garde movies are still premièred here, often followed by in-house debates with the directors and actors.

Le Studio 28, 10 rue de Tholozé, 18ᵉ (M° Blanche/Abbesses). In its early days, after one of the first showings of Buñuel's *L'Age d'Or*, this was done over by extreme right-wing Catholics who destroyed the screen and the paintings by Dali and Ernst in the foyer. The cinema still hosts avant-garde premières, followed occasionally by discussions with the director, as well as regular festivals.

Cinémathèques and vidéothèques

For the seriously committed film-freak, the best movie venues in Paris are the cinémathèques, in the Salle Garance on the top floor of Beaubourg, 4ᵉ (M° Rambuteau; closed until 2000); the Salle du Palais Chaillot, 7 av Albert-de-Mun, 16ᵉ (M° Trocadéro); and the Salle Grands Boulevards, 42 bd Bonne Nouvelle, 10ᵉ (M° Bonne-Nouvelle; closed Mon; ☎01.56.26.01.01). These give you a choice of more than fifty different films a week, many of which would never be shown commercially, and tickets are only 28F (17F for students and members). The Cinémathèque Française, formerly in the Palais de Chaillot, is in the process of moving to the Maison du Cinéma, a grand project in Bercy which will also house a museum and library.

The Vidéothèque de Paris, in the Forum des Halles (see p.349), is another excellent-value venue for the bizarre or obscure on celluloid or video. Their repertoires are always based around a particular theme with some connection to Paris.

The largest screen: Omnimax

For more details of La Villette, see p.359.

There is one cinematic experience that has to be recommended, however trite and vainglorious the film – and that's the 180-degree projection system called Omnimax, which works with a special camera and a 70mm horizontally progressing – rolling loop – film.

There are fewer than a dozen Omnimax cinemas in existence, of which two are to be found in Paris. One is La Géode, the mirrored globe bounced off the Cité des Sciences at La Villette; and the other, its offspring, is the new Dôme-Imax on the Colline de l'Automobile beside the Grande Arche at La Défense.

Unfortunately, Omnimax owners are not the sort to produce brilliant plots. What you get is a *Readers' Digest* view of natural and man-made wonders and breathtaking shots taken from the front of moving trains, bobsleighs, cars and so on.

There are several screenings a day at both places, but you usually need to book in advance (La Géode: Tues–Sun 10am–9pm; tickets 57F/44F or 92F/79F for combined ticket with Cité des Sciences; programme details on ☎01.40.05.12.12; avoid the queues by going at 9.30am for the first showing; M° Porte-de-la-Villette/Corentin-Cariou; Le Dôme-Imax: daily 12.30–8.15pm; tickets 57F/44F; information ☎08.36.67.06.06; M°/RER line A, Grande-Arche-de-la-Défense). The films are the same for months at a time (listed in *Pariscope*, etc). Don't worry if you don't understand French – in this instance it's a positive advantage.

Also in the Parc de la Villette is the Cinaxe, which shows high-resolution action film with seats that move in synchronization with the image (part of the Cité des Sciences; Tues–Sun 11am–6pm; 34F/29F or 29F supplement to Cité des Sciences ticket; not recommended if you're pregnant or have a weak heart; no admission for under-4s).

Finally, from mid-July to mid-Aug, epics, musicals, westerns and old-time Hollywood classics are shown in the open air on the Prairie du Triangle in the Parc de la Villette (free).

Television

At the other end of the scale of screen size, French TV has six channels – three public, F2, Arte/La Cinq and F3; one subscription, Canal Plus (with some unencrypted programmes); and two commercial open broadcasts, TF1 and M6.

In addition there are the **cable** networks, including France Infos (French news), CNN, the BBC World Service, Euronews with news in the original version from around Europe, MTV and Planète specializing in documentaries.

Arte and La Cinq are two different channels sharing the same frequency. La Cinq, an educational channel, broadcasts during the day, then at 7pm, Arte, a joint Franco-German cultural venture, takes over. Its highbrow programmes, daily documentaries, Horizon from the BBC, art criticism, serious French and German movies and complete operas are transmitted simultaneously in French and German.

Canal Plus is the main **movie channel** (and financer of the French film industry), with repeats of foreign films usually shown at least once in the original language. F3 screens a fair selection of serious movies, with its Cinéma de Minuit slot late on Sunday nights good for foreign, undubbed films.

The main French **news broadcasts** are at 8.30pm on Arte and at 8pm on F2 and TF1. At 7am on Canal Plus (unencrypted) you can watch the American CBS evening news.

Theatre

Certain directors in France do extraordinary things with the medium of **theatre**. Classic texts are shuffled into theatrical moments, where spectacular and dazzling sensation takes precedence over speech. Their shows are overwhelming: huge casts, vast sets (sometimes real buildings never before used for theatre), exotic lighting effects, original music scores. It adds up to a unique experience, even if you haven't understood a word.

Ariane Mnouchkine, whose **Théâtre du Soleil** is based at the Cartoucherie in Vincennes, is the director par excellence of this form. Her production of *Les Atrides* (*The House of Atreus* in her own translation from Euripides and Aeschylus)

stunned and delighted audiences in France, Britain and the USA. It lasted ten hours – relatively short for the Théâtre du Soleil, some of whose performances have gone on for several days. In 1996 she again dazzled French and foreign critics with her interpretation of Molière's *Tartuffe*, set in a contemporary North African city with Tartuffe as a young mullah.

Peter Brook, the English director based at the Bouffes du Nord theatre, is another great magician of the all-embracing several-day show. Also a big name, though often involved in films rather than the theatre, is **Patrice Chéreau**. Any show by these three should not be missed, and there are likely to be other weird and wonderful productions by younger directors, such as Jérôme Savary, following their example.

At the same time, bourgeois farces, postwar classics, Shakespeare, Racine and the like, are staged with the same range of talent, or lack of it, that you'd find in London or New York. What you'll rarely find are the home-grown, socially concerned and realist dramas of the sort that have in the past kept theatre alive in Britain. An Edward Bond or David Edgar play crops up in translation often enough, although, frequently, such adaptations are not very successful because of the enormous differences between the British and French ways of thinking. The French equivalent, however, hardly exists.

The great generation of French or Francophone dramatists, which included Anouilh, Genet, Camus, Sartre, Adamov, Ionesco and Cocteau, came to an end with the death of **Samuel Beckett** in 1990 and Ionesco in 1994. Their plays, however, are still frequently performed. The Huchette has been playing Ionesco's *La Cantatrice Chauve* every night since October 1952, and Genet's *Les Paravents*, which set off riots on its opening night, can now be included alongside Corneille and Shakespeare in the programme of the **Comédie Française**, the national theatre for the classics.

Film, theatre and dance

Film, theatre and dance

One of the encouraging things about France and its public authorities is that they take their culture, including the theatre, seriously. Numerous theatres and theatre companies in Paris are subsidized, either wholly or in part, by the government or the Ville de Paris. And the suburbs are not left out, thanks to the ubiquitous **Maisons de Culture**, which were the brainchildren of André Malraux, man of letters, de Gaulle's wartime aide, and, eventually, in the 1960s, his Minister of Culture. Ironically, however, although they were designed to bring culture to the masses, their productions are often among the most "difficult" and intellectually inaccessible.

Another plus is the openness to **foreign influence** and foreign work. There is little xenophobia in Paris theatre; Argentinian Jorge Lavelli and Catalan Lluis Pasqual direct at the Théâtre National de la Colline and at the Odéon, and foreign artists are as welcome as they've always been. In any month there might be an Italian, Mexican, German or Brazilian production playing in the original language, or offerings by radical groups from Turkey, Iraq or China, who have no possibilities of a home venue.

The best time of all for theatre lovers to come to Paris is for the **Festival d'Automne** from end-September to December (see p.35), an international celebration of all the performing arts, which attracts stage directors of the calibre of the American Bob Wilson, who directed the Opéra Bastille's highly successful *Magic Flute*, and Polish director Tadeusz Kantor.

Noteworthy venues

Bouffes du Nord, 37bis bd de la Chapelle, 10ᵉ; ☎01.46.07.34.50 (Mᵒ La Chapelle). Peter Brook has made this his Paris base, where he occasionally produces epic events. The rest of the time the theatre invites renowned international directors as well as hosts jazz concerts.

Cartoucherie, rte du Champ-de-Manoeuvre, 12ᵉ (Mᵒ Château-de-Vincennes). As well as the Théâtre du Soleil (see p.316; ☎01.43.74.24.08), the Cartoucherie is home to the French-Spanish troupe, Théâtre de l'Épée de Bois (☎01.43.08.39.74), the Théâtre de la Tempête (☎01.43.28.36.36), the Théâtre du Chaudron (☎01.43.28.97.04) and the Théâtre de l'Aquarium (☎01.43.74.99.61).

Comédie Française (national theatre), 2 rue de Richelieu, 1ᵉʳ; ☎01.44.58.15.15 (Mᵒ Palais-Royal). The national theatre for the classics. However, the trend now seems to be to cut down on traditional productions, with the exception of

Molière and Feydeau, in favour of more contemporary work and modernized versions of the classics.

Maison des Arts de Créteil, place Salvador-Allende, Créteil; ☎01.45.13.19.19 (M° Créteil-Préfecture). As well as its movie programmes (see box on p.314), this also serves as a lively suburban theatre with a festival near the beginning of May, Festival Exit, of multi-cultural performance.

Maison de la Culture de Bobigny, 1 bd Lénine, Bobigny; ☎01.41.60.72.72 (M° Pablo-Picasso). The resident company, MC93, succeeds with highly challenging productions, for example a dramatization of *De Rerum Natura (The Nature of Things)* a scientific treatise by the first-century BC Roman poet Lucretius, using the auditorium as stage, considerable amounts of Latin, a boxing match, mime and giant swings.

Odéon Théâtre de l'Europe (national theatre), 1 place Paul-Claudel, 6e; ☎01.44.41.36.36 (M° Odéon). Contemporary plays, as well as *version originale* productions by well-known foreign companies. During May 1968, this theatre was occupied by students and became an open parliament with the backing of its directors, Jean-Louis Barrault (of Baptiste fame in *Les Enfants du Paradis* and who died in 1994) and Madeleine Renaud, one of the great French stage actresses. Promptly sacked by de Gaulle's Minister for Culture, they formed a new company and moved to the disused Gare d'Orsay. Their final years in the Théâtre du Rond-Point gave Paris its best performances of Beckett.

Théâtre des Amandiers, 7 av Pablo-Picasso, Nanterre, 92; ☎01.46.14.70.00 (RER Nanterre-Université and theatre bus). Renowned as the suburban base for Jean-Paul Vincent's exciting productions.

Théâtre des Artistic-Athévains, 45bis rue Richard-Lenoir, 11e; ☎01.43.56.38.32 (M° Voltaire). Small company heavily involved in community and educational theatre.

Théâtre de la Bastille, 79 rue de la Roquette, 11e; ☎01.43.57.42.14 (M° Bastille). One of the best places for new work and fringe productions.

Théâtre de la Colline (national theatre), 15 rue Malte-Brun, 20e; ☎01.44.62.52.52 (M° Gambetta). Most of the work put on by Jorge Lavelli is twentieth-century and innovative, and nearly always worth seeing.

Théâtre de la Commune, 2 rue Edouard-Poisson, Aubervilliers; ☎01.48.33.93.93 (M° Aubervilliers). Suburban theatre with an excellent reputation based on the work of director Brigitte Jacques.

Théâtre de l'Est Parisien, 159 av Gambetta, 20e; ☎01.43.64.80.80 (M° Gambetta). Well respected for its innovative work.

Théâtre de Gennevilliers, Centre Dramatique National, 41 av des Grésillons, Gennevilliers; ☎01.41.32.26.26 (M° Gabriel-Péri). Several stimulating productions by Bernard Sobel have brought acclaim – and audiences – to this suburban venue in recent years.

Théâtre de la Main-d'Or, 15 passage de la Main-d'Or, 11e; ☎01.48.05.67.89 (M° Bastille). An interesting experimental space, with occasional classics and English productions including a festival of English theatre in the spring.

Théâtre National de Chaillot (national theatre), Palais de Chaillot, place du Trocadéro, 16e; ☎01.53.65.30.00 (M° Trocadéro). The great Antoine Vitez may be no more, but the mega-spectacles go on under the directorship of Jérôme Savary. Roger Planchon from Lyon has some of his Parisian showings here, which even in French are accessible to foreign audiences with an innovative individual translation system.

Théâtre de Nesle, 8 rue de Nesle, 6e; ☎01.46.34.61.04 (M° Odéon). New French work, as well as English and American.

Théatre Silvia-Montfort, Parc Georges-Brassens, 106 rue Briançon, 15e;

Film, theatre and dance

**Film,
theatre and
dance**

☎01.45.31.10.96 (M° Porte-de-Vanves).
A pyramidal theatre, playing "classics"
such as Anouilh, but also dedicated to
staging original works.

Café-théâtre

Literally a revue, monologue or mini-play
performed in a place where you can
drink, and sometimes eat, **café-théâtre** is
probably less accessible than a Racine
tragedy at the Comédie Française. The
humour or puerile dirty jokes, wordplay,
and allusions to current fads, phobias
and politicians can leave even a fluent
French speaker in the dark.

To give it a try, the main **venues** are
concentrated around the Marais. Tickets
average around 80F, and it's best to
book in advance – the spaces are small
– though you have a good chance of
getting in on the night during the week.

Blancs-Manteaux, 15 rue des Blancs-
Manteaux, 4e; ☎01.48.87.15.84 (M°
Hôtel-de-Ville/Rambuteau). Somewhat
cramped venue, beneath a restaurant.

Café de la Gare, 41 rue du Temple, 4e;
☎01.42.78.52.51 (M° Hôtel-de-
Ville/Rambuteau). This may not be operating its turn-of-the-wheel admission
price system any more, but it has
retained a reputation for novelty.

Point Virgule, 7 rue Ste-Croix-de-la-
Bretonnerie, 4e; ☎01.42.78.67.03 (M°
Hôtel-de-Ville/St-Paul). With a policy for
giving unknown performers a go, you
can sometimes strike lucky, sometimes
not.

Dance and mime

In the 1970s all the dancers left Paris for
New York, and only **mime** remained as
the great performing art of the French,
thanks to the Lecoq School of Mime and
Improvisation, and the famous practition-
er **Marcel Marceau** and his school.
Marceau, now in his 70s, continues to
perform and remains incomparable, with
no new pure mime artists of his stature
to have appeared. Lecoq foreign graduates return to their own countries, while
the French incorporate their skills into

dance, comedy routines and improvisation. While this cross-fertilization has
given rise to new standards in performing art, it's still a pity that mime by itself
is rarely seen.

The best-known and loved French
performance artist, **Coluche**, died in a
motorcycle accident in 1986. Most of his
acts were incomprehensible to foreigners, save jests such as starting a campaign for the presidency, for which he
posed nude with a feather up his bum.
A troupe of mimes and **clowns** who
debunk the serious in literature rather
than politics are La Clown Kompanie,
famous for their Shakespearean
tragedies turned into farce. Joëlle Bouvier
and Régis Obadia trained both at dance
school and at Lecoq; their company,
L'Esquisse, combines both disciplines,
takes inspiration from paintings, and por-
trays a dark, hallucinatory world.

The renaissance of French **dance** in
the 1980s was not, on the whole, Paris-
based. Subsidies have gone to regional
companies expressly to decentralize the
arts. But all the best contemporary practi-
tioners come to the capital regularly.
Names to look out for are Régine
Chopinot's troupe from La Rochelle, Jean-
Claude Gallotta's from Grenoble, Roland
Petit's from Marseille, Dominique
Bagouet's from Montpellier, and Joëlle
Bouvier and Régis Obadia's from Angers.
Creative choreographers based in or
around Paris include Maguy Marin,
Karine Saporta, François Verret, Jean-
François Duroure and the Californian
Carolyn Carlson.

Humour, everyday actions and obses-
sions, social problems, and the darker
shades of life find expression in the myriad of current dance forms. A multi-
dimensional performing art is created by
combinations of movement, mime, ballet,
music from the medieval to contemporary jazz-rock, speech, noise, and theatrical effects. The Gallotta-choreographed
film *Rei-Dom* opened up a whole new
range of possibilities. Many of the traits
of the modern epic theatre are shared
with dance, including crossing international frontiers.

Many of the **theatres** listed above (see pp.318–319) include both mime and dance in their programmes: the Théâtre de la Bastille shows works by young dancers and choreographers; Maguy Marin's company is based at the Créteil Maison des Arts and François Verret's at the Maison de la Culture in Bobigny, where a prestigious competition for young choreographers is held in March; and the Théâtre des Amandiers in Nanterre hosts major contemporary works.

Plenty of space and critical attention are also given to **tap**, **tango**, **folk** and **jazz dancing**, and to visiting traditional dance troupes from all over the world. There are also a dozen or so black African companies in Paris, who, predictably, find it hard to to compete with Europeans and the fashionable Japanese *butoh* for venues, as well as several Indian dance troupes, the Ballet Classique Khmer, and many more from exiled cultures.

As for **ballet**, the principal stage is at the newly renovated Opéra Garnier, home to the Ballet de l'Opéra National de Paris. After a troubled period under the directorship of the late, great Rudolf Nureyev, many of the best French classical dancers have returned to the company, with the exception, however, of the ravishing superstar Sylvie Guillem who is determined to plough her own independent furrow. Paris has also lost Maurice Béjart – wooed back to his home town of Marseille – who used to run the Ballet du XXᵉ Siècle. But ballet fans can still be sure of masterly performances, at the Opéra Garnier, the Opéra Bastille, the Théâtre des Champs-Élysées and the Théâtre Musical de Paris.

The highlight of the year for dance is the **Concours International de Danse de Paris** in October and November, which involves contemporary, classical and different national traditions (☎01.45.22.28.74). Other festivals combining theatre, dance, mime, classical music and its descendants include the Festival Exit in Créteil, the Paris Quartier

d'Été from mid-July to mid-August (☎01.44.94.98.00) and the Festival d'Automne from mid-September to mid-December (☎01.53.45.17.00), where Trisha Brown always makes an appearance.

Venues

Centre Beaubourg, rue Beaubourg, 4ᵉ; ☎01.44.78.13.15 (Mᵒ Rambuteau/RER Châtelet-Les Halles). The Grande Salle in the basement is used for dance performances by visiting companies.

Centre Mandapa, 6 rue Wurtz, 13ᵉ; ☎01.45.89.01.60 (Mᵒ Glacière). The one theatre dedicated to traditional dances from around the world.

L'Espace Kiron, 10 rue la Vacquerie, 11ᵉ; ☎01.44.64.11.50 (Mᵒ Voltaire). Venue for experimental dance and performance art.

Ferme du Boisson, 77 allée de la Ferme, Noisiel; ☎01.64.62.77.77 (RER Noisiel). A suburban venue renowned for avant-garde perfomances.

Opéra de Bastille, place de la Bastille, 12ᵉ; ☎01.40.01.17.89 (Mᵒ Bastille). Stages some productions by the Ballet de l'Opéra National de Paris, but in general its programme moves away from the classics.

Opéra de Paris Garnier, place de l'Opéra, 9ᵉ; ☎01.40.01.17.89 (Mᵒ Opéra). Main home of the Ballet de l'Opéra National de Paris and the place to see ballet classics.

Regard du Cygne, 210 rue de Belleville, 20ᵉ; ☎01.43.58.55.93 (Mᵒ Place-des-Fêtes). Innovative and exciting new work by companies such as Fabrice Dugied's troupe are performed here.

Théâtre de la Bastille, 76 rue de la Roquette, 11ᵉ; ☎01.43.57.42.14 (Mᵒ Bastille). As well as more traditional theatre, there are also dance and mime performances including productions by the Théâtre Contemporain de la Danse.

Théâtre des Champs-Élysées, 15 av Montaigne, 8ᵉ; ☎01.49.52.50.50 (Mᵒ Alma-Marceau). Forever aiming to outdo

Film, theatre and dance

**Film,
theatre and
dance**

the Opéra with even grander and more expensive ballet productions. Recently welcomed the National Ballet of Cuba.

Théâtre Musical de Paris, place du Châtelet, 4e; ☎01.40.28.28.40 (M° Châtelet). It was here, in 1910, that Diaghilev put on the first season of Russian ballet, assisted by Cocteau. Though mainly used for classical con-

certs and opera, it hosts top-notch visiting ballet companies.

Théâtre de la Ville, 2 place du Châtelet, 4e; ☎01.42.74.22.77 (M° Châtelet). The height of success for dance productions is to end up here. Karine Saporta's work is regularly featured as is Maguy Marin and Pina Bausch, together with modern theatre classics, comedy and concerts.

Chapter 16

Shops and markets

Flair for style and design is as evident in the shops of Paris as it is in other aspects of the city's life. Parisians' fierce attachment to their small local traders, especially when it comes to food, has kept alive a wonderful variety, despite pressures to concentrate consumption in gargantuan underground and multi-storey complexes.

Even if you don't plan – or can't afford – to buy, Parisian **shops** can be one of the chief delights of the city. Some of the most entertaining and tempting are those small, cluttered affairs that reflect their owners' particular passions. You'll find traders in offbeat merchandise in every quartier.

Markets, too, are a grand spectacle. Mouthwatering arrays of food from half the countries of the globe, intoxicating in their colour, shape and smell, assail the senses in even the drabbest parts of town. In Belleville and the Goutte d'Or, North Africa predominates; Southeast Asia in the 13ᵉ arrondissement. Though the food is perhaps the best offering of the Paris markets, there are also street markets dedicated to second-hand goods

(the *marchés aux puces*), clothes and textiles, flowers, birds, books and stamps.

Shops

The most distinctive and unusual shopping possibilities are in the nineteenth-century arcades of the *passages* in the 2ᵉ and 9ᵉ arrondissements, almost all now smartly renovated. On the streets proper, the square kilometre around **place St-Germain-des-Près** is hard to beat, packed with books, antiques, gorgeous garments, artworks and playthings.

Les Halles is another well-shopped district, with its focus the submarine shopping complex of the Forum des Halles, good for everything from records through to designer clothes. The aristocratic **Marais** and the trendy quartier of the **Bastille** and northeastern Paris to **Ménilmontant** have filled up with dinky little boutiques, arty and specialist shops and galleries. For window-shopping Parisian **haute couture** – Hermès and the like – the two traditional areas are av Montaigne, rue François-1ᵉʳ and rue

Toy shops, and shops selling children's clothes and books, are detailed in Chapter 18.

Opening hours

The majority of shops in Paris now stay **open all day** from Monday to Saturday. Most tend to close comparatively late – 7 or 8pm as often as not. Some smaller businesses still close for up to two hours at lunchtime, somewhere between noon and 3pm. Most shops are closed on Sunday and many on Monday as well, though many food shops, such as boulangeries, will open on Sunday morning, and other shops, such as clothes or book shops, will take only Monday morning off.

Shops and markets

For a list of late-night pharmacies, see p.369.

Late-night shopping

The **Drugstore** at 133 av Champs-Élysées, 8ᵉ (Mᵒ Charles-de-Gaulle/Étoile), is open for books, newspapers, tobacco and all kinds of gift gadgetry daily from 10am until 2am every night.

In addition, you could try:

Prisunic supermarket, 109 rue de la Boétie, 8ᵉ (Mᵒ Franklin-D-Roosevelt). Open till midnight Mon–Sat.

Boulangerie de l'Ancienne-Comédie, 10 rue de l'Ancienne-Comédie, 6ᵉ (Mᵒ Odéon). Open 24hr daily.

Kiosque, place Charles-de-Gaulle, 8ᵉ (Mᵒ Charles-de-Gaulle/Étoile). Newsagents open 24hr daily.

TABACS

La Favourite, 3 bd St-Michel, 5ᵉ (Mᵒ St-Michel). Daily to 2am.

Old Navy, 150 bd St-Germain, 6ᵉ (Mᵒ St-Germain-des-Près). Open till 5am.

Shell Garage, 6 bd Raspail, 7ᵉ (Mᵒ Rue-du-Bac). 24hr food shop and garage.

PETROL STATIONS

There are two dozen or so petrol stations in the city that stay open 24hr. The following are some central addresses:

Esso, 336 rue St-Honoré, 1ᵉʳ.

Garage St-Bernard, 36 rue des Fossés-St-Bernard, 5ᵉ.

Shell, underground car park, place de la Bourse, 2ᵉ; 10 rue de Bailleul, 1ᵉʳ; and 6 bd Raspail, 7ᵉ.

---

du Faubourg-St-Honoré in the 8ᵉ, and av Victor-Hugo in the 16ᵉ. The fashionable newer designers, led by the Japanese, are to be found around place des Victoires in the 1ᵉʳ and 2ᵉ.

For **food** and essentials, the cheapest supermarket chain is Ed l'Épicier. Other last-minute or convenience shopping is probably best at FNAC shops (for books and records) and the big department stores (for everything else).

Art and design

The **commercial art galleries** are concentrated in four main areas: in **the 8ᵉ**, especially in and around av Matignon; in the Marais; around the Bastille; and in St-Germain. A new crop of next-generation conceptual art galleries are located in **rue Louise-Weiss** in the 13ᵉ, just west of the new Bibliotheque Nationale de France-Mitterand.

There are literally hundreds of galleries, and for an idea of who is being exhibited where, *Pariscope* carries details of major exhibitions under "Expositions". Or look in *L'Officiel des Spectacles* under "Galeries". Entry to commercial galleries is free to all.

ART SUPPLIES

Paris American Art, 2 & 4 rue Bonaparte, 6ᵉ; ☎01.43.26.09.93 (Mᵒ St-Germain-des-Près). Local art suppliers for the Beaux-Arts students residing around the corner. Tues–Sat 10am–1pm & 2–6.30pm.

DESIGN

A small selection of places where contemporary and the best of twentieth-century **design** can be seen is listed below. Also worth checking out are the shops of the art and design museums, and the **rue Oberkampf** in Ménilmontant with a particularly high concentration of shops specializing in particular periods.

En Attendant les Barbares, 50 rue Étienne-Marcel, 2ᵉ; ☎01.45.39.59.40 (Mᵒ Châtelet-Les Halles). The style known as neo-Barbarian: Baroque gilding on bizarre experimental forms. Nothing you'd actually trust your weight to, but fun to look at. Tues–Fri 10.30am–7pm, Mon 10.30am–1pm & 2–7pm, Sat 11am–6.30pm.

Décalage, 33 rue des Francs-Bourgeois, 4ᵉ; ☎01.42.77.55.72 (Mᵒ St-Paul).

Beautiful hand-crafted jewellery – unusual, yet reasonably priced. Also, a good range of lights, from antique to contemporary. Sun & Mon 2–7pm, Tues–Sat 11am–7pm.

Dream On, 31 rue de Charonne, 11e; ☎01.47.00.41.44 (M° Ledru-Rollin). Corner shop that specializes in 1960s furniture. Mon–Sat 10.30am–7.30pm.

Le Chat Huant, 50–52 rue Galande, 5e; ☎01.46.33.67.56 (M° Maubert-Mutualité). Classy shop crammed full of beautiful, covetable Eastern objects, from ceramics to dressing gowns. Mon 1–7pm, Tues–Sun 11am–7pm.

Eugénie Seigneur, 16 rue Charlot, 3e; ☎01.48.04.81.96 (M° République). The place to take your print or original for a highly unique frame. Also sells one-off beautiful old floral tiles (120F), mirrors and interesting brooches. Mon–Fri 10am–7pm, Sat 10am–1pm & 3–7pm.

Fiesta Galerie, 45 rue Vieille-du-Temple, 4e; ☎01.42.71.53.34 (M° Hôtel-de-Ville). A big selection of twentieth-century kitsch objects. Thurs–Sat noon–7pm, Sun & Mon 2–7pm.

Galerie Documents, 53 rue de Seine, 6e; ☎01.43.54.50.68 (M° Odéon). Best antique posters. Mon 2.30–7pm, Tues–Sat 10.30am–7pm.

Galerie Maeght, 42 rue du Bac, 7e; ☎01.45.48.45.15 (M° Rue-du-Bac). Famous gallery that makes its own beautifully printed art books. Tues–Sat 9.30am–7pm.

Louvre des Antiquaires, 2 place du Palais-Royal, 1er; ☎01.42.97.27.00 (M° Palais-Royal/Musée-du-Louvre). An enormous antiques and furniture hypermarket where you can pick up anything from a Mycenaean seal ring to an Art Nouveau vase – for a price. Tues–Sun 11am–7pm; closed Sun in July and Aug.

Lulu Berlu, 27 rue Oberkampf, 6e; ☎01.43.55.12.52 (M° Oberkampf). Crammed with twentieth-century toys and curios, most with their original packaging. Mon–Sat noon–9pm, Sun 3–9pm.

Le Viaduc des Arts, 9–129 av Daumesnil, 12e (M° Bastille/Gare de Lyon). Practically the entire north side of the street is dedicated to an extremely high standard of skilled workmanship and craft. Each arch of this old railway viaduct houses a shop front and workspace for the artists within. Walk the length of the viaduct for a show of contemporary metalwork, ceramics, tapestry, sculpture and much more.

Bookshops

Books are not cheap in France – foreign books least of all. But don't let that stop you browsing. The best areas are the Seine **quais** with their rows of stalls perched against the river parapet and the narrow streets of the **Quartier Latin**, but don't neglect the array of specialist shops listed below.

ENGLISH-LANGUAGE

English-language bookshops operate as home-away-from-home for expats, often with readings from visiting writers, and sometimes handy notice boards for apartment-shares, language lessons and work. The Australian Bookshop and Abbey's in particular operate as cultural ambassadors for Australia and Canada respectively, with a large range of the national literature available in French translation.

Abbey Bookshop/La Librairie Canadienne, 29 rue de la Parcheminerie, 5e; ☎01.46.33.16.24 (M° St-Michel). A Canadian bookshop round the corner from Shakespeare & Co. with lots of second-hand British and North American fiction; good social and political science sections; knowledgeable and helpful staff – and free coffee. Mon–Sat 10am–7pm.

Australian Bookshop, 33 Quai des Grands Augustins, 6e; ☎01.43.29.08.65 (M° St-Michel). Friendly Australian-run place in a great spot right opposite the Seine. Australian books in French and in English, mostly new, a few second-hand. They often have Australian authors reading here – call for details. Tues–Sun 11am–7pm.

Shops and markets

Shops and markets

Brentano's, 37 av de l'Opéra, 2ᵉ; ☎01.42.61.52.50 (M° Opéra). English and American books. Good section for kids, with storytelling on Wednesday afternoons and Saturday mornings. Mon–Sat 10am–7pm.

Galignani, 224 rue de Rivoli, 1ᵉʳ; ☎01.42.60.76.07 (M° Concorde). Good range, including fine art and children's books, in a business that claims to be the first English bookshop established on the Continent way back in 1802. Mon–Sat 10am–7pm.

Gibert Joseph, see Gibert Jeune, below.

San Francisco Bookshop, 17 rue Monsieur le Prince, 6ᵉ; ☎01.43.29.15.70. (M° Odéon). American-run second-hand bookshop with a selection of contemporary literature that would be impressive anywhere. Quite a collection of books on jazz, and sections for everything from gay and lesbian to Latin American studies. Well-organized and calm – not a social hang-out. Mon–Sat 11am–9pm, Sun 2–9pm; in summer extended hours on Fri & Sat until 11pm.

Shakespeare & Co., 37 rue de la Bûcherie, 5ᵉ; ☎01.43.26.96.50 (M° Maubert-Mutualité). A cosy, friendly, famous American-run literary haunt, with the biggest selection of second-hand English books in town, plus a selection of new titles, staffed by young would-be writers. Also poetry readings and such. There's a huge and useful notice board outside. Noon–midnight every day.

Tea and Tattered Pages, 24 rue Mayet, 6ᵉ; ☎01.40.65.94.35 (M° Duroc). American-run second-hand bookshop with more than 15,000 titles in English. You can munch on cheesecake, brownies and the like in the small attached *salon de thé*, and there's a bookish Sunday brunch for 85F. Daily 11am–7pm.

Village Voice, 6 rue Princesse, 6ᵉ; ☎01.46.33.36.47 (M° Mabillon). Principally poetry and modern literature, both British and American, and regular poetry readings. Mon 2–8pm, Tues–Sat 11am–8pm.

W H Smith, 248 rue de Rivoli, 1ᵉʳ; ☎01.44.77.88.99 (M° Concorde). Parisian outlet of the British chain. Wide range of new books, newspapers and magazines. Mon–Sat 9.30am–7pm.

GENERAL FRENCH

For general **French titles**, the biggest and most convenient shop has to be the FNAC in the Forum des Halles, though it's hardly the most congenial of places. If you fancy a prolonged session of browsing, the other general bookshops below are probably more suitable.

FNAC, at the Forum des Halles, *niveau 2*, Porte Pierre-Lescot (M°/RER Châtelet-Les Halles). Also at 136 rue de Rennes, 6ᵉ (M° Montparnasse); 26 av des Ternes, 17ᵉ (M° Ternes); and CNIT, 2 place de la Défense (M° La Défense). Lots of *bandes dessinées*, guidebooks and maps, among everything else. Mon–Sat 10am–7.30pm.

Gallimard, 15 bd Raspail, 7ᵉ (M° Sèvres-Babylone). The shop of the great French publisher. Mon–Sat 10am–7pm.

Gibert Jeune, 6 place St-Michel, 5ᵉ and 27 quai St-Michel, 5ᵉ (both M° St-Michel). With lots of sales, some English books and second-hand, too. These are the number-one suppliers of school and university set books. Their chain of shops now stretches up bd St-Michel. For English literature, go to Gibert Joseph at 26 bd St-Michel. Mon–Sat 9.30am–7.30pm.

La Hune, 170 bd St-Germain, 6ᵉ (M° St-Germain-des-Prés). One of the biggest and best. Mon–Sat 10am–midnight.

La Terrasse de Gutenberg, 9 rue Émilio-Castelar, 12ᵉ; ☎01.43.07.42.15 (M° Ledru-Rollin). Excellent collection of fine and graphic art, including *bandes dessinées*, plus photographs, postcards and general books. Near the place d'Aligre market. Tues–Sun 10am–8pm.

ETHNIC FRENCH

L'Harmattan, 16 rue des Écoles, 5ᵉ; ☎01.43.26.04.52 (M° Maubert-Mutualité). Excellent, very knowledgeable bookshop, especially good for Arab/North

African literature in French, with a few titles in English. Publisher, too. Mon–Sat 10am–12.30pm & 1.30–7pm.

Présence Africaine, 25bis rue des Écoles, 5ᵉ; ☎01.43.54.13.74 (Mᵒ Maubert-Mutualité). Specialist black African bookshop, with titles ranging from literature to economics and philisophy by Caribbean and North American as well as African writers. All in French, either in translation or written by black Francophones. Mon–Sat 10am–7pm.

SECOND-HAND AND ANTIQUARIAN

In addition to the *bouquinistes* lining the Left Bank quais of the Seine, and the second-hand English-language bookshops mentioned above, you might try:

Albert Petit Siroux, Galerie Vivienne, 2ᵉ (Mᵒ Bourse). New and second-hand books, including musty leather-bound volumes on Paris and France. Mon–Sat 11am–7pm.

Gibert Jeune, see opposite

Giraud-Badin, 22 rue Guynemer, 6ᵉ (Mᵒ St-Sulpice). These are books that belong in museum collections – with prices to match. Mon–Sat 9am–1pm & 2–6pm; closed Aug.

L'Introuvable, 23 rue Juliette-Dodu, 10ᵉ (Mᵒ Colonel-Fabien). All sorts stocked, but particular specialization is detective, crime, spy and SF stories. Tues, Thurs & Fri 3–7pm, Wed 4–7pm, Sat 3.30–7pm.

Librairie Ulysse, 26 rue St-Louis-en-L'Ille, 4ᵉ; ☎01.43.25.17.35 (Mᵒ Pont-Marie/Sully-Morland). Antiquarian travel bookshop in a charming location. Tues–Sat 2–8pm.

ART AND ARCHITECTURE

Artcurial, 9 av Matignon, 8ᵉ; ☎01.42.99.16.16 (Mᵒ Franklin-D-Roosevelt). *The* art bookshop in Paris – French and foreign editions. There is also a gallery, which puts on interesting exhibitions. 10am–7.15pm; closed Mon and two weeks in Aug.

Librairie de l'École Superieure des Beaux Arts, 17 quai Malaquais, 6ᵉ;

☎01.47.03.50.70 (Mᵒ St-Germain-des-Près). The bookshop of the national Fine Art school: own publications, posters, reproductions, postcards, etc. Mon–Fri 10am–6pm; closed Aug.

Librairie du Musée d'Art Moderne de la Ville de Paris, Palais de Tokyo, 11 av du Président-Wilson, 16ᵉ (Mᵒ Iéna). Specialist publications on modern art, including foreign works. Tues–Sun 10am–5.30pm.

Librairie du Musée des Arts Décoratifs, 107 rue de Rivoli, 1ᵉʳ; ☎01.42.96.21.31 (Mᵒ Palais-Royal). Design, posters, architecture, graphics, etc. Daily 10am–7pm.

AUTOGRAPHS

Librairie de l'Abbaye, 27 rue Bonaparte, 6ᵉ; ☎01.43.54.89.99 (Mᵒ St-Germain-des-Près). Signatures of the famous. Good for a browse. Tues–Sat 10am–12.30pm & 2–7pm; closed Aug.

COMICS/BANDES DESSINÉES

Album, 60 rue Monsieur-le-Prince, 6ᵉ; ☎01.43.26.19.32 (Mᵒ Odéon). Also at 6–8 rue Dante, 5ᵉ (Mᵒ Maubert-Mutualité). Vast collection of French, US and other comics, some of them the rarest editions with original artwork. Tues–Sat 10am–8pm.

Boulinier, 20 bd St-Michel, 6ᵉ; ☎01.43.26.76.96 (Mᵒ St-Michel). Renowned for its selection of new and second-hand comics, including many that are difficult to obtain. Good collection of second-hand CDs as well. Mon–Sat 9am–midnight, Sun 2pm–midnight.

Librairie d'Images, 84 bd St-Germain, cnr rue St-Jaques, 6ᵉ; ☎01.43.25.25.68 (Mᵒ Cluny-La-Sorbonne/Maubert-Mutualité). Big range of new comic books and luxury editions but the best thing about this place is the comic-related paraphernalia: posters, t-shirts, models, from Asterix through to Tweety Bird and The Simpsons. Mon–Sat 10am–8pm, Sun noon–7pm.

Thé-Troc, 52 rue Jean-Pierre-Timbaud, 11ᵉ; ☎01.43.55.54.80 (Mᵒ Parmentier).

Shops and markets

Shops and markets

The friendly owner publishes *The Fabulous Furry Freak Brothers* in French (*Les Fabuleux Freak Brothers*) and English; he is a friend of the author of the famous Seventies comics, Gilbert Shelton, who lives nearby. There are other comic books on sale, too, among Freak Bros books, T-shirts and posters, as well as a wide selection of teas and tea pots, second-hand records, jewellery and assorted junk. The attached *salon de thé* (until 7pm) is comfy, colourful and restful, with board-games to play. Mon–Fri 9am–8pm, Sat 11am–8pm.

COOKERY, GARDENING, CRAFTS

Librairie Gourmande, 4 rue Dante, 6e; ☎01.43.54.37.27 (M° Maubert-Mutualité). The very last word in books about cooking. Daily 10am–7pm, Sun 2.30–7pm.

La Maison Rustique, 26 rue Jacob, 6e; ☎01.43.25.67.00 (M° St-Germain-des-Près). Books – many in English – on all kinds of country and outdoor interests, from gardening to pruning olive trees and identifying wild flowers and birds. Mon–Sat 10am–7pm.

FEMINIST

Librarie des Femmes, 74 rue de Seine, 6e; ☎01.43.29.50.75 (M° Mabillon). Large bookshop run by Antoinette Fouque's political group. Mon–Sat 10am–7pm.

GAY AND LESBIAN

Les Mots à la Bouche, 6 rue Ste-Croix-de-la-Bretonnerie, 4e; ☎01.42.78.88.30 (M° Hôtel-de-Ville). Selling mainly gay-interest books, guides and magazines, plus some lesbian titles. There's a section with English-language literature, and the staff speak English well. A handy place for contacts, with a good notice board and a stack of free listings magazines. Mon–Sat 11am–11pm, Sun 2–8pm.

LEFTIST AVANT-GARDE

Actualités, 38 rue Dauphine, 6e; ☎01.43.26.35.62 (M° Odéon). Literature (foreign included), philosophy, *bandes dessinées* (especially US comic books), etc. Tues–Sat 11am–1pm & 2–7pm.

Parallèles, 47 rue St-Honoré, 1er; ☎01.42.33.62.70 (M° Châtelet-Les Halles). The place to go for green, feminist, anti-racist, and socialist publications. As well as most of the "underground" press, you can pick up info on current events, demos and more. Good, too, on music and comics. Mon–Sat 10am–7pm.

PERFORMING ARTS

Les Feux de la Rampe, 2 rue de Luynes, 7e (M° Bac). Books, scripts, stills, etc. Tues–Sat 11am–1pm & 2.30–7pm; closed three weeks in July and Aug 15.

Librairie Bonaparte, 31 rue Bonaparte, 6e; ☎01.43.26.97.56 (M° St-Germain-des-Près). Exhaustive stock of books on ballet, theatre, opera, puppets, music hall, *chansonniers* and the like, and some prints. Mon–Sat 10am–7pm; closed Aug.

POETRY

L'Arbre Voyageur, 55 rue Mouffetard, 5e; ☎01.47.07.98.34 (M° Monge). Poetry from all over the world, plus readings, discussions and exhibitions. Tues–Thurs 11am–8pm, Fri & Sat 11am–midnight, Sun 11am–8pm.

L'Envers du Miroir, 19 rue de Seine, 6e; ☎01.43.54.45.13 (M° Mabillon). Some fine and rare editions of modern poetry, as well as periodicals. Tues–Sat 2–7pm; closed Aug.

TRAVEL

L'Astrolabe, 46 rue de Provence, 9e; ☎01.42.85.42.95 (M° Le-Peletier). Every conceivable map, French and foreign; guidebooks; climbing and hiking guides; sailing, natural history, etc. Mon–Sat 9.30am–7pm.

Institut Géographique National (IGN), 107 rue La-Boétie, 8e; ☎01.43.98.85.00 (M° Miromesnil). The French Ordnance Survey: the best for maps of France and the entire world, plus guidebooks, satellite photos, day packs, map holders, etc. Mon–Fri 9.30am–7pm, Sat 12.30–6.30pm.

Clothes

There may be no way you can get to see the haute couture shows (see the box below), but there's nothing to prevent you trying on fabulously expensive creations by famous **couturiers** in rue du Faubourg-St-Honoré, av François-1er and av Victor-Hugo – apart from the intimidating air of the assistants and the awesome chill of the marble portals. Likewise, you can visit the **younger designers** round place des Victoires and in the Marais and St-Germain area. The long-time darling of the glitterati is **Azzedine Alaïa**, who is to fashion what Jean Nouvel is to architecture and Philippe Starck to interior design – together they form the triumvirate of Paris style. **Jean-Paul Gaultier** remains as popular as ever for his anti-fashion fash-

ion and former model **Inès de la Fressange** produces her own lines. Foreign designers like **Jil Sander** from Germany are competing with the wares of Japanese stylists, while two of Paris' most written about and talented designers are in fact British – **John Galliano** at Dior and the controversial **Alexander McQueen** at Givenchy. Another young British designer recently transferred to Paris and receiving plenty of column inches is **Stella McCartney** at Chloé.

End-of-line and old stock of the couturiers are sold all year round in discount shops (listed on p.331). For clothes without the fancy labels, the best area is the 6e: round rue de Rennes, rue de Sèvres and, in particular, rue St-Placide and rue St-Dominique in the neighbouring 7e. The **department stores** Galeries Lafayette and Au Printemps have good selections of

Shops and markets

The common signs you see in clothes stores, vente en gros *and* vente en détail *(or* vente aux particuliers*), mean "wholesale" and "retail", respectively.*

The haute couture shows

Invitations to the January and July **haute couture shows** go out exclusively to the élite of the world's fashion editors and to the 2000 or so clients who don't flinch at price tags between £10,000 and £100,000 for a dress. The world's press have a field day as the top hotels, restaurants and palace venues disgorge famous bodies cloaked in famous names. Mrs ex-Trump thrills the press by saying husbands come and go but couturiers are worth hanging onto, and every arbiter of taste and style maintains the myth that fashion is the height of human attainment. The truth, of course, is that the catwalks and the clientele are there to promote more mass-consumed luxuries, *prêt-à-porter* (ready-to-wear) lines and perfumes.

During the early 1990s, with the Gulf War keeping Gulf princesses away and the fear of terrorist bombs deterring Americans, fashion-house accountants began to question the cost-effectiveness of haute couture collections; fewer clothes were shown and some couturiers switched to producing videos. But the super-rich have weathered the

recessions as they always do and are happily flocking to the lavish shows of Dior's John Galliano, Givenchy's Alexander McQueen, Chanel's Karl Lagerfeld, Yves St-Laurent, Christian Lacroix and Valentino. The Carrousel du Louvre has a subterranean space specially designed for fashion shows, but designers have taken to making their statements in sports stadiums, the Grande Arche de la Défense or, in the case of Alexander McQueen's 1998 show for Givenchy, in Paris' indoor circus, the Cirque d'Hiver, the interior transformed into an Amazonian jungle, with the show opening with a Lady Godiva-like naked model on a white horse. In the same year, John Galliano's showing for Dior, was held on a closed-off platform at Gare d'Austerlitz, which was transformed into a Moroccan scene. Models now command mega-fees – about forty percent of the budget for most shows – and music is as important as visual effects. The requisite minimum of 75 garments has been reduced to 50, but they must still all be hand-sewn by a minimum of twenty production workers.

Shops and markets

Big names in Paris fashion

Prices at Paris' big-name fashion emporia are well into the stratosphere. The addresses below are those of the main or most conveniently located shops.

Agnès B, 6 rue du Jour, 1er (M° Châtelet-Les Halles).

Azzedine Alaïa, 7 rue de Moussy, 4e (M° Hôtel-de-Ville).

Balenciaga, 12 rue François-1er, 8e (M° George-V).

Balmain, 44 rue François-1er, 8e (M° George-V).

Cacharel, 5 place des Victoires, 2e (M° Bourse).

Calvin Klein, 45 av Montaigne, 8e (M° Franklin-D-Roosevelt).

Carven, 6 rond-point des Champs-Élysées-M-Daussault, 8e (M° Franklin-D-Roosevelt).

Castelbajac, 5 rue des Petits-Champs, 1er (M° Pyramides).

Cerruti, 3 place de la Madeleine, 8e (M° Madeleine).

Chanel, 31 rue Cambon, 1er (M° Madeleine).

Chloë, 54 rue du Faubourg-St-Honoré, 8e (M° Madeleine).

Christian Lacroix, 73 rue du Faubourg-St-Honoré, 8e (M° Concorde).

Claude Montana, 3 rue des Petits-Champs, 1er (M° Bourse/Pyramides).

Comme des Garçons, 40–42 rue Étienne-Marcel, 2e (M° Étienne-Marcel).

Courrèges, 40 rue François-1er, 8e (M° George-V).

Dior, 30 av Montaigne, 8e (M° Franklin-D-Roosevelt).

Dolce e Gabbana, 2 av Montaigne, 8e (M° Alma-Marceau).

Emmanuelle Khan, 45 av Victor-Hugo, 16e (M° Victor-Hugo).

Gianni Versace, 62 rue du Faubourg-St-Honoré, 8e (M° Concorde).

Giorgio Armani, 25 place Vendôme, 1er (M° Opéra).

Givenchy, 8 av George-V, 8e (M° Alma-Marceau).

Gucci, 2 rue du Faubourg-St-Honoré, 8e (M° Concorde).

Guy Laroche, 30 rue du Faubourg-St-Honoré, 8e (M° Concorde).

Inès de la Fressange, 14 av Montaigne, 8e (M° Alma-Marceau).

Issey Miyake, 3 place des Vosges, 4e (M° St-Paul).

Jean-Louis Scherrer, 51 av Montaigne, 8e (M° Franklin-D-Roosevelt).

Jean-Paul Gaultier, 30 rue du Faubourg-St-Antoine, 12e (M° Bastille) & 6 rue Vivienne, 2e (M° Bourse).

Jil Sander, 52 av Montaigne, 8e (M° Franklin-D-Roosevelt).

Junko Shimada, 54 rue Étienne-Marcel, 2e (M° Les Halles/RER Châtelet-Les Halles).

Karl Lagerfeld, 14 bd Madeleine, 9e (M° Opéra).

Kenzo, 3 place des Victoires, 1er (M° Bourse).

Lanvin, 22 rue du Faubourg-St-Honoré, 8e (M° Concorde).

Louis Féraud, 88 rue du Faubourg-St-Honoré, 8e (M° Madeleine).

Myrène de Prémonville, 24 rue Boissy d'Anglas, 8e (M° Madeleine).

Nina Ricci, 39 av Montaigne, 8e (M° Alma-Marceau).

Paco Rabanne, 7 rue du Cherche-Midi, 6e (M° Sèvres-Babylone).

Pierre Cardin, 83 rue du Faubourg-St-Honoré, 8e (M° Madeleine).

Prada, 10 av Montaigne, 8e (M° Alma-Marceau).

Sonia Rykiel, 175 bd St-Germain, 6e (M° St-Germain-des-Près).

Ted Lapidus, 5 rue du Faubourg-St-Honoré, 8e (M° Concorde).

Thierry Mugler, 49 av Montaigne, 8e (M° Alma-Marceau).

Ungaro, 2 av Montaigne, 8e (M° Alma-Marceau).

Valentino, 17–19 av Montaigne, 8e (M° Alma-Marceau).

Yves Saint-Laurent, 6 place St-Sulpice, 6e (M° St-Sulpice/Mabillon).

designer *prêt-à-porter*, the **Forum des Halles** is chock-a-block with clothes shops but at less competitive prices; and individual **boutiques** have taken over more and more of the Marais and the Bastille around rue de la Roquette and there are several interesting young designers with shops on nearby rue Keller.

The Les Halles end of rue de Rivoli has plenty of **chain stores**, including a Monoprix supermarket for essentials, or you can get even better bargains in the **rag-trade district** round place du Caire or place de la République, with a Printemps on the north side, Tati on the south, and the adjacent rues Meslay and Notre-Dame-de-Nazareth full of **shoe** and **clothes** shops respectively. For **jewellery** – gems and plastic – try rue du Temple and rue Montmorency.

The **sales** take place in January and July, with reductions of up to forty percent on designer clothes. This still leaves prices running into hundreds of pounds, but if you want to blow out on something bizarre and beautiful, these are the months to do it. The sales in the more run-of-the-mill shops don't offer significant reductions.

DISCOUNT

The best areas to wander for shops selling end-of-line and last year's models at thirty- to fifty-percent reductions are in rue d'Alésia in the 14ᵉ, west of place Victor-Blasch; bd Victor in the 15ᵉ between rue Lecourbe and rue Desnouettes (M° Balard); for shoes rue Meslay in the 3ᵉ; and rue St-Placide in the 6ᵉ. Before you get too excited, however, remember that twenty percent off £500 still leaves a hefty bill – not that all items are this expensive. The best times of year to join the scrums are after the new collections have come out in January and October.

L'Annexe, 48 rue St-Placide, 6ᵉ (M° St-Placide) & 138 bd St-Germain 6ᵉ (M° St-Germain-des-Près). Popular discount store for men – annexe of Le Mouton à Cinq Pattes, below – with discounts on a wide range of big names. Mon–Sat 10am–7pm.

Cacharel Stock, 114 rue d'Alésia, 14ᵉ, ☎01.45.42.53.04 (M° Alésia). Forty to fifty percent off last season's stock. Men, women and kids. Mon–Sat 10am–7pm.

La Clef des Marques, 99 rue St-Dominique, 7ᵉ; ☎01.47.05.04.55 (M° Varenne). Huge store with wide choice of clothes for men and women, from Ungaro to Paco Rabanne, and lots of lingerie. Mon–Sat 10am–2pm & 3–7pm.

Kookai Stock, 82 rue Réamur, 2ᵉ; ☎01.45.08.51.00 (M° Réamur-Sebastopol). Trendy young women's clothes, up to 70 percent off end of line and old stock.

Le Mouton à Cinq Pattes, 8 rue St-Placide, 6ᵉ; ☎01.45.48.20.29. Helmut Lang and Vivienne Westwood are among the names discounted here.

Stock 2, 92 rue d'Alésia, 14ᵉ; ☎01.45.41.65.57 (M° Alésia). Forty percent off on Daniel Hechter's end-of-line items. Mon–Sat 10am–7.30pm.

SECOND-HAND AND RÉTRO

Rétro means "period clothes", mostly unsold factory stock from the 1950s and 1960s, though some shops specialize in expensive high fashion articles from as far back as the 1920s. Plain second-hand stuff is referred to as *fripe* – not especially interesting compared with London or New York, and dominated by the US combat-jacket style. The best place to look is probably the Porte de Montreuil flea market (see p.341).

Derrière les Fagots, 8 rue des Abbesses, 18ᵉ; ☎01.42.59.72.53 (M° Abbesses). A gold mine of 1920s to 1960s clothes and accessories in (on the whole), very good condition. Reasonable prices. Tues–Sat 11am–12.30pm & 2.30–7.30pm.

Ding Dong Bazaar, 24 rue Mouffetard, 5ᵉ; ☎01.43.37.58.68 (M° Place Monge). Tiny store specializing in clothes and paste jewellery from the 1920s to the 1940s. Also does a nice line in creative recycling: interesting new brooches fashioned from bits of old jewellery and scarves created from past-it vintage

Shops and markets

For shops selling children's clothes, see Chapter 18.

Shops and markets

Kiliwatch, 64 rue Tiquetonne, 2ᵉ; has an interesting range of second-hand clothes among its clubwear. See 'Trendy' below.

clothes. Noon–2pm & 4–8pm, closed Tues.

Rag Time, 23 rue du Roule, 1ᵉʳ; ☎01.42.36.89.36 (Mᵒ Louvre-Rivoli). A veritable museum of superb dresses and high-fashion articles from the turn of the century to the 1950s. Some for hire. Expensive. Mon–Sat 2–7.30pm.

Réciproque, 89, 92, 93–97, 101 & 123 rue de la Pompe, 16ᵉ; ☎01.47.04.30.28 (Mᵒ Pompe). Haute couture: for women at no. 93–95; accessories and coats for men at no. 101; more accessories and coats for women at no. 123. Tues–Sat 11am–7.30pm.

TATI

Tati is in a class by itself, the cheapest-of-cheap clothes stores and always thronged with people. Addresses are: 2–30 bd Rochechouart, 18ᵉ (Mᵒ Barbès-Rochechouart); 140 rue de Rennes, 6ᵉ (Mᵒ Montparnasse-Bienvenüe); and 13 place de la République, 11ᵉ (Mᵒ République). Tatis have also flummoxed the city's well-established jewellers by opening their own Tati D'Or shops around town selling gold jewellery at cut-rate prices, and they have even branched out into phone cards for cheap international calls (see Basics, p.31).

TRENDY

Agnés Hekpazo, 75 rue Vieille du Temple, 3ᵉ; ☎01.44.59.84.19. (Mᵒ Rambuteau/St-Paul). A young designer whose grandparents hail from Benin in West Africa, Agnés Hekpazo marries old African traditions with a modern look in her brightly coloured pure cotton clothes. The cotton is grown and woven in West Africa and hand-dyed – many of the dyes are natural. Agnés has an interesting take on combat trousers, some in bright yellow, others dyed naturally with grass and clay. The clothes are well-made and the prices reasonable, with trousers from 350F, and reversible dresses at 490F. Daily 10.30am–7.30pm.

APC, 3 (*femme*) & 4 (*homme*) rue de Fleurus, 6ᵉ; ☎01.42.22.12.77 (Mᵒ St-

Placide). Hip collection for the young and stylish. Mon–Sat 10.30am–7pm.

Bonnie Cox, 38 rue des Abbesses, 18ᵉ; ☎01.42.54.95.68 (Mᵒ Abbesses). Young fashion names and recent graduates have their sartorial creations on show here and they now also have their own label. Affordable clothes, with dresses from 490F. Mon–Sat 10.30am–8pm, Sun 11am–7pm.

Kabuki, 25 rue Étienne-Marcel, 1ᵉʳ; ☎01.42.33.55.65 (Mᵒ Étienne-Marcel). For all your Prada, Issey Miyaké and Calvin Klein needs. Mon 1pm–7.30pm, Tues–Sat 10.30am–7pm.

Kiliwatch, 64 rue Tiquetonne, 2ᵉ; ☎01.42.21.17.37 (Mᵒ Étienne-Marcel). No problems coming up with an original clubbing outfit here: a clubbers' mecca, where rails of new cheap 'n' chic youth streetwear and a slew of trainers meet the best range of unusual second-hand clothes and accessories in Paris. Mon 1–7pm, Tues–Sat 10.30am–7pm.

Miss China, 4 rue Française, 1ᵉʳ; ☎01.40.41.08.07 (Mᵒ Étienne-Marcel). Beautiful shop creating a *look-chinoise* for Western girls, with exquisite shoes and gags to match. Children's range to open in boutique directly opposite. Mon–Sat 11am–7pm.

Nina Jacob, 23 rue des Francs-Bourgeois, 4ᵉ; ☎01.42.77.41.20 (Mᵒ St-Paul). A jumble of colourful and original party/club clothes and quirky paste jewellery; not pricey but interesting. Dresses from 299F, pants from 249F. Daily 10am–7pm.

SHOES

Freelance, 30 rue du Four, 6ᵉ; ☎01.45.48.14.78 (Mᵒ Mabillon). Unique shoe store featured in all the French fashion mags. Mon–Sat 10am–7pm.

Menkes, 12 rue Rambuteau, 6ᵉ; ☎01.40.27.91.81 (Mᵒ Rambuteau). Flamenco shoes (and outfits) plus a huge selection of wild platforms and stilettos in larger sizes – good for drag acts.

Patrick Cox, 62 rue Tiquetonne, 2ᵉ; ☎01.40.26.66.55 (Mᵒ Étienne-Marcel).

The chic and friendly Paris outlet of the London-based shoe designer. Clothes to match. Mon–Sat 10am–7pm.

Swingtap, 21 rue Keller, 11e; ☎01.48.06.38.18. (M° Ledru-Rollin). The hoofers' mecca: tap shoes, CDs to dance along to, and details on tap-dancing classes and shows around town. Tues–Sat 2–7pm.

ACCESSORIES

Cécile et Jeanne, 49 av Daumesnil, 12e; ☎01.43.41.24.24 (M° Gare-de-Lyon). Innovative jewellery design in one of the Viaduc des Arts showrooms. Mon–Fri 11am–7pm, Sat & Sun 2–7pm.

Didier Lavilla, 47 rue du Faubourg-St-Antoine, 11e; ☎01.53.33.85.55 (M° Bastille). Beautiful bags in vibrant colours. Also at 15 rue du Cherche-Midi, 6e. Mon–Sat 11am–7pm.

Divine, 39 rue Daguerre, 14e; ☎01.43.22.28.10 (M° Denfert-Rochereau). With a big selection of both new and second-hand hats, this is a fun place to try out a few of your fantasy Parisian looks with a rakishly angled beret or a coquettish cloche. Tues–Sat 10.30am–1pm & 3–7pm.

Hermès, 24 rue du Faubourg-St-Honoré, 8e; ☎01.40.17.47.17 (M° Concorde). Luxury clothing and accessory store. Come here for the ultimate silk scarf – at a price.

Stephane Plassier, 19 bd Raspail, 7e; ☎01.45.44.62.62 (M° Rue-du-Bac). Underwear only for men and women. Also at 2 rue des Blancs-Manteaux, 4e. Tues–Sat 11am–7.30pm, Sun & Mon 2.30–7pm.

Tati Or, 19 rue de la Paix, 1er; ☎01.40.07.06.76 (M° Opéra) & 42 av Général-Leclerc, 14e (M° Denfert-Rochereau). The well-known cheap clothing chain, Tati, is now selling gold jewellery, priced well below other Parisian jewellers. Mon–Sat 10am–7pm.

Ursule Beaugeste, 15 rue Oberkampf, 11e; ☎01.49.23.02.48 (M° Oberkampf). Handbag designer Ann Grand-Clement's delicious trade-mark crocheted handbags, some made on old looms, are influenced by a childhood spent abroad. Beautifully engraved leather bags and cloth hats (and raffia bags in summer) are presented in a simple industrial-chic decor. Although Ann's designs have been featured in all the top international fashion magazines, the open, approachable owner prefers the creativity of the Ménilmontant scene to a grander address, and the store is not the least bit snobby. Mon–Fri 11am–7.30pm, Sat 3–7pm.

Shops and markets

Department stores and hypermarkets

Paris' two largest **department stores**, Printemps and Galeries Lafayette, are right next door to each other near the St-Lazare station, and between them there's not much they don't have. Less enticing for its wares, perhaps, but a visual knockout, is the renovated Samaritaine. Best for food is Au Bon Marché.

In addition, Paris has its share of **hypermarkets** – giant shopping complexes – of which the Forum des Halles, in the 1er; the Centre Maine-Montparnasse, in the 14e; and the Quatre-Saisons, in La Défense, are the biggest.

Bazar de l'Hôtel de Ville (BHV), 52–64 rue de Rivoli, 4e (M° Hôtel-de-Ville). Only two years younger than the Bon Marché and noted in particular for its DIY department and cheap self-service restaurant overlooking the Seine. Less elegant in appearance than some of its rivals, perhaps, but the value for money is pretty good. Mon–Sat 9.30am–7pm, except Wed till 10pm.

Au Bon Marché, 38 rue de Sèvres, 7e (M° Sèvres-Babylone). Paris' oldest department store, founded in 1852. The prices are lower on average than at the more chic Galeries Lafayette and Printemps, and the tone is more mass-market middle-class. It has an excellent kids' department and a renowned food hall. Mon–Sat 9.30am–7pm.

Shops and markets

Galeries Lafayette, 40 bd Haussmann, 9ᵉ (Mᵒ Havre-Caumartin). The store's forte is high fashion. Two complete floors are given over to the latest creations by leading designers for men and women, and there is a large section devoted to clothes for children on the fourth floor. Then there's household stuff, tableware, furniture, a host of big names in men's and women's accessories, a whole floor devoted to lingerie, a huge parfumerie, etc – all under a superb 1900 dome. Mon–Sat 9.30am–6.45pm, Thurs till 9pm.

Au Printemps, 64 bd Haussmann, 9ᵉ (Mᵒ Havre-Caumartin). Books, records, a parfumerie even bigger than the rival Galeries Lafayette's. Excellent fashion department for women – less so for men. Mon–Sat 9.30am–7pm, Thurs till 10pm.

La Samaritaine, 19 rue de la Monnaie, 1ᵉʳ (Mᵒ Pont-Neuf/Louvre). The biggest of the department stores, spread over three buildings, whose boast is to provide anything anyone could possibly want. It aims downmarket of the previous two. Magasin 3 is wholly devoted to sport. You get a superb view of the Seine from the eleventh-floor rooftop (open all year) and the tenth-floor terrace restaurant, which is closed from Oct–March – take the lift from building two to the ninth floor then walk up the old wrought-iron staircase. Daily 9.30am–7pm, Thurs till 10pm.

Food and drink

The general standard of **food shops** throughout the capital is remarkably high, both in quality and presentation: a feast for the eyes quite as much as the palate. These listings are for the **specialist places**, many of which are veritable palaces of gluttony, and very expensive. Markets are detailed in a separate section at the end of this chapter.

Food halls to equal that of Harrods are to be found at Fauchon's, on place de la Madeleine, and the Grande Épicerie, in the Bon Marché department store – each with exhibits to rival the best of the capital's museums. In addition, there are **one-product specialists** for whom gourmets will cross the city:

Poilâne's or Ganachaud's for bread, Barthélémy for cheese, La Maison de l'Escargot for snails, Émile's for fish.

As for buying food with a view to **economic eating**, you will be best off shopping at the street markets or supermarkets – though save your bread-buying at least for the local boulangerie and let yourself be tempted once in a while by the apple *chaussons, pains aux raisins, pains au chocolat, tartes aux fraises* and countless other goodies. Useful **supermarkets** with branches throughout the city are Félix Potin, Prisunic and Monoprix. The cheapest supermarket chain is Ed l'Épicier; choice, inevitably, is limited, but they do some things very well – jams, for instance.

Next door to the Tang Frères emporium in Chinatown (see under "Markets", p.344) is the Supermarché Paris Store, 21 av d'Ivry, 13ᵉ (Mᵒ Porte-d'Italie). Open daily 9.30am–7pm, this is one of the best **Chinese supermarkets**, selling everything from teacups to ampoules of royal jelly and ginseng. Other branches are at 12 bd de la Villette, 19ᵉ (Mᵒ Belleville), and 8–10 rue de l'Evangile, 18ᵉ (Mᵒ Marx-Dornoy).

BREAD

La Flûte Gana, 226 rue des Pyrénées, 20ᵉ (Mᵒ Gambetta). Run by the daughters of Ganachaud. Start the day with a *pain biologique* and you'll live a hundred years, guaranteed. Tues–Sat 7.30am–8pm.

Ganachaud, 150–154 rue de Ménilmontant, 20ᵉ (Mᵒ Pelleport). Although father Ganachaud has left the business, the new owners continue his recipes, and the bread is still out of this world. Tues 2.30–8pm, Wed–Sat 7.30am–8pm, Sun 7.30am–1.30pm; closed Mon & Aug.

Poilâne, 8 rue du Cherche-Midi, 6ᵉ (Mᵒ Sèvres-Babylone). More marvellous bread, which is baked by hand to ancient and secret Poilâne family recipes. These are shared with Lionel's brother Max, who has a shop at 87 rue Brancion, 15ᵉ (Mᵒ Porte-de-Vanves), and Max's daughter Sophie at 29 rue de

Any list of food shops in Paris has to have at its head the two **palaces**:

Fauchon, 26 place de la Madeleine, 8ᵉ (Mᵒ Madeleine). Mon–Sat 9.40am–7pm. An amazing range of extravagantly beautiful groceries, fruit and veg, charcuterie, wines both French and foreign – almost anything you can think of, all at exorbitant prices. The quality is assured by blind testing, which all suppliers have to submit to. Just the place for presents of tea, jam, truffles, chocolates, exotic vinegars, mustards and so forth. A self-service counter for pâtisseries and *plats du jour*, and a *traiteur*

which stays open a little later, until 8.30pm, too.

Hédiard, 21 place de la Madeleine, 8ᵉ (Mᵒ Madeleine). Since the 1850s, the aristocrat's grocer, with sales staff as deferential as servants, as long as you don't try to reach for items for yourself. Superlative quality. Among the other branches are those at 126 rue du Bac, 7ᵉ; 106 bd de Courcelles, 17ᵉ; and Forum des Halles, level-1, 1ᵉʳ. Mon–Sat 8am–10pm.

Shops and markets

l'Ouest, 14ᵉ (Mᵒ Gaîté/Pernety). Mon–Sat 7.15am–8.15pm.

Poujauran, 20 rue Jean-Nicot, 7ᵉ (Mᵒ Latour-Maubourg). The shop itself is exquisite, with its original painted glass panels and tiles. The bread is excellent – there are several different kinds – and so too are the pâtisseries. Tues–Sat 8am–8.30pm; closed Aug.

CHARCUTERIE

Divay, 4 rue Bayen, 17ᵉ (Mᵒ Ternes). *Foie gras, choucroute, saucisson* and suchlike. 8am–1.30pm & 3.30–7.30pm; closed Wed & Sun afternoon, Mon & Aug.

Aux Ducs de Gascogne, 4 rue du Marché-St-Honoré, 1ᵉʳ (Mᵒ Pyramides). An excellent chain with numerous southwestern products like preserved fruits in Armagnac, *foie gras*, conserves, hams, and so forth. Mon–Sat 10am–7pm. Further branches at 112 bd Haussmann, 8ᵉ (Mᵒ St-Augustin; 10am–7pm; closed Sun & Mon am); 111 rue St-Antoine, 4ᵉ (Mᵒ St-Paul; 9.30am–2pm & 3–8pm; closed Sun & Mon am); 21 rue de la Convention, 15ᵉ (Mᵒ Boucicaut; 9.30am–1pm & 4–8pm; closed Sun & Mon am); 41 rue des Gatines, 20ᵉ (Mᵒ Gambetta; 9am–12.45pm & 3–8pm; closed Sun & Mon am).

Ets Bruneau, 6 rue Montmartre, 1ᵉʳ (Mᵒ Châtelet-Les Halles). Specialist in products from the Landes region, pâtés in

particular: Bayonne hams, goose and duck pâtés, conserves, etc. Tues–Sun 8am–6pm.

Flo Prestige, 42 place du Marché-St-Honoré, 1ᵉʳ (Mᵒ Pyramides). All sorts of super delicacies, plus wines, champagne and exquisite ready-made dishes. Daily 8am–11pm.

Maison de la Truffe, 19 place de la Madeleine, 8ᵉ (Mᵒ Madeleine). Truffles, of course, and more from the Dordogne and Landes. Mon 9am–8pm, Tues–Sat 9am–9pm.

Sacha Finkelsztajn, 27 rue des Rosiers, 4ᵉ (Wed–Sun 10am–2pm & 3–7pm; closed Aug) & 24 rue des Écouffes, 4ᵉ (10am–1pm & 3–7pm, closed Wed). Both Mᵒ St-Paul. Marvellous Jewish deli for takeaway snacks and goodies: gorgeous East European breads, cakes, *gefilte* fish, aubergine purée, tarama, *blinis* and *borscht.*

Aux Vrais Produits d'Auvergne, 46–48 rue Daubenton, 5ᵉ (Mᵒ Censier-Daubenton). An excellent chain, with numerous outlets across the city, selling genuine Auvergne fare. 8.30am–12.30pm & 4–7.30pm; closed Sun pm, Mon & July 15–Sept.

CHEESE

Androuët, 6 rue Arsène-Houssaye, 8ᵉ (Mᵒ Charles-de-Gaulle-Etoile). One of the most famous food shops in Paris, spe-

Shops and markets

cializing in cheese – dozens of types. A rather expensive restaurant adjoining the shop, whose menu features . . . lots of cheese. Mon–Fri 10am–8pm, Sat 9am–8pm, closed Aug.

Barthélémy, 51 rue de Grenelle, 7e (M° Rue-du-Bac). Purveyors of cheeses to the rich and powerful; orders can be faxed on ☎01.45.49.25.16. Tues–Sat 8.30am–1pm & 4–7.30pm; closed Aug.

Carmès et Fils, 24 rue de Lévis, 17e (M° Villiers). In the rue de Lévis market. A family of experts, who bring on many of the cheeses in their own cellars and can advise you exactly which one is ripe for the picking. Said to be the only place in Paris where you can buy (whole) Cheddar cheeses. Tues–Sat 8.30am–1pm & 4–7.30pm, Sun 8.30am–1pm; closed Aug.

Maison du Fromage, 62 rue de Sèvres, 6e (M° Sèvres-Babylone). Specializes in goat, sheep and mountain cheeses. Mon–Fri 9am–1pm & 3–7.30pm, Sat 9am–7.45pm.

CHOCOLATES AND PÂTISSERIES

Debauve et Gallais, 30 rue des Sts-Pères, 6e (M° St-Germain-des-Prés). A beautiful and ancient shop, specializing since time began in chocolate and elaborate sweets. Mon–Sat 9am–7pm; closed Aug.

Ladurée, 16 rue Royale, 8e (M° Franklin-D-Roosevelt). Delectable and pricey pâtisseries. and an attached *salon de thé.* Mon–Sat 8.30am–7pm.

A la Mère de Famille, 35 rue du Faubourg-Montmartre, 9e (M° Le-Peletier). A nineteenth-century *confiserie* selling *marrons glacés*, prunes from Agen, dried fruit, sweets, chocolates and even some wines, and delicious own-label jams. Tues–Sat 8.30am–1.30pm & 3–7pm.

Le Moule à Gâteaux, at several addresses including 111 rue Mouffetard, 5e (M° Censier-Daubenton) 47 rue St-Louis-en-l'Ille, 4e (M° Pont-Marie); 18 rue Quentin-Bauchart, 8e (M° George-V); 17 rue Daguerre, 14e (M° Denfert-Rochereau); 243 rue des Pyrénnées, 20e (M° Gambetta). A chain of pâtisseries. All open daily 8.30am–8pm.

Pâtisserie Stohrer, 51 rue Montorgueil, 2e (M° Sentier). Bread, pâtisseries, chocolate and charcuterie baked here for more than 250 years. Discover what standard-fare *pain aux raisins* should really taste like. Daily 7.30am–8pm; closed first two weeks Aug.

HERBS, SPICES AND DRIED FOODS

Aux Cinq Continents, 75 rue de la Roquette, 11e (M° Bastille). Boxes, trays, sacks of rice, pulses, herbs, spices, tarama, vine leaves, alcohol, etc, from the world over. Tues–Fri 9.30am–1.30pm & 3.30–10pm, Sun 9.30am–1.30pm, Mon 3.30–10pm.

Izraêl, 30 rue François-Miron, 4e (M° St-Paul). Another cosmopolitan emporium of goodies from all round the globe. Tues–Fri 9.30am–1pm & 2.30–7pm, Sat 9.30am–7pm.

HEALTH FOOD

Naturalia, 52 rue St-Antoine, 4e; ☎01.48.87.87.50 (M° St-Paul/Bastille). Feel like you need a vitamin boost? Or after too many rich meals you fancy some rice cakes and seaweed? This is where to come. Several other branches. Mon–Sat 10am–7.30pm.

HONEY

Les Abeilles, 21 rue Butte-aux-Cailles, 13e (M° Corvisart/Place d'Italie). Honey from all over France and further afield, sold by an experienced beekeeper. Tues–Sat 11am–8pm.

KITCHEN EQUIPMENT

Au Bain Marie, 10 rue Boissy-d'Anglas, 8e (M° Concorde). An Aladdin's cave of things for the kitchen: pots, pans, books, antiques, napkins. Mon–Sat 10am–7pm.

E Dehillerin, 18–20 rue Coquillière, 1er (M° Châtelet-Les Halles). Laid out like a traditional ironmonger's: no fancy displays, prices buried in catalogues, but good-quality stock at reasonable prices. In business since 1820. Mon 8am–12.30pm & 2–6pm, Tues–Sat 8am–6pm.

MORA, 13 rue Montmartre, 1er (M° Châtelet-Les Halles). An exhaustive collection of tools of the trade for the top professionals. Mon–Fri 8.30am–5.45pm, Sat 8.30am–1pm.

La Vaissellerie, 80 bd Haussmann, 8e; ☎01.45.22.32.47 (M° Hauvre-Caumartin). Simple inexpensive French crockery, mostly in white, but they also stock the cheerful bright-yellow Chocolat Menier and Banania range. Also branches at 85 rue de Rennes, 6e; 79 rue St-Lazare, 9e; 332 rue St-Honoré, 1er; and 92 rue St-Antoine, 4e. Mon–Sat 9.30am–7pm.

SALMON, CAVIAR AND OTHER SEAFOOD

In addition to the establishments below, more caviar, along with truffles, *foie gras*, etc, is to be found at the lower end of rue Montmartre by the Forum des Halles in the 1er.

Caviar Kaspia, 17 place de la Madeleine, 8^e (M° Madeleine). Blinis, smoked salmon and Beluga caviar. 9am–12.30am.

Comptoir du Saumon, 60 rue François-Miron, 4^e (M° St-Paul), and several other addresses. Salmon especially, but eels, trout and all things fishy as well. Plus a delightful little restaurant in which to taste the fare. Mon–Sat 10am–10pm.

Petrossian, 18 bd de Latour-Maubourg, 7^e (M° Latour-Maubourg). More gilt-edge fish eggs, but other Russian and French delicacies, too. 10am–7pm.

SNAILS

La Maison de l'Escargot, 79 rue Fondary, 15e (M° Dupleix). The most delicious snails and stuffings in town. Here they sauce and re-shell them while you wait. There is a restaurant for *dégustation* opposite at no. 70 (60–70F, with a glass of wine). Tues–Sat 9am–7.30pm, Sun 9am–1pm closed mid-July to Sept.

VEGETARIAN

Diététique D J Fayer, 45 rue St-Paul, 4e (M° St-Paul). Tiny shop, one of the city's oldest specialists, selling dietary, macrobiotic and vegetarian products. Mon–Sat 9.30am–1.30pm & 2.30–8.45pm.

WINE

Le Baron Rouge, 1 rue Théophile-Roussel, 12e (M° Ledru-Rollin). A good selection of dependable lower-range French wines; 7F for a small tasting glass. Very drinkable Merlot at 16F a litre, if you bring your own containers. Tues–Fri 10am–2pm & 5–9.30pm, Sat 10am–9.30pm, Sun 10.30am–1pm.

Caves Michel Renaud, 12 place de la Nation, 12^e (M° Nation). Established in 1890 and purveying superb-value French and Spanish wines, champagnes and Armagnac. 9.30am–1pm & 2–8.30pm; closed Sun pm and Mon am.

Aux Caves Royales, 137 bd de l'Hôpital, 13^e (M° Campo-Formio). Another good selection of wines, from 17F a litre. 9.30am–1pm, 3.30–7.45pm; closed Mon in Aug & Sun pm.

Les Caves St-Antoine, 95 rue St-Antoine, 4^e (M° St-Paul). Another small, amicable outfit. Tues–Fri 9am–1pm, 3–8pm, Sat 9am–8pm, Sun 9am–1pm.

Maison de la Vigne et du Vin de France, 21 rue François-1er, 8^e; ☎01.47.20.20.76 (M° Franklin-D-Roosevelt). The headquarters of the French wine industry, with free wine tasting, a shop, and information about all the wine regions. English spoken. Mon–Thurs 10am–12.30pm & 1.30–6.30pm, Fri until 5.30pm.

Nicolas, 31 place de la Madeleine, 8^e (M° Madeleine). A reliable merchant, with dozens of shops across the city. A good general selection. Mon–Sat 9am–8pm.

Le Repaire de Bacchus, 112 rue Mouffetard, 5^e (M° Censier-Daubenton), and several other addresses. A good chain to look out for, with many lesser-known and cheaper wines. Tues–Sat 9.30am–1pm & 3.30–8pm.

A miscellany

Abdon, 24 bd Beaumarchais, 11^e; ☎01.47.00.67.27 ((M° Chemin-Vert). New and second-hand photographic equipment.

Shops and markets

Shops and markets

Archives De La Presse, 51 rue des Archives, 3ᵉ; ☎01.42.72.63.93 (Mᵒ Rambuteau). A fascinating shop for a browse, trading in old French newspapers and magazines. The window always has a display of outdated newspapers corresponding to the current month, and there are bewildering piles upon piles of old magazines inside, with vintage *Vogues* giving a good insight into the changing fashion scene. Mon–Sat 10.30am–7pm.

Diptyque, 34 bd St-Germaine, 5ᵉ; ☎01.43.26.45.27 (Mᵒ Maubert-Mutualité). Luxurious scented candles and other fragrant products. Tues–Sat 10am–7pm.

Au Facteur Cheval, 66 rue de Javel, 15ᵉ; ☎01.45.79.59.93 (Mᵒ Charles-Michels). Small antiques shop with reasonably priced glass and chinaware, perfume bottles, knick-knacks and furniture. Tues–Sat 9.30am–1.30pm & 3–7pm.

Le Laguiole de Marais, 6 rue du Pas de la Mule, 3ᵉ; ☎01.48.87.46.88 (Mᵒ Chemin-Vert). Tiny shop selling a large range of the celebrated knives from Laguiole in the Massif Central. Mon–Sat 10am–12.30pm & 1.30–7pm, Sun 2–7pm.

La Maison du Collectionneur, 137 av Émile-Zola, 15ᵉ (Mᵒ Émile-Zola). Old books, hats, newspapers of the wartime liberation, and assorted junk.

La Maison de la Fausse Fourrure, 34 bd Beaumarchais, 11ᵉ; ☎01.43.55.24.21 (Mᵒ Chemin-Vert). Sumptuous lengths of fake fur draped and pinned over every surface imaginable. Mon–Sat 10am–7pm.

Marché St-Pierre, 2 rue Charles-Nodier, 18ᵉ; ☎01.46.06.92.25 (Mᵒ Anvers). Five floors of fabrics. Very cheap and definitely worth a visit. Mon 2–7pm, Tues–Sat 10am–7pm.

Milles Fêtes, 60 rue du Cherche-Midi, 6ᵉ; ☎01.42.22.09.43 (Mᵒ Sèvres-Babylone/St-Placide). Everything you need for a party, from invitations to fireworks.

Pentagram, 15 rue Racine, 6ᵉ (Mᵒ Cluny). Hand-blown glass pens, pharaonic board games, stationery and PCs for kids.

Le Petit Bleu, 21 rue Jean-Pierre Timbaud, 11ᵉ; ☎01.47.00.90.73 (Mᵒ Oberkampf). An excellent place for a last minute present-buying expedition, this unclassifiable shop sells all things fragrant and delicious – wines, oils, teas, soaps, candles – and other gifts for the home. Mon noon–8pm, Tues–Sat 10.30am–8pm, closed two weeks Aug.

Pylones, 57 rue St-Louis-en-l'Ile, 4ᵉ; ☎01.46.34.05.02 (Mᵒ Sully-Morland), and many other branches. Playful and silly things, including inflatable fruit bowls, grasshopper can crushers, hand-puppet face-washers and sparkly resin jewellery. Daily 11am–7.30pm.

Séphora, 70 av des Champs-Élysées, 8ᵉ; ☎01.53.93.22.50 (Mᵒ Franklin-D-Roosevelt). Huge perfumerie with related books, an exhibition and a sampling area, and a big range of cosmetics. Also branches at Forum des Halles, level-3, 1ᵉʳ, 1 rue Pierre Lescot, 1ᵉʳ, and 30 av d'Italie, 13ᵉ.

Travelingue, 20 rue Boulard, 14ᵉ (Mᵒ Denfert-Rochereau). Lots of bizarre accessories: ties, earrings, kitchenware and socks.

Trousselier, 73 bd Haussmann, 8ᵉ; ☎01.42.66.16.16 (Mᵒ St-Augustin). Described in French *Vogue* as *the* artificial flower shop. Every conceivable species of flora fashioned from man-made fibre. Decadent and pricey, but fun. Mon–Sat 10am–7pm.

Music

Records, cassettes and **CDs** are not particularly cheap in Paris, but there are plenty of second-hand bargains, and you may come across selections that are novel enough to tempt you. Brazilian, Caribbean, Antillais, African and Arab albums that would be **specialist rarities** in London or the States, as well as every kind of jazz, abound in Paris. **Rue Keller** and **rue des Taillandeurs**, in the 11ᵉ (Mᵒ Bastille), have a wide range of offbeat record shops selling current trends. Second-hand traders offer up scratchy treats – anything from the Red Army choir singing the *Marseillaise* to African drummers on skins made from spider ovaries. The **flea markets** (St-Ouen especially), and the *bouquinistes* along the Seine, are good places to look for old records.

In the **classical** department, the choice of interpretations is generous and multi-national. For all new and mainstream records, FNAC Musique (see below) usually has the best prices.

Also listed below are a couple of **bookshops** selling sheet music, scores and music literature, and some that sell instruments. Victor-Massé, Douai, Houdon, bd Clichy and other streets in the **Pigalle** area are full of instrument and soundsystem shops. Guitarists especially will enjoy a look in at 16 rue V-Massé, 9e – afternoons only – where François Guidon builds jazz guitars for the greats and amateurs. For instruments and scores, head for Paul Beuscher, at the Bastille, which has amazing sales in spring.

Afric' Music, 3 rue des Plantes, 14e; ☎01.45.42.43.52 (M° Mouton-Duvernet). A small shop with an original selection of African, Caribbean and reggae discs. Mon–Sat 10am–7pm.

BPM Records, 1 rue Keller, 11e; ☎01.40.21.02.88 (M° Bastille). Specialists in house, including acid, hiphop, rap, techno and dub. A good place to pick up club flyers. Mon–Sat noon–8pm.

Camara, 45 rue Marcadet, 18e; ☎01.42.51.33.18 (M° MarcadetPoissonnière). Paris' best selection of West African music on cassette and video. Mon–Sat noon–8pm.

La Chaumière, 5 rue de Vaugirard, 6e; ☎01.43.54.07.25 (M° Odéon). Exclusively classical music, with more than 10,000 CD recordings to choose from, many discounted. You can listen before you buy, and the staff are happy to give advice. Mon–Sat 11am–8pm, Sun 2–8pm.

Cinq Planetes, 10 rue Saint-Sébastian, 11e; ☎01.43.55.00.10 (M° SaintSébastian-Froissart). World music specialists, with imports from as far afield as Australia. Mon–Fri 11am–7pm, Sat 10am–7pm.

Crocodisc, 40–42 rue des Écoles, 5e; ☎01.43.54.47.95 (M° MaubertMutualité). Folk, oriental, Afro-Antillais, funk, reggae, soul, new and secondhand. Some of the best prices in town. Tues–Sat 11am–7pm.

Crocojazz, 64 rue de la Montagne-SteGeneviève, 5e; ☎01.46.34.78.38 (M° Maubert-Mutualité). Jazz, blues, gospel and country: mainly new imports. Tues–Sat 11am–1pm & 2–7pm.

Disc' Inter, 2 rue des Rasselins, 20e; ☎01.43.73.63.48 (M° Porte-deMontreuil). Wide-ranging stock of AfroCaribbean music on CD, cassette, video and vinyl. Mon–Sat 10am–7pm.

Dream Store, 4 place St-Michel, 6e; ☎01.43.26.49.75 (M° St-Michel). Good discounted prices on blues and jazz in particular but also rock and folk. Mon 1.30pm–7.15pm, Tues–Sat 9.30am–7.15pm.

FNAC Musique, 4 place de la Bastille, 12e, next to the opera house; ☎01.49.54.30.00 (M° Bastille). Extremely stylish shop in black, grey and chrome with computerized catalogues, every variety of music, books, and a concert booking agency. Mon–Sat 10am–8pm, Wed till 10pm. The other FNAC shops (see under "Bookshops") also sell music and hi-fi. The branch at 24 bd des Italiens, 9e (☎01.48.01.02.03, M° Richelieu-Drouot), has a greater emphasis on rock and popular music, and stays open until midnight. Try FNAC-Étoile, at 26 av des Ternes, 17e (M° Ternes), Mon–Sat 10am–7pm, for jazz.

Hamm, 135–139 rue de Rennes, 6e; ☎01.44.39.35.35 (M° St-Placide). The biggest general music shop in Paris, selling instruments new and old, sheet music, scores, manuals, librettos, etc. Mon 2–7.30pm, Tues–Sat 10am–7.30pm.

Librairie Musicale de Paris, 68bis rue Réaumur, 3e; ☎01.40.29.18.18 (M° Réaumur-Sébastopol). Huge selection of books on music and of music, from Baroque oratorios to heavy metal. Mon–Fri 10am–12.45pm & 2–7pm, Sat 10am–7pm.

Shops and markets

The Cité de la Musique (see p.197) has a range of shops devoted to all things musical.

Shops and markets

Maison Sauviat, 124 bd de la Chapelle, 18e; ☎01.46.06.31.84 (M° Barbès). Wonderful shop that's been going strong since the 1920s. Now specializing in African and Arab music. Mon–Sat 9am–7.30pm.

Moby Disques, 28 rue Monge, 5e; ☎01.43.29.70.51 (M° Cardinal-Lemoine). Passionate jazz fans will like this small shop; jazz on vinyl – many collectors' items – bought, sold and exchanged at reasonable prices.

Parallèles, 47 rue St-Honoré, 1er; ☎01.42.33.62.70 (M° Châtelet-Les Halles). The bookshop (see p.328) also sells records and cheap second-hand CDs.

Paul Beuscher, 15–29 bd Beaumarchais, 4e; ☎01.44.54.36.00 (M° Bastille). A music department store that's been going strong for more than 100 years. Instruments, scores, books, recording equipment, etc. Mon–Fri 9.45am–12.30pm & 2–7pm, Sat 9.45am–7pm.

Rough Trade, 30 rue de Charonne, 11e; ☎01.40.21.61.62 (M° Ledru-Rollin). Indie labels and fanzines – an offshoot of London's Portobello Road store. Mon–Wed noon–7pm, Thurs–Sat 11am–8pm.

Virgin Megastore, 56–60 av des Champs-Élysées, 8e (M° Franklin-D-Roosevelt); and Carrousel du Louvre, under the Louvre, 1er (M° Palais-Royal/Musée-du-Louvre). Virgin has trumped all Paris' music shops. It's the biggest and the trendiest, but lacks the wax rock heroes of the London store. Concert-booking agency and expensive Internet connection. Mon–Sat 10am–midnight, Sun noon–midnight.

Sport

Bicloune, 7 rue Froment, 11e; ☎01.48.05.47.75 (M° Bréguet-Sabin). A bike shop with some bizarre models on show. Repairs carried out. Tues–Fri 10.30am–1.30pm & 2–7pm, Sat 10am–1pm & 2–6.30pm.

La Boutique des Gardien de But, 89 ter rue de Charenton, 12e; ☎01.43.45.99.66 (M° Gare-de-Lyon). "The Goalkeeper": a very friendly, young shop specializing in French soccer. Stock includes shirts of every French club. Tues–Sat 10am–1pm & 2–7pm.

Le Ciel est à Tout le Monde, 10 rue Gay-Lussac, 5e; ☎01.46.33.21.50 (RER Luxembourg). The best kite shop in Europe also sells frisbees, boomerangs and anything else that flies without a motor. Also, material for making your own plus traditional toys and the complete Petit Prince and Babar gift range. Mon–Sat 10am–7pm; closed Mon in Aug.

Décathlon, Parc Aquatic, 4 rue Louis-Armand, 15e ☎01.45.72.66.88 (M° Balard/RER Bd-Victor). A brilliant selection of sports gear and swimming costumes. Mon–Sat 10am–8pm, Sun 10.30am–7.30pm.

La Haute Route, 33 bd Henri-IV, 4e; ☎01.42.72.38.43 (M° Bastille). Mainly skiing and mountaineering equipment: to rent or to buy – new and second-hand. Mon 2–7pm, Tues–Sat 9.30am–1pm & 2–7pm.

La Maison du Vélo, 11 rue Fénelon, 10e; ☎01.42.81.24.72 (M° Poissonnière). Classic models, mountain bikes, tourers and racers. Tues–Sat 10am–7pm.

Marathon, 6 rue de Lyon, 12e; ☎01.42.27.48.18 (M° Gare-de-Lyon). Specialists in running shoes. The shop is owned by an experienced marathon runner. Tues–Sat 10am–7pm.

Nomades, 37 bd Bourdon, 4e; ☎01.44.54.07.44 (M° Bastille). The place to buy and hire rollerblades and equipment, with its own bar out back where you can find out about the scene. See also Rollerblading p.352. Mon–Fri 11am–7pm, Sat & Sun 10am–7pm.

La Roue d'Or, 60 bd de Strasbourg, 10e; ☎01.40.34.48.88 (M° Gare-de-l'Est). Another cycling enthusiasts' gold mine. Tues–Sat 9am–6.30pm; closed Aug.

Au Vieux Campeur, 48 rue des Écoles, 5e; ☎01.43.29.12.32 (M° Maubert-Mutualité). The main shop of this enormous outdoor and sporting equipment outfitter. Here you'll find climbing, hiking and camping gear – and a climbing wall for kids downstairs. Ask here for the exact location of its various mushrooming departments – selling maps and guides, ski gear, walking shoes, swimming things, jogging paraphernalia, rollerblades, kites and any other sporting gear you could think of. Mon 2–7pm, Tues & Thurs–Fri 9.30am–7.30pm, Wed 10.30am–9pm, Sat 9.30am–8pm, closed Mon in Aug.

Markets

Several of the markets listed below are described in the text of Chapters 1–11. These, however, are the details – and the highlights. The map on p.342 shows the location of them all.

Books, stamps and art

As well as the specialized book markets listed below, you should of course remember the wide array of books and all forms of printed material on sale from the **bouquinistes**, who hook their green padlocked boxes onto the riverside quais of the Left Bank.

Marché aux Cartes Postales Anciennes, Marché St-Germain, 3 ter rue Mabillon, 6ᵉ (M° Mabillon). Old postcards. Wed & Thurs 9am–1pm & 4–6.30pm.

Marché de la Création Mouton-Duvernet, cnr rues Mouton-Duvernet, Boulard & Brézin, 14ᵉ (M° Mouton-Duvernet). Artists, many with studios nearby, display and sell their work here. Sun 10.30am–5pm.

Marché du Livre Ancien et d'Occasion, Pavillon Baltard, Parc Georges-Brassens, rue Brancion, 15ᵉ (M° Porte-de-Vanves). Second-hand and antiquarian books. Sat & Sun 9am–6pm.

Marché aux Timbres, junction of avs Marigny & Gabriel, on the north side of place Clemenceau in the 8ᵉ (M° Champs-Élysées–Clemenceau). The stamp market. Thurs, Sat, Sun & hols 10am–dusk.

Marché aux Vieux Papiers de St-Mandé, av de Paris (M° St-Mandé). Old

books, postcards and prints. Wed 10am–6pm.

Clothes and flea markets

Paris has three main flea markets (*marchés aux puces*) of ancient descent gathered about the old gates of the city. No longer the haunts of the flamboyant gypsies and petty crooks of literary tradition, they are nonetheless good entertainment, and if you go early enough you might just find something special. Some of the food markets have spawned second-hand clothes and junk stalls, notably the place d'Aligre, in the 12ᵉ, and the place des Fêtes, in the 20ᵉ.

Carreau du Temple, between rue Perrée & rue du Petit-Thouars, 3ᵉ (M° République/Temple). Specializes in plain and practical new clothes. Tues–Fri until noon, Sat & Sun until 1pm.

Porte de Montreuil, 20ᵉ (M° Porte-de-Montreuil). Cheap new clothes have begun to dominate what was the best of flea markets for second-hand clothes – still cheapest on Mon when leftovers from the weekend are sold off. Also old furniture, household goods and assorted junk. Sat, Sun & Mon 7am–7pm.

Porte de Vanves, av Georges-Lafenestre/av Marc-Sangnier, 14ᵉ (M° Porte-de-Vanves). The obvious choice for bric-a-brac searching, with professional dealers operating alongside amateurs. See also p.162. Sat & Sun 7am–7pm.

St-Ouen/Porte de Clignancourt, 18ᵉ (M° Porte-de-Clignancourt). The biggest and most touristy, with stalls selling new and second-hand clothes, shoes, records, books and junk of all sorts as well as expensive antiques. Trading usually starts well before the official opening hour – as early as 5am. Sat, Sun & Mon 7.30am–7pm.

Flowers and birds

Paris used to have innumerable flower markets around the streets, but today just the three listed below remain. Throughout the week, however, there's

Shops and markets

For a detailed description of the Puces de St-Ouen, see pp.180–182.

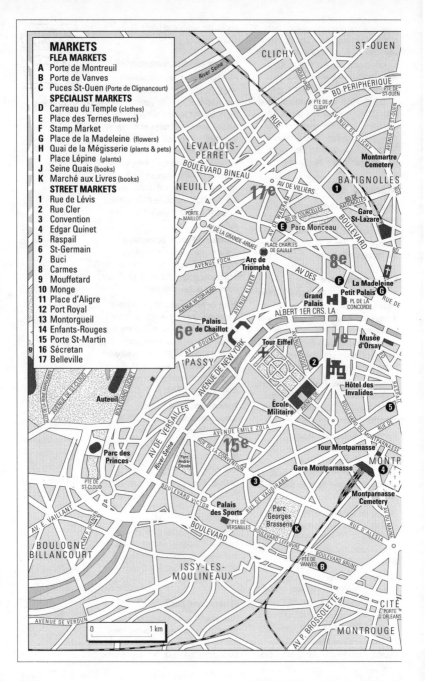

MARKETS

FLEA MARKETS
A Porte de Montreuil
B Porte de Vanves
C Puces St-Ouen (Porte de Clignancourt)

SPECIALIST MARKETS
D Carreau du Temple (clothes)
E Place des Ternes (flowers)
F Stamp Market
G Place de la Madeleine (flowers)
H Quai de la Mégisserie (plants & pets)
I Place Lépine (plants)
J Seine Quais (books)
K Marché aux Livres (books)

STREET MARKETS
1 Rue de Lévis
2 Rue Cler
3 Convention
4 Edgar Quinet
5 Raspail
6 St-Germain
7 Buci
8 Carmes
9 Mouffetard
10 Monge
11 Place d'Aligre
12 Port Royal
13 Montorgueil
14 Enfants-Rouges
15 Porte St-Martin
16 Sécretan
17 Belleville

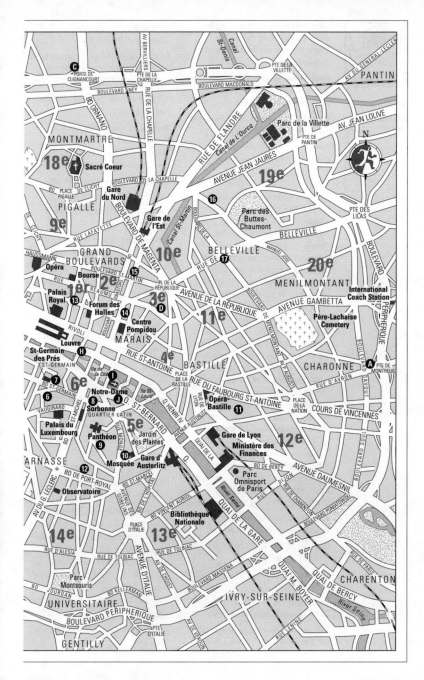

Shops and markets

also the heavy concentration of plant and pet shops along the quai de la Mégisserie, between Pont-Neuf and Pont-au-Change.

Place Lépine, Île de la Cité, 1er. On Sunday flowers give way to birds and pets. Daily 8am–7.30pm.

Place de la Madeleine, 8e. Flowers and plants. Tues–Sun 8am–7.30pm.

Place des Ternes, 8e. Flowers and plants. Tues–Sun 8am–7.30pm.

Food

The street **food markets** provide one of the capital's more exacting tests of willpower. At the top end of the scale, there are the Satanic arrays in rue de Lévis in the 17e and rue Cler in the 7e, both of which are more market street than street market, with their stalls mostly metamorphosed into permanent shops. The **real street markets** include a tempting scattering in the Left Bank – in rue de Buci (the most photographed) near St-Germain-des-Prés, rue Mouffetard, place Maubert and place Monge. Bigger ones are at Montparnasse, in bd Edgar-Quinet, and opposite Val-de-Grâce in bd Port-Royal. The largest is in rue de la Convention, in the 15e.

For a different feel and more exotic foreign produce, take a look at the **Mediterranean/Oriental** displays in bd de Belleville and rue d'Aligre.

Markets usually start between 7am and 8am and tail off around 1pm. The covered markets have specific **opening hours**, which are given below along with details of locations and days of operation.

Belleville, bd de Belleville, 20e (M° Belleville/Ménilmontant). Tues & Fri.

Buci, rue de Buci & rue de Seine, 6e (M° Mabillon). Tues–Sun.

Carmes, place Maubert, 5e (M° Maubert-Mutualité). Tues, Thurs & Sat.

Convention, rue de la Convention, 15e (M° Convention). Tues, Thurs & Sun.

Dejean, place du Château-Rouge, 18e (M° Château-Rouge). Tues–Sun.

Edgar-Quinet, bd Edgar-Quinet, 14e (M° Edgar-Quinet). Wed & Sat.

Enfants-Rouges, 39 rue de Bretagne, 3e (M° Filles-du-Calvaire). Tues–Sat 8am–1pm & 4–7.30pm, Sun 9am–1pm.

Monge, place Monge, 5e (M° Monge). Wed, Fri & Sun.

Montorgueil, rue Montorgueil & rue Montmartre, 1er (M° Châtelet-Les Halles/Sentier). Tues–Sat 8am–1pm & 4pm–7pm, Sun 9am–1pm.

Mouffetard, rue Mouffetard, 5e (M° Censier-Daubenton). Tues–Sun.

Place d'Aligre, 12e (M° Ledru-Rollin). Tues–Sat until 1pm.

Port-Royal, bd de Port-Royal, near Val-de-Grâce, 5e (RER Port-Royal). Tues, Thurs & Sat.

Porte-St-Martin, rue du Château-d'Eau, 10e (M° Château-d'Eau). Tues–Sat 8am–1pm & 4–7.30pm, Sun 8am–1pm.

Raspail, bd Raspail, between rue du Cherche-Midi & rue de Rennes, 6e (M° Rennes). Tues & Fri. Organic on Sun.

Rue Cler, 7e (M° École-Militaire). Tues–Sat.

Rue de Lévis, 17e (M° Villiers). Tues–Sun.

Rue du Poteau, 18e (M° Jules-Joffrin). Tues–Sat.

St-Germain, rue Mabillon, 6e (M° Mabillon). Tues–Sat 8am–1pm & 4–7.30pm, Sun 8am–1pm.

Secrétan, av Secrétan/rue Riquet, 19e (M° Bolivar). Tues–Sat 8am–1pm & 4–7.30pm, Sun 8am–1pm.

Tang Frères, 48 av d'Ivry, 13e (M° Porte-d'Ivry). Not really a market, but a vast emporium of all things Oriental, where speaking French will not help you discover the nature and uses of what you see before you. In the same yard, there is also a Far Eastern flower shop. Tues–Sun 9am–7.30pm.

Ternes, rue Lemercier, 17e (M° Ternes). Tues–Sat 8am–1pm & 4–7.30pm, Sun 8am–1pm.

Chapter 17

Daytime amusements and sports

When it's cold and wet, and you've had enough of peering at museums, monuments, the dripping panes of shop fronts and café vistas, don't despair or retreat back to your hotel. There are saunas to soak in, rollerblading and ice-skating rinks to fall on, music halls inviting you to dance the tango, bowling alleys, billiards, swimming pools and gyms. You can call up a choice of music and videos on CD-ROM or examine, in old-fashioned style, obscure picture books in medieval libraries.

If you're feeling brave, you could also change your hairstyle, indulge in a total body tonic, take up yoga or take your first steps as a ballerina. You could even learn how to concoct sublime French dishes at a professional cookery school. And when the weather isn't so bad, you can go for a ride in a boat or perhaps even a helicopter if you've had a successful flutter on the horses in the Bois de Boulogne.

Paris' range of **sports**, both for spectators and participants, is also outlined below. For additional possibilities, *L'Officiel des Spectacles* has the best listings of **sports facilities** (under "Activités sportives"). Information on municipal facilities is also available from Allo Sports (Mon–Fri 10.30am–5pm; ☎01.42.76.54.54) or Direction Jeunesse et Sports, 25 bd Bourdon, 4ᵉ (Mon–Fri noon–7pm; ☎01.42.76.22.60; Mº Bastille), while the Mairie de Paris give

away a weighty free book, *Le Guide du Sport à Paris* (ask for it at the tourist office, town halls or the Direction Jeunesse et Sports), which provides an arrondissement-by-arrondissement list of sporting facilities. For current **sporting events** there's the daily sports paper *L'Équipe*. The highlight of the calendar is, of course, the triumphal arrival of cycling's *Tour de France* in July.

Boat trips, balloon and heli rides

Seeing Paris by boat is one of the city's most popular and durable tourist experiences – and a lot of fun. Seeing it from the air is even better.

Bateaux-Mouches

From the quais or the bridges, after night has fallen, the sudden appearance of a bulging **Bateau-Mouche**, blaring its multi-lingual commentaries and dazzling with its floodlights, can come as a nasty shock to anyone indulging in romantic contemplations. One way of avoiding the ugly sight of these hulking hulls is to get on one yourself. You may not be able to escape the trite narration, but the evening rides certainly give a superb and very glamorous close-up view of the classic buildings along the Seine.

Bateaux-Mouches **boat trips** start from the Embarcadère du Pont de l'Alma, on the Right Bank in the 8ᵉ (reservations

For details on the cinemas of Paris, see Chapter 15.

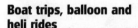

Daytime amusements and sports

☎ 01.42.25.96.10, information
☎ 01.40.76.99.99 M° Alma-Marceau).
The rides, which usually last an hour,
depart at 11am, 11.30am, 12.15pm, 1pm
and every half hour from 2pm to 10pm;
winter departure times are reduced (40F,
under-14s 20F). Avoid the outrageously
priced lunch and dinner trips, for which
"correct" dress is mandatory. The main
competitors to the Bateaux-Mouches are
Bateaux Parisiens, Bateaux-Vedettes de
Paris and Bateaux-Vedettes du Pont
Neuf. They're all much of a muchness,
and can be found detailed in *Pariscope*
under "Croisières" in the "Visites-
Promenades" section and in *L'Officiel des
Spectacles* under "Promenades" in the "À
Travers Paris" section.

An alternative way of riding on the
Seine, which spares you the commentaries, is the **Batobus**, a river transport
system operating from May to
September between port de la
Bourdonnais by the Eiffel Tower and the
quai du Louvre by the Musée du Louvre
stopping along the way at quai de
Solférino (by the Musée d'Orsay), quai
Malaquais on the Left Bank for St-
Germain-de-Prés (by the Pont des Arts,
the footbridge to the Louvre), quai de
Montebello (by Notre-Dame) and quai de
l'Hôtel-de-Ville. The service runs every
half-hour or so from 10am to 7pm: total
journey time is 21 minutes and tickets
cost 20F for the first stop, 10F for subsequent stops, or 60F for a day pass.

Canal trips

Less overtly tourist fodder than the
Bateaux-Mouches and their clones are
the **canal boat trips**. Canauxrama (reservations ☎ 01.42.39.15.00) chugs up and
down between the Port de l'Arsenal
(opposite 50 bd de la Bastille, 12ᵉ; M°
Bastille) and the Bassin de la Villette (13
quai de la Loire, 19ᵉ; M° Jaurès) on the
Canal St-Martin. Daily departures are at
9.45am and 2.45pm from La Villette and
at 9.45am and 2.30pm from the Bastille.
At the Bastille end is a long tunnel from
which you don't surface till the 10ᵉ
arrondissement. The ride lasts three
hours – not a bad bargain for 75F (stu-

dents 60F, under-12s 45F, under-6s free;
no reductions weekends or holiday afternoons). The company also runs day trips
along the Canal de l'Ourcq, west as far
as Meaux, with a coach back (200F;
meal extra).

A more stylish vessel for exploring the
canal is the **catamaran** of Paris-Canal,
with trips between the Musée d'Orsay
(quai Anatole-France by the Pont
Solférino, 7ᵉ; M° Solférino) and the Parc
de la Villette (La Folie des Visites
Guidées, on the canal by the bridge
between the Grande Salle and the Cité
des Sciences, 19ᵉ; M° Porte-de-Pantin),
which also last three hours. The catamaran departs from the Musée d'Orsay at
9.30am daily. Parc de la Villette departures are at 2.30pm. Trips cost 95F,
12–25s 70F (except Sun and holiday
afternoons), 4–11s 55F; reservations
☎ 01.42.40.96.97.

Paris by helicopter or balloon

Having seen Paris from the water, the
next step up is Paris from the air. A **helicopter tour** above all the city's sights is
somewhat pricey, but if whirlygig rides
turn you on as much or more than a
four-star meal or a stalls seat at the theatre, then a quick loop around La
Défense is on: Héli-France at the Héliport
de Paris, 4 av de la Porte-de-Sèvres, 15ᵉ
(☎ 01.45.54.95.11, Mon–Fri 8am–8pm,
Sat & Sun 9am–6pm; M° Balard). A
thirty-minute trip will set you back an
astronomical 850F for each passenger,
and a minimum of five is required.

For a far more extravagant overview,
you can opt to go up in an **air balloon**.
Air Atmosphère Dirigeable Montgolfière
(87bis bd de la République, 92100
Boulogne; ☎ 01.46.09.44.22) or France
Montgolfière (16 passage de la Main
d'Or, 75011 Paris; ☎ 01.47.00.66.44) can
oblige.

Afternoon tangos

A less obvious but very Parisian way to
fill the afternoon hours is at a **bal
musette**. The dance halls where they
take place were the between-the-wars

solution in the down-and-out parts of *Gay Paree* to depression, dole and the demise of the Popular Front. They crossed social scales, too, with film stars and jaded aristocrats coming to indulge in a bit of rough. Three or four generations of owners later, only **Balajo** remains in the rue de Lappe, still attracting a partially working-class clientele, and running both afternoon and evening sessions. Turn up on a Friday afternoon and you'll find people dancing to the accordion, cheek-to-cheek, couple squashed against couple. Their clothes aren't smart, their French isn't academy, men dance with women, and everyone drinks.

Less conducive to participation, but potentially entertaining, are the **tea dances**, a much more genteel or camp experience than the *bals musettes*.

Balajo, 9 rue de Lappe, 11e; ☎01.47.00.07.87 (M° Bastille). The original *bal musette* venue. Music, all recorded, is a mixture of waltz, tango and cha cha; 50F, or 60F with a drink. Sun & hols 3–7pm; closed Aug.

Chalet du Lac, Bois de Vincenes, 11e; ☎01.43.28.09.89 (M° St-Mandé-Tourelles). Elegant Sunday afternoon dancing with an orchestra, 3–7.30pm; 70F.

Chez Gégène, 162bis quai de Polangis, Joinville-Le-Pont; ☎01.48.83.29.43 (RER Joinville-Le-Pont). Just across the Marne from the Bois de Vincennes. Sunday *bals musettes* 3–6pm from March to Oct, but ring first to check. High-class rétro dancing in a 1900-style *guinguette*. 80F.

La Coupole, 102 bd Montparnasse, 14e; ☎01.43.20.14.20 (M° Vavin). Definitely for the older generation. Sat 3–7pm, 40F; Sun & hols 3–9pm, 80F includes a drink and a pâtisserie.

Divan du Monde, 165 rue des Martyrs, 18e ; ☎01.44.92.77.66 (M° Pigalle). One Sunday each month, a friendly 'bal des familles' is held 4–9pm. Children under 13 are free; teenagers and adults 60F.

Le Palace, 8 rue du Faubourg-Montmartre, 9e; ☎01.42.46.10.87 (M°

Rue-Montmartre). Gay tea dance every Sun afternoon, Oct–May 4–11pm, rest of year from 5pm; 60F including a drink. Strictly men only.

Le Rétro, 23 rue du Faubourg-du-Temple, 10e; ☎01.42.08.54.06 (M° République). Daily 2–6.30pm; 30F including drink.

Libraries, vidéothèques and musical discoveries

The city's libraries offer unexpected delights, while you can listen to CDs or watch videos all day in public places in Paris, too.

Libraries: municipal collections

Some of the collections below require day passes (around 20F). You don't have to pay to browse through the **BPI-Brantôme** collection, near the Pompidou Centre, however, and it keeps foreign newspapers in case you're pining for news from home.

Bibliothèque André Malraux, 78 bd Raspail, 6e (M° Rennes). Named after the novelist and art critic who fought with the Republicans in Spain and the French Resistance during World War II, later becoming a minister in de Gaulle's government and Minister of Cultural Affairs throughout the 1960s. The library is notable for its collection of books on cinema on the sixth floor. Tues–Fri 2–7pm, Sat 10am–noon & 2–5pm.

Bibliothèque des Femmes Marguerite Durand, 79 rue Nationale, 13e (M° Nationale/Tolbiac). A feminist library with books, journals, photos, posters and original manuscripts and letters. Tues–Sat 2–6pm.

Bibliothèque du Film, 100 rue du Faubourg-St-Antoine, 12e (M° Ledru-Rollin). New library devoted to film with magazines, books, stills, posters, videos and CD-Roms. Mon–Fri 10am–7pm; 20F day pass, 10 entries 100F.

Bibliothèque Forney, Hôtel de Sens, 1 rue du Figuier, 4e (M° Pont-Marie). Medieval building filled with volumes on

Daytime amusements and sports

For details of evening activities at Balajo *and* Chez Gégène, *see p.303.*

Daytime amusements and sports

fine and applied arts. Tues–Sat 1.30–8pm; 20F.

Bibliothèque Historique de la Ville de Paris, Hôtel Lamoignon, 24 rue Pavée, 4e (M° St-Paul). Sixteenth-century mansion housing centuries of texts and picture books on the city. Mon–Sat 9.30am–6pm.

Bibliothèque Mazarine, Institut de France, 23 quai de Conti, 6e (M°.St-Michel). History of France and of books; genaology. The setting, in a magnificent seventeenth-century building, with fine views across the Seine to the Louvre, is the real lure here. Some identification is required.

Bibliothèque Nationale de France François Mitterand, quai François-Mauriac, 13e (M° Quai-de-la-Gare). Tues–Sat 10am–7pm, Sun noon–6pm; 20F day pass, annual pass 200F. The massive new national library was officially opened in 1996 as the last of the late President Mitterand's *Grand Projets*. Reversing the usual library format, it is the readers (room for 3000) who are kept underground while the books – at least ten million of them – live in four controversial (and troublesome) glass towers. The public library gives access to books, newspapers and magazines, and there is an audio-visual room where you can look at photos, documentaries and listen to sound recordings. The specialist research library is not open to the general public – and unfortunately only researchers have access to the impressive central gardens.

Bibliothéque Ste-Geneviève, 10 pl du Panthéon, 5e (RER Luxembourg). Reference library with beautiful murals in the foyer and a gorgeous reading room. You need to be keen to get in: you have to register, bringing identification and a photo. Mon–Sat 10am–10pm.

BPI-Brantôme (Bibliothèque Publique d'Information), 11 rue Brantôme, 3e (M° Rambuteau). The smaller, temporary home of the nearby Pompidou Centre's library, scheduled to move back home

early in 2000. The vast collection includes the foreign press, videos and a language lab to brush up on your French. Mon & Wed–Fri noon–10pm, Sat, Sun & pub hols 10am–10pm; closed Tues & 1 May; free.

Sources d'Europe, base of La Grande Arche, La Défense, 18e (M° La Défense). French- and European-sponsored centre, with documents and videos on the EU. Mon–Fri 11am–5pm.

English-language libraries

If you're in Paris for any length of time, you might want to join one of the paying English-language libraries detailed below.

American Library in Paris, 10 rue du Général-Camou, 7e; ☎01.53.59.12.60 (M° École-Militaire). Hundreds of American magazines and newspapers and a vast range of books, plus readings and other events. Day pass 70F, annual 570F. Tues–Sat 10am–7pm.

British Council, 9 rue de Constantine, 7e; ☎01.49.55.73.23 (M° Invalides). Daily British newspapers, but a much smaller collection of books than at the American Library. Internet access. Day pass 30F, annual membership 250F. Mon–Fri 11am–6pm except Wed until 7pm.

FNAC, Virgin Megastore and the Vidéothèque de Paris

FNAC, 4 place de la Bastille, 12e, next to the opera house (M° Bastille). Extremely stylish music shop has touch-screen access to a limited but interesting selection of CDs. Once you've donned the headphones, touch the square on the screen reading "*Touchez l'écran*". If you then touch first "*Répérages FNAC*", then "*Variétés Françaises*", then "*Rock*", you'll end up with a list of recent French rock recordings which you can listen to, adjusting the volume or flicking forwards by touching arrows. "*Sommaire*" takes you back to the previous list. Of course you can choose medieval church music, jazz or Pierre Boulez instead – it's very simple, and when the shop isn't crowded you can spend as long as you like for free. Mon–Sat 10am–8pm, Wed until 10pm.

Vidéothèque de Paris, 2 Grande Galerie, Porte St-Eustache, Forum des Halles, 1er; ☎01.44.76.63.44 (RER Châtelet-Les Halles/M° Châtelet). Tues–Sun 1–9pm, Thurs till 10pm. For 30F you can watch any of the four videos or films screened each day, and, in the Salle Pierre Emmanuel, make your own selection from thousands of film clips, newsreel footage, commercials, documentaries, soaps and the like, from 1896 to the present day. All the material is connected to Paris in some way, and you can make your choice – on your individual screen and keyboard – via a Paris place name, an actor, a director, a date, and so on. Don't be put off by the laboratory atmosphere. All are welcome, and there are instructions in English at the desk and a friendly "librarian" to help you out. Once you're in the complex you can go back and forth between the projection rooms, the Salle Pierre Emmanuel and a Cyber Café. The café – open 1–9pm – allows you to hook up to the Internet for half an hour with the price of the Vidéothèque entry; after that, it's 25F per hour.

Virgin Megastore, 52 av des Champs-Élysées, 8e (M° George-V). No sophisticated computers here: just grab the headphones of whichever one of the hundred hooked-up CDs takes your fancy, or the headphones for one of the feature film videos being screened, and pretend you're on a transatlantic flight. Expensive Internet connection, too. Mon–Sat 10am–midnight, Sun noon–midnight.

Cookery and wine appreciation courses

Paris is, of course, the perfect place to try to get to grips with French gastronomy and wines. There are a large number of places offering courses which can extend your knowledge, a couple of which we've listed below.

Centre d'Information, de Documentation et de Dégustation (CIDD), 30 rue de la Sabliéne, 14e; ☎01.45.45.32.20 or 01.43.27.67.21 (M° Pernéty). Free "Porte-Ouvertes" days with tastings, and runs wine-tasting courses in English (four 3hr sessions for 1240F).

Cordon Bleu, at 8 rue Léon-Delhomme, 15e; ☎01.53.68.22.50, fax 01.48.56.03.96 (M° Vaugirard/Convention). Offers cookery demonstrations followed by tastings (morning or afternoon sessions, some in English. 48hr advance booking; 250F), or day-long hands-on sessions (again some in English, 2 weeks' advance booking required; 750F). You can make your reservations in London (☎0171/935 3503, fax 935 7621) or in Canada/USA (toll free 1-800/457-CHEF). Web site: *cordonbleu.net*

Hairdressing salons

The range of **hairdressing salons** is as wide – style-wise and price-wise – as you'd expect in this supremely fashion-conscious city.

Alexandre, 3 av Matignon, 8e; ☎01.42.25.57.90 (M° Franklin-D-Roosevelt). For men and women. The long-established haute-coiffeur of Paris could be an intimidating experience unless you're wearing Yves St-Laurent or Gaultier. Wash, cut and blow-dries for women are not that expensive considering the clientele – around 500F. Manicure and pedicure also offered.

Jacques Dessange, *women* at 43 av Franklin-D-Roosevelt, 8e; ☎01.43.59.31.31; *men* at no. 37 ☎01.43.59.21.21 (M° Franklin-D-Roosevelt). And at thirteen other addresses around Paris. Less classic, but still very smart; around 480–530F for women, 360F for men for wash, cut and blow-dry.

Jean-Marc Maniatis, 35 rue de Sèvres, 6e; ☎01.45.44.16.39 (M° Sèvres-Babylone). Younger and less-established beauties come here for the renowned and meticulous cutting. You can have a free cut by a trainee; phone ☎01.47.20.00.05 to make an appointment.

Daytime amusements and sports

Daytime
amusements
and sports

For shops selling sporting gear and equipment, see p.340.

Schools and cheaper cuts

Around **Les Halles**, the **Bastille** and **St-Germain** many salons go for maximum visibility, so you can watch what's being done and take your pick. It's always a gamble, but it can be fun trying out your French in the intimate trivial chitchat that many hairdressers insist on. Book a couple of days in advance.

Various salons or schools offer low fee or free wash, cut and blow-dries to those bold enough to act as guinea-pigs for new cuts or inexperienced trainees. These include the following:

Jean-Louis David, 5 rue Cambon, 1er; ☎01.42.97.51.71 (Mº Concorde). You need to go to the salon to make an appointment – Mon–Fri 9.30am–5.30pm – for a free cut by a trainee.

Jean-Louis Déforges Académie, 71 bd Richard-Lenoir, 11e; ☎01.43.55.56.67 (Mº Richard-Lenoir). Monsieur Déforges may be wandering around criticizing his trainees, in which case your cut will take much longer. Around 60F. Mon–Thurs 9.30am, 1.30pm & 3.30pm, Fri 9.30am & 1.30pm.

Jean-Marc Maniatis. See overleaf.

Les Salons Jean-Claude Biguine, 50 salons around the city; ☎01.44.76.88.10 for addresses. No need to make an appointment. From 120F for men, 180F for women. Good value. Also trainee cuts and colouring from 30F.

Fitness clubs and gyms

The body beautiful is big business in Paris. You'll find any number of aerobics classes, dance workouts and anti-stress fitness programmes offered, along with yoga, t'ai chi and martial arts.

Fitness venues

Many **fitness clubs** organize their activities in courses or require a minimum month's or year's subscription (big gym chains like Garden Gym and Gymnase Club are financially prohibitive), but if your last meal has left you feeling you need it, here are some options.

Centre de Danse du Marais, 41 rue du Temple, 4e; ☎01.42.72.15.42 (Mº Hôtel-de-Ville). Try out rock 'n' roll, folkloric dance classes from the East, tap dancing, modern dance, physical expression or flamenco. You'll find a board advertising all the workshops in the alleyway. Expect to pay around 80F per session. Mon–Sat 9am–10pm, Sun 9am–2pm.

Centre de Yoga Sivananda Vedanta, 123 bd de Sébastopol, 2e; ☎01.40.26.77.49 (Mº Strasbourg-St-Denis). First lesson – Tues 8pm – is free. Daily 11am–9.30pm.

Club Quartier Latin, 19 rue de Pontoise, 5e; ☎01.43.25.31.99 (Mº Maubert-Mutualité). Dance, gym, swimming and squash; 60F day pass for the pool and gym. Mon–Fri 9am–10pm, Sat & Sun 9.30am–7pm.

Espace Vit'Halles, place Beaubourg, 48 rue Rambuteau, 3e; ☎01.42.77.21.71 (Mº Rambuteau). Fanatics can spend a day doing every kind of tendon-shattering gyration. It's divided into four "work zones": the dance floor, gym floor, body-building room, and multi-gym room. *Détente* – relaxation – is also provided for with a sauna, Turkish baths, solarium and diet bar. For a 100F day pass you can have access to these and one floor session. Daily 8am–10pm.

Swimming pools

For around 16F, you can go swimming in many of Paris' **municipal pools** (we have indicated those that are more expensive). **Non-municipal pools** are usually twice as expensive.

Municipal pools

As varying hours are given over to schools and clubs, its best to choose a pool nearby and consult their timetable in advance. Many are closed on Monday. The following are among the best.

Les Amiraux, 6 rue Hermann-Lachapelle, 18e (Mº Simplon). Pool where Juliette Binoche memorably swam in the Kieslowski film *Three Colours Blue*.

Armand-Massard, 66 bd Montparnasse, 15e (M° Vavin). 25m pool. Closed Mon.

Bernard-Lafay, 79 rue de la Jonquière, 17e (M° Guy-Môquet). Two 25m pools. Closed Mon.

Butte aux Cailles, 5 place Paul-Verlaine, 13e (M° Place-d'Italie). Housed in a spruced-up 1920s brick building with an Art Deco ceiling for one of the most pleasant swims in the city. There's a children's pool outside. Rules are strict here: both sexes must wear bathing caps, and men must wear Speedo-style swimming briefs, not trunks.

Château-Landon, 31 rue du Château-Landon, 10e (M° Louis-Blanc). Two 25m pools and one for children. Closed Mon.

Georges-Vallerey Tourelles, 148 av Gambetta, 20e (M° Porte-des-Lilas). Two pools – one 37m– and a solarium; 24F.

Henry-de-Montherlant, 32 bd Lannes, 16e (M° Porte-Dauphine). Two 25m pools and one for children, a terrace for sunbathing, a solarium – and the Bois de Boulogne close by. Closed Mon.

Jean Taris, 16 rue Thouin, 5e (M° Cardinal-Lemoine). A 25m unchlorinated pool in the centre of the Latin Quarter and a student favourite. There's a small pool for children, too.

Piscine des Halles Susanne Berlioux, 10 place de la Rotonde, *niveau 3*, Porte du Jour, Forum des Halles, 1er (RER Châtelet-Les Halles/M° Châtelet). A 50m pool with a vaulted concrete ceiling and a glass wall looking through to a tropical garden; 25F.

Privately run pools

Aquaboulevard, 4 rue Louis-Armand, 15e ☎01.40.60.10.00 (M° Balard/RER Bd-Victor). An American-style vast multi-sports complex. The pool has wave machines and water slides, and a grassy outdoor sunning area, and costs 56F daily before 11am, 69F after 11am weekdays, 77F weekends (for children 3–11 50F weekdays, 56F weekends) for a 4hr session. Each extra hour you stay incurs a charge of 10F. Mon–Thurs

9am–11pm, Fri 9am–midnight, Sat 8am–midnight, Sun 8am–11pm.

Pontoise-Quartier Latin, 19 rue de Pontoise, 5e (M° Maubert-Mutualité). Art Deco architecture, beautiful blue mosaic interior and a 33m pool. Features night sessions from 9pm until midnight Mon–Thurs for 44F, and sometimes nude swimming. Ordinary rates 23F. Gym and squash courts, too – see Club Quartier Latin, opposite.

Roger-Le Gall, 34 bd Carnot, 12e (M° Porte-de-Vincennes). Most of the extras are reserved for club members, but anyone can swim in the 50m pool (open in summer; covered in winter); 23F.

Hammams

The **hammams**, or Turkish baths, are one of the unexpected delights of Paris. Much more luxurious than the standard Swedish sauna, these are places to linger and chat.

Les Bains du Marais, 31–33 rue des Blancs-Manteaux, 4e; ☎01.44.61.02.02 (M° Rambuteau/St-Paul). Completely restored hammam with Moroccan-style mosaic interior. 180F for sauna and massage. *Women* Mon 10am–8pm & Tues 10am–11pm; *men* Thurs 10am–11pm, Fri & Sat 10am–7pm; *mixed* Wed & Sat 8pm–midnight, Sun 11am–11pm.

Cleopatra Club, 53 bd de Belleville, 11e; ☎01.43.57.34.32 (M° Belleville). Women only. 80F for a sauna, 130F for massage. Very relaxed *hammam* with beautiful tiling; mint tea served. Tues–Sun 10am–6.30pm; closed Aug.

Les Grands Bains d'Odessa, 5 rue d'Odessa, 14e; ☎01.43.20.91.21 (M° Montparnasse). The oldest *hammam* in the city, which you reach through a courtyard decorated with shells and cupids. *Women*: Mon & Thurs–Sat 9.30am–9pm; *men*: Mon, Tues & Thurs–Sat 9.30am–9pm. 106F for steam-bath and sauna; jacuzzi 120F, massage 150F.

Hammam de la Mosquée, 39 rue Geoffroy-St-Hilaire, 5e; ☎01.43.31.18.14

Daytime amusements and sports

Daytime amusements and sports

(M° Censier-Daubenton). You can order mint tea and honey cakes after your baths, around a fountain in a marble and cedarwood-covered courtyard. It's very good value for 85F (massage 55F extra), and a very unintimidating experience if you've never taken a public bath before. Daily 10am–9pm. Hours and days for men and women change, so phone first, but generally women on Mon & Wed, Thurs & Sat and men on Fri & Sun; closed Aug.

Participatory sports

Ice-skating, rollerblading, skateboarding, jogging, bowling, billiards, boules – it's all here to be enjoyed.

One sport that is not really worth trying in Paris, however, is **horse riding** (*equitation*). You need to have all the gear with you and a licence, the Carte Nationale de Cavalier, before you can mount.

Rollerblading and skateboarding

Rollerblading takes over the streets every Friday night from 9.45pm, when between 5000 and 10,000 in-line skaters meet on place d'Italie in the 13ᵉ (M° Place-d'Italie) for a 40km circuit of the city, accompanied by rollerblading police officers and tag-along cyclists. If you want to join in, you can find out more information and **hire** skates or blades at Nomades (37 bd Bourdon, 4ᵉ; ☎01.44.54.07.44; M° Bastille), open Mon–Fri 11am–7pm, Sat & Sun 10am–7pm, with its own bar out back where you can meet other bladers. Hire is a reasonable 50F per day on a weekday, 60F on the weekend (half-day 30F/40F), but the deposit is 1000F and hiring the recommended protective pads will cost another 30F. Bike 'n' Roller (6 rue St-Julien-Le-Pauvre, 5ᵉ; ☎01.44.07.35.89), open Wed–Sat 10am–7.30pm, Sun 9am–8pm, also hires rollers and blades from 25F per hour (or 75F per day), and the owner sometimes gives rollerblading tours of the Latin Quarter.

The main official outdoor arena for rollerblading and **skateboarding** is the concourse of the Palais de Chaillot (M° Trocadéro), though Les Halles (around the Fontaine des Innocents), the Beaubourg piazza, the place du Palais-Royal and the Pont au Double outside Notre-Dame are also popular spots. On Sundays, the central quais along the Seine and the stretch of road along the Canal St Martin are car-free between 10am and 4pm, making way for a stream of rollerbladers and cyclists.

There's also a special disco **roller-skating rink**, La Main Jaune (place de la Porte-de-Champerret, 17ᵉ; M° Porte-de-Champerret), open Wed, Sat & Sun 2.30–7pm, 50F plus 15F skate hire. Fri & Sat disco sessions 10pm–dawn; 80F plus 15F skate hire.

Ice skating

You can get on the ice year round at the city's permanent **ice rink**: the Patinoire des Buttes-Chaumont (30 rue Edouard-Pailleron, 19ᵉ; ☎01.42.08.72.20; M° Bolivar) is open Mon, Tues & Thurs 3–9pm, Wed 10am–9pm, Fri 3pm–midnight, Sat 10am–midnight, Sun 10am–6pm. Entry including skate rental is around 50F.

From November to March, a small rink is set up in the Tuileries gardens by the Orangerie (M° Place-de-la-Concorde); open Mon, Tues, Thurs & Fri noon–1.30pm & 4–7pm, Wed, Sat & Sun 10am–7pm; 50F including skate hire.

Jogging – and the Marathon

The **Paris Marathon** is held in May over a route from place de la Concorde to Vincennes. If you want to join in and need details and equipment, the best place for information is a shop owned by a dedicated marathon runner, Marathon (6 rue de Lyon, 12ᵉ; ☎01.42.27.48.18; M° Gare-de-Lyon). A shorter race, "Les 20km de Paris", takes place mid-October and begins and ends at the Eiffel Tower.

To go running or **jogging** solo any other time, take great care with the traffic. The Jardin du Luxembourg, Tuileries and Champs de Mars, which are particularly popular with Parisian joggers, all provide decent, varied runs, and are more or less flat. If you want to run hills, head for the Parc des Buttes-Chaumont in the 19ᵉ or Parc Montsouris in the 14ᵉ for plenty of suitably punishing gradients. If you have easy access to them, the Bois de Boulogne and the Bois de Vincennes are the largest open spaces, though both are cut through by a number of roads.

Cycling

Since 1996 the Mairie de Paris has made great efforts to introduce dedicated **cycle lanes** in the city, which now add up to 100km. You can pick up a free leaflet, *Paris à Vélo*, outlining the routes, from town halls, the tourist office, or bike hire outlets (see below). If you prefer cycling in a more natural environment, the Bois de Boulogne and the Bois de Vincennes have extensive bike tracks. On Sundays cycling by the Seine is popular, when its central quais (and along the Canal St-Martin) are closed to cars between 10am and 4pm.

Several outlets detailed below **rent bikes**, by the hour, day, weekend or week. Prices depend on the type of bike, but usually start from about 80–120F a day, 400–575F a week with a *caution* (deposit) of 1000–2500F or your credit card details. If you want a bike for Sunday, when all of Paris takes to the quais, you'll need to book in advance.

Some companies also offer **bike trips**. Excellent half-day tours and night tours of the city are offered by Paris à Vélo C'est Sympa (see below). For sorties into the outlying countryside, phone Escapade à Vélo for information about a variety of expeditions.

Bike 'n' Roller, 6 rue St-Julien-Le-Pauvre, 5ᵉ ; ☎01.44.07.35.89 (Mº/RER St-Michel). Also hires out rollerblades. Wed–Sat 10am–7.30pm, Sun 9am–8pm.

Bois de Boulogne near the Porte de Sablons entrance (Mº Les Sablons). For rides through the wood.

Escapade à Vélo ☎01.53.17.03.18. As well as tours within Paris, their day trips

further afield can take in the Canal de l'Ourcq, Chantilly, Fontainebleu or Versailles; 250F including hire of bike, train ticket, guide and admission costs.

Maison du Vélo, 11 rue Fénélon, 10ᵉ; ☎01.42.81.24.72 (Mº Gare-du-Nord/Poissonnière). Tues–Sat 10am–7pm.

Paris À Vélo C'est Sympa, 37 bd Bourdon, 4ᵉ; ☎01.48.87.60.01 (Mº Bastille). One of the cheapest and most helpful for bike hire. Their excellent half-day tours of Paris cost 170F – under-26s 150F. Also night-time tours, which are especially enjoyable (190F, under-26s 170F). For details, consult their Web site: *www.parisvelosympa.com*. Daily 9am–7pm, closed weekdays 1–2pm.

Paris-Vélo, 2 rue du Fer-à-Moulin, 5ᵉ; ☎01.43.37.59.22; (Mº Censier-Daubenton). 21-speed and mountain bikes. Mon–Sat 10am–12.30pm & 2–7pm.

Bowling alleys

There's nothing particularly Parisian about **bowling** alleys, but they exist and they're popular, should the urge take you. Prices vary between 15F and 35F a session, being more in the evenings and at weekends, plus there's an 8–10F charge for shoe hire.

Bowling de Montparnasse, 25 rue du Commandant-Mouchotte, 14ᵉ; ☎01.43.21.61.32 (Mº Montparnasse-Bienvenue). A complex with sixteen lanes, plus a bar, brasserie, pool tables and video games. Daily 10am–2am.

Bowling Mouffetard, Centre-Commercial Mouffetard-Monge, 73 rue Mouffetard, 5ᵉ; ☎01.43.31.09.35 (Mº Monge). The cheapest in town, frequented by students, with bar and billiards. Daily 11am–2am.

Bowling de Paris, Jardin d'Acclimatation, Bois de Boulogne 16ᵉ; ☎01.53.64.93.00 (Mº Les Sablons). Popular with chic types west of town. Daily 11am–2am.

Le Stadium, 66 av d'Ivry, 13ᵉ; ☎01.45.86.55.52 (Mº Porte-d'Ivry). Entrance by escalators to Olympiades.

Daytime amusements and sports

Daytime amusements and sports

Attracts a young clientele to roll the balls in Chinatown. With bar billiards and pool alongside. Daily 10am–2am.

Billiards and pool

Unlike bowling, **billiards** (*billard*) is an original and ancient French game played with three balls and no pockets. Pool, or *billard américain* as the French call it, is also played. If you want to watch or try your hand (for around 55F per hour for the French game, and 60–65F for the American, plus an average of 100F deposit), head for one of the following:

Académie de Billard Clichy-Montmartre, 84 rue de Clichy, 9e (M° Place-de-Clichy). The chicest billiard hall in Europe, where the players look like they've stepped out of a 1940s movie (or a *Men in Vogue* ad) and the decor is all ancient gilded mirrors, high ceilings and panelled walls. Daily 10am–4am.

Blue-Billard, 111 rue St-Maur, 11e (M° Parmentier). Cocktails, chess and backgammon as well as billiards, in arty-intellectual café-bar close to Belleville. If you have at least a 50F *formule* at lunchtime, you can have a game for free. Daily 11am–2am.

Bowling Mouffetard, 73 rue Mouffetard, 5e (M° Monge). See under "Bowling alleys" overleaf. Daily 11am–2am.

Salle de Billard des Halles, *niveau 2*, 14 rue Porte-du-Jour, Forum des Halles, 1er (RER Châtelet-Les Halles). Mon–Fri 10am–10pm, Sat & Sun 2–10pm.

Le Stadium, 66 av d'Ivry, 13e (M° Tolbiac). See under "Bowling alleys" overleaf. Daily 10am–2am.

Boules

The classic French game involving balls, **boules** (or *pétanque*), is best performed or watched at the Arènes de Lutèce (see p.128) and the Bois de Vincennes (see p.213). The principle is the same as British bowls but the terrain is always rough (never grass) and the area much smaller. The metal ball is usually thrown upwards from a distance of about 10m, to land and skid towards the wooden marker (*cochonnet*). It's very male-dominated, and socially the equivalent of darts or perhaps pool: there are café or neighbourhood teams and endless championships. On balmy summer evenings it's a common sight in the city's parks and gardens.

Rock climbing

The best training wall for **rock climbing** (*escalade*) in Paris is at the Centre Sportif Poissonnier, 2 rue Jean-Cocteau, 18e; ☎01.42.51.24.68 (M° Porte-de-Clignancourt); the wall is 21m high, with corridors and chimneys, and is accessible Mon–Fri noon–2pm, Sat & Sun noon–4pm. There's another wall in Aquaboulevard (see p.351) and one for kids in the sports and camping shop, Au Vieux Campeur (see "Kids' Paris" on p.367).

Other sports

Tennis, squash, golf, dry-slope skiing, archery, canoeing, fishing, windsurfing, water-skiing and parachuting – you name it, you can do it, in or around the city. Whether you'll want to spend the time and money on booking and renting equipment is another matter. If you're determined, you'll find some details in *L'Officiel des Spectacles*, *Pariscope* or *Le Guide du Sport à Paris*. Alternatively you can ring Allo Sports (see p.345) or pay a visit to Direction Jeunesse et Sports (p.345). These are both municipal outfits, so the places they have listed will all be subsidized and cheapish.

A lovely spot to play **tennis** is on one of the six asphalt courts at the Jardins du Luxembourg (daily 8am–9pm; hourly rates are 37F by day, 53F by night; reservations only on Minitel 3615; M° Notre-Dame-des-Champs). However, to play on municipal courts such as these, you need first to apply for a Carte Paris-Tennis from the Mairie, while private clubs demand steep membership fees. It's much easier to play **squash**, with several dedicated centres, including Squash Montmartre (14 rue Achille-

Martinet, 18e; ☎01.42.55.38.30; M°
Lamarck-Caulaincourt), who charge 30F
for a novice first half-hour, while the Club
Quartier Latin (see p.350) has some
squash courts which cost 60–75F for
40min to an hour.

Of the private clubs and complexes,
Aquaboulevard, 4 rue Louis-Armand, 15e
(M° Balard/RER Boulevard-Victor) is the
newest and biggest and easiest to use
casually, with squash and tennis courts,
a climbing wall, golf tees, aquatic diversions, *hammams*, dance floors, shops,
restaurants and other money-extracting
paraphernalia.

Spectator sports

Paris St-Germain (Paris-SG) is one of
France's most rich and powerful **football**
teams, owned by the French cable station Canal-Plus. That said, it hardly
enjoys a local following. The capital's
teams retain a special status, too, in the
rugby, cycling and tennis worlds. Horse
racing is as serious a pursuit as in
Britain, Australia or North America.

Cycling

The sport the French are truly mad about
is **cycling**, and the biggest event of the
French sporting year is the grand finale
of the **Tour de France**, which ends in a
sweep along the Champs-Élysées in the
third week of July with the French president himself presenting the *maillot jaune*
(the winner's yellow jersey).

It was, after all, in Paris' Palais Royale
gardens in 1791 that the precursor of the
modern bicycle, the *célerifière*, was presented, and seventy years later that the
Parisian father-and-son team of Pierre and
Ernest Michaux constructed the *véloci-
pede* (hence the modern French term
vélo for bicycle), the first really efficient
bicycle. The French can also legitimately
claim the sport of cycle racing as their
own, with the first event, a 1200 metre
sprint, held in Paris' Parc St Cloud in 1868
– sadly for national pride, however, the
first champion was an Englishman.

The Tour de France was inaugurated
in 1903; France, though, hasn't had a

victory since Bernard Hinault in 1985. In
theory the last day of the 4000-odd-kilo-
metre, 25-stage, three-week race is a
competitive time trial, but most years this
amounts to a triumphal procession, the
overall winner of the Tour having long
since been determined. Only very rarely
does Paris witness memorable scenes
such as those of 1989, when American
Greg Lemond snatched the coveted
maillot jaune on the final day. Requiring
what seems like inhuman endurance,
around 200 riders usually start the race
but sometimes less than 150 finish, and
in 1998 the event was rocked by drug
scandals. Nicholas Chaine, of the Crédit
Lyonnais bank, which sponsored the
race, supplied this unusually honest
quotable quote: "Let's not be hypocrites.
You just don't do that on fizzy mineral
water and salads."

Other classic long-distance bike races
which end or begin in Paris include the
600-km **Bordeaux–Paris**, the world's
longest single-stage race, first held in
1891; the **Paris–Roubaix**, instigated in
1896, which is reputed to be the most
exacting one-day race in the world; the
Paris–Brussels held since 1893; and the
rugged six-day **Paris–Nice** event, covering more than 1100km.

The Palais Omnisport de Bercy (see
p.356) holds cycling events including
time trails.

Football (*le foot*) and rugby

The Parc des Princes (24 rue du
Commandant-Guilbaud, 16e;
☎01.42.88.02.76; M° Porte-de-St-Cloud)
is the capital's main stadium for both
rugby union and domestic **football**
events, and home ground to the first-
division Paris football team Paris-SG (St-
Germain) and the rugby team, Le Racing.
In 1998 France hosted – and won – the
World Cup and the action in Paris
(including the final where they beat
Brazil 3–0) centred around the specially
built Stadé de France, on rue Francis de
Pressensé in St-Denis (☎01.55.93.00.00;
RER Stade-de-France-St-Denis) – now the
venue for international football matches
and rugby Five Nations' Cup matches.

Daytime
amusements
and sports

Daytime amusements and sports

Tennis

The French equivalent of Britain's Wimbledon complex, Roland-Garros, lies between the Parc des Princes and the Bois de Boulogne, with the ace address of 2 av Gordon-Bennett, 16ᵉ (☎01.47.43.48.00; Mᵒ Porte-d'Auteuil). The French Tennis Open, one of the four major events which together comprise the Grand Slam, takes place in the last week of May and first week of June, and tickets need to be reserved before February. A few are sold on each day of the tournament, but only for the unseeded matches. Unlike Wimbledon, you can't get near the main courts once inside the turnstiles.

Athletics and other sports

The Palais des Omnisports Paris-Bercy (POPB) at 8 bd Bercy, 12ᵉ (☎01.40.02.61.60; Mᵒ Bercy) hosts all manner of sporting events, including athletics, cycling, handball, dressage and show-jumping, ice hockey, ballroom dancing, judo and motocross. Keep an eye on the sports pages of the newspapers (except *Le Monde*, which has no sports coverage at all), and you might find something on that interests you. The complex holds 17,000 people, so you've a fair chance of getting a ticket at the door, championships excepted.

HORSE RACING

The **biggest races** are the Prix de la République and the Grand Prix de L'Arc de Triomphe, held on the first and last Sundays in October at Auteuil and Longchamp. The week starting the last Sunday in June sees nine big events, at Auteuil, Longchamp, St-Cloud and Chantilly (see p.391). If you want to fathom the **betting system**, any bar or café with the letters PMU will take your money on a three-horse bet, known as *le tiercé*.

St-Cloud Champ de Courses is in the Parc de St-Cloud off Allée de Chamillard. Auteuil is off the route d'Auteuil, and Longchamp off the route des Tribunes, both in the Bois de Boulogne. *L'Humanité* and *Paris-Turf* carry details, and admission charges are less than 30F.

Trotting races, with the jockeys in chariots, run from August to September on the Route de la Ferme in the Bois de Vincennes.

Chapter 18

Kids' Paris

Paris is often considered a strictly adult city, with little to engage or entertain energetic kids. Keeping teenagers amused may be as hard in Paris as it is anywhere, but for the younger ones there is a lot on offer, in addition to Disneyland Paris (see Chapter 21).

You shouldn't underestimate the sheer attraction of Paris' vibrant sense of life, with its diversity of sights and sounds so far removed from typical British, Australasian and American cities.

But neither should you expect kids to be enthralled by the Louvre, Notre-Dame and the Invalides. There are museums and monuments to excite most children, as well as playgrounds, puppet shows, wonderful shops and high-tech treats. The French are also extremely welcoming to children, so there's never a problem taking them into cafés, bars or restaurants, most of which will cook simpler food on request. Hotels charge by the room – there's a small supplement

A full account of Disneyland Paris is given in Chapter 21.

Paris with babies

You will have little problem in getting hold of essentials for **babies**. Familiar brands of baby food are available in the supermarkets, as well as disposable nappies (*couches à jeter*), etc. After hours, you can get most goods from late-night pharmacies.

Getting around with a pushchair poses the same problems as in most big cities. The métro is particularly bad, with its constant flights of stairs (and few escalators), difficult turnstiles and very stiff doors. One particular place to avoid is the Louvre: taking a buggy in there is like trying to pothole with a rucksack. Unfortunately the majority of parks are gravelled rather than grassed, and when there are lawns they are often out of bounds (*"perlouse interdite"*), so sprawling horizontally with toddlers and napping babies is usually not an option.

For emergency medical care, see under "Health and insurance".

Baby-sitters
Inter-service Parents (☎01.44.93.44.93) is a very handy phone service giving up-to-date advice on **baby-sitting agencies**. Reliable agencies include Ababa, 8 av du Maine, 15ᵉ (☎01.45.49.46.46; 31F per hour plus agency fees of 62F and taxis home after 11pm), which has English speakers; and Kid Services, 75 bd Pereire, 17ᵉ (☎01.47.66.00.52; 33F per hour plus 60F fees). Otherwise, try individual notices at the American Church, 65 quai d'Orsay, 6ᵉ (Mᵒ Invalides), the Alliance Française, 101 bd Raspail, 6ᵉ (Mᵒ St-Placide), or CIDJ, 101 quai Branly, 15ᵉ; ☎01.44.49.12.00 (Mᵒ Bir-Hakeim).

Kids' Paris

Sporting amusements: swimming, rollerblading and other family activities

One of the most fun things a kid can do in Paris – and it's just as enjoyable for the minders – is to have a wet and wild day at **Aquaboulevarde**, a giant leisure complex with a landscaped wave pool, slides and a grassy outdoor park. Details are given on p.351. Many municipal **swimming pools** in Paris have dedicated children's pools. We have listed four such on p.351 – Jean Taris in the 5ᵉ, Château-Landon in the 10ᵉ, Butte aux Cailles in the 13ᵉ and Henry-de-Montherlant in the 16ᵉ.

Cycling and **rollerblading** are other fun undertakings for the whole family. Sunday is now the favoured day to be *en famille* on wheels in Paris, when the central quais of the Seine and the Canal St-Martin are closed to traffic between 10am and 4pm. One of the most thrilling wheelie experiences is the mass rollerblading that occurs on Friday nights. Ten thousand rollerbladers and tag-along cyclists do a 40-kilometre circuit of Paris, and it's all kept safe by accompanying rollerblading policemen. See p.352 for more details. We have listed bike and rollerblade hire places on the same page. Paris à Vélo C'est Sympa has a good range of kid-sized bikes as well as baby carriers and tandems, and they also offer bicycle tours of Paris.

Children get a free introduction to **rock climbing** at the Mur d'Escalade Poissoniers, and they can also practise it for free at the outdoor shop Au Vieux Campeur (see below, p.367). **Bowling** and **billiards** are both popular in Paris and might amuse your teenagers (see p.354).

---

for an additional bed or cot. You'll have no difficulty finding disposable nappies, baby foods and milk powders (see box overleaf). The SNCF (French Railways) charge half-fare for kids aged 4–11, and the RATP (Paris Transport) charge half-fares for 4–10s; under-4s travel free.

If your offspring know that **Disneyland Paris** is just outside the city, you probably won't be able to do anything with them until they've been there. If you can keep its existence a secret, so much the better, but at least take them to the **Cité des Sciences**, at La Villette, for a contrast.

For older kids, a good start is a visit to **Paristoric**, at 11 rue Scribe, 9ᵉ (Mᵒ Opéra/Chaussée-d'Antin; daily: April–Oct hourly 9am–8pm; Nov–March 9am–6pm; adults 50F, children over 6 and students 30F, second child free). This 45-minute wide-screen film (with headphones giving an English version) illustrating the history of the city is breathy-voiced and romantic, but informative and fun to watch. Performances are on the hour, every hour. There's also a new permanent exhibition in the foyer illustrating different styles of Parisian architecture through the ages.

The most useful **sources of information**, for current shows, exhibitions and events, are the special sections in the listings magazines: "Enfants" in *Pariscope* and "Jeunes" in *L'Officiel des Spectacles*. The best place for **details of organized activities**, whether sports, courses or local youth clubs, is the Centre d'Information et de Documentation de la Jeunesse (CIDJ), 101 quai Branly, 15ᵉ; ☎01.43.06.15.38 (Mᵒ Bir-Hakeim; Mon–Fri 9.30am–6pm & Sat 9.30am–1pm). The Mairie of Paris also provides information about sports and special events at the Kiosque Paris-Jeunes, 25 bd Bourdon, 4ᵉ; ☎01.42.76.22.60 (Mᵒ Bastille; Mon–Fri noon–7pm). The tourist office also publish a free booklet in French, *Paris-Ile-de-France avec des Yeux Enfants*, with lots of ideas and contacts.

It's worth remembering that **Wednesday afternoons**, when primary school children have free time, and

Saturdays are the peak times for children's activities and entertainment; Wednesdays continue to be child-centred even during the school holidays.

Parks, gardens and zoos

Younger kids are well catered for by the **parks and gardens** within the city, though some may find the activities too structured or even twee. The most standard forms of entertainment are puppet shows and **Guignol**, the French equivalent of Punch and Judy; these usually last about 45 minutes and cost around 15F, and are most common on Wednesday, Saturday and Sunday afternoons. Children under about eight seem to appreciate these shows most, with the puppeteers eliciting an enthusiastic verbal response from them; even though it's all in French, the combined excitement of a room full of kids should rub off, and the stories are easy enough to follow.

Adventure playgrounds hardly exist, and there aren't, on the whole, any open spaces for spontaneous games of football, baseball or cricket, but most parks have an enclosed playground with swings, climbing frames and perhaps a sandpit, while there's usually a netted enclosure where older children play casual ballgames. Otherwise, French sport tends to be thoroughly organized (see Chapter 17, "Daytime amusements and sports").

The real star attractions for young children have to be the **Jardin d'Acclimatation** and the **Parc de la Villette**, though you can also let your kids off the leash at the **Jardin des Plantes**, 57 rue Cuvier, 5e (M° Jussieu/Monge). Open from 7.30/8am until dusk, it contains a small **zoo**, the **Ménagerie** (summer Mon–Sat 9am–6pm, Sun till 6.30pm; winter Mon–Sat 9am–5pm, Sun till 6.30pm; 30F/20F), a playground, hothouses and plenty of greenery. Paris' top zoo is at the **Bois de Vincennes**, the **Parc Zoologique**, at 53 av de St-Maurice, 12e (M° Porte-Dorée; April–Sept Mon–Sat 9am–6pm, Sun & hols 9am–6.30pm;

Oct–March Mon–Sat 9am–5pm, Sun & hols 9am–5.30pm; 40F/30F, under-4s free). This zoo was one of the first in the world to get rid of cages and use landscaping to give the animals more room to exercise.

The Jardin d'Acclimatation

In the Bois de Boulogne, by Porte des Sablons (M° Les Sablons/Porte-Maillot). 12F, child 6F, under-3s free; rides from 10F. Daily: Oct–May 10am–6pm, June–Sept 10am–7.30pm, with special attractions Wed, Sat, Sun & all week during school hols, including a little train to take you there from M° Porte-Maillot (behind L'Orée du Bois restaurant; every 10min, 1.30–6pm; 5F one way, 10F return).

The garden is a cross between a funfair, a zoo and an amusement park, with temptations ranging from bumper cars, go-karts, pony and camel rides, sea lions, birds, bears and monkeys, to a magical mini-canal ride (*la rivière enchantée*; 11F), distorting mirrors, scaled-down farm buildings, and a puppet theatre with free guignol stagings at 3 & 4pm daily. Astérix and friends may be explaining life in their Gaulish village, or Babar the world of the elephants in the created-for-children **Musée en Herbe** (Mon–Fri & Sun 10am–6pm, Sat 2–6pm; 16F, aged 4–18 13F, under-4s free). The museum also has a permanent interactive exhibition aimed at 4- to 12-year-olds, introducing them to the history of art. There'll be game sheets (also available in English), workshops and demonstrations of traditional crafts. And if they just want to watch and listen, the **Théâtre du Jardin pour l'Enfance et la Jeunesse** puts on musicals and ballets.

Outside the *jardin*, in the **Bois de Boulogne**, older children can amuse themselves with mini-golf and bowling, or boating on the Lac Inférieur. By the entrance to the *jardin* there's **bike rental** for roaming the wood's 14km of cycle trails.

Parc de la Villette

In the 19e between avs Jean-Jaurès and Corentin-Cariou; ☎ 01.40.03.75.75 (M°

The Jardin des Plantes and its attractions – the Ménagerie and the Grand Galerie d'Evolution – are detailed more fully on pp.126–127.

More information about the Bois de Vincennes and the Parc Zoologique is given on pp.213–215.

Kids' Paris

Porte-de-Pantin/Porte-de-la-Villette). Daily 6am–1am; entry to park free.

As well as the Cité des Sciences, various satellite attractions (see below), and wide open spaces to run around or picnic in, the **Parc de la Villette** has a series of ten themed gardens, some specially designed for kids.

Polished steel monoliths hidden amongst the trees and scrub cast strange reflections in the Jardin des Miroirs, while Le Jardin des Brouillards has jets and curtains of water at different heights and angles. Formalized shapes of dunes and sails, windmills and inflated mattresses make up the Jardin des Vents et des Dunes (under-12s only and their accompanying adults). Strange music creates a fairy tale or horror-story ambience in the imaginary forests of the Jardin des Frayeurs Enfantines. The Jardin des Voltiges has an obstacle course with trampolines and rigging. Small bronze figures lead you through the vines and other climbing plants of the Jardin de la Treille; and the Jardin des Bambous is filled with the sound of running water. On the north side of the canal de l'Ourcq is the popular **Dragon Slide**.

Some of the park's "follies" have activities for kids: video editing in the Folie Vidéo and a game-filled crèche for 2–5-year-olds in the Petite Folie, both on the south bank of the canal de l'Ourcq; and arts activities for 7- to 10-year-olds in the Folie des Arts Plastiques, by the northeast corner of the Grande Halle (details on ☎01.40.03.75.00).

Parc Floral

In the Bois de Vincennes, on rte de la Pyramide (M° Château-de-Vincennes, then bus #112 or a ten-minute walk past the Château Vincennes). Daily: March–Sept 9.30am–8pm; Oct–Feb 9.30am–5pm; admission 10F, 6- to 10-year-olds 5F plus supplements for some activities, under-6s free.

There's always fun and games to be had at the **Parc Floral**, on the other side of the Bois de Vincennes to the

zoo. The excellent playground has slides, swings, ping-pong (racket and ball 30F) and pedal carts (42–60F per half-hour), mini-golf modelled on Paris monuments (from 1.45pm; 30F, children under 12 15F), an electric car circuit, and a little train touring all the gardens (April–Oct daily 10.30am–5pm; 6F). Tickets for the paying activities are sold at the playground between 1.45pm and 5.30pm weekdays and until 7pm on weekends; activities stop fifteen minutes afterwards. On Wednesdays at 2.30pm (May–Sept) there are free performances by clowns, puppets and magicians. Also in the park is a children's theatre, the **Théâtre Astral**, which has mime, clowns or other not-too-verbal shows for small children aged 3 to 8 (Wed 3pm, Sun & public hols 4.30pm & during school hols Mon–Fri 3pm; 33F; ☎01.42.41.88.33). There are also a series of pavilions with child-friendly educational exhibitions (free entry) which look at nature in Paris; the best is the **butterfly garden** (mid-May to mid-Oct Mon–Fri 1.30–5.15pm, Sat & Sun 1.30pm–6pm).

Jardin des Enfants aux Halles

105 rue Rambuteau, 1ᵉʳ ☎01.45.08.07.18 (M°/RER Châtelet-Les Halles). 7–11-year-olds only except Sat am; summer Tues–Thurs & Sat 10am–7pm, Fri 2–5pm, Sun 1–7pm, winter till 4pm; closed Mon & during bad weather; 2.50F per hour.

Right in the centre of town, just west of the Forum des Halles, the **Jardin des Enfants aux Halles** is great if you want to lose your charges for the odd hour. A whole series of fantasy landscapes fill this small but cleverly designed space. On Wednesday, animators organize adventure games; and at all times the children are supervised by professional child-carers. You may have to reserve a place an hour or so in advance. On Saturday mornings (10am–2pm) adults too can go in and play while they take charge of their under-seven-year-olds – the only time the little ones have access. Several lan-

Kids' Paris

Food for kids

Junk-food addicts no longer have any problems in Paris. *McDonald's, Quick Hamburger* and their clones are to be found all over the city. The French-style *"fast foude"* chain, *Hippopotamus*, is slightly healthier (branches throughout the centre of the city, including 1 bd des Capucines, 2ᵉ; ☎01.47.42.75.70; Mᵒ Opéra; daily 11am–5am; 47F *menu enfants*). At *Chicago Meatpackers* (8 rue Coquillière, 1ᵉʳ; ☎01.40.28.02.33; Mᵒ Les Halles; daily 11.30am–1am; 69F children's *menu*) a dining room with giant electric trains is reserved for kids. They're given balloons and drawing equipment, and on Wednesday, Saturday and Sunday lunchtimes at 1pm & 2pm (weekends only in summer) there are mime, music or magic shows.

Other restaurants are usually good at providing small portions or allowing children to share dishes. *Dame Tartine*, 2 rue Brisemiche, 4ᵉ (Mᵒ Rambuteau/Hôtel-de-Ville), open daily noon–11.30pm, is family-friendly, relaxed and affordable in a great spot overlooking the Stravinsky Fountain, right beside the Pompidou Centre. Kids can share things from the menu like the delicious open toasted sandwiches (from 30F), or there's a special kids' *menu* at 49F. Some other eating places we have listed in the *Guide* which offer kids' menus include *Chez Jenny*, an Alsatian restaurant at 39 bd du Temple, 3ᵉ (see p.272) and *Chez Imogéne*, a Breton crêperie on the corner of rue Jean-Pierre-Timbaud and rue du Grand-Prieuré, 11ᵉ (see p.292).

Keeping away from ice creams (rather than finding them) is the main problem in Paris. One thing to remember when ordering a steak, hamburger, etc, is that the French will serve it rare unless you ask for it *"bien cuit"*.

---

guages are spoken, including English. Opening times vary a bit in the middle of the day, so it might be best to phone ahead.

Other parks, squares and public gardens

All of these assorted **open spaces** can offer play areas, puppets or, at the very least, a bit of room to run around in, and are open from 7.30 or 8am till dusk. **Guignol and puppet shows** take place on Wednesday and weekend afternoons (and more frequently in the summer holidays).

Buttes-Chaumont, 19ᵉ; ☎01.42.40.88.66 (Mᵒ Buttes-Chaumont/Botzaris). Puppets, grassy slopes to roll down (see p.198).

Champs-de-Mars, 7ᵉ; ☎01.48.56.01.44 (Mᵒ École-Militaire). Puppet shows.

Jardin du Luxembourg, 6ᵉ; ☎01.43.26.46.47 (Mᵒ St-Placide/Notre-Dame-des-Champs/RER Luxembourg). A large playground, pony rides, toy boat rental, bicycle track, rollerblading rink, and puppets (see p.133).

Jardin du Ranelagh, av Ingres, 16ᵉ (Mᵒ Muette). *Guignol*, cycle track, rollerblading rink and playground.

Jardins du Trocadéro, place du Trocadéro, 16ᵉ (Mᵒ Trocadéro). Rollerblading, skateboarding and aquarium.

Jardin des Tuileries, place de la Concorde/rue Rivoli, 1ᵉ (Mᵒ Place-de-la-Concorde/Palais-Royal/Musée-du-Louvre). Pony rides, marionettes, ice rink (in winter), funfair in July.

Parc Georges-Brassens, rue des Morillons, 15ᵉ (Mᵒ Convention/Porte-de-Vanves). Climbing rocks, puppets, artificial river, playground and scented herb gardens (see p.159).

Parc de Monceau, bd de Courcelles, 17ᵉ; ☎01.42.67.04.63 (Mᵒ Monceau). Rollerblading rink (see p.224).

Parc Montsouris, bd Jourdan, 14ᵉ (Mᵒ Glacière/RER Cité-Universitaire). Puppet shows by the lake (see p.162).

Kids' Paris

Funfairs

There are three big **funfairs** (*fête foraines*) held in Paris each year. The season kicks off in late March with the Fête du Trône in the Bois de Vincennes (running until late May), followed by the funfair in the Tuileries gardens in mid-June to late August, with more than forty rides including a giant ferris wheel, and ending up with the Fête à Neu Neu, held near the Bois de Boulogne from early September to the beginning of October. Look up "Fête Populaires" under "Agendas" in *Pariscope* for details if you're in town at these times. Very occasionally, rue de Rivoli around M° St-Paul hosts a mini-fairground.

There's usually a **merry-go-round** at the Forum des Halles and beneath Tour St-Jacques at Châtelet, with carousels for smaller children on place de la République, at the Rond-Point des Champs-Élysées by av Matignon, at place de la Nation, and at the base of the Montmartre funicular in place St-Pierre. The going rate for a ride is 10F. There is also a funfair museum, the privately owned **Musée des Arts Forains**, on the edge of the Parc de Bercy at 53 av des Terroirs de France, 12ᵉ. It's a treat, located within one of the old Bercy wine warehouses, with working merry-go-rounds as well as fascinating relics from nineteenth-century fairs which are restored here. At the moment, the museum is only opened to groups of at least ten, but if you're keen you could try to tag along on a tour, and it may be open to the public by 1999 (bookings and enquiries ☎01.43.40.16.22; guided tour 1hr to 1hr 30min includes rides on attractions; 75F, child 25F; M° Bercy then bus #24).

Theme parks

Disneyland Paris (see Chapter 21) has put all Paris' other fantasy worlds and **theme parks** into the shade. And unfortunately it's the only one with direct transport links. But, if you're prepared to make the effort, **Parc Astérix** is better mind-fodder and cheaper than Disney.

Parc Astérix

In Plailly, 38km north of Paris off the A1 autoroute, most easily reached by half-hourly shuttle bus from RER Roissy-Charles-de-Gaulle (line B). Roughly April–June Mon–Fri 10am–6pm, weekends 9.30am–7pm; July & Aug daily 9.30am–7pm; Sept Wed & weekends only 10am–6pm, Oct one Wed & two weekends only 10am–6pm. Closed most of Oct to early April, and for several days in May, June and Sept, so it's best to phone to check times on ☎03.44.62.34.04. Admission is 170F, 3–12s 120F, under-3s free; at most RER and métro stations you can buy an inclusive transport and admission fee ticket for 198F/148F.

A Via Antiqua shopping street, with buildings from every country in the Roman Empire, leads to a Roman town where gladiators play comic battles and dodgem chariots line up for races. There's a legionaries' camp where incompetent soldiers attempt to keep watch, and a wave-manipulated lake which you cross on galleys and long-ships. In the Gaulish village, Getafix mixes his potions, Obelix slavers over boars, Astérix plots further sorties against the occupiers, and the dreadful bard is exiled up a tree. In another area, street scenes of Paris show the city changing from Roman Lutetia to the present-day capital. All sorts of rides are on offer (with long queues for the best ones); dolphins and sea lions perform tricks for the crowds; there are parades and jugglers; restaurants for every budget; and most of the actors speak English (even if they occasionally get confused with the variations on the names). Information about Parc Astérix in the UK is available on ☎01538/702200; in Paris, ☎01.44.62.34.04.

Circus, theatre and cinema

Language being less of a barrier for smaller children, the younger your kids, the more likely they are to appreciate Paris' many special theatre shows and films. There's also mime and the circus, which need no translations.

Circus (*Cirque*)

Circuses, unlike funfairs, are taken seriously in France. They come under the heading of culture as performance art (and there are no qualms about performing animals).

Some circuses have permanent venues, of which the most beautiful in Paris is the nineteenth-century Cirque d'Hiver Bouglione (see below). You'll find details of the seasonal ones under "Cirques" in the "Jeunes" section of *L'Officiel des Spectacles* and under the same heading in the "Enfants" section of *Pariscope*, and there may well be visiting circuses from Warsaw or Moscow.

Cirque Diana Moreno Bormann. This touring circus sets up at the Grands Sablons at the Jardin d'Acclimatation, 16ᵉ; ☎01.45.00.23.01 (M° Sablons), during its two seasons: April–June & Sept–Dec. From 70F, children under 4 free.

Cirque d'Hiver Bouglione, 110 rue Amelot, 11ᵉ; ☎01.47.00.12.25 (M° Filles-du-Calvaire); details in *Pariscope*, etc. Strolling players and fairy lights beneath the dome welcome circus-goers from Oct to Jan (and TV and fashion shows the rest of the year).

Cirque National Alexis Gruss. Performs at various venues between Oct and mid-Feb. Phone ☎01.40.36.08.00 for details.

Cirque de Paris in Villeneuve-La Garenne in the Parc des Chanteraines, 115 bd Charles-de-Gaulle; ☎01.47.99.40.40 (RER Gennevilliers/St-Denis). This dream day out allows you to spend an entire day at the circus (Oct–June Wed, Sun & school hols 10am–5pm; 295F/children under 12 230F, includes a meal). In the morning you are initiated into the arts of juggling, walking the tightrope, clowning and make-up. You have lunch in the ring with your artist tutors, then join the spectators for the show, after which, if you're lucky, you might be taken round to meet the animals. You can, if you prefer, just attend the show at 3pm (70–155F/under 12 45–95F), but if so, you'd better not let the kids know what they have missed.

Theatre and magic

Several **theatres**, apart from the ones in the Parc Floral and the Jardin d'Acclimatation, specialize in shows for children.

Au Bec Fin, 6 rue Thérese, 1ᵉʳ (☎01.42.96.29.35; M° Palais-Royal). Blancs-Manteaux (see p.320) and Point Virgule (see p.320) in the Marais have excellent reputations for occasional programming for kids, while the Théâtre des Jeunes Spectateurs in Montreuil (26 pl Jean Jaurès; ☎01.48.70.48.91; M° Mairie-de-Montreuil) specializes in children's theatre, but it's doubtful how much pleasure your children will get unless they're bilingual. Magic, mime, dance or music shows are probably more promising and it's worth checking under "Spectacles" in the "Enfants" section of *Pariscope*.

The magician's venue, Le Double-Fond, 1 pl du marché Ste-Catherine, 4e (☎01.42.71.40.20), has a special children's magic show every Saturday at 3.30pm, but it's very pricey at 60F for a child or adult, and there's a lot of chat in French along with the sleight of hand. If your kids are really into magic they should visit the Musée de la Curiosité (see p.114), where a magician performs throughout the day.

Cinema

There are many **cinemas** showing cartoons and children's films, but if they're foreign they are inevitably dubbed into French. Listings of the main Parisian cinemas are given in Chapter 15. The pleasure of an Omnimax projection at La Géode in La Villette or Dôme-Imax at La Défense, however, is greatly enhanced by not understanding the commentary. The Cinaxe projection at La Villette simulates motion to accompany high-definition film (see p.316). Films at the Louis-Lumière cinema (also in the Cité des Sciences – see overleaf) may be less accessible, but you can ask at the enquiry desk for advice.

Kids' Paris

Kids' Paris

*The Cité des
Sciences et de
l'Industrie is
described in
full on p.195.*

*Details of the
Dôme-Imax
are given on
p.316.*

Museums

The best treat for children of every age from three upwards is the **Cité des Sciences** in the Parc de la Villette. All the other museums, despite entertaining collections and special activities and workshops for children, pale into insignificance. So beware that, if you visit the Cité on your first day, your offspring may decide that's where they want to stay.

Given kids' particular and sometimes peculiar tastes, the choice of other museums and monuments is best left to them, though the **Musée des Enfants** itself, purveying sentimental images of childhood, is certainly one to avoid. On the other hand, don't forget the gargoyles of Notre-Dame, the tropical fish- and crocodile-filled aquarium at the **Musée des Arts Africains et Océaniens** (see p.214), and the **Grande Galerie de l'Évolution** (see p.127), which also has a children's discovery room on the first floor with child-level microscopes, glass cases with live caterpillars and moths and a burrow of Mongolian rodents. The **Musée de la Poupée** (see p.103) should please children who like dolls; and the **Musée de la Curiosité** (see p.114) should appeal to most kids. Excursions to the **catacombs** or even the **sewers** will also delight some children.

If outer space is the kids' prime interest, then bear in mind the two **planetariums**, in the Palais de la Découverte (see p.74) and the Cité des Sciences.

Certain museums have **children's workshops**. For a current programme, look under "Animations" in the "Enfants" section of *Pariscope*. The **Musée d'Art Moderne de la Ville de Paris** has special exhibitions and workshops in its children's section (Wed, Sat & Sun; entrance 14 av de New-York; 50F). The **Musée d'Orsay** provides worksheets (English promised) for 8- to 12-year-olds that make them explore every aspect of the building; plus the house runs children's workshops (☎01.40.20.52.63 to reserve a place; 25F). Other museums with sessions for kids include the **Musée**

Carnavalet, Musée de la Mode et du Costume, Musée des Arts Décoratifs, Institut du Monde Arabe, the **Louvre** and the **Petit Palais**; costs are around 25F.

Full details of all the state museums' activities for children, which are all included in the admission charge, are published in *Objectif Musée*, a booklet available from the museums or from the Direction des Musées de France (34 quai du Louvre, 1er; closed Tues).

Cité des Sciences et de l'Industrie

Parc de la Villette, 30 av Corentin-Cariou, 19e (Mº Porte-de-la-Villette). Tues–Sat 10am–6pm, Sun 10am–7pm; everything closed Mon. Cité pass giving access to Explora and its temporary exhibitions, planetarium, Cinéma Louis-Lumière, Salle Jean-Painlevé and mediathèque screens, aquarium and Argonaute: 50F, reduced tarrif 35F, under-7s free; Géode hourly shows 10am–9pm: 57F/44F, combined ticket with Cité 92F/79F (available from Géode only); Cité des Enfants and Techno Cité 25F, combined ticket with the Cité des Sciences 55F adult, 45F child; Cinaxe (screenings every 15 min 11am–6pm) 34F/29F.

The **Cité des Enfants** (90min sessions; Tues, Thurs & Fri 11.30am, 1.30pm & 3.30pm; Wed, Sat, Sun & public hols 10.30am, 12.30pm, 2.30pm & 4.30pm; special sessions school hols; advance reservations at the Cité des Sciences ticket office advised to avoid disappointment), the Cité's special section for children, divided between 3–5s and 6–12s, is totally engaging. The kids can touch and smell and feel inside things, play about with water, construct buildings on a miniature construction site (complete with cranes, hard hats and barrows), experiment with sound and light, manipulate robots, race their own shadows, and superimpose their image on a landscape. They can listen to different languages by inserting telephones into the appropriate country on a globe, and put together their own television news. Everything, including the butterfly park, is on an appropriate scale, and the whole area is beautifully organized and managed. If you haven't got a child, it's worth borrowing one to get in here.

On the ground floor, **Techno Cité** (sessions and times as for Cité des Enfants), for over-11s only, offers hands-on application of technology to industry. You can write a programme for a robotic videotape selector, design a prototype racing bike, manufacture a plastic puzzle and package it using a laser-guided cutter, and set up a control system for an assembly line.

The rest of the museum is also pretty good for kids, particularly the planetarium, the various film shows, the *Argonaute* submarine (Tues–Fri 10.30am–5.30pm, Sat & Sun 10.30am–6pm; 25F or free entry with day pass), children's médiathèque (noon–8pm; free) and the frequent temporary exhibitions designed for the young. In the Parc de la Villette (see p.359), there's lots of wide open green space, the dragon slide and seven themed gardens featuring mirrors, trampolines, water jets and spooky music.

The catacombs and the sewers

Horror fanatics and ghouls should get a really satisfying shudder from the **catacombs** at 1 place Denfert-Rochereau, 14e (Tues–Fri 2–4pm, Sat & Sun 9–11am & 2–4pm; closed Mon & hols; 27F/19F; M° Denfert-Rochereau), though perhaps you should read p.153 first.

The archetypal pre-teen fixation, on the other hand, can be indulged in the sewers – **les égouts** – at place de la Résistance, on the corner of quai d'Orsay and the Pont de l'Alma (Sat–Wed 11am–4/5pm; closed Thurs, Fri & last 3 weeks in Jan; 25F/20F; M° Alma-Marceau). For further details, see p.141.

Shops

If your offspring belong to the modern breed of sophisticated consumers, then keeping them away from **shops** will be your biggest saving. This can be difficult given the Parisian art of enticing window displays, practised to the full on every other street. Children with an eye for

clothes are certain to spy boots, gloves or dresses without which life will not be worth living. Huge cuddly animals, gleaming models, and the height of fashionable sports equipment will beckon them from every turn, not to mention ice-creams, waffles, chips and pancakes. The only goodies you are safe from are high-tech toys, of which France seems to offer a particularly poor selection. Below is a small selection of shops to seek out, be dragged into or to avoid at all costs.

Books

The following are among a number of shops stocking a good selection of English books, but be warned: they're expensive.

Brentano's, 37 av de l'Opéra, 2e; 01.42.61.52.50 (M° Opéra). Storytelling sessions, singing and crafts on Wednesday afternoons and Saturday mornings. Call first to check. Mon–Sat 10am–7pm.

Chantelivre, 13 rue de Sèvres, 6e; 01.45.48.87.90 (M° Sèvres-Babylone). A huge selection of everything to do with and for children, including good picture books for the younger ones, an English section, and a play area. Mon 1–6.50pm, Tues–Sat 10am–6.50pm; closed mid–Aug.

Galignani, 224 rue de Rivoli, 1er; 01.42.60.76.07 (M° Tuileries). Mon–Sat 10am–7pm.

W H Smith, 248 rue de Rivoli, 1er (M° Concorde). Mon–Sat 9.30am–7pm.

Toys and games

As well as the wide assortment of shops listed below, it's worth bearing in mind that if children have enjoyed a museum they'll probably want what's on offer in the museum shops. The boutique at the **Cité des Sciences** have wonderful books, models, games, scientific instruments and toys covering a wide price range.

Art et Joie, 74 rue de Maubeuge, 9e; 01.48.78.27.72 (M° Poissonnière). Everything you need for painting, model-

Kids' Paris

The whole family can go dancing one Sunday afternoon a month at the friendly Divan du Monde *"bal des familles", in the 18e. See* p.302.

Kids' Paris

ling, graphic design, pottery and every other art and craft. Mon–Fri 9.30am–6.30pm, Sat 10am–12.30pm; closed Aug.

Le Ciel Est à Tout le Monde, 10 rue Gay-Lussac, 5e; ☎01.46.33.21.50 (RER Luxembourg); 7 av Trudaine, 9e (M° Anvers). The best kite shop in Europe also sells frisbees, boomerangs, etc, and, next door, books, slippers, mobiles and traditional wooden toys. Mon–Sat 10am–7pm; closed Sun.

Au Cotillon Moderne, 13 bd Voltaire, 11e; ☎01.47.00.43.93 (M° Oberkampf). Celluloid and supple plastic masks of animals and fictional and political characters, plus there are trinkets, festoons and other party paraphernalia. Mon–Fri 9.30am–6.30pm, Sat 10am–12.30pm & 2–6pm; closed Aug.

Les Cousins d'Alice, 36 rue Daguerre, 14e; ☎01.43.20.24.86 (M° Gaîté/Edgar-Quinet). *Alice in Wonderland* decorations, toys, games, puzzles and mobiles, plus a general range of books and records. Tues–Sat 10am–1pm & 3–5pm, Sun 11am–1pm; closed Mon & Aug.

FNAC Junior, 19 rue Vavin, 6e; ☎01.56.24.03.46 (M° Vavin). Multimedia store – books, videos, CD-ROMs, educational games and toys for the pre-teens – where you can try before you buy, plus special Wednesday afternoon and Saturday entertainment and activities.

Mayette Magie Moderne, 8 rue des Carmes, 5e; ☎01.43.54.13.63 (M° Maubert-Mutualité). The oldest French magic shop, founded in 1808. A magician's paradise. There is usually someone here who speaks English. Tues–Sat 10am–8pm, Mon 2–8pm.

Au Nain Bleu, 406–410 rue St-Honoré, 8e; ☎01.42.60.39.01 (M° Concorde). The Paris equivalent of London's Hamley's – a large store completely devoted to toys of all kinds – which has been in business since the 1830s. Mon–Sat 9.45am–6.30pm; closed Mon in Aug.

Pains d'Épices, 29 passage Jouffroy, 9e; ☎01.47.70.82.65 (M° Grands-

Boulevards). Fabulous doll's house necessities from furniture to wine glasses, and puppets. Mon 2–7pm, Tues–Sat 10am–7pm.

La Pelucherie, 84 av des Champs-Élysées, 8e; ☎01.43.59.49.05 (M° George-V/Franklin-D-Roosevelt). The top cuddly toy consortium. Expensive, but worth a look. Mon 10am–7.30pm, Tues–Sat 10am–11pm, Sun & hols noon–8pm.

Puzzles d'Art, 116 rue du Château, 14e; ☎01.43.22.28.73 (M° Pernéty). Exactly what the name says; with workshop on the premises. Mon–Fri 8.30am–8pm, Sat 10am–8pm.

Si Tu Veux, 68 galerie Vivienne, 2e; ☎01.42.60.59.97 (M° Bourse). Well-made traditional toys plus do-it-yourself and ready-made costumes. Mon–Sat 10.30am–7pm.

Virgin Megastore, 56–60 av des Champs-Élysées, 8e; ☎01.49.53.50.00 (M° George-V); and Carrousel du Louvre, 1er (M° Louvre–Rivoli). As well as all the cassettes and CDs to listen to, there's a Nintendo Gameboy to play with. Mon–Sat 10am–midnight, Sun noon–midnight.

Clothes

Besides the specialist shops we list here, most of the big department stores and the discount stores have children's sections (see Chapter 15). Of the latter, Tati and Monoprix are the cheapest places to go for vital clothing purchases.

ABC Carnaval et Fêtes, 22 av Ledru-Rollin, 12e; ☎01.43.47.06.08 (M° Gare-de-Lyon). Need something a little different? Fancy dress galore, gimmicks, masks, accessories and stage make-up all for hire or purchase. Tues–Sat 10am–7pm.

Agnès B, 2 rue du Jour, 1er; ☎01.40.39.96.88 (M°/RER Châtelet-Les Halles). Very fashionable, desirable and unaffordable, with lovely animal rocking chairs for the kids to sit in and contemplate their image. Mon–Sat 10am–7pm.

Kids' Paris

Baby Dior, 30 av Montaigne, 8ᵉ; ☎01.40.73.54.44 (Mᵒ Alma-Marceau/Franklin-D-Roosevelt). Even more unaffordable, but entertaining – especially the prices. Mon–Sat 10am–6.30pm.

Bill Tournade, 32 rue du Four, 6ᵉ; ☎01.45.44.39.58 (Mᵒ St-Germain-des-Près). All the top-name designers for kiddies. Good stuff, though not cheap. Mon–Fri 10.30am–7pm, Sat 10.30am–7.30pm.

Dipaki, 46 rue de l'Université, 7ᵉ; ☎01.42.97.49.89 (Mᵒ Bac). Also at 23 other addresses. Dependable, hard-wearing and reasonably priced clothes for up to 14-year-olds. Mon–Sat 10am–7pm.

Lara et les Garçons, 60 rue St-Placide, 6ᵉ; ☎01.45.44.01.89 (Mᵒ St-Placide). One of several samples and seconds clothes shops for children on this street. Cute little 'Marin' blue-and-white sailors' caps from 20F to make your baby look very French. Mon noon–7pm, Tues–Sat 10am–7pm.

Menkes, 12 rue de Rambuteau, 3ᵉ; ☎01.40.27.91.81 (Mᵒ Rambuteau). A vibrant selection of Spanish flamenco outfits, sombreros, fans and footwear for boys and girls. Classes also on offer. Tues–Sat 10am–12.30pm & 2–7pm.

Du Pareil au Même, 122 rue du Faubourg-St-Antoine, 12ᵉ; ☎01.43.44.47.66 (Mᵒ Ledru-Rollin). Beautiful kids' clothing at very good prices. Gorgeous inexpensive floral dresses. Branches all over Paris. Mon–Sat 10am–7pm.

Pom d'Api, 13 rue du Jour, 1ᵉʳ; ☎01.42.36.08.87 (Mᵒ/RER Châtelet-Les Halles). The most colourful, imaginative and well-made shoes for kids in Paris (up to size 40/UK7, and from 250F), plus exquisite chairs in the shapes of swans and dogs for the little ones to sit on. Mon–Sat 10.30am–7pm. Also at 28 rue du Four, 6ᵉ (Mᵒ St-Germain-des-Près; Mon–Sat 10am–7pm).

Le Refuge Enfants, 34 rue St-Placide; ☎01.42.22.23.29 (Mᵒ St-Placide). Affordable sports clothes for children, with a good range of swimming costumes. Mon noon–7pm, Tues–Sat 10am–7pm.

Unishop, 4 rue Rambuteau, 3ᵉ; ☎01.42.78.07.81 (Mᵒ Hôtel-de-Ville). Very cheap and cheerful kids' clothes: vibrant selection of zebra leggings, teeny hooded sweatshirts and floral dresses. Branch also at 42 rue de Rivoli, 4ᵉ (Mᵒ Hôtel-de-Ville). Tues–Sat 10.15am–7pm.

Au Vieux Campeur, 48 rue des Écoles, 5ᵉ; ☎01.43.29.12.32 (Mᵒ Cluny-La Sorbonne). The best camping and sporting equipment range in Paris, spread over several shops in the quartier. The special attraction for kids is a climbing wall. Mon 2–7pm, Tues, Thurs & Fri 10.30am–7.30pm, Wed 10.30am–9pm, Sat 10am–7.30pm.

Chapter 19

Directory

AIDS/HIV Information in English from FACTS-LINE (☎01.44.93.16.69 Mon, Wed & Fri 6–10pm). FACTS (Free AIDS Counselling Treatment Support) offers support groups and free counselling at 190 bd de Charonne, 20ᵉ (☎01.44.93.16.32; M° Alexandre-Dumas). SIDA info service ☎08.00.84.08.00.

AIRLINES Aer Lingus, 47 av de l'Opéra, 2ᵉ (☎01.47.42.12.50); Air Canada, 31 rue Falguière 15ᵉ (☎01.44.50.20.20); Air France, 119 av des Champs-Élysées, 8ᵉ (☎08.02.80.28.02); British Airways, 12 rue Castiglione, 1ᵉʳ (☎08.02.80.29.02); British Midland, 4 pl de Londres, Roissy-en-France 95700 (☎01.48.62.55.52); Delta, 4 rue Scribe, 9ᵉ (☎01.47.68.92.92); Qantas, 7 rue Scribe, 9ᵉ (☎01.44.55.52.05).

AMERICAN EXPRESS, 11 rue Scribe, 9ᵉ (☎01.47.77.79.79; M° Opéra). Bureau de change open Mon–Fri 9am–6.30pm, Sat 9am–5pm, Sun 10am–6pm, public hols 9am–5pm.

BANKS Barclays, 6 Rond Point-des-Champs-Élysées, 8ᵉ (☎01.44.95.13.80; M° Franklin-D-Roosevelt); Mon–Fri 9.15am–4.30pm; branches throughout the city (info. on ☎01.42.92.39.08). Western Union Money Transfer, CCF Change, 4 rue du Cloître-Notre-Dame, 4ᵉ (☎01.43.54.46.12; M° Cité); daily 9am–5.15pm.

CAR RENTAL Europcar (☎01.30.43.82.82); Hertz (☎01.39.38.38.38); Eurodollar

(☎01.44.38.61.61). Or some good local firms are: Acar, 99 bd Auguste-Blanqui, 13ᵉ (☎01.45.88.28.38; M° Place-d'Italie); Dergi, 133bis rue de Paris, 20ᵉ (☎01.43.68.55.55; M° Liberté); Locabest, 3 rue Abel, 12ᵉ (☎01.43.46.05.05; M° Gare-de-Lyon), and at 104 bd Magenta, 10ᵉ (☎01.44.72.08.05; M° Gare-du-Nord). Look up "*location*" in the yellow pages for others.

CUSTOMS With the Single European Market you can bring in and take out most things as long as you have paid tax on them in an EU country, and they are for personal consumption. Customs may be suspicious if they think you are going to resell goods (or break the chassis of your car). At the time of writing, limits still apply to drink and tobacco bought in duty free shops: 200 cigarettes or 250g tobacco or 50 cigars; 1 litre spirits or 2 litres fortified wine, or 2 litres sparkling wine; 2 litres table wine; 50gm perfume and 250ml toilet water.

ELECTRICITY 220V out of double, round-pin wall sockets. If you haven't bought the appropriate converter (*adapteur*) or transformer (*transformateur* – for US appliances) before leaving home, head for the electrical section of a department store, where someone is also more likely to speak English; cost is around 60F.

EMERGENCIES Fire brigade (Sapeurs-Pompiers) ☎18; Ambulance (Service d'Aide Médicale Urgente – SAMU) ☎15; Doctor call-out (SOS Médecins)

☎01.47.07.77.77 or 01.43.37.77.77;
Rape crisis (SOS Viol; Mon–Fri
10am–6pm) ☎08.00.05.95.95; SOS Help
(crisis line/any problem: 3–11pm) in
English ☎01.47.23.80.80. English-speaking hospitals: The American Hospital in
Paris, 63 bd Victor-Hugo, Neuilly-sur-
Seine (M° Porte-Maillot, then bus #82 to
terminus; ☎01.46.41.25.25) and The
Hertford British Hospital, 3 rue Barbès,
Levallois-Perret (M° Anatole-France;
☎01.46.39.22.22). In the event of a car
breakdown, call SOS Dépannage
(☎01.47.07.99.99) for round-the-clock
assistance.

EXCHANGE Some of the more conveniently located bureaux de change are:
at Charles-de-Gaulle airport (daily
6.30am–11.30pm) and Orly airport (daily
6.30am–11pm); at Gare d'Austerlitz
(Mon–Fri 7am–9pm), Gare de l'Est (summer 6.45am–10pm; winter
6.45am–7pm), Gare de Lyon
(6.30am–11pm), Gare du Nord
(6.30am–11pm), Gare St-Lazare (summer
8am–8pm; winter 8am–6.45pm); at the
Office de Tourisme de Paris (127 av
Champs-Élysées, 8ᵉ; 9am–7.30pm; M°
Charles-de-Gaulle–Etoile); and at CCF
(115 av Champs-Élysées, 8ᵉ;
8.30am–8pm; M° George-V). Try also the
main banks, American Express (see
above) or branches of Thomas Cook, eg
at 52 av des Champs-Élysées, 8ᵉ (daily
8.30am–10.30pm; ☎01.42.89.80.32; M°
Franklin-D-Roosevelt).

LAUNDRY You shouldn't have any trouble finding a laundry in Paris. If you can't
immediatley spot one near your hotel,
look in the phone book under "Laveries
Automatiques". They're often unattended,
so come pre-armed with small change.
The smallest machines cost around 12F
for a load, though some laundries only
have bigger machines and charge
around 20F. The alternative *blanchisserie*,
or pressing services, are likely to be
expensive, and hotels in particular
charge very high rates. If you're doing
your own washing in hotels, keep quantities small as most forbid doing any
laundry in your room.

LEFT LUGGAGE As an anti-terrorist security measure, only the left-luggage lockers, with heavy security, at the Gare du
Nord are operating.

LOST BAGGAGE Airports: Orly
(☎01.49.75.04.53); Charles de Gaulle
(☎01.48.62.10.86).

LOST PROPERTY Bureau des Objets
Trouvés, Préfecture de Police, 36 rue des
Morillons, 15ᵉ; ☎01.55.76.20.00 (M°
Convention). Mon, Wed & Fri
8.30am–5pm, Tues & Thurs till 8pm. For
property lost on public transport, phone
the RATP on ☎01.40.06.75.27.

PEDESTRIANS French drivers pay no
heed to pedestrian/zebra crossings,
marked with horizontal white stripes on
the road. It's very dangerous to step out
onto one and assume drivers will stop
as is usually the case at home. Take just
as great care as you would crossing at
any other point, even at traffic lights.

PETROL 24hr filling stations: 336 rue St-
Honoré, 1ᵉʳ; place de la Bourse, 2ᵉ; 42
rue Beaubourg, 3ᵉ; 36 rue des Fossés-
St-Bernard, 5ᵉ; 6 bd Raspail, 7ᵉ; 118 av
des Champs-Élysées and place de la
Madeleine, 8ᵉ; 1 bd de la Chapelle, 2
rue Louis-Blanc, 166 rue du Faubourg St-
Martin, 152 rue Lafayette, 10ᵉ; 55 quai
de la Rapée, 12ᵉ; Porte d'Ivry and Porte
d'Italie, 13ᵉ; Porte d'Orléans and av du
Maine (nr junction with av Gal-Leclerc),
14ᵉ; rue Linois and 95 bd Lefebvre, 15ᵉ;
Porte de St-Cloud and 24 av Paul-
Doumer, 16ᵉ; Porte de Champerret and
Porte de Clichy, 17ᵉ; Porte de la
Chapelle, 18ᵉ; Porte de Pantin, 19ᵉ; and
av de la Porte de Vincennes, 20ᵉ.

PHARMACIES All pharmacies, signalled
by an illuminated green cross, are
equipped to give first aid on request (for
a fee). When closed, they all display the
address of the nearest open pharmacy.
Pharmacies open at night include
Dérhy/Pharmacie des Champs-Élysées,
84 av des Champs-Élysées, 8ᵉ
☎01.45.62.02.41; 24hr; M° George-V);
Pharmacie Européenne, 6 place de
Clichy, 9ᵉ (☎01.48.74.65.18; 24hr; M°
Place-de-Clichy); Pharmacie des Halles,

Directory

Directory

10 bd Sébastopol, 4ᵉ (☎01.42.72.03.23; Mon–Sat 9am–midnight, Sun noon–midnight; Mᵒ Châtelet); Pharmacie Matignon, 2 rue Jean-Mermoz, 8ᵉ (☎01.43.59.86.55; daily 8.30am–2am; Mᵒ Franklin-D-Roosevelt); Pharmacie Azouley, 5 pl Pigalle, 9ᵉ (☎01.48.78.38.12; daily to 1am; Mᵒ Pigalle); Lagarce, 13 place de la Nation, 11ᵉ (☎01.43.73.24.03; Mon noon–midnight, Tues–Sat 8am–midnight, Sun 8pm–midnight; Mᵒ Nation).

PUBLIC TRANSPORT RATP information on ☎08.36.68.77.14 (6am–9pm; premium rate); SNCF information in English ☎01.45.82.08.41.

SAFER SEX A warning: Paris has the highest incidence of AIDS of any city in Europe; people who are HIV positive are just as likely to be heterosexual as homosexual. Condoms (*préservatifs*) are readily available in chemists, supermarkets, clubs, from dispensers on the street – often outside pharmacies – and in the métro. From pharmacies you can also get spermicidal cream and jelly (*dose contraceptive*), plus suppositories (*ovules, suppositoires*), and (with a prescription) the pill (*la pillule*), a diaphragm or IUD (*le sterilet*). Pregnancy test kits (*tests de grossesse*) are sold by chemists; if you need the morning-after pill (the RU624), you will have to go to a hospital.

SALES TAX What is called VAT (Value Added Tax) in Britain is referred to as TVA in France (*taxe sur la valeur ajoutée*). The standard rate in France is 20.6 percent; it's higher for luxury items and lower for essentials, but there are no exemptions (books and children's clothes are therefore a lot more expensive than in the UK). However, non-EU residents who have been in the country for less than six months are entitled to a refund (*détaxe*) of some or all of this amount (but usually around 14 percent) if you spend at least 2000F in one shop. The procedure is rather complicated: present your passport to the shop while paying and ask for the three-paged *bordereau de détaxe* form. They should help you fill it in and provide you with a self-

addressed envelope. When you leave the EU, get customs to stamp the filled-in form; they will send two of the pages back to the shop in the envelope; the shop will then transfer the refund through your credit card or bank.

SMOKING Laws requiring restaurants to have separate smokers' (*fumeurs*) and non-smokers' (*non-fumeurs*) areas are widely ignored. Non-smokers may well find themselves eating elbow to elbow alongside smokers, and waiters are not that likely to be sympathetic. Smoking is not allowed on public transport, including suburban trains, or in cinemas. Most office reception areas are non-smoking. But smoking is still a socially acceptable habit in France, and cigarettes are cheap in comparison with Britain, for example. Note that you can only buy tobacco in tabacs: a list of late-night tabacs is given on p.324.

STUDENT INFORMATION CROUS, 39 av Georges-Bernanos, 5ᵉ (☎01.40.51.36.00; Mᵒ Port-Royal).

TAXIS Try Taxis Bleus (☎01.49.36.10.10), Alpha Taxis (☎01.45.85.85.85), Artaxi (☎01.42.41.50.50) or G7 (☎01.47.39.47.39). Aero Taxis (☎01.41.27.66.66) specialze in trips to the airports.

TIME France is one hour ahead of Britain (Greenwich Mean Time), six hours ahead of Eastern Standard Time (eg New York), and nine hours ahead of Pacific Standard Time (eg Los Angeles). Australia is eight–ten hours ahead of France, depending on which part of the continent you're in. Remember also that France uses a 24hr clock, with, for example, 2am written as 2h and 2.30pm written as 14h30. The most confusing are noon and midnight – respectively 12h and 00h. **Talking clock** ☎36.99. **Alarm** ☎36.88, or with a digital phone dial *55* then the time in four figures (eg 0715 for 7.15am) then #. To annul, dial #55* then the time, then # (costs around 3.70F).

TOILETS Ask for *les toilettes* or look for signs for the WC (pronounced "vay say"); when reading the details of facilities outside hotels, don't confuse *lavabo*, which means washbasin, with lavatory. French toilets in bars are still often of the hole-in-the-ground squatting variety, and tend to lack toilet paper. Standards of cleanliness aren't always high. Toilets in railway stations and department stores are commonly staffed by attendants who will expect a bit of spare change. Some have coin-operated locks, so always keep 50 centimes and 1F and 2F pieces handy for these and for the frequent tardis-like public toilets found on the streets. These beige- or brown-coloured boxes have automatic doors which open when you insert coins to the value of two francs, and are cleaned automatically once you exit. Children under ten aren't allowed in on their own.

TOURS The best **walking tours** of Paris in English are those offered by Paris Walking Tours (☎01.48.09.21.40; 1hr 30min; 60F), with subjects ranging from "Hemingway's Paris" to "Historic Marais". A full list of times, meeting points and prices can be found in *Pariscope* in the "Time Out Paris" English-language section. The Paris transport authority, RATP, also runs numerous **excursions**, some to quite far-flung places, that are far less expensive than those offered by commercial operators. Details are available from RATP's Bureau de Tourisme, place de la Madeleine, 1ᵉ (☎01.40.06.71.45; Mᵒ Madeleine).

TRAFFIC & ROAD CONDITIONS For Paris' traffic jams listen to 105.1 FM (FIP) on the radio; for the boulevard péripherique and main routes in and out of the city, ring ☎01.48.99.33.33.

TRAVELLING ON Buses to all European destinations: Eurolines, gare routière, 28 av du Général-du-Gaulle, Bagnolet (Mᵒ Gallieni; ☎01.49.72.51.51). **Hitching agency**: Allostop-Provoya, 8 rue Rochambeau (square Montholon), 9ᵉ (Mᵒ Cadet/Poissonnière; ☎01.53.20.42.42, fax 01.53.20.42.44; can be e-mailed on *allostop@ecritel.fr*; Mon–Fri 9am–7.30pm, Sat 9am–1pm & 2–6pm).

WEATHER Paris and Île de France ☎08.36.68.02.75; rest of France ☎01.36.68.01.01.

YOUTH INFORMATION CIDJ (Centre d'Information et de Documentation de la Jeunesse), 101 quai Branly, 15ᵉ (Mon–Fri 9.30am–6pm & Sat 9.30am–1pm; ☎01.43.06.15.38; Mᵒ Bir-Hakeim).

Directory

Beyond the City

Chapter 20

Day trips from Paris

The region that surrounds Paris – known as the Île de France – and the borders of the neighbouring provinces are studded with large-scale **châteaux.** In this chapter, we detail a select few of them. Many were royal or noble retreats for hunting and other leisured pursuits; some, such as **Versailles,** were for more serious state show. However, if you have limited time and even the slightest curiosity about church buildings, your first priority should be to make instead for the **cathedral of Chartres.** Also, much closer in, on the edge of the city itself, **St-Denis** has a cathedral second only to Notre-Dame among Paris' churches. A visit to it could be combined with an unusual approach to the city: a walk back along the banks of the **St-Denis canal.**

Note that Disneyland Paris has a chapter to itself, starting on p.397.

Whether the various outlying **museums** deserve your attention will depend on your degree of interest in the subjects they represent. Several, however, have authoritative collections: **china** at Sèvres, **French prehistory** at St-Germain-en-Laye, the **history of flying machines** at Le Bourget, and the **Île de France** at Sceaux.

But the most satisfying experience is undoubtedly **Monet's garden** at Giverny, the inspiration for all his waterlily canvases in the Marmottan and Musée d'Orsay.

Cathedrals

An excursion to **Chartres** can seem a long way to go from Paris just to see one building; but then you'd have to go a very long way indeed to find any edifice to beat it. The cathedral of **St-Denis,** right on the edge of Paris, predates Chartres and represents the first break-throughs in Gothic art. It is also the burial place of almost all the French kings.

Chartres

The small and relatively undistinguished city of **Chartres** lies 80km southwest of Paris. The hour-long train journey from Paris brings an immediate reward in the moment you approach, when you first see

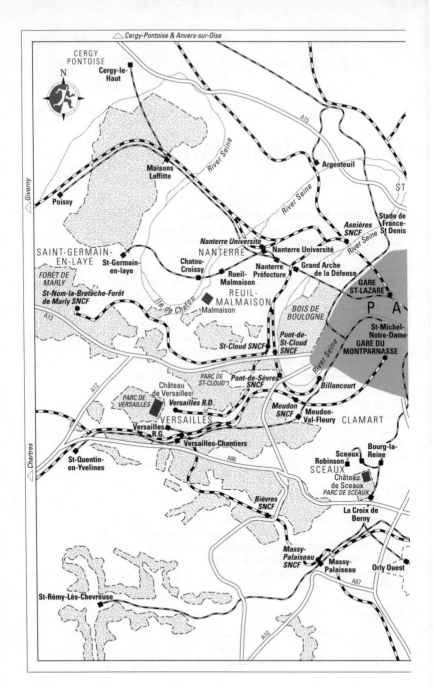

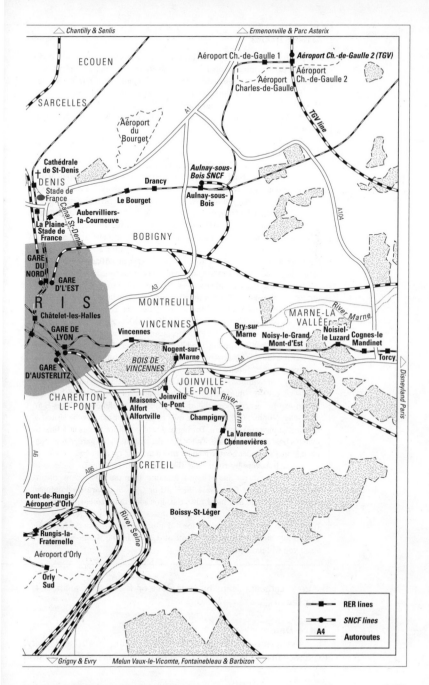

Artistic Haunts

For painters in search of visual inspiration, the countryside around Paris began to take a primary role in the late nineteenth-century art and attracted many a Parisian-based artist, either on a day jaunt or on a more permanent basis. The towns along the banks of the Seine read like a roll-call of Musée d'Orsay paintings, and pockets of unchanged towns and scenery remain. Local museums, set up to record these pioneering artistic days, are well worth a visit.

AUVERS-SUR-OISE

On the banks of the River Oise, about 35km northwest of Paris, **Auvers** makes an attractive rural excursion. It is the place where Van Gogh spent the last two months of his life, in a frenzy of painting activity, producing more canvases than the days of his stay. The church at Auvers, the portrait of Dr Gachet, black crows flapping across a wheat field – many of Van Gogh's best-known works belong to this period. He died, in his brother's arms after an incompetent attempt to shoot himself, in the tiny attic room he rented in the *Auberge Ravoux*. The **auberge** still stands, repaired and renovated, on the main street. A visit to Van Gogh's room (Tues–Sun 10am–6pm; 30F) is surprisingly moving. There is a short video about his time in Auvers.

You can also make a rather special and fascinating tour of the world that the Impressionists lived, an infra-red helmet on your head, at the **Château d'Auvers**, at the entrance to the village (May–Oct Tues–Sun 10am–8pm; Nov–April 10am–6.30pm; 50F; ☎05.34.48.48.48). Most evocative of all is a walk through the old part of the village, past the church and the red lane into the famous wheat field and up the hill to the cemetery where, against the far left wall in a humble ivy-covered grave, the Van Gogh brothers lie side by side.

Auvers boasts further artistic connections – Van Gogh's predecessor Daubigny, contemporary of Corot and Daumier. A small museum (Wed–Sun: April–Oct 2.30–6.30pm; Nov–March 2–5.30pm; 20F) dedicated to him and his art can be visited above the tourist office. His studio-house (Tues–Sun: April–Oct 2–6pm; 20F), built to his own requirements, can also be visited at 61 rue Daubigny. From here, Daubigny would go off for weeks at a time to take his boat and go painting. Today the boat that sits in the garden is a replica of Monet's smaller boat, which he would take out on day trips.

To reach Auvers **by road**, take the autoroute A15 from La Défense to Pontoise, the exit for Saint-Ouen-L'Aumône, then the SD4 to Auvers-sur-Oise. Trains depart from Gare du Nord or Gare St-Lazare for Pontoise, where you change and head for Creil. For something **to eat**, there's the reasonably priced *salon de thé, Les Roses Écossaises*, in a street that turns up to the church (salads for 45F), or the *Hostellerie du Nord* for something more substantial (*menu* at 120F). In the *Auberge Ravoux* itself you will pay upwards of 140F.

the great cathedral standing as if alone on the slight rise above the River Eure.

Notre-Dame

The mysticism of medieval thought on life, death and deity, expressed in material form by the glass and masonry of the **cathedral**

CHATOU

A long narrow island in the Seine, the Île de Chatou was once a rustic spot where Parisians came on the newly opened rail line to row on the river, and to dine and flirt at the *guinguettes*. A favourite haunt of many artists was the **Maison Fournaise**, just below the Pont de Chatou road bridge, which is now once again a restaurant (daily except Sun in winter: lunch & eve until 10pm; *menu* 150F, *carte* 200–250F; ☎01.30.71.41.91), with a small **museum** of memorabilia (Wed–Sun 11am–5pm; permanent exhibition 15F, temporary exhibition 25F). One of Renoir's best-known canvases, *Le Déjeuner des Canotiers*, shows his friends lunching on the balcony, which is still shaded by a magnificent riverside plane tree. As well as many Impressionists, Vlaminck and his fellow Fauves, Derain and Matisse, were also habitués.

Access to the island is from the Rueil-Malmaison RER stop. Take the Sortie av Albert-1er, go left out of the station and right along the dual carriageway onto the bridge – a ten-minute walk. Bizarrely, the island hosts a twice-yearly **ham and antiques fair** (March & Sept), which is fun to check out.

BARBIZON

The landscape and country living around Barbizon, southeast of Paris, inspired painters such as Rousseau and Millet to set up camp here, initiating an artistic movement, the Barbizon group. More painters followed as well as writers and musicians, all attracted by the lifestyle and community. The *Auberge du Père Ganne*, on the main road, became the place to stay, not unrelated to the fact that the generous owner accepted the artists' decorations of his inn and furniture as payment. Now home to a **museum** (Mon & Wed–Fri 10am–12.30pm & 2–5/6pm, Sat & Sun 10am–5/6pm; 25F), the inn still contains the original painted furniture as well as many Barbizon paintings.

MEUDON

The tranquil suburb of **Meudon**, to the southwest of Paris, was where **Rodin** spent the last years of his life. In 1895, he acquired the **Villa des Brillants** (19 av Rodin, Meudon; ☎01.45.34.13.09; May–Oct Fri–Sun 1–6pm; 10F; RER line C to Meudon-Val Fleury, then 15min walk along avs Barbusse and Rodin), and installed his studio in the first room you encounter as you enter through the veranda. It was here that he used to dine with his companion, Rose Beuret, on summer evenings, and here that he married her, after fifty years together, just a fortnight before her death in February 1917. His own death followed in November, and they are buried together on the terrace below the house, beneath a version of *The Thinker*. The classical façade behind them masks an enormous pavilion containing plaster casts of many of his most famous works.

at Chartres (open for services only Sat after 5.45pm & Sun until 1pm), should best be experienced on a cloud-free winter's day. The low sun transmits the stained-glass colours to the interior stone, the quiet scattering of people leaves the acoustics unconfused, and the exterior is unmasked for miles around.

The best-preserved medieval cathedral in Europe is, for today's

Chartres' cathedral is open Mon–Sat 7.30am– 7.15pm, Sun 8.30am– 7.15pm.

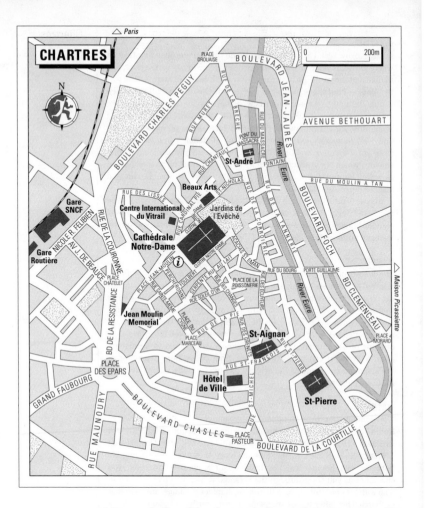

CHARTRES

PLACE DROUAISE
BOULEVARD JEAN-JAURES

0   200m

N

BOULEVARD CHARLES PEGUY

AVENUE BETHOUART

RUE MURET

RUE DE LA BRECHE

RUE DU MASSACRE

PONT DU MASSACRE

River Eure

FONTAINE

RUE CHANTAULT

St-André

RUE DU MOULIN A TAN

RUE DES LISSES

RUE NICHOLAS

Beaux Arts

RUE CARDINAL PIE

BOULEVARD FOCH

Gare SNCF

Centre International du Vitrail

RUE DE LA CORRO...

Jardins de l'Evêché

RUE CLOITRE

RUE DE LA TANNERIE

RUE DE LA COURONNE

NICOLE R. FELIBIEN

Gare Routière

AV. J. DE BEAUCE

Cathédrale Notre-Dame

RUE CLOITRE NOTRE-DAME

RUE JEAN-MOULIN

RUE PERCHERONNE

RUE AU LAIT

RUE ST-YEMAN

PLACE CHATELET

ⓘ

RUE DU BOURG

PORTE GUILLAUME

BD DE LA RESISTANCE

PLACE JEAN-MOULIN

RUE SAINTE-MÈME

RUE SERPENTE

PLACE DE LA POISSONERIE

RUE DES CHANGES

RUE DES ECUYERS

Jean Moulin Memorial

RUE SOLEIL D'OR

River Eure

BD CLEMENCEAU

RUE DE LA PIE

St-Aignan

RUE DE LA PETITE CORDONNERIE

PLACE MARCEAU

RUE DES GRENETS

PLACE MORARD

PLACE DES EPARS

RUE ST-PIERRE

GRAND FAUBOURG

RUE MAUNOURY

RUE ST-FRANÇOIS

RUE ST-MICHEL

Hôtel de Ville

BOULEVARD CHASLES

PLACE PASTEUR

St-Pierre

BOULEVARD DE LA COURTILLE

△ Maison Picassiette

visitors, only flawed by changes in Roman Catholic worship. The immense distance from the door to the altar which, through mists of incense and drawn-out harmonies, emphasized the distance that only priests could mediate between worshippers and worshipped, has been abandoned. The central altar undermines (from a secular point of view) the theatrical dogma of the building and puts cloth and boards where the coloured lights should play.

A less recent change, that of allowing the congregation to use chairs, covers up the labyrinth on the floor of the nave – an original thirteenth-century arrangement and a great rarity, since the authorities at other cathedrals had them pulled up as distracting frivolities. The **Chartres labyrinth** traces a path over 200m long, enclosed within a diameter of 13m, the same size as the rose window above the main doors. The centre used to have a bronze relief of Theseus and the Minotaur and the pattern of the maze was copied from classical texts – the medieval Catholic idea of the path of life to eternity echoing Greek myth. During pilgrimages, when the chairs are removed, you may be lucky enough to see the full pattern.

But any medieval pilgrims who were projected to contemporary Chartres would think the battle of Armaggedon had been lost. For them, the cathedral would seem like an abandoned shrine with its promise of the New Jerusalem shattered. In **the Middle Ages** all the sculptures above the doors were painted and gilded while inside the walls were whitewashed. The colours in the clean stained-glass windows would have been so bright they would have glittered from the outside along with the gold of the crowns and halos of the statuary. Inside, the reflected patterns from the windows on the white walls would have jewelled the entire building.

It is difficult now to appreciate just how important **colour** used to be, when the minerals or plant and animal extracts to make the different shades cost time, effort and considerable amounts of money to procure. Perhaps, in a later age, the statues will again be painted. Demands for whitewash are occasionally made and ignored. Cleaning the windows does go on, but each one takes years and costs run into millions.

There remain, however, more than enough wonders to enthral modern eyes: the geometry of the building, unique in being almost unaltered since its consecration in the thirteenth century; the details of the stonework, most notably the western façade which includes the Portail Royal saved from the cathedral's predecessor, destroyed by fire in 1195, the Renaissance choir screen, and the hosts of sculpted figures above each transept door; and the shining circular symmetries of the transept windows.

There are separate admission fees for various of the less public parts of the cathedral. Probably the best value of these, preferable to

---

Cathedral tours

One of the best ways to appreciate the detail of the Cathédrale Notre-Dame is to join a **guided tour** given by the erudite Englishman Malcolm Miller (April–Nov daily except Sun noon & 2.45pm; rest of the year, days and times vary – call ☎02.37.21.75.02; 40F; tour starts just inside the West door). This is no ordinary patter, but a labour of love from someone who has studied, written and lectured about Chartres for decades. Mr Miller's performance as the eccentric academic is impeccably done and he knows so much about the cathedral that you can follow several consecutive tours without fear of repetition. His explanation for the endless scope is that the cathedral is a library in which the windows and the statuary are the books. He reveals the storylines with fascinating digressions into the significance, past and present, of symbols, shapes and numbers.

---

the crypt and the treasures, is the climb up the **north tower** (crowds permitting; times vary, check in the cathedral; price 25F), for its bird's-eye view of the sculptures and structure of the cathedral. There are gardens at the back from where you can contemplate the complexity of stress factors balanced by the flying buttresses.

The Town

Though the cathedral is the main attraction, a wander round the town of Chartres also has its rewards.

The Centre International du Vitrail is open Mon–Fri 9.30am–12.30pm & 1.30–6pm, Sat & Sun 10am–12.30pm & 2.30–6pm; 20F.

Occasionally, stunning exhibitions of stained glass are displayed in a medieval wine and grain store, now the **Centre International du Vitrail**, at 5 rue du Cardinal-Pie on the north side of the cathedral. The **Beaux Arts Museum** in the former episcopal palace just north of the cathedral has some beautiful tapestries, a room full of Vlaminck, and Zurbaran's *Sainte Lucie*, as well as good temporary exhibitions. Behind it, rue Chantault leads past old town houses to the River Eure and Pont des Massacres. You can follow this reedy river lined with ancient wash-houses upstream via **rue du Massacre** on the right bank. On the left bank you'll see the Romanesque **church of St-André**, now used for art exhibitions, concerts, and so on.

The Beaux Arts Museum is open May–Oct 10am–noon & 2–6pm except Sun am & all Tues; Nov–April same days 10am–noon & 2–5pm; 10F.

A left turn at the end of rue de la Tannerie, then third right, will bring you to one of Chartres' more eccentric tourist attractions. The **Maison Picassiette**, at 22 rue du Repos, has been decorated by Raymond Isidore with mosaics using bits of pottery and glass and is a fine example of Naïve art. Back at the end of rue de la Tannerie, the bridge over the river brings you back to the **medieval town**. At the top of rue du Bourg there's a turreted staircase attached to a house, and at the eastern end of place de la Poissonnerie, a carved salmon decorates an entrance. The **food market** takes place on place Billard and rue des Changes, and there's a **flower market** on place du Cy (Tues, Thurs & Sat).

Cloître-Notre-Dame, along the south side of the cathedral, has mainly expensive eating places, an exception being the popular *Café Serpente*, at no. 2. The best meals are at *La Truie qui File*, place de la Poissonnerie (☎02.37.21.53.90; closed Sun eve, Mon & Aug); *Le Buisson Ardent*, 10 rue du Lait (☎02.37.34.04.66; closed Sun eve). There are also innumerable *faste foude* joints. The liveliest place to drink on market days is *Le Brazza*, on place Billard.

The Maison Picassiette is open daily except Tues and Sun am April–Oct 10am–noon & 2–6pm; 10F.

At the edge of the old town, on the junction of bd de la Résistance and rue Collin-d'Arleville (to the right as you're coming up from the station), stands a memorial to **Jean Moulin**, Prefect of Chartres until he was sacked by the Vichy government in 1942. When the Germans occupied the town in 1940, Moulin refused under torture to sign a document to the effect that black soldiers in the French army were responsible for Nazi atrocities. He later became de Gaulle's number-one man on the ground, coordinating the Resistance. He died at the hands of Klaus Barbie in 1943.

Chartres practicalities

Trains run roughly every two hours to Chartres from Paris-Montparnasse (140F return), with a journey time of just under an hour. From the station, av J-de-Beauce leads up to place Châtelet. Diagonally opposite, past all the parked coaches, is rue Ste-Même, which meets place Jean-Moulin. Turn left and you'll find the cathedral, and the tourist office (☎02.37.21.50.00; April–Sept Mon–Sat 9am–7pm, Sun 9.30am–5.30pm; Oct–March Mon–Sat 10am–6pm, Sun 10am–1pm & 2.30–4.30pm), on place de la Cathédrale. They can supply free maps and help with accommodation. There's also a youth hostel in town.

St-Denis

St-Denis, just 10km north of the centre of Paris and accessible by métro, remains a very distinct community, focused around its magnificent cathedral, the **basilica of St-Denis**. Numbering 30,000 in 1870, 100,000 strong today, its people have seen their town grow into the most heavily industrialized community in France, bastion of the Red suburbs and stronghold of the Communist Party, with nearly all the principal streets bearing some notable left-wing name. Today, recession and the advance of the Pacific Rim have taken a heavy toll, though the decision to stage the 1998 Football World Cup finals in St-Denis brought temporary fame and fortune. A vast hi-tech stadium was built in honour of the occasion, just south of town, and two new RER stops for the thousands of fans passing through. The decision as to whether it will house a team, or not, is still undecided, but in the meantime, plans are going ahead to install a wind and wave machine for windsurfing competitions, and international pop and rock stars such as Celine Dion and the Rolling Stones are managing to pack it out.

Although the centre of St-Denis still retains traces of its small town origins, the area immediately abutting the cathedral has been transformed in the last ten years into a fortress-like housing and shopping complex. The thrice-weekly **market**, however (Tues, Fri & Sun), still takes place in the square by the Hôtel de Ville and in the covered *halles* nearby. It is a multi-ethnic affair these days, and the quantity of offal on the butchers' stalls – ears, feet, tails and bladders – shows this is not rich folks' territory.

The cathedral

Begun by Abbot Suger, friend and adviser to kings, in the first half of the twelfth century, **St-Denis cathedral** is generally regarded as the birthplace of the Gothic style in European architecture. Though its west front was the first ever to have a rose window, it is in the choir that you see the clear emergence of the new style: the slimness and lightness that comes with the use of the pointed arch, the ribbed vault and the long shafts of half-column rising from pillar to roof. It

St-Denis is open April–Sept Mon–Sat 10am–7pm, Sun noon–7pm; Oct–March Mon–Sat 10am–5pm, Sun noon–5pm; closed Jan 1, May 1, Nov 1, Nov 11 & Dec 25

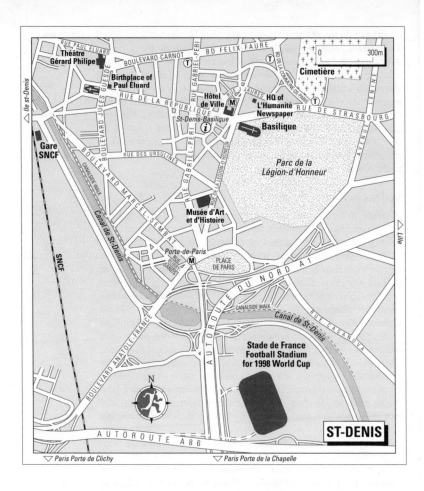

RUE PAUL ELUARD
**Théâtre
Gérard Philipe**
BOULEVARD CARNOT
BD FELIX FAURE
Cimetière
**Birthplace of
Paul Eluard**
RUE DE LA RÉPUBLIQUE
**Hôtel
de Ville** Ⓜ
**HQ of
L'Humanité
Newspaper**
RUE DE STRASBOURG
St-Denis-Basilique ⓘ
Basilique
**Gare
SNCF**
RUE DES URSULINES
*Parc de la
Légion-d'Honneur*
SNCF
Canal de St-Denis
CANALSIDE WALK
**Musée d'Art
et d'Histoire**
Porte-de-Paris
Ⓜ
PLACE
DE PARIS
AUTOROUTE DU NORD A1
Lille
CANALSIDE WALK
Canal de St-Denis
RUE CASANOVA
**Stade de France
Football Stadium
for 1998 World Cup**
N
AUTOROUTE A86
ST-DENIS

BOULEVARD JULES GUESDE
BOULEVARD MARCEL-SEMBAT
BOULEVARD ANATOLE-FRANCE
Île st-Denis
RUE GABRIEL-PÉRI
RUE J. JAURÈS
BD DE LA COMMUNE-DE-PARIS
AVENUE LÉNINE
RUE DE LA LÉGION-D'HONNEUR
RUE DE LA LÉGION-D'HONNEUR
RUE JUDE SANDS

0   300m

▽ Paris Porte de Clichy   ▽ Paris Porte de la Chapelle

is a remarkably well-lit church too, thanks to the clerestory being almost wholly glass – another first for St-Denis – and the transept windows being so big that they occupy their entire end walls.

Once the place where the kings of France were crowned, since 1000 AD the cathedral has been the burial place of all but three. Their very fine **tombs and effigies** are deployed about the transepts and ambulatory (32F). Among the most interesting are the enormous Renaissance memorial to François 1er on the right just beyond the entrance, in the form of a triumphal arch with the royal family perched on top and battle scenes depicted below, and the tombs of Louis XII, Henri II and Catherine de Médicis on the left side of the church. Also on the left, close to the altar steps, Philippe the Bold's is one of the earliest lookalike portrait statues, while to the right of the ambulatory steps you can see the stocky little general, Bertrand du Guesclin, who gave the English a run-around after the death of the Black Prince; and on the level above him, invariably graced by bouquets of flowers from the royalist contingent, the undistinguished statues of Louis XVI and Marie-Antoinette. Around the corner on the far side of the ambulatory is Clovis himself, king of the Franks way back in 500AD, a canny little German who wiped out Roman Gaul and turned it into France, with Paris for a capital.

The **tourist office** is located directly opposite.

The Musée d'Art et d'Histoire

Not many minutes' walk away on rue Gabriel-Péri is the **Musée d'Art et d'Histoire de la Ville de St-Denis**. The quickest route is along rue de la Légion-d'Honneur, then take the third right.

The museum is housed in a former Carmelite convent, rescued from the clutches of the developers and carefully restored. The exhibits on display are not of spectacular interest, though the presentation is excellent. The **local archeology** collection is good, and there are some interesting paintings of nineteenth- and twentieth-century industrial landscapes, including the St-Denis canal. The one unique collection is of documents relating to **the Commune**: posters, cartoons, broadsheets, paintings, plus an audiovisual presentation. There is also an exhibition of manuscripts and rare editions of the Communist poet, Paul Éluard, native son of St-Denis.

The Musée d'Art et d'Histoire de la Ville de St-Denis is open Mon & Wed–Sat 10am–5.30pm, Sun 2–6.30pm; 15F.

Canal St-Denis

To get to the canal – at the St-Denis end – follow rue de la République from the Hôtel de Ville to its end by a church. (To the right, at 46 bd Jules-Guesde, is the birthplace of the poet Paul Éluard.) Go down the left side of the church until you reach the canal bridge. Turn left, and you can walk all the way back to Paris along the towpath, taking something between ninety minutes and two hours. You come out at Porte de la Villette. There are stretches where it looks as if you're probably not supposed to be there. Just pay no attention and keep going.

Not far from the start of the walk, past some peeling villas with lilac and cherry blossom in their unkempt gardens, you come to a cobbled ramp on the left by a now-defunct restaurant, *La Péniche* (The Barge). Rue Raspail leads thence to a dusty square where the town council named a side street for IRA hunger-striker Bobby Sands. The whole neighbourhood is calm, poor and forgotten.

Continuing along the canal, you pass patches of greenery, sand and gravel docks, waste ground where larks rise above rusting bedsteads and doorless fridges, lock-keepers' cottages with roses and vegetable gardens, decaying tenements and improvised shacks, derelict factories and huge sheds where trundling gantries load bundles of steel rods onto Belgian barges. Barge traffic is regular and the life appears attractive, for these barges are proper family homes, with a dog at the prow, lace curtains at the window, potted plants, a bike propped against the cabin side, a couple of kids. But the keynote is decay and nothing looks set to last.

Châteaux

The mansions and palaces around the capital are all very impressive on first sight, and most have played an integral part in French history – none more so than **Versailles**, an overwhelming monument to the reign of Louis XIV.

That said, **Vaux-le-Vicomte**'s classical magnificence and **Fontainebleau**'s Italianate decoration are easy to appreciate; **Chantilly** has a gorgeous Book of Hours and a bizarre horse connection; and **Malmaison** is interesting for its former occupants. You can also enjoy the country air by taking a stroll in the **gardens, parks and forests** that surround the châteaux, and being able to get back to Paris comfortably in a day. If you are inspired to see other châteaux, there are many more places in addition to those detailed in this section. Some, whose principal function these days is to house museums, are described later in this chapter, while the tourist office in Paris can provide full lists of others.

Versailles

The **Palace of Versailles** is one of the three most visited monuments in France. It was inspired by the young Louis XIV's envy of his finance minister's château at Vaux-le-Vicomte (see p.388), which he was determined to outdo. He recruited the design team of Vaux-le-Vicomte architect Le Vau, painter Le Brun and gardener Le Nôtre, and ordered something a hundred times the size. Versailles is the apotheosis of French regal indulgence, and even if its grotesque decor and blatant self-propaganda of the Sun King are not to your liking, its historical significance and anecdotes will enthral.

In the park, a mere four square kilometres in area, the fountains only gush on selected days (Sun mid April–mid Oct), bringing the gardens to life. The rest of the time the statues on the empty pools look rather bereft of purpose. Versailles' notoriety, however, ensures a steady stream of tourists, and the château is always a crush of bodies.

The château

Open May–Sept Tues–Sun 9am–6.30pm; Oct–April Tues–Fri 9am–5.30pm; closed Mon & hols. Last admission 30min before closing. Grands Appartements and Chambre du Roi 70F; Grands Appartements only 45F, 35F after 3.30pm.

Visitors to the château have a choice of itineraries, and whether to be guided or not. Apart from the state apartments of the king and queen and the Galerie des Glaces (the Hall of Mirrors, where the Treaty of Versailles was signed to end World War I), which you can visit on your own, most of the palace can only be viewed by guided tour. Don't set out to see all the palace in one day – it's impossible not simply because of the building's size, but because tours of some of the apartments run concurrently.

There are four **entrances, each catering to different agendas**: **entrance A** is for those who want to visit the Grands Appartements only, which can be done either on your own or with an audioguide (30F); **entrance B** is for pre-booked groups; at **entrance C** you can hire an audioguide and gain access to Louis XIV's apartments, the Dauphin's apartments and the Hall of Mirrors, as well as being able to use your ticket to enter via entrance A and visit the Grands Appartements; **entrance D** organizes various guided tours for individual visitors with varying prices. Places can be booked for **guided tours** on the same day, but it's wise to arrive early. Information on which tours will be running is available by ringing the day before (Bureau d'Action Culturelle for information ☎01.30.84.76.20; group reservations ☎01.30.84.76.18 or 01.30.84.76.41). A word of warning, however, about guided tours: first, there are often several going on around you simultaneously in a distracting babel of languages; second, the guides' spiel consists largely of anecdotes about court life with a heavy emphasis on numbers of mistresses and details of the cost, weight and so on of various items of furniture.

The construction of the château began in 1664 and lasted virtually until Louis XIV's death in 1715. It was never meant to be a home; kings were not homely people. Second only to God, and the head of an immensely powerful state, Louis XIV was an institution rather than a private individual. His risings and sittings, comings and goings, were minutely regulated and rigidly encased in ceremony, attendance at which was an honour much sought after by courtiers. Versailles was the headquarters of every arm of the state. More than twenty thousand people – nobles, administrative staff, merchants, soldiers and servants – lived in the palace in a state of unhygienic squalor according to contemporary accounts.

Following Louis XIV's death, the château was abandoned for a few years before being reoccupied by Louis XV in 1722. It remained the residence of the royal family until the Revolution of 1789, when the furniture was sold and the pictures dispatched to the Louvre. Thereafter it fell into ruin and was nearly demolished, until 1837 when Louis-Philippe donated funds to turn it into a museum to the glory of France. In 1871, during the Paris Commune, it became the seat of the nationalist government, and the French parliament continued to meet in Louis XV's opera building until 1879. Restoration only began in earnest between the two world wars.

In 1961, a law was passed requiring the return of all the original furniture in existence to Versailles. The process still continues.

*The park is
open daily
7am–dusk;
free except on
Sun (28F).
Fountains
play May–
Sept Sun
11.15–
11.45am &
3.30–5pm.*

The park

The **park** scenery is better the further you go from the palace. There are even informal groups of trees near the lesser outcrops of royal mania: the Italianate **Grand Trianon** (Tues–Sun: summer 10am–6.30pm, winter 10am–12.30pm & 2–5.30pm; 25F), designed by Hardouin-Mansart in 1687 as a "country retreat" for Louis XIV, and the more modest Greek **Petit Trianon** (same hours; 15F, combined ticket for both Petit and Grand Trianon 30F), built by Gabriel in the 1760s.

More charming and rustic than either of these is **Le Hameau de Marie-Antoinette**, a play-village and farm built in 1783 for Louis XVI's queen to indulge the fashionable Rousseau-inspired fantasy of returning to the natural life.

Distances in the park are considerable. If you can't manage them on foot, a *petit train* shuttles between the terrace in front of the château and the Trianons (32F). There are **bikes** for hire at the Grille de la Reine, Porte St-Antoine and by the Grande Canal, and **boats** for hire on the Grande Canal, within the park.

Versailles practicalities

Much the simplest way to get to Versailles from Paris is to take the RER line C5 to Versailles-Rive Gauche (40min). Once there, turn right out of the station and almost immediately left; the château itself, as big as a small town, is in front of you (10min walk). The **tourist office** is at 7 rue des Réservoirs (☎01.39.50.36.22; daily May–Oct 9am–7pm, Nov–April 9am–noon & 2–6pm). In summer there are additional information booths in the place d'Armes in front of the château.

The town of Versailles has a wonderfully posh place to take **tea**: the *Hôtel Palais Trianon*, where the final negotiations for the Treaty of Versailles took place in 1919. Near the park entrance at the end of boulevard de la Reine, it offers trayfuls of pâtisseries to the limits of your desire for about 100F. The style of the hotel is very much that of the town in general. The dominant population is aristocratic, with those holding pre-revolutionary titles disdainful of those dating merely from Napoléon. On Bastille Day both lots show their colours, with black ribbons and ties in mourning for the guillotined monarchy.

Oddly enough, though, Versailles' **markets** offer excellent bargains, both for food (Sun, Tues & Fri 8am–1pm) in the Marché Notre-Dame, and for second-hand stuff (Fri, Sat & Sun 10am–7pm, Thurs 2–7pm) in the passage de la Geôle.

Vaux-le-Vicomte

Of all the great mansions within reach of a day's outing from Paris, the classical **château of Vaux-le-Vicomte** is the most architecturally harmonious, the most aesthetically pleasing and the most human in scale. It stands isolated in the countryside amid fields and woods, and its gardens make a lovely place to picnic.

The château was built between 1656 and 1661 for **Nicolas Fouquet**, Louis XIV's finance minister, to the designs of three of the finest French artists of the day. Fouquet, however, had little chance to enjoy his magnificent residence. On August 17, 1661, he invited the king and his courtiers to a sumptuous housewarming party. Three weeks later he was arrested – by d'Artagnan of Musketeer fame – charged with embezzlement, and clapped into jail for the rest of his life. Thereupon, the design team of Le Vau, Le Brun and Le Nôtre were carted off to build the king's own piece of one-upmanship, the palace of Versailles.

Stripped of much of its furnishings by the king, the château remained in the possession of Fouquet's widow until 1705, when it was sold to the Maréchal de Villars, an adversary of the Duke of Marlborough in the War of Spanish Succession. In 1764 it was sold, again, to the Duc de Choiseul-Praslin, Louis XV's navy minister. His family kept it until 1875, when, in a state of utter dereliction – the gardens had vanished completely – it was taken over by Alfred Sommier, a French industrialist, who made its restoration and refurbishment his life's work. It was finally opened to the public in 1968.

Vaux-le-Vicomte

Vaux-le-Vicomte is open April–Oct daily 10am–6pm; Nov–March group bookings only on ☎01.64.14.41. 90; 56F château, gardens and museum, 30F gardens and museum only.

The château and gardens

Seen from the entrance the **château** is a rather austere grey pile built on a stone terrace surrounded by an artificial moat and flanked by two matching brick courtyards. It is only when you go through to the south side, where the gardens decline in measured formal patterns of grass and water, clipped box and yew, fountains and statuary, that you can look back and appreciate the very harmonious and very French qualities of the building – the combination of steep, tall roof and central dome with classical pediment and pilasters. It is a building which manages to have charm in spite of its size.

As to the interior, the predominant impression as you wander through is inevitably of opulence and monumental cost. The main artistic interest lies in the work of **Le Brun**. He was responsible for the two fine **tapestries** in the entrance, made in the local workshops set up by Fouquet specifically to adorn his house (and subsequently removed by Louis XIV to become the famous Gobelins works in Paris), as well as numerous **painted ceilings**, notably in Fouquet's bedroom, the Salon des Muses, his *Sleep* in the Cabinet des Jeux, and the so-called King's bedroom, whose decor is the first example of the style that became known as Louis Quatorze. The two oval marble tables in the Salle d'Hercule are the only pieces of furniture never to have left the château.

Other points of interest are the **kitchens**, which have not been altered since construction, and – if you read French – a room displaying **letters** in the hand of Fouquet, Louis XIV and other notables. One, dated November 1794 (ie in mid-Revolution), addresses the incumbent Duc de Choiseul-Praslin as *tu*. "Citizen," it says, "you've got a week to hand over one hundred thousand pounds . . ." and signs off with, "Cheers and brotherhood". You can imagine the shock to the aristocratic system.

The **Musée des Équipages** in the stables comprises a collection of horse-drawn vehicles, including the method of transport used by Charles X fleeing Paris and the Duc de Rohan retreating from Moscow (a Russian model).

Every Saturday evening from May to mid-October, between 8pm and midnight, the state rooms are illuminated with a thousand candles, as they probably were on the occasion of Fouquet's fateful party (75F entrance). **The fountains and other waterworks** can be seen in action on the second and last Saturdays of each month between April and October, from 3pm until 6pm.

Vaux-le-Vicomte practicalities

By road, Vaux-le-Vicomte is 7km east of Melun, which is itself 46km southeast of Paris by the A4 autoroute (exit Melun-Sénart) or a little further by the A6 (exit Melun). **By rail** there are regular services from Gare de Lyon as far as Melun (40min), but, short of walking, the only means of covering the last 7km is **by taxi** (approximately 100–120F). There is a taxi rank on the forecourt of the train station, with telephone numbers to call if there are no taxis waiting.

Fontainebleau

Fontainebleau is open daily except Tues May–Oct 9.30am–5pm; Nov–April 9.30am–12.30pm & 2–5pm; 35F. The Musée Chinois opens sporadically, depending on staff availability. The Musée Napoléon offers guided tours mornings only, and the Petits Appartements has guided tours afternoons only – although both are prone to changes. Ring for details: ☎01.60.71.50.70.

The **château of Fontainebleau**, 60km south of Paris, owes its existence to its situation in the middle of a magnificent forest, which made it the perfect base for royal hunting expeditions. Its transformation into a luxurious palace only took place in the sixteenth century on the initiative of François 1er, who imported a colony of Italian artists to carry out the decoration: among them Rosso il Fiorentino and Niccolò dell'Abate. It continued to enjoy royal favour well into the nineteenth century; Napoléon spent huge amounts of money on it, as did Louis-Philippe. And, after World War II, when it was liberated from the Germans by General Patton, it served for a while as Allied military HQ in Europe. The town in the meantime has become the seat of INSEAD, a prestigious and elite multi-lingual business school.

The **buildings**, unpretentious and attractive despite their extent, have none of the architectural unity of a purpose-built residence like Vaux-le-Vicomte. Their distinction is the sumptuous interiors worked by the Italians, notably the celebrated **Galerie François-1er** – which had a seminal influence on the subsequent development of French aristocratic art and design – the Salle de Bal, the Salon Louis-XIII, and the Salle du Conseil with its eighteenth-century decoration.

The **gardens** are equally luscious. If you want to escape into the relative wilds, head for the surrounding **Forest of Fontainebleau**, which is full of walking and cycling trails, all marked on Michelin map 196 (*Environs de Paris*). Its rocks are a favourite training ground for Paris-based climbers.

Getting to Fontainebleau from Paris is straightforward. By road it is 16km from the A6 autoroute (exit Fontainebleau). By train, it is 50 minutes from the Gare de Lyon to Fontainebleau-Avon station, whence bus #B takes you to the château gates in a few minutes. For further information, contact the SI at 4 rue Royale (Mon–Sat 10am–6.30pm, Sun 10am–4pm; ☎01.60.74.99.99).

Chantilly

The main association with **Chantilly**, a small town 40km north of Paris, is horses. Some 3000 thoroughbreds prance the forest rides of a morning, and two of the season's classiest flat races are held here. The stables in the château are given over to a **museum** dedicated to live horses.

The château

The Chantilly estate used to belong to two of the most powerful clans in France: first to the Montmorencys, then through marriage to the Condés. The present château was put up in the late nineteenth century. It replaced a palace, destroyed in the Revolution, which had been built for the Grand Condé, who smashed Spanish military power for Louis XIV in 1643. It's a beautiful structure, graceful and romantic, surrounded by water and looking out in a haughty manner over a formal arrangement of pools and pathways designed by the busy Le Nôtre.

The château is open March–Oct daily except Tues 10am–6pm; Nov–Feb Mon & Wed–Fri 10.30am–12.45pm & 2–5pm, Sat & Sun 10.30am–5pm; 39F.

The entrance to the château is across a moat past two realistic bronzes of hunting hounds. The visitable parts of the château are all museum, comprising mainly an enormous collection of paintings and drawings, of which only the *galeries de peinture* on the first floor are accessible without a guided tour. The paintings are displayed in a rather muddled way (their donor, Henri d'Orléans, stipulated that they remain as he had organized them), with ranks of good, bad and indifferent, deployed as if of equal value. Highlights of the collection include Piero di Cosimo's *Simonetta Vespucci* and Raphaël's *Madone de Lorette*, both in the Rotunda of the picture gallery. Raphaël is also well represented in the so-called Sanctuary, with his *Three Graces* displayed alongside Filippo Lippi's *Esther and Assuerius*, and forty miniatures from a fifteenth-century Book of Hours attributed to the French artist Jean Fouquet. Pass through the Galerie de Psyche with its series of sepia stained glass illustrating Apuleius' *Golden Ass*, to the room known

Chantilly

as the Tribune, where Italian art, including Botticelli's *Autumn*,
takes up two walls; works by Ingres and Delacroix fill the other
walls.

*Sleeping
Beauty's castle
at Disneyland
Paris is based
on an illustra-
tion in* Les
Très Riches
Heures.

A free guided tour will take you round the main **apartments**. The
first port of call is the well stocked **library**, where the museum's single greatest treasure is kept: *Les Très Riches Heures du Duc de
Berry*, the most celebrated of all the Books of Hours. The illuminated pages illustrating the months of the year with representative
scenes from contemporary (early 1400s) rural life – like harvesting
and ploughing, sheep-shearing and pruning – are richly coloured and
drawn with a delicate naturalism. Only facsimiles are on view, but
these give an excellent idea of the original.

The Horse Museum

*The Horse
Museum is
open April–Oct
Mon &
Wed–Fri
10.30am–
5.30pm, Sat &
Sun till 6pm;
May & June
also open Tues
10.30am–
5.30pm; July
& Aug also
open Tues
2–5.30pm;
Nov–March
Mon–Fri
2–5pm,
Sat & Sun
10.30am–5pm;
50F.*

Five minutes' walk along the château drive at Chantilly, the colossal
stable block has been transformed into a museum of the horse, the
Musée Vivant du Cheval. The building was erected at the beginning
of the eighteenth century by the incumbent Condé prince, who
believed he would be reincarnated as a horse and wished to provide
fitting accommodation for 240 of his future relatives.

In the main hall horses of different breeds from around the world
are stalled, with a ring for **demonstrations** (April–Oct 11.30am,
3.30pm & 5.15pm; Nov–March weekends & public hols 11.30am,
3.30pm & 5.15pm, weekdays 3.30pm only), followed by a series of
life-size models illustrating the various activities horses are used for.
In the rooms off the hall are collections of paintings, horseshoes, vet-
erinary equipment, bridles and saddles, a mock-up of a blacksmith's,
children's horse toys (including a chain-driven number, with handles
in its ears, which belonged to Napoléon III), and a fanciful Sicilian
cart painted with scenes of Crusader battles.

Chantilly practicalities

Trains take about thirty minutes from Paris' Gare du Nord to
Chantilly. Occasional free buses pass from the station to the château,
though it's an easy walk. **Footpaths** GR11 and 12 pass through the

château park and its surrounding forest, offering a peaceful and leisurely way of exploring this bit of country.

A rather unique view of the château can be experienced by going up in a hot-air balloon (March–Oct daily 10am–7pm, departure every 10min, duration 10min; 45F), the *aérophile*, which is moored in the park. You can also take a 25min commentated boat trip (Feb 15–Nov 15 daily 10am–7pm; 45F, 65F for both the boat and the balloon) all the way round the château and be dropped off at the entrance to the museum

By the entrance-gate to the grounds of the château is a caravan selling the local delight, Chantilly cream. It's basically whipped, sugared cream and delicious.

Malmaison

The relatively small and surprisingly enjoyable **château of Malmaison** is set in the beautiful grounds of the Bois-Préau, about 15km west of central Paris. This was the home of the Empress Josephine. During the 1800–1804 Consulate, Napoléon would drive out at weekends, though by all accounts his presence was hardly guaranteed to make the party go with a bang. Twenty minutes was all the time allowed for meals, and when called upon to sing in party games, the great man always gave a rendition of *Malbrouck s'en Vat'en Guerre* (*Malbrouck Goes to War*), out of tune. A slightly odd choice, too, when you remember that it was Malbrouck, the Duke of Marlborough, who had given the French armies a couple of drubbings 100 years earlier. According to his secretary, Malmaison was "the only place next to the battlefield where he was truly himself". After their divorce, Josephine stayed on here, occasionally receiving visits from the emperor, until her death in 1814.

Malmaison is open for guided tours only Mon & Wed–Fri 10am–noon & 1.30–5/6pm, Sat & Sun 10am–5/6pm; 30F, Thurs–Sun ticket includes entrance to Bois-Préau museum.

Visits today include private and official apartments, with some of their original furnishings, as well as Josephine's clothes, china, glass and personal possessions. During the Nazi occupation, the imperial chair in the library was rudely violated by the fat buttocks of Reichsmarschall Goering, dreaming perhaps of promotion or the conquest of Egypt. There are other Napoleonic bits in the **Bois-Préau museum** (open Thurs–Sun) nearby.

On a high bump of ground behind the château, and not easy to get to without a car, is the 1830s fort of **Mont Valérien**. It was once a place of pilgrimage, but the Germans killed 4500 hostages and Resistance people there during the war. It is again a national shrine, though the memorial itself is not much to look at.

To reach Malmaison, either take the métro to Grande-Arche-de-la-Défense, then bus #258 to Malmaison-Château, or, if you don't mind a walk, take the RER direct to Rueil-Malmaison and walk from there. To make a feature of the walk, follow the GR11 footpath from the Pont de Chatou along the left bank of the Seine and into the château park.

Other museums

Of the assortment of museums in the general vicinity of Paris, the one with the widest appeal must be the **Musée de l'Île-de-France** at Sceaux, with its delightfully eclectic collection of mementos of the region. But for specialist interest, the **ceramics** at Sèvres, **prehistory** at St-Germain-en-Laye, and **aviation** at Le Bourget are all excellent. Some of the museums also provide a good excuse for wanderings in the countryside.

Musée de l'Air et de l'Espace

The Musée de l'Air et de l'Espace is open Tues–Sun 10am–5/6pm; 30F.

The French were always adventurous, pioneering aviators, and the name of **Le Bourget** is intimately connected with their earliest exploits. Lindbergh landed here after his epic first flight across the Atlantic. From World War I until the development of Orly in the l950s, it was Paris' principal airport.

Today Le Bourget is used only for internal flights (and for international arms fairs), while some of the older buildings have been turned into the museum of flying machines. It consists of five adjacent hangars and a Grande Galerie, taking you from the earliest attempts to fly through to the latest spacecrafts. A room dedicated to the Montgolfier brothers, inventors of the first successful hot-air balloon, shows society going balloon crazy before real airplane madness begins in the Grande Galerie; the first contraption to fly 1km, the first cross channel flight, the first aerobatics . . . successes and failures are all on display here. Post-1918 continues in the hangars: the majority of the planes from the two world wars are indefinitely closed to the public. Highlights of the WWII planes are on display with the first Concorde prototype in the Hall Concorde, while **Hangars C and D** cover the years from 1945 to the present day. Having lost eighty percent of its capacity in 1945, the French aviation industry has recovered to the extent that it now occupies a pre-eminent position in the world. Its high-tech achievement is represented here by the super-sophisticated best-selling Mirage fighters and two Ariane space-launchers, Ariane I and the latest, Ariane V (both parked on the tarmac outside). **Hangar E** contains light and sporty aircraft and **Hangar F**, nearest to the entrance, is devoted to **space**, with rockets, satellites, space capsules, etc. Some are mock-ups, some the real thing. Among the latter are a Lunar Roving Vehicle, the Soyuz craft in which a French astronaut flew, and France's own first successful

At **Drancy**, near the Aéroport du Bourget, the Germans and the French Vichy regime had a transit camp for Jews en route to Auschwitz – this was where the poet Max Jacob, among others, died. A cattle wagon and a stone stele in the courtyard of a council estate commemorate the nearly 100,000 Jews who passed through here, of whom only 1518 returned.

space rocket. Everything is accompanied by extremely good explanatory panels – though in French only.

To get to the Musée de L'Air et de l'Espace **from Paris**, take RER line B from Gare du Nord to Gare du Bourget, then bus #152 to Le Bourget/Musée de l'Air. Alternatively, take bus #350 from Gare du Nord, Gare de l'Est and Porte de la Chapelle, or #152 from Porte de la Villette.

Musée des Antiquités Nationales

The unattractively renovated château of St-Germain-en-Laye, 10km west of Malmaison and a total of 20km out of Paris, was one of the main residences of the French court before the construction of Versailles. It now houses the extraordinary **national archeology museum**, which will prove of immense interest to anyone who has been to the prehistoric caves of the Dordogne.

The presentation and lighting make the visit a real pleasure. The extensive Stone Age section includes a mock-up of the **Lascaux caves** and a profile of Abbé Breuil, the priest who first published studies on paleolithic art and its meanings, as well as a beautiful collection of decorative objects, tools and so forth. All ages of prehistory are covered, right on down into historical times with Celts, Romans and Franks: abundant evidence that the French have been a talented arty lot for a very long time. The end piece is a room of **comparative archeology**, with objects from cultures across the globe.

The Musée des Antiquités Nationales is open daily except Tues 9am–5.15pm; 25F.

From right outside the château, a **terrace** – Le Nôtre arranging the landscape again – stretches for more than 2km above the Seine with a view over the whole of Paris. All behind it is the **forest of St-Germain**, a sizable expanse of woodland, but crisscrossed by too many roads to be convincing as wilderness.

Musée de l'Île-de-France

The **château of Sceaux**, 10km south of Paris, is a nineteenth-century replacement of the original – demolished post-Revolution – which matched the now-restored Le Nôtre grounds. If you fancy a stroll, you can get off the RER line B at La-Croix-de-Berny at the southern end of the surrounding park – the usual classical geometry of terraces, water and woods. Otherwise, it's a five- to ten-minute walk from Parc-de-Sceaux station (15min from Denfert-Rochereau): turn left on avenue de la Duchesse-du-Maine, right into avenue Rose-de-Launay, and right again on avenue Le-Nôtre: the château gates are on your left.

The Musée de l'Île-de-France is open April–Sept Mon & Wed–Sun 10am–6pm; Oct–March closes 5pm; 23F.

The recently restored château was a country residence, and the **museum** inside evokes the Paris countryside of the *ancien régime* with its aristocratic and royal domains of the nineteenth century, and with its riverside scenes and eating and dancing places, the *guinguettes*, that inspired so many artists. The collection consists of paintings, prints, and ceramics from various bygone Île-de-France manufacturers.

Musée
National de
la
Céramique

Temporary exhibitions and a summer **festival of classical chamber music** (mid-July to third week in Sept) are held in the Orangerie,
which, along with the Pavillon de l'Aurore (in the northeast corner of
the park), survives from the original residence (details of the concerts on ☎01.46.60.07.79). In the summer you can get snacks and
drinks in the park.

Musée National de la Céramique

A ceramics museum may possibly seem a bit too rarefied an attraction to
justify a trip out of Paris, but if you do have the time, there is much to be
savoured at Sèvres' **Musée National de la Céramique**. As well as French
pottery and china, there's also Islamic, Chinese, Italian, German, Dutch
and English produce, though the displays inevitably centre around a
comprehensive collection of Sèvres ware, as the stuff is made right here.

Right by the museum is the **Parc de St-Cloud**, good for fresh air
and visual order, with a geometrical sequence of pools and fountains.
You could, if you wanted, take a train from St-Lazare to St-Cloud and
head south through the park to the museum.

To get to the museum, take the métro to the Pont-de-Sèvres terminus, cross the bridge and spaghetti junction – the museum is the
massive building facing the river bank on your right.

*The Musée
National de la
Céramique is
open daily
except Tues
10am–5pm;
22F.*

Giverny

Monet's gardens in Giverny are in a class by themselves. They are a long
way out from Paris (65km), in the direction of Rouen, and you'll need to
take train and bus to reach them (see below). If you're planning a future
holiday in Normandy, or if you're visiting in winter, leave them for another time. But, if not, consider making the effort – the rewards are great.

Monet lived in Giverny from 1883 till his death in 1926, and the gardens he laid out leading down from his house towards the river were
considered by most of his friends to be his greatest masterpiece. Each
month is reflected in a dominant colour, as are each of the rooms,
hung as he left them with his collection of Japanese prints. May and
June, when the rhododendrons flower round the lily pond and the wisteria winds over the Japanese bridge, are the best of all times to visit.
But any month, from spring to autumn, is overwhelming in the beauty
of this arrangement of living shades and shapes. Although you have to
contend with crowds photographing images of the waterlilies far
removed from Monet's renderings, there's no place like it.

Without a car, the easiest **approach to Giverny** is by train to
Vernon from Paris-St-Lazare (45min; 3 daily, last one to get you
there in time is at 2.20pm; 134F). Buses meet each train (20F) for
the 6km ride to the gardens or you can rent a bike (1000F deposit)
or **walk** (1hr), in which case cross the river and turn right on the D5;
take care as you enter Giverny to follow the left fork, otherwise you'll
make a long detour to reach the garden entrance.

*Giverny is
open April–Oct
Tues–Sun
10am–6pm;
house and gar-
den 35F, gar-
den only 25F.*

*Painters are
allowed into
the garden on
Mon but by
appointment
only: ☎01.32.
51.28.21.*

Chapter 21

Disneyland Paris

C hildren will love Disneyland Paris, 25km east of the capital – there are no two ways about it. What their minders will think of it is another matter. For a start, there has to be the question of whether it's worth the money. Quite why American parents might bring their charges here is hard to fathom: even British parents might well decide that it would be easier, and cheaper, to buy a family package to Florida, where sunshine is assured, where Disney World has better rides, and where the conflict between enchanted kingdom and enchanting city does not arise.

Unless it's a weekend, a Wednesday afternoon or the school holidays, French visitors to the park are rare, as are American accents at any time, and you'll find yourself in a polyglot European community of mostly Italian, Spanish, British and Belgian familiies. In fact, foul north European weather does have its advantages. On an off-season wet and windy weekday (Mon & Thurs are the best), you can probably get round every ride you want. Otherwise, one-hour waits for the popular rides are common in the middle of the day.

Getting to Disneyland Paris

From Paris, take RER line A (Châtelet-Les Halles, Gare-de-Lyon, Nation) to Marne-la-Vallée/Chessy, the Disneyland Paris stop. The journey takes about 40min, and costs 76F round-trip (38F child, under-3s free). For prices of one-, two- and three-day Paris Visite transport card including Disneyland Paris, see p.401.

If you're coming straight from the airport, there is a **shuttle bus** from Charles de Gaulle and Orly (times and frequencies change seasonally, but roughly every 45min 8.30am–8pm; for recorded information call ☎01.64.30.66.56; 85F one-way, children 65F, under-3s free). Marne-la-Vallée/Chessy also has its own TGV train station, linked to Lille, Lyon and London: Eurostar run trains direct from London Waterloo and Ashford in Kent (see p.6 for details).

By car, the park is 32km east of Paris along the A4 (exit 13 for Ranch Davy Crockett and exit 14 for the park and the hotels); from Calais follow the A26 changing to the A1, the A104 and finally the A4.

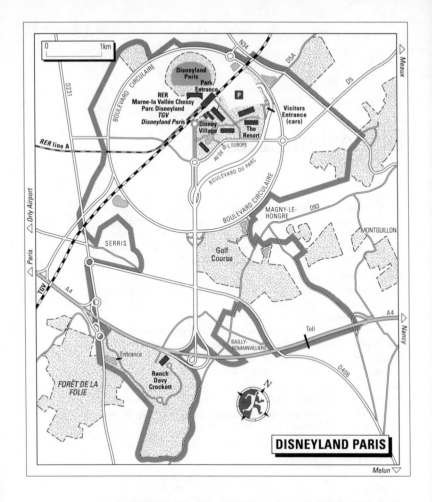

With the opening of Space Mountain, Disneyland Paris does now provide a variety of good fear and thrill rides, though the majority of attractions remain very safe and staid. It takes its inspiration from film sets, not funfairs or big tops, which is why it's so wonderful for children. These sets are "real" – you can go into them and round them and the characters talk to you. All the structures are incredibly detailed, and their shades and textures have been worked out with the precision of a brain surgeon. But if you're not a child, solid three-dimensional buildings masquerading as flimsy film sets and constantly being filmed by swarming hordes of camcorder operators can well fail to fulfil any kind of escapist fantasy.

Besides the **Disneyland Paris Park**, the complex includes **Festival Disney** – the evening entertainments complex – and the

Disney **hotels**. These, unlike the park, are radically different from their US or Japanese counterparts, having been designed especially for Europeans, who, according to Disney executives, invented fairy tales and castles, but have run out of good ideas since.

Michael Eisner, Chair and Chief Executive of Disney USA, stated that "Euro Disney introduces a new level of design and innovation to Europe". Paris can take such bombast; it has existed for about 27 times as long as Mr Eisner's company has been in business, and at the end of two millennia of sustained design achievement it remains the most innovative and stylish capital city in Europe. Disney's publicizing of Paris as a sideline tourist attraction is perhaps the most objectionable feature of the whole enterprise.

The Park

The introduction to Disneyland Paris is the same as in Florida, LA and Tokyo. **Main Street USA** is a mythical vision of a 1900s American town, West Coast with a dash of East Coast, but more the mishmash memories of a thousand and one American movies – without the mud.

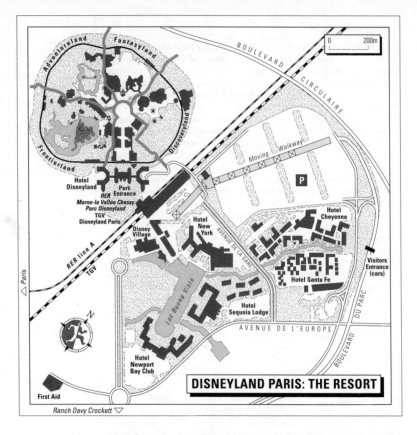

DISNEYLAND PARIS: THE RESORT

Main Street leads to **Central Plaza**, the hub of the standard radial layout. Clockwise from Main Street are **Frontierland**, **Adventureland**, **Fantasyland** and **Discoveryland**. The **castle**, directly opposite Main Street across Central Plaza, belongs to Fantasyland. A steam train **Railroad** runs round the park with stations at each "land" and at the entrance.

Information and access

You enter the park under Main Street Station. **City Hall** is to the left, where you can get **information** about the day's programming of events and about the hotels and evening's entertainments. For people in **wheelchairs** there's the *Guest Special Services Guide* that details accessibility of the rides. All the loos, phones, shops and restaurants have wheelchair access. Wheelchairs and pushchairs can be rented (30F, plus 20F deposit if you wish to leave the park) in the building opposite City Hall (you are allowed to bring in your own).

Admission fees for the park

	Low season Oct–March excl Christmas hols	High season April–Sept & 3rd week Dec–1st week Jan
1 day	160/130F	200/155F
2 days	305/250F	385/300F
3 days	415/335F	545/420F

Reduced tariff: children aged 3–11; under-3s free.

Passes, known as "passports", can be purchased in advance at the Paris Tourist Office and at all Disney shops, or you can buy admission passes and train tickets in Paris at all RER line A and B stations and in major métro stations. You can come and go during the day – your wrist is stamped with invisible ink when you leave the park, allowing you to return. Multi-day passes don't have to be used on consecutive days.

Opening hours vary greatly depending on the season and whether it's a weekend. Generally, low season Mon–Fri 10am–6pm, Sat & Sun till 8pm; high season daily 9am–11pm – but check exact opening hours before you buy your ticket (you can check the Internet on *www.disneylandparis.com*).

The **lost property office** is in City Hall. You can enquire about lost children here, too, or there's a **Lost Children** area in the First Aid complex by the Plaza Gardens Restaurant on Central Plaza (in the block between Main Street and Discoveryland). Next door, you can change nappies, breast-feed and heat baby-food in the Baby Care Centre. **Luggage** can be left in lockers in "Guest Storage" under Main Street Station (10F).

Food and drink

The former Disney policy of no alcohol has been abandoned. Adults can now sip wine or beer at any of the park's restaurants, at a considerable price, of course. Coke, fruit juices, tea, coffee, chocolate, mineral water, fizzy drinks and alcohol-free cocktails are also readily available, and coffee away from Main Street is reasonably priced, if a bit weak compared to the French café norm. The **food** in Disneyland Paris, however, tastes as if it's been first cooked, then sterilized, then put on your plate. This is certainly not the place to blow precious meal money, so avoid the restaurants on Main Street and go for hamburgerish snacks at the various themed eateries around the park. Best value is the generous fish and chips meal at Toad Hall.

Officially, you're not allowed to bring any refreshments into the park, but, if you don't want to spend anything more than the entrance fee, eat a good Parisian breakfast and smuggle in some discreet snacks. Whether Goofy will turn nasty if he sees you eating a brand name not on the list of Disney sponsors is anyone's guess. Though there are a few green patches, there is no lawn to loll on, a bad sign in a park designed for families, so opportunites for after-

noon naps are limited, which shows by late afternoon in the general
frayed tempers and high incidence of exhausted squalling children:
hiring a pushchair for even an older child might be a good idea.

Smoking is allowed in the park, but not in the queues for the rides.
The park no longer has the same high American standards with
which it commenced, when all litter was swept up instantaneously –
scandalously you will probably see cigarette butts littering the pavements.

Main Street USA

On the corner of **Main Street**, Town Square Photography rents out
still and video cameras, and sells film, lenses, cameras and tripods
amid a collection of museum pieces. Kodak is one of Disney's main
sponsors, and kiosks throughout the park sell film and offer two-
hour print developing.

If you succumb at this stage to the idea of takeaway snapshots and
the Disneyland Paris home movie, you'll be in serious financial trouble by the end of the day. As a practice run, see if you can get down
Main Street without buying one of the following: a balloon, a hat with
your name embroidered on it, an ice-cream, bag of sweets, silhouette
portraits of your kids, the *Wall Street Journal* of 1902, a Disney
version of a children's classic in hardback, an evening dress and suit
and tie, a Donald Duck costume, a model rocket, a tea service and set
of crystal glasses, some muffins, a Coke, a few cakes, a limited edition Disney lithograph, and a complete set of Disney characters in
ceramics, metal, plastic, rubber or wool.

Leaving Main Street is quickest on foot (crowds permitting),
although omnibuses, trams, horse-drawn streetcars, fire trucks and
police vans are always on hand, plus the Disney *pièce de résistance*,
the Railroad, for which **Main Street Station** has the longest queues.

The Railroad

The "attraction" on the circular Railroad is the **Grand Canyon
Diorama** between Main Street and Frontierland. You enter a tunnel,
and there below you, in all its tiny glory, is a miniature plastic Grand
Canyon. While you ruminate on the fact that it is the *size* of the real
Grand Canyon that is the source of its fascination, you can look out
the window and appreciate how enormous Disneyland Paris is. Once
you've been in the park a few hours, however, you may begin to find
yourself unable to imagine any fantasy, discovery, adventure or
"frontier experience" other than those created by the scenes laid out
before you.

The parades

La Parade Disney happens every day at 3pm and lasts for half an
hour. This is not a bad time to go on the most popular rides, but if
you have kids they will no doubt force you to press against the barri-

ers for the ultimate Disney event. One of the best vantage spots is on the queuing ramp for *It's a Small World*, right by the gates through which the floats appear. You can even see them over the fence "backstage", but Disney cast members are too well trained to be frowning and smoking a fag before their entrance. From here, the parade progresses, very slowly, to Town Square. The best seating is in front of the Fantasyland Castle, one of the points where the floats stop and the characters put on a performance.

The parade floats represent all the top box-office Disney movies – *Dumbo, Snow White, Cinderella, Pinocchio, The Jungle Book, Peter Pan, Mary Poppins, Beauty and the Beast, Aladdin* and *Hercules*, with Mickey and Minnie Mouse and Donald Duck making an appearance. Everyone waves and smiles, characters on foot shake hands with the kids who've managed to get to the front, and Mary Poppins' chimney sweeps engage some lucky children in a dance.

The night-time parades that feature in Florida are not a regular event here. They do have **Electrical Parades**, with characters' costumes strung with light bulbs, but not every night. **Firework displays** happen about twice a week during the summer (and have had to be toned down because of complaints by people living in villages 15km away). Check with the *Programme des Spectacles* available at City Hall for dates and times.

The rides

The listings below are a selection of the best and worst rides, or "attractions", as they like to be called. As the guide you get on entry covers the park in a clockwise direction, this does the opposite in the hope that you might be competing with slightly fewer of your fellow RER travellers on the first few rides.

Apart from some height restrictions, there is little guidance about the suitability of rides for small children, and two rides in particular stand out: the *Pirates of the Caribbean* might frighten little ones, and *Big Thunder Mountain* is too physically shattering for any child

---

Queues

Disney's claim of average 15min queues are hard to believe. One-hour waits for the popular rides are common – don't be fooled by the length of the visible queues; they often snake for a further 100m or more inside. Make sure your kids have all been to the toilet recently before you begin to queue, as once you're in, it's very hard to get out; keep snacks and drinks handy, too. Some outdoor rides, such as the hideously popular *Dumbo the Flying Elephant*, where you can wait up to an hour for a 25-second spin, do not offer shade or shelter as you queue, so bring sunhats and umbrellas. The shortest waits are first thing in the morning (though Disney hotel guests can enter the park up to an hour earlier than the general public), during the 3pm afternoon parade and after 5pm.

---

under about eight. For the youngest kids, **Fantasyland** is likely to
hold the most thrills. There are no height restrictions here, and rides
are mostly gentle. **Adventureland** has the most outlandish sets. Boat
trips in canoes, keelboats and a paddle-steamer are to had in
Frontierland, where *Big Thunder Mountain* provides a ripper of a
roller-coaster ride. The one and only real heart-stopper, *Space
Mountain*, is in **Discoveryland**.

Discoveryland

Space Mountain

The star attraction and not for the faint-hearted. You're catapulted
upwards, suspended weightless and then spun through an interstel-
lar world at speeds of up to 40km, with a 360 degree sidewinder loop
and corkscrew loop. The inspiration for the decor is Jules Verne's
From the Earth to the Moon. Minimum height is 1.40m, and pregnant women and people with health problems are advised not to ride.
When you emerge from the ride, video screens show close-up images
of terrified faces captured moments before: while it's fun to hang
around until you spot your own twisted visage, buying a photographic copy will set you back a steep 45F.

Le Visionarium

A slow build-up to a 360 degree film (shot with nine cameras and
screened with nine projectors), presented by a robotic timekeeper
host and his nervous android assistant. The story involves their travelling through time and picking up Jules Verne at the 1900
Exposition Universelle in Paris just as he and H G Wells, played by
Jeremy Irons, are discussing time travel. They show Jules Verne all
the wonders of contemporary life (TGVs and Mirages mainly), with bit
parts for the likes of Gérard Depardieu as an airport baggage handler.
You stand to watch the film, wearing headphones for the English
translation, so you are free to turn this way and that to fully appreciate the complete surround film. The duration of the film is 19 minutes.

Les Mystères du Nautilus

More Jules Verne fetish, with a visit in a miniature *Nautilus* submarine – Captain Nemo's vessel in *20,000 Leagues Under the Sea* –
through an oversize *Nautilus*. Apart from the giant squid attack on
the big *Nautilus*' porthole window, what's supposed to impress you
is the faithfulness of the decor to the original Disney set: the organ is
even an exact replica.

Orbitron

The "rockets" on this hideous structure go round and round extremely slowly and go up (at your control) even more laggardly to a daring
30 degrees above the horizontal. Only suitable for small kids and for

those who hate more violent rides (whatever the special boarding restrictions say).

Star Tours

Simulated ride in a spacecraft (with 60 other people all in neat rows) piloted by friendly incompetent C3PO of *Star Wars* fame. The projection of what you're supposed to be careering through is from the film, which is the only thing that makes this superior to space tour simulations elsewhere. When you come off the ride there's an arcade of video games, which only those adept at this kind of entertainment can work out how to use. Pregnant women and those with health problems are advised not to board.

Cinémagique

A Michael Jackson Sci-Fi movie, with Jackson playing one Captain Eo commanding a spaceship and a troupe of fluffy toys and with a cameo wicked-witch appearance by Angelica Huston. Impressive animations, deafening sound, Thrilleresque choreography and 3-D specs turn it from film into stage. Not for those with sensitive eyes or ears, nor for those whose sensitivities don't extend to adoring Mr Jackson. Duration of the film is 17 minutes.

Autopia

Miniature futuristic cars to drive on rails with no possibility of any dodgems stratagems. Minimum height to drive is 1.32m.

Fantasyland

Le Château de la Belle au Bois Dormant

Sleeping Beauty was originally *La Belle au Bois*, heroine of a seventeenth-century French tale. Disney is very smug about having based the design of the castle on an illustration in the medieval manuscript *Les Très Riches Heures du Duc de Berry* (see p.392). In the picture, the château is a veritable fortress, grey and forbidding. In the foreground grumpy peasants till the fields. The château here copies the shapes of some of the turrets and the blue of the roof tiles, but that's about it. In fact, it has about the same connection as the originals of *Alice in Wonderland*, *The Jungle Book* and *La Belle au Bois* to the Disney versions.

You might wonder why after a hundred years' enforced slumber, finally rescued by the Prince's kiss, Sleeping Beauty should decide to turn her place of torment into a shopping arcade – but she has. The one thing you can't buy are the tapestries of Disney scenes that adorn the walls; these are genuine one-offs, painstakingly manufactured by the d'Aubusson workshops. Down below, in the dungeon, you'll find one of the better bits of fantasy apparatus: a huge dragon with red eyes that wakes on cue to snap its jaws and flick its tail.

Peter Pan's Flight

Disney must have cursed the appearance of *Hook* in the same year that Disneyland Paris opened. Anyone who has seen Spielberg's movie will have problems returning to the Disney version. But the very young will probably appreciate the jerky ride above Big Ben and the lights of London to Never-Never Land.

Le Pays des Contes de Fées

An unenthralling boat ride through fairytale scenes: *Alice in Wonderland, Pinocchio*, etc. Fine for little kids.

Le Carrousel de Lancelot

No complaints about this stately merry-go-round, whose every horse has its own individual medieval equerry in glittering paint.

Blanche-Neige et les Sept Nains

Unlike *Peter Pan, Snow White and the Seven Dwarfs* no longer exist as anything but their Disney manifestations. So this ride, through lots of menacing moving trees, swinging doors and cackling witches, is less grating than some of the others.

Mad Hatter's Tea Cups

These look wonderful – great big whirling teacups sliding past each other on a chequered floor – even if the connection with *Alice* is a little strained. Again, not a whizzy ride, but fun for younger ones.

Dumbo the Flying Elephant

Dumbo and his clones provide yet another safe, slow, aerial ride – you can regulate the rise and fall of the revolving elephants yourself with a lever. One of the most popular rides in Fantasyland, though it only lasts a measly 25 seconds.

Alice's Curious Labyrinth

The best things about this maze are the slow-motion fountains spurting jets of water over your head. There are passages that only those under 1m can pass through, and enough false turns and exits to make it an irritatingly good labyrinth. You'll encounter the Disneyized White Rabbit, Tweedledum and Tweedledee and the Cheshire Cat along the way.

It's a Small World

This is a quintessential Disney experience: there's one in every Disneyland, and Walt considered it to be the finest expression of his corporation's philosophy. For jaded adults, it's certainly one of the most entertaining of all the "attractions". It is quite definitively, and spectacularly, revolting. Your boat rides through a polystyrene and

Working for Disney

Daily deodorant, clipped fingernails, unbleached hair, no jewellery of any kind, no facial hair, hair neither short nor long – these were just some of the conditions imposed at the outset on Disneyland Paris "cast members". However, you'll see the odd staff-member with cropped and bleached hair now, and the place feels more laissez-faire French and less squeaky clean.

The cardinal rule here is to be in character – in sweet, smiley, have-a-good-day persona – all the time. Yet pay is not brilliant, accommodation is neither provided nor subsidized, and turnover, not surprisingly, is very high. Several costumed characters walked out in late 1998, bruised and tempers frayed by the constant pinching and poking of curious children, demanding that conditions and working hours be improved to limit the harrassment.

In the nearby village of Neufmoutiers-en-Brie, a monastery was set up specifically to give a stress-free space to Disney cast members. The priests who work there have described Disney world as "a fortress", "a world of money and imitation", where everything is passive except the shooting gallery.

Another Roman Catholic priest has been a major irritant to Disney (and to his bishop). He joined the CGT (the Communist trade union) and got a job on the Disney railway where he managed to unionize his workmates. CGT members among the cleaning staff have staged strikes and caused serious embarrassment during visits by VIPs.

glitter world, where animated dolls in national/ethnic/tribal costumes dance beside their most famous landmarks or landscapes, singing the song *It's a Small World*. The lyrics and the context make it clear that what unites the human race is the possibility that every child could have its imagination totally fed by Disney products. What a relief that the global telecommunications network trumpeted by France Telecom, who sponsor this "attraction", does not in fact reach every corner of the globe.

Adventureland

Le Passage enchanté d'Aladdin
A magic carpet ride – of course, with the film's soundtrack and all the highlights of the film, which rather lose their charm in three dimensions.

Pirates of the Caribbean
This satisfyingly long ride is one of Disneyland Paris' finest, consisting of an underground ride on water and down waterfalls, past scenes of evil piracy. The animated automata are the best yet, to the extent that it's hard to be convinced that they're not actors (perhaps they are) – be warned that they set small children whimpering and crying immediately. Baddies in jail try coaxing a dog who has the

keys in its mouth, sitting just out of reach. Battles are staged across the water, skeletons slide into the water, parrots squawk, chains rattle and a treasure trove is revealed. Note that queues for this one can be horrendous, and once you're inside there's still a very long way to go through darkened tunnels.

Indiana Jones and the Temple of Doom (Le Temple du Péril)

This is a fast and quite violent roller-coaster with the first 360 degree loop on a Disney ride. Impressive stone vipers wait for you above the flame torches after you've lined up through tents filled with fossils and the ruined temple. Visually one of the best, though the ride itself doesn't last long. The minimum height is 1.40m, and pregnant women and people with health problems should steer clear.

La Cabane des Robinson

The 27-metre mock banyan tree at the top of Adventure Isle is one of Disneyland Paris' most obsessively detailed creations, complete with hundreds of thousands of false leaves and blossoms. It's reached by walkways and a series of more than 170 steps, so it's best avoided by pram-pushers and toddler-haulers. For dedicated Swiss Family Robinson fans only.

Adventureland Bazaar

This is a clever bit of shopping mall, disguised as a *souk*, with traditional Arab latticed walls, desert pastel colours, and all sorts of genuine Hollywood details. In the alleyway to the right of the archway (with Adventureland behind you) there's an inset in the wall where a laughing genie appears out of Aladdin's lamp every few minutes.

Frontierland

Big Thunder Mountain

A proper heart-in-the-mouth funfair thrill, this is a roller-coaster mimicking a runaway mine train round the "mining mountain", under the lake to the other island and back again, with wicked twists and turns, splashes and collapsing roofs. Also, all the mining bits and pieces are genuine articles, bought up by Disney from museums and old mines in California and Nevada. Not suitable for small children.

Phantom Manor

This starts off very promisingly: a *Psycho*-style house on the outside and Hammer Horror Edwardian mansion within. Holographic ghosts appear before cobweb-covered mirrors and ancestral portraits. But horror is not part of Disney's world; the dead bride story suddenly switches to a Wild West graveyard dance, and any lurking heebie-jeebies are well and truly scuttled. The other problem with Disney doing a Ghost Train ride is that the last thing they want to do is to scare you. So nothing jumps out and screams at you, no deathly hand skims your hair.

Rustler Roundup Shootin' Gallery
The only "attraction" for which there's a fee (10F), because, without some check, people stay for hours and hours when they might otherwise be consuming.

River Rogue Keelboats and Indian Canoes
Northern European weather is a problem here. If it's raining and there's more than a ripple on the lake's surface, the boats don't go out.

Disney Village and the hotels

When the park gates close, you're not supposed to hop it back to Paris. Oh no. It's festival time in the **Disney Village** entertainment and restaurant complex next to the RER station. *Buffalo Bill's Wild West Show, Billy Bob's Country Western Saloon, Hurricanes, Annette's Diner, Rock 'n' Roll America*, the *Champions Sports Bar*, and a *Planet Hollywood Restaurant* await you with live music on summer nights: bluegrass bands, rock 'n' roll and the Top 40 hits. And don't forget the new multiplex cinema.

When you're nearing exhaustion from so much enchantment, you can return to your themed **hotel** and have a sauna, a jacuzzi or a whirlpool dip, eat and drink some more, purchase more "giftware", play video games and be in bed in time to feel fresh and fit to meet Mickey and Minnie again over breakfast. Then out for a round of golf, a workout, some pony or bike riding or serious team sports. You can skate (in winter), sail (in summer), jog on a special "health circuit", shop some more, and return to the park for another go at the queues.

In reality, partaking of this end of the resort on top of the park is well beyond most people's budgets. The cheapest hotel room off season is 435F (for 2 adults, 2 children); the Davey Crockett Ranch is 300F for a self-catering cabin (again low season, sleeping 4–6) but is only feasible if you have a car; and entertainments such as *Buffalo Bill's Wild West Show* (real guns, horses, bulls and bison) cost 325F (nightly 6.30pm & 9.30pm; 195F for 3–11-year-olds) for the dinner and show. Accommodation is based on a family of four sharing a room or campsite. Special accommodation and entry packages are available in advance (for details call ☎01.60.30.60.53 in France, ☎1-407/WDISNEY in the US, and ☎0990/030303 in the UK).

Even if you don't stay, you may be intrigued enough to take a look at the state of **contemporary American architecture,** as patronized by the Disney Corporation. Producing some way-out buildings with big signatures was an important ploy in persuading the French cultural establishment to accept Disneyland Paris. Two hundred internationally renowned architects were invited to compete. Only one,

James Stirling, turned down the offer, and only one non-American won a contract. The star of the show is the fashionable architect **Frank D. Gehry**, the man responsible for the Bilbao art museum.

A tour of Disney Village and the **six hotels** would be quite an effort on foot – the whole site is twice that of the park. Fortunately, you can get around by hopping in and out of the free bright yellow shuttle buses.

Festival Disney

This is the shops, shows, bars and restaurants complex between the station and the lake. It's Frank Gehry's work, and looks as though a bomb has carried off the circus top tent, in case you were wondering what all the wires and zigzag towers were. There are also a huge great red thing, a shiny white rocket cone thing, some greenhouses, and lots of slanting roofs and fairy lights.

Disneyland Hotel

Situated over the entrance to the park with wings to either side, the *Disneyland Hotel* is in the Main Street *à la Hollywood* style, and is the most upmarket. Rooms vary from 1550F off season to 2500F in peak season.

Hotel New York

The architect of the *Hotel New York*, Michael Graves, says things like "The idea of two dimensions versus three is something that Disney, in a sense, teaches in a very solemn way." A peculiar state-ment for anyone, even an architect and one who has spectacularly failed to translate the skyline of New York onto the outline of this hotel. It is a very ugly building, mixing Mickey-ear-shapes with post-modernist triangles, stripes and upright tombs in ochres and greys. Within, the furnishings are pseudo Art Deco with lots of apples – in case you'd failed to recognize New York from outside. The rooms are 950–1600F.

Newport Bay Club

This "New England seaside resort circa 1900" spreads like a game of dominoes, with no apparent reason why the wings have turned one way rather than another. Blue and white striped canopies over the balconies fail to give it that cosy guesthouse feel, while the cupola roof resembles a cross between a Kaiser Wilhelm and a Nazi helmet. Robert Stern is the architect. Rooms start at 725F; 995F peak season.

Sequoia Lodge

Prison blocks, minus fence and watchtowers, masquerading as the National Parks of the western United States, by the only non-

American architect, Antoine Grumbach. Rooms from 695F to over 1200F.

Hotel Cheyenne

Along with *Sante Fe*, *Cheyenne* deals with the scale problem by breaking into small units: the film-set buildings of a Western frontier town, complete with wagons, cowboys, a hanging tree and scarecrows. The architect is again Robert Stern. Rooms from 535F to 925F.

Hotel Santa Fe

Accommodation in the *Hotel Santa Fe* takes the form of smooth, mercifully unadorned, imitation sun-baked mud buildings in various shapes and sizes. Between them are tasteful car wrecks, a cactus in a glass case, irrigation systems, strange geological formations, ancient desert ruins and other products of the distinctly un-Disney imagination of New Mexican architect Antoine Predock. He cites Wim Wenders' film *Paris, Texas*, the Roman archeological site in Marne-la-Vallée and UFOs as part of his reference material. But the dominant icon, visible from the autoroute, is a scowling cheroot-chewing Clint Eastwood. This gigantic mural creates the drive-in movie entrance to *Santa Fe*. This is the cheapest hotel, at 435F (low season) to 780F.

Davy Crockett Ranch and camping

The log cabin experience at the *Davy Crockett Ranch* costs from 300F to 800F for a self-catering log cabin (4–6 people). The ranch is a 15-minute drive from the park, with no transport laid on.

To really economize, you can **camp** at the nearby *Camping du Parc de la Colline*, Route de Lagny, 77200 Torcy (☎01.60.05.42.32), which is open all year.

Contexts

Paris in history

Two thousand years of compressed history – featuring riots and revolutions, shantytowns, palaces, new street plans, sanitation and the Parisian people.

Beginnings

It was **Rome** that put Paris on the map, as it did the rest of western Europe. When Julius Caesar's armies arrived in 52 BC, they found a Celtic settlement confined to an island in the Seine – the Île de la Cité. It must already have been fairly populous, as it had sent a contingent of eight thousand men to stiffen the Gallic chieftain Vercingétorix's doomed resistance to the invaders.

Under the name of Lutetia, it remained **a Roman colony** for the next three hundred years, prosperous commercially because of its commanding position on the Seine trade route, but insignificant politically. The Romans established their administrative centre on the Île de la Cité, and their town on the Left Bank on the slopes of the Montagne Ste-Geneviève. Though no monuments of their presence remain today, except the baths by the *Hôtel de Cluny* and the amphitheatre in rue Monge, their **street plan**, still visible in the north–south axis of rue St-Martin and rue St-Jacques, determined the future growth of the city.

When Roman rule disintegrated under the impact of **Germanic invasions** around 275 AD,

Paris held out until it fell to **Clovis the Frank** in 486. In 511 Clovis' son commissioned the cathedral of St-Étienne, whose foundations can be seen in the *crypte archéologique* under the square in front of Notre-Dame. Clovis' own conversion to Christianity hastened the **Christianization** of the whole country, and under his successors Paris saw the foundation of several rich and influential monasteries, especially on the Left Bank.

With the election of **Hugues Capet,** Comte de Paris, as king in 987, the fate of the city was inextricably identified with that of the **monarchy**. The presence of the kings, however, prevented the development of the middle-class, republican institutions that the rich merchants of Flanders and Italy were able to obtain for their cities. The result was recurrent political tension, which led to open **rebellion**, for instance, in 1356, when Étienne Marcel, a wealthy cloth merchant, demanded greater autonomy for the city. Further rebellions, fuelled by the hopeless poverty of the lower classes, led to the king and court abandoning the capital in 1418, not to return for more than a hundred years.

The Right Bank, Latin Quarter and Louvre

As the city's livelihood depended from the first on its river-borne trade, commercial activity naturally centred round the place where the goods were landed. This was the **place de Grève** on the **Right Bank**, where the Hôtel de Ville now stands. Marshy ground originally, it was gradually drained to accommodate the business quarter. Whence the continuing association of the Right Bank with commerce and banking today.

The **Left Bank**'s intellectual associations are similarly ancient, dating from the growth of schools and student accommodation round the two great **monasteries** of Ste-Geneviève and St-Germain-des-Prés. The first, dedicated to the city's patron saint who had saved it from destruction by Attila's raiders, occupied the site of the present Lycée Henri-IV on top of the hill behind the Panthéon. In 1215 a papal licence allowed the formation of what gradually became the renowned **University of Paris**, eventually to be known as **the Sorbonne**, after Robert de Sorbon, founder of a college for poor scholars. It was the fact that Latin was the language of the schools both inside and outside the classroom that gave the district its name of Latin Quarter.

To protect this burgeoning city, Philippe Auguste (king from 1180 to 1223) built the Louvre fortress (whose excavated remains are now on display beneath the Louvre museum) and a wall, which swung south to enclose the Montagne Ste-Geneviève and north and east to encompass the Marais. The administration of the city remained in the hands of the king until 1260, when St Louis ceded a measure of responsibility to the leaders of the Paris watermen's guild, whose power was based on their monopoly control of all river traffic and taxes thereon. The city's government, when it has been allowed one, has been conducted ever since from the place de Grève/place de l'Hôtel-de-Ville.

Civil wars and foreign occupation

From the mid-thirteenth to mid-fourteenth centuries Paris shared the same unhappy fate as the rest of France, embroiled in the long and destructive **Hundred Years War** with the English. Étienne Marcel let the enemy into the city in 1357, the Burgundians did the same in 1422, when the Duke of Bedford set up his government of northern France here. Joan of Arc made an unsuccessful attempt to drive them out in 1429 and was wounded in the process at the Porte St-Honoré. The following year the English king, Henry VI, had the cheek to have himself crowned king of France in Notre-Dame.

It was only when the English were expelled – from Paris in 1437 and from France in 1453 – that the economy had the chance to recover from so many decades of devastation. It received a further boost when **François 1er** decided to re-establish the royal court in Paris in 1528. Work began on reconstructing the Louvre and building the Tuileries palace for Cathérine de Médicis, and on transforming Fontainebleau and other country residences into sumptuous Renaissance palaces.

But before these projects reached completion, war again intervened, this time **civil war** between Catholics and Protestants, in the course of which Paris witnessed one of the worst atrocities ever committed against French Protestants. Some

three thousand of them were gathered in Paris for the wedding of Henri III's daughter, Marguerite, to Henri, the Protestant king of Navarre. On August 25, 1572, St Bartholomew's Day, they were massacred at the instigation of the Catholic Guise family. When, through this marriage, Henri of Navarre became heir to the French throne in 1584, the Guises drove his father-in-law, Henri III, out of Paris. Forced into alliance, the two Henris laid siege to the city. Five years later, Henri III having been assassinated in the meantime, Henri of Navarre entered the city as king **Henri IV**. "Paris is worth a Mass", he is reputed to have said to justify renouncing his Protestantism in order to soothe Catholic susceptibilities.

The Paris he inherited was not a very salubrious place. It was overcrowded. No domestic building had been permitted beyond the limits of Philippe-Auguste's twelfth-century walls because of the guilds' resentment of the unfair advantage enjoyed by craftsmen living outside the jurisdiction of the city's tax regulations. The population had doubled to around 400,000, causing an acute housing shortage and a terrible strain on the rudimentary water supply and drainage system. It is said that the first workmen who went to clean out the city's cesspools in 1633 fell dead from the fumes. It took seven months to clean out 6420 cartloads of filth that had been accumulating for two centuries. The overflow ran into the Seine, whence Parisians drew their drinking water.

Planning and expansion

The first systematic attempts at **planning** were introduced by Henri IV at the beginning of the seventeenth century: regulating street lines and uniformity of façade, and laying out the first geometric squares. The **place des Vosges** dates from this period, as does the **Pont Neuf**, the first of the Paris bridges not to be cluttered with medieval houses. Henri thus inaugurated a tradition of grandiose public building, which was to continue to the Revolution and beyond, that perfectly symbolized the bureaucratic, centralized power of the newly self-confident state concentrated in the person of its absolute monarch.

The process reached its apogee under **Louis XIV**, with the construction of the **boulevards** from the Madeleine to the Bastille, the places Vendôme and Victoire, the Porte St-Martin and St-

Denis gateways, the Invalides, Observatoire and the Cour Carrée of the Louvre – not to mention the vast palace at **Versailles**, whither he repaired with the court in 1671. The aristocratic *hôtels* or mansions of the Marais were also erected during this period, to be superseded early in the eighteenth century by the Faubourg St-Germain as the fashionable quarter of the rich and powerful.

The underside of all this bricks and mortar self-aggrandizement was the general neglect of the living conditions of the ordinary citizenry of Paris. The centre of the city remained a densely packed and insanitary warren of medieval lanes and tenements. And it was only in the years immediately preceding the 1789 Revolution that any attempt was made to clean it up. The buildings crowding the bridges were dismantled as late as 1786. Pavements were introduced for the first time and attempts were made to improve the drainage. A further source of pestilential infection was removed with the emptying of the overcrowded cemeteries into the catacombs. One gravedigger alone claimed to have buried more than ninety thousand people in thirty years, stacked "like slices of bacon" in the charnel house of the innocents, which had been receiving the dead of 22 parishes for 800 years.

In 1786 Paris also received its penultimate ring of fortifications, the so-called wall of the Fermiers Généraux, with 57 *barrières* or toll gates (one of which survives in the middle of place Stalingrad), where a tax was levied on all goods entering the city.

The 1789 Revolution

The immediate cause of the Revolution of 1789 was a campaign by the privileged classes of the clergy and nobility to protect their status, especially exemption from taxation, against erosion by the royal government. The revolutionary movement, however, was quickly taken over by the middle classes, relatively well off but politically underprivileged. In the initial phases this meant essentially the provincial bourgeoisie. It was they who comprised the majority of the representatives of the **Third Estate**, the "order" that encompassed the whole of French society after the clergy, who formed the First Estate, and the nobility who formed the Second. It was they who took the initiative in setting up the **National Assembly** on June 17, 1789. The majority of them would probably have been content with

constitutional reforms that checked monarchical power on the English model. But their power depended largely on their ability to wield the threat of a Parisian popular explosion.

Although the effects of the Revolution were felt all over France and indeed Europe, it was in Paris that the most profound changes took place. Being as it were on the spot, the people of Paris discovered themselves in the Revolution. They formed the revolutionary shock troops, the driving force at the crucial stages of the Revolution. They marched on Versailles and forced the king to return to Paris with them. They stormed and destroyed the Bastille on July 14, 1789. They occupied the Hôtel de Ville, set up an insurrectionary Commune and captured the Tuileries palace on August 10, 1792. They invaded the Convention in May 1793 and secured the arrest of the more conservative Girondin faction of deputies.

Where the bourgeois deputies of the Convention were concerned principally with political reform, the **sans-culottes** – literally, the people without breeches – expressed their demands in economic terms: price controls, regulation of the city's food supplies, and so on. In so doing they foreshadowed the rise of the working-class and socialist movements of the nineteenth century. They also established by their practice of taking to the streets and occupying the Hôtel de Ville a tradition of revolutionary action that continued through to the 1871 Commune.

Napoléon – and the barricades

Apart from some spectacular bloodletting, and yet another occupation of the city by foreign powers in 1814, Napoléon's chief legacy to France was a very centralized, authoritarian and efficient **bureaucracy** that put Paris in firm control of the rest of the country. In Paris itself, he left his share of pompous architecture – in the **Arcs de Triomphe** and **Carrousel**, rue de Rivoli and rue de la Paix, the Madeleine and façade of the Palais-Bourbon, plus a further extension for the Louvre and a revived tradition of court flummery and extravagant living among the well-to-do. For the rest of the nineteenth century after his demise, France was left to fight out the contradictions and unfinished business left behind by the Revolution of 1789. And the arena in which these conflicts were resolved was, literally, the streets of the capital.

On the one hand, there was a tussle between the class that had risen to wealth and power as a direct result of the destruction of the monarchy and the old order, and the survivors of the old order, who sought to make a comeback in the 1820s under the restored monarchy of **Louis XVIII** and **Charles X**. This conflict was finally resolved in favour of the new bourgeoisie. When Charles X refused to accept the result of the 1830 National Assembly elections, Adolphe Thiers – who was to become the veteran conservative politician of the nineteenth century – led the opposition in revolt. Barricades were erected in Paris and there followed three days of bitter street fighting, known as **les trois glorieuses**, in which 1800 people were killed (they are commemorated by the column on place de la Bastille). The outcome was the election of **Louis-Philippe** as constitutional monarch, and the introduction of a few liberalizing reforms, most either cosmetic or serving merely to consolidate the power of the wealthiest stratum of the population. Radical republican and working-class interests remained completely unrepresented.

The other, and more important, major political conflict was the extended struggle between this enfranchised and privileged bourgeoisie and the heirs of the 1789 *sans-culottes*, whose political consciousness had been awakened by the Revolution but whose demands remained unsatisfied. These were the people who died on the barricades of July to hoist the bourgeoisie firmly into the saddle.

As their demands continued to go unheeded, so their radicalism increased, exacerbated by deteriorating living and working conditions in the large towns, especially Paris, as the Industrial Revolution got underway. There were, for example, twenty thousand deaths from cholera in Paris in 1832, and 65 percent of the population in 1848 were too poor to be liable for tax. Eruptions of discontent invariably occurred in the capital, with insurrections in 1832 and 1834. In the absence of organized parties, opposition centred on newspapers and clandestine or informal political clubs in the tradition of 1789. The most notable – and the only one dedicated to the violent overthrow of the regime – was Auguste Blanqui's *Société Républicaine*.

In the 1840s the publication of the first Socialist works like Louis Blanc's *Organization of Labour* and Proudhon's *What is Property?* gave an additional spur to the impatience of the opposition. When the lid blew off the pot in **1848** and the **Second Republic** was proclaimed in Paris, it looked for a time as if working-class demands might be at least partly met. The provisional government included Louis Blanc and a Parisian manual worker. But in the face of demands for the control of industry, the setting up of co-operatives and so on, backed by agitation in the streets and the proposed inclusion of men like Blanqui and Barbès in the government, the more conservative Republicans lost their nerve. The nation returned a spanking reactionary majority in the April elections.

Revolution began to appear the only possible defence for the radical left. On June 23, 1848, **working-class Paris** – Poissonnière, Temple, St-Antoine, the Marais, Quartier Latin, Montmartre – rose in **revolt**. Men, women and children fought side by side against fifty thousand troops. In three days of fighting, nine hundred soldiers were killed. No-one knows how many of the *insurgés* – the insurgents – died. Fifteen thousand people were arrested and four thousand sentenced to prison terms.

Despite the shock and devastation of civil war in the streets of the capital, the ruling classes failed to heed the warning in the events of June 1848. Far from redressing the injustices which had provoked them, they proceeded to exacerbate them – by, for example, reducing the representation of what Adolphe Thiers called "the vile multitude". The Republic was brought to an end in a coup d'état by **Louis Napoléon**, who within twelve months had himself crowned Emperor Napoléon III.

Rewards of colonialism

There followed a period of **foreign acquisitions** on every continent and of **laissez-faire capitalism** at home, both of which greatly increased the economic wealth of France, then lagging far behind Britain in the industrialization stakes. Foreign trade trebled, a huge expansion of the rail network was carried out, investment banks were set up, and so forth. The rewards, however, were very unevenly distributed, and the regime relied unashamedly on repressive measures – press censorship, police harassment and the forcible suppression of strikes – to hold the underdogs in check.

The response was entirely predictable. Opposition became steadily more organized and determined. In 1864, under the influence of Karl Marx in London, a French branch of the International was established in Paris and the youthful trade union movement gathered its forces in a federation. In 1869 the far from socialist Gambetta, briefly deputy for Belleville, declared, "Our generation's mission is to complete the French Revolution."

During these nearly twenty years of the Second Empire, while conditions were ripening for the most terrible of all Parisian revolutions, the 1871 Commune, the city itself suffered the greatest ever shock to its system. **Baron Haussmann**, appointed Prefect of the Seine department with responsibility for Paris by Napoléon III, undertook the total transformation of the city. In love with the straight line and grand vista, he drove 135km of broad new streets through the cramped quarters of the medieval city, linking the interior and exterior boulevards, and creating north–south, east–west cross-routes. His taste dictated the uniform grey stone façades, mansard roofs and six to seven storeys that are still the architectural hallmark of the Paris street today. In fact, such was the logic of his planning that construction of his projected streets continued long after his death, boulevard Haussmann itself being completed only in 1927.

While it is difficult to imagine how Paris could have survived without some Haussmann-like intervention, the scale of demolitions entailed by such massive redevelopment brought the direst social consequences. The city boundaries were extended to the 1840 fortifications where the boulevard périphérique now runs. The prosperous classes moved into the new western arrondissements, leaving the decaying older properties to the poor. These were divided and subdivided into ever smaller units as landlords sought to maximize their rents. Sanitation was nonexistent. Water standpipes were available only in the street. Migrant workers from the provinces, sucked into the city to supply the vast labour requirements, crammed into the old villages of Belleville and Ménilmontant. Many, too poor to buy furniture, lived in barely furnished digs or *demi-lits*, where the same bed was shared by several tenants on a shift basis. Cholera and TB were rife. Attempts to impose sanitary regulations were resisted by landlords as covert socialism. Many considered even connection to Haussmann's water mains an unnecessary luxury. Until 1870 refuse was thrown into

the streets at night to be collected the following morning. When in 1884 the Prefect of the day required landlords to provide proper containers, they retorted by calling the containers by his name, *poubelle* – and the name has stuck as the French word for "dustbin".

Far from being concerned with Parisians' welfare, Haussmann's scheme was at least in part designed to keep the workers under control. Barracks were located at strategic points like the place du Château-d'Eau, now République, controlling the turbulent eastern districts, and the broad boulevards were intended to facilitate troop movements and artillery fire. A section of the Canal St-Martin north of the Bastille was covered over for the same reason.

The Siege of Paris and the Commune

In September 1870, Napoléon III surrendered to Bismarck at the border town of Sedan, less than two months after France had declared war on the well-prepared and superior forces of the **Prussian** state. The humiliation was enough for a Republican government to be instantly proclaimed in Paris. The Prussians advanced and by September 19 were laying **siege** to the capital. Gambetta was flown out by hot-air balloon to rally the provincial troops but the country was defeated and liaison with Paris almost impossible. Further balloon messengers ended up in Norway or the Atlantic; the few attempts at military sorties from Paris turned into yet more blundering failures. Meanwhile, the city's restaurants were forced to change menus to fried dog, roast rat or peculiar delicacies from the zoos. For those without savings, death from disease or starvation became an ever more common fate. At the same time, the peculiar conditions of a city besieged gave a greater freedom to collective discussion and dissent.

The government's half-hearted defence of the city – more afraid of revolution within than of the Prussians – angered Parisians, who clamoured for the creation of a 1789-style Commune. The Prussians meanwhile were demanding a proper government to negotiate with. In January 1871, those in power agreed to hold elections for a new national assembly with the authority to surrender officially to the Prussians. A large monarchist majority, with Thiers at its head, was returned, again demonstrating the isolation from the countryside of the Parisian leftists, among whom many prominent old-timers, veterans of 1848 and the empire's jails like Blanqui and Delescluze, were still active.

On March 1, Prussian troops marched down the Champs-Élysées and garrisoned the city for three days while the populace remained behind closed doors in silent protest. On March 18, amid growing resentment from all classes of Parisians, Thiers' attempt to take possession of the National Guard's artillery in Montmartre (see p.162) set the barrel alight. The Commune was proclaimed from the Hôtel de Ville and Paris was promptly subjected to a second siege by Thiers' government, which had fled to Versailles, followed by all the remaining Parisian bourgeoisie.

The **Commune** lasted 72 days – a festival of the oppressed, Lenin called it. Socialist in inspiration, it had no time to implement lasting reforms. Wholly occupied with defence against Thiers' army, it succumbed finally on May 28, 1871, after a week of street-by-street warfare, in which three thousand Parisians died on the barricades and another twenty to twenty-five thousand men, women and children were killed in random revenge shootings by government troops. Thiers could declare with satisfaction – or so he thought – "Socialism is finished for a long time."

Among the non-human casualties were several of the city's landmark buildings, including the Tuileries palace, Hôtel de Ville, Cours des Comptes (where the Musée d'Orsay now stands) and a large chunk of the rue Royale.

The Belle Époque

Physical recovery was remarkably quick. Within six or seven years few signs of the fighting remained. Visitors remarked admiringly on the teeming streets, the expensive shops and energetic nightlife. Charles Garnier's Opéra was opened in 1875. Aptly described as the "triumph of moulded pastry", it was a suitable image of the frivolity and materialism of the so-called naughty Eighties and Nineties. In 1889 the **Eiffel Tower** stole the show at the great Exposition. For the 1900 repeat, the **Métropolitain** (métro) – or *Nécropolitain*, as it was dubbed by one wit – was unveiled.

The lasting social consequence of the Commune was the confirmation of the them-and-us divide between bourgeoisie and working class. Any stance other than a revolutionary one

after the Commune appeared not only feeble, but also a betrayal of the dead. None of the contradictions had been resolved. The years up to World War I were marked by the increasing organization of the Left in response to the unstable but thoroughly conservative governments of the Third Republic. The trade union movement unified in 1895 to form the **Confédération Générale du Travail** (CGT), and in 1905 Jean Jaurès and Jules Guesde founded the **Parti Socialiste** (also known as the SFIO). On the extreme right, fascism began to make its ugly appearance with Maurras' proto-Brownshirt organization, the Camelots du Roi, which inaugurated another French tradition, of violence and thuggery on the far Right.

Yet despite – or maybe in some way *because of* – these tensions and contradictions, Paris provided the supremely inspiring environment for a concentration of **artists and writers** – the so-called **Bohemians**, both French and foreign – such as Western culture has rarely seen. Impressionism, Fauvism and Cubism were all born in Paris in this period, while French poets like Apollinaire, Laforgue, Max Jacob, Blaise Cendrars and André Breton were preparing the way for Surrealism, concrete poetry and symbolism. Film, too, saw its first developments. After World War I, Paris remained the world's art centre, with an injection of foreign blood and a shift of venue from Montmartre to Montparnasse.

In the postwar struggle for recovery the interests of the urban working class were again passed over, with the exception of Clemenceau's eight-hour day legislation in 1919. An attempted general strike in 1920 came to nothing, and workers' strength was again weakened by the irredeemable split in the Socialist Party at the 1920 Congress of Tours. The pro-Lenin majority formed the **French Communist Party**, while the minority faction, under the leadership of Léon Blum, retained the old SFIO title.

As **Depression** deepened in the 1930s and Nazi power across the Rhine became more menacing, fascist thuggery and anti-parliamentary activity increased in France, culminating in a pitched battle outside the Chamber of Deputies in February 1934. (Léon Blum was only saved from being lynched by a funeral cortege through the intervention of some building workers who happened to notice what was going on in the street below.) The effect of this fascist activism was to unite the Left, including the Communists, led by the Stalinist Maurice Thorez, in the

Popular Front. When they won the 1936 elections with a handsome majority in the Chamber, there followed a wave of strikes and factory sit-ins – a spontaneous expression of working-class determination to get their just deserts after a century and a half of frustration. Frightened by the apparently revolutionary situation, the major employers signed the Matignon Agreement with Blum, which provided for wage increases, nationalization of the armaments industry and partial nationalization of the Bank of France, a forty-hour week, paid annual leave and collective bargaining on wages. These reforms were pushed through parliament, but when Blum tried to introduce exchange controls to check the flight of capital the Senate threw the proposal out and he resigned. The Left returned to Opposition, where it remained, with the exception of coalition governments, until 1981. Most of the Popular Front's reforms were promptly undone.

The German Occupation

During the occupation of Paris in World War II, the Germans found some sections of Parisian society, as well as the minions of the Vichy government, only too happy to hobnob with them. For four years the city suffered fascist rule with curfews, German garrisons and a Gestapo HQ. Parisian Jews were forced to wear the star of David and in 1942 were rounded up – by other Frenchmen – and shipped off to Auschwitz (see p.385).

The **Resistance** was very active in the city, gathering people of all political persuasions into its ranks, but with communists and socialists, especially of East European Jewish origin, well to the fore. The job of torturing them when they fell into Nazi hands – often as a result of betrayals – was left to their fellow citizens in the fascist militia. Those who were condemned to death – rather than the concentration camps – were shot against the wall below the old fort of Mont Valérien above St-Cloud.

As Allied forces drew near to the city in 1944, the FFI (armed Resistance units), determined to play their part in driving the Germans out, called their troops onto the streets – some said, in a Leftist attempt to seize political power. To their credit, the Paris police also joined in, holding their Île de la Cité HQ for three days against German attacks. Liberation finally came on August 25, 1944.

Postwar Paris – one more try at Revolution

Postwar Paris has remained no stranger to **political battles** in its streets. Violent demonstrations accompanied the Communist withdrawal from the coalition government in 1947. In the Fifties the Left took to the streets again in protest against the colonial wars in Indochina and Algeria. And, in 1961, in one of the most shameful episodes in modern French history, some two hundred Algerians were killed by the police during a civil rights demonstration.

This **"secret massacre"**, which remained covered by a veil of total official silence until the 1990s, took place during the Algerian war. It began with a peaceful demonstration against a curfew on North Africans imposed by de Gaulle's government in an attempt to inhibit FLN resistance activity in the French capital. Whether the police were acting on higher orders or merely on the authority of their own commanders is not clear. What is clear from hundreds of eyewitness accounts, including some from horrified policemen, is that the police went berserk. They opened fire, clubbed people and threw them in the Seine to drown. Several dozen Algerians were killed in the courtyard of the police HQ on the Île de la Cité. For weeks afterwards, corpses were recovered from the Seine, but the French media remained silent, in part through censorship, in part perhaps unable to comprehend that such events had happened in their own capital. Maurice Papon, the police chief at the time, was subsequently decorated by de Gaulle. He is now finally under investigation for war crimes.

The state attempted censorship again during the events of **May 1968**, though with rather less success. Through this extraordinary month, a radical, libertarian, Leftist movement spread from the Paris universities to include, eventually, the occupation of hundreds of factories across the country and a general strike by nine million workers. The old-fashioned and reactionary university structures that had triggered the revolt were reflected in the hierarchical and rigid organizations of many other institutions in French life. The position of women and of youth, of culture and modes of behaviour, were suddenly highlighted in the general dissatisfaction with a society in which big business ran the state.

There was no revolutionary situation on the 1917 model. The vicious battles with the paramilitary CRS police on the streets of Paris shook large sectors of the population – France's silent majority – to the core, as the government cynically exploiting the scenes for TV knew full well. There was no shared economic or political aim in the ranks of the opposition. With the exception of Michel Rocard's small Parti Socialiste Uni, the traditional parties were taken completely by surprise and uncertain how to react. The French Communist Party, stuck with its Stalinist traditions, was far from favourably disposed to the adventurism of the students and their numerous Maoist, Trotskyist and anarchist factions or *groupuscules*. Right-wing and "nationalist" demonstrations orchestrated by de Gaulle left public opinion craving stability and peace; and a great many workers were satisfied with a new system for wage agreements. It was not, therefore, surprising that the elections called in June returned the Right to power.

The occupied buildings emptied and the barricades in the Latin Quarter came down. For those who thought they were experiencing The Revolution, the defeat was catastrophic. But French institutions and French society did change, shaken and loosened by the events of May 1968. And most importantly it opened up the debate of a new road to socialism, one in which no old models would give all the answers.

The Mitterrand Era, 1981–95

The **Socialists'** first government after 23 years in opposition included four Communist ministers: an alliance reflected in the government commitments to expanded state control of industry, reduction of the hours in the working week, high taxation for the rich, support for liberation struggles around the world, and a public spending programme to raise the living standards of the least well-off. By 1984, however, the government had done a complete volte-face with Laurent Fabius presiding over a cabinet of centrist to conservative "socialist" ministers, clinging desperately to power.

The commitments had come to little. Attempts to bring private education under state control were defeated by mass protests in the streets; ministers were implicated in cover-ups and corruption; unemployment continued to rise. Any idea of peaceful and pro-ecological intent was dashed, as far as international opinion was concerned, by the French Secret Service's murder of

a Greenpeace photographer on the *Rainbow Warrior* in New Zealand.

There were sporadic achievements – in labour laws and women's rights, notably – but no cohesive and consistent socialist line. The Socialists' 1986 election slogan was "Help – the Right is coming back", a bizarrely self-fulfilling tactic. **Jacques Chirac** became prime minister (and continued as Mayor of Paris).

Throughout 1987 the chances of François Mitterrand's winning the presidential election in 1988 seemed very slim. But Chirac's economic policies of privatization and monetary control failed to deliver the goods. Millions of first-time investors in "popular capitalism" lost all their money on Black Monday. Terrorists planted bombs in Paris and took French hostages in Lebanon. Unemployment steadily rose and Chirac made the fatal mistake of flirting with the extreme right. Several leading politicians of the centre-right, among them Simone Weil, a concentration-camp survivor, denounced Chirac's concessions to Le Pen, and a new alignment of the centre started to emerge. **Mitterrand**, the grand old man of politics, with decades of experience, played off all the groupings of the Right in an all-but-flawless campaign, and a mandate.

His party, however, failed to win an absolute majority in the parliamentary elections soon afterwards. The austerity measures of Mitterrand's new prime minister, **Michel Rocard**, upset traditional Socialist supporters in the public-service sector, with nurses, civil servants, teachers and the like quick to take industrial action. Though Chirac's programmes were halted, they were not reversed.

In 1991, Mitterrand sacked Michel Rocard and appointed **Édith Cresson** as prime minister. Initially the French were happy to have their first woman prime minister, who promised to wage economic war against the Germans and the Japanese. The Left, including the Communists, were pleased with Cresson's socialist credentials. But she soon began to turn a few heads with her comments about special charters for illegal immigrants; her dismissal of the stock exchange as a waste of time; her description of the Japanese as yellow ants and British males as homosexual; and by attacks on her own ministers. Cresson became the most unpopular prime minister in the history of the Fifth Republic.

Cresson's worst move was to propose a tax on everyone's insurance contributions to pay for compensation to haemophiliacs infected with HIV. The knowing use of infected blood in transfusions in 1985 became one of the biggest scandals of the Socialist regime.

Pierre Bérégovoy succeeded Cresson in 1992. Universally known as *Béré*, and mocked for his bumbling persona, he survived strikes by farmers, dockers, car workers and nurses, the scandals touching the Socialists, and the Maastricht referendum. But then a private loan was revealed from one Roger-Patrice Pelat, a friend of Mitterrand's accused of insider dealing. Mitterrand distanced himself from his prime minister, who then shot himself, on May 1, two months after losing the elections, leaving no note of explanation.

The new prime minister, **Edouard Balladur**, a fresh and fatherly face from the Right, started off with great popularity. But a series of U-turns after demonstrations by Air France workers, teachers, farmers, fishermen and school pupils, and the state's rescue of the Crédit Lyonnais bank after spectacular losses, wiped away his successes over GATT and keeping the franc strong and inflation down.

His home affairs minister, **Charles Pasqua** (who served in the same post under Chirac), was a highly unpopular right-winger with a strong anti-immigration and anti-immigrant line. In 1992, Pasqua joined forces with another senior Gaullist bully boy, Philippe Séguin, and the extreme UDF right-winger Philippe de Villiers, to oppose the Maastricht treaty. Opposition to the treaty also came from the PCF, the breakaway socialist Jean-Pierre Chevènement and the Front National. Clearly, the long-established certainty of the absolute divide between Right and Left loyalties was no longer tenable. The actual voters divided along the lines of the poorer rural areas voting "No" and the rich urbanites voting "Yes". In Paris the "Yes" vote was overwhelming. Disillusionment with the established parties was confirmed in the 1994 Euro elections. The RPR/UDF lost votes to the anti-Europeans and for the Parti Socialiste it was a total disaster. Rocard had to resign as the party secretary – his attempts to "modernize" the party had failed.

Meanwhile Mitterrand tottered on to the end of his presidential term, looking less and less like the nation's favourite uncle. Two months after Bérégovoy's suicide, Réné Bousquet, who was head of police in the Vichy government and supervised the rounding up of Jews in 1942, was murdered. He was a friend of Mitterrand's and thought to have known shady secrets about the president. The following year a secret service agent and close adviser and friend, Jacques Attali, had to resign from the European Bank for Reconstruction and Development, suspected for wasting the bank's money on a luxury lifestyle.

On the twentieth anniversary of President Pompidou's death in April 1994, there was a wave of nostalgia for a time when "things were right and proper". A month later, a leading French businessman was arrested for corruption, soon followed by other corruption scandals touching businesspeople and politicians, including ministers. Cracks had opened up in the French establishment and the recession was biting.

In 1995, with **Mitterrand dying from cancer** but refusing to step down before the end of his term, revelations surfaced in Pierre Péan's biography, *Une Jeunesse Français*, about his war record as an official in the Vichy regime before he joined the Resistance. Another biography of Mitterrand, *Le Grand Secret*, by Mitterrand's doctor, detailing a whole host of scandals, was banned in France but published on the Internet.

François Mitterrand's presidency came to an end in April 1995. He had been the French head of state for fourteen years, presiding over two Socialist and two Gaullist governments. When he won the elections in 1981, he embodied all the hopes of a generation of socialists who had never seen their party in power. The last years of his presidency saw him becoming ill and aged, his reputation tarnished and his party's popularity reduced to an all-time low. But on his death in January 1996, despite everything, Mitterrand was genuinely mourned as a man of culture and vision, a supreme political operator, with unwavering commitment to the European Union.

Modern developments of the city

Until World War II, Paris remained pretty much as Haussmann had left it. Housing conditions showed little sign of improvement. There was even an outbreak of bubonic plague in Clignancourt in 1921. In 1925 a third of the houses still had no sewage connection. Of the seventeen worst blocks of slums designated for clearance, most were still intact in the 1950s, and even today they have some close rivals in parts of Belleville and elsewhere.

Migration to the suburbs continued, with the creation of **shantytowns** to supplement the hopelessly inadequate housing stock. Post-World War II, these became the exclusive territory of **Algerian** and other **North African immigrants**. In 1966 there were 89 of them, housing 40,000 immigrant workers and their families.

Only in the last thirty years have the authorities begun to grapple with the housing problem, though not by expanding possibilities within Paris, but by siphoning huge numbers of people into a ring of **satellite towns** encircling the greater Paris region.

In Paris proper this same period has seen the final breaking of the mould of Haussmann's influence. Intervening architectural fashions, like Art Nouveau, Le Corbusier's International style and the Neoclassicism of the 1930s, had little more than localized cosmetic effects. It was devotion to the needs of the motorist – a cause unhesitatingly espoused by Pompidou – and the devel-

opment of the high-rise tower that finally did the trick, starting with the **Tour Maine-Montparnasse** and **La Défense**, the redevelopment of the 13e and, in the 1970s, projects like **Beaubourg**, the **Front de Seine** and **Les Halles**. In recent years, new colossal public buildings in myriad conflicting styles have been inaugurated at an evermore astounding rate. At the same time, the fabric of the city – the streets, the métro and the graffitied walls – have been ignored.

When the Les Halles flower and veg market was dismantled, it was not just the nineteenth-century architecture that was mourned. As a sign posted during the redevelopment of Les Halles lamented, "The centre of Paris will be beautiful. Luxury will be king. But we will not be here." The city's social mix has changed more in 25 years than in the previous 100. Gentrification of the remaining working-class districts has accelerated, and the population has become essentially middle-class and white-collar.

The political present

Mitterrand's avuncular fourteen-year presidency was well-calculated and a hard act to follow, but general unease demanded a change of direction. The ensuing presidential elections marked a homecoming for French politics, bringing the right-wing candidate, Chirac, into the presidential seat.

The Socialist Party was desperate for **Jacques Delors**, chair of the European Commission, to stand as their presidential candidate. When he finally refused, it looked as if the party was doomed. But **Lionel Jospin**, the uncharismatic former education minister, performed remarkably well, topping the poll in the first round – in which right-wing votes were split between Balladur, Chirac, the extreme-right Le Pen and the anti-European Philippe de Villiers. Le Pen scored 15.5 percent and called on his followers to abstain in the second round run-off between Jospin and Chirac. Chirac stole the Left's clothes by placing **unemployment and social exclusion** at the top of the political agenda, and heaped promises of better times on every section of the electorate. He won, by a small margin, and was inaugurated as the new president of France in May 1995.

The recession started to take hold during Mitterrand's presidency, official unemployment figures passed three million, and scandals touched the president, politicians of all parties and businesspeople. Socialist Lionel Jospin did surprisingly well in the presidential elections, but it was a foregone conclusion that Jacques Chirac, former Mayor of Paris, would win.

Chirac's presidency

Mitterrand had predicted that Jacques Chirac as president would become the laughing stock of the world. But it was international condemnation rather than derision that greeted the first significant act of his presidency, the decision to resume **nuclear testing** on the Pacific island of Muroroa. A typically Gaullist move, it provoked boycotts of French produce and a revival of the French peace and environmental movements.

Municipal elections in June 1995 gave the Front National control of three towns, including the major port of Toulon. The Socialists, who did not

do too badly, accused the Right of refusing tactical alliances to defeat Le Pen. The increasing popularity of racist measures was noted by the political establishment in Paris, but it was happy to ignore the shock of Le Pen's best ever electoral success.

Chirac's new prime minister, replacing Balladur who had treacherously stood against Chirac in the presidentials, was **Alain Juppé**, a clever, clinical technocrat to whom the French could not warm easily. It was down to him to square the circle of Chirac's election pledges of job creation, maintaining the value of pensions and welfare benefits and reducing the number of homeless, with tax cuts, a continuing strong franc and a reduction in the budget deficit to stay on course for monetary union.

Juppé was in trouble right from the start due to allegations of **corruption** concerning his luxury flat in Paris (see p.430). A summer of **bomb attacks** by Islamic fundamentalists diminished public confidence in the government as guardians of law and order. By October Juppé had broken all records for prime ministerial unpopularity. Having sacked his finance minister, Alain Madelin, for proposing tax cuts and radical reductions in public spending, Juppé raised VAT along with other taxes and provoked a round of strikes with an austerity budget freezing public sector pay.

But that was nothing compared to the **strikes of November and December 1995**, sparked off by Juppé's announcement of dramatic changes in social security provision and a restructuring of the state-owned railways involving job losses and branch line closures. Suddenly, and en masse, the French decided they had had enough of arrogant, elitist politicians, their false election promises and the austerity measures demanded by a free-market approach to European union. Students, teachers and nurses, workers in the transport, energy, post and telecommunications industries, bank clerks and civil servants – all took to the streets with the strong support of private sector employees struggling to get to work. Even the police showed sympathy to the strikers.

With five million people out over a period of 24 days, it was the strongest show of protest in

Parties and politicians

ON THE LEFT

PS (Parti Socialiste). The Socialist Party to which **François Mitterrand** belonged but whose difficulties he chose to ignore during the "cohabitation" years of right-wing governments in his second presidential term. The party had its all-time electoral low in 1993 followed by a very poor showing in the Euro elections of 1994. Corruption in Socialist-controlled town halls was revealed and party secretary **Henri Emmanuelli** charged with fraud. Though it has not exactly cleaned up its act, the party's fortunes have been restored by the creditable performance in the presidential elections of **Lionel Jospin** and his subsequent election and popularity as prime minister. Other key figures include **Michel Rocard**, prime minister 1988–91, who tried to push the party towards the centre ground; **Laurent Fabius**, prime minister 1984–86 and now leader of the parliamentary group; and **Martine Aubry**, minister for jobs and solidarity, who is seen as a possible future first woman president. The party has a coalition with the Greens, the Communists and the Mouvement des Radicaux de Gauche (MRG).

PCF (Parti Communiste Français). Robert Hue succeeded the veteran Stalinist leader **Georges Marchais** as party leader. Hue has proposed a new broad coalition with progressive Greens, Socialists, community groups, churches, etc, which forms a big break from the old line, but has probably come too late to get very far. The PCF remains influential with the country's trade unions and also in local government.

Mouvement des Citoyens (MDC). Small radical socialist grouping led by **Jean-Pierre Chevènement**, who resigned as defence minister in protest at the Gulf War, and is now Minister of the Interior.

Lutte Ouvrière. Trotskyist party whose presidential candidate, **Arlette Laguillier**, has stood in every contest since 1974 (with an identical workers' revolutionary programme). In 1995 she was credited with being the only honest candidate and won five percent of the vote in the first round – her highest ever score.

ON THE RIGHT

The parties on the right are in constant flux as post-election reorganization continues. What follows is a general overview.

UDF (Union pour la Démocratie Française). Confederation of centre-right parties in alliance with the RPR (see below) created by aloof, aristocratic **Valéry Giscard d'Estaing**, French president 1974–81. It failed to put up a presidential candidate in 1995 after Giscard decided not to stand and members split their support

France since May 1968. The mood this time, however, was not joyful liberation but anxiety about unemployment and social welfare, and disillusionment with politicians of both Right and Left, seen as lackeys of the global financial markets. There were no positive demands; indeed no united voice at all from the protestors who ranged from working-class Front National supporters to middle-class Gaullists to Communist trade unionists. But it was the clearest indication in Europe to date that there are limits to people's acceptance of neoliberalism, and that dressing up the free pay of market forces as "modernization" or "realism" does not wash.

Amazingly Juppé survived this "winter of discontent", abandoning some proposals, such as upping the public sector retirement age, but only delaying others. A new tax to pay off the social security deficit has been imposed; cuts in the health service are going ahead along with a market restructuring along British lines; shortening the working week was ruled out.

With a very comfortable right-wing majority in both houses of parliament at the presidential elections, Chirac's position was a happy one, for the time being. However, with the general election looming in 1998, and the possibility of a left government being elected, Chirac decided to surprise the electorate, while the going was good. Chirac's call for a **general election** a year early in May 1997 was an error of judgement, as the left bounded in, joining forces with the Communists and the Greens, to create a **Socialist coalition government**, with **Jospin** as Prime Minister. Chirac was left in a difficult position; having to preside over a left-wing government for the between Balladur and Chirac. It was then embroiled in a leadership battle after Giscard stepped down in 1996. **François Bayrou**, national education minister under Chirac, is now the leader. **Raymond Barre**, mayor of Lyon and prime minister under Giscard, is an old stalwart who may yet return to high office.

DL (Démocratie Libérale). Old Parti Républican. Key figures are Léotard, who supported Balladur in the presidentials, and the leader, **Alain Madelin**, one time finance minister sacked by Juppé, who headed the pro-Chirac camp.

RPR (Rassemblement Pour la République). Gaullist, conservative party once headed by **Jacques Chirac**, mayor of Paris 1977–95, prime minister 1974–76 and 1986–88 and president since 1995. **Edouard Balladur**, prime minister 1993–95 and known by his opponents in the media as "Ballamou" (Balla-wimp), stood against Chirac in the presidentials. After the demise of **Alain Juppé**, **Philippe Séguin**, is now no. 1 of the RPR and a strong anti-European. **Charles Pasqua** still plays a major role in the party, but is no longer a contender for leader. He was home affairs minister under Chirac and Balladur, renowned for his hard line on immigration and law and order. Unlike the two prime ministers he has served, Pasqua is another anti-European.

Mouvement Pour La France. Anti-European party created by former Gaullist **Philippe de Villiers**, a Catholic aristocrat **against abortion, divorce, immigration, state education**, etc, and by UK industrialist **James Goldsmith**. De Villiers won twelve percent of the vote in the 1994 Euro elections but did not fare as well in the presidentials.

FN (Front National). Extreme-right party led by arch-racist **Jean-Marie Le Pen** and his unspeakable deputy **Bruno Mégret**. Following troubles during the regional elections, a bitter power struggle between Le Pen and Mégret is unfolding. Mégret, a more diplomatic character, has the support of key members, including Le Pen's daughter, and may well take control of the FN or create a new party, taking his support with him. The FN currently has eleven MEPs, several hundred local councillors, controls four town halls and scored over fifteen percent in the first round of the presidential elections.

GREEN PARTIES

Les Verts. Part of the Socialist coalition led by **Dominique Voynet**, minister of the environment. All eight Green European seats were lost in 1994, and Voynet scored very badly in the 1995 presidentials. Unofficial coalitions at local level take place with left-wing socialists, anti-racists, reforming communists, etc. Many Greens, including 1988 presidential candidate **André Waechter**, now stand independently from Les Verts.

ensuing five years, and paving the way for both presidential and general elections in 2002.

The current Socialist Government, and Jospin in particular, has never been so popular. The economy is strong and unemployment has gone down, albeit very little, for the first time in years. The government is committed to helping people under the age of 25 into jobs by creating three hundred and fifty thousand *emplois jeunes* in the public sector by the end of 1999. But the problem of long-term unemployment has yet to be tackled as figures continue to rise. Reduction of the hours in the working week from 39 hours to 35 hours, due to begin in 2000, is a less popular attempt to combat unemployment. The signs are that people are happy to work less and create new jobs but not if it means taking a cut in salary. The economics of this radical move have yet to be finalized. The government's other major priority is education, with the plans for the biggest shake-up from primary school to university on the drawing-board.

Meanwhile, on the Right, the election defeat has given them the chance to regroup. Coalitions with the Front National have been much-publicized successes in the 1998 regional elections, proving that for some members of right-wing parties, the Front National is no longer an extremist party against which to stand but a party with which to join forces.

Political issues in Paris

In the twenty years that Paris has had its own Mairie (Town Hall), it has always been in the hands of the Right. Indeed, from 1977 to 1995 there was only one mayor, Jacques Chirac. Over the same period, the mairies of the arrondissements have also been controlled by Gaullists or UDF members, and Paris deputies have rarely been from the Left. It was only in the suburbs that voters chose Socialist or Communist representatives.

But in the local elections of 1995, the Left tripled its number of councillors and won the 3^e, 10^e, 11^e, 18^e, 19^e and 20^e arrondissements, with several ecologists, communists and members of the Mouvement des Citoyens elected. Though still the largest party, the Gaullists lost their absolute majority in the Mairie de Paris, where the real power resides. The arrondissement Mairies have tiny budgets, their main function being to distribute grants to local organizations. In theory they do have a veto over planning consents, in practice, however, the city mairie gets its way.

The Fabric of the city

Presidents of France traditionally make their mark on the capital, though none has left such a notable legacy as François Mitterrand. His "*grands projets*" included the Parc de la Villette (inherited from Giscard), the Louvre Pyramid, the Grande Arche de la Défense, the Institut du Monde Arabe, the Opéra Bastille and the Bibliothèque Nationale de France.

Parisians may be proud of their ever-evolving and architecturally innovative city, but they have begun to question the massive drain on public funds represented by these projects, particularly as the numbers of poor and homeless in the city have rocketed.

Neighbourhood action against the demolition of familiar and much-loved landmarks of Paris has had its successes. The Enfants-Rouge covered market, which the former right-wing mayor of the 3^e *arrondissement* wanted to pull down and replace with a concrete mall, was saved by determined local campaigning. The gardens of square Villemin, in the 8^e, have been preserved for public use, and groups of "*amis du quartier*" have sprung up in several areas to combat unwelcome development.

For the first time since World War II, the population of the city has started to drop. Single people are occupying flats that would previously have housed families, as people with children move out in search of more generous living space and a cleaner environment. Those who can work from home are beginning to doubt whether the charms of the city outweigh its congestion and, most of all, the air pollution that is said to kill several hundred Parisians a year. Many businesses are beginning to relocate away from the city, along the TGV lines, to lower tax zones, faster communications and environments more attractive to the thirtysomething generation.

The City of Light is not going to empty overnight. But Parisians may be forced, not before time, to rethink their relationship with the motor car; and the tourist industry that fills the city centre with poison-belching coaches will have to consider whether Paris as a collection of monuments and museums is, in the end, as attractive as Paris as a city in which people can live and bring up their kids.

Racism

The fate of immigrants and their French descendants has never been so precarious. Fury and frustration at discrimination, assault, abuse and economic deprivation has erupted into battles on the street. Several young blacks have died at the hands of the police, while the right-wing media have revelled in images of violent Arab youths.

Parisians of Algerian origin have long been used to frequent identity checks and harassment by the police. However, since the 1995 bombing campaign in Paris, thought to be the work of Algerian fundamentalists, in which seven people died and over a hundred were injured, their experiences at the hands of the law have deteriorated dramatically; the assumption that Arabs must be fundamentalist sympathizers has added another layer to the burden of racist treatment.

In 1992, tent cities were erected by homeless Africans in the 13^e *arrondissement* and in the Bois de Vincennes to protest against discrimination in housing allocation. There was some public sympathy, but the issue was used as a political football between Mitterrand as president and Chirac as mayor of Paris, and a clear distinction promoted between the "deserving" and the "undesirable undeserving".

In March 1996, three hundred Malian immigrants, many of them failed asylum seekers, sought refuge in the church of St-Ambroise, in the 11e arrondissement. On the eve of the International Day Against Racism, they were forcibly evicted by truncheon-wielding riot police with the complicity of the local bishop and the curé of the church who had even provided the police with the keys. There was considerable outrage, though aimed more against the Church than the "Pasqua Law" of 1993, which took away the automatic entitlement to French citizenship of those born in France and made it far harder for legal immigrants' families to enter France, for asylum seekers and for long-term students.

In its annual report, the National Commission on Human Rights underlined a dramatic increase in racist assaults in 1995 and said that France had gone backwards ten years, with xenophobic opinions becoming accepted platitudes. Following the success of the Front National in the local elections of 1995, the government announced plans to deport 20,000 illegal immigrants a year on charter planes. Only in 1998, has the government got round to relaxing the hard-line "Pasqua law", with Guigou, the Minister of Justice, changing the criteria for obtaining French citizenship. An immigrant married to a French citizen only has to have been married for one year, as opposed to the prior three years, to be eligible for French citizenship, and immigrants under the age of eighteen, arriving and living in France, are automatically entitled to French citizenship when they turn eighteen. However, as far as getting into France and an immigrant's rights while waiting for official status, much progress has yet to be made.

The "excluded"

Unemployment in Paris, standing at around thirteen percent, is significantly higher than the national average. The problem is even worse in many of the suburbs, some of which have a youth unemployment rate of over fifty percent. The numbers of homeless (SDF – *Sans Domicile Fixe*) in Paris has continued to grow – reaching an estimated 250,000 – along with the numbers of people with no option but to beg on the streets and in the métro.

Despite the visibility of poverty in the city, Parisians like to imagine that all the associated problems of drugs, violence and delinquency belong to *la banlieue* (the suburbs). Whenever trouble occurs on the capital's streets, it is *banlieusards* who are blamed.

In July 1996, Prime Minister Juppé announced yet another package of measures to create jobs in the most deprived suburban estates. But the experience of residents is that tax incentives

used to lure in businesses tended to attract fast-food companies and ended up employing outsiders. Nor have they found much comfort in the extra police contingents, armed with plastic bullets. The widely shared view, strongly expressed in the winter strikes of 1995, is that the problems of the dissaffected younger generation go right to the heart of the general malaise of French society, something that needs a much more profound solution than the creation of enterprise zones. The date set for further discussions on combating exclusion coincided with the day Chirac called the general election and had to be abandoned. In 1998, the issue was put back on the agenda by the minister of employment and solidarity, Martine Aubry, who has committed a sum of 21 billion francs to combating exclusion. The target is youth employment, with 350,000 new jobs for young people in the public sector to have been created by the end of 1999.

There are small-scale initiatives that give some hope; like the projects in Argenteuil and Gennevilliers where young people, equipped with a battered old van, buy fresh food directly from the producers in the countryside to sell on the estates. The producers get a better price, the food is sold more cheaply than in supermarkets, and the young people earn a living. But such "self-help" ideas receive no media coverage and fall well outside the conventional framework of the political parties.

The 1995 winter strikes

Other cities in France saw larger demonstrations than Paris, but that was largely because public transport stoppages in the capital made it virtually inaccessible. Roads into the city were blocked with traffic jams 100km long. People walked, cycled, roller-skated and hitched to work, and, despite the cold and the traffic-snarled streets, the majority of Parisians gave the strikers their full support.

The first Paris demonstrations, in November, were by students demanding more money for understaffed and overcrowded universities. As is always the case, a minority indulged in looting and car-burning, but even café and shop owners whose windows had been smashed remained sympathetic to the strike. There were typical scenes of French revolt: railway sleepers being burnt by the Arc de Triomphe; tear-gas canisters, petrol bombs and stones flying between students and riot police; jazz bands, balloons and food stalls in place de la République. On one day 120 women's groups demonstrated for equal pay and tougher action against anti-abortion campaigners. A call by the government for a counter-demonstration brought out a miserable straggle.

Rubbish continued to be collected, the dead to be buried and bread to be baked. Parisians found themselves talking animatedly to strangers on the streets; the final mood was elation that the city's tradition of public protest was still alive.

Town hall scandals

In 1994 it was revealed that Chirac, then mayor of Paris, was renting – at half the going rate – an apartment in the 7e belonging to an obscure civic trust controlled by the Mairie. Since then revelations of town hall officers and politicians being awarded desirable municipal residences have multiplied.

Soon after Jean Tiberi became mayor in 1995, it was discovered that his two children were living in council flats for next to nothing while raking in market rents from apartments they owned. (The waiting list for Paris council flats is around 60,000.) In addition, city funds were used for an extravagant refit of Tiberi's son's property.

Prime Minister Juppé, formerly deputy mayor of Paris in charge of finances, was living in a St-Germain mansion owned by the Mairie, again paying below market rents. In 1993 he reduced the rent on his son's flat and found prestigious homes owned by the Mairie for other family members.

In addition, there have been allegations of bribery by construction companies seeking contracts from the city's housing department, headed at the time by Tiberi, and of misappropriation of municipal funds earmarked for public housing. The money, it was said, was finding its way into RPR party funds.

The magistrate examining the case raided Tiberi's home in June 1996, but corruption proceedings against the mayor have since been shelved and the magistrate in question taken off the case. This has led to another row about the impartiality of the Minister for Justice, fellow Gaullist Jacques Toubon, who went on to sack the head of the anti-corruption agency whose investigations into the homes-for-the-boys scandal were paving the way for a prosecution against Juppé.

Juppé is still being investigated; he has had to move out of his mansion, but has kept his position as mayor of Bordeaux. Nothing has come from the two senior prosecutors, Gaullist sympathizers appointed in July 1996 to examine whether fraud proceedings should go ahead against Tiberi and others – what went on remains unclear.

In the past, politicians feathering their own nests never roused much public anger. But times have changed. People are disgusted at seeing the "elites" profiting from subsidized housing while hundreds of thousands are homeless. Even the normally obsequious right-wing press has been asking questions about the judiciary's independence. Despite Chirac's promises to uphold this independence in his election manifesto, he has kept his mouth shut throughout the affairs. The scandal typifies the increasing gap between the governors and the governed, which was one of the key themes of the 1995 strikes.

Meanwhile, a struggle for the seat of mayor is going on behind the scenes. At the beginning of 1998, Jacques Toubon, currently mayor of the 13e arrondissement and Chirac's other protégée along with Tiberi, attempted to pull the carpet from under Tiberi, by gathering allies in the Municipal Council. At the risk of looking ridiculous, the affair has gone quiet, but the tensions remain.

Books

An extraordinary number of books have been written about Paris and all things Parisian. In the selected listing of books below, publishers are detailed in the form of British publisher/American publisher. Where books are published in one country only, UK or US follows the publisher's name.

History

Richard Cobb, *The French and their Revolution* (John Murray, UK). A selection of expert essays on the French Revolution, with a personal touch.

Alfred Cobban, *A History of Modern France* (3 vols: 1715–99, 1799–1871 and 1871–1962; Penguin/Viking). Complete and very readable account of the main political, social and economic strands in French – and inevitably Parisian – history.

Norman Hampson, *A Social History of the French Revolution* (Routledge). An analysis that concentrates on the personalities involved. Its particular interest lies in the attention it gives to the *sansculottes*, the ordinary poor of Paris.

Christopher Hibbert, *The French Revolution* (Penguin, UK). Good, concise popular history of the period and events.

Alistair Horne, *How Far from Austerlitz* (Macmillan/Griffin) and *The Fall of Paris* (Papermac, UK). The first an excellent, modern history of Napoleon, catching him at his zenith and recounting his subsequent demise. The second, rather less readable but essential for an understanding of the events of the Paris Commune.

Colin Jones, *The Cambridge Illustrated History of France* (Cambridge UP). A political and social history of France from prehistoric times to the mid-1990s, concentrating on issues of regionalism, gender, race and class. Good illustrations and a friendly, non-academic writing style.

Lissagaray, *Paris Commune* (o/p). A highly personal and partisan account of the politics and fighting by a participant. Although Lissagaray himself is reticent about it, history has it that the last solitary Communard on the last barricade – in the rue Ramponneau in Belleville – was in fact himself.

Karl Marx, *Surveys from Exile* (Penguin); *On the Paris Commune* (Pathfinder, US). *Surveys* includes Marx's speeches and articles at the time of the 1848 Revolution and after, including an analysis, riddled with jokes, of Napoléon III's rise to power. *Paris Commune* – more rousing prose – has a history of the Commune by Engels.

Paul Webster, *Pétain's Crime: The Full Story of French Collaboration in the Holocaust.* (Papermac/Ivan R Dee). The fascinating and alarming story of the Vichy regime's more than willing collaboration with the German authorities' campaign to implement the "final solution" in occupied France, and the bravery of those, especially the Communist resistance, who attempted to prevent it. A mass of hitherto unpublished evidence.

Theodore Zeldin, *A History of French Passions, 1848–1945* (2 paperback vols; Oxford UP). French history tackled by theme, such as intellect and taste – a good read.

Society, culture and politics

John Ardagh, *France Today* (Penguin). Comprehensive journalistic overview, covering food, film, education and holidays as well as politics and education. Good on detail about the urban suburbs (and the shift there from the centre) of Paris.

Roland Barthes, *Mythologies* and *Selected Writings; (A Barthes Reader)* (both Vintage/Noonday). The first, though dated, is the classic: a brilliant description of how the ideas, prejudices and contradictions of French thought and behaviour manifest themselves, in food, wine, cars, travel guides and other cultural offerings. Barthes' piece on the Eiffel Tower doesn't appear, but it's included in the *Selected Writings*, published in the US as *A Barthes Reader* (ed Susan Sontag).

Simone de Beauvoir, *The Second Sex* (Vintage). One of the prime texts of Western feminism, written in 1949, covering women's inferior status in history, literature, mythology, psychoanalysis, philosophy and everyday life.

Denis Belloc, *Slow Death in Paris* (Quartet, UK). A harrowing account of a heroin addict in Paris. Not recommended holiday reading, but if you want to know about the seamy underbelly of the city, this is the book.

James Campbell, *Paris Interzone* (Minerva, UK). The feuds, passions and destructive lifestyles of Left Bank writers 1946–60 are evoked here. The cast includes Richard Wright, James Baldwin, Samuel Beckett, Boris Vian, Alexander Trocchi, Eugene Ionesco, Sartre, de Beauvoir, Nabokov and Allan Ginsberg.

Richard Cobb, *Paris and Elsewhere* (ed. David Gilmour; John Murray, UK). Selected writings by the acclaimed historian of the Revolution reveal his unique encounter with the French.

Robert Cole, *A Traveller's History of Paris* (Windrush Press/Interlink). This brief history of the city from the first Celtic settlement to today is an ideal starting point for those wishing to delve into the historical archives.

Christopher Flood & Laurence Bell (eds), *Political Ideologies in Contemporary France* (Pinter/Cassell). Beginners' guide to the current political trends in France.

Gisèle Halim, *Milk for the Orange Tree* (Quartet). Born in Tunisia, daughter of an Orthodox Jewish family; ran away to Paris to become a lawyer; defender of women's rights, Algerian FLN fighters and all unpopular causes. A gutsy autobiographical story.

Peter Lennon, *Foreign Correspondents: Paris in the Sixties* (Picador/McClelland & Stewart). Irish journalist Peter Lennon went to Paris in the early 1960s unable to speak a word of French. He became a close friend of Samuel Beckett and was a witness to the May 1968 events.

François Maspero, *Roissy Express* (Blackwell/W W Norton & Co.), photographs Anaïk Frantz. A "travel book" along the RER line B from Roissy to St-Rémy-lès-Chevreuse (excluding the Paris stops). Brilliant insights into the life of the Paris suburbs, and fascinating digressions into French history and politics.

Andrea Kupfer Schneider, *Creating the Musée d'Orsay (The Politics of Culture in France)* (Pennsylvania State UP). Interesting and sometimes amusing account of the struggles involved in transforming the Gare d'Orsay into one of Paris' most visited museums. An original insight revealing French attitudes towards such grand cultural projects.

William Wiser *The Great Good Place* (o/p). An account of American expatriate women in Paris, from the Impressionist painter Mary Cassatt, through to writer Edith Wharton, publisher Caresse Crosby, the sad socialite novelist's wife Zelda Fitzgerald and finally the singer Josephine Baker.

Theodore Zeldin *The French* (Harvill). A coffee-table book without the pictures, based on the author's conversations with a wide range of people, about money, sex, phobias, parents and everything else.

Art, architecture and photography

Brassaï, *Le Paris Secret des Années 30* (Gallimard, France) Extraordinary photos of the capital's nightlife in the 1930s – brothels, music halls, street cleaners, transvestites and the underworld – each one a work of art and a familiar world (now long since gone) to Brassaï and his mate, Henry Miller, who accompanied him on his nocturnal expeditions.

Robert Doisneau, *Three Seconds of Eternity* (Neues Publishing Co.). The famous *Kiss in front of the Hôtel de Ville* takes the front cover, but there's more to Doisneau than this. A collection chosen by himself of photographs taken in France, but mainly Paris, in the 1940s and 50s. Beautifully nostalgic.

Norma Evenson, *Paris: A Century of Change, 1878–1978* (Yale UP). A large illustrated volume which makes the development of urban planning and the fabric of Paris an enthralling subject, mainly because the author's concern is always with people, not panoramas.

John James, *Chartres* (D S Brewer, UK). The story of Chartres cathedral, with insights into the medieval context, the character and attitudes of the masons, the symbolism, and the advanced mathematics of the building's geometry.

William Mahder (ed), *Paris Arts: The '80s Renaissance* (o/p), *Paris Creation: Une Renaissance* (o/p). Illustrated, magazine-style survey of French arts. The design and photos are reason enough in themselves to look it up.

Willy Ronis, *Belleville Ménilmontant* (o/p). Misty black-and-white photographs of people and streets in the two "villages" of eastern Paris in the 1940s and 1950s.

Vivian Russell, *Monet's Garden* (Frances Lincoln/Stewart, Talson & Chang). An exceptional book illustrated with sumptuous colour photographs by the author, old photographs of the artist and reproductions of his paintings. Superb opening chapter on Monet as "poet of nature", plus a detailed description of the garden's evolution, seasonal cycle and current maintenance, which will delight serious gardeners.

Edward Lucie-Smith, *Concise History of French Painting* (o/p). If you're after an art reference book, then this will do as well as any, though there are of course dozens of other books available on particular French artists and art movements.

Yves St-Laurent, *Forty Years of Creation* (Distributed Art Publishers). Glossy pages of the best of Y-S-L's stylish fashion photography and creations.

Anthony Sutcliffe, *Paris – An Architectural History* (Yale UP). Excellent overview of Paris' changing cityscape, as dictated by fashion, social structure and political power.

Cookery

Linda Dannenberg, *Paris Bistro Cooking* (C N Potter). *Poule au Pot* and *Rum Baba* among other delicious French traditional dishes as cooked by some of Paris' best *bistrots*.

Patricia Wells, *Joël Robuchon – Cuisine Actuelle* (Macmillan, UK). Paris' most famous chef reveals some basic and some more advanced recipes from his restaurant.

Paris in literature

British/American

Charles Dickens, *A Tale of Two Cities* (Penguin). Paris and London during the 1789 Revolution and before. The plot's pure Hollywood, but the streets and at least some of the social backdrop are for real.

Robert Ferguson, *Henry Miller* (o/p). Very readable biography of the old rogue and his rumbustious doings, including his long stint in Paris and affair with Anaïs Nin.

Brion Gysin, *The Last Museum* (Olympia Marketing Corp, US). The setting is the *Hôtel Bardo*, the Beat hotel: the co-residents are Kerouac, Ginsberg and Burroughs. Published posthumously, this is 1960s Paris in its most manic mode.

Ernest Hemingway, *A Moveable Feast* (Arrow/Touchstone). Hemingway's American-in-Paris account of life in the 1930s with Ezra Pound, F. Scott Fitzgerald, Gertrude Stein, etc. Dull, pedestrian stuff, despite its classic and best-seller status.

Jack Kerouac, *Satori in Paris* (Flamingo/Grove Press) . . . and in Brittany, too. Uniquely inconsequential Kerouac experiences.

Ian Littlewood, *Paris: A Literary Companion* (John Murray, UK). A thorough account of which literary figures went where, and what they had to say about it.

Herbert Lottman, *Colette: A Life* (Little, Brown & Co., UK). An interesting if somewhat dry account of this enigmatic Parisian writer's life.

Henry Miller, *Tropic of Cancer; Quiet Days in Clichy* (both Flamingo/Grove Press). Again 1930s Paris, though from a more focused angle – sex, essentially. Erratic, wild, self-obsessed writing, but with definite flights of genius.

Anaïs Nin, *The Journals 1931–1974* (7 vols) (Peter Owen/Harcourt Brace). A detailed literary narrative of French and US artists and fiction-makers from the first half of this century – not least, Nin herself – in Paris and elsewhere. The more famous *Erotica* was also written in Paris, for a local connoisseur of pornography.

George Orwell, *Down and Out in Paris and London* (Penguin/Harcourt Brace). Documentary account of breadline living in the 1930s – Orwell at his best.

Paul Rambali, *French Blues* (o/p). Movies, sex, down-and-outs, politics, fast food, bikers – a cynical, streetwise look at modern urban France.

Jean Rhys, *Quartet* (Penguin/Norton). A beautiful and evocative story of a lonely young woman's existence on the fringes of 1920s Montparnasse society.

French (in translation)

Paul Auster (ed), *The Random House Book of Twentieth Century French Poetry* (Random House). Bilingual anthology containing the major French poets of this century, most of whom were based in Paris. Apollinaire and Cendrars; Aragon, Eluard and Prévert.

Honoré de Balzac, *Le Père Goriot* (Oxford UP). Cornerstone of his *Comédie Humaine* in which nineteenth-century Paris is the principal character.

Baudelaire's Paris, translated by Laurence Kitchen (Forest, UK). Gloom and doom by Baudelaire, Gérard de Nerval, Verlaine and Jiménez – in bilingual edition.

André Breton, *Nadja* (Grove Press). A surrealist evocation of Paris. Fun.

Louis-Ferdinand Céline, *Death on Credit* (J Calder, UK). A landmark in twentieth-century French literature, along with his earlier *Voyage to the End of the Night* (Calder/Cambridge UP) Céline recounts the delirium of the world as seen through the eyes of an adolescent in working-class Paris at the beginning of the twentieth century.

Blaise Cendrars, *To the End of the World* (Peter Owen/Dufour). An outrageous bawdy tale of a randy septuagenarian Parisian actress, having an affair with a deserter from the Foreign Legion.

Didier Daeninckx, *Murder in Memoriam* (Serpent's Tail). A thriller involving two murders: one of a Frenchman during the massacre of the Algerians in Paris in 1961, the other of his son twenty years later. The investigation by an honest detective lays bare dirty tricks, corruption, racism and the cover-up of the massacre.

Alexandre Dumas, *The Count of Monte Cristo* (Penguin). One hell of a good yarn, with Paris and Marseilles locations.

Gustave Flaubert, *Sentimental Education* (Oxford UP). A lively, detailed 1869 reconstruction of the life, manners, characters and politics of Parisians in the 1840s, including the 1848 Revolution.

Victor Hugo, *Les Misérables* (Penguin). A racy, eminently readable novel by the French equivalent of Dickens, about the Parisian poor and low-life in the first half of the nineteenth century. Book Four contains an account of the barricade fighting during the 1832 insurrection.

François Maspero, *Le Sourire du Chat* (translated as *Cat's Grin*) (Penguin/New Amsterdam Books). Semi-autobiographical novel of the young teenager Luc in Paris during World War II, with his adored elder brother in the Resistance, his parents taken to concentration camps as Paris is liberated, and everyone else busily collaborating. An intensely moving and revealing account of the war period.

Guy de Maupassant, *Bel-Ami* (Penguin/Viking). Maupassant's chef-d'oeuvre reveals the double standards of Paris during the Belle Époque with a keen observer's eye.

Daniel Pennac, *The Scapegoat* and *The Fairy Gunmother* (both Harvill). Finally two of the series of four have been translated into English. Pennac has long been Paris' favourite contemporary writer, with his hilarious crime stories set among the chaos and colour of multi-ethnic Belleville.

Georges Perec *Life: A User's Manual* (Harvill/David R Godine). An extraordinary literary jigsaw puzzle of life, past and present, human, animal and mineral, extracted from the residents of an imaginary apartment block in the 17e arrondissement of Paris.

Édith Piaf, *My Life* (Penguin,UK). Piaf's dramatic story told pretty much in her words.

Marcel Proust, *Remembrance of Things Past* (Penguin). Written in and of Paris: absurdly long but bizarrely addictive.

Jean-Paul Sartre, *Roads to Freedom Trilogy* (Vintage). Metaphysics and gloom, despite the title.

Georges Simenon, *Maigret at the Crossroads* (Penguin/Harcourt Brace), or any other of the Maigret novels. Literary crime thrillers; the Montmartre and seedy criminal locations are unbeatable.

Michel Tournier, *The Golden Droplet* (Harper Collins, UK). A magical tale of a Saharan boy coming to Paris, where strange adventures, against the backdrop of immigrant life in the slums, overtake him because he never drops his desert oasis view of the world.

Émile Zola, *Nana* (Penguin/Viking). The rise and fall of a courtesan in the decadent times of the Second Empire. Not bad on sex, but confused on sexual politics. A great story nevertheless, which brings mid-nineteenth-century Paris alive, direct, to present-day senses. Paris is also the setting for Zola's *L'Assommoir*, *L'Argent* and *Thérèse Raquin*.

Language

French can be a deceptively familiar language because of the number of words and structures it shares with English. Despite this it's far from easy, though the bare essentials are not difficult to master and can make all the difference. Even just saying "Bonjour Madame/Monsieur" and then gesticulating will usually get you a smile and helpful service. People working in tourist offices, hotels and so on almost always speak English and tend to use it when you're struggling to speak French – be grateful, not insulted.

French pronunciation

One easy rule to remember is that **consonants** at the end of words are usually silent. *Pas plus tard* (not later) is thus pronounced "pa-plu-tarr". But when the following word begins with a vowel, you run the two together: *pas aprés* (not after) becomes "pazapray".

Vowels are the hardest sounds to get right. Roughly:

a	as in hat		*i*	as in machine
e	as in get		*o*	as in hot
é	between get and gate		*o/au*	as in over
è	between get and gut		*ou*	as in food
eu	like the **u** in hurt		*u*	as in pursed-lip version of **use**

More awkward are the **combinations** in/im, en/em, on/om, un/um at the ends of words, or followed by consonants other than n or m. Again, roughly:

in/im	like the **an** in an**x**ious		*on/om*	like the **on** in **Don**caster said by
an/am,	like the **on** in **Don**caster when said			someone with a heavy cold
en/em	with a nasal accent		*un/um*	like the **u** in **u**nderstand

Consonants are much as in English, except that ch is always sh, h is silent, th is the same as t, ll is like the y in "yes", w is v, and r is growled (or rolled).

Learning materials

Rough Guide French Phrasebook (Rough Guides). Mini dictionary-style phrasebook with both English–French and French–English sections, along with cultural tips for tricky situations and a menu reader.

Get By In French (BBC Publications). Phrasebook and cassette. A good stepping-stone before tackling a complete course.

Mini French Dictionary (Harrap/Prentice Hall). French–English and English–French, plus a brief grammar and pronunciation guide.

Breakthrough French and **Further Breakthrough French** (Pan; book and two cassettes). Excellent teach-yourself course.

A Comprehensive French Grammar Byrne & Churchill (Blackwell). Easy to follow reference grammar.

French and English Slang Dictionary (Harrap). A bit large to carry, but the key to understanding everyday French.

Verbaid (Verbaid, Hawk House, Heath Lane, Farnham, Surrey GF9 0PR). CD-size laminated paper "verb wheel" giving tense endings for regular verbs.

A Vous La France; Franc Extra; Franc Parler (BBC Publications; each has a book and two cassettes). BBC radio courses, running from beginners' to fairly advanced language.

Basic words and phrases

French nouns are divided into masculine and feminine. This causes difficulties with adjectives, whose endings have to change to suit the gender of the nouns they qualify. If you know some grammar, you will know what to do. If not, stick to the masculine form, which is the simplest – it's what we have done in this glossary.

today	*aujourd'hui*	that one	*celà*
yesterday	*hier*	open	*ouvert*
tomorrow	*demain*	closed	*fermé*
in the morning	*le matin*	big	*grand*
in the afternoon	*l'après-midi*	small	*petit*
in the evening	*le soir*	more	*plus*
now	*maintenant*	less	*moins*
later	*plus tard*	a little	*un peu*
at one o'clock	*à une heure*	a lot	*beaucoup*
at three o'clock	*à trois heures*	cheap	*bon marché*
at ten-thirty	*à dix heures et demie*	expensive	*cher*
at midday	*à midi*	good	*bon*
man	*un homme*	bad	*mauvais*
woman	*une femme*	hot	*chaud*
here	*ici*	cold	*froid*
there	*là*	with	*avec*
this one	*ceci*	without	*sans*

Accommodation

a room for one/ two people	*une chambre pour une/ deux personnes*	do laundry	*faire la lessive*
a double bed	*un lit double*	sheets	*draps*
a room with a shower	*une chambre avec douche*	blankets	*couvertures*
		quiet	*calme*
a room with a bath	*une chambre avec salle de bain*	noisy	*bruyant*
		hot water	*eau chaude*
For one/two/ three nights	*Pour une/deux/ trois nuit(s)*	cold water	*eau froide*
		Is breakfast included?	*Est-ce que le petit déjeuner est compris?*
Can I see it?	*Je peux la voir?*	I would like breakfast	*Je voudrais prendre le petit déjeuner*
a room in the courtyard	*une chambre sur la cour*		
a room over the street	*une chambre sur la rue*	I don't want breakfast	*Je ne veux pas le petit déjeuner*
		Can we camp here?	*On peut camper ici?*
first floor	*premier étage*	campsite	*un camping/ terrain de camping*
second floor	*deuxième étage*		
with a view	*avec vue*	tent	*une tente*
key	*clef*	tent space	*un emplacement*
to iron	*repasser*	youth hostel	*auberge de jeunesse*

Days and dates

January	*janvier*	May	*mai*	September	*septembre*
February	*février*	June	*juin*	October	*octobre*
March	*mars*	July	*juillet*	November	*novembre*
April	*avril*	August	*août*	December	*décembre*

Sunday	*dimanche*	August 1	*le premier août*
Monday	*lundi*	March 2	*le deux mars*
Tuesday	*mardi*	July 14	*le quatorze juillet*
Wednesday	*mercredi*	November 23, 1998	*le vingt-trois novembre,*
Thursday	*jeudi*		*dix-neuf-cent-quatre-*
Friday	*vendredi*		*vingt-dix-huit*
Saturday	*samedi*		

Numbers

1	*un*	12	*douze*	30	*trente*	95	*quatre-*
2	*deux*	13	*treize*	40	*quarante*		*vingt-*
3	*trois*	14	*quatorze*	50	*cinquante*		*quinze*
4	*quatre*	15	*quinze*	60	*soixante*	100	*cent*
5	*cinq*	16	*seize*	70	*soixante-dix*	101	*cent-et-un*
6	*six*	17	*dix-sept*	75	*soixante-*	200	*deux cents*
7	*sept*	18	*dix-huit*		*quinze*	300	*trois cents*
8	*huit*	19	*dix-neuf*	80	*quatre-*	1000	*mille*
9	*neuf*	20	*vingt*		*vingts*	2000	*deux milles*
10	*dix*	21	*vingt-et-un*	90	*quatre-vingt-*	5000	*cinq milles*
11	*onze*	22	*vingt-deux*		*dix*	1,000,000	*un million*

Talking to people

When addressing people you should always use *Monsieur* for a man, *Madame* for a woman, *Mademoiselle* for a girl. Plain *bonjour* by itself is not enough. This isn't as formal as it seems, and it has its uses when you've forgotten someone's name or want to attract someone's attention.

Excuse me	*Pardon*	OK/agreed	*d'accord*
Do you speak English?	*Vous parlez anglais?*	please	*s'il vous plaît*
		thank you	*merci*
How do you say in French?	*Comment ça se dit en français?*	hello	*bonjour*
		goodbye	*au revoir*
What's your name?	*Comment vous appelez-vous?*	good morning/ afternoon	*bonjour*
My name is . . .	*Je m'appelle . . .*	good evening	*bonsoir*
I'm English/	*Je suis anglais(e)/*	good night	*bonne nuit*
Irish/	*irlandais(e)/*	How are you?	*Comment allez-vous?/*
Scottish/	*écossais(e)/*		*Ça va?*
Welsh/	*gallois(e)/*	Fine, thanks	*Très bien, merci*
American/	*américan(e)/*	I don't know	*Je ne sais pas*
Australian/	*australien(ne)/*	Let's go	*Allons-y*
Canadian/	*canadien(ne)/*	See you tomorrow	*A demain*
a New Zealander	*néo-zélandais(e)*	See you soon	*A bientôt*
yes	*oui*	Sorry	*Pardon, Madame/*
no	*non*		*je m'excuse*
I understand	*Je comprends*	Leave me alone	*Fichez-moi la paix!*
I don't understand	*Je ne comprends pas*	(aggressive)	
Can you speak slower?	*S'il vous plaît, parlez moins vite?*	Please help me	*Aidez-moi, s'il vous plaît*

Questions and requests

The simplest way of asking a question is to start with *s'il vous plaît* (please), then name the thing you want in an interrrogative tone of voice. For example:

Where is there a bakery?	*S'il vous plaît, la boulangerie?*	Which way is it to the Eiffel Tower?	*S'il vous plaît, la route pour la Tour Eiffel?*

Similarly with requests:

We'd like a room for two.	*S'il vous plaît, une chambre pour deux.*	Can I have a kilo of oranges?	*S'il vous plaît, un kilo d'oranges.*

Question words:

where?	*où?*	when?	*quand?*
how?	*comment?*	why?	*pourquoi?*
how many/ how much?	*combien?*	at what time?	*à quelle heure?*
		what is/which is?	*quel est?*

Getting around

bus	*autobus, bus, car*	on foot	*à pied*
bus station	*gare routière*	Where are you going?	*Vous allez où?*
bus stop	*arrêt*		
car	*voiture*	I'm going to . . .	*Je vais à . . .*
train/taxi/ferry	*train/taxi/ferry*	I want to get off at . . .	*Je voudrais descendre à . . .*
boat	*bâteau*		
plane	*avion*	the road to . . .	*la route pour . . .*
railway station	*gare*	near	*près/pas loin*
platform	*quai*	far	*loin*
What time does it leave?	*Il part à quelle heure?*	left	*à gauche*
		right	*à droite*
What time does it arrive?	*Il arrive à quelle heure?*	straight on	*out droit*
		on the other side of	*à l'autre côté de*
a ticket to . . .	*un billet pour . . .*	on the corner of	*à l'angle de*
single ticket	*aller simple*	next to	*à côté de*
return ticket	*aller retour*	behind	*derrière*
validate your ticket	*compostez votre billet*	in front of	*devant*
valid for	*valable pour*	before	*avant*
ticket office	*vente de billets*	after	*aprés*
how many kilometres?	*combien de kilomètres?*	under	*sous*
		to cross	*traverser*
how many hours?	*combien d'heures?*	bridge	*pont*
hitchhiking	*autostop*		

Cars

garage	*garage*	put air in the tyres	*gonfler les pneus*
service	*service*	battery	*batterie*
to park the car	*garer la voiture*	the battery is dead	*la batterie est morte*
car park	*un parking*	plugs	*bougies*
no parking	*défense de stationner/ stationnement interdit*	to break down	*tomber en panne*
		petrol can	*bidon*
petrol station	*poste d'essence*	insurance	*assurance*
petrol	*essence*	green card	*carte verte*
fill it up	*faire le plein*	traffic lights	*feux*
oil	*huile*	red light	*feu rouge*
air line	*ligne à air*	green light	*feu vert*

French and architectural terms: a glossary

These are either terms you'll come across in this book, or come up against on signs, maps, etc, while travelling around. For food items see p.258 onwards.

ABBAYE abbey

AMBULATORY covered passage around the outer edge of a choir of a church

APSE semicircular termination at the east end of a church

ARRONDISSEMENT district of the city

ASSEMBLÉE NATIONALE the French parliament

AUBERGE DE JEUNESSE (AJ) youth hostel

BAROQUE High Renaissance period of art and architecture, distinguished by extreme ornateness

BEAUX ARTS fine arts museum (and school)

CAR bus

CAROLINGIAN dynasty (and art, sculpture, etc) founded by Charlemagne, late eighth to early tenth centuries

CFDT Socialist trade union

CGT Communist trade union

CHASSE, CHASSE GARDÉE hunting grounds

CHÂTEAU mansion, country house, castle

CHÂTEAU FORT castle

CHEMIN path

CHEVET end wall of a church

CIJ (Centre d'Informations Jeunesse) youth information centre

CLASSICAL architectural style incorporating Greek and Roman elements – pillars, domes, colonnades, etc – at its height in France in the seventeenth century and revived in the nineteenth century as **NEOCLASSICAL**

CLERESTORY upper storey of a church, incorporating the windows ·

CODENE French CND

CONSIGNE luggage consignment

COURS combination of main square and main street

COUVENT convent, monastery

DÉFENSE DE . . . It is forbidden to . . .

DÉGUSTATION tasting (wine or food)

DÉPARTEMENT county – more or less

ÉGLISE church

EN PANNE out of order

ENTRÉE entrance

FERMETURE closing period

FLAMBOYANT florid form of Gothic

FN (Front National) fascist party led by Jean-Marie Le Pen

FO Catholic trade union

FRESCO wall painting – durable through application to wet plaster

GALLO-ROMAIN period of Roman occupation of Gaul (first to fourth centuries AD)

GARE station; **ROUTIÈRE** – bus station; **SNCF** – train station

GOBELINS famous tapestry manufacturers, based in Paris; its most renowned period was in the reign of Louis XIV (seventeenth century)

GRANDE RANDONÉE (GR) long-distance footpath

HALLES covered market

HLM public housing development

HÔTEL a hotel, but also an aristocratic townhouse or mansion

HÔTEL DE VILLE town hall

JOURS FÉRIÉS public holidays

MAIRIE town hall

MARCHÉ market

MEROVINGIAN dynasty (and art, etc), ruling France and parts of Germany from the sixth to mid-eighth centuries

NARTHEX entrance hall of church

NAVE main body of a church

PCF Communist Party of France

PLACE square

PORTE gateway

PS Socialist party

POSTE post office

QUARTIER district of a town

RENAISSANCE art/architectural style developed in fifteenth-century Italy and imported to France in the early sixteenth century by François 1er

RETABLE altarpiece

REZ-DE-CHAUSSÉE (RC) ground floor

RN (Route Nationale) main road

ROMANESQUE early medieval architecture distinguished by squat, rounded forms and naive sculpture

RPR Gaullist party led by Philippe Seguin

SI (Syndicat d'Initiative) tourist information office; also known as OT, OTSI and Maison du Tourisme

SNCF (Société Nationale des Chemins de Fer) French railways

SOLDES sales

SORTIE exit

STUCCO plaster used to embellish ceilings, etc

TABAC bar or shop selling stamps, cigarettes, etc

TOUR tower

TRANSEPT cross arms of a church

TYMPANUM sculpted panel above a church door

UDF centre-right party headed by François Bayrou

VAUBAN seventeenth-century military architect – his fortresses still stand all over France

VILLA a mews or a series of small residential streets, built as a unity

VOUSSOIR sculpted rings in an arch over church door

ZONE BLEUE restricted parking zone

ZONE PIÉTONNE pedestrian zone

Index

S

Stay in touch with us!

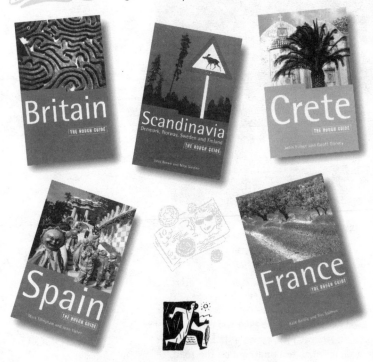

¿Qué pasa?

WHAT'S HAPPENING?
A ROUGH GUIDES SERIES –
ROUGH GUIDES PHRASEBOOKS

**Rough Guide Phrasebooks
represent a complete shakeup
of the phrasebook format.
Handy and pocket sized, they
work like a dictionary to get you
straight to the point. With clear
guidelines on pronunciation,
dialogues for typical situations,
and tips on cultural issues, they'll
have you speaking the language
quicker than any other
phrasebook.**

Czech, French, German, Greek,
Hindi & Urdu, Hungarian, Indonesian,
Italian, Japanese, Mandarin Chinese,
Mexican Spanish, Polish, Portuguese,
Russian, Spanish, Thai, Turkish,
Vietnamese

Further titles coming soon...

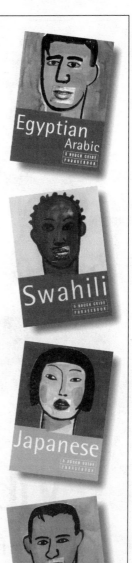

the perfect getaway vehicle

low-price holiday car rental.

rent a car from holiday autos and you'll give yourself real freedom to explore your holiday destination. with great-value, fully-inclusive rates in over 4,000 locations worldwide, wherever you're escaping to, we're there to make sure you get excellent prices and superb service.

what's more, you can book now with complete confidence. our £5 undercut* ensures that you are guaranteed the best value for money in holiday destinations right around the globe.

drive away with a great deal, call holiday autos now on **0990 300 400** and quote ref RG.

holiday autos
miles ahead

*in the unlikely event that you should see a cheaper like for like pre-paid rental rate offered by any other independent uk car rental company before or after booking but prior to departure, holiday autos will undercut that price by a full £5. we truly believe we cannot be beaten on price.

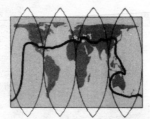

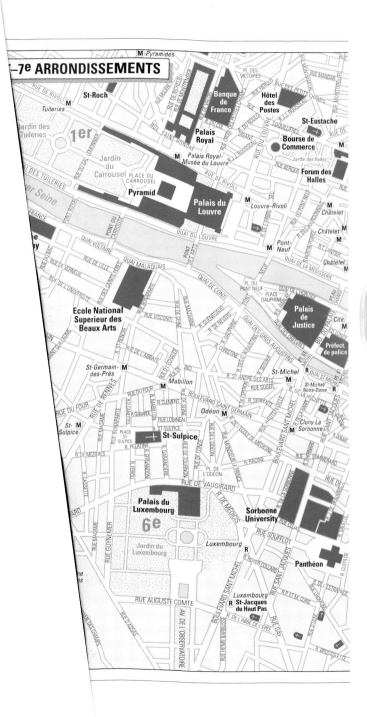

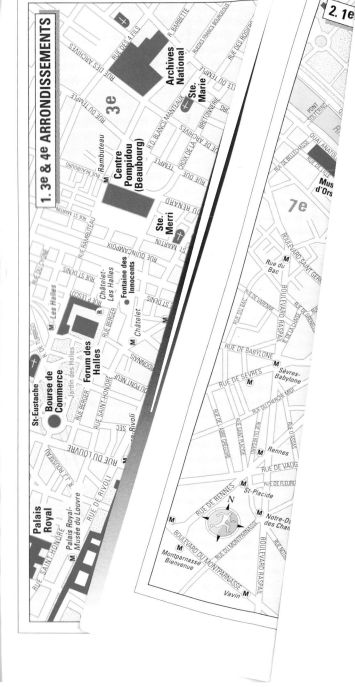

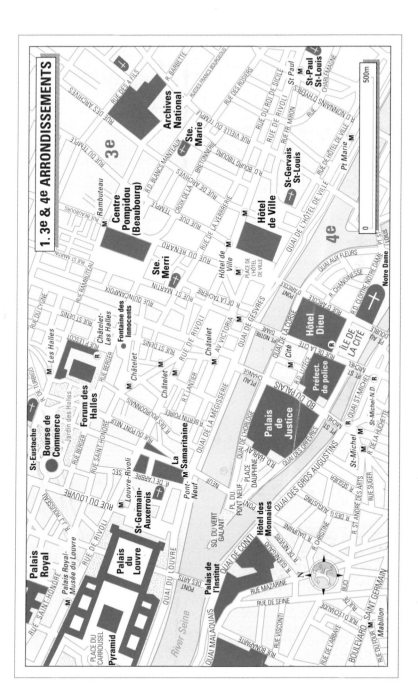

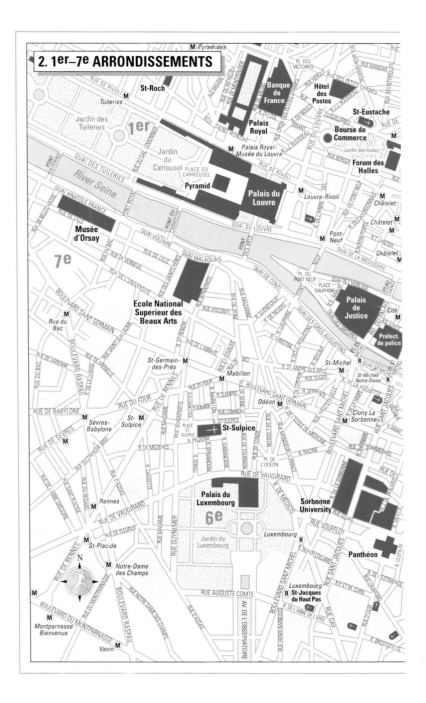

2. 1er–7e ARRONDISSEMENTS

St-Roch

Tuileries

Jardin des Tuileries

1er

Banque de France

Hôtel des Postes

St-Eustache

Palais Royal

Bourse de Commerce

Jardin du Carrousel

PLACE DU CARROUSEL

Palais Royal-Musée du Louvre

Forum des Halles

Jardin des Halles

Pyramid

Palais du Louvre

Louvre-Rivoli

Châtelet

River Seine

Musée d'Orsay

Louvre-Rivoli

Pont-Neuf

Châtelet

Châtelet

7e

PLACE DAUPHINE

Palais de Justice

Cité

Préfect. de police

Ecole National Superieur des Beaux Arts

Rue du Bac

St-Germain-des-Prés

Mabillon

St-Michel

St-Michel Notre-Dame

Cluny La Sorbonne

Sèvres-Babylone

St-Sulpice

Odéon

St-Sulpice

PLACE ST-SULPICE

PL. DE L'ODÉON

Rennes

St-Placide

Palais du Luxembourg

6e

Sorbonne University

Luxembourg

Panthéon

Jardin du Luxembourg

Notre-Dame des Champs

N

Luxembourg

St-Jacques du Haut Pas

RUE AUGUSTE COMTE

Montparnasse Bienvenue

Vavin